Making War
Making Peace

The Social Foundations
of Violent Conflict

ADVISING EDITOR IN SOCIOLOGY

Charles M. Bonjean
University of Texas–Austin

Making War
Making Peace

The Social Foundations
of Violent Conflict

EDITED BY

Francesca M. Cancian
University of California at Irvine

James William Gibson
Southern Methodist University

WADSWORTH PUBLISHING COMPANY
Belmont, California
A Division of Wadsworth, Inc.

Sociology Editor: Serina Beauparlant
Editorial Assistant: Marla Nowick
Production Editor: Angela Mann
Managing Designer: MaryEllen Podgorski
Print Buyer: Barbara Britton
Designer: Lisa S. Mirski
Copy Editor: Melissa Andrews
Compositor: Omegatype Typography, Inc.
Cover: Lisa S. Mirski

Printed in the United States of America   49

1 2 3 4 5 6 7 8 9 10—94 93 92 91 90

Library of Congress Cataloging in Publication Data

Making war/making peace : the social foundations of violent conflict /
  edited by Francesca M. Cancian, James William Gibson.
      p.   cm.
  ISBN 0-534-12348-1
  1. Peace.   2. War.   3. International relations.   4. Social
movements.   5. Peace movements.   I. Cancian, Francesca M.
II. Gibson, James William.
JX1952.M224   1990   89-22432
303.6′6—dc20   CIP

Contents

Preface

Societies make war and peace, not disembodied foreign policies. Long before battle begins, states must recruit armies and raise the money to fund them, industries have to produce arms, munitions, transportation and communication systems, and a war culture is necessary to create images of heroic warriors and evil enemies. War requires a "war system" implicating virtually all aspects of social structure and culture. Conversely, peacemaking is also a social process involving different social patterns and values.

Making War/Making Peace provides a broad overview of all the major social institutions that contribute to making war or making peace, including childhood socialization, gender roles, popular culture, social stratification, and education. Although this reader has sections on military weapons and strategy, it offers an expanded definition of the parameters of war and peace studies. Our reader bridges the gap between conventional international relations approaches to foreign policy and traditional sociological approaches to the study of society as a domestic or internal system. A wide selection of readings offers instructors and students a variety of substantive issues and theoretical debates appropriate for courses in the social sciences or interdisciplinary peace and war studies.

To make the issue of war and peace emotionally real, we begin in Part One with oral histories from soldiers, civilian war victims, and peace activists. These accounts challenge the popular notions that soldiers always find war to be a romantic adventure and that peacemakers are foolhardy dreamers.

Part Two, Socialization, shows how children's experiences of being dominated and being socialized to traditional gender roles are linked to war, while experiences of affection and closeness with their fathers contribute to peace. Part Three, Culture, analyzes images of military heroism, nationalism, and evil enemies in war movies and other mass media. We also explore how the language used by the weapons designers, strategic theorists, and soldiers responsible for nuclear weapons and war make nuclear war seem like a game or a reasonable way to defend ourselves.

Part Four, Inequality, discusses relations of domination based on class, ethnicity, and gender. The articles present both empirical evidence and theoretical arguments debating whether social inequality contributes to war and peace processes. Part Five, Political Economy of the Armaments Industry, explores the formation of the military-industrial complex after World War II and the development of weapons systems by the military and industry.

Part Six considers the contribution of education and scientific research to war and peace. American universities and research institutions create weapons and policy studies for practicing warfare, but they are also the place where students are often exposed to facts and ideas that challenge the status quo. In Part Seven, our discussion of the peace movement begins with a historical overview of peace movements in the United States and is followed by discussions of the Vietnam anti-war movement and the government's attempt to repress it. Considerable attention is paid to the 1980s anti-nuclear movements in both the United States and Europe.

In Part Eight, we analyze modern military strategies, tracing the development of guerilla warfare in Vietnam and other Third World countries, the failure of U.S. conventional warfare in Vietnam, and the subsequent development of "low-intensity conflict" by the United States. Additional articles evaluate the current policy of nuclear deterrence and consider alternative defense measures. Part Nine, The Nation and the International System, explores how nationalism, the industrialization of war, and the threat of nuclear war reinforce each other to undermine democracy. Several articles suggest that a more peaceful international system could be created by weakening national sovereignty and strengthening the capacities of international organizations for peace making and peace keeping.

Articles in *Making War/Making Peace* have different levels of accessibility to readers; some are more complex than others. But we have only picked authors whose writing style runs from plain to very good and have avoided authors who are overly dependent on jargon. A long introduction provides a more in-depth frame for the collected readings by discussing the common belief that war is inevitable, the history of modern warfare, and the major causes of war and peace. In addition, each part has its own short introduction that presents the major issues and debates in that part. In these ways we have tried to create a useful tool for understanding the dynamics of peace and war.

Acknowledgments

For their helpful suggestions, we would like to thank the members of the Center for Global Peace and Conflict Studies at the University of California, Irvine, especially Lawrence Howard, Jon Lawrence, and Julius Margolis. Reviewers Robert Benford, University of Nebraska; Russell R. Dynes, University of Delaware; William A. Gamson, Boston College; Lester Kurtz, University of Texas, Austin; David R. Segal, University of Maryland; Robin M. Williams, Cornell University; Nigel Young, Colgate University, all provided helpful comments. We thank Karole Nylander for valuable assistance in locating articles, and we appreciate the excellent job done by Linda Cleland who, with care and a friendly spirit, obtained the permissions to reprint the articles in this volume.

INTRODUCTION

Is War Inevitable?

Wars are part of our everyday world. Wars in the 1980s included the Iran–Iraq war (together with the U.S. Navy on patrol in the Persian Gulf), the Israeli invasion of Lebanon and prolonged conflict with Palestinians, the Russian invasion of Afghanistan, the U.S. invasion of Grenada, and various revolutionary guerrilla wars and counterinsurgency campaigns in Nicaragua, El Salvador, Angola, South Africa, and dozens of other Third World countries.

New nuclear weapons have been developed: a new intercontinental ballistic missile (ICBM), first called "MX" and then "Peacekeeper"; "Poseidon" nuclear missiles with multiple warheads; "B–1" and "Stealth" nuclear bombers; and "Star Wars," or the "Strategic Defense Initiative," the system for ostensibly defending against ballistic missile attack with a vast complex of ground-based radar sets, antimissile missiles, and spectacular nuclear-bomb–powered antimissile lasers orbiting the earth in outer space.

War in Early Societies

It is tempting to resign oneself to this world of destruction, to accept these wars and weapons as necessary evils, modern reminders that humans are primitive, violent animals, always threatening to destroy the civilization that they have created. To many, this tragic view of human nature is reassuring. In their view, the good in humans is inextricably, biologically connected to the bad, and there is no need to struggle for peace because nothing can be done; war is part of the natural order of things.

In our view, war is not inevitable. We (and you) study peace and war because we believe that what we learn can be used to help us create a more peaceful world. Just as those who study medicine value health over illness and take action to promote health, we value peace over war and believe that informed action can promote peace.

Comparative research on all kinds of human societies from the first hunting and gathering communities to the modern era does not support the view that war is natural and consequently more wars are inevitable. "Despite the popular image of violence and anarchy in the most primitive societies," concludes political scientist Marc Ross, "available studies show that those societies at the simplest level of technological complexity are no more prone to violence than those which are high on complexity" (Ross, in this volume). Some hunting and gathering and horticultural societies have little conflict within the community, whereas others have frequent fights and killings (Chagnon 1967; Draper 1978).

Even in those hunting and gathering societies that were highly combative, war chiefs only had command of individual raiding parties; the routine affairs of the group followed different leadership patterns (Turney-High 1971). Wars of conquest were not useful because such societies could not control many slaves for economic exploitation. Most battles had a limited scope and often were highly ritualized affairs with many rules governing combat. Many early societies saw killing of "enemies" as necessary either to renew the fertility cycle of the seasons or to certify the transition from boyhood to manhood (Mails 1972). However, this ritually necessary violence was fulfilled by a handful of enemy deaths either on the battlefield or in torture of prisoners.

Hunting of animals was in turn contained by the recognition that enough game animals needed to survive and reproduce if continued hunting was to be feasible. The hunt was not the breeding ground for the total destruction of other societies.

Wars in which one social group wages sustained combat against another with many casualties and destruction of the enemy's social order are a relatively modern social institution, at most 9,000 to 12,000 years old, with few examples before 4000 B.C. (Dyer 1985; Fromm 1973). Only after agriculture had developed to a sophisticated enough level that part of the population could grow enough "surplus" food to feed the rest did a centralized state with a system of commanding men and resources to fuel war become feasible.

Classes of war lords and warriors came to own or control the land and the peasants who worked the land. The peasants gave part of their food to the war lords because the warriors both threatened them and promised to protect them from other war lords. Over generations these ruling war lords and their subordinate warriors became hereditary kings and nobility, such as the pharaohs and royal families of Egypt, the nobility of Western Europe, and the dynastic empires of Rome, China, and Japan. For centuries, warfare was mostly limited to conflict among these relatively small warrior groups (McNeil 1982). If peasants fought, the agriculture that sustained the nobility

was disrupted. It also created risks that the peasants would not always fight the declared enemy but would instead leave the battlefield or use their arms against the nobility who ruled them.

The History of Modern Warfare

The first mass warfare of the modern era began with the revolution of French peasants, urban workers, and part of the merchant class against the old feudal order in 1789. When threatened in 1793 by the monarchs of Austria, Prussia, and Hungary, the revolutionary government responded with romantic manifestos (legitimating compulsory state actions) to mobilize the entire society for war:

> *All Frenchmen are permanently requisitioned for service into the armies. Young men will go forth to battle; married men will forge weapons and transport munitions; women will make tents and clothing and serve in hospitals; children will make lint from old linen; and old men will be brought to the public squares to arouse the courage of the soldiers, while preaching the unity of the Republic and hatred against the Kings. (Quoted by McNeil 1982, p. 192)*

Over a million men eventually served in the French Army from 1793 to 1799, a force much larger than any previous army. France's armies under the revolution and Napoleon created a modern bureaucratic organization. It abolished the feudal practice of aristocratic right to officer ranks and instead established a merit system for promotion of enlisted men into officers. Primary schools were established for its low-level leaders so that the men could read written orders and maps. A highly elaborate military division of labor came into existence, with especially skilled "staff" officers for planning strategy and logistics and for testing new weapons and tactics.

Industrial capitalism's rapid advance in the United States caused another radical change in war. The U.S. government's arsenal at Springfield, Massachusetts had pioneered the use of machine-made interchangeable parts in guns. By the 1850s the American gun industry led the world. England

and the rest of Europe soon imported "the American system of manufacture." These new industries could produce many thousands of weapons and millions of cartridges a year.

Industrialism and the nation-state made huge armies financially possible: Civilians could be conscripted at low wages and armed with weapons that were at once state of the art and relatively cheap. Mass-manufactured food and clothing helped solve the traditional problems of sustaining an army in the field, while the new railroads and telegraphs facilitated transportation and communication over vast distances.

In 1863 the U.S. Civil War gave the world a good look at industrialized warfare. Armies on each side were armed with rifles accurate for several hundred yards, creating a "killing zone" far larger than those of previous battlegrounds. Traditional frontal assaults designed to seize the other side's position led to thousands of casualties per battle.

The industrialization of warfare in turn helped create an awareness that the economy was a crucially important target. President Lincoln issued the Emancipation Proclamation abolishing slavery to deprive the Confederacy of their labor, and the commanding U.S. general, Ulysses S. Grant, ordered his field commanders to lay waste to the southern countryside. Such a massive war, featuring both huge casualties among soldiers and destruction of the opponent's industry, buildings, and whole social order marks the advent of what historians call "total war."

Britain and France made further advances both in industry and in warfare in the 19th century. Their imperial control over African and Asian societies was aided by their superior weapons. For example, at the 1898 Battle of Omdurman in the Sudan, British troops armed with six "Maxim" machine guns killed 11,000 Dervish in a few hours.

When World War I started in 1914 all the combating states envisioned a short war, but instead the integration of industrial capitalism with the nation-state created an unprecedented destructive system. Armies soon found themselves ensconced in trench systems stretching for hundreds of miles. At first industry could not keep up with demand for artillery shells. France had anticipated firing 12,000 shells a

day; its army soon averaged over 100,000 a day. In 1915 the Russian army fired more shells in a day than its factories produced in a month.

Governments soon took over industry, dictating what would be produced and the prices that would be paid for war materials and labor. Each side created sophisticated propaganda agencies to control its populace and make them want to support the war effort. The distinction between civilian and soldier began to vanish. President Woodrow Wilson explained in 1917 that "there are entire nations armed. Thus the men [and women] who remain to till the soil and man the factories are not less a part of the army than the men beneath the battle flags" (Weigley 1977, p. 210).

Frontal assaults across the "no man's land" that divided the opposing trenches led to incredible casualties from artillery and machine guns. In 1916 British generals argued that because they had more men than the Germans, that even by trading one for one, the British would win. At the battle of Somme in France in 1918 the British took 415,000 casualties in a five-month period. Of the 65 million men who fought in World War I, 9 million were killed and 22 million wounded.

The war might well have gone on past 1918 had the politicians and generals had their way. But the first phase of the Russian revolution began in March 1917, when Russian peasant soldiers who had been starved and abused by their noblemen officers took Russia out of the war. The next month one half of the French Army mutinied after another failed offensive; 25,000 men were court-martialed by their commanding officers in an effort to regain control. Four hundred thousand Italian soldiers walked away from the battle at Caporetto in May. German troops stationed in Russia began to talk with Communist revolutionaries. By mid-1918 when the U.S. Army arrived in Europe, the war in many places along the front had already ended in a series of tacit truces. None of the losing governments in Germany, Russia, Austria, and the Ottoman Empire survived the war, and even in the "victorious" countries, the human and material sacrifices led to deep public disenchantment with their power structures.

Thus from both political and military standpoints, the "problem" was how to break through the trenches and end the next war quickly. Fast-moving armored warfare was one solution: This was the route taken by the German military with its development of the *blitzkrieg,* or rapid attack. In 1939 the world's first such assault destroyed the Polish Army in 9 days and conquered Holland, Belgium, and France in 3 weeks.

The United States and Great Britain also developed armored warfare, but they specialized in another solution, strategic bombing by aircraft. "Strategic" bombing meant attacking the opponent's industries, military headquarters, and communications centers far behind the battlefield. As Russian emigré and aircraft designer Alexander Seversky theorized this new strategy in his 1942 book, *Victory Through Air Power,"* ... the will to resist can be broken in a people only by destroying effectively the essentials of their lives—the supply of food, shelter, light, water, sanitation and the rest.... Advanced peoples, must, if possible, be reduced to impotence beyond easy recovery, through annihilation of the industrial foundations of their life" (Seversky 1942, pp. 146 and 101).

For the first few years of World War II the Americans and the British followed different bombing strategies. The British followed Seversky by deliberately targeting German cities for terror bombing at night, with large formations of bombers dropping incendiary fire bombs in an effort to break the German "will to resist." For example, in July 1942 the Royal Air Force killed about 42,000 people in Hamburg, Germany during four night attacks. U.S. strategists most often favored "precision" daylight bombing against German factories and oil refineries. German civilians were killed in such attacks, but civilian casualties were not the direct objective in American daylight bombing.

However, the U.S. air war against Japan resembled the British approach. In February 1945 Major General Curtis E. LeMay ordered B-29 bombers to drop incendiary bombs on the city of Kobe as an experiment. Because Japanese built their cities and homes largely from wood and paper, Kobe burned fiercely; a "firestorm" was created in which the burning city sucked in wind that fueled an even larger fire. Army Air Corps experiments with incendiary bombing raids continued. On March 9 LeMay ordered 324 B-29s loaded with

2,000 tons of fire bombs to attack Tokyo. One quarter of the city's buildings were destroyed, and over 1 million were left homeless; 83,793 residents died in the attack, and another 40,918 were injured. All told, the conventional bombing campaign against Japanese cities killed 300,000 people and left one third of the population, some 22 million people, homeless (Dyer 1985, p. 95).

American atomic attacks on Hiroshima and Nagasaki in August 1945 followed this strategy of annihilation. The two bombs dropped killed over 140,000 people at Hiroshima and 80,000 at Nagasaki, wounding tens of thousands more. With strategic conventional and nuclear bombing, the trend to total war that began with the armies of the French revolution reached a new level of mass murder. The famous German military theorist Carl von Clausewitz defined strategy as the theory of using military forces to achieve a state's political objectives (von Clausewitz 1968, p. 86). According to von Clausewitz, the benefits gained through a particular strategy of war must be in some proportion to the costs. But if combat totally destroys the enemy's society, then what is left for the victor? As military historian Russell Weigley has noted, atomic weapons so totally destroyed society that they could not serve what von Clausewitz called "the object of the War," "unless the object of war was to transform the enemy's country into a desert" (Weigley 1977, p. 365).

Many scholars have concluded that if there is a third world war using thousands of nuclear weapons, then the collateral damages—widespread fires, high levels of radioactive fallout (perhaps creating a "nuclear winter" by blocking sunlight), damage to the earth's ozone layer (which protects life from dangerous ultraviolet rays), and breakdown of all complex social organization—might be extensive enough to destroy the entire world (Schell 1982).

Although the United States drastically reduced its forces in 1945 after World War II ended, by 1950 the struggle between the United States and Western Europe on one side and the Soviet Union and its allies on the other side resulted in military buildups. Each of the major belligerent nations mobilized its domestic social institutions and culture for warfare; the "war system" became more firmly institutionalized. In the United States, for example, putting the nation on a permanent war footing meant the creation of a peacetime draft, the allocation of billions of dollars for a permanent military–industrial complex to create new weapons systems, formation of the Central Intelligence Agency (CIA) to conduct covert operations (and thus preserve the aura of peace), and emphasis in Hollywood on war movies and westerns.

Thus the move toward total war is not a throwback to our animal or primitive beginnings but is part of our "progress" as an industrial nation-state. The war system of institutions is something that we have created and therefore is something that we may be able to abolish.

The possibility of eliminating war is also supported by some positive developments in world history. From the broad historical perspective of several centuries, public support for war as a normal state of affairs has tended to decline (Wright 1964, p. 45). Moreover, the world has moved much closer to an effective world government since World War II. The United Nations is far from able to keep the world at peace, but it has had some successes in defusing international tensions, and it has set a precedent for international cooperation (Lash, in this volume; Moskos, in this volume).

The international peace movement has a long history, and once again became a powerful political force in the Western democracies during the 1980s (Howlett and Zeitzer, in this volume). Activists in Great Britain, the United States, and West Germany have increased public understanding of the dangers of nuclear war and have thus helped push their political leaders toward negotiations with the Soviet Union to reduce nuclear weapons. Although the Soviet Union did not permit autonomous movements to develop prior to the recent policy of "glasnost" (openness), it does have several popular organizations concerned with creating a more peaceful international order. Soviet officials have met many of the West's peace movement leaders for discussions.

Long-standing evils have been eradicated before in human history after the prolonged efforts of social movements: The abolition of slavery in the 19th century is probably the best example. Now, the terror and pointlessness of nuclear holocaust may goad us to abolish war. The task of abolishing war calls for men and women to rethink and remake their social institutions. We need theory and research that will clarify how domestic and international social relations contribute to war or peace.

Defining War and Peace

Webster's Ninth New Collegiate Dictionary defines *war* as "open and declared armed hostile conflict between states or nations." This definition is too narrow; it excludes all U.S. military activity since World War II, such as the Korean War, the Vietnam War, and the U.S. participation in the "contra" guerrilla war in Nicaragua. We define war more broadly as "organized armed conflict between groups," including undeclared wars, civil and guerrilla wars, covert operations, and lower levels of violence such as terrorism or the killing of political activists by the police or "death squads" (Wright 1964, pp. 5–7).

A "war system" refers to those components of social institutions of cultural beliefs and practices that tend to promote the development of warriors, weapons, and war as a normal part of a society and its foreign policy. For example, the research presented in this book suggests that using harsh, authoritarian childrearing methods creates people who both are intolerant toward others and have a strong will to dominate. This disposition can be readily mobilized by government for supporting or participating in warfare.

In contrast to the relative clarity of war, there is no agreed-on set of people, objects, and actions or events that forms the core meaning of peace. The fact that peace is also widely accepted as a desirable, ideal state contributes to the complexity of the concept because people tend to associate peace with their particular goals and beliefs. Left-wing groups associate peace with economic equality and socialism, whereas right-wing groups associate peace with military strength and a balance of power. Others identify peace with a utopian heaven on earth, a world of harmony without any conflict. Vague and unrealistic conceptions of peace make it difficult to work toward peace or even talk about it.

We define *peace* as "the absence of war." "Peace system" refers to social patterns that promote peace. For example, developing a civilian economy tends to promote peace in contrast to economies in which a substantial number of jobs and technological innovations are dependent on high military expenditures for weapons. A cultural tradition that encourages skepticism toward government and its rationales for instigating war would also be considered part of a "peace system." Spelling out the social arrangements that make up peace systems will provide us with concrete visions and models of a peaceful world. This is the most important research task for achieving a peaceful world; we need some idea of where we are going before we can set out to get there.

Many peace researchers use an alternative approach to conceptualizing peace. They reject our definition of peace as "the absence of war": They consider this a "negative" definition of peace. They instead focus on "positive" peace, which includes social justice, economic well-being, and the freedom to develop one's potential (Galtung 1985). Their approach was developed to deal with the fact that more people are killed by hunger, preventable illness, and repression—what such researchers call "structural violence"—than by the direct violence of war.

According to this reasoning, people who work for "negative" peace often inadvertently support the status quo and the privileges of ruling groups and dominant nations. Sometimes extreme repression and structural domination—such as existed in the American South's slave system—creates a "peaceful" society, that is, a society not at war. To avoid this problem, many researchers refuse to separate peace from social justice.

We define peace as the absence of war and *do* separate peace from social justice because we believe that treating them as the same thing creates more confusion than clarity. A revolutionary movement that makes war to overthrow an unjust, repressive regime is still making war, even if the war is justified. And there is a risk that the violence of war may devour the revolution's liberating intentions, creating a new militarized system of rule in place of the old one. We doubt the usefulness of defining all "good" things with the same word, *peace*. Peace and justice are both desirable, but they sometimes conflict. Peace may also conflict with economic prosperity for some groups and with political freedom, self-determination, and other valued goals.

Causes of Peace and War

What aspects of our society are part of a war system and what aspects contribute to peace? Nationalism, the military-industrial complex, and relations of domination are the three factors that seem most important.

A major cause of war in recent centuries is the growing power of the nation-state, accompanied by popular feelings of patriotism. Being an American or a Russian gives many people a sense of identity and meaning in life, and many men experience their most intense feelings of being alive, important, and connected to others by becoming warriors and killing and dying "for their country."

As warfare became increasingly destructive of civilian life in the 17th and 18th centuries, it became imperative for political elites to persuade their populaces both to participate in mass war and to endure the causalities and economic hardships of war mobilization. In *A Study of War* (1964, pp. 51–52), Quincy Wright concludes "Since popular support became more necessary with the new technology, the management of opinion became increasingly important. Development of the sentiment of nationalism, identifying the citizen with the state, made it possible to arouse popular enthusiasm for war. . . . National sovereignty, defined by the new international law, became the prevailing value, the dominant sentiment, the political objective and the leading cause of war in the modern period."

Modern nationalism has its origins with the French Revolution—the struggle of the merchant class, workers, and peasants against the feudal aristocracy. The revolution was made in the name of the French people, the nation as a whole, as opposed to a highly privileged elite. But the struggle for "liberty, equality, fraternity" connected to a sense of belonging to a national community did not lead to a peaceful international community.

National pride in the emerging 18th-century European nation-states became transformed into a sense of national superiority in relation to other countries and peoples. The ruling elites of the dominant class in European countries soon used the doctrine of national superiority to legitimate their political, economic, and cultural domination of other peoples in colonial empires they created around the world. Nationalism became the rhetoric of imperialism, as well as a major theme justifying the struggle of one imperial state against another. Nationalism and patriotism were also used by ruling elites to divert people's attention away from inequalities and injustices at home.

To be sure, nationalism has also been the rallying cry of all colonized peoples revolting against foreign domination, from the 1776 American Revolution against Britain through the many post-World War II independence movements and revolutionary wars in Third World countries. But even in its best, most liberating moments of aiding a people to overthrow tyranny, nationalism as a meaningful belief system requires an "enemy," an Other against whom the nation struggles. Americans, Russians, Germans, Chinese, and Kenyans all come to know themselves in relation to past, present, and future potential "enemies." Nation-states "mirror" each other in this respect; each constructs national cultural identities and visions of each other that make military de-escalation and peace making difficult (Bronfenbrenner, in this volume; Dower, in this volume). Only if love of country were combined with respect for other countries and their diverse ways of life could nationalism become part of a peace system.

Nationalism begins in our schools, with the morning pledge of allegiance and with history books that glorify the United States and our military heroes. It is strengthened and renewed by the movies, songs, and newspaper stories that teach us to love the abstraction called "our country," rank many other countries as somehow inferior, and see still other nations as "the enemy" (Gibson, in this volume). A peaceful alternative to nationalism is internationalism, or greater power for international organizations, and feelings of solidarity with the whole earth. Schools that give students sympathetic views of other cultures and parents that give their sons toys that don't require enemies to conquer in play are part of a peace system.

The military-industrial complex, or more accurately, the military-industrial-scientific complex, is another major component of the war system in the United States, the Soviet Union, and many other countries. Making war is the goal and raison d'être for the armed forces, arms industry, and scientific researchers specializing in military research. According to political economist Seymour Melman, the United States spent $2001 billion dollars on defense from 1946 to 1981 and another $2089 billion from 1981 to 1988. This cumulative sum is equal to the nation's "reproducible national wealth, which means *the money value of everything man-made on the surface of the United States,* excluding the money value assigned to the land." By 1987 the United States spent $87 on the military for every $100 spent on both private investments such as factories and civilian government investments such as schools, hospitals, and roads (Cockburn and Ridgeway, from an original speech by Melman, in this volume).

The large corporations that manufacture weapons, the university researchers who provide the scientific knowledge needed to make them, and the millions of workers who work for military contractors have strong reasons to support a foreign policy that emphasizes military force. These people receive more money, job opportunities, and respect when war seems likely. If peace was assured, they would be out of work. These groups, more than others, are key actors in the war system. Even though they believe that they are working for peace by "keeping America strong," they are the people most directly involved in making war, not peace (Singer, in this volume).

Peace "conversion" would replace the military-industrial complex with a much smaller military organized for defense rather than for foreign intervention and global nuclear war. Such a defensive strategy possibly would be based on greater civilian participation (Sharp, in this volume). A defensive strategy would use war technology not readily adaptable to attacking an opponent and would reduce the constant technological innovation and planned obsolescence of weaponry that characterize today's military (Forsberg, in this volume).

Government expenditures could help many military contractors convert their factories to make civilian goods and help employees of military firms learn new job skills. Only if a sizable proportion of business and/or labor see another way to survive and prosper without massive military production will the paralyzing grip of "jobs blackmail" be broken and the war system changed to a peace system. A redirected American government and economy would rebuild U.S. industry for producing consumer goods and satisfying public needs such as health, education, and environmental protection. Scientific research in universities and think tanks would focus on solving human problems. Parts of the peace movement are working to achieve these goals.

Domination as opposed to democracy is the third factor that distinguishes peace systems from war systems. It is our hypothesis that relationships that are dominating and disrespectful will contribute to war, whereas democratic relationships of equal power and mutual empathy will lead to peace. Domination versus democracy is an aspect of all social relations between individuals or groups. It is a broad concept that overlaps with other ideas such as "oppression versus liberation," "authoritarianism," and "power over" other people versus "power with" others (Adorno et al. 1964; Friere 1970; Starhawk 1987). In relations of domination, members of one group monopolize resources and power, regard themselves as intellectually and morally superior, and attempt to impose their will and their ideas on the subordinate group. In the extreme, the dominant group views subordinates as dehumanized objects and has no feelings of empathy or responsibility for them; thus subordinates can be killed without serious regret.

Domination *between nations* clearly contributes to modern warfare. The 20th century has witnessed many colonial or imperialistic wars aimed at dominating another country and anti-colonial struggles against foreign domination (the United States in Vietnam and Nicaragua or the Soviet Union in Hungary and Afghanistan). Propaganda portraying the home country as morally superior in contrast to the monstrous or inhuman enemy is a standard feature of warfare.

However, the importance of domination or inequality *within* a nation has been a controversial issue among scholars and peace activists for generations (see Howlett and Zeitzer, in this volume). Politically conservative internationalists argue that domestic inequality is not a significant cause of war; relations between governing elites are most important, and the road to peace is through arms control treaties and international law. In contrast, socialists and pacifists maintain that domestic inequality is a major cause of war.

We think that domestic inequality based on social class, ethnicity, and gender is one of the social foundations of modern war. Domination by a ruling class promotes war because the elite have much to gain (such as increased profits from access to foreign markets and natural resources) and little to lose (because most of the dying will be done by sons of the working class and minority ethnic groups). A ruling elite may also promote war to maintain their political power; war can deflect popular unrest with the class hierarchy and undermine foreign revolutionary regimes whose success might inspire political changes at home. A more democratic distribution of political power and economic resources would reduce the perceived gains of war to decision makers and increase the costs—especially the costs of protracted war, since public support often declines as casualties and material costs mount over time. A more powerful populace could more readily challenge the elite at any stage of the war-making process.

The domination of women by men encourages war by promoting military values and a militarized ideal of masculinity. "Real" men and soldiers are both trained to be tough, aggressive, and—most important—not like women, who are seen as tender, peace loving, and inferior (Arkin and Dobrofsky, in this volume; Cancian, in this volume).

Domination versus democracy in other spheres is also part of making war or making peace. An important new political movement in the 1980s—called the Greens or eco-pacifists—sees domination of people, land, and nature as the basic cause of war (Bahro, in this volume). Bringing together elements of the ecology, peace, and feminist movements, they argue that they are suffering from a pervasive "culture of domination" in which nature is destroyed, disadvantaged groups are oppressed, and the extermination of the world is threatened. In their view, the road to peace requires a commitment to decentralized democracy and preservation of all life.

There is substantial evidence that domination in *some* relationships is linked to war, especially the relationships between parents and children, men and women, and natives and foreigners. In peaceful societies, parents are warmer and more permissive toward their children than parents in warlike societies; men and women are relatively equal in power and respect; and people perceive foreigners as humans similar to themselves (Bronfenbrenner, in this volume; Dower, in this volume; Fabbro, in this volume; Rohrer 1985; Ross, in this volume; Sanday 1981).

We believe that more democratic relations in other spheres as well probably contribute to peace—relations between teachers and students, governments and citizens, managers and workers, "First World" and "Third World" nations. But the evidence is unclear. For example, with the rise of nations with partially democratic political systems in the past two centuries, warfare intensified, as we have described. Clarifying the links between domination and war should be a high priority for future research.

Domination versus democracy is an important concept because it identifies aspects of everyday life that contribute to peace and war, such as childrearing patterns and gender roles. In addition, the concept points to a common thread linking acts of war. Making war requires domination: generals ordering a bomb raid that will kill many people; recruits in boot camp being drilled in instant obedience; civilians who are taught to see the "enemy" as subhuman (but dangerous) and who gladly accept the authority of rulers who "defend" them.

In contrast, making peace requires democratic relationships: soldiers who refuse to fight in a war they do not support; citizens who claim the right to participate in making decisions instead of accepting rule by elites who make decisions in secret; newspaper reporters, magazine editors, movie makers, and others in the mass media who question the necessity of casting another nation as an "enemy" and instead look for ways to communicate with other human beings who are potentially our friends.

James William Gibson
Francesca M. Cancian

References

Adorno, T. W., Elsa Frenkel-Brunswick, Daniel Levinson, and R. Nevitt Sanford. 1964. *The Authoritarian Personality.* New York: Science Editions.

Brock-Utne, Birgit. 1985. *Educating for Peace: A Feminist Perspective.* New York: Pergamon Press.

Chagnon, Napoleon. 1967. "Yanomamo Social Organization and Warfare." Pp. 109–159 in *War: The Anthropology of Armed Conflict and Aggression,* edited by Morton Fried, M. Harris, and R. Murphy. Garden City, NY: Natural History Press.

Draper, Patricia. 1978. "The Learning Environment for Aggression and Anti-Social Behavior among the Kung." In *Learning Non-Aggression,* edited by Ashley Montagu. New York: Oxford University Press.

Dyer, Gwynne. 1985. *War.* New York: Crown.

Friere, Pablo. 1970. *Pedagogy of the Oppressed.* New York: Continuum.

Fromm, Eric. 1973. *The Anatomy of Human Destructiveness.* New York: Holt, Rinehart & Winston.

Galtung, Johann. 1985. "25 Years of Peace Research." *Journal of Peace Research* 22:141–158.

Mails, Thomas E. 1972. *The Mystic Warriors of the Plains.* New York: Doubleday.

McNeil, William H. 1982. *The Pursuit of Power: Technology, Armed Force, and Society since A.D. 1000.* Chicago: The University of Chicago Press.

Rohrer, John H. 1985. *The Warmth Factor.* Beverly Hills, CA: Sage.

Sanday, Peggy Reeves. 1981. *Female Power and Male Dominance.* New York: Cambridge University Press.

Schell, Jonathan. 1982. *The Fate of the Earth.* New York: Alfred A. Knopf.

Seversky, Major Alexander P. de. 1942. *Victory Through Air Power.* New York: Simon and Schuster.

Starhawk. 1987. *Truth or Die: Encounters with Power, Authority, and Mystery.* San Francisco: Harper & Row.

Turney-High, Harry Hughes. 1971. *Primitive War: Its Practice and Concepts.* Columbia: University of South Carolina Press.

von Clausewitz, Carl. 1968. *On War,* translated by Col. J. J. Graham. New York: Barnes and Noble.

Weigley, Russell Frank. 1977. *The American Way of War.* Bloomington: University of Indiana Press.

Wright, Quincy (abridged by Louise Wright). 1964. *A Study of War.* Chicago: The University of Chicago Press.

PART ONE

Experiencing Peace and War

The experiences of peace activists, combat soldiers, and war victims described in this section help us see that "peace" and "war" are neither distant abstractions found only in history books and newspaper headlines nor heroic epics of legends and modern movies. Instead, both peace and war consist of actions and feelings by people like ourselves. To understand the stories men and women tell about their experiences makes the intellectual debates about peace and war seem more real and more important.

Peace often seems like a vague and unrealistic ideal. We think of peacemakers in the tradition of Jesus Christ, Gandhi, and Martin Luther King, Jr., men who either were fully divine according to religion (Christ) or became semidivine martyrs through their sacrificed lives. Although this tradition of sacrifice in the search for peace is vitally important, it makes it difficult to conceive of peacemakers and peace in a more worldly sense of organizing society and living everyday life. We have no clear image of the people, objects, and events that form the core meaning of peace. What does "experiencing peace" mean, besides being a peace activist?

As children, most of us learned to identify peace with being obedient, quiet, and "good."

Thus, part of the hidden attractions of war are the ways in which war is perceived as a liberation from conventional moral restraints and submission to authority. Teenagers usually equate peace with general ideals of freedom and equality and believe that peace is unattainable, and consequently, "unreal."[1] Thus the tacit definitions of peace found in our culture are not helpful in pointing to how we might create a peaceful world.

War, in contrast, calls up concrete, exciting images of battles, weapons, and destruction. The war hero who risks his life for his buddies and his country is an inspiring model for many men. Yet another popular image of war is a web of anonymous experts, directing a vast, computerized network of stunning war machines that we can watch but cannot control and for which we have no responsibility. Neither image inspires collective action to abolish war.

The following personal accounts present alternative images of warmakers and peacemakers. By focusing on everyday experiences, they suggest that we can all understand critical aspects of war and peace; we do not have to leave decisions determining who lives and who dies to experts. Also, understanding peace and war on an emotional level as well as an intellectual level makes us more likely to take responsibility for the future. As peace activist Kristina Selvig says, "I didn't *want* to know about the bomb . . . you have to act on what you know (in this volume, p. 17).

In the first selection, "Constructing Peace as a Whole System," Mark Sommer tries a new way to define peace through functioning "peace systems," including, for example, the balanced ecology of a farm community and the international mail system. Sommer defines peace as "an imperfect and evolving" system that channels "potentially destructive conflicts into processes that dissipate their violence and release their latent creativity" (in this volume, p. 13). In the next selection, two peace activists describe how they have worked against nuclear war, one by nonviolent direct actions that led to her imprisonment and one by working "within the system" to organize American and Soviet doctors opposed to nuclear war.

Our selections on war describe experiences of combat, killing, and bombing—all part of the core meaning of "war." These personal accounts also suggest that many of our images of war are romantic myths that do not represent the actual experience of war. We should remember that the war system also includes other kinds of experiences that are less dramatic but are connected to killing, such as the decision of government leaders to station nuclear arms abroad, or working in a

scientific laboratory that creates new weapons (see Cohn, in this volume; Gray and Payne, in this volume).

In Mark Baker's selection, "Making War: Soldiers in Vietnam," different Vietnam veterans talk about their efforts to survive, their pride in being Marines, and their cynicism about the war. Their experiences rarely fit the myth of military heroes. Real combat, as opposed to the romantic myth, seems to focus on fatigue, fear, and endurance; on painful, often grotesque injuries; and on death.

In another selection, Vietnam veteran William Broyles asks the controversial question, "Why do men love war?" and presents in reply a much more positive account of combat. Some of the hidden attractions of warfare, he argues, are the thrill of killing and the beauty and sexuality of making war. If he is right that many men love war, then understanding and redirecting these attractions will promote peace. But Broyles seems to make war more attractive by implying that it is inevitable and by covering up the pointless horror of real war with dramatic and sexual images and tender stories of tearful comrades and newborn rabbits. The horror of civilian death during war is clearly conveyed in the next selection—the matter-of-fact diary of Michihiko Hachiya, a Japanese doctor who lived through the atom bomb attack of Hiroshima.

---

1. See Julliete Burstermann, "Let's Listen to Our Children and Youth," in *Education for Peace,* ed. George Henderson (Washington D.C.: Association for Supervision and Curriculum Development, 1973), 63–80.

Constructing Peace as a Whole System
Making the World Safe for Conflict

Mark Sommer

For the past ten years, I have been looking for a way to think about peace. What's odd is that when you try to think about peace, you end up mostly thinking about war. Peace itself has no positive identity. It's what you walk by on the way to something interesting. But surely peace is something more than the mere absence of something else. It must be something in itself, a real experience. How will we ever find it if we don't know what it looks like?

It occurred to me recently that maybe we've been looking in the wrong place for peace. Perhaps it's not somewhere in the sky above us, where we've always expected to find it, but more at eye level in many of the processes, institutions, and events we take most for granted. Peace is not the rarefied and unblemished state of our fondest imaginings, but a more common experience that includes conflict but is not consumed by it. Peace is not a fixed or final state of being but an experimental and evolving process, necessarily imperfect and always tending toward a harmony that it may never fully attain.

To this understanding of peace as an imperfect and evolving process, I have recently added another simple notion: the idea of peace as a whole system, with qualities resembling other whole systems. Both as they occur in nature and as they are designed by man, peace systems (as I call them) channel potentially destructive conflicts into processes that dissipate their violence and release their latent creativity. Peace is an organic rather than mechanical concept, a live rather than manufactured process. This distinction has many implications for the kind of peace we get when we try making it. Peace can be of many kinds, and not all of them are sustaining. War is often the consequence of a forced peace. For example, the badly conceived Treaty of Versailles, which negotiated a peace among the Allies and Germany in 1919, doomed Europe to a return engagement 20 years later. Likewise, the repressive peace of the Marcos regime in the Philippines first spawned guerrilla war and then a sudden and bloodless "evolution" into what one hopes will become a more genuine peace.

It is vital to sustain this distinction between a true and an illusory peace, a healthy and an unhealthy state of calm, since one constitutes freedom, the other tyranny. Peace based on repression is no peace at all. A forced peace has its systems, too. They are all too easy to describe because there have been so many of them.

Sometimes they may penetrate the institutions of a genuine peace system and turn it toward war, all the while mouthing the rhetoric of peace. In the end they become war systems. Though they differ widely in structure and circumstance, false peace systems all ultimately depend on the threat of violence to enforce their brand of order.

They share, too, a mechanistic view of the universe—fixed, hierarchical, highly regulated with linear patterns of thought and belief, and viewing history as a forced march toward perfection. The ideologies used to justify false peace systems envision a future point in time when their doctrine will triumph and history will end.

Peace systems already exist in society on every scale and circumstance. These systems represent peace played out in its most mundane contexts. City traffic is a peace system and a remarkably good one. In the absence of lights and laws, the streets would be paralyzed within minutes by accidents and arguments. But in the presence of a set of rules, a means to determine violations, and the machinery to enforce the law, city traffic has become an astonishingly effective peace system. What is most remarkable about city traffic is its nonpartisan nature. It is a system without a leader other than the technology itself, which simply enforces a pattern and rhythm of traffic based on easing the flow throughout the network. To my knowledge, no one has ever sought to take over city traffic and run it for personal advantage.

Pedestrian as it may be, traffic provides an extraordinarily useful precedent for peace systems at the global level. Indeed, it is already a global system since it links every nation with every other. Howard Kurtz, author of a proposal to create a global satellite monitoring agency, uses this metaphor in likening the function of such an institution to that of an air traffic control system. Satellites would not be maintained by adversaries but by an independent and nonpartisan global authority, and the information gathered would be made available to the world community. The maintenance of a nonpartisan source of data would balance the often biased accounts kept by the contending parties.

There are many other nonpartisan peace systems already present at the global level—the international mail system and the telephone network, for examples. These are largely open systems with access available to most all who wish to use them. Blockages are inevitable from time to time, and constrictions in communications between East and West continue to impair the health of the global peace system. Nevertheless we have something here to build upon. Peace systems already operate in dozens of little-known roles at the global level, but their dependability leads us to forget them.

"How could this be peace?" we ask ourselves. "It's so ordinary!"

The components of a peace system are all around us. Even where conflict is endemic, peace systems of a very imperfect variety thrive. Within their jurisdictions, most cities, towns, counties, states, and nations carry on the prosaic process of negotiating conflicts that constitute the everyday nature of a political peace system. The essential elements are all present: a set of laws, a court system, a set of sanctions, and norms of behavior that incline toward self-restraint. The machinery of democratic government allows for conflicts to be played out largely without cataclysm in domestic politics.

There is obviously much that is stifling and inequitable in many political peace systems. All too easily they can be disfigured into systems of bureaucratic inertia or private gain, and they can be swallowed by systems of war or war preparation. Then, in Orwellian fashion, war itself comes packaged as a kind of peace system (Pax Americana, Pax Sovieticus). Yet in their more ordinary expressions, domestic peace systems (at least in democratic nations) provide us with imperfect but remarkably sturdy models for the kinds of structures and processes we will need for a successful global peace system.

Nature may provide the clearest example of a working peace system. Though nature lurches to extremes, its cycles revolve around a moderate center. It is unpredictable in its details, but reliable in its larger patterns. In a cultivated state, nature is sometimes a peace system, sometimes not. Monocultural farming, for example, is a kind of forced peace in which natural diversity is replaced by a single crop dependent upon the heavy use of chemical fertilizers and pesticides that eliminate benign along with troublesome organisms in soil, thus threatening one of the most essential qualities of living systems—accommodating conflict. The organic gardening and farming movement aims to strengthen these qualities of natural living systems by multiplying rather than replacing life, adding to its already abundant natural variety still more diversity and vitality.

Both the promise and problems of consciously designing a peace system have been brought home to me by the challenge of establishing a self-sufficient organic farm. My wife, Sandi, and I have been living on the edge of the woods for fifteen years now. We arrived with our baggage stuffed with the principles we hoped to uphold—to live lightly on the earth and to do no harm to any creature. Along the way we've had occasion to recall those words with more than a little irony and amusement.

We located ourselves in a meadow surrounded by deep wilderness. By planting several hundred fruit trees and ornamentals, we seem to have quickened the pace of life here. There are more birds in the trees, more worms in the ground, more wildflowers and lusher grasses. Planting willows, pines, eucalyptus and redbuds in a raw gully, Sandi has nursed it back to health and initiated what has now become a spontaneous process of healing in which grasses and trees she did not plant have begun to reseed themselves. A planned synergy is at work among the ornamentals she has planted, since they serve simultaneously as shelterbelts to break the wind, habitats for birds and other small creatures, forage for bees, and pleasure for people.

Yet we still need to consider defenses. Coons, skunks, and porcupines are common and deer run free in large herds. We succeeded in screening out the deer without harming them by building a six-foot-high fence around the perimeter of the meadow, but the coons and porcupines were undeterred. One porcupine harvested an entire year's strawberry crop. Jays saucily nibbled peaches they didn't even help to grow. Our neighbor, Jack, a devoted student of Zen, was beset one summer by several families of coons intent on harvesting his corn and fruit trees. Having been counseled by a Buddhist teacher in Sri Lanka that he had accumulated five hundred additional lifetimes on the Great Wheel for the murder of a porcupine a few years earlier, he proceeded with a heavy heart to accumulate six thousand more in the course of saving a remnant of his devastated crops.

We've given a lot of thought to how we might protect our creatures without threatening or killing their predators. Ultimately Sandi came up with a solution, a defense that protects without threat-

ening: an Akbash livestock guardian dog. For centuries, the great white Akbash has protected herds of sheep from both wolves and bears on the steppes of Asia Minor, often in the absence of the shepherd. But it is neither a herder nor a hunter. While the Akbash is extraordinarily strong, it is also uncommonly gentle. If raised with the animals it is to protect, the dog will bond with them as if it were their own mother. She will fiercely protect them from anything sensed as a threat, but only if it enters her territory. She has no impulse to initiate attack.

Have we established a successful peace system? "Peaceable kingdom, ha!" cried Sandi one afternoon a few years ago as she held up the corpse of a duckling, while Hannah, our terrier mix, cringed forlornly, in a corner of the garden, wondering what she'd done wrong. "Some peace system!," we laugh ruefully as we load the air gun to scatter the jays that peck at our just-ripe apricots. To be truthful, we've accumulated a few thousand extra lifetimes ourselves in the course of building this homestead peace system.

Despite the obvious disparity of scale and circumstance between a remote rural homestead and a global political system, there may be several clues to use in designing that larger system. The first is that despite one's best intentions, there is inevitably some violence in any system of human design. The second is that while one can't wholly eliminate such violence, one can do much to minimize it, not least of all by devising strategies which, like our Akbash, protect without threatening.

Observing natural systems at work around us on this farm, I've noticed several essential qualities. Peace as a whole system is:

> *Diverse:* A peace system at the global level would need to be extraordinarily flexible and open to a vast range of interests.

> *Evolutionary:* Evolution is a thoroughly experimental process, learning from its own mistakes and tending always toward greater complexity and connection throughout the system. Healthy political evolution, like its biological counterpart, is a highly imperfect process, but it is also self-correcting. Popularly elected parliaments and well-rooted

spontaneous citizen activism are two tools for self-correction.

Resilient, robust: Robust political peace systems inevitably contain small accumulations of "social diseases" that corrupt and abuse their institutions. Yet if they are resilient, they can withstand such minor plagues without losing their essential vitality.

Abundant, redundant: A wisely structured political peace system makes allowance for misfortune and mischief and builds redundancy into itself. Rather than depending on any single institution or group, it seeks to broaden and decentralize responsibilities so particular components may fail for periods of time without paralyzing the functions of the larger system. Successful complex systems are built on the integration of many simple systems. A global peace system must base itself on local peace systems that are already alive and thriving.

Symbiotic and synergistic: Just as the Pentagon, defense contractors, and academia coalesce in the synergistic war system popularly known as the "military–industrial complex," so it is possible to strengthen the synergy of a global peace system by improving communications and mutual aid among the myriad groups and institutions operating at the grassroots level. Together they could achieve far more than the sum of all their efforts made in isolation from one another.

Kristina Selvig and James Muller, Anti-Nuclear Activists

Sam Totten • Martha Wescoat Totten
With the Editorial Assistance of Brad Edmondson

Kristina Selvig

I am in Pacific Life Community, and my main interest is to stop nuclear arms proliferation and reverse the arms race. Currently, my energy is focused on the Trident missile and submarine system.

When I was seven years old my family moved from California to Mexico City, and I was suddenly confronted by a lot of poverty. In our country, we stick the poor people away in ghettos and never see them; but in Mexico, rich and poor are side by side, and that had quite an impact on me. I was about ten years old when I met a young woman my age who was of the peasant class. She lived down the street from me in a ravine, with no house or

Kristina Selvig and James Muller interviews from *Facing the Danger* ©1984 Sam Totten and Martha W. Totten. Published by The Crossing Press, Freedom CA. Reprinted by permission of the publisher.

anything; just some cardboard boxes strung together. I really liked her a lot. She had a wonderful, exuberant personality. But she was a secret friend, because I knew that I would get in trouble if I brought her into the house.

One day, when I was at my parents' country club, I happened to see her walk by and I invited her to come swimming with me. I was the only one in the pool. She had never been in a full body of water before, and she was just delighted—jumping and screaming and splashing. I was teaching her how to hold her breath under water, and we were having a great time.

But then the guard found us and he began yelling at her, telling her to get out. He was really cruel to her, and I think I really identified with the rejection and oppression she felt at the time. I think of this as a crucial moment in my life; for the first time, I had a sense of injustice and oppression and I wanted to do something about it.

I grew up with the desire to be a social worker, and I started school as a sociology major but I got really disillusioned. It was all theory, nothing real in the way of helping people. So I dropped out of school and began doing volunteer work teaching Indian children in Arizona.

I went back to school in 1978; I took classes in Black Studies at Cal State in L.A., reading about racism and slavery. Now prior to that, I had done a bit of reading about Nazi Germany. Because I come from a Christian perspective, one of the things that disturbed me was the question, "Where were the Christians?" Most of them, it turns out, were in their churches saying, "Heil Hitler." I was very upset to find this out and I said to myself, "If I were there, I hope I would have resisted. I would have done whatever I could to change that terrible situation." When I was studying about slavery, I found myself asking again: "Where were the Christians?" And by and large, most of them were in church saying, "Slaves, obey your masters." So this made a big impression on me; I didn't want to be a hypocritical Christian. And then I began asking myself, "Where is the crisis today?"

At that time, about three years ago, my husband brought home some tapes from a conference. These were speeches given by a radical

Christian named Clarence Jordan who, in the forties, had started an inter-racial community in Americus, Georgia. In the forties!

So I began listening to these tapes, and it's no exaggeration to say that they absolutely revolutionalized my life. Here was a Christian actually *doing* something about injustice. He started an integrated community at great cost to himself; the Klan burned down his barns, threatened his life and shot at him numerous times. He was boycotted to the extent that when his children were sick, no local doctor would see them. No one would buy their farm products, and he was thrown into jail countless times. Jordan's example really gave me a lot of hope, and he helped me to interpret Christianity in a different way. I began asking myself, "How do we change society?" And I thought, it's got to be a personal risk that does it. Anything less is not going to work.

Then I met Phil Berrigan when he came to L.A. to do a week-long conference on nuclear weapons. Phil talked to me about civil disobedience and it seemed very right to me—it just seemed to click. And it was through Phil that I began to find out about nuclear weapons. I knew nothing about them previously except once, when my husband had come home from a rally and began talking to me about reversing the arms race. I told him, "You're crazy. Why don't you pick something that would be a possibility?"

So I was skeptical, but I did go to one demonstration at Seal Beach, where they have nuclear weapons stored right next to an earthquake fault. There were about 200 of us there marching around and I was saying, "Well, this is ridiculous! What are we doing here?" It was a negative, depressing experience, but it was out of that sense of hopelessness that I came to feel that our only hope lies in some kind of spiritual revolution.

But at the same time, I didn't *want* to know about the bomb. I was very involved in black rights and anti-racism work at that time, and I didn't want to leave it. I believe that you're responsible for what you know and you have to act on what you know. So what I try to do is not know things! I couldn't avoid it, however. I made myself join Pacific Life Community.

Last April we went to the Pentagon for a week with 52 other activist groups; the protest was organized by Jonah House, a Baltimore community where Phil Berrigan lives. Each group had their own emphasis and their own concern, and we brought our concern for Trident. We went to the Pentagon every day for a week, and it was quite an experience. It deepened my commitment to the disarmament movement, but I was still fighting it. I was arrested and jailed on August 6, 1980 for pouring ashes and blood on the steps of the Lockheed building as a remembrance of Hiroshima.

Then on March 11, 1981, four of us from Pacific Life Community climbed over a security fence and entered Lockheed Building 182, where they make parts for the Trident missile. We got past two guard stations and an unlocked door that was supposed to be locked; we were looking for a section of the missile called the Interstage. Eventually we found it—in a huge room with gigantic sliding doors. There were big signs on the wall that said, "Keep these doors closed at all times," but they were wide open.

There were no workers in the room, but there were four interstage sections. We had bottles of our own blood which we used as a symbol to signify that these are weapons of death. We use symbols because words don't mean anything anymore. You can talk and talk and.... We feel that the symbols say things that words cannot. We do our actions in hopes that the symbols will penetrate into people's hearts.

We found an unlocked cabinet full of blueprints and order forms, and we pulled stacks of them out and labelled them with blood. People were walking by and watching us, but no one did anything. Then we poured blood on ourselves, again as a symbol to the workers that this will be the end result of their work. Then we sat in a circle and prayed for an end to the arms race. Eventually we were arrested and led out of the building—and as we left, all the workers were watching us.

We were charged with trespassing, which is a misdemeanor. The next day they added a charge of burglary, which has a maximum three year

sentence, and vandalism, which added another possible year. A few days later they added conspiracy—three years—and another trespassing count for six months. We were facing an eight year maximum possible sentence.

We pleaded not guilty at the arraignment, but at the preliminary hearing we decided to admit to what we did, as part of our commitment to truth and nonviolence. We pleaded no contest, which is admitting it without admitting guilt. You see, we feel that Lockheed is the guilty party here. They ended up dropping some of the charges, and now we face a three and a half year maximum sentence. We'll be sentenced this Friday.

We won't accept probation. This is why: we feel that these weapons exist because in our own lives, we have replaced a spirit of love and truth with a spirit of hate and mistrust and discord. And we feel that one way to reverse that is to speak truthfully, whatever the consequences. To accept probation would be to accept silence, and when you accept silence, the spirit of truth dies. We will not agree to probation because we won't be silenced. To agree to silence is to allow the evil to continue.

Gandhi has taught us that the means and the ends are the same; if your end is truth, your means also have to be truth. If we accept probation and silence, we compromise the truth and we undermine everything we believe to be true.

I believe that the truth is what makes a person free, whether or not he or she is in jail. I'm discovering that the more I commit myself to the truth, no matter what it's going to cost, the freer I become. That has been an exciting discovery for me; it has released tremendous feelings of exhilaration.

I think it's my Christian and human duty to address the problems of the bomb. I have great qualms about obeying laws which are unjust and life-threatening, even if we *are* taught from birth to obey the law. Blind obedience to unjust laws is creating a nation of zombies, who are following their leaders and willingly drinking at the nuclear kool-aid vat. And so, I never ask if I'm successful. I ask, "Am I faithful and am I truthful?" I leave the success up to God.

James Muller

I am 40 years old. People of my generation have a different attitude toward nuclear weapons; we grew up hiding from bombs under our school desks. I think that we're the generation which will have to remove nuclear weapons from this planet.

I went to college at Notre Dame, starting as a physics major and then switching to pre-med. I had no interest whatsoever in nuclear weapons or the arms race, but I did study Russian to fulfill a language requirement. I attended med school at Johns Hopkins, and during my second year I heard a lecture by the president, Russell Nelson, on his trip to the Soviet Union. I had six months of elective time, so I thought to myself why not go to the Soviet Union? So I went to the president of the hospital and he said that it was a wonderful idea—he began looking for a way for me to go.

He found an exchange program for graduate students in Slavic studies through the State Department; I was accepted, and once I knew I was going, I began to read up on nuclear weapons. I found *Sanity and Survival* by Dr. Jerome Frank, an extremely valuable book. Then, I guess, I began to think a lot about nuclear war. I began getting a picture of what it would be like. Working in the emergency room, I saw a couple of severely burned patients—their bodies and the awful smell. I saw only two patients, but I began to multiply that times thousands; I began to get a sense of what a nuclear war would be.

Once this idea struck me, I became an absolute idiot; I couldn't eat well for six months, I lost a lot of weight and I began talking with everyone I knew about the necessity of preventing nuclear war. They all said, "You're crazy. Why bother? Don't worry about it." So I was like an outcast, a Don Quixote figure. In 1967, I felt like I had to prevent nuclear war—that it was up to me.

I also read Senator Fulbright's book, *The Arrogance Of Power,* which argued that the way to prevent nuclear war is to build areas of common interest with the Soviet Union. So I thought what more common area of interest is there than medicine?

So eventually I made an appointment to see Senator Fulbright. I went down to Washington and essentially volunteered my services to enlarge the Soviet–American health exchange. He said, "What do you want me to do about it?" I said, "I don't know; I read your book and liked your ideas, and I'm asking for your advice." He said, "Well, I can't do anything about it. That's an executive branch decision." And he sort of shuffled me out of the office.

So I started investigating the Soviet–American health exchange on my own, and I found that it was very small; the people who administered it were very anti-Soviet, and they were basically trying to keep the Russians from getting access to American medical technology. I went back to President Nelson at Hopkins and persuaded him to let me set up an independent medical exchange program with the Soviets.

I went to the Soviet Union and spent six months there; I lived with Russian students, stood in the streets and watched the missiles go by during their parades. I talked with the people about nuclear war and found out that they don't want it any more than we do, despite all our propaganda. They remember World War II. I came back to America totally committed to building up these exchange programs.

When I got back, Martin Luther King and Bobby Kennedy had been shot and I'd missed six months of med school. I went from being one of the best students to being the worst. It was a very depressing time for me; I felt as if my outside activism had diminished my professional career. The exchange program I wanted to set up fell apart; I got back to studying and put the nuclear war issue out of my mind.

Then about two years later, when I was in the Public Health Service, I worked with the Assistant Secretary of Health, Education and Welfare just before he was to make a trip to Moscow. I mentioned my health exchange idea to him and he was excited by it—in fact, he took me with him. I met the Russian Minister of Health and all the Russian health officials. In 1970, we proposed a broad expansion of health exchange programs with the Russians. The time was right.

In 1972 the Soviet–American Health Exchange was enlarged and we announced a joint war on heart disease, cancer and environmental problems. I was the aide for those delegations. I set all that up, and the primary reason I did it was to prevent nuclear war.

I went back to my internal medicine residency at Hopkins, and in 1973 I came here to Harvard to do research on heart disease. I worked for Dr. Eugene Braunwald, a famous cardiologist and professor here. Braunwald arranged for some joint Soviet–American research on heart attacks through Brezhnev's doctor, Eugene Chazov. In 1975 I went to Russia again to direct a study of heart attacks in five Russian hospitals. The study went very well and I thought, "Isn't this wonderful. I got a chance to give an interview to the *Washington Post* showing how nations can work together to prevent a war." But the headlines on the story read, "American Doctor Experiments on Soviet Patients." It was reinforcing all the old Cold War stereotypes. A very distressing experience.

About two and a half years ago I was walking from the hospital to my office and I began thinking about the arms race, the neutron bomb and this new movement toward first-strike capability. And I thought we simply have to do something. So I tried again. I went to Dr. Bernard Lown, a professor at the School of Public Health here who has worked with the Russians on health cooperation programs. Lown admitted that he'd been having similar thoughts that the Russian doctors might work with us. So he wrote a letter to Brezhnev's doctor to propose that American and Soviet physicians join in the struggle against nuclear weapons. We got a wonderful letter back from Dr. Chazov saying yes, they would like to try. And this was the beginning of the International Physicians for the Prevention of Nuclear War.

In the early stages of the group Lown and I wrote to Chazov. Then we were joined by Dr. Eric Chivian who had run the first Harvard symposium on nuclear weapons and their health effects. The fourth to become involved was Dr. Herbert Abrams, who is a professor of radiology here. We four wrote to some leading American physicians and asked if they would like to join an effort against the nuclear arms race; most of them said yes. So we put their names on the letter and sent it out to more leaders, and more people said yes. Then we went to the press and said, "Here's the group." The press found it extremely interesting; we got articles in the *Boston Globe* and *Time,* and *The New York Times* has carried three or four articles on our movement. All of this attention culminated in the first conference in March of 1981; we had doctors there from twelve countries.

So the effort has gone incredibly well so far. We did it initially with no money, but when we started getting attention, we began to contact foundations. We raised about $200,000 and hired a full-time staff. It really took off! Now, Canada, France, Israel, Japan, the Netherlands, Norway, Sierra Leone, Sweden, the United Kingdom, the Soviet Union, West Germany and the United States are all members of the IPPNW. We're adding more countries all the time.

I believe that this group's greatest strength is that we are bilateral—Soviet and American. We have prominent doctors on both sides agreeing that these weapons should be eliminated. It's extraordinary. We have tried to maintain our position as a group of medical professionals, not as apologists for one country or another. We're not being painted into a corner by the press or anyone else, either, because we're concerned about the whole nuclear arms race.

There are about four hundred people out there playing nuclear chess right now, and there are about three billion people whose lives are in jeopardy. We're the spokesmen for the three or four billion who say that the arms race should not go on.

In May of '82, Dr. Lown and I were on an airplane bound for Washington to receive a message from Brezhnev at the Soviet Embassy. The IPPNW had asked him, "When we go to Moscow for the World Congress on Cardiology, what could we do that might help the nuclear weapons cause?" We decided to try to go on Soviet national television.

So we met with Ambassador Dobrynin and proposed the idea; he said, "Why not try it?" We got a call several weeks later from the representa-

TOTTEN & TOTTEN / KRISTINA SELVIG AND JAMES MULLER, ANTI-NUCLEAR ACTIVISTS

tive of Soviet TV in the United States, and he said that the show had been approved and was scheduled. I called the producers of the show in Moscow, and they asked for us to send a proposal.

So I sent a letter—an unbelievably arrogant letter, really. I said that we wanted an hour of prime time on national television, uncensored and unedited. I asked for the American press to be there to watch the filming. I said that we would discuss the topics of limited nuclear war, the medical effects of Hiroshima, accidental nuclear war, the economics of the arms race, and on and on. I also proposed that a Russian doctor should make a speech to the American people, and that I would speak to the Russian people. And it turned out that when we went to Moscow, that's exactly what we got. The Soviets were *extremely* positive about this idea. So I immediately began to draft my speech; I felt that this was something I had been waiting to do for many, many years. I was ecstatic over the opportunity.

The show was considered an historic event by the American correspondents in Moscow. We had a close call where the Soviets almost didn't allow American press into the studio. *That* would have been a disaster, because it would have erased the show's credibility in the eyes of Americans. But after a flurry of midnight calls the night before, we did get the opportunity to let American press in and about twenty correspondents attended.

Six of us spoke. There were three Americans and three from the Soviet Union; it was estimated that over 50 million people watched the original telecast. There was a repeat broadcast and worldwide distribution—it's now estimated that over 200 million people have seen it.

The response to the show, in general, has been extremely positive. The Soviets we talked to say that it was just an extremely important event for them; we were told that the phones weren't ringing for an hour when the show ran, because so many were watching it. I have a friend from Johns Hopkins who saw it in Central Asia. So it really did go out. That speech may have been the most important thing I've ever done.

While still in the Soviet Union I went around and asked people if they had heard of the doctor's movement against nuclear weapons, and most of them had. I remember one conversation I had with a woman in the Aeroflot office, the airline office; she said, "We began realizing the danger when the doctors started talking about it. As a matter of fact, my mother now cries every night when she goes to bed because of the threat of war. She says that if the doctors are warning against it, then it must be a real danger. She says she thinks it's going to happen." So it's there! The feeling is there among the Soviet people.

Now Dr. Chazov has told us that he is a national hero in the Soviet Union because of the speech. The Supreme Soviet gave him a standing ovation, and when he went back to his home town there were crowds chanting his name.

All of these events have had a profound effect on me. I'm convinced now that we are in the midst of an effort to change the way that people think about force and security; especially since the Catholic Church hierarchy has gotten involved in the disarmament movement, I believe that a basic shift in consciousness is occurring now, worldwide. Somebody ought to be screaming that this is wrong: to build weapons and hold four billion hostages with the threat of being burned to death is just plain wrong! It's immoral. And I think that more than anything else, this issue of morality will be the thing that stops the arms race. People stopped slavery because it was *wrong*. This nuclear arms race is wrong!

What gives me the energy to keep going is my own vision of the event of a nuclear war; I think that anyone who sees that and *really* thinks about it would have a hard time working on anything else. At certain times, I've been very frightened. When we first started this movement with the Russian doctors, none of us could sleep at night. We'd wake up dreaming of nuclear war; we'd see the burned patients, the whole disaster. Now I don't feel the same fear. Our organization is firm, it's got a good image and there are thousands of doctors working on the problem. We're not alone.

Making War: Soldiers in Vietnam

Mark Baker

Six Vietnam veterans describe their experiences: being recruited, working as "grunts" or foot soldiers in Vietnam, and becoming victors and victims.

Recruitment: Ask Not . . .

It's just a little town where I grew up. I played some football and baseball like everybody else. I was kind of a hard-ass in school. I didn't know how good I had it then. I took little odd jobs and saved up enough money to buy an electric guitar and an amplifier. I started playing in a band.

Near the end of high school, everybody's saying, "What you going to do? What you going to do?" I didn't know. I said, "I'm going to join the service." After I graduated, I went into the Marine Corps. They were supposed to be the best. To me, they were. They helped me grow up. I grew up in Vietnam.

■

My old man, when the war came, he says, "Oh, go. You'll learn something. You'll grow up to be a man. Go."

Shit, if my folks had to send their little poodle, they would have cried more tears over that than over me. But I'm supposed to go, because I'm a man.

■

The bus pulls into the receiving area. There's a guy with a Smokey Bear hat out there really looking lean and mean. He gets on the bus and starts reeling this shit off, "All right, you'll grab your bag. You'll get off the bus. You'll fall into the yellow footprints painted on the pavement . . ."

It was really funny, a take-off from *Gomer Pyle*. The guy within arm's reach of the Marine was laughing just like everybody else. Smokey Bear whipped around and smacked him right in the face, knocked him halfway through the window. His head bounced off the luggage rack and he reeled back out in the aisle.

Smiles froze on faces. My heart stopped. We realized, "Hey, this guy isn't fooling around. He's going to come through this bus and kick all our asses." People started flying out of the door.

I came down with a couple of guys who were Puerto Rican street gang material from the big city and they thought they were bad news. They fell down the steps on top of me. We all stumble into the right footprints on the ground and Smokey marches us into some barracks and stands us at attention. He's yelling and screaming, really intimidating. You dumped all of your stuff out on a table and he went by and just threw everything away. We were too scared to say anything to him.

I was next to this big Puerto Rican dude. Smokey catches the dude looking at him out of the corner of his eye. He says, "Are you eye-fucking me, boy? I don't want your scuzzy eyes looking at me. You think this is funny? I hope you fuck up. I hate you Puerto Rican cocksuckers."

Eyes in the back of his head, Smokey sees a guy's eyes flick and he's there to punch him in the chest, five feet to the wall and back again. My knees were shaking. "What the fuck have I gotten myself into?"

Then they march us into some barracks. Bare mattresses and springs. It's like a concentration camp. They turn the lights on and leave us there. My stomach is in a knot. I'm lying there thinking, "What happened to my world?" Reality has suddenly turned to liquid shit before my very eyes. Kids were crying, rolling in their bunks. I'm so depressed, I can't believe this is happening to me.

We're there for a couple of hours. You're in your civilian clothes and you've been in them for a couple of days. You feel like shit. When they march you out, all of a sudden it's by the numbers. All your hair's gone. You don't even know who you are. You get a duffel bag and they're dumping things in it. Everybody hates you and they're fucking with you left and right. You get your shots. You stand at attention. People are passing out on their feet. Going rigid and falling on their faces and the corpsmen are laughing at them. Nobody talks to you, they scream. Nothing they give you fits. You look like shit and you feel like shit. A bunch of drill instructors put you back in receiving and that's when the shit really hits the fan.

■   ■   ■

Grunts in Vietnam

It'd get daylight. You get water out of a shell hole and throw your halazone tablets in there so you could brush your teeth. We were pretty ragged, but you sweat yourself clean every day. Then you pull out a piece of C4—plastic explosive—and light it up to heat your food.

I get out the map. Okay, we've got to go up the blue line, which would be a river. We'd walk down the side of the mountain into the valley. It was harder walking down mountains than walking up.

There were scout snipers with us, so I would use the scope on one of their rifles to check out where we were going. You could see the veins on leaves with those things. I'd send out the flanks for protection of the main body, so we couldn't be

ambushed from the sides. It was tough on the flanks, because they had to hack through the bush. The rest of us would be walking down by the river bank, so we had to wait up for the guys out there on either side from time to time.

You'd hump your God damn brains out, up hills, over rocks, through water. Sometimes it was hand over hand through the roots of trees. You sweat your balls off with the sun beating down on your head.

Ninety percent of the time, nothing happened, just boring, a walk in the sun, like sightseeing. But you're always aware that you could get blown away. You always protect yourself tactically to make sure your ass is covered. Just the dispersion of your people insures that you can put down suppressing fire.

You're hunting the smartest animal there is and that's a human being. You can't believe how fucking smart a man is. If you get one, it's blind luck. In the entire time I was over there, we got one confirmed kill on a day patrol out of battalion. It's their show, you're in their backyard.

Hump through the paddies and into the villes. A ville would just be a few bamboo hooches with dirt floors in a little clearing. Each one had a little shrine inside. There would always be cooking. Their diet was very hot, fish heads and peppers, that type of thing. You never saw any men or even teen-agers, just small children, women and old men.

They pray to their Buddha, go out to work the paddy. Come home, go to sleep. A very simple life. A water buffalo was the family car.

"Honcho, hey honcho," the kids come running out of the ville. "Cigmo, you got cigmo, Joe? Chop-chop, you got chop-chop?"

You tell them, *"Didi, didi mao."* Get the fuck away. They'd swear up and down at you. The war had been going on so long there that these kids never had a childhood. You'd be in a fire fight in the middle of a paddy someplace and they would just go right on about their business—a woman and her son with a bucket tied to a rope whipping water over a dike from one paddy to another, old women humping what looked like 150 pounds of brush across their backs.

Westmoreland used to make me crazy with all that bullshit about winning the hearts and minds of the people. Sometimes you felt like trash walking through these villes. Some of the people were beautiful, aristocratic, more civilized than you ever thought of being. They'd come up to you and say, "America and Americans are No. 1. Vietnam is No. 10. You got girl friend? You should be with her. We don't want you here." Who was it that wanted us there?

Sometimes it was beautiful. We were in a bamboo forest and came upon an old Buddhist temple with vines climbing all over it, big Buddhas, brightly colored with reverse swastikas and leaf designs. It felt like being the first explorer to walk into the ruins of Angkor Wat. The monks came out to meet me. I set out some security and made everybody entering the compound take off their weapons. I knew we weren't going to get any trouble from them. They were very educated men, very holy men.

I was constantly fatigued. The killing part is easy but you're just so fucking tired all the fucking time. Your strength is zapped out of your body by the heat. Waiting in a column going down a hill, you go to sleep leaning against a tree. Every day you're out on patrol. Intelligence says they're out there, so here you go walking around in little geometric triangles. Go to this checkpoint, go to that checkpoint, go here, go there. Day in, day out, day in, day out. You get into a mind-numbing routine and before long you're a fucking zombie.

Humans are out there watching you. They know where you're going before you even get there. You see them running very far away in their straw hats and black outfits.

We had a constant attrition from booby traps, seven out of ten casualties a month were traumatic amputees. On a sweep you all get in a long line and walk in. You're watching every place you step wondering who's going to hit it. You know someone is going to. Sweep and sweep and sweep, halfway through the day and nothing's happened. Are we going to hit a booby trap today? Who will it be? It was mentally draining.

Boom! Just like that and a guy is missing a leg, somebody is missing a foot. Everything stops for a second and there's a lot of action on the radio. A chopper comes down to pick him up. *Zoom,* he's gone. I thought, "Boy, there's going to be a lot of people walking around after this war with no feet." But I still haven't seen them. Where are they?

Then you're back at it again, hunting humans. I hope one shows up, man. I'm going to blow that motherfucker to kingdom come. If the world could only see me now. This is bad news out here and I am bad. We are armed to the teeth. If I could get back to the States with my platoon intact, I could take over the world. Somebody fuck with me, just somebody fuck with me. Come and get me.

When they came to get you—holy shit. I can't even talk on the radio to call in the fire mission. I'm warbling like a kid going through puberty. You swallow slowly and force yourself to say the coordinates. Everything hits slow motion, like you're in your own movie. You try to be cool, calm and collected, and you are... kind of. You certainly ain't John Wayne.

Where's it coming from? Who's getting hit? I don't want to die. You can see everything that's happening in immediate terms—life-and-death terms.

When something went right in a fire fight—you call in a fire mission real good, you get your fields of fire right, deploy your men so that you outflank them and you stand up and walk right through them—it's thrilling. There's nothing like it. It's so real. Talk about getting high, this is beyond drugs—ultrareality.

There's nothing like a confirmed kill either. They make you crazy. You want more. You know everybody back at battalion will look at you with envy when you get back in. You scored a touchdown in front of the hometown fans. You get a lot of respect from your peers who are all doing the same thing. When somebody else got one, you'd go, "Son of a bitch, the lucky bastards. Why couldn't we have been there?"

All of a sudden that's over with. It's something everybody talks about to mark the days. A point of reference. You tell the new guys about it. "Hey, remember the day that motherfucker, Jay-Jay, jumped up in the middle of that fire fight, man?"

Then you go back to the mind-numbing routine. You're a zombie again. Take a walk in the boonies.

It starts getting dark, you occupy the high ground. You set up the perimeter, send out the LPs—guys on watch called listening posts. No big deal. I was always near the radio, nothing much happened anyway.

But then the sun would go down and I could feel my stomach sinking. There goes the light. There goes one of your senses, the most important one. Life stops. There's no electricity. There's no technology. It's just hovels made out of corrugated tin and Coke boxes, cardboard, sticks, thatch. There's nothing else over there. The only technology you have is death: M-16s—black plastic rifles—grenades, pocket bombs, Claymores, M-79s, M-60s, mortars, jungle utilities, flak jackets, jungle boots, C4, radios and jet planes to drop the napalm. That was the only technology happening.

You think about people back in the world walking around downtown, going out to get a beer. You'd be staring into the dark so hard, you'd have to reach up and touch your eyes to make sure they were still open.

You try to sleep out there on operations. I'd take off my helmet and my flak jacket and arrange the plates in the jacket just right to fit my back. Then I'd tip my helmet and get my head just right in the webbing. I never went anywhere without my lucky green towel. I'd wrap it around my face with just a little hole for my nose. Put on my long sleeve utilities, tuck my hands up under my armpits and just listen to the mosquitoes whine all night long. You know one is going to fly right up your nose and suck the blood out of your brain. It was miserable.

You know it's going to be the same tomorrow as it was today. . . only maybe it might be worse. It won't be any better. We had a saying about how bad a thing could be: As bad as a day in the Nam.

· · ·

Victors

I was enjoying the feel. There was a couple of guys saying they didn't enjoy the feel. That was junk. We had a sense that we was no longer that GI who had to march, who had to salute. That was shit. We didn't have to salute nobody. We dressed the way we wanted to dress. If I wanted to wear the boony hat, I wore the boony hat. If I wanted one sleeve up and one sleeve down, I did it. If I didn't want to shave, I didn't. Nobody fucked with nobody in the field. An officer knows if he messed with you in the field, in a fire fight you could shoot him in the head. This was standard procedure in any infantry unit. Anybody tells you differently, he's shitting you.

If you mess with my partner as an NCO or something like that, in the unwritten code there, I had the right to blow your brains out. And the guys would do it. Those lieutenants and the CO didn't mess with nobody in the field. They didn't say, "Hey, soldier, why is your boot unbloused? Why is your hair long?" Everybody just said fuck it.

I had a sense of power. A sense of destruction. See, now, in the United States a person is babied. He's told what to do. You can't carry a gun, unless you want to go to jail. If you shoot somebody, it's wrong. You're constantly babied till you go to the grave. The only people's got the authority is the judges or the Establishment.

But in the Nam you realized that you had the power to take a life. You had the power to rape a woman and nobody could say nothing to you. That godlike feeling you had was in the field. It was like I was a god. I could take a life, I could screw a woman. I can beat somebody up and get away with it. It was a godlike feeling that a guy could express in the Nam.

· · ·

Victims

When I changed divisions, I started catching all kinds of shit. First I was wearing a bush hat, which they weren't quite ready for. Plus I had a Fu-Manchu and they said that was too long. What about my boots? They weren't shiny enough. And I had something around my neck that wasn't my dog tags. My dog tags were stuck in my boots. You unlace your boot and put one dog tag on each foot so they don't make no sound at night when you're moving.

These guys all thought that I was a short-timer. I *was* salty. But you could also tell the difference in the units I had been with. By the time I got there, I had seen a lot of action. I got me a Bronze Star. I forgot how many fire fights I'd been in. Some of these guys could count their fire fights on one hand without using three fingers. Never saw anybody. Some of them had no kills. And they was tedious about the boots and uniform. That seems like a small thing, but it annoyed me.

The first fire fight, the gun squad leader panicked. He don't know if either one of his guns opened up. He don't know where he is supposed to set up his guns at. The gunner was stationary doing nothing but freezing.

Instinct for survival took over. I snatched the gun out of his hand and started working with it. I told the a-gunner, "Get up and walk with me! Do something! But get up and get me some more ammo." I yelled, "Ammo up! Ammo up! There's no ammo coming to me. They are shooting from behind these little rocks—but nobody is bringing ammo to me. I had to run around back to where they were and tell them, "Give me this God damn ammo."

I got recommended right there and they made me the squad leader. They demoted my man and got rid of him.

Later, the gun-team leader, name of Browne, and his best friend and brother-in-law, White—they both had these funny color names—came over to see me. They was from the same neighborhood, real college kids, the whole works. Browne didn't like me being the squad leader, because he thought he was going to be promoted automatically when the guy that panicked left. He said, "Well, you're short, so I'm going to get squad leader anyway. You're going to leave soon."

"I ain't that short," I said, "I got me awhile to go." Come to find out we came in-country a month apart. I had him by a month. "But don't worry," I told him, "one day you can have the gun squad. I plan to get the fuck out of here. I don't want the fucking machine gun anyway."

I started working my gun squad. They were breaking down the guns and cleaning them, but they would take their time and bullshit around, always cleaning them in daylight. I had them breaking down and cleaning the gun blindfolded. "Why we doing this?" they ask me.

"Because I say so. If I get any lip, you suckers are running."

"We're what?" I was a madman to them.

"You're not going to get me killed. I already seen what you guys can do in a fire fight. Which is nothing."

The gunny was with me, so pretty soon the whole platoon is cracking down their weapons and putting them back together, doing what they're told and not questioning, responding to sounds, listening. The lieutenant we had, he thought it was kind of funny. I looked at him and thought to myself, that fool is going to get killed. I knew he wasn't going to make it. He didn't.

The captain started volunteering us for a lot of bullshit. Any time something came up—like going to find somebody to kill—he volunteered us. Before, the company wasn't really finding nothing. So the captain was getting desperate. He wanted to make major and he could only do that by getting into fire fights and getting the body counts.

I just wanted my men to survive. If I got to count on these men and all they know how to do is hide behind rocks, they are going to get me killed. I ain't ready for it.

About this time, a kid came in-country and for some reason I took him under my wing. He was one skinny fellow, Stanley. He was a rich kid, sure-enough rich. He would tell me about when he turned eighteen his family bought him a home on so much acres, about his Jaguar XKE and shit.

I couldn't understand this guy. He would take his drinking water and wash his hands before he'd eat. I said, "When you run out of water, what you going to have to drink? You're going to be sorry. What you going to do, ask somebody for some of their water? They ain't going to give it to you. It's one thing if you drink your water. If you need more, they'll give it to you. There's no doubt about that. But you take your drinking water and waste it washing, that's different. You're going to have to learn to eat with dirty hands."

"Well, okay. I'll see," was all he said. He was

funny because he couldn't grow a beard—had this scraggly beard. Stanley didn't drink and he had had sex once in his life up to that point. The only black person he remembered seeing in his life was the maid and the chauffeur. He claimed there was three black brothers in his school, but he said you couldn't tell they were black.

"I saw your guys rioting and stuff on TV," Stanley said, "and that's all I know." It tickled him that when we sat down and talked, he found out, hey, we were people just like him. We had different life-styles, but we're still people. He got an education that he would have never got if he hadn't been in the service. It was beneficial to him. He started understanding.

For instance, the Vietnamese used to ask us, "Why are you over here fighting when you can't even live where you want back in America?" That was a true statement. We all understood it, but Stanley couldn't understand. It was a matter of me trying to explain to him and trying to get him to not see color when he sees me or any of the other men in his platoon. His life depended on that. If he sees color, then he's never going to help some black dude. "Oh, that's just a nigger, I don't know if I'm going to risk my life for that." If he let the black dudes know how he felt, then they may say, "Why should I help him? He's into the prejudice thing." We didn't have time for that. Color over there was petty. I had pride in being black. But I also had pride in being a Marine. A lot of men had to have their lives thrown on the line to relate to that.

I made corporal when we took this hill called Razor Back about three times. We would go up there, spend a week and leave. Each time we lost men. There ain't nothing on the stupid-ass hill. It's out in the middle of bullshit. Walk up it getting killed and walk down the other side again. We did that three times.

Then we decided to do our own Tet on that area. Our recon had spotted units all over the place and we were going all out on a Search and Destroy. When we pulled into the staging area, as far as the eye could see was Marines and the sky was full of choppers. The choppers were picking them up and taking them to the damn hills, running out and running back as fast as they could.

You could hear sniper fire hitting the chopper as we came to the LZ. The chopper gunners were firing down. I did my praying. Everybody was making the Sign of the Cross or closing their eyes to pray like me. I said, "This is the big one now." I been in a lot of fire fights, but this one scared the hell out of me. I was more scared than I had been in my very first fire fight. And I was *scared* then.

As we ran off, we hit the ground. I seen gooks running up the hill firing, our guys running after them like a damn movie. They'd pop their heads up, guys were taking potshots at them. Everybody had 200 rounds of ammunition for the machine gunners, one or two rockets, M-16 ammo and one mortar round. We were throwing the mortar rounds over to the mortarmen, taking the M-60 ammo to the gunner, trying to get the rockets over to the rocket men. They were going to get us killed delivering this crap to each other. The guys were in their holes. We were losing a lot of men but there were gooks falling a lot, too.

We finally wound up securing the hill just as it's starting to get dark. I looked at Stanley and this other kid named Donald who wasn't in-country even three months. Stanley had taken a liking to him, tried to take him under his wing. I was just telling them, "I want you to keep your heads down. Keep your eyes open. We got snipers up here."

Stanley responded like I was telling him. Donald took his time and was laughing. They were sitting behind a little knoll. Donald sits up facing away from the outside of the perimeter. As I was telling him to keep his eyes open, all of a sudden there's this pow!

The bullet went through Donald's upper shoulder, came out of his chest and went through Stanley's arm. Stanley panicked.

When it hit the kid, he didn't die right away. His guts were hanging out his mouth and nose. He like coughed them up when he was shot. That hurt me. I didn't really have a chance to be working with him, to teach him how to stay alive, because by the time he came, we was on the run constantly. He didn't learn how to do what you told him instantly, when he was told to do it.

He looked at me and all I could see were the tears in his eyes. It was like he was saying, "I'm alive, but what do I do? I'm dying."

I debated whether I should put a bullet in his head and take him out of his misery. For some reason, I couldn't do it. I looked at him, he was a young kid. He was seventeen when his parents signed for him to get in the service.

Stanley went into shock. I yelled at him, "Get down to the chopper, get out of here! You're going home." Stanley was groggy. He kept asking, "What? What happened to Donnie? What?"

I was getting Stanley out of there, because I took a liking to him. I grabbed him by his collar and started yanking him and running him down to the chopper. He yelled, "No! Wait!"

"There ain't no waiting," I said. "There's nothing up on this hill that you want." He kept looking at the other kid. See, Stanley got close to him. If Stanley had stayed there, he would have died.

I ran him down to where the chopper had landed to pick up the wounded. I threw Stanley toward it and said, "Write me one day. But now you're going home." The chopper took off and he looked back at me and started to wave. I turned away. You know, fuck it. Lay down. Then I got the fuck back up the hill.

By then Donald was dead and we laid him over and got him in a poncho. I said, "Get him out of here. I don't want him up here. Get him down." I wanted him away from the top of that knoll . . . So I could have somebody else up to cover that spot.

We wound up getting the sniper and a couple of others.

The next day, Browne, the lieutenant and that particular squad he was hooked up with went on patrol around the area. Our mortars sitting up on top of the hill said they saw movement in the valley but didn't check with a living soul to find out if we had a patrol out or not. They opened up on them.

They fucked up Browne and killed the lieutenant and a couple of other guys. When we tried to get to them, the Viet Cong had their snipers nearby. Every time one of our people got near, the snipers would pick them off one at a time. So we had to leave Browne down there overnight, alive.

When we went down the next morning trying to get Browne, he was trying to wave the corpsmen off, like don't touch me. But before we could tell them not to touch him, they flipped him over. He was booby trapped. It blew out his side. They didn't mean to hurt him. They thought they was doing right. They had on gas masks because we had opened up the tear gas. The glass in the eyepieces of the masks busted on their eyes, so about four of them were blinded instantly. Besides that they killed Browne really. He was still alive when we pulled him out—but he was dead. His whole side was blown out, there was nothing there.

I'll never forget Browne's eyes. He looked at me and he tried to smile. White, his brother-in-law, looked at him. I had to send White home—he cracked. They had been too close. I felt sorry for both of them. But Browne was eventually going to be out of his misery. White, his man, was going to have to live with the whole idea. They thought they was going to go home together. A lot of guys got hurt bad trying to take that stupid hill.

Why Men Love War

William Broyles, Jr.

I last saw Hiers in a rice paddy in Vietnam. He was nineteen then—my wonderfully skilled and maddeningly insubordinate radio operator. For months we were seldom more than three feet apart. Then one day he went home, and fifteen years passed before we met by accident last winter at the Vietnam Veterans Memorial in Washington. A few months later I visited Hiers and his wife, Susan, in Vermont, where they run a bed-and-breakfast place. The first morning we were up at dawn trying to save five newborn rabbits. Hiers built a nest of rabbit fur and straw in his barn and positioned a lamp to provide warmth against the bitter cold.

"What people can't understand," Hiers said, gently picking up each tiny rabbit and placing it in the nest, "is how much fun Vietnam was. I loved it. I loved it, and I can't tell anybody."

∎

Hiers loved war. And as I drove back from Vermont in a blizzard, my children asleep in the back of the car, I had to admit that for all these years I also had loved it, and more than I knew. I hated war, too. Ask me, ask any man who has been to war about his experience, and chances are we'll say we don't want to talk about it—implying that we hated it so much, it was so terrible, that we would rather leave it buried. And it is no mystery why men hate war. War is ugly, horrible, evil, and it is reasonable for men to hate all that. But I believe that most men who have been to war would have to admit, if they are honest, that somewhere inside themselves they loved it too, loved it as much as anything that has happened to them before

or since. And how do you explain that to your wife, your children, your parents, or your friends?

That's why men in their sixties and seventies sit in their dens and recreation rooms around America and know that nothing in their life will equal the day they parachuted into St. Lô or charged the bunker on Okinawa. That's why veterans' reunions are invariably filled with boozy awkwardness, forced camaraderie ending in sadness and tears: you are together again, these are the men who were your brothers, but it's not the same, can never be the same. That's why when we returned from Vietnam we moped around, listless, not interested in anything or anyone. Something had gone out of our lives forever, and our behavior on returning was inexplicable except as the behavior of men who had lost a great—perhaps the great—love of their lives, and had no way to tell anyone about it.

In part we couldn't describe our feelings because the language failed us: the civilian-issue adjectives and nouns, verbs and adverbs, seemed made for a different universe. There were no metaphors that connected the war to everyday life. But we were also mute, I suspect, out of shame. Nothing in the way we are raised admits the possibility of loving war. It is at best a necessary evil, a patriotic duty to be discharged and then put behind us. To love war is to mock the very values we supposedly fight for. It is to be insensitive, reactionary, a brute.

But it may be more dangerous, both for men and nations, to suppress the reasons men love war than to admit them. In *Apocalypse Now* Robert

Duvall, playing a brigade commander, surveys a particularly horrific combat scene and says, with great sadness, "You know, someday this war's gonna be over." He is clearly meant to be a psychopath, decorating enemy bodies with playing cards, riding to war with Wagner blaring. We laugh at him—Hey! nobody's like that! And last year in Grenada American boys charged into battle playing Wagner, a new generation aping the movies of Vietnam the way we aped the movies of World War II, learning nothing, remembering nothing.

Alfred Kazin wrote that war is the enduring condition of twentieth-century man. He was only partly right. War is the enduring condition of man, period. Men have gone to war over everything from Helen of Troy to Jenkins's ear. Two million Frenchmen and Englishmen died in muddy trenches in World War I because a student shot an archduke. The truth is, the reasons don't matter. There is a reason for every war and a war for every reason.

For centuries men have hoped that with history would come progress, and with progress, peace. But progress has simply given man the means to make war even more horrible; no wars in our savage past can begin to match the brutality of the wars spawned in this century, in the beautifully ordered, civilized landscape of Europe, where everyone is literate and classical music plays in every village café. War is not an aberration; it is part of the family, the crazy uncle we try—in vain—to keep locked in the basement.

Consider my own example. I am not a violent person. I have not been in a fight since grade school. Aside from being a fairly happy-go-lucky carnivore, I have no lust for blood, nor do I enjoy killing animals, fish, or even insects. My days are passed in reasonable contentment, filled with the details of work and everyday life. I am also a father now, and a man who has helped create life is war's natural enemy. I have seen what war does to children, makes them killers or victims, robs them of their parents, their homes, and their innocence—steals their childhood and leaves them marked in body, mind, and spirit.

I spent most of my combat tour in Vietnam trudging through its jungles and rice paddies without incident, but I have seen enough of war to know that I never want to fight again, and that I would do everything in my power to keep my son from fighting. Then why, at the oddest times—when I am in a meeting or running errands, or on beautiful summer evenings, with the light fading and children playing around me—do my thoughts turn back fifteen years to a war I didn't believe in and never wanted to fight? Why do I miss it?

■

I miss it because I loved it, loved it in strange and troubling ways. When I talk about loving war I don't mean the romantic notion of war that once mesmerized generations raised on Walter Scott. What little was left of that was ground into the mud at Verdun and Passchendaele; honor and glory do not survive the machine gun. And it's not the mindless bliss of martyrdom that sends Iranian teenagers armed with sticks against Iraqi tanks. Nor do I mean the sort of hysteria that can grip a whole country, the way during the Falklands war the English press inflamed the lust that lurks beneath the cool exterior of Britain. That is vicarious war, the thrill of participation without risk, the lust of the audience for blood. It is easily fanned, that lust; even the invasion of a tiny island like Grenada can do it. Like all lust, for as long as it lasts it dominates everything else; a nation's other problems are seared away, a phenomenon exploited by kings, dictators, and presidents since civilization began.

And I don't mean war as an addiction, the constant rush that war junkies get, the crazies mailing ears home to their girlfriends, the zoomies who couldn't get an erection unless they were cutting in the afterburners on their F-4s. And, finally, I'm not talking about how some men my age feel today, men who didn't go to war but now have a sort of nostalgic longing for something they missed, some classic male experience, the way some women who didn't have children worry they missed something basic about being a woman, something they didn't value when they could have done it.

I'm talking about why thoughtful, loving men can love war even while knowing and hating it.

Like any love, the love of war is built on a complex of often contradictory reasons. Some of them are fairly painless to discuss; others go almost too deep, stir the caldron too much. I'll give the more respectable reasons first.

Part of the love of war stems from its being an experience of great intensity; its lure is the fundamental human passion to witness, to see things, what the Bible calls the lust of the eye and the Marines in Vietnam called eye fucking. War stops time, intensifies experience to the point of a terrible ecstasy. It is the dark opposite of that moment of passion caught in "Ode on a Grecian Urn": "For ever warm and still to be enjoy'd/ For ever panting, and for ever young." War offers endless exotic experiences, enough "I couldn't fucking believe it!" 's to last a lifetime.

Most people fear freedom; war removes that fear. And like a stern father, it provides with its order and discipline both security and an irresistible urge to rebel against it, a constant yearning to fly over the cuckoo's nest. The midnight requisition is an honored example. I remember one elaborately planned and meticulously executed raid on our principal enemy—the U.S. Army, not the North Vietnamese—to get lightweight blankets and cleaning fluid for our rifles, repeated later in my tour, as a mark of my changed status, to obtain a refrigerator and an air-conditioner for our office. To escape the Vietnamese police we tied sheets together to let ourselves down from the top floor of whorehouses, and on one memorable occasion a friend who is now a respectable member of our diplomatic corps hid himself inside a rolled-up Oriental rug while the rest of us careered off in the truck, leaving him to make his way back stark naked to our base six miles away. War, since it steals our youth, offers a sanction to play boys' games.

War replaces the difficult gray areas of daily life with an eerie, serene clarity. In war you usually know who is your enemy and who is your friend, and are given means of dealing with both. (That was, incidentally, one of the great problems with Vietnam: it was hard to tell friend from foe—it was too much like ordinary life.)

War is an escape from the everyday into a special world where the bonds that hold us to our duties in daily life—the bonds of family, community, work—disappear. In war, all bets are off. It's the frontier beyond the last settlement, it's Las Vegas. The men who do well in peace do not necessarily do well at war, while those who were misfits and failures may find themselves touched with fire. U.S. Grant, selling firewood on the streets of St. Louis and then four years later commanding the Union armies, is the best example, although I knew many Marines who were great warriors but whose ability to adapt to civilian life was minimal.

I remember Kirby, a skinny kid with JUST YOU AND ME LORD tattooed on his shoulder. Kirby had extended his tour in Vietnam twice. He had long since ended his attachment to any known organization and lived alone out in the most dangerous areas, where he wandered about night and day, dressed only in his battered fatigue trousers with a .45 automatic tucked into the waistband, his skinny shoulders and arms as dark as a Montagnard's.

One day while out on patrol we found him on the floor of a hut, being tended by a girl in black pajamas, a bullet wound in his arm.

He asked me for a cigarette, then eyed me, deciding if I was worth telling his story to. "I stopped in for a mango, broad daylight, and there bigger'n hell were three NVA officers, real pretty tan uniforms. They got this map spread out on a table, just eyeballin' it, makin' themselves right at home. They looked at me. I looked at them. Then they went for their nine millimeters and I went for my .45."

"Yeah?" I answered. "So what happened?"

"I wasted 'em," he said, then puffed on his cigarette. Just another day at work, killing three men on the way to eat a mango.

"How are you ever going to go back to the world?" I asked him. (He didn't. A few months later a ten-year-old Vietcong girl blew him up with a command-detonated booby trap.)

War is a brutal, deadly game, but a game, the best there is. And men love games. You can come back from war broken in mind or body, or not come back at all. But if you come back whole you bring with you the knowledge that you have explored regions of your soul that in most men will always remain uncharted. Nothing I had ever studied was as complex or as creative as the small-unit tactics of Vietnam. No sport I had ever played brought me to such deep awareness of my physical and emotional limits.

One night not long after I had arrived in Vietnam, one of my platoon's observation posts heard enemy movement. I immediately lost all saliva in my mouth. I could not talk; not a sound would pass my lips. My brain erased as if the plug had been pulled—I felt only a dull hum throughout my body, a low-grade current coursing through me like electricity through a power line. After a minute I could at least grunt, which I did as Hiers gave orders to the squad leaders, called in artillery and air support, and threw back the probe. I was terrified, I was ashamed, and I couldn't wait for it to happen again.

■

The enduring emotion of war, when everything else has faded, is comradeship. A comrade in war is a man you can trust with anything, because you trust him with your life. "It is," Philip Caputo wrote in *A Rumor of War,* "unlike marriage, a bond that cannot be broken by a word, by boredom or divorce, or by anything other than death." Despite its extreme right-wing image, war is the only utopian experience most of us ever have. Individual possessions and advantage count for nothing; the group is everything. What you have is shared with your friends. It isn't a particularly selective process, but a love that needs no reasons, that transcends race and personality and education—all those things that would make a difference in peace. It is, simply, brotherly love.

What made this love so intense was that it had no limits, not even death. John Wheeler, in *Touched with Fire,* quotes the Congressional Medal of Honor citation of Hector Santiago-Colon: "Due to the heavy volume of enemy fire and exploding grenades around them, a North Vietnamese soldier was able to crawl, undetected, to their position. Suddenly, the enemy soldier lobbed a hand grenade into Sp4c. Santiago-Colon's foxhole. Realizing that there was not time to throw the grenade out of his

position, Sp4c. Santiago-Colon retrieved the grenade, tucked it into his stomach, and, turning away from his comrades, absorbed the full impact of the blast." This is classic heroism, the final evidence of how much comrades can depend on each other. What went through Santiago-Colon's mind for that split second when he could just as easily have dived to safety? It had to be this: my comrades are more important to me than my most valuable possession—my own life.

Isolation is the greatest fear in war. The military historian S.L.A. Marshall conducted intensive studies of combat incidents during World War II and Korea and discovered that at most, only 25 percent of the men who were under fire actually fired their own weapons. The rest cowered behind cover, terrified and helpless—all systems off. Invariably, those men had felt alone, and to feel alone in combat is to cease to function; it is the terrifying prelude to the final loneliness of death. The only men who kept their heads felt connected to other men, a part of something, as if comradeship were some sort of collective life-force, the power to face death and stay conscious. But when those men came home from war, that fear of isolation stayed with many of them, a tiny mustard seed fallen on fertile soil.

When I came back from Vietnam I tried to keep up with my buddies. We wrote letters, made plans to meet, but something always came up and we never seemed to get together. For a few years we exchanged Christmas cards, then nothing. The special world that had sustained our intense comradeship was gone. Everyday life—our work, family, friends, reclaimed us, and we grew up.

But there was something not right about that. In Vietnam I had been closer to Hiers, for example, than to anyone before or since. We were connected by the radio; our lives depended on it, and on each other. We ate, slept, laughed, and were terrified together. When I first arrived in Vietnam I tried to get Hiers to salute me, but he simply wouldn't do it, mustering at most a "Howdy, Lieutenant, how's it hanging?" as we passed. For every time that he didn't salute I told him he would have to fill a hundred sandbags.

We'd reached several thousand sandbags

when Hiers took me aside and said, "Look, Lieutenant, I'll be happy to salute you, really. But if I get in the habit back here in the rear I may salute you when we're out in the bush. And those gooks are just waiting for us to salute, tell 'em who the lieutenant is. You'd be the first one blown away." We forgot the sandbags—and the salutes. Months later, when Hiers left the platoon to go home, he turned to me as I stood on our hilltop position, and gave me the smartest salute I'd ever seen. I shot him the finger, and that was the last I saw of him for fifteen years. When we met by accident at the Vietnam memorial it was like a sign; enough time had passed—we were old enough to say goodbye to who we had been and become friends as who we had become.

For us and for thousands of veterans the memorial was special ground. War is theater, and Vietnam had been fought without a third act. It was a set that hadn't been struck; its characters were lost there, with no way to get off and no more lines to say. And so when we came to the Vietnam memorial in Washington we wrote our own endings as we stared at the names on the wall, reached out and touched them, washed then with our tears, said goodbye. We are older now, some of us grandfathers, some quite successful, but the memorial touched some part of us that is still out there, under fire, alone. When we came to that wall and met the memories of our buddies and gave them their due, pulled them up from their buried places and laid our love to rest, we were home at last.

■

For all these reasons, men love war. But these are the easy reasons, the first circle, the ones we can talk about without risk of disapproval, without plunging too far into the truth or ourselves. But there are other, more troubling reasons why men love war. The love of war stems from the union, deep in the core of our being, between sex and destruction, beauty and horror, love and death. War may be the only way in which most men touch the mythic domains in our soul. It is, for men, at some terrible level the closest thing to what childbirth is for women: the initiation into the power of life and death. It is like lifting off the corner of the universe and looking at what's underneath. To see war is to see into the dark heart of things, that no-man's-land between life and death, or even beyond.

And that explains a central fact about the stories men tell about war. Every good war story is, in at least some of its crucial elements, false. The better the war story, the less of it is likely to be true. Robert Graves wrote that his main legacy from World War I was "a difficulty in telling the truth." I have never once heard a grunt tell a reporter a war story that wasn't a lie, just as some of the stories that I tell about the war are lies. Not that even the lies aren't true, on a certain level. They have a moral, even a mythic, truth, rather than a literal one. They reach out and remind the tellers and listeners of their place in the world. They are the primitive stories told around the fire in smoky teepees after the pipe has been passed. They are all, at bottom, the same.

Some of the best war stories out of Vietnam are in Michael Herr's *Dispatches*. One of Herr's most quoted stories goes like this: "But what a story he told me, as one-pointed and resonant as any war story I ever heard, it took me a year to understand it:

" 'Patrol went up the mountain. One man came back. He died before he could tell us what happened.'

"I waited for the rest, but it seemed not to be that kind of story; when I asked him what had happened he just looked like he felt sorry for me, fucked if he'd waste time telling stories to anyone as dumb as I was."

It is a great story, a combat haiku, all negative space and darkness humming with portent. It seems rich, unique to Vietnam. But listen, now, to this:

"We all went up to Gettysburg, the summer of '63: and some of us came back from there: and that's all except the details." That is the account of Gettysburg by one Praxiteles Swan, onetime captain in the Confederate States Army. The language is different, but it is the same story. And it is a story that I would imagine has been told for as long as men have gone to war. Its purpose is not to enlighten but to exclude; its message is not its content but putting the listener in his place. I suffered, I was there. You were not. Only those facts matter. Everything else is beyond words to tell. As was said after the worst tragedies in Vietnam: "Don't mean nothin'." Which meant, "It means everything, it means too much." Language overload.

War stories inhabit the realm of myth because every war story is about death. And one of the most troubling reasons men love war is the love of destruction, the thrill of killing. In his superb book on World War II, *The Warriors,* J. Glenn Gray wrote that "thousands of youths who never suspected the presence of such an impulse in themselves have learned in military life the mad excitement of destroying." It's what Hemingway meant when he wrote, "Admit that you have liked to kill as all who are soldiers by choice have enjoyed it at some time whether they lie about it or not."

My platoon and I went through Vietnam burning hooches (note how language liberated us—we didn't burn houses and shoot people; we burned hooches and shot gooks), killing dogs and pigs and chickens, destroying, because, as my friend Hiers put it, "We thought it was fun at the time." As anyone who has fired a bazooka or an M-60 machine gun knows, there is something to that power in your finger, the soft, seductive touch of the trigger. It's like the magic sword, a grunt's Excalibur: all you do is move that finger so imperceptibly, just a wish flashing across your mind like a shadow, not even a full brain synapse, and *poof!* in a blast of sound and energy and light a truck or a house or even people disappear, everything flying and settling back into dust.

There is a connection between this thrill and the games we played as children, the endless games of cowboys and Indians and war, the games that ended with "Bang bang you're dead," and everyone who was "dead" got up and began another game. That's war as fantasy, and it's the same emotion that touches us in war movies and books, where death is something without consequence, and not something that ends with terrible finality as blood from our fatally fragile bodies flows out onto the mud. Boys aren't the only ones prone to this

fantasy; it possesses the old men who have never been to war and who preside over our burials with the same tears they shed when soldiers die in the movies—tears of fantasy, cheap tears. The love of destruction and killing in war stems from that fantasy of war as a game, but it is the more seductive for being indulged at terrible risk. It is the game survivors play, after they have seen death up close and learned in their hearts how common, how ordinary, and how inescapable it is.

I don't know if I killed anyone in Vietnam, but I tried as hard as I could. I fired at muzzle flashes in the night, threw grenades during ambushes, ordered artillery and bombing where I thought the enemy was. Whenever another platoon got a higher body count, I was disappointed: it was like suiting up for the football game and then not getting to play. After one ambush my men brought back the body of a North Vietnamese soldier. I later found the dead man propped against some C-ration boxes. He had on sunglasses, and a *Playboy* magazine lay open in his lap; a cigarette dangled jauntily from his mouth, and on his head was perched a large and perfectly formed piece of shit.

I pretended to be outraged, since desecrating bodies was frowned on as un-American and counterproductive. But it wasn't outrage I felt. I kept my officer's face on, but inside I was . . . laughing. I laughed—I believe now—in part because of some subconscious appreciation of this obscene linkage of sex and excrement and death; and in part because of the exultant realization that he—whoever he had been—was dead and I—special, unique me—was alive. He was my brother, but I knew him not. In war the line between life and death is gossamer thin; there is joy, true joy, in being alive when so many around you are not. And from the joy of being alive in death's presence to the joy of causing death is, unfortunately, not that great a step.

A lieutenant colonel I knew, a true intellectual, was put in charge of civil affairs, the work we did helping the Vietnamese grow rice and otherwise improve their lives. He was a sensitive man who kept a journal and seemed far better equipped for winning hearts and minds than for a combat command. But he got one, and I remember flying out to visit his fire base the night after it had been attacked by an NVA sapper unit. Most of the combat troops had been out on an operation, so this colonel mustered a motley crew of clerks and cooks and drove the sappers off, chasing them across the rice paddies and killing dozens of these elite enemy troops by the light of flares. That morning, as they were surveying what they had done and loading the dead NVA—all naked and covered with grease and mud so they could penetrate the barbed wire—on mechanical mules like so much garbage, there was a look of beautific contentment on the colonel's face that I had not seen except in charismatic churches. It was the look of a person transported into ecstasy.

And I—what did I do, confronted with this beastly scene? I smiled back, as filled with bliss as he was. That was another of the times I stood on the edge of my humanity, looked into the pit, and loved what I saw there. I had surrendered to an aesthetic that was divorced from that crucial quality of empathy that lets us feel the sufferings of others. And I saw a terrible beauty there. War is not simply the spirit of ugliness, although it is certainly that, the devil's work. But to give the devil his due, it is also an affair of great and seductive beauty.

Art and war were for ages as linked as art and religion. Medieval and Renaissance artists gave us cathedrals, but they also gave us armor, sculptures of war, swords and muskets and cannons of great beauty, art offered to the god of war as reverently as the carved altars were offered to the god of love. War was a public ritual of the highest order, as the beautifully decorated cannons in the Invalides in Paris and the chariots with their depictions of the gods in the Metropolitan Museum of Art so eloquently attest. Men love their weapons, not simply for helping to keep them alive, but for a deeper reason. They love their rifles and their knives for the same reason that the medieval warriors loved their armor and their swords: they are instruments of beauty.

War *is* beautiful. There is something about a firefight at night, something about the mechanical elegance of an M-60 machine gun. They are everything they should be, perfect examples of their form. When you are firing out at night, the red

tracers go out into the blackness as if you were drawing with a light pen. Then little dots of light start winking back, and green tracers from the AK-47s begin to weave in with the red to form brilliant patterns that seem, given their great speeds, oddly timeless, as if they had been etched on the night. And then perhaps the gunships called Spooky come in and fire their incredible guns like huge hoses washing down from the sky, like something God would do when He was really ticked off. And then the flares pop, casting eerie shadows as they float down on their little parachutes, swinging in the breeze, and anyone who moves in their light seems a ghost escaped from hell.

Daytime offers nothing so spectacular, but it also has its charms. Many men loved napalm, loved its silent power, the way it could make tree lines or houses explode as if by spontaneous combustion. But I always thought napalm was greatly overrated, unless you enjoy watching tires burn. I preferred white phosphorus, which exploded with a fulsome elegance, wreathing its target in intense and billowing white smoke, throwing out glowing red comets trailing brilliant white plumes. I loved it more—not less—because of its function: to destroy, to kill. The seduction of war is in its offering such intense beauty—divorced from all civilized values, but beauty still.

■

Most men who have been to war, and most women who have been around it, remember that never in their lives did they have so heightened a sexuality. War is, in short, a turn-on. War cloaks men in a costume that conceals the limits and inadequacies of their separate natures. It gives them an aura, a collective power, an almost animal force. They aren't just Billy or Johnny or Bobby, they are soldiers! But there's a price for all that: the agonizing loneliness of war, the way a soldier is cut off from everything that defines him as an individual—he is the true rootless man. The uniform did that, too, and all that heightened sexuality is not much solace late at night when the emptiness comes.

There were many men for whom this condition led to great decisions. I knew a Marine in Vietnam who was a great rarity, an Ivy League graduate. He also had an Ivy League wife, but he managed to fall in love with a Vietnamese bar girl who could barely speak English. She was not particularly attractive, a peasant girl trying to support her family. He spent all his time with her, he fell in love with her—awkwardly, formally, but totally. At the end of his twelve months in Vietnam he went home, divorced his beautiful, intelligent, and socially correct wife, and then went back to Vietnam and proposed to the bar girl, who accepted. It was a marriage across a vast divide of language, culture, race, and class that could only have been made in war. I am not sure that it lasted, but it would not surprise me if, despite great difficulties, it did.

Of course, for every such story there are hundreds, thousands, of stories of passing contacts, a man and a woman holding each other tight for one moment, finding in sex some escape from the terrible reality of the war. The intensity that war brings to sex, the "let us love now because there may be no tomorrow," is based on death. No matter what our weapons on the battlefield, love is finally our only weapon against death. Sex is the weapon of life, the shooting sperm sent like an army of guerrillas to penetrate the egg's defenses—the only victory that really matters. War thrusts you into the well of loneliness, death breathing in your ear. Sex is a grappling hook that pulls you out, ends your isolation, makes you one with life again.

Not that such thoughts were anywhere near conscious. I remember going off to war with a copy of *War and Peace* and *The Charterhouse of Parma* stuffed into my pack. They were soon replaced with *The Story of O.* War heightens all appetites. I cannot describe the ache for candy, for taste; I wanted a Mars bar more than I had wanted anything in my life. And that hunger paled beside the force that pushed us toward women, any women; women we would not even have looked at in peace floated into our fantasies and lodged there. Too often we made our fantasies real, always to be disappointed, our hunger only greater. The ugliest prostitutes specialized in group affairs, passed among several men or even whole squads, in communion almost, a sharing more than sexual. In sex even more than in killing I could see the beast, crouched drooling on its haunches, could see it mocking me for my frailties, knowing I hated myself for them but that I could not get enough, that I would keep coming back again and again.

After I ended my tour in combat I came back to work at division headquarters and volunteered one night a week teaching English to Vietnamese adults. One of my students was a beautiful girl whose parents had been killed in Hué during the Tet Offensive of 1968. She had fallen in love with an American civilian who worked at the consulate in Da Nang. He had left her for his next duty station and promised he would send for her. She never heard from him again. She had a seductive sadness about her. I found myself seeing her after class, then I was sneaking into the motor pool and commandeering a deuce-and-a-half truck and driving into Da Nang at night to visit her. She lived in a small house near the consulate with her grandparents and brothers and sisters. It had one room divided by a curtain. When I arrived, the rest of the family would retire behind the curtain. Amid their hushed voices and the smells of cooking oil and rotted fish we would talk and fumble toward each other, my need greater than hers.

I wanted her desperately. But her tenderness and vulnerability, the torn flower of her beauty, frustrated my death-obsessed lust. I didn't see her as one Vietnamese, I saw her as all Vietnamese. She was the suffering soul of war, and I was the soldier who had wounded it but would make it whole. My loneliness was pulling me into the same strong current that had swallowed my friend who married the bar girl. I could see it happening, but I seemed powerless to stop it. I wrote her long poems, made inquiries about staying on in Da Nang, built a fantasy future for the two of us. I wasn't going to betray her the way the other American had, the way all Americans had, the way all men betrayed the women who helped them through the war. I wasn't like that. But then I received orders sending me home two weeks early. I drove into Da Nang to talk to her, and to make definite plans. Halfway there, I turned back.

At the airport I threw the poems into a trash can. When the wheels of the plane lifted off the soil of Vietnam, I cheered like everyone else. And as I pressed my face against the window and watched Vietnam shrink to a distant green blur and finally disappear, I felt sad and guilty—for her, for my comrades who had been killed and wounded, for everything. But that feeling was overwhelmed by my vast sense of relief. I had survived. And I was going home. I would be myself again, or so I thought.

But some fifteen years later she and the war are still on my mind, all those memories, each with its secret passages and cutbacks, hundreds of labyrinths, all leading back to a truth not safe but essential. It is about why we can love and hate, why we can bring forth life and snuff it out, why each of us is a battleground where good and evil are always at war for our souls.

The power of war, like the power of love, springs from man's heart. The one yields death, the other life. But life without death has no meaning; nor, at its deepest level, does love without war. Without war we could not know from what depths love rises, or what power it must have to overcome such evil and redeem us. It is no accident that men love war, as love and war are at the core of man. It is not only that we must love one another or die. We must love one another *and* die. War, like death, is always with us, a constant companion, a secret sharer. To deny its seduction, to overcome death, our love for peace, for life itself, must be greater than we think possible, greater even than we can imagine.

■

Hiers and I were skiing down a mountain in Vermont, flying effortlessly over a world cloaked in white, beautiful, innocent, peaceful. On the ski lift up we had been talking about a different world, hot, green, smelling of decay and death, where each step out of the mud took all our strength. We stopped and looked back, the air pure and cold, our breath coming in puffs of vapor. Our children were following us down the hill, bent over, little balls of life racing on the edge of danger.

Hiers turned to me with a smile and said, "It's a long way from Nam, isn't it?"

Yes.

And no.

Hiroshima Diary
The Journal of a Japanese Physician August 6–7, 1945

Michihiko Hachiya, M.D.

Translated and Edited by Warner Wells, M.D.

6 August 1945

The hour was early; the morning still, warm, and beautiful. Shimmering leaves, reflecting sunlight from a cloudless sky, made a pleasant contrast with shadows in my garden as I gazed absently through wide-flung doors opening to the south.

Clad in drawers and undershirt, I was sprawled on the living room floor exhausted because I had just spent a sleepless night on duty as an air warden in my hospital.

Suddenly, a strong flash of light startled me—and then another. So well does one recall little things that I remember vividly how a stone lantern in the garden became brilliantly lit and I debated whether this light was caused by a magnesium flare or sparks from a passing trolley.

Garden shadows disappeared. The view where a moment before all had been so bright and sunny was now dark and hazy. Through swirling dust I could barely discern a wooden column that had supported one corner of my house. It was leaning crazily and the roof sagged dangerously.

Moving instinctively, I tried to escape, but rubble and fallen timbers barred the way. By picking my way cautiously I managed to reach the *rōka* and stepped down into my garden. A profound weakness overcame me, so I stopped to regain my strength. To my surprise I discovered that I was completely naked. How odd! Where were my drawers and undershirt?

What had happened?

All over the right side of my body I was cut and bleeding. A large splinter was protruding from a mangled wound in my thigh, and something warm trickled into my mouth. My cheek was torn, I discovered as I felt it gingerly, with the lower lip laid wide open. Embedded in my neck was a sizable fragment of glass which I matter-of-factly dislodged, and with the detachment of one stunned and shocked I studied it and my blood-stained hand.

Where was my wife?

Suddenly thoroughly alarmed, I began to yell for her: "Yaeko-san! Yaeko-san! Where are you?"

Blood began to spurt. Had my carotid artery been cut? Would I bleed to death? Frightened and irrational, I called out again: "It's a five-hundred-ton bomb! Yaeko-san, where are you? A five-hundred-ton bomb has fallen!"

Yaeko-san, pale and frightened, her clothes torn and bloodstained, emerged from the ruins of our house holding her elbow. Seeing her, I was reassured. My own panic assuaged, I tried to reassure her.

"We'll be all right," I exclaimed. "Only let's get out of here as fast as we can."

She nodded, and I motioned for her to follow me.

The shortest path to the street lay through the house next door so through the house we went—running, stumbling, falling, and then running again until in headlong flight we tripped over something and fell sprawling into the street. Getting to my feet, I discovered that I had tripped over a man's head.

"Excuse me! Excuse me, please!" I cried hysterically.

There was no answer. The man was dead. The head had belonged to a young officer whose body was crushed beneath a massive gate.

We stood in the street, uncertain and afraid, until a house across from us began to sway and then with a rending motion fell almost at our feet. Our own house began to sway, and in a minute it, too, collapsed in a cloud of dust. Other buildings caved in or toppled. Fires sprang up and whipped by a vicious wind began to spread.

It finally dawned on us that we could not stay there in the street, so we turned our steps toward the hospital.* Our home was gone; we were wounded and needed treatment; and after all, it was my duty to be with my staff. This latter was an irrational thought—what good could I be to anyone, hurt as I was.

We started out, but after twenty or thirty steps I had to stop. My breath became short, my heart pounded, and my legs gave way under me. An overpowering thirst seized me and I begged Yaeko-san to find me some water. But there was no water to be found. After a little my strength somewhat returned and we were able to go on.

I was still naked, and although I did not feel the least bit of shame, I was disturbed to realize that modesty had deserted me. On rounding the corner we came upon a soldier standing idly in the street. He had a towel draped across his shoulder, and I asked if he would give it to me to cover my nakedness. The soldier surrendered the towel quite willingly but said not a word. A little later I lost the towel, and Yaeko-san took off her apron and tied it around my loins.

Our progress towards the hospital was interminably slow, until finally, my legs, stiff from drying blood, refused to carry me farther. The strength, even the will, to go on deserted me, so I told my wife, who was almost as badly hurt as I, to go on alone. This she objected to, but there was no choice. She had to go ahead and try to find someone to come back for me.

Yaeko-san looked into my face for a moment, and then, without saying a word, turned away and began running towards the hospital. Once, she looked back and waved and in a moment she was swallowed up in the gloom. It was quite dark now, and with my wife gone, a feeling of dreadful loneliness overcame me.

I must have gone out of my head lying there in the road because the next thing I recall was discovering that the clot on my thigh had been dislodged and blood was again spurting from the wound. I pressed my hand to the bleeding area and after a while the bleeding stopped and I felt better.

Could I go on?

I tried. It was all a nightmare—my wounds, the darkness, the road ahead. My movements were ever so slow; only my mind was running at top speed.

In time I came to an open space where the houses had been removed to make a fire lane. Through the dim light I could make out ahead of me the hazy outlines of the Communications Bureau's big concrete building, and beyond it the hospital. My spirits rose because I knew that now someone would find me; and if I should die, at least my body would be found.

I paused to rest. Gradually things around me came into focus. There were the shadowy forms of people, some of whom looked like walking ghosts. Others moved as though in pain, like scarecrows, their arms held out from their bodies with forearms and hands dangling. These people puzzled me until I suddenly realized that they had been burned and were holding their arms out to prevent the painful friction of raw surfaces rubbing together. A naked woman carrying a naked baby came into view. I averted my gaze. Perhaps they had been in the bath. But then I saw a naked man, and it occurred to me that, like myself, some

---

*Dr. Hachiya's home was only a few hundred meters from the hospital.

strange thing had deprived them of their clothes. An old woman lay near me with an expression of suffering on her face; but she made no sound. Indeed, one thing was common to everyone I saw—complete silence.

All who could were moving in the direction of the hospital. I joined in the dismal parade when my strength was somewhat recovered, and at last reached the gates of the Communications Bureau.

Familiar surroundings, familiar faces. There was Mr. Iguchi and Mr. Yoshihiro and my old friend, Mr. Sera, the head of the business office. They hastened to give me a hand, their expressions of pleasure changing to alarm when they saw that I was hurt. I was too happy to see them to share their concern.

No time was lost over greetings. They eased me onto a stretcher and carried me into the Communications Building, ignoring my protests that I could walk. Later, I learned that the hospital was so overrun that the Communications Bureau had to be used as an emergency hospital. The rooms and corridors were crowded with people, many of whom I recognized as neighbors. To me it seemed that the whole community was there.

My friends passed me through an open window into a janitor's room recently converted to an emergency first-aid station. The room was a shambles; fallen plaster, broken furniture, and debris littered the floor; the walls were cracked; and a heavy steel window casement was twisted and almost wrenched from its seating. What a place to dress the wounds of the injured.

To my great surprise who should appear but my private nurse, Miss Kado, and Mr. Mizoguchi, and old Mrs. Saeki. Miss Kado set about examining my wounds without speaking a word. No one spoke. I asked for a shirt and pajamas. They got them for me, but still no one spoke. Why was everyone so quiet?

Miss Kado finished the examination, and in a moment it felt as if my chest was on fire. She had begun to paint my wounds with iodine and no amount of entreaty would make her stop. With no alternative but to endure the iodine, I tried to divert myself by looking out the window.

The hospital lay directly opposite with part of the roof and the third floor sunroom in plain view, and as I looked up, I witnessed a sight which made me forget my smarting wounds. Smoke was pouring out of the sunroom windows. The hospital was on fire!

"Fire!" I shouted, "Fire! Fire! The hospital is on fire!"

My friends looked up. It was true. The hospital *was* on fire.

The alarm was given and from all sides people took up the cry. The high-pitched voice of Mr. Sera, the business officer, rose above the others, and it seemed as if his was the first voice I had heard that day. The uncanny stillness was broken. Our little world was now in pandemonium.

I remember that Dr. Sasada, chief of the Pediatric Service, came in and tried to reassure me, but I could scarcely hear him above the din. I heard Dr. Hinoi's voice and then Dr. Koyama's. Both were shouting orders to evacuate the hospital and with such vigor that it sounded as though the sheer strength of their voices could hasten those who were slow to obey.

The sky became bright as flames from the hospital mounted. Soon the Bureau was threatened and Mr. Sera gave the order to evacuate. My stretcher was moved into a rear garden and placed beneath an old cherry tree. Other patients limped into the garden or were carried until soon the entire area became so crowded that only the very ill had room to lie down. No one talked, and the ominous silence was relieved only by a subdued rustle among so many people, restless, in pain, anxious, and afraid, waiting for something else to happen.

The sky filled with black smoke and glowing sparks. Flames rose and the heat set currents of air in motion. Updrafts became so violent that sheets of zinc roofing were hurled aloft and released, humming and twirling, in erratic flight. Pieces of flaming wood soared and fell like fiery swallows. While I was trying to beat out the flames, a hot ember seared my ankle. It was all I could do to keep from being burned alive.

The Bureau started to burn, and window

after window became a square of flame until the whole structure was converted into a crackling, hissing inferno.

Scorching winds howled around us, whipping dust and ashes into our eyes and up our noses. Our mouths became dry, our throats raw and sore from the biting smoke pulled into our lungs. Coughing was uncontrollable. We would have moved back, but a group of wooden barracks behind us caught fire and began to burn like tinder.

The heat finally became too intense to endure, and we were left no choice but to abandon the garden. Those who could fled; those who could not perished. Had it not been for my devoted friends, I would have died, but again, they came to my rescue and carried my stretcher to the main gate on the other side of the Bureau.

Here, a small group of people were already clustered, and here I found my wife. Dr. Sasada and Miss Kado joined us.

Fires sprang up on every side as violent winds fanned flames from one building to another. Soon, we were surrounded. The ground we held in front of the Communications Bureau became an oasis in a desert of fire. As the flames came closer the heat became more intense, and if someone in our group had not had the presence of mind to drench us with water* from a fire hose, I doubt if anyone could have survived.

Hot as it was, I began to shiver. The drenching was too much. My heart pounded; things began to whirl until all before me blurred.

"*Kurushii,*" I murmured weakly. "I am done."

■

The sound of voices reached my ears as though from a great distance and finally became louder as if close at hand. I opened my eyes; Dr. Sasada was feeling my pulse. What had happened?

Miss Kado gave me an injection. My strength gradually returned. I must have fainted.

Huge raindrops began to fall. Some thought a thunderstorm was beginning and would extinguish the fires. But these drops were capricious. A few fell and then a few more and that was all the rain we saw.†

The first floor of the Bureau was now ablaze and flames were spreading rapidly towards our little oasis by the gate. Right then, I could hardly understand the situation, much less do anything about it.

An iron window frame, loosened by fire, crashed to the ground behind us. A ball of fire whizzed by me, setting my clothes ablaze. They drenched me with water again. From then on I am confused as to what happened.

I do remember Dr. Hinoi because of the pain, the pain I felt when he jerked me to my feet. I remember being moved or rather dragged, and my whole spirit rebelling against the torment I was made to endure.

My next memory is of an open area. The fires must have receded. I was alive. My friends had somehow managed to rescue me again.

A head popped out of an air-raid dugout, and I heard the unmistakable voice of old Mrs. Saeki: "Cheer up, doctor! Everything will be all right. The north side is burnt out. We have nothing further to fear from the fire."

I might have been her son, the way the old lady calmed and reassured me. And indeed, she was right. The entire northern side of the city was completely burned. The sky was still dark, but whether it was evening or midday I could not tell. It might even have been the next day. Time had no meaning. What I had experienced might have been crowded into a moment or been endured through the monotony of eternity.

---

*The water mains entered the city from the north and since the Communications Bureau was in the northern edge of the city, its water supply was not destroyed.

†There were many reports of a scanty rainfall over the city after the bombing. The drops were described as large and dirty, and some claimed that they were laden with radioactive dust.

Smoke was still rising from the second floor of the hospital, but the fire had stopped. There was nothing left to burn, I thought; but later I learned that the first floor of the hospital had escaped destruction largely through the courageous efforts of Dr. Koyama and Dr. Hinoi.

The streets were deserted except for the dead. Some looked as if they had been frozen by death while in the full action of flight; others lay sprawled as though some giant had flung them to their death from a great height.

Hiroshima was no longer a city, but a burnt-over prairie. To the east and to the west everything was flattened. The distant mountains seemed nearer than I could ever remember. The hills of Ushita and the woods of Nigitsu loomed out of the haze and smoke like the nose and eyes on a face. How small Hiroshima was with its houses gone.

The wind changed and the sky again darkened with smoke.

Suddenly, I heard someone shout: "Planes! Enemy planes!"

Could that be possible after what had already happened? What was there left to bomb? My thoughts were interrupted by the sound of a familiar name.

A nurse calling Dr. Katsube.

"It is Dr. Katsube! It's him!" shouted old Mrs. Saeki, a happy ring to her voice. "Dr. Katsube has come!"

It was Dr. Katsube, our head surgeon, but he seemed completely unaware of us as he hurried past, making a straight line for the hospital. Enemy planes were forgotten, so great was our happiness that Dr. Katsube had been spared to return to us.

Before I could protest, my friends were carrying me into the hospital. The distance was only a hundred meters, but it was enough to cause my heart to pound and make me sick and faint.

I recall the hard table and the pain when my face and lip were sutured, but I have no recollection of the forty or more other wounds Dr. Katsube closed before night.

They removed me to an adjoining room, and I remember feeling relaxed and sleepy. The sun had gone down, leaving a dark red sky. The red flames of the burning city had scorched the heavens. I gazed at the sky until sleep overtook me.

7 August 1945

I must have slept soundly because when I opened my eyes a piercing hot sun was shining in on me. There were no shutters or curtains to lessen the glare—and for that matter no windows.

The groans of patients assaulted my ears. Everything was in a turmoil.

Instruments, window frames, and debris littered the floor. The walls and ceilings were scarred and picked as though someone had sprinkled sesame seeds over their surfaces. Most of the marks had been made by slivers of flying glass but the larger scars had been caused by hurtling instruments and pieces of window casements.

Near a window an instrument cabinet was overturned. The head piece had been knocked off the ear, nose, and throat examining chair, and a broken sunlamp was overturned across the seat. I saw nothing that was not broken or in disorder.

Dr. Sasada, who had looked after me yesterday, lay on my left. I had thought he escaped injury, but now I could see that he was badly burned. His arms and hands were bandaged and his childish face so obscured by swelling that I would not have recognized him had it not been for his voice.

My wife lay to my right. Her face was covered with a white ointment, giving her a ghostly appearance. Her right arm was in a sling.

Miss Kado, only slightly wounded, was between me and my wife. She had nursed all of us throughout the night.

My wife, seeing that I was awake, turned and said: "Last night, you seemed to be suffering."

"Yes," said Miss Kado, chiming in. "I don't know how many times I examined your breathing."

I recognized Dr. Fujii's wife sitting motionless on a bench near the wall. Her face bore an expression of anguish and despair. Turning to Miss Kado, I asked what the matter was, and she replied: "Mrs. Fujii was not hurt very much, but her baby was. It died during the night."

"Where is Dr. Fujii?" I inquired.

"Their older daughter is lost," she answered. "He's been out all night looking for her and hasn't returned."

Dr. Koyama came in to inquire how we were. The sight of him, with his head bandaged and an arm in a sling, brought tears to my eyes. He had worked all night and was even now thinking of others before himself.

Dr. Katsube, our surgeon, and Miss Takao, a surgical nurse, were with Dr. Koyama, who was now deputy director. They all looked tired and haggard, and their white clothes were dirty and blood-stained. I learned that Mr. Iguchi, our driver, had contrived to rig up an emergency operating light from a car battery and headlight with which they had managed to operate until the light went out just before day.

Dr. Koyama, observing my concern, remarked: "Doctor, everything is all right."

Dr. Katsube looked me over and after feeling my pulse, said: "You received many wounds, but they all missed vital spots."

He then described them and told me how they had been treated. I was surprised to learn that my shoulder had been severely cut but relieved at his optimism for my recovery.

"How many patients are in the hospital?" I asked Dr. Koyama.

"About a hundred and fifty," he replied. "Quite a few have died, but there are still so many that there is no place to put one's foot down. They are packed in everywhere, even the toilets."

Nodding, Dr. Katsube added: "There are about a half dozen beneath the stairway, and about fifty in the front garden of the hospital."

They discussed methods for restoring order, at least to the extent of making the corridors passable.

In the space of one night patients had become packed, like the rice in *sushi,* into every nook and cranny of the hospital. The majority were badly burned, a few severely injured. All were critically ill. Many had been near the heart of the city and in their efforts to flee managed to get only as far as the Communications Hospital before their strength failed. Others, from nearer by, came deliberately to seek treatment or because this building, standing alone where all else was destroyed, represented shelter and a place of refuge. They came as an avalanche and overran the hospital.

There was no friend or relative to minister to their needs, no one to prepare their food.* Everything was in disorder. And to make matters worse was the vomiting and diarrhea. Patients who could not walk urinated and defecated where they lay. Those who could walk would feel their way to the exits and relieve themselves there. Persons entering or leaving the hospital could not avoid stepping in the filth, so closely was it spread. The front entrance became covered with feces overnight, and nothing could be done for there were no bed pans and, even if there had been, no one to carry them to the patients.

Disposing of the dead was a minor problem, but to clean the rooms and corridors of urine, feces, and vomitus was impossible.

The people who were burned suffered most because as their skin peeled away, glistening raw wounds were exposed to the heat and filth. This was the environment patients had to live in. It made one's hair stand on end, but there was no way to help the situation.

This was the pattern conversation took as I lay there and listened. It was inconceivable.

"When can I get up?" I asked Dr. Katsube. "Perhaps I can do something to help."

"Not until your sutures are out," he answered. "And that won't be for at least a week."

With that to think about they left me.

I was not left long with my thoughts. One

---

*It is customary in Japan for the hospital patient to provide his own bedding, food, cooking utensils, and charcoal stove or *konro*. A member of the family or a friend stays with the patient to prepare the food and provide practical bedside nursing.

after another the staff came in to express their concern over my injuries and to wish me a speedy recovery. Some of my visitors embarrassed me, for they appeared to be as badly injured as myself. Had it been possible, I would have concealed my whereabouts.

Dr. Nishimura, President of the Okayama Medical Association, came all the way from my native city,* ninety miles away, to see me. He had been crew captain of the boat team when we were classmates in Medical School. As soon as he saw me, tears welled up in his eyes. He looked at me a moment, and then exclaimed: "I say, old fellow, you are alive! What a pleasant surprise. How are you getting along?"

Without waiting for an answer, he continued: "Last night, we heard that Hiroshima had been attacked by a new weapon. The damage was slight, they told us, but in order to see for myself and to lend a hand if extra physicians were needed, I secured a truck and came on down. What a frightful mess greeted us when we arrived. Are you sure *you* are all right?"

And again, without stopping for me to reply, he went on to tell about the heartbreaking things he witnessed from the truck as he entered the city. These were the first details any of us had heard, so we listened intently.

While he talked, all I could think of was the fear and uncertainty that must be preying on my old mother who lived in the country near Okayama. When he had finished, I asked Dr. Nishimura if he would get word to my mother, and also to a sister who lived in Okayama, that Yaeko-san and I were safe. He assured me that he would, and before leaving he also promised to organize a team of doctors and nurses to come down and help as soon as he could get them together.

Dr. Tabuchi, an old friend from Ushita, came in. His face and hands had been burned, though not badly, and after an exchange of greetings, I asked if he knew what had happened.

"I was in the back yard pruning some trees when it exploded," he answered. "The first thing I knew, there was a blinding white flash of light, and a wave of intense heat struck my cheek. This was odd, I thought, when in the next instant there was a tremendous blast.

"The force of it knocked me clean over," he continued, "but fortunately, it didn't hurt me; and my wife wasn't hurt either. But you should have seen our house! It didn't topple over, it just inclined. I have never seen such a mess. Inside and out everything was simply ruined. Even so, we are happy to be alive, and what's more Ryoji, our son, survived. I didn't tell you that he had gone into the city on business that morning. About midnight, after we had given up all hope that he could possibly survive in the dreadful fire that followed the blast, he came home. Listen!" he continued, "why don't you come on home with me? My house is certainly nothing to look at now, but it is better than here."

It was impossible for me to accept his kind offer, and I tried to decline in a way that would not hurt his feelings.

"Dr. Tabuchi," I replied, "we are all grateful for your kind offer, but Dr. Katsube has just warned me that I must lie perfectly still until my wounds are healed."

Dr. Tabuchi accepted my explanation with some reluctance, and after a pause he made ready to go.

"Don't go," I said. "Please tell us more of what occurred yesterday."

"It was a horrible sight," said Dr. Tabuchi. "Hundreds of injured people who were trying to escape to the hills passed our house. The sight of them was almost unbearable. Their faces and hands were burnt and swollen; and great sheets of skin had peeled away from their tissues to hang down like rags on a scarecrow. They moved like a line of ants. All through the night, they went past our house, but this morning they had stopped. I found them lying on both sides of the road so thick that it was impossible to pass without stepping on them."

I lay with my eyes shut while Dr. Tabuchi was

---

*Dr. Hachiya was born and educated in Okayama, a large city and cultural center near the Inland Sea east of Hiroshima.

talking, picturing in my mind the horror he was describing. I neither saw nor heard Mr. Katsutani when he came in. It was not until I heard someone sobbing that my attention was attracted, and I recognized my old friend. I had known Mr. Katsutani for many years and knew him to be an emotional person, but even so, to see him break down made tears come to my eyes. He had come all the way from Jigozen* to look for me, and now that he had found me, emotion overcame him.

He turned to Dr. Sasada and said brokenly: "Yesterday, it was impossible to enter Hiroshima, else I would have come. Even today fires are still burning in some places. You should see how the city has changed. When I reached the Misasa Bridge† this morning, everything before me was gone, even the castle. These buildings here are the only ones left anywhere around. The Communications Bureau seemed to loom right in front of me long before I got anywhere near here."

Mr. Katsutani paused for a moment to catch his breath and went on: "I *really* walked along the railroad tracks to get here, but even they were littered with electric wires and broken railway cars, and the dead and wounded lay everywhere. When I reached the bridge, I saw a dreadful thing. It was unbelievable. There was a man, stone dead, sitting on his bicycle as it leaned against the bridge railing. It is hard to believe that such a thing could happen!"

He repeated himself two or three times as if to convince himself that what he said was true and then continued: "It seems that most of the dead people were either on the bridge or beneath it. You could tell that many had gone down to the river to get a drink of water and had died where they lay. I saw a few live people still in the water, knocking against the dead as they floated down the river. There must have been hundreds and thousands who fled to the river to escape the fire and then drowned.

"The sight of the soldiers, though, was more dreadful than the dead people floating down the river. I came onto I don't know how many, burned from the hips up; and where the skin had peeled, their flesh was wet and mushy. They must have been wearing their military caps because the black hair on top of their heads was not burned. It made them look like they were wearing black lacquer bowls.

"And they had no faces! Their eyes, noses and mouths had been burned away, and it looked like their ears had melted off. It was hard to tell front from back. One soldier, whose features had been destroyed and was left with his white teeth sticking out, asked me for some water, but I didn't have any. I clasped my hands and prayed for him. He didn't say anything more. His plea for water must have been his last words. The way they were burned, I wonder if they didn't have their coats off when the bomb exploded."

It seemed to give Mr. Katsutani some relief to pour out his terrifying experiences on us; and there was no one who would have stopped him, so fascinating was his tale of horror. While he was talking, several people came in and stayed to listen. Somebody asked him what he was doing when the explosion occurred.

"I had just finished breakfast," he replied, "and was getting ready to light a cigarette, when all of a sudden I saw a white flash. In a moment there was a tremendous blast. Not stopping to think, I let out a yell and jumped into an air-raid dugout. In a moment there was such a blast as I have never heard before. It was terrific! I jumped out of the dugout and pushed my wife into it. Realizing something terrible must have happened in Hiroshima, I climbed up onto the roof of my storehouse to have a look."

Mr. Katsutani became more intense and, gesticulating wildly, went on: "Towards Hiroshima, I saw a big black cloud go billowing up, like a puffy summer cloud. Knowing for sure then that something terrible had happened in the city, I

*A village on the Inland Sea about 10 miles southwest of Hiroshima.
†A large bridge which crosses the Ōta River not far from the old Hiroshima Castle in the northern part of the city and only a few blocks from the Communications Hospital.

jumped down from my storehouse and ran as fast as I could to the military post at Hatsukaichi.* I ran up to the officer in charge and told him what I had seen and begged him to send somebody to help in Hiroshima. But he didn't even take me seriously. He looked at me for a moment with a threatening expression, and then do you know what he said? He said, 'There isn't much to worry about. One or two bombs won't hurt Hiroshima.' There was no use talking to that fool!

"I was the ranking officer in the local branch of the Ex-officer's Association, but even I didn't know what to do because that day the villagers under my command had been sent off to Miyajima† for labor service. I looked all around to find someone to help me make a rescue squad, but I couldn't find anybody. While I was still looking for help, wounded people began to stream into the village. I asked them what had happened, but all they could tell me was that Hiroshima had been destroyed and everybody was leaving the city. With that I got on my bicycle and rode as fast as I could towards Itsukaichi. By the time I got there, the road was jammed with people, and so was every path and byway.

"Again I tried to find out what had happened, but nobody could give me a clear answer. When I asked these people where they had come from, they would point towards Hiroshima and say, 'This way.' And when I asked where they were going, they would point toward Miyajima and say, 'That way.' Everybody said the same thing.

"I saw no badly wounded or burned people around Itsukaichi, but when I reached Kusatsu, nearly everybody was badly hurt. The nearer I got to Hiroshima the more I saw until by the time I had reached Koi,‡ they were all so badly injured, I could not bear to look into their faces. They smelled like burning hair."

Mr. Katsutani paused for a moment to take a deep breath and then continued: "The area around Koi station was not burned, but the station and the houses nearby were badly damaged. Every square inch of the station platform was packed with wounded people. Some were standing; others lying down. They were all pleading for water. Now and then you could hear a child calling for its mother. It was a living hell, I tell you. It was a living hell!

"Today it was the same way.

"Did Dr. Hanaoka come to the hospital yesterday? I saw him cross the streetcar trestle at Koi and head in this direction, but I can't believe that he could have made his way through that fire."

"No, we haven't seen him," someone answered.

Mr. Katsutani nodded reflectively and went on: "I left Koi station and went over to the Koi primary school. By then, the school had been turned into an emergency hospital and was already crowded with desperately injured people. Even the playground was packed with the dead and dying. They looked like so many cod fish spread out for drying. What a pitiful sight it was to see them lying there in the hot sun. Even I could tell they were all going to die.

"Towards evening, I was making my way back to the highway when I ran into my sister. My sister, whose home had been in Tokaichi, must surely have been killed. But here she was—alive! She was so happy, she couldn't utter a word! All she could do was cry. If ever anyone shed tears of joy, she did. Some kind people lent me a hand in making a stretcher and helped carry her back to my home in Jigozen near Miyajima Guchi. Even my little village, as far removed as it was from Hiroshima, had become a living hell. Every shrine, every temple was packed and jammed with wounded people."

*The next village towards Hiroshima from Jigozen.
†Miyajima, or "Sacred Island," one of the seven places of superlative scenic beauty in Japan, where the magnificent camphor-wood *torii* of the Itsukushima Shrine rises majestically from the sea as a gateway to the island, is plainly visible to the south of Jigozen.
‡A railroad station on the very western limits of the city where the slopes of Chausu-yama merge with the Hiroshima delta.

Mr. Katsutani had said all he had in him to say. He left our room, but instead of going home, he stayed to help with the wounded.

∎ ∎ ∎

All day I had listened to visitors telling me about the destruction of Hiroshima and the scenes of horror they had witnessed. I had seen my friends wounded, their families separated, their homes destroyed. I was aware of the problems our staff had to face, and I knew how bravely they struggled against superhuman odds. I knew what the patients had to endure and the trust they put in the doctors and nurses, who, could they know the truth, were as helpless as themselves.

By degrees my capacity to comprehend the magnitude of their sorrow, to share with them the pain, frustration, and horror became so dulled that I found myself accepting whatever was told me with equanimity and a detachment I would have never believed possible.

In two days I had become at home in this environment of chaos and despair.

I felt lonely, but it was an animal loneliness. I became part of the darkness of the night. There were no radios, no electric lights, not even a candle. The only light that came to me was reflected in flickering shadows made by the burning city. The only sounds were the groans and sobs of the patients. Now and then a patient in delirium would call for his mother, or the voice of one in pain would breathe out the word *eraiyo*—"the pain is unbearable; I cannot endure it!"

What kind of a bomb was it that had destroyed Hiroshima? What had my visitors told me earlier? Whatever it was, it did not make sense.

There could not have been more than a few planes. Even *my* memory would agree to that. Before the air-raid alarm there was the metallic sound of one plane and no more. Otherwise why did the alarm stop? Why was there no further alarm during the five or six minutes before the explosion occurred?

Reason as I would, I could not make the ends meet when I considered the destruction that followed. Perhaps it *was* a new weapon! More than

one of my visitors spoke vaguely of a "new bomb," a "secret weapon," a "special bomb," and someone even said that the bomb was suspended from two parachutes when it burst! Whatever it was, it was beyond my comprehension. Damage of this order could have no explanation! All we had were stories no more substantial than the clouds from which we had reached to snatch them.

One thing was certain—Hiroshima was destroyed; and with it the army that had been quartered in Hiroshima. Gone were headquarters, gone the command post of the Second General Army and the Military School for young people, the General Headquarters for the Western Command, the Corps of Engineers, and the Army Hospital. Gone was the hope of Japan! The war was lost! No more help would come from the gods!

American forces would soon be landing; and when they landed, there would be streetfighting; and our hospital would become a place of attack and defense. Had I not heard earlier that soldiers were coming to set up headquarters in the Communications Bureau? Would we be turned out?

Were there no answers?

Dr. Sasada, Miss Kado, and my wife were asleep. That was good, but there was no sleep for me.

I heard footsteps, and a man appeared at the door, outlined in the flickering darkness. His elbows were out and his hands down, like the burned people I had seen on my way to the hospital. As he came nearer, I could see his face—or what had been his face because this face had been melted away by the fire. The man was blind and had lost his way.

"You are in the wrong room!" I shouted, suddenly stricken with terror.

The poor fellow turned and shuffled back into the night. I was ashamed for having behaved as I did, but I was frightened. Now more awake than ever, every nerve taut, I could find no sleep.

To the east there was a perceptible lightening of the sky.

My shouting must have wakened my wife because she got up and left the room, I suppose to find the toilet. Before long she was back.

"What is the matter, Yaeko-san?" I asked, sensing she was upset.

"*O-tōsan,* the hall was so full of patients that I could find nowhere to walk without disturbing someone," she answered, trying to suppress her agitation. "I had to excuse myself every step I took. Oh! it was terrible. Finally, I stepped on somebody's foot, and when I asked to be excused, there was no answer. I looked down; and do you know what I had done?"

"What?" I asked.

"I had stepped on a dead man's foot," she said and with a shudder moved nearer.

PART TWO

Socialization

How important is childhood socialization in promoting peace? We begin to explore this question with Marc Ross's important study of childrearing and adult violence in 90 preindustrial societies. Preindustrial societies, remember, are the legendary lands of constant war, according to those who believe that war is biologically rooted in the species. But according to Ross's findings, rates of warfare in preindustrial societies vary according to the quality of *social relationships*. Societies with harsh, unaffectionate relations between parents and children and little contact between fathers and sons tend to have high levels of warfare and internal violence.

These childhood experiences create a personality disposed to violence, Ross finds, but social structure determines the target of the violence. For example, societies that are unified by many social connections or ties that cut across diverse social groupings usually direct their violence to warfare with another society rather then feuding with each other. Those societies with fewer cross-cutting ties tend to have internal factions that fight each other.

Studies in modern societies suggest that childhood suffering also leads to adult violence. Children abused by their parents and elders usually repress their hurt and anger (as a coping mecha-

nism) and instead idealize their parents. When they grow up, this repressed rage surfaces in the form of hostility to either their own children or outsiders.[1]

In the next selection, "A Conversation on War, Peace, and Gender," Francesca Cancian argues that socialization to the masculine role is directly linked to war. Teaching boys to be aggressive and dominant, to endure pain, and to avoid expressing tenderness or empathizing with the enemy prepares them to be effective soldiers. These same masculine virtues are the prevailing ethos in business, government, universities, and other institutions run by men. Interestingly enough, the traditional feminine role also contributes to war, according to Cancian, since "weak" and tender women often desire men who appear tough to protect them. Since men want women to desire them, this further reinforces the dominant masculine role.

Military socialization intensifies the warrior aspects of the masculine role, according to William Arkin and Lynne Dobrofsky in the selection "Military Socialization and Masculinity." Boys are told to join the armed services to "become a man." The military's ability to confer manhood status is an extremely important aspect of its cultural power, since in modern Western societies there are virtually no other public ceremonies that confer manhood. Instead, "being a man" is always in doubt. Military socialization teaches recruits that "real" men are tough, effective kill-ers and are contemptuous of all that is "soft" or "feminine."

None of these articles asks how gender socialization might contribute to peace. We leave this question to the reader.

----

1. See T. W. Adorno et al., *The Authoritarian Personality* (New York: Science Editions, 1964) and Alice Miller, *For Your Own Good: Hidden Cruelty in Childrearing and the Roots of Violence* (New York: Farrar Straus Giroux, 1983).

Childrearing and War in Different Cultures

Marc Howard Ross

Introduction

It is difficult to conceive of a human community where there is no conflict among members, or between persons in the community and outsiders. At the same time, the degree to which conflict is physically violent varies widely. Cases such as the Yanomamo of lowland South America (Chagnon 1967), where feuding and warfare are an ongoing condition of daily life, contrast with the Fore of New Guinea, where open physical expression of differences is rare and strongly discouraged (Sorenson 1978). How can we best understand the variation both in the amount of violence and in the choice of targets?

The research reported here contrasts two explanations for societal variation in conflict behavior. One emphasizes the ways in which the social structure of a society creates divergent interests around which conflicts develop. The other focuses on psychocultural dispositions, explaining violent conflict as a result of culturally learned behaviors and of personality configurations typical in a society. To examine these two different perspectives on violent conflict, hypotheses based on each perspective are tested using data from a world-wide sample of 90 small scale, preindustrial societies.

The study suggests that psychocultural dispositions rooted in early childhood learning experiences determine a society's overall level of violent conflict. But while psychocultural dispositions affect the propensity to engage in open conflict, they do not determine very precisely who argues, contests, and fights with whom. The structural features of the social, economic, and political system determine whether the people with whom one cooperates and with whom one fights are within one's society, in another society, or both.

The conflict behavior addressed in this article is group behavior, not that of individuals acting alone. It involves efforts of two or more mutually opposed parties to obtain scarce resources at each other's expense through destroying, injuring, thwarting, or otherwise controlling other parties (Mack and Snyder 1957). Societies can differ greatly in their levels of conflict behavior, the ways in which conflicts are played out, and the mechanisms for dispute settlement which are utilized to control or direct conflicts when they occur. My goal is to explain this variation. Why are conflicts in some societies or between members of a society and outsiders violent, while in other cases, where there are clearly disagreements and differences, open violence is rare? Political violence, from this perspective, is not simply present or absent in a society. Rather we need to think about a continuum. At one end violence is common, perhaps endemic; at the midpoint conflict is common, but it takes more institutionalized forms: at the low end conflict rarely becomes physically violent.

This article is a revised and shortened version of Marc Howard Ross, "A Cross-Cultural Theory of Political Conflict and Violence," *Political Psychology*, 1986 (7): 427-469.
Reprinted by permission of the author.

Hypotheses About Conflict and Violence

In the extensive literature on violence and conflict there are at least three major explanations of observed variations in violence. Some international relations theorists argue that nations which differ in terms of internal or external conflict are not necessarily very different in terms of their internal characteristics and that conflict is best explained by alliances, constraints in the international system, and status inconsistency, and not by national characteristics (Midlarsky 1975; Zinnes 1980).

In contrast, the two explanations considered in this paper focus on internal characteristics. One framework explains violence and warfare in terms of structural features of society (e.g., Hibbs 1973; Otterbein 1968, 1970), identifying aspects of the social, economic, or political system with patterns of conflict. The other emphasizes psychological factors, or what I call psychocultural dispositions (Montagu 1978). I investigate these two explanations for conflict behavior, first by identifying several major hypotheses from each framework, and then by testing them using data coded from ethnographic reports on a world-wide sample of 90 preindustrial societies. My results suggest that *both* social structural and psychocultural factors are important in understanding differences in the levels and targets of conflict across societies.

Social Structural Hypotheses

Social structural hypotheses see the social, economic, or political structure of a society as crucial in creating interests which shape the organization and level of conflict. Different theories, however, identify a wide range of social structural elements as central. The most common ones are cross-cutting ties, fraternal interest group theory, and socioeconomic complexity. In each case the structure of society is seen to be related to patterns of conflict within the society and between a society and outside groups.

Cross-Cutting Ties. Cross-cutting ties such as marriage and trading partnerships, connect individuals and communities within a society. The best known structural hypothesis is that these ties limit the severity of overt conflict, and promote the settlement of disputes, by creating shared interests among groups and individuals (Coleman 1957; Colson 1953). For example, marriage can link members of different kinship groups; and religious cults can bring people together from different regions to participate in common ritual activities. One explanation for the relative stability of the American political system is that differences based on religion, age, political ideology and economic interests, for example, create few enduring groups and link different members of a community together in different ways as new issues arise. Divided or multiple loyalties connect diverse and often dispersed members of a society; conversely, the presence of such ties makes it difficult to organize coalitions of persons and factions who will be at odds with others for extended periods of time, for there are primary bonds across social units, producing less suspicion, more trust, and greater cooperation (LeVine and Campbell 1972:53).

While cross-cutting ties can limit the severity of conflict within a society, they might increase overt conflict between a society and outsiders. By providing a social basis for political unity, they can emphasize the boundaries of a society. The growth of solidarity, of course, might have roots either within the society, or in the actions of outsiders, but for the moment the point is that internal social links, whatever their origin, have important consequences for the stance adopted towards outsiders (LeVine and Campbell 1972).

But what produces cross-cutting ties? Marriage patterns, residence patterns, trade between communities, and groups whose membership cuts across local communities all shape the cross-cutting ties in a society.

a. *Marriage.* Anthropological theory (and sociobiological theory as well) begins, not surprisingly, by looking at kinship and marriage alliances. There are varying viewpoints as to how kinship and marriage influence the expression of conflict. Kinship bonds create mutual obligation and solidarity, while the absence of these ties makes for potentially hostile relationships. In this view a preference for marriage outside the local community inhibits conflict among different communities of the same society because people will not want to fight with those with whom they share kinship and other affective bonds. Of course, internal peace may have a price in terms of external strife as societies with strong bonds among local communities may become more ethnocentric and brazen when facing outsiders. When alliances with neighbors are easily mobilized, attacks against outsiders may be more common. While this view of marriage ties sounds plausible, it has some weaknesses as well. Just because fighting with close kin is potentially disadvantageous does not mean it won't occur. Alliances and exchanges have their own tensions, as the mother-in-law jokes in western society clearly reveal. After all, statistics from our own society show that the vast majority of violent crimes are committed among kin and close friends.

b. *Residence*. Anthropologists pay a good deal of attention to where a new couple resides after marriage. In terms of the impact on violence and conflict, anthropologists have focused particular attention on the dispersion or concentration of related men in a society since they are almost universally dominant in overt fighting and warfare (LeVine and Campbell 1972:52). Matrilocal or uxorilocal residence (where men live with their wives' kin after marriage) disperses male kin among local communities; some argue this inhibits conflict among communities of the same society while promoting external fighting against external groups (Murphy 1957; LeVine 1965). Data from cross-cultural samples show that matrilocality is associated with external warfare, while patrilocality is more common when internal fighting is high (Ember and Ember 1971; Divale 1974). Exactly why this is the case is the subject of disagreement, however. The Embers, interestingly, hypothesize that warfare patterns shape residence rules. Divale (1974), on the other hand, places a primary role on the effects of migration: patrilocal groups which migrate into previously populated areas adopt matrilocal residence to increase internal peace and to be better united in facing outside enemies (Divale 1974). Some contend there is less internal

conflict in matrilocal societies because organized power groups are not present, while others, in contrast, give a crucial role to psychodynamic, as well as structural, factors in the choice of targets for aggression.

c. *Intercommunity trade*. The functionalist school in international relations advocates the exchange of persons and goods as crucial to inhibiting warfare among nations (Haas 1964). Developing interdependencies among communities will, in this view, inhibit overt fighting between them and encourage the development of peaceful mechanisms for resolving disputes when they do arise.

d. *Cross-community organized groups*. In some societies there are important groups which link members of different residential and kinship units together. For example, among the Ndembu, Turner (1957) describes cult groups which unite individuals who might otherwise be opposed to one another on other structural grounds. Age-sets provide the same kind of cross-cutting linkages in many societies. Where such groups are present, linkages can have political relevance in enhancing the internal unity of society, in inhibiting internal conflict, and in facilitating defense against perceived outside enemies.

Fraternal Interest Group Theory. Fraternal interest groups are power groups made up of male kin who live together and have common interests to protect. Where such fraternal interest groups are present, internal conflict is likely to be high, for it is easy to rapidly mobilize them into collective action which is often violent (van Velzen and van Wetering 1960). In several tests of this hypothesis, Otterbein (1968) and Otterbein and Otterbein (1965) found that in politically uncentralized societies the levels of feuding and internal warfare (armed conflict between different communities of the same society) are related to the presence of fraternal interest groups. However, the strength of fraternal interest groups is not related to external warfare (Otterbein 1970).

Polygynous systems (where men have more than one wife) are commonly viewed as warlike and conflict ridden. One view is that polygyny is usually supported by patrilocality, and conflict is high because related males with common interests are grouped together, as spelled out in fraternal interest group theory. On the other hand, Melvin Ember (1974), in a study of polygyny, argues that warfare and unbalanced sex ratios lead to polygyny, not the other way around, and that polygyny is a response to high male mortality as the community needs to replenish its members (1974:204).

3 *Socioeconomic Complexity.* Despite the popular image of violence and anarchy in the most primitive societies, available studies show that societies at the simplest level of technological complexity are no more prone to violence than highly complex ones. Some of the writing on hunters and gatherers stresses the ways in which coordination and cooperation of the entire community in activities such as hunting are essential for survival, and outbreaks of severe conflict within the community are rare (Marshall 1961; Draper 1978; but also see Knauft, 1987). At the same time, some of the most conflict-ridden societies are groups with a similarly low level of complexity such as the Yanomamo in South America or various groups in New Guinea (Chagnon 1967; Meggitt 1977; Koch 1974). Here societies lacking mechanisms of coordination and control also have few means for limiting open conflicts once they break out. The relation between internal conflict and complexity is unclear.

However, external conflict is more prevalent in more complex societies. There is good support for the hypothesis that societies that have been more warlike and more successful in warfare have displaced those that lack such traits (LeVine and Campbell 1972:72–77). Looking at modern nations there is also a modest tendency for more developed nations to have higher levels of external conflict (Haas 1965).

Political complexity—the rise of a centralized state—has received more attention as a correlate of conflict and warfare than socioeconomic complexity. As the state develops, warfare increases and the type of warfare changes (Wright 1942; Broch and Galtung 1966). Some argue that the develop-

ment of military leadership produces political leaders and subsequent centralization, while others put the causal arrow in the opposite direction (Service 1975). Materialist interpretations of the rise of the state argue that the development of stratification and wealth creates the need for a military to protect privileged interests against internal and external predators (Fried 1967). Theories of the state as a mechanism of conquest posit the growth of military sophistication as a way to control neighboring people and resources (Adams 1966).

A somewhat different perspective suggests that even if more centralized systems are more militarily sophisticated, the concentration of political power in a few hands places greater control over the outbreak of violence. This view emphasizes the role of the state as a conflict inhibitor through its control over the instruments of violence (Service 1975). If the state is effective in controlling the overall level of violence as well as its targets, then political centralization will be associated with lower violence both internally and externally.

To summarize, the social structural hypotheses identify different ways in which the organization of a society affects conflict behavior: weak cross-cutting ties and strong fraternal interest groups are expected to raise internal and lower external conflict, while the effects of complexity are more likely to increase the level of both internal and external conflict.

Psychocultural Hypotheses

Early socialization influences adult behavior by shaping the personality of the individual (Harrington and Whiting 1972). Shaping cognition as well as deeper motivations, early learning experiences prepare individuals for patterns of conflict and cooperation in their society. LeVine and Campbell (1972) review psychocultural theories in the area of ethnocentrism and provide three key hypotheses relevant to internal violence and external warfare: harsh socialization, warmth and affection, and male gender identity conflict.

Harsh Socialization. Several psychological approaches associate harsh and severe child training practices with later aggressiveness: psychoanalytic theory (and the authoritarian personality work derived from it), social learning theory, and frustration–aggression theory.

One psychonalytic theory focuses on the development of a superego that monitors behaviors and feelings. As part of psychological maturation, individuals come to repress impulses that are too frightening to be acknowledged at a conscious level. Repression is a normal part of psychological functioning. However, when parents are very hostile and punitive, the child develops an overly harsh superego, leading to severe repression. The repressed, pent up feelings can be highly destructive for either the individual or those around him or her. Identification with aggressive parents and severe repression are the raw material for the expression of violence, according to this psychoanalytic theory. In some cases the feelings are turned inward, while in others they are projected onto others and one's own aggressive feelings are displaced onto available targets (Adorno 1950).

Other theories identify different mechanisms, but the predictions are similar (Zigler and Child 1969). For example, where psychoanalytic and frustration–aggression theory connect severe physical punishment of children with later displacement onto outgroups, social learning theory emphasizes imitation, modeling, and reinforcement. In either case, however, the argument is that children who experience harsh socialization become aggressive adults who engage in overt conflict more readily.

A number of specific cross-cultural studies find a positive association between harsh socialization practices and physical aggression, bellicosity, or warfare (Levinson and Malone 1980:249). Slater (1968) finds a connection between sexual repression, sadism, and militarism. Others argue that children who are forced to repress their private feelings later identify with aggression by the state. "War," conclude Durbin and Bowlby, "is due to the transformed aggressiveness of individuals" (1939:41). This is an illustration of the psychoanalytic concept of "identification with the aggressor"; children identify with harsh, punitive parents and become like their parents (Anna Freud 1937).

Warmth and Affection. Affection, warmth, and love-oriented child rearing practices are associated with low violence and conflict. Several studies show that variables measuring harsh socialization practices are *distinct* from indicators of warmth and affection (Ross 1986); these two dimensions are *not* simply opposite poles on the same continuum.

Greater expression of affection toward children, greater emphasis on values such as trust, honesty, and generosity, and closer father–child ties all lead individuals toward cooperation, rather than animosity and aggressiveness. The healthy psychosocial development of the individual in early relationships with parental figures prepares the way for socially cooperative experiences later in life (Winnicott 1965; Greenberg and Mitchell 1983).

Winnicott (1965) uses the term "good enough mother" to refer to the caretaker who provides a child with early experiences resulting in a positive sense of self, and trust and openness toward others. In contrast, if early relationships are highly negative and threatening, psychological growth remains fixated at an early developmental stage, and bonds to others cannot develop. Attachment to others is crucial later in life whether we are speaking about the ability of individuals to form intimate relationships or to join with others in socially cooperative ventures (Bowlby 1969).

The profiles of seven small-scale societies, all low on internal conflict and aggression, present some good examples of this pattern (Montagu 1978). In these societies, great affection is frequently directed toward the child, whose overall feelings of security are high. Overt expression of aggression is discouraged, but not through physical punishment. Finally, these societies lack models of highly aggressive persons whom the child can imitate. Affectionate parent–child relationships are associated with lower conflict, both within one's society and in dealing with outsiders, just as harsh socialization is associated with higher conflict.

3 *Male Gender Identity Conflict.* Men who are uncertain about their gender identity tend to be more aggressive, according to several theories. In male dominated cultures, where fathers are distant and aloof from their children, frustration develops when young boys grow up with especially strong bonds to their mothers, anthropologists have theorized (Whiting 1965; Whiting and Whiting 1975a). At adolescence, and sometimes earlier, these bonds may be severed by severe initiation rites or other rituals, so that boys can meet the societal expectations of adult male behavior, but some frustration and insecurity about gender identity remain (Herdt 1987; Munroe, Munroe, and Whiting 1981).

A second source of frustration is maternal ambivalence. Women living in patrilocal, polygynous societies have neither strong ties to their natal families nor strong affective bonds with their husbands. Slater and Slater call this "diluted marriage" (1965). Women in these settings develop strong bonds with their children, but also take out frustration on them, and the male child is "alternatively seduced and rejected" (Slater and Slater, 1965:242). The result is that males in such cultures develop very ambivalent feelings toward females; narcissistic personalities that are preoccupied with early developmental tasks, pride, and self-enhancement are common, and the males are prone to aggressive actions (Herdt 1987; Huyghe 1986). Despite cultural attempts to deal with male gender ambivalence, the solutions are only partial so that compensatory behaviors seen in bellicosity, aggressive display behavior, and open fighting are common.

Distant father-child ties promote aggressivity, while close, affectionate bonds are associated with low overt conflict according to the male gender identity hypothesis. Many studies support this hypothesis (Ember 1980:561–62), although several critics have suggested that the same data might be better explained by other theories (e.g., Young 1965; Paige and Paige 1981). A major finding from *The Authoritarian Personality* research was that distant fathers produce children (particularly boys) who are insecure in interpersonal relationships and are more ready to engage in open aggression against outgroups (Adorno et al. 1950).

Detailed observations of children in six cultures show that children are more authoritarian and aggressive in the cultures in which the father is present less, and child-father contact is lower (Whiting and Whiting 1975a). The highest rates of physical assault and homicide occurred in the two cultures in which children spent the least time with adult males, Beatrice Whiting found (1965). She also notes that the absence of fathers is often correlated with juvenile delinquency in industrial societies. Distant fathering is associated with training boys to be warriors, and societies in which fathers are distant are likely to have a high incidence of warfare (Whiting and Whiting 1975b; West and Konner 1976:203). Among both human and nonhuman primates, close father–child ties are associated with lower aggression and conflict, according to Alcorta (1982). She says that there is noticeably less stress among infants, particularly among males, and lower subsequent aggression, the more that adult males are involved in child rearing.

In summary, the psychocultural hypotheses are: when socialization is harsh and punishing, low in affection and warmth, and when male gender conflict is high, there is a high level of both internal and external conflict.

Results

Procedures

These social structural and psychocultural hypotheses were tested with data obtained from coding ethnographic reports on 90 preindustrial societies located throughout the world. The societies were scored on a number of variables based on reports about politics, socioeconomic organization, and child training. The political codes are described in Ross (1983), while the socioeconomic and child training variables are found in Barry and Schlegel (1980).

Internal violence and conflict was measured by seven variables. Beginning with the most important, they are (1) the severity of conflict between residents of different communities in the same society, (2) the acceptability of using violence against members of the same society but outside the local community, (3) the frequency of internal warfare, (4) the severity of conflict within local communities in the society, (5) the degree to which physical force is used as a mechanism for dispute settlement, (6) the acceptability of violence against members of the community, and (7) the variability of compliance with norms and decisions on the part of members of the local community. Societies on the high end of this scale, such as the Jivaro or Somali, have frequent violent conflict and internal warfare both within and between communities of the same society. Societies at the middle of the scale, such as the Kikuyu or Comanche, have regular conflict, but internal warfare and the use of violence in local disputes is less common. At the low point are societies where conflict itself is milder and physical violence infrequent. The Mbuti Pygmies, Semang, and Papago fall here.

Three variables make up the external warfare and conflict scale: the frequency of external warfare, the degree of hostility expressed to other societies (not just in war), and the acceptability of violence directed to people in other societies. Societies such as the Buganda, Maori, Comanche, and Jivaro are high on this dimension, while low external conflict societies are the !Kung Bushmen, the Lepcha, and the Trobriand Islanders.

Findings

Multiple regression is used in the analysis. Because there are many moderate correlations among the independent variables, it is especially useful in showing how each of the independent variables is related to the dependent variables after the effects of the other independent variables are removed. With this procedure, we arrive at results different from, and more straightforward than, those we get from simply looking at the bivariate correlations.

The regression results are presented in Table 1. They show that both structural and psychocultural variables are significantly related to internal and external conflict and in combination explain conflict better than either set of variables alone. A closer look shows that low affection, harsh socialization, and male gender identity conflict increase internal *and* external violence and conflict, but the specific structural factors associated with internal and external conflict differ. To explain these results we propose a dispositional basis for aggression and violence rooted in early learning and personality formation, while the targets of aggression are shaped by the structural features of a society. In some cases the targets will be outside one's society, in some they will be inside it, while in many situations both forms of violence will occur. Before elaborating on the general argument, it is useful to first examine the specific results.

Internal Violence and Conflict. Two psychocultural and two structural variables are significantly related to the level of violence and conflict within a society. The more affectionate and warm and the less harsh the socialization in a society, the lower the level of political violence and conflict. This finding suggests that early experiences become critical in establishing an individual's capacity to cooperate with others and provide a framework for interpreting their behavior. Individuals who have experienced early lack of affection and harsh treatment will have much more trouble in establishing warm cooperative bonds with others as adults and will be more prone to view the behavior of others as hostile and threatening. Projecting threat and aggression onto others then provides an easy justification for one's own aggressive actions.

The results concerning structural variables show that the weaker the cross-cutting ties in a society, and the stronger fraternal interest groups are in uncentralized societies, the greater the level of internal violence and conflict. Cross-cutting ties, by providing social and political links among different groups, offer a brake on the expansion of conflict, limit polarization, and lessen the possibility of widespread violence. Fraternal interest groups do the opposite, bringing related males together where it is easy for them to organize violent actions, either defending their own perceived interests or attacking others.

TABLE 1   Multiple regressions: Internal and external conflict

	Standardized Regression Coefficient (Beta)	Standard Error of Beta	Pearson Corr. #	
Internal violence and conflict				
Structural variables				
Strength of cross-cutting ties scale	-.29**	.11	-.24**	(90)
Marital endogamy	.01	.10	.04	(90)
Fraternal interest group strength in uncentralized societies	.22*	.10	.26**	(90)
Political power concentration	-.11	.14	-.03	(90)
Polygyny	.12	.10	.20*	(90)
Intercommunity trade	.04	.11	.03	(89)
Socioeconomic complexity	.09	.14	.08	(90)
Matrilocality #	-.07	.10	.05	(90)
Psychocultural variables				
Affectionate socialization practices	-.31**	.10	-.35***	(89)
Harsh socialization practices	.22*	.10	.33***	(82)
Male gender identity conflict	.13	.10	.05	(68)

Multiple R = .60 R Square = .36

	Standardized Regression Coefficient (Beta)	Standard Error of Beta	Pearson Corr. #	
External violence and conflict				
Structural variables				
Strength of cross-cutting ties in uncentralized societies	.21*	.10	.20*	(90)
Marital endogamy in uncentralized societies	.43***	.11	.28**	(90)
Fraternal interest group strength	.07	.12	.24**	(87)
Political power concentration	-.12	.12	.11	(90)
Polygyny	-.12	.09	.03	(90)
Socioeconomic complexity	.27*	.13	.24**	(90)
Matrilocality	.11	.09	.14	(90)
Psychocultural variables				
Affectionate socialization practices	-.39***	.09	-.41***	(89)
Harsh socialization practices	.19*	.09	.30**	(82)
Male gender identity conflict	.32***	.08	.29**	(68)

Multiple R = .69 R Square = .47

Definitions of the variables are provided in the Appendix below.

***statistically significant at the .001 level

**statistically significant at the .01 level

*statistically significant at the .05 level

##sample sizes in parentheses; Sample size = 90 in the regressions

Means have been substituted for missing data in the regression

#results are the same when matrilocality is substituted for patrilocality; but the sign is reversed

###correlations are for all cases, not just uncentralized societies

APPENDIX   Measures and sources for the independent variables

In all cases the specific measures used begin with published data for the societies in the Standard Cross-Cultural Sample (Murdock and White 1969). The measurement of the two dependent variables is explained in the text. Included here are brief descriptions of each independent variable; greater detail about the technical aspects of the measures is provided in Ross (1983, 1985). The sources for the nonpolitical variables are found in Barry and Schlegel (1980).

Strength of cross-cutting ties is a scale made up of seven variables including the extent to which individuals living in different communities of the same society are linked together in politically relevant ways, the strength of in-group or we feelings directed toward the wider society—i.e., beyond the local community, the strength of kinship organizations and ritual groups that link different communities, and the extent to which there is intervention in disputes as they develop and community pressures work toward settlement (see Ross 1983).

Intercommunity marriage is a five point measure of the extent to which marriage in a society favors local exogamy vs. endogamy.

Matrilocality and *patrilocality* classifies societies as patrilocal if there is a preference for patrilocal or virilocal residence, otherwise patrilocality is absent; similarly, matrilocality is scored as present if the society is matrilocal or uxorilocal, absent if it is not.

Intercommunity trade is a seven point measure of the extent to which a community in the society trades for foodstuffs.

Fraternal interest group strength is based on Paige and Paige's (1981) measure and includes the presence or absence of brideprice, the presence or absence of patrilineality, and a trichotomized measure of the size of effective kin-based political subunits.

Polygyny is a three point measure—monogamous, less than 20% polygynous marriage, and more than 20% polygynous.

Socioeconomic complexity is a scale made up of eight different highly associated measures: importance of agriculture as a contribution to subsistence, importance of animal husbandry, low importance of hunting, low importance of gathering, the degree to which food is stored, the size of the average community in the society, the degree of social stratification, and cultural complexity.

Political complexity is a thirteen variable scale originally called *political power concentration* (Ross, 1983). The crucial variables are: the extent to which leaders act independently in a community, the presence or absence of checks on political leaders, the degree of political role differentiation in a society, the importance of decision making bodies, and the level of taxation.

Harsh socialization is a scale made up of the following socialization measures: severity of pain infliction, extent to which corporal punishment is used, the degree to which children are not indulged, the extent to which children are scolded, the importance of caretakers other than the mother, the degree to which fortitude is stressed as a value, and the degree to which aggressiveness is stressed as a value.

Affectionate socialization is a scale made up of the following socialization measures: the degree to which trust is emphasized as a value during childhood, the degree to which honesty is stressed as a value during childhood, the closeness of the father in childhood, the degree to which generosity is stressed as a value during childhood, the degree to which affection is expressed toward the child, and the extent to which children are valued by the society.

Male gender identity conflict is a seven point measure of the length of abstinence from sexual intercourse by the mother after birth, described as the cultural norm. The seven point measure is from Barry and Paxson (1971). Another measure which Whiting has also used is polygyny (see above).

External Warfare and Hostility. The results for external warfare show the same psychocultural basis for external as for internal conflict—lack of affectionate, and presence of harsh, socialization—and there is strong support for the male gender identity hypothesis as a predictor of external violence. Structural factors are important here too, but they are different from those involved in internal violence. Finally, there are some important differences between centralized and uncentralized societies. In uncentralized societies only, external violence is related to a preference for intracommunity marriage and strong cross-cutting ties.

This study of internal and external conflict in 90 preindustrial societies shows *both* psychocultural and structural variables are important. Socialization creates dispositions toward high or low violence in a society. Particular structural conditions then determine the ways in which the violence is directed at others within the society, at outsiders, or in both directions.

The psychocultural argument supported here is rooted in the notion that early relationships provide a template for perceiving the world and for intra- and inter-group cooperation and conflict later in life (Fornari 1975:101). Dispositional patterns emphasize *cultural* constructions and are more than individual personality configurations; they are culturally learned and approved methods for dealing with others. Although participants have little trouble citing "objective" bases for conflict, "She [he] took my toy [land, water, women cows]," what is striking to the outsider is the number of times the same supposedly provocative action occurs and is *not* followed by any overt violence. This is crucial. It means that objective situations alone do not cause conflict; *interpretations* of such situations also play a central role, while the structural features of a society affect who the targets of hostility are likely to be.

Group, and not just individual, processes are especially important as individuals seek to answer difficult questions about the meaning of their lives. Groups, after all, provide social support telling people both that they are not alone and that particular answers are right. Because there cannot be certainty concerning the meaning of many social actions, building social consensus and support become crucial. For Whiting (1980) areas such as religion and the interpretation of illness are areas of human behavior producing projective behaviors that are best understood as psychological products. I suggest that conflict and violence should frequently be seen in this same framework as well. Conflict situations are often crucial and very ambiguous. There is great room for individuals to interpret them in terms of their own needs. Conflicts often begin with scanty information concerning a supposedly objective situation, and therefore encourage projective processes.

In this way a full understanding of war and peace within and between societies seems to require an integration of psychocultural and social factors. This should not be very surprising for after all conflict behavior is one of the things that is distinctively human. It is not something we do in a trivial way; it involves and absorbs so much of our emotional energy and resources. Perhaps from looking at the behavior of those human groups who seem most different from ourselves we can learn something about the range of possible human behavior, as well as gain better understanding of ourselves.

References

Adams, Robert McC. 1966. *The Evolution of Urban Society.* Chicago: Aldine.

Adorno, T. W. et al. 1950. *The Authoritarian Personality.* New York: John Wiley.

Alcorta, Candace Storey. 1982. "Paternal Behavior and Group Competition." *Behavior Science Research* 17:3–23.

Barry, Herbert H. III, Irwin L. Child, and Margaret K. Bacon. 1959. "Relations of Child Training to Subsistence Economy." *American Anthropologist* 61:51–63.

Barry, Herbert H. III and Lenora M. Paxson. 1971. "Infancy and Early Childhood: Cross-Cultural Codes 2." *Ethnology* 10:466–508.

Barry, Herbert III and Alice Schlegel (eds.). 1980. *Cross-Cultural Samples and Codes.* Pittsburgh: University of Pittsburgh Press.

Bowlby, John. 1969. *Attachment and Loss.* New York: Basic Books.

Broch, Tom and Johan Galtung. 1966. "Belligerence among the Primitives.." *Journal of Peace Research* 3:33–45.

Bronfenbrenner, Urie. 1960. "Freudian Theories of Identification and Their Derivation. *Child Development* 31:15–40.

Chagnon, Napoleon. 1967. "Yanomamo Social Organization and Warfare." Pp. 109–159 in *War: The Anthropology of Armed Conflict and Aggression,* edited by Morton Fried, Marvin Harris, and Robert Murphy. Garden City, New York: Natural History Press.

Chodorow, Nancy. 1978. *The Reproduction of Mothering: Psychoanalysis and the Sociology of Gender.* Berkeley and Los Angeles: University of California Press.

Coleman, James S. 1957. *Community Conflict.* New York: Free Press.

Colson, Elizabeth. 1953. "Social Control and Vengeance in Plateau Tonga Society." *Africa* 23:199–211.

Divale, William T. 1974. "Migration, External Warfare and Matrilocal Residence." *Behavior Science Research* 9:75–133.

Draper, Patricia. 1978. "The Learning Environment for Aggression and Anti-Social Behavior among the !Kung." Pp. 31–53 in *Learning Non-Aggression,* edited by Ashley Montagu. New York: Oxford University Press.

Durbin, E. F. M. and John Bowlby. 1939. *Personal Aggressiveness and War.* New York: Columbia University Press.

Ember, Carol R. 1974. "An Evaluation of Alternative Theories of Matrilocal Versus Patrilocal Residence." *Behavior Science Research* 9:135–149.

————. 1980. "A Cross-Cultural Perspective on Sex Differences." Pp. 531–580 in *Handbook of Cross-Cultural Human Development,* edited by Ruth H. Munroe et al. New York: Garland STPM Press.

Ember, Melvin. 1974. "Warfare, Sex Ratio, and Polygyny." *Ethnology* 13:197–206.

Ember, Melvin and Carol R. Ember. 1971. "The Conditions Favoring Matrilocal Versus Patrilocal Residence." *American Anthropologist* 73:571–594.

Fisher, Seymour and Robert P. Greenberg. 1977. *The Scientific Credibility of Freud's Theories and Therapy.* New York: Basic Books.

Fornari, Franco. 1975. *The Psychoanalysis of War.* Bloomington: Indiana University Press.

Freud, Anna. 1937 [1966]. *The Ego and the Mechanisms of Defense.* New York: International Universities Press.

Freud, Sigmund. 1914 [1963]. "On Narcissism: An Introduction." *General Psychological Theory.* New York: Macmillan, 56–82.

————. 1922 [1922]. *Group Psychology and the Analysis of the Ego.* New York: Norton.

————. 1917 [1963]. "Mourning and Melancholia." *General Psychological Theory.* New York: Macmillan, 164–179.

Fried, Morton H. 1967. *The Evolution of Political Society.* New York: Random House.

Greenberg, Jay R. and Stephen A. Mitchell. 1983. *Object Relations in Psychoanalytic Theory.* Cambridge: Harvard University Press.

Greenstein, Fred I. 1967. "The Impact of Personality and Politics: An Attempt to Clear Away the Underbrush." *American Political Science Review.* 61:629–641.

————. 1965. *Children and Politics.* New Haven: Yale University Press.

Gurr, Ted Robert. 1970. *Why Men Rebel.* Princeton: Princeton University Press.

Haas, Ernst. 1964. *The Uniting of Europe.* Stanford: Stanford University Press.

Haas, Michael. 1965. "Societal Approaches to the Study of War." *Journal of Peace Research* 4:307–323.

Harrington, Charles and John W. M. Whiting. 1972. "Socialization Processes and Personality." Pp. 469–507 in *Psychological Anthropology,* second ed., edited by Francis L. K. Hsu. Cambridge: Schenkman.

Hendrix, Lewellen. 1985. "Economy and Child Training Reexamined." *Ethos* 13:246–261.

Herdt, Gilbert. 1987. *The Sambia: Ritual and Gender in New Guinea.* New York: Holt, Rinehart & Winston.

Hess, Robert D. and David Easton. 1960. "The Child's Changing Image of the President." *Public Opinion Quarterly* 24:632–644.

Hibbs, Douglas. 1973. *Mass Political Violence: Cross-National Causal Analysis.* New York: John Wiley.

Huyghe, Bernard. 1986. "Toward a Structural Model of Violence: Male Initiation Rituals and Tribal Warfare." Pp. 25–48 in *Peace and War in Cross-Cultural Perspective,* edited by Mary LeCron

Foster and Robert A. Rubinstein. New Brunswick: Transaction Books.

Knauft, Bruce. 1987. "Reconsidering Violence in Simple Human Societies: Homicide Among the Gebusi of New Guinea." *Current Anthropology* 28:457–500.

Koch, Klaus Frierich. 1974. *War and Peace in Jalemo.* Cambridge: Harvard University Press.

Lamb, Michael E. (ed). 1976. *The Role of the Father in Child Development.* New York: John Wiley.

LeVine, Robert A. 1965. "Socialization, Social Structure and Intersocial Images." Pp. 43–69 in *International Behavior: A Social-Psychological Analysis,* edited by Herbert Kelman. New York: Holt, Rinehart & Winston.

LeVine, Robert A. and Donald Campbell. 1972. *Ethnocentrism: Theories of Conflict, Ethnic Attitudes and Group Behavior.* New York: John Wiley.

Levinson, David and Martin J. Malone. 1980. *Toward Explaining Human Culture: A Critique of the Findings of Worldwide Cross-Cultural Research.* New Haven: HRAF Press.

Mack, Raymond W. and Richard Snyder. 1957. "The Analysis of Social Conflict: Toward an Overview and Synthesis." *Journal of Conflict Resolution* 1:212–248.

Mahler, Margaret S., Fred Pine, and Anni Bergman. 1975. *The Psychological Birth of the Human Infant: Symbiosis and Individuation.* New York: Basic Books.

Marsh, David. 1971. "Political Socialization: The Implicit Assumptions Questioned." *British Journal of Political Science* 1:453–465.

Marshall, Lorna. 1961. "Sharing, Talking and Giving: The Relief of Social Tension Among the !Kung Bushmen." *Africa* 31:231–249.

Meggitt, Mervyn. 1977. *Blood Is Their Argument: Warfare among the Mae Enga Tribesmen of the New Guinea Highlands.* Palo Alto: Mayfield.

Midlarsky, Manus. 1975. *On War: Political Violence in the International System.* New York: Free Press.

Montagu, Ashley (ed). 1978. *Learning Non-Aggression.* New York: Oxford Univ. Press.

Munroe, Robert L., Ruth H. Munroe, and John W. M. Whiting. 1981. "Male Sex-Role Resolutions." Pp. 611–632 in *Handbook of Cross-Cultural Human Development,* edited by Ruth H. Munroe, Robert L. Munroe, and Beatrice B. Whiting. New York and London: Garland STPM Press.

Murdock, George Peter and Douglas R. White. 1969. "Standard Cross-Cultural Sample." *Ethnology* 8:329–369.

Murphy, Robert F. 1957. "Intergroup Hostility and Social Cohesion." *American Anthropologist* 59:1018–1035.

Otterbein, Keith. 1968. "Internal War: A Cross-Cultural Comparison." *American Anthropologist* 70:277–289.

————. 1970. *The Evolution of War.* New Haven: HRAF Press.

————. 1977. "Warfare as a Hitherto Unrecognized Critical Variable." *American Behavioral Scientist* 20:693–710.

Otterbein, Keith F. and Charlotte Swanson Otterbein. 1965. "An Eye for an Eye, a Tooth for a Tooth: A Cross-Cultural Study of Feuding." *American Anthropologist* 67:1470–1482.

Paige, Karen Ericksen and Jeffrey M. Paige. 1981. *The Politics of Reproductive Ritual.* Berkeley: University of California Press.

Ross, Marc Howard. 1981. "Socioeconomic Complexity, Socialization, and Political Differentiation: A Cross-Cultural Study." *Ethos* 9:217–247.

————. 1983. "Political Decision Making and Conflict: Additional Cross-Cultural Codes and Scales." *Ethnology* 22:169–192.

————. 1985. "Internal and External Violence and Conflict: Cross-Cultural Evidence and a New Analysis." *Journal of Conflict Resolution* 29:547–579.

————. 1986. "A Cross-Cultural Theory of Political Confict and Violence." *Political Psychology.* 7:427–69.

Schafer, Roy. 1968. *Aspects of Internalization.* New York: International Universities Press.

Searing, Donald, Joel J. Schwartz, and Alden F. Lind. 1973. "The Structuring Principle: Political Socialization and Belief Systems." *American Political Science Review* 67:415–432.

Service, Elman R. 1975. *Origins of the State and Civilization.* New York: Norton.

Slater, Phillip E. 1968. *The Glory of Hera.* Boston: Beacon.

Slater, Phillip E. and Dori A. Slater. 1965. "Maternal Ambivalence and Narcissism: A Cross-Cultural Study." *Merrill-Palmer Quarterly* 11:241–259.

Sorenson, Richard E. 1978. "Cooperation and Freedom among the Fore of New Guinea." In *Learning Non-Aggression,* edited by Ashley Montagu. New York: Oxford.

Turner, Victor. 1957. *Schism and Continuity in an African Society.* Manchester: Manchester University Press.

van Velzen, H. U. E. Thoden and W. van Wetering. 1960. "Residence, Power Groups and Intra-Societal Aggression." *International Archives of Ethnography* 49:169–200.

Weisner, Thomas S. and Ronald Gallimore. 1977. "My Brother's Keeper: Child and Sibling Caretaking." *Current Anthropology* 18:169–190.

West, Mary Maxwell and Melvin J. Konner. 1976. "The Role of the Father: An Anthropological Perspective." In *The Role of the Father in Child Development,* edited by Michael E. Lamb. New York: Wiley-Interscience, 185–216.

Whiting, Beatrice B. 1965. "Sex Identity Conflict and Physical Violence: A Comparative Study." *American Anthropologist* 67, part 2:123–140.

————. 1980. "Culture and Social Behavior: A Model for the Development of Social Behavior." *Ethos* 8:95–116.

Whiting, Beatrice B. and John W. M. Whiting. 1975a. *Children of Six Cultures: A Psycho-Cultural Analysis.* Cambridge: Harvard University Press.

Whiting, John W. M. and Beatrice B. Whiting. 1975b. "Aloofness and Intimacy Between Husbands and Wives." *Ethos* 3:183–207.

Whiting, John W. M., Richard Kluckhohn, and Albert S. Anthony. 1958. "The Function of Male Initiation Ceremonies at Puberty." In *Readings in Social Psychology,* edited by Eleanor E. Maccoby, T. M. Newcomb, and Eugene L. Hartley. Third Ed. New York: Holt, Rinehart & Winston, 359–370.

Wilkenfeld, Jonathan and Dina A. Zinnes. 1973. "A Linkage Model of Domestic Conflict Behavior." In *Conflict Behavior and Linkage Politics,* edited by Jonathan Wilkenfeld. New York: David McKay.

Winnicott, Donald W. 1965. *The Maturational Process and the Facilitating Environment.* New York: International Universities Press.

Wright, Quincy. 1942. *A Study of War.* 2 vols. Chicago: University of Chicago Press.

Young, Frank. 1965. *Initiation Ceremonies: A Cross-Cultural Study of Status Dramatization.* New York: Bobbs-Merrill.

Zigler, Edward and Irwin L. Child. 1969. "Socialization." In *Handbook of Social Psychology,* second ed., edited by Gardner Lindzey and Elliot Aronson. Reading, Mass.: Addison-Wesley.

Zinnes, Dina A. 1980. "Why War? Evidence on the Outbreak of International Conflict." In *Handbook of Political Conflict,* edited by Ted Robert Gurr. New York: Free Press.

A Conversation on War, Peace, and Gender

Francesca M. Cancian

The conversation is part of a videotaped interview by John Whiteley, as part of his series of interviews and readings, "The Quest For Peace." Used with permission.

John: An important factor as you think about "The Quest for Peace" is gender. What do you learn about peace from studying gender?

Francesca: Let me start with the male role. Robert Brannon has identified what he calls four main dimensions of the male role: (1) no sissy stuff—don't do anything feminine; (2) big wheel—be a success, have people look up to you; (3) sturdy oak—be tough, stand up to pain, don't back down when people attack you; and finally (4) give 'em hell—be violent and daring. I think the "no sissy stuff" dimension, the avoiding anything feminine, is a lot more important than people often realize.[1]

John: How is it important?

Francesca: Many of the qualities that our culture defines as "feminine" are important to peacemaking: being able to love someone else, being able to care for them, being able to experience and share feelings of weakness and empathy with others, being able to compromise. So if you tell a man, "The first thing you have to do, young man, you never do anything feminine." Well, it becomes very dangerous to engage in a lot of peacemaking activities.

John: What about aggression? You've indicated that this is an important part of the male role. How is that related to the prospects for peace or war?

Francesca: Well, I think it's interesting to see how violence is often the ultimate test of whether you are really a man, and often it's connected with avoiding being feminine. When men are trained in the military to be more violent—of course that is what the military has to train people to do—they play very much on "don't be a girl," "go out there and get that person or you're a faggot or a woman." The same thing happens when boys in football are trained to be violent.

John: What are the implications for the injunction to be a big wheel?

Francesca: The way we seem to identify success in our society is not only being a big wheel but also being competitive and independent: I succeed and you don't. It's not being successful in terms of me together with you, let us build a better world, but me over you, me against you. The same thing happens with the sturdy oak role; again that is defined in terms of not caring for others, standing there and being the rock, not showing pain.

John: How does that keep you from being peaceful?

Francesca: Well, one way is that it's obviously very convenient if you want to train someone to be a soldier. Being a soldier is a horrible thing to have to be, and you really have to be able to endure pain and suffering and not express weakness and just keep going. Another important way it ties up with war and peace is that it's probably very hard either to defend war as a policy or to engage in war if you experience empathy with the enemy. I don't think you could actually kill people repeatedly unless those feelings were really pushed down—feelings of your own vulnerability and how you're not really that different from that other person. Insisting on men not experiencing those feelings, especially in times of crisis, very much feeds into the whole war system.

John: What are the major components of the feminine role: How does the female gender role impact the prospects for peace and war?

Francesca: Well, a lot of people look at the feminine role and say, "Oh what a picture of a peacemaking person: loving, tender, and empathic, able to express feelings of vulnerability." But there are important elements that encourage war, not peace. One of them is the stereotype of a woman being tender, sweet, and only concerned with other people, not a person who can protect herself. This kind of feminine woman needs a sturdy oak; she needs someone to act like a tree to protect her because she can't protect herself. Part of raising girls to be feminine is raising them to need men who will be strong and will take care of them because they can't take care of themselves.

John: So that contributes to women being helpless and encourages men to be aggressive?

Francesca: That's right. I think there is another way that the feminine role may encourage aggression in men. The feminine stereotype is aggression-phobic: "I don't want to do anything ugly; I don't want to do anything bloody." I think women are trained to some extent to push down their own aggression and lustiness so much that they kind of egg men on to do it for them and are attracted to that dangerous aspect of men. Not that women want violent men, but there is some truth in the feeling that men express that, if I am too sensitive, she won't think that I'm sexy.

John: And that reinforces men's aggression.

Francesca: High school is when gender roles are the most rigid and you can see it most clearly. At football games guys are dying of pain, but not saying it, trying to kill each other. And then there are these very gorgeous girls, the cheerleaders, getting turned on by these guys; it is the basic dance.

I think there is another way that the feminine role contributes to war, and that is that we think of peace as something women do, and we associate women with the home. So we don't think of peace as something that important people do when things

get really serious out in the real world. Our attitude is: "There, there dear, you be loving and sweet at home; when it gets down to things like guns and missiles and foreign policy, you have to leave that to the men." And I think women have often bought into that and have felt "yes I am devoted to love and caring for other people, but only at home."

There is a nice historical example of that in the 1920s, when women won the right to vote and the expectation of a lot of people was, "Oh now women are going to get to vote: they are going to take their values of peace and caring for others into the political sphere, and boy are we going to see a political change." So in fact, Congress passed a law to protect children right away because they anticipated the impact of women's vote.[2] But there was no impact of women having a vote at first because women were unable to carry this "peace and love" orientation into the public sphere. They often did not vote, and if they voted they did what their husbands or their fathers told them to do. Lately, though, there has been a promising change; women are starting to take their peace-loving attitudes into the public sphere. Women are now voting as much as men, and we are now seeing a "gender gap" where women are voting for peace issues. For example, when Reagan ran for president, about 10% more women voted against him than men. So we are starting to see a breaking away from confining peace to the private sphere, but it's just beginning.

John: One part of your analysis has been to focus on the importance of the male gender role as it relates to peace on three of the dominant institutions of our society: the military, government, and higher education. I'd like to present those to you one at a time and ask you to share with us what you have in mind. First, what is the impact of the male role on the military?

Francesca: The military in some ways gets a bum rap because *societies* go to war, and then the military has to go and do it. I think the war-making values that are in the military are in the rest of society too. Nonetheless, we've got to focus on the military because they are the ones that go to war. The connection between the military and the male role is a two-way street. On the one hand, the male gender role feeds into being a soldier: the emphasis on enduring pain and on being violent, and all the emphasis on athletics in high school. As a Vietnam veteran said, "I've been in basic training since I was 6 years old." On the other hand, the military also defines the masculine role. Boys go into the army to become men, and what the military does is define masculinity in such a way as to emphasize being violent and suppressing feelings of vulnerability and of empathy with other people. Also the military obviously emphasizes obedience enormously because that is the core of the army. This emphasis on violence and on suppressing feelings is something men pick up in the army through military training and carry with them in later life.

John: In your view that reinforces something that has already been socialized?

Francesca: That's right, it reinforces that.

John: What is the impact of gender roles on the government?

Francesca: It is interesting to look at gender in government. I don't think of it so much as the impact of gender on government because, you know, where are gender roles? To some extent I think they exist within each of us. They are in our personalities, and we carry them around wherever we go. But in another way I think gender exists in our social institutions. We have divided the world up into what historians often call the feminine sphere and the masculine sphere, and institutions like government and higher education belong to the masculine sphere, so the way you are supposed to behave in those places is according to the male gender role, whether you are a man or a woman.

Now in government, you can, I think, see the emphasis on being tough, on not showing feelings of vulnerability, on not backing down. You see that especially in foreign policy crises. There is a nice account of President Kennedy, when he was getting ready to go to a summit meeting with Khrushchev.[3] This was right after the Bay of Pigs, where we had not done very well, and Harriman was counseling

Kennedy, using a more androgynous model of how to behave.

So Harriman was telling Kennedy, "Look, Khrushchev is going to bait you and threaten you, but the thing is to be gentle and don't take it too seriously and try to joke. Don't retaliate." So Kennedy goes to the summit and does not follow Harriman's advice. Khrushchev attacks him, and he counterattacks immediately. Afterward, he sends another military division to Berlin, and in explaining this to a reporter, Kennedy said: "The reason Khrushchev attacked me was because I just lost in the Bay of Pigs. He thought I was young, I had no guts. I had to show him I had guts. That is the only way I could get anywhere, and so what I had to do is to send the division to Berlin." Kennedy also described how he saw Vietnam as an opportunity to demonstrate that he had guts. So the President's view was: "I have to prove that I am a real man," not, "I have to get certain foreign policy objectives accomplished for the United States."

John: What is the impact of female gender behavior on government?

Francesca: I think primarily as a negative reference point—don't be sissy—such as when Muskie cried during his presidential campaign, and that destroyed his chances. Why is it so terrible to cry? I am not suggesting that this is what people should do all the time, but I think crying is condemned in politics because it's seen as feminine. So the main impact of the feminine role on the ideals of how you're supposed to behave in government and the distributions of punishments and rewards is, if you act feminine, you lose.

John: You've given considerable thought to gender, peace, and war in institutions of higher education. What is the thrust of that analysis?

Francesca: I focus on higher education because I am a professor; that is where I am doing my life. Gender permeates everything that each of us does, and I think it's important to focus on the institution that you're in. My own experience in research universities is that the masculine values are the dominant values. The way you win is to be tough, to not show pain, to compete, and to not spend too much time worrying about weak people. My own most vivid experience as a graduate student was an experience where I was in danger of losing my macho image. This was a situation where I flunked an exam, and I was going to talk to a professor about it, and my greatest effort before this meeting was worrying about if I was going to cry. I did cry, and I still dream about that. Why was that so important? There were a lot of important things happening in that situation, my career, what I was learning, what I wasn't learning, but it was this emblem of my toughness that was the most important thing. That suggests to me that the same values of being tough and winning dominate in the academic setting as well as in government and in all our public institutions.

John: The heart of your analysis is that gender behavior creates a cycle of war. How do you break that cycle? Where do you intervene?

Francesca: Well, I think you begin all at once, simultaneously, at all the places that we believe create these gender roles, given our current knowledge. One place is obviously socialization of children by families.

John: Within the family, what should parents do differently?

Francesca: It looks like it's important that fathers participate in raising their girls and boys. It looks like part of the reason why males are so insecure about whether they're real men, part of why they're so worried about, "Gee, did I do something sissy," is that they often don't grow up with a real male role model close by. So it would be helpful to have a male parent present. Also parents need to resist repeating these roles; for example, if parents know their son is being a bully and beating up on the little kids, parents should take a stern line with that. This is very difficult to do because a lot of parents are worried that their boys are not going to be real masculine. We need to get our boys to be more caring, as well as being powerful, and we need to get our girls to be more powerful, more out there in the world, as well as caring for people at home.

---

1. Brannon, Robert. 1976. "The Male Sex Role." Pp. 1–45 in *The Forty-Nine Percent Majority: The Male Sex Role,* edited by Deborah David and Robert Brannon. New York: Addison-Wesley.
2. Chafe, William. 1972. *The American Woman,* New York: Oxford University Press.

3. Fasteau, M. F. 1974. *The Male Machine.* New York: McGraw-Hill.

Military Socialization and Masculinity

William Arkin • *Lynne R. Dobrofsky*

The relationship between the military and the "masculine mystique" (Komisar 1976) is apparent in the process of adult or secondary socialization. As a monolithic organization experienced by a substantial part of American society—23.7 million veterans and almost half of the employed male population having served an average of 27 months of active duty (Young, Note 1; President's Commission 1970)—the military occupies a unique position in the spectrum of adult socialization. Although the average age of entry into the military varies with the degree of mobilization for war, when we consider that entry comes between the ages of 17 and 20, a transition period between adolescence and adulthood, we can understand the impact of secondary socialization on the recruit's vaguely defined and minimally experienced role of adult. Recognizing not only the individual's position in the life cycle but that entry into the military is entry into a relatively closed and monolithic social system where the individual experiences a coordinated and controlled range of work, living, and emotional experiences, we can begin to understand the dimensions and the potential impact of the secondary socialization processes that operate in and through the military.

The military provides a social environment which is a hybrid of family and social groups as well as work and reference groups that become interwoven through a network of primary and secondary interactions. Analogous to the life cycle, the sequence and pattern of socialization unfolds in the military—from entry as a skinned-head recruit through the warrior's initiation rites and

finally, for some, badged and rewarded retirement. Potential for resistance to military socialization only comes from values, attitudes, and definitions of early primary socialization or from pre- or non-military relationships and group identities; these civilian influences and bonds reduce with time, mobility, and distance of the recruit from his civilian counterpart. The significant impact of military socialization on civilian society is only minimized by the fact that the majority of those who have served to date tend to return to civilian society after two years of active duty, yet even this population carries with it elements of military socialization.

The potential of the impact of military socialization was recognized in the 1970 report of the President's Commission on an All Volunteer Armed Force (AVAF): "Military life is thought to have a discernible and beneficial impact on an individual's capabilities, attitudes, and behavior patterns as they are carried over into the veteran's civilian life." Alleged differences between veterans and nonveterans centered around patriotism, concern with foreign and domestic affairs, as well as self-discipline, neatness, and hygiene, and greater participation in community social and political activities. No firm conclusions were made regarding all veterans because intervening variables of race, education, age, and ability interacted with the military experience and clouded the issue. The primary concern of this article, the secondary socialization processes that influence and shape masculine role definitions and attitudes that are implicit in the military experience, was not examined in the commission's report. Rather than explicit goals, objectives, and examples put forth by the military, we are here concerned with patterns of implicit definitions and attitudes existing in a social environment that is mutually reinforcing to them since it is the implicit rather than the explicit that is often the basic force of socialization and social control.

It is our purpose to analyse the major dimensions of a secondary socialization process that influences a large number of men as young adults, with an eye towards a deeper, more complete understanding of adult male roles. This analysis is largely based on that process which underlies the traditional male role, where major forms of achievement which validate masculinity are physical (Pleck 1976). Important changes evidenced in the "modern" or "emerging" male role are now beginning to appear in society at large, but not within the military system's rules of conduct. "The interpersonal skills which promote collaboration with others towards achievement, as in management," (Pleck 1976) are definitely part of the new image which the AVAF wishes to establish. Yet the traditional male role is still dominant and even a contemporary analysis of the military must focus on the traditional processes and images of masculinity upon which the system is based. Whether the military is reflecting civilian movements regarding male role changes or whether the changes are demanded by the AVAF in peace time, with an emphasis on jobs and occupations that must mimic civilian changes in order to succeed, remains an empirical question ripe for research.

The question of military socialization in general and the impact on civilian institutions in the specific was considered a moot point with the shift to the AVAF in 1973. The assumption that with the AVAF, significantly fewer people would experience the military and recycle into civilian life is currently not valid. While the active strength of the military has decreased from 2.7 million in 1964 (pre-Vietnam) to 2.1 in 1977 (Goldich, Note 2), the military still must currently recruit one out of every 5.6 18-year-old males and a projected one out of every 4.6 by the end of the 1980s. The increasing percentage of 18-year-old males who

will serve in the military is the result of the declining birth rate that began in the 1960s (Goldich, Note 2).

When we consider that, based on current standards, 32.6% of the 18-year-old population are physically, mentally, or morally unqualified for the AVAF and 16% are college students and will probably not volunteer, we can understand why the military is currently developing policy for standby selective service or national conscription. Although the AVAF has not been in existence for a sufficient period to totally evaluate its impact on civilian society, it is clear that the military experience will, in the absence of war, minimally socialize 20% of our annual 18-year-old male population, who will be cycled back into civilian society on a regular basis.

It is impossible to determine total military influence and socialization on the civilian sector when we consider those who leave or are forced out early as well as those who retire and enter private and government employment as second careers. But it is estimated that retired military personnel constitute 5% of civilian federal employees alone.

Recruitment

Prior to the initial training, recruitment reveals the military's definition of who is to carry out its objectives or mission. Although definitions change with the extent of crises, war mobilization, and budgets (variables which define for the military those populations to be recruited), certain patterns do emerge.

In addition to entry requirements, we have seen a major shift in recruitment policies, reflected in providing an option of occupations to potential recruits. This change has been experimented with in the past when the military was encouraging primarily re-enlistment or attempting to bolster lagging enlistment. The current policy, along with increased wages, is the result of the AVAF and the military's desire to assure a sufficient population of recruits. Additionally, technological trends in war-making result in modifications towards "civilianization," a trend which modifies but doesn't eliminate civil–military differences. The trend towards civilianization is applicable to occupations within the military, however, and not to the military as an occupation; the military is attempting to professionalize the military image but not necessarily socialization therein.

Until recently, young males have either been lured or drafted into the military with the promise of becoming a man: "Join the army, Be a man"; "The army will make a man out of you"; or, from the marines: "We only take a few good men." In general, the military has been defined as an opportunity to grow up, a belief that youth leaving home will return as men. Because there has been evidence enough in the form of medals, honors, recognition, jobs, education, and success for those who have served, popular expectations have reinforced the military's role as patriarch under whose influence and discipline a doubtless man emerges.

As a result of the AVAF, today we find becoming a man being defined in terms of learning an occupation or a skill, but basically the recruitment message of turning a boy into a man has only added the traditional work ethic dimension of masculinity, which equates masculinity with productivity, occupation, and breadwinning. This shift does not change one of the primary objectives of the military, that of turning boys into (fighting) men, but rather it attempts to widen the military appeal. As the result of the negative publicity that was spotlighted by Vietnam, this new appeal further represents a typical peacetime pattern where the masculine warrior appears superfluous to the population.

Overall, socially and personally joining the military is viewed as not only an opportunity for boys to become men but the opportune time for the military to make men out of boys. The secondary socialization and indoctrination processes occur at a time in one's life when our society both expects and requires formalization of an adult sex-role identity. Hauser (1973) suggests that because the military may easily be characterized as an organization "where they holler at you," some men probably join to find discipline in the not uncommon belief that they must undergo some kind of

hardship ritual in search of maturity. Independent of obligatory or voluntary recruitment, however, the military is committed to fulfill one of the promises that young boys will develop into mature men. The military operationalizes the equation of masculinity-warrior, not through the process of anticipating maturity but with a more efficient aggressive conditioning model of creating the masculine male. Recruits end up internalizing much of the ethos of masculinity and then begin to place value on their training experience:

> I can see how subtle and how insidious...the changes are. Because as determined as we were not to change, we certainly were changed. ... Unless you had this pressure on you...somebody beating you... well, it was good in a way [in that] you found you were capable of doing much more than you've even anticipated you could do.... So you know, this was a valuable thing. (Lifton 1973)

The acceptance of a recruit depends upon a classification system which includes measurements of physical, moral, and mental standards as well as number of dependents, age, and other criteria. The Armed Forces Qualification Test rejects the lower 10% as part of the mental criteria; criminal records as well as sexual preference serve as major moral variables for rejection. However, by far, emphasis is still on physical criteria and a series of classifications identify the individuals who are physically 1A overall but still have physical defects which would preclude certain types of assignments. The pre-entrance physical, where there is only minimal and symbolic emotional testing, represents a milestone in the progression into masculinity. The physical classification represents the prerequisite for masculinity and emphasis on high physical standards contrasted with minimal emotional and attitudinal standards implicitly carries with it the military's belief that masculinity is determined primarily by a healthy body not a healthy mind.

The initial physical status of the recruit sets the pattern of stratification within the military structure, as the prime "A" profiles have been traditionally designated for combat careers and training while the lower status physical profiles are tagged for support or administrative functions. The importance of the physical classification can be seen throughout the military structure; those belonging to or assigned combat occupational categories are deferred to or given more privileges than those of equal and higher formal rank who have support occupational roles. The emphasis on physical fitness and combat roles can further be seen in the current dispute on women and combat, as well as the undue emphasis on the absence of upper-body strength in women without ever establishing the relation of upper-body strength to combat. Promotion is difficult without having served in a combat or line unit; officers are periodically rotated into line units to assure probability of retention and promotion. Having experienced combat obviously increases the individual's status; special combat marks on the uniform sleeve, organization patches, service ribbons, and badges are authorized to identify the status of the individual.

Even though the emphasis on "be a man" is drawn largely from civilian culture, it is given special interpretation in the combat situation, for it is in combat that the core of masculinity is demonstrated:

> *Courage, endurance and toughness, lack of squeamishness when confronted with shocking or distasteful stimuli, avoidance of display of weakness in general, reticence about emotional or idealistic matters, sexual competency . . . (Stouffer et al. 1949)*

Status is derived from the role of combat soldier (proof of manhood) in the extreme case of war (test of manhood). Even when we look at those of equal rank who have not experienced combat, we still find the drill sergeant receiving more informal status deference than the equally ranked support personnel. Implicit in this structure is not the test of manliness in battle, since combat conditions or war are not constant, but the physical prerequisite of manliness and the supremacy of physical attributes over either intellectual or emotional ones. It

should be noted that the pre-acceptance physical is the primary determinant of military acceptance, with the majority of the in-depth intelligence and skill tests not being administered until after the recruit has been sworn in.

Basic Training

All recruits are subjected to varying degrees of basic training depending upon the branch of service and the individual's projected occupational assignment. Currently, there are an estimated 2 million persons in the armed forces—777 thousand army, 581 thousand air force, 526 thousand navy, and 188 thousand marines (Goldich, Note 2). Basic training represents a one time experience, occurring immediately after recruitment, for the purpose of being indoctrinated into military life and of learning the rudimentary combat skills. Its success is difficult to measure since the turnover rate at the end of the first enlistment or conscription period varies with peace and war, economic crises, and relative composition of volunteers and draftees. However, in projecting the AVAF, the military estimates a 20% turnover rate, indicating that the majority of 17- to 20-year-old volunteers find the initial period satisfactory. It also implies that basic training, where initial definitions are learned, is highly successful in developing secondary or institutional socialization where the individual's values, behavior, and definitions are the objective roles and status defined by the institution. In effect, the military's definition and expectations become the individual's definitions and expectations. Masculinity, particularly as defined by prescribed rules of conduct, is and/or becomes the major emphasis of basic training (see also Eisenhart 1975).

Form and content of basic training varies little from service to service; however, intensity of the experience and weapons skill does vary with the service. Those services whose primary mission is direct confrontation of the enemy in combat (the marines and army) receive a more intense basic training experience than the navy and the air force, who are perceived of as combat units engaged in support missions. Intensity of the training common to all services does have an effect on socialization, since intensity and frequency of interaction produces stronger socialization patterns as well as increasing the probability of socialization. The difference between the esprit de corps of the marines with its tough, macho image and the relaxed easy-going sailor in the navy reflects a difference in intensity and not in the form or content of the basic training experience.

By definition, basic training is combat training. The justification for basic "combat" military training for all—even though a large percentage of recruits will subsequently be shuffled off to noncombative specialization training—is that the primary mission of the military is combat, and all members must be prepared to fight in the event an emergency war situation requires it. The expressed military purpose, however, does not reflect the degree of manliness training that each recruit must receive before qualifying for "manhood."

Basic training is a rite of passage for a young American "boy"—with the key phrase (goal) being "a civilian into a soldier, and a boy into a man" (Yarmolinsky 1971). Basic training is thus a carefully executed process which supports "the intentional disruption of civilian patterns of adjustment, replacement of individual gratifications with group goals, inculcation of unquestioning acceptance of authority and development of conformity of official attitudes and conduct" (Yarmolinsky 1971).

Military discipline is of central importance to basic training and is often conceptually interchangeable with processes of socialization. While it might be difficult to isolate what is meant by military discipline, the demands center on appearance, cleanliness, exactitude of detail, respect for tradition and rank. Military discipline refers to and thus encompasses the total individual's conformity to a prescribed role, including one's behavior, attitudes, beliefs, values, and definitions. Conformity to the prescribed rules of conduct is the focal point for change within the military processes of indoctrination.

The objective of basic training is to shape the total person into being a disciplined cog within the military machine. Ultimately, basic training is where the most profound changes must be made; it functions as the military's agency for primary socialization. As the primary force of socialization, the military operationalizes an ideal of masculinity in basic training through instrumental archetypes: the male, the female, the team archetype, and the family archetype. Basic training, as a sharp contrast with civilian life, places the emphasis upon establishing a high degree of social solidarity and it is clear that basic training will often have a traumatic impact on the recruit (Yarmolinsky 1971). In this context, it also becomes obvious why a heretofore closed male social system has been necessary to insure a controlled environment in which to reinforce and reward the fundamental archetypes to be acquired in the weeks of basic training.

The Male Archetype

The end product of basic training—becoming a strong, silent, self-reliant man who functions as a loyal member of a team—is primarily created through the indoctrination of values and a mentality which have nothing to do with the military mission (Eisenhart 1975). All of the exercises and assignments of basic training are designed to build the man whose sex-role identity is molded under conditions similar to the controlled environment of a laboratory:

> These "leaders" are the men; that pretty much makes you the "pussies"—at the very most "boys." You have to conform to a hard core, tough image or you're a punk. And I began to believe it because of my insecure state of mind, which was so encouraged in training. I was real insecure. ... The pressures of assuming manhood are very heavy. (Anonymous 1974)

Thus the training program for the masculine sex role is operationalized via skills and techniques deemed necessary for a man's survival in combat; combat training and masculine sex-role socialization are never separated from one another. Today's emphasis on occupational opportunities only extends the domains in which a certain set of skills and techniques are necessary for the male role.

The values which underlie the basic training techniques are "tradition, esprit de corps, unity and community" (Goertzel and Hengst 1971). Combined, these values, techniques, and pressures for manhood define the formal image of military discipline—"duty, honor, country" (Spencer 1973). The mind and image of the military are sustained through discipline, the heart of the military social system (Hauser 1973); and basic training is where and when they are collectively operationalized. For example, the regulation of shaving heads or shortening hair which the recruit immediately experiences serves the dual purpose of exposing him to discipline while simultaneously removing the extra frills of longer hair often associated with individual vanity (vanity being believed to be the prerogative of women). As a preparation for resocialization, the military used hair-shaving long before movements such as Synanon and Hare Krishnas devised it as a symbol of resocialization and the new individual.

Along with disciplinary measures are psychological controls used to shape masculine behaviors. Levy (1971) points out that even though "the marines heard lectures about Vietnamese men expressing friendship among themselves and with other men through physical contact," once in Vietnam their need to relate these gestures to their own culture manifested itself in defining such behavior as homosexuality.

> In the case of the American marines ... homosexuality appeared in two contradictory themes of basic training. ... On the one hand, homosexuals were the enemy. ... On the other hand, marine recruits were called "faggots" by their drill instructors during boot camp. (Levy 1971)

The long grueling marches are particularly suited to building a man under high stress conditions, where marching is the means not the end of this objective. A variety of verbal practices are also used by drill instructors to train recruits to withstand stress while relinquishing personal controls:

> By compelling these men to accept [derogatory] labels, the drill instructors achieved on a psychological level the same control that they had on a physical level when, for example, the men were not permitted a bowel movement for the first week of boot camp. (Levy 1971)

The emphasis on inspections and drills fosters conformity to discipline and to authority. Discipline and authority are also reinforced by uniformity in dress and activities, yet clearly differentiated by rank. Many boot camp rituals are coupled with violence:

> The violence towards trainees was merged with the learning how to do violence, so that "We used to be disgusted with the other services because we considered them unagressive." Aggression meant learning how to protect not only their lives, but also their masculinity. Accordingly, after boot camp they referred to the Marine Corps as "the crotch," while the other military branches were callled "the sister services." (Levy 1971)

Inspections and drills form the strong, silent, obedient man. It is deeply rooted belief that obedience in training is the prerequisite to discipline under fire on the battlefield (Hauser 1973).

Disciplinary methods used in training are not confined to the physically strenuous exercises of marches and obstacle courses. Psychologically, as punitive measures for various policy infractions or violations of ground rules, military discipline simultaneously embarrasses and reminds the recruit of his penis-as-power link by requiring him to hold his rifle in one hand while his other hand grasps his crotch and to shout:

> Sir: This is my rifle
> This is my gun
> This is for pleasure
> This is for fun!

(For violent disciplinary measures linking sexuality and military mission, see also Eisenhart 1975):

"In the purely masculine surroundings of the Army, the values associated with the ideal of virility play a determining role in molding the soldier's image of himself and in creating his inner tensions and the channels for their release" (Elkin 1946). Thus, mechanisms of social control are constantly operating to reinforce the appropriate masculine self-image by negating menaces (like showing emotions) or threats (like homosexuality) to that image. Official reasons given by the army and the navy for fearing homosexuals, for example, are stated thus:

> *The Army considers homosexuals to be unfit for military service because their presence impairs the morale and discipline of the Army, and that homosexuality is a manifestation of a severe personality defect which appreciably limits the ability of such individuals to function effectively in society. . . .*
>
> *Homosexuals and other sexual deviates are military liabilities who can not be tolerated in a military organization. (Williams and Weinberg 1971)*

The Female Archetype

While some disciplinary themes explicitly refer to the male image, other themes found in sex-oriented rhymes which function for cadence counts, are reserved for the female image:

> *I don't know but I've been told*
> *Eskimo pussy is mighty cold*
>
> *I got a gal in Kansas City*
> *She's got gumdrops on her titties*
> *When I get back to Kansas City*
> *Gonna suck those gumdrops off her titties*
>
> *Momma's on the bottom, Poppa on the top*
> *Baby in the middle yelling give it to her pop!*

The relationships of masculinity and violence and masculinity and sex dominate formal as well as informal military socialization patterns. Even the chaplain's speeches stress masculinity in terms of male sexuality and dominance by warning men to leave "good" women alone, in the recognition that masculinity and sexual conquest go hand in hand. The underlying assumption in pre-leave "chaplain's orientations" is that men must and will seek out women for sexual conquest after long periods of abstention. The primary theme of these orientations is that all men have strong sex drives and when denied access to women, their desire for immediate gratification may interfere with good judgement—"So watch out for the good women who may not understand and watch out for the bad women who may roll you or give you VD."

In basic training, recruits are shown sex-education films which reinforce themes and images of women as objects for men's sexual exploitations and which "educate" men in the evils and dangers of VD, fostering a distrust in those who communicate sexual diseases, women. Additionally, many weapons training films impose or use women to sustain interest and attention in the instructive content. Naming equipment by women's names further reveals the function that objectifying women has for confirming male's values of dominance and power. Land mines named Bouncing Betty which are designed to explode at groin height smack of the female castration theme; ships, planes, and tanks as war equipment are named after females who do not represent wives at home but symbolize sex objects or goddesses. Instruments of war, like bombs and guns, are commonly referred to as "her" and "she," telling of man's habit of using women as a means to accomplishing his ends. The joystick (slang for penis) as the control lever for female-named combat aircraft such as "Betty Boob" further exemplifies this. The sanctioned use and abuse of women (and the ability to impress others with one's sexual exploits) is a common means of confirming one's manliness, power, strength, and dominance by removing any doubt as to one's own virility in heterosexual encounters.

> *In basic training...people talked about fucking sheep and cows and women with about the same respect for them all. (Anonymous 1974)*

A consequence of using the imagery of females in basic training to strengthen the intended masculine imagery is sexual and often violent use and abuse.

The military's image of the role women should play in the life of the military man is that of receptacle for his sex drives too long held in check and as an object of distrust that the chaplain warns may be the source of venereal disease and a conspiracy to entrap one into marriage and a monthly allotment check. As a result, discussions of intimate relationships between men and women, of marriage and the family are conspicuously absent. But the emphasis on heterosexual exploitation and women as sex objects derives from another need to dismiss any possible doubts about the gender identity of the male. As Stouffer (1949) wrote of being a soldier in World War II: if one were not socially defined as a man there was a strong likelihood of being branded a woman.

The Team Archetype

A major aim of basic training is to foster maximum individual identity with the group, in the form of loyalty, esprit de corps, and a team work orientation, while minimizing the fostered anxiety, paranoia, and fear of expressions of homosexuality. The "buddy system" designed for keeping track of one another and for companionship is not to be confused with sanctioning intimacy. In fact,

> *When a recruit mentioned that he and a friend had been separated in violation of the "buddy system" under which they joined, the drill instructor is reported to have asked, "Do you like Private R?" The next question was, "Do you want to fuck him?" (Levy 1971)*

The emphasis on team work enables a viable balance of group identity and loyalty, dependence on the group and on the military, while preserving values of competition and aggression necessary to one's definition as a self-reliant male. While training is often a traumatic experience, one gains a sense of morale. There is fellowship; knowing there are others in the same situation makes for easier adjustment (Wagner 1975). Identity with the group is not an accident; loyalty to the group is planned for as an objective of basic socialization. Promoting a team-work image does not conflict with masculine values of competition, aggression, and fighting to win, nor does such an orientation in any way imply relations more intimate than masculine camaraderie or companionship, survival relations considered integral to the buddy system. Keeping in mind that basic training is primarily training for combat, the military effectively structures both formal and informal factors to promote the dependence of the individual on the group.

During training situations, the military promotes the team concept through a division of labor where the combined weapons or skills of the team represent the highest probability of survival. Constant badgering, company punishment, and peer pressure are utilized when drill instructors loudly identify individual errors as costing the life of a team member, or the lives of a squad, platoon, company, or regiment. Guilt and survival are the bases of the team concept, but individual competition is promoted through rank, medals, assorted rewards and assignments. In order to foster both team cooperation and individual competition, the military uses a mixed bag of reinforcers. In one situation an individual will be punished for improper behavior or attitude; in another situation the whole squad, barracks, platoon, or company can be punished for one individual's error. The undefined rewards and punishments—first individual, next group—quickly get translated into a belief that one can only compete within the conformity of the team concept. Conformity, competition, and aggression are the keys, not creativity, innovation, or spontaneity. The military man is, in effect, a corporate man where the greater the sacrifices for the good of the corps, the greater the likelihood for status, promotion, reward, and recognition.

It is within this cooperative–competitive model of team work that the military is able successfully to prevent intimate relationships between males. One's buddy is one who may get a coveted assignment, promotion, or leave; he may also cause you to lose similar rewards. Since a buddy is one's competitor as well as a necessary resource for survival during combat, all signs of weakness must be concealed, including personal problems, doubts, fears, or concerns. As a result, intimacy even with constant physical proximity and shared experiences rarely emerges.

The Family Archetype

Basic Training is also designed to condition the man for a particular relationship with his family. This socialization begins with total separation from family except for emergency leaves, defined by the birth of a child or a death in the immediate family. Men go through training independent of family ties or even military family recognition except for minimal dependency allotments. The near denial of familial relations is in the form of insulating the recruit from his family, coupled with a noticeable absence of films or other recognition of the stress families go through during the recruits' absence. During basic, families of members in training are consequently also being prepared for the military as a support system for the man and, ultimately, for the military (Dobrofsky, Note 3; Dobrofsky and Batterson 1977).

Starting with basic training, the only communication patterns that exist with one's family or future wife are reliance on mail or an occasional phone call, where the latter is controlled by access and availability of a phone. In severing this intimate interaction, the military believes that the recruit's self-reliance is increased. Seeking advice from parents or spouses is considered characteristic of a sissy or cry baby, one who is tied to his mother's or wife's apron string. Women in the family are perceived as potential threats until they themselves have been absorbed into the military community. Out of sight, out of mind is the military model. However, when this backfires and a soldier receives a "Dear John" letter, it becomes evidence

of either the woman's insincerity or selfishness. The ideal woman remains at home; her support is demonstrated by sending letters and gift packages in tribute to the deprivation the recruit is undergoing for her own well-being and that of the nation's. The interpersonal relationship between recruit and family is defined in terms of symbolic martyrdom. The separation is difficult but justified because he is forsaking all for the good of the nation, which translates into the good of the family or the woman. The initial separation is never defined as his socialization and her or family preindoctrination, but always in terms of sacrifice for a higher good and those who do not endure experience the pangs of guilt.

The discouragement and/or denial of privileges to families or recruits in training are attempts to keep social distance between the man and his family, ultimately to minimize their influence. This practice also serves as a training period for the family in learning to handle family routines as well as crises independent of the male. Married women must become sacrificing heads of households and learn to assume the male's responsibility. (It should be noted that the chaplain is the appropriate advice and counseling source regarding personal and, in particular, family problems; the equation of religious and family difficulties stems from a belief that the feminine domain includes religious and domestic concerns.)

The weeks of basic training, then, are also used to socialize the man as not being integral to his family life and the family into being an understanding support system for the military. Not only is contact with family severed during basic, but any interest in integrating one's family during the first tour of enlistment is seriously discouraged—by not making on-base housing available, in contrast to accommodations designed especially for military families after one's first tour. The interruption of intimate family relations which basic training accomplishes, the separation from family which basic training enforces, and the distance from one's family which the first enlistment tour encourages are all processes intended to insure that the man is fully socialized (disciplined) by the military before re-introducing civilian and intimate influences of family. The preferred practice of not welcoming families into the military community until one has re-enlisted allows the man to prove his military commitment in the form of re-enlistment and thus demonstrate that he is a self-affirmed instrument now capable of folding his family into the military for their socialization.

With the shift away from the imagery of a "single man's military," the military had to socialize families into their society as effectively as it accomplished this with individual recruits. By creating an elaborate network of social, psychological, recreational, religious, economic, and educational services and facilities marked by convenience and reduced prices, the military has managed to isolate wives and children from civilian influences while using them to free the man to maintain a relatively uninterrupted relationship with his work and with the military.

Conclusion

In the ways discussed here, the military represents not only the primary traditional sex-role identity for American men, but it has been the instrumental force of socialization for this identity. Through relative physical isolation, community insulation, and behavior modification, the traditional prototype of masculinity is molded by the military in the belief that war and military are masculine domains and, as inherently masculine domains, success is dependent upon the degree to which the military person conforms to the defined archetypes. The purpose of basic training is to militarize, which means to give a military character or to adapt for military use. This represents the primary purpose of basic training, not training in occupational or combat skills. The individual's proficiency at using sophisticated equipment and weapons comes after he has been militarized. The combat equipment and techniques of basic training are notoriously obsolete and inadequate for the military's primary mission. In effect, militarization translates into socialization into a masculine domain, which requires a definition of what a male should be. Masculinity supported by various archetypes rep-

resents the military definition of who is qualified to occupy the masculine domain.

Because of reliance on the techniques and processes used to create the masculine archetype of behavior and the rejection of intimacy and warmth, neither basic training nor the military community can ever provide for primary group relations which are mutually personal, intimate, supportive, and interactive. The relations and feelings characterized by the military are conditioned as a team where emotions and character are controlled and/or positioned by rank, authority, cooperation and competition, aggressiveness, and self-reliance. As a result, it is difficult to gauge the effects of military socialization on any one individual although the dynamics are readily apparent in the total society.

The military has socialized millions of men according to the same traditional masculine blueprint. As such, the dominant adult male-role model could largely be the product of the military, particularly in as much as those who are thus socialized have returned to society. Formal and informal social relations in society at large replicate the archetypes of male, female, team, and family that are used by the military to socialize the recruit. Even the universality of this traditional male-gender role is telling as exhibited in visual, dramatic, and novel representations of war, depictions which are accepted as reality. The various media presentations stress disciplinary efforts to fit the character into the model soldier, rather than developing the individual character of the soldier. Thus, to date, we witness the formal and informal impact of a dominant militarization process.

All indications are that the military blueprint of masculinity has not changed with the AVAF, and the military can point with pride to increasing ROTC programs as well as increasing enlistments. The military has not become a haven for the undereducated, poor, and minorities, though unemployment trends do cause surges in enlistments.

What we are seeing is not a dramatic change in the military as many expected, but a series of fissures which could threaten the military infrastructure. The navy (Navy Desertions 1977) reported that more than 1100 sailors per month are jumping ship, the highest desertion rate in navy history including Vietnam. In addition, the navy estimates 17,000 single parents, with 75% being male, while the army and air force have yet to recognize this growing population. The influx of women in all traditional male occupations, with the exception of combat, can only serve to challenge the military socialization in masculinity since the military has yet to develop a female warrior model. Military women tend to represent a neutered or "little brother" role model. But whether a feminine or little brother model of socialization is used for women, it is questionable if the military model of masculinity can be preserved when shared.

---

1. Young, D. E. 1976. Personal Communication, August 16.

2. Goldich, R. L. 1977. *Military Manpower Policy and the All-Volunteer Force* (Issue Brief No. IB77032). Washington, D.C.: Congressional Research Service.

3. Dobrofsky, L. R. 1977. "The Wife: From Military Dependent to Feminist?" In *Changing Families in a Changing Military System,* edited by E. J. Hunter. San Diego: Naval Health Research Center.

References

Anonymous. 1974. "Life in the Military." In *Men and Masculinity,* edited by J. Pleck and J. Sawyer. Englewood Cliffs, NJ: Prentice-Hall.

Dobrofsky, L. R. and C. Batterson. 1977. "The Military Wife and Feminism." *Signs* 2: 675–684.

Eisenhart, R. W. 1975. "You Can't Hack It Little Girl, A Discussion of the Covert Psychological Agenda of Modern Combat Training." *Journal of Social Issues* 31 (4): 13–23.

Elkin, H. 1946. "Aggressive and Erotic Tendencies in Army Life." *American Journal of Sociology* 51: 408–413.

Goertzel, T. and A. Hengst. 1971. "A Military Socialization of University Students." *Social Problems* Fall: 258–267.

Hauser, W. L. 1973. *America's Army in Crisis.* Baltimore: The Johns Hopkins Press.

Komisar, L. 1976. "Violence and the Masculine Mystique." In *The Forty-Nine Percent Majority: The Male Sex Role,* edited by D. S. David and R. Brannon. Reading, MA: Addison-Wesley.

Levy, C. J. 1971. "ARVN as Faggots: Inverted Warfare in Vietnam." *Transaction* October: 18–27.

Lifton, R. J. 1973. *Home from the War—Vietnam Veterans: Neither Victims nor Executioners.* New York: Simon & Schuster.

"Navy Desertions Hit All-Time High." The *Washington Post,* July 16, 1977, p. 2.

Pleck, J. H. 1976. "The Male Sex Role: Definitions, Problems, and Sources of Change." *Journal of Social Issues* 32 (3): 155–164.

President's Commission. 1970. *The Report of the President's Commission on an All-Volunteer Armed Force.* London: Collier Books/The Macmillan Co.

Spencer, G. 1973. "Methodological Issues in the Study of Bureaucractic Elites: A Case Study of West Point." *Social Problems* Summer: 90–103.

Stouffer, S. A., et al. 1949. *The American Soldier (Volume 2): Combat and Its Aftermath.* Princeton, NJ: Princeton University Press.

Wagner, J. 1975. "The Impact of Military Service on the Male Adolescent." *Adolescence* Spring: 71–74.

Williams, C. J. and M. S. Weinberg. 1971. *Homosexuals and the Military: A Study of Less than Honorable Discharge.* New York: Harper and Row.

Yarmolinsky, A. 1971. *The Military Esatblishment.* New York: Harper and Row.

PART THREE

Culture

Because war and peace are such vital parts of world history, societies have created cultures that make war and peace "meaningful" to their lives. There can be no war without stories of heroic warriors and horrible enemies. To motivate men for war, war must be portrayed as desirable, something for which killing and dying seem worthwhile. And conversely, there can be no lasting peace without developing positive images of peace and learning to see the "enemy" as human beings, not just as soldiers of adversary nations.

This part begins with an investigation of how the peoples of both the United States and the Soviet Union have come to see each other as very similar kinds of enemies, what Urie Bronfenbrenner calls "the mirror image" process. Perceiving each other as always the aggressive enemy creates a self-fulfilling prophecy.

In "American Paramilitary Culture and the Reconstitution of the Vietnam War," James William Gibson presents an analysis of American paramilitary culture in the 1980s: the world of war movies, novels, magazines, and war games that celebrate the male warrior as the epitome of manhood and the symbol of national strength. Gibson sees these mythic attempts to overcome the trauma of defeat in Vietnam as related to how the original wars

against the American Indians were portrayed in American culture as "regenerating" the entire society.

John Dower's essay, "Apes and Others," examines the American image of the Japanese as apelike savages during World War II. Transforming and dehumanizing the enemy through such racial stereotypes was in part responsible for the atrocities of the Pacific campaign.

Carol Cohn's essay, "Nuclear Language and How We Learned to Pat the Bomb," shows how the men who create U.S. nuclear strategy and who operate the nuclear missile submarines and other weapons have developed a special *language* about nuclear weapons and war that frames war as a sexually exciting but relatively safe game. Such language makes the massive death and destruction of nuclear war seem remote and disconnected from the "game" of war. This disjunction of war language from the reality of war makes fighting such a war more thinkable.

Finally, in "Making Peace with Music," *New York Times* reporter Thomas Friedman reminds us that culture is a mosaic of different kinds of symbolic communications; although "enemies" hate each other at some levels, they can also come to respect and enjoy one another through different aspects of cultural communication. His story details the popularity of Israeli music in many Arab countries. To share music together shows that the "enemy" has a human side. Music contributes to friendship, and although friendship does not eliminate the causes of war, it can both create limits to hostility and help find a way to peace.

The Mirror Image in Soviet–American Relations

Urie Bronfenbrenner

I should explain by way of introduction that I was in the Soviet Union during the summer of 1960, about a month after the U-2 incident. The primary purpose of my trip was to become acquainted with scientific developments in my field, which is social psychology. But in addition to visiting laboratories at universities and institutes, I wanted also to become acquainted with *living* social psychology—the Soviet people themselves. It was my good fortune to be able to speak Russian. I was traveling with a tourist visa on a new plan which permitted me to go about alone without a guide. Accordingly, after spending the first two or three days of my visit in a particular city at scientific centers, I would devote the remaining days to walking about the town and striking up conversations with people in public conveyances, parks, stores, restaurants, or just on the street. Since foreigners are a curiosity, and I was obviously a foreigner (though, I quickly learned, not obviously an American), people were eager to talk. But I also went out of my way to strike up conversations with people who weren't taking the initiative—with fellow passengers who were remaining silent, with strollers in the park, with children and old people. Or I would enter a restaurant deciding in advance to sit at the third table on the left with whoever should turn out to be there. (In Soviet restaurants it is not uncommon to share a table with strangers.)

These conversations convinced me that the great majority of Russians feel a genuine pride in the accomplishments of their system and a conviction that communism is the way of the future not only for themselves but for the rest of the world as well. For several reasons my Soviet journey was a deeply disturbing experience. But what frightened me was not so much the facts of Soviet reality as the discrepancy between the real and the perceived. At first I was troubled only by the strange irrationality of the Soviet view of the world—especially their gross distortion of American society and American foreign policy as I knew them to be. But then, gradually, there came an even more disquieting awareness—an awareness which I resisted and still resist. Slowly and painfully, it forced itself upon me that *the Russian's distorted picture of us was curiously similar to our view of them—a mirror image.* But of course our image was real. Or could it be that our views too were distorted and irrational—a mirror image in a twisted glass?

It was—and is—a frightening prospect. For if such reciprocal distortion exists, it is a psychological phenomenon without parallel in the gravity of its consequences. For this reason, the possibility deserves serious consideration.

The Mirror Image Magnified

Let us then briefly examine the common features in the American and Soviet view of each other's societies. For the Russian's image I drew mainly, not on official government pronouncements, but on what was said to me by Soviet citizens in the course of our conversations. Five major themes stand out.

Excerpted from "The Mirror-Image in Soviet–American Relations: A Social Psychologist's Report," *Journal of Social Issues* 16 (3): 45–56. Reprinted by permission of The Society for the Psychological Study of Social Issues and the author.

1. They Are the Aggressors

The American view: Russia is the warmonger bent on imposing its system on the rest of the world. Witness Czechoslovakia, Berlin, Hungary, and now Cuba and the Congo. The Soviet Union consistently blocks Western proposals for disarmament by refusing necessary inspection controls.

The Soviet view: America is the warmonger bent on imposing its power on the rest of the world and on the Soviet Union itself. Witness American intervention in 1918; Western encirclement after World War II with American troops and bases on every border of the USSR (West Germany, Norway, Turkey, Korea, Japan); intransigence over proposals to make Berlin a free city; intervention in Korea, Taiwan, Lebanon, Guatemala, Cuba. America has repeatedly rejected Soviet disarmament proposals while demanding the right to inspect within Soviet territory—finally attempting to take the right by force through deep penetration of Soviet airspace.

2. Their Government Exploits and Deludes the People

The American view: Convinced communists, who form but a small proportion of Russia's population, control the government and exploit the society and its resources in their own interest. To justify their power and expansionist policies they have to perpetuate a war atmosphere and a fear of Western aggression. Russian elections are a travesty, since only one party appears on the ballot. The Russian people are kept from knowing the truth through a controlled radio and press, and conformity is insured through stringent economic and political sanctions against deviant individuals or groups.

The Soviet view: A capitalistic–militaristic clique controls the American government, the nation's economic resources, and its media of communication. The group exploits the society and its resources. It is in their economic and political interest to maintain a war atmosphere and engage in militaristic expansion. Voting in America is a farce, since candidates for both parties are selected by the same powerful interests leaving nothing to

choose between. The American people are kept from knowing the truth through a controlled radio and press and through economic and political sanctions against liberal elements.

3. The Mass of Their People Are Not Really Sympathetic to the Regime

The American view: In spite of the propaganda, the Soviet people are not really behind their government. Their praise of the government and the party is largely perfunctory, a necessary concession for getting along. They do not trust their own sources of information and have learned to read between the lines. Most of them would prefer to live under our system of government if they only could.

The Soviet view: Unlike their government, the bulk of the American people want peace. Thus, the majority disapproved of American aggression in Korea, the support of Chiang Kai-shek, and above all, of the sending of the U-2. But of course they could do nothing, since their welfare is completely under the control of the ruling financier-militaristic clique. If the American people were allowed to become acquainted with communism as it exists in the USSR, they would unquestionably choose it as their form of government. ("You Americans are such a nice people; it is a pity you have such a terrible government.")

4. They Cannot Be Trusted

The American view: The Soviets do not keep promises and they do not mean what they say. Thus, while they claim to have discontinued all nuclear testing, they are probably carrying out secret underground explosions in order to gain an advantage over us. Their talk of peace is but a propaganda maneuver. Everything they do is to be viewed with suspicion, since it is all part of a single coordinated scheme to further aggressive communist aims.

The Soviet view: The Americans do not keep promises and they do not mean what they say. Thus, they insist on inspection only so that they can look at Soviet defenses; they have no real intention of disarming. Everything the Americans do is to be viewed with suspicion (e.g., they take advantage of Soviet hospitality by sending in spies as tourists).

5. Their Policy Verges on Madness

The American view: Soviet demands on such crucial problems as disarmament, Berlin, and unification are completely unrealistic. Disarmament without adequate inspection is meaningless; a "free Berlin" would be equivalent to a Soviet Berlin; and a united Germany without free elections is an impossibility. In pursuit of their irresponsible policies the Soviets do not hesitate to run the risk of war itself. Thus, it is only due to the restraint and coordinated action of the Western alliance that Soviet provocations over Berlin did not precipitate World War III.

The Soviet view: The American position on such crucial problems as disarmament, East Germany, and China is completely unrealistic. They demand to know our secrets before they disarm; in Germany they insist on a policy which risks the resurgence of a fascist Reich; and as for China, they try to act as if it did not exist while at the same time supporting an aggressive puppet regime just off the Chinese mainland. And, in pursuit of their irresponsible policies, the Americans do not hesitate to run the risk of war itself. Were it not for Soviet prudence and restraint, the sending of a U-2 deep into Russian territory could easily have precipitated World War III.

It is easy to recognize the gross distortions in the Soviet views summarized above. But is our own outlook completely realistic? Are we correct, for example, in thinking that the mass of the Soviet people would really prefer our way of life and are unenthusiastic about their own? Certainly the tone and tenor of my conversations with Soviet citizens hardly support this belief.

But, you may ask, why is it that other Western observers do not report the enthusiasm and commitment which I encountered?

I asked this very question of newspapermen and embassy officials in Moscow. Their answers were revealing. Thus one reporter replied somewhat dryly, "Sure, I know, but when a communist

acts like a communist, it isn't news. If I want to be sure that it will be printed back home, I have to write about what's wrong with the system, not its successes." Others voiced an opinion expressed most clearly by representatives at our embassy. When I reported to them the gist of my Soviet conversations, they were grateful but skeptical: "Professor, you underestimate the effect of the police state. When these people talk to a stranger, especially an American, they *have* to say the right thing."

The argument is persuasive, and comforting to hear. But perhaps these very features should arouse our critical judgment. Indeed, it is instructive to view this argument against the background of its predecessor voiced by the newspaperman. To put it bluntly, what he was saying was that he could be sure of getting published only the material that the *American people wanted to hear.* But notice that the second argument also fulfills this objective, and it does so in a much more satisfactory and sophisticated way. The realization that "Soviet citizens *have* to say the right thing" enables the Western observer not only to discount most of what he hears but even to interpret it as evidence in direct support of the West's accepted picture of the Soviet Union as a police state.

It should be clear that I am in no sense here suggesting that Western reporters and embassy officials deliberately misrepresent what they know to be the facts. Rather, I am calling attention to the operation, in a specific and critical context, of a phenomenon well known to psychologists—the tendency to assimilate new perceptions to old, and unconsciously to distort what one sees in such a way as to minimize a clash with previous expectations. In recent years, a number of leading social psychologists, notably Heider (1958), Festinger (1957), and Osgood (1960), have emphasized that this "strain toward consistency" is especially powerful in the sphere of social relations—that is, in our perceptions of the motives, attitudes, and actions of other persons or groups. Specifically, we strive to keep our views of other human beings compatible with each other. In the face of complex social reality, such consistency is typically accomplished by obliterating distinctions and organizing the world in terms of artificially simplified frames of reference. One of the simplest of these, and hence one of the most inviting, is the dichotomy of good and bad. Hence we often perceive others, be they individuals, groups, or even whole societies, as simply "good" or "bad." Once this fateful decision is made, the rest is easy, for the "good" person or group can have only desirable social characteristics and the "bad" can have only reprehensible traits. And once such evaluative stability of social perception is established, it is extremely difficult to alter. Contradictory stimuli arouse only anxiety and resistance. When confronted with a desirable characteristic of something already known to be "bad," the observer will either just not "see" it, or will reorganize his perception of it so that it can be perceived as "bad." Finally, this tendency to regress to simple categories of perception is especially strong under conditions of emotional stress and external threat. Witness our readiness in times of war to exalt the virtues of our own side and to see the enemy as thoroughly evil.

Still one other social–psychological phenomenon has direct relevance for the present discussion. I refer to a process demonstrated most dramatically and comprehensively in the experiments of Solomon Asch (1956), and known thereby as the "Asch phenomenon." In these experiments, the subject finds himself in a group of six or eight of his peers, all of whom are asked to make comparative judgments of certain stimuli presented to them; for example, identifying the longer of two lines. At first the task seems simple enough; the subject hears others make their judgments and then makes his own. In the beginning he is usually in agreement, but then gradually he notices that more and more often his judgments differ from those of the rest of the group. Actually, the experiment is rigged. All the other group members have been instructed to give false responses on a predetermined schedule. In any event, the effect on our subject is dramatic. At first he is puzzled, then upset. Soon he begins to have serious doubts about his own judgment, and in an appreciable number of cases, he begins to "see" the stimuli as they are described by his fellows.

What I am suggesting, of course, is that the Asch phenomenon operates even more forcefully

outside the laboratory where the game of social perception is being played for keeps. *Specifically, I am proposing that the mechanisms here described contribute substantially to producing and maintaining serious distortions in the reciprocal images of the Soviet Union and the United States.*

My suggestion springs from more than abstract theoretical inference. I call attention to the possible operation of the Asch phenomenon in the Soviet–American context for a very concrete reason: I had the distressing experience of being its victim. While in the Soviet Union I deliberately sought to minimize association with other westerners and to spend as much time as I could with Soviet citizens. This was not easy to do. It was no pleasant experience to hear one's own country severely criticized and to be constantly outdebated in the bargain. I looked forward to the next chance meeting with a fellow westerner so that I could get much-needed moral support and enjoy an evening's invective at the expense of Intourist and the "worker's paradise." But though I occasionally yielded to temptation, for the most part I kept true to my resolve and spent many hours in a completely Soviet environment. It was difficult but interesting. I liked many of the people I met. Some of them apparently liked me. Though mistaken, they were obviously sincere. They wanted me to agree with them. The days went on, and strange things began to happen. I remember picking up a Soviet newspaper which featured an account of American activities in the Near East. "Oh, what are they doing now!" I asked myself, and stopped short; for I had thought in terms of "they," and it was my own country. Or I would become aware that I had been nodding to the points being made by my Soviet companion where before I had always taken issue. In short, when all around me saw the world in one way, I too found myself wanting to believe and belong.

And once I crossed the Soviet border on my way home, the process began to reverse itself. The more I talked with fellow westerners, especially fellow Americans, the more I began to doubt the validity of my original impressions. "What would you expect them to say to an American?" my friends would ask. "How do you know that the person talking to you was not a trained agitator?" "Did you ever catch sight of them following you?" I never did. Perhaps I was naive. But then, recently I reread a letter written to a friend during the last week of my stay. "I feel it is important," it begins, "to try to write to you in detail while I am still in it, for just as I could never have conceived of what I am now experiencing, so, I suspect, it will seem unreal and intangible once I am back in the West." The rest of the letter, and others like it, contain the record of the experiences reported in this account.

In sum, I take my stand on the view that there *is* a mirror image in Soviet and American perceptions of each other and that this image represents serious distortions by *both* parties of realities on either side.

The Mirror Image Projected

And if so, what then? Do not distortions have adaptive functions? Especially in war is it not psychologically necessary to see the enemy as thoroughly evil and to enhance one's self-image? And are we not engaged in a war, albeit a cold war, with the Soviet Union?

But is not our hope to bring an end to the cold war and, above all, to avoid the holocaust of a hot one? And herein lies the terrible danger of the distorted mirror image, for *it is characteristic of such images that they are self-confirming;* that is, each party, often against its own wishes, is increasingly driven to behave in a manner which fulfills the expectations of the other. As revealed in social–psychological studies, the mechanism is a simple one: if A expects B to be friendly and acts accordingly, B responds with friendly advances; these in turn evoke additional positive actions from A, and thus a benign circle is set in motion. Conversely, where A's anticipations of B are unfavorable, it is the vicious circle which develops at an accelerating pace. And as tensions rise, perceptions become more primitive and still further removed from reality. Seen from this perspective, the primary danger of the Soviet–American mirror image is that it impels each nation to act in a manner which confirms and enhances the fear of the other to the point that even deliberate efforts to reverse the process are reinterpreted as evidences of confirmation.

Manifestations of this mechanism in Soviet–American relations are not difficult to find. A case in point is our policy of restricting the travel of Soviet nationals in the United States by designating as "closed areas" localities that correspond as closely as possible to those initially selected by Soviet authorities as "off limits" to Americans in the USSR. As was brought home to me in conversations with Soviet scientists who had visited the United States, one of the effects of this policy is to neutralize substantially any favorable impressions the visitor might otherwise get of American freedoms.

To take another example in a more consequential area: in a recent issue of *Atlantic Monthly* (August 1960), Dr. Hans Bethe, an American physicist who participated in negotiations at the Geneva Conference on nuclear testing, reports that our tendency to expect trickery from the Soviets led us into spending considerable time and energy to discover scientific loopholes in their proposals which could have permitted them to continue nuclear tests undetected. As a result, our scientists did succeed in finding a theoretical basis for questioning the effectiveness of the Soviet plan. It seems that if the Soviets could dig a hole big enough, they could detonate underground explosions without being detected. Says Dr. Bethe:

> *I had the doubtful honor of presenting the theory of the big hole to the Russians in Geneva in November 1959. I felt deeply embarrassed in so doing, because it implied that we considered the Russians capable of cheating on a massive scale. I think they would have been quite justified if they had considered this an insult and walked out of the negotiations in disgust.*
>
> *The Russians seemed stunned by the theory of the big hole. In private, they took Americans to task for having spent the last year inventing methods to cheat on a nuclear test cessation agreement. Officially, they spent considerable effort in trying to disprove the theory of the big hole. This is not the reaction of a country that is bent on cheating.*

But the most frightful potential consequence of the mirror image lies in the possibility that it may confirm itself out of existence. For if it is possible for either side to interpret concessions as signs of treachery, it should not be difficult to recognize an off-course satellite as a missile on its way. After all, we, or they, would be expecting it.

But it is only in the final catastrophe that the mirror image is impartial in its effects. Short of doomsday, we have even more to lose from the accelerating vicious circle than do the Soviets. Internally, the communist system can justify itself to the Soviet people far more easily in the face of external threat than in times of peace. And in the international arena, the more the United States becomes committed to massive retaliation and preventive intervention abroad, the more difficult it becomes for uncommitted or even friendly nations to perceive a real difference in the foreign policies of East and West.

Breaking the Mirror Image

How can we avoid such awesome consequences? One step seems clearly indicated: we must do everything we can to break down the psychological barrier that prevents both us and the Russians from seeing each other and ourselves as we really are. If we can succeed in dispelling the Soviet Union's bogeyman picture of America, we stand to gain, for to the same degree that militant communism thrives in a context of external threat, it is weakened as this threat is reduced. And as the raison d'être for sacrifice, surveillance, and submission disappears there arises opportunity for the expression of such potential for liberalization as may still exist in Russian society.

American Paramilitary Culture and the Reconstitution of the Vietnam War

James William Gibson

The Vietnam War was the United States' first military defeat. It was not a small one. When Vietnam declared its independence from French colonial domination in 1945, the United States backed British and French troops in their effort to regain control. From 1946 to 1954 the United States supported France in its colonial war to crush the Vietnamese independence movement, the Vietminh; after 1950 it paid 80 per cent of France's costs. After the French defeat in 1954, the United States created a government in southern Vietnam, and sent hundreds of millions of dollars in assistance and several hundred advisers and intelligence agents.

In the early 1960s, President John Kennedy escalated US involvement to over 15,000 counter-

From Jeffrey Walsh and James Auslich, eds., *Vietnam Images: War and Representation*. New York: St. Martin's Press. Reprinted by permission of the author.

insurgency troops, advisers and logistics specialists fighting the Vietnamese revolutionary organization called the National Liberation Front. President Johnson began main-force escalation in 1965. By 1969 over 550,000 US soldiers were in Vietnam. At its peak the Vietnam War involved 40 per cent of all US Army combat-ready divisions, more than half of all Marine Corps divisions, a third of US naval forces, roughly half of the fighter bombers, and between a quarter and a half of all B-52 bombers in the US Air Force Strategic Air Command.

About 58,000 Americans died in Vietnam. (The exact number changes from year to year as some of the 800 servicemen listed as missing in action are reclassified as dead.) Over 300,000 men were wounded; how many Vietnam veterans have later died from medical conditions connected to the war is not known. Over 2.5 million Vietnamese and Laotians were killed. Much of South East Asia was destroyed.

Defeat in Vietnam broke a long tradition of American military victories. All of the land-conquest wars fought against the American Indians from the first skirmishes in the 1700s through to the final battles in the late 1880s ended with the "Americans" victorious. US forces defeated Spain during the Spanish–American War, and subsequent imperial interventions to protect US corporate interests in Central America and the Caribbean during the 1920s and 1930s also resulted in US victories.

And, in a sense, the United States was the only country to win the Second World War. American allies, particularly the Soviet Union with its 20 million dead, suffered far more than the United States, with 300,000 dead. No combat occurred on American soil; instead the economy expanded tremendously through war production. After the war, the Central Intelligence Agency (CIA) staged coups and successfully manipulated politics in many Third World countries, establishing reliable "client" regimes favourable to US corporate and political interests. Only the Korean War in the early 1950s ended in stalemate, a return to the pre-war division between North and South.

Debate over why the United States lost the Vietnam War has been confined to two positions. Some liberals have claimed that the great lesson to be learned concerned "the limits of power." The United States had expended too many men and too much money fighting in a country that wasn't so important after all. Other liberals viewed the war as a tragic drama fuelled by hubris. The US political leadership, the best and brightest of the land, made a series of "small decisions," each being "reasonably regarded at the time as the last that would be necessary." Historian Arthur M. Schlesinger, Jr, concluded that Vietnam was simply a "tragedy without villains."[1]

In contrast, conservatives say that the United States lost the war because of "self-imposed restraints." During the war, US generals had constantly complained that political leaders kept them from fighting in the way they wanted to fight, even as troop allotments escalated in "packages" of 50,000–100,000 combat and support troops and as bombing campaigns in North and South Vietnam and Laos reached levels far beyond the 2.1 million tons dropped by the United States in the Second World War.

After the 1975 debacle this claim became more pronounced. The most famous analysis is Colonel Harry Summers's book *On Strategy*.[2] Summers recapitulates the military's position that there was no peasant social revolution in South Vietnam seeking land reform and national reunification with the North. Instead, guerrilla war, pacification and building a government that enjoyed popular support were all false idols that distracted US forces from the true enemy, North Vietnamese who were determined to conquer the South and expand the Communist empire. Summers says the United States should have lined up its forces like a wall in southern Laos to keep the foreign invaders out. Other US military men have said that in retrospect a *land invasion* of North Vietnam, taking the chief port, Haiphong, and the capital city, Hanoi, would have ended the war.[3]

But neither the liberal "Vietnam-as-mistake" nor the conservative "self-imposed restraint" theory explains what happened. By the technical and economic standards that US war-managers thought were the only appropriate measures in warfare, the United States should have won. After the Second World War the US military reconceptualised and reorganised itself along corporate lines. Officers became "managers," the enlisted men "workers," and the product was enemy deaths, the famous "body count." Just as the US economy prospered from high-technology, capital-intensive production systems, "technowar" would produce so many enemy deaths that the other side would be driven "bankrupt."[4] General William Westmoreland called this the "cross-over point," when the North Vietnamese would no longer be able to replace casualties fast enough to maintain a stable force.[5] After the cross-over point had been reached, the North Vietnamese would recognise US superiority and begin negotiations on that basis.

From the technowar paradigm, Vietnamese history, social structure and cultural arrangements did not appear important. Thus neither "liberals" of the Kennedy and Johnson administrations nor "conservatives" of the Nixon administration ever saw the significance of traditional Vietnamese resistance to foreign invaders. For thousands of years Vietnamese fought against the Chinese; then they fought against the French from the 1880s until their victory in 1954. Most Vietnamese cultural heroes were nationalist warriors.

Nor did the technological-production orientation towards warfare consider that most Vietnamese were poor peasants with little or no land. Under French rule, land-ownership had become concentrated in a small land-owning and merchant class. Frequently members of this ruling class converted to Catholicism, while the overwhelming peasant majority practised Buddhism, often mixed with Confucianism. The South Vietnamese ruling class in turn monopolised army leadership, using its position both as a way to appropriate American aid and as a way to collect rents from the peasantry at gunpoint.[6]

Such crucial social dynamics have not been considered in the post-Vietnam liberal–conservative debate on why the United States lost. Both sides remain within the "technowar" perspective. Within the confines of the debate, the conservative

"self-imposed restraint" school has achieved political hegemony. After Ronald Reagan won the presidential election in 1980, he called the Vietnam War a "noble cause." His Secretary of Defense, Caspar Weinberger, officially endorsed the self-imposed restraint position when he announced that the United States would never again ask its men to "serve in a war that we did not intend to win."[7]

To overcome these imaginary "self-imposed restraints" the Reagan administration radically increased military expenditure. By 1984, military spending reached over $200 billion (thousand million) and plans were made for spending $1800 billion between 1984 and 1988. (Historically, major weapons systems have cost over three times their original estimates, and recent systems much more.) Weapons procurement constitutes $670.8 billion of this $1800 billion. In economic expenditures, the United States fought a more intense war in the early and mid 1980s than it did in the 1960s and plans to fight an even greater one in the late 1980s. By 1988 the US military will receive $87 for every $100 spent in the civilian economy for fixed capital formation.[8]

Some of these funds have gone to expand conventional US military forces for new expeditions in the Third World. The Central Command or Rapid Deployment Force, created in the early 1980s, now totals between 200,000 and 300,000 men, besides ships and aircraft. New long-range air transports and aerial-refuelling tankers have been ordered, as have amphibious warfare vessels and floating warehouses called "near-term prepositioning ships." Extensive air bases and port facilities have been prepared in Honduras for rapid US escalation in a war against Nicaragua or leftist guerrillas in El Salvador. Other US bases have been prepared in Egypt and Somalia as staging areas for military deployment in the Middle East.[9]

Overt military operations and "covert" paramilitary operations have also increased during the Reagan administration. Marines were sent to Lebanon in 1982. US military forces invaded Grenada and overthrew the government there in 1983. Libya was bombed by US planes. Covertly, the Mujahadeen in Afghanistan have received massive assistance in their war to drive out Russian invaders. Former Nicaraguan dictator Anastasio Somoza's National Guard, now commonly known as the Contras, has received extensive US support in its war against the Sandinista revolution. Over 1000 sophisticated anti-tank missiles, together with jet-fighter and anti-aircraft missile parts, were covertly shipped to Iran in 1986 at a time when the United States was publicly calling for an arms embargo against Iran because of its support for terrorist groups.

Thus, just over a decade after defeat in Vietnam, the United States has expanded its military economy and is engaging in extensive covert operations and "sub-limited" warfare. How did this happen? How did the massive military defeat in Vietnam become so inconsequential? How did US foreign policy return so quickly to the same basic directions it followed before and during the Vietnam War? Why have the American people supported this political-military direction when the record of expeditionary forces intervening in Third World revolutions and civil wars has been so poor in recent years?

To answer these questions it is necessary to examine not only US economic interests in Third World countries—the traditional question asked when investigating imperialism—but also the mythical place of war in American culture. According to historian Richard Slotkin, "Myth describes a process, credible to its audience, by which knowledge is transformed into power; it provides a scenario or prescription for action, defining and limiting the possibilities for human response to the universe."[10] The Indian wars formed a fundamental American myth: to justify taking away Indian lands, first colonists and later "American" explorers and settlers developed a national mythology in which "American" technological and logistic superiority in warfare became culturally transmitted as signs of cultural–moral superiority. European and "American" "civilisation" morally deserved to defeat Indian "savagery." Might made right and each victory recharged the culture and justified expansion—what Sloktin calls "regeneration through violence."[11]

Primary American mythology survived the closing of the frontier and the final subordination of the Indians by changing to incorporate new enemies at the very same time US economic and political interests wanted an overseas empire. No one knew for sure why the battleship *Maine* exploded in Havana harbour: Spanish soldiers could have mined it or its steam boiler could have blown up, a common occurrence among steamships. Both the newspapers and the film industry claimed that the Spaniards were responsible. Early "motion pictures" re-created the sinking by constructing a model battleship out of a rowboat, filling it with explosives and photographing the subsequent explosion. These special-effects films were highly effective in raising the 125,000 recruits needed for the war.[12]

On 20 April 1898, when President McKinley called for volunteers, he also authorised formation of the First US Volunteer Cavalry, "to be composed exclusively of frontiersmen possessing special qualifications as horsemen and marksmen." He immediately offered the unit to Theodore Roosevelt, Assistant Secretary of the Navy, who had long wanted to command a troop of "harum-scarum rough-riders."[13]

The name "Rough Riders"—what the regiment was soon called—was already internationally famous. The original "rough-riders" were the "cowboys and Indians" of William Cody's (Buffalo Bill's) Wild West Show. Hundreds of dime novels and thousands of short stories had been written about Cody; he had succeeded Daniel Boone and Davy Crockett as the mythical Western hero. When Cody shot Chief Yellow Hand at Warbonnet Creek in 1876, he wore a Mexican black velvet suit trimmed in silver buttons and lace. As historian Henry Nash Smith notes in *Virgin Land,* by the 1870s the blending of the real Cody with his theatrical role had reached "the point where no one—least of all the man himself—could say where the actual left off and where the dime novel fiction began."[14]

Some Wild West show members enlisted in the First Cavalry under a special contract whereby Cody was assured they would return to the show once the war was over (Cody did not enlist). Roosevelt filled the unit with the frontier's last generation of cowboys and a sprinkling of Ivy

League college men. He also took with him to Cuba two motion-picture photographers from the Vitagraph Corporation.

San Juan Hill has long been remembered as the Rough Riders' great victory. Although the First Cavalry was there, so too were several black infantry and cavalry units, and other white units. Nevertheless, Roosevelt got the glory (via Vitagraph) and successfully campaigned for the presidency as a war hero. Once in office he initiated the "walk softly and carry a big stick" school of gunboat diplomacy in the Caribbean and Central America.

Roosevelt also helped transform frontier mythology into the twentieth-century war movie. Stuart Blackton, a partner in Vitagraph, wanted to make a movie based on Hudson Maxim's *Defenseless America,* a book about how easily the United States could be invaded. (Hudson Maxim's brother, Sir Hiram Maxim, had invented smokeless gunpowder, the machine gun, and a high explosive for torpedoes—he worked for E. I. Dupont de Nemours Company, a munitions firm.) Roosevelt arranged a special meeting for Blackton with "the mayor of New York, Admiral Dewey, Major General Leonard Wood, Elihu Root, president of the War College and Brigadier General Cornelius Vanderbilt, of the National Guard."[15] All became enthused about the prospect of such a magnificent sequel to Vitagraph's first feature film, D. W. Griffith's *Birth of a Nation.*

Battle Cry for Peace was released in 1915. A foreign agent named Emanon ("no name" spelled backwards) ideologically seduces a millionaire named Vandergriff to espouse peace. When Vandergriff makes his pro-peace speech in New York City, it is shelled by ships, bombed by planes, and invaded by foreign troops wearing Kaiser Wilhelm moustaches. Vandergriff is shot and his fiancée's mother kills her two daughters and then herself to avoid rape. Fifty million people saw the movie in the United States and Britain.

Vitagraph went on to make many war films based on novels by Sir Gilbert Parker, British

Director of Propaganda. The sinking of the passenger liner *Lusitania* in 1915 enlisted the rest of the film industry. *Lusitania* films and the many heirs to *Battle Cry for Peace* formed a war-movie genre soon called "Hate-the-Hun" films: Germans became a race apart, specialists in rape (allowing lurid sexual encounters) and general mayhem and murder. . . .

■ ■ ■

Mythic warriors and war culture became even more important during the Second World War. Hollywood and the Defense Department (successor to the War Department) formed a vital working relationship. Hollywood produced thousands of military training films—subjects ranged from political topics such as why Hitler was bad, to basic hygiene, to instruction on how to operate a radio. (Ronald Reagan spent the war making such films.) Hollywood also created war movies to boost American morale. John Wayne films such as *They Were Expendable* (1945) and *Back to Bataan* (1945) showed American soldiers valiantly fighting delaying actions against superior Japanese forces.

After the great American victory in 1945, Hollywood and the Defense Department reaffirmed their relationship, with the military providing either free or low-cost technical advisers, tanks, planes, ships, guns and often soldiers to Hollywood film-makers. In exchange the Defense Department had the right to demand script changes to ensure favourable portrayal. According to various estimates, 5000 war movies were made between 1945 and 1965 and 1200 received major assistance from the Defense Department.[16*]

This massive film celebration of US war success began just as the United States entered the Cold War. Selective Service initiated a draft for the Korean War that was retained throughout the 1950s. Naval and air forces obtained massive funding to fight strategic nuclear war. New military bases were constructed around the world to "contain Communism." A permanent war economy evolved to provide more advanced weapons systems.

---

*[Footnotes have been renumbered because portions of the original work have been deleted—EDS.]

In 1947 the House Un-American Activities Committee (HUAC) investigated "Hollywood Communism." Major studios, broad-casting networks and other media outlets, together with film-industry organizations such as the Screen Actors Guild (Ronald Reagan was its president) all co-operated with HUAC, the Federal Bureau of Investigation (FBI) and "private" security firms in blacklisting politically left-of-centre media workers. Making war movies and Westerns was politically safe, a sign of alignment with Cold War politics.

War movies and Westerns are not varieties of the same genre; each type has its complexities, and both changed from 1945 to 1965. Nevertheless, war movies and Westerns presented a highly coherent view of American war (with rare exceptions) that encompassed the Western wars against the Indians and the foreign battles of the Second World War.

First, war films show the United States always fighting on the morally correct side. While killing enemies is rarely shown as pleasurable, it is seldom portrayed as causing sorrow either.

Second, US soldiers win almost all battles and always win the war. Good American soldiers, with relatively egalitarian relationships with each other (even between formal ranks), shoot better than bad Indians, Japanese or Germans, who are regimented in a hierarchy and ultimately controlled by a dictator chief. Might and right go together in the war-movie code.

Third, war movies show good guys and bad guys, but few innocents. Warfare is portrayed as a clean fight between two forces; rarely are civilians caught in crossfire. When civilians are killed, they die at the hands of the bad guys.

Fourth, war does not appear dangerous. In most cases the principal American heroes and most of the secondary heroes survive battle. In those rare cases where the hero is killed, as John Wayne's Sergeant Stryker character is in *The Sands of Iwo Jima* (1949), his martial spirit passes on to a younger soldier. Bullet and shrapnel entry and exit holes appear as small red dots. No one screams in agony. The dead die quickly; the camera pans over the body and returns to the living.

Finally, war movies portray war as a crucial ritual transition from male adolescence into manhood. Boys arrive at basic training camp, where a harsh but secretly loving drill instructor forces them to bond together. Recruits abandon their shallow class, ethnic and regional prejudices, replacing them with egalitarian mutual respect for their achievements in training as they collectively approach manhood. Soldiers then go off to war (where they bond even tighter) and the surviving victors are certified men. In Westerns the master warrior or warriors don't "go home." In war movies, however, soldiers frequently talk of going home. War movies imply that the soldiers' victories will be well respected since they have both defended their society and embody the society's highest ideals; their war success infuses society with their powers.[17]

Baby-boomers grew up on this war and Western mythology. Around 3.5 million men went to Vietnam. Memoirs, oral histories, novels and poems by veterans make frequent mention of the war movies and Westerns they watched as teenagers. Ron Kovic writes in his memoir *Born on the Fourth of July,* "Every Saturday afternoon we'd go down to the movies in the shopping center and watch gigantic prehistoric birds breathe fire, and war movies with John Wayne and Audie Murphy. . . . I'll never forget Audie Murphy in *To Hell and Back.*"[18] Kovic enlisted after recruiters visited his high school. Philip Caputo entered Marine Officers Candidate School for similar reasons: "For me, the classroom work was mindnumbing. I wanted the romance of war, bayonet charges, and desperate battles against impossible odds. I wanted the sort of thing I had seen in *Guadalcanal Diary* and *Retreat, Hell!*"[19]

Most combat soldiers quickly learned the difference between war-movie fantasy and real war. On Kovic's first operation he accidentally killed an American corporal. Another man's movie dissolved when he killed an enemy soldier: "I felt sorry. I don't know why I felt sorry. John Wayne never felt sorry."[20] US military headquarters in Saigon was satirised as "Hollywood West" and John Wayne's name soon was taken in vain, either as a metaphor for a foolish act, as in one sergeant's instruction to newcomers, "Now, we don't want to see no John Wayne performances out there," or as an invective against war horror, as in Charles Anderson's *The Grunts:* "There was no longer any doubt about what warfare in the modern industrial era had come to mean. The grunts—newbys, short-timers, and lifers alike—could see now that what happens to human beings in mechanized warfare has absolutely no poetic. Fuck you, John Wayne!"[21]

But politicians further removed from battle did not learn. President Richard Nixon saw *Patton* several times in spring 1970. George C. Scott portrayed the Second World War general as a brilliant eccentric whose vision and valour saved an American airborne division under siege from a German offensive. According to former Secretary of State William Rogers and White House Chief of Staff H. R. Haldeman, Nixon talked incessantly about the movie while deciding that US forces should invade Cambodia. Nixon even ordered American military chaplains to pray for a change in weather, just as Patton did.[22]

■ ■ ■

Defeat in Vietnam created a twofold crisis for the United States. First, its inability successfully to exert its power ended US dominance in world affairs. Second, defeat created a cultural crisis among the American people. There had been no "regeneration through violence." Assumptions about what was right and how the world operated became problematic—and domestic challenges to the natural order of things had already been raised by the civil rights, anti-war and feminist movements.

American culture did not have any mythical narratives and visual symbols to explain why US forces had not achieved victory. There was no popular cultural archetype to account for successful Vietnamese resistance to foreign invaders—the Indians had always lost. Nor did the major news media, especially network television news, provide any different framework for interpreting the war. For the most part, network news correspondents and politicians reported what leading US generals and politicians said about the war. News cameras in turn showed thousands of images of sophisticated American technology such as jet fighter bombers, helicopters, tanks and ships. Once ABC

television news contrasted the immense power of the newly recommissioned battleship *New Jersey* to the "Vietcong Flying Trashcan," a homemade rocket (looking like a trashcan) on a stick mounted in the mud along a river bank.[23] Weekly bodycount summaries always showed Vietcong losses as several times greater than those of US and allied forces. Relatively few bodies and almost no blood were shown. Technowar appeared clean and productive on the news; of course the United States would win.

But "self-imposed restraint" offered the American people a way to make sense of failure in Vietnam; that position plunges into the core of American mythology. In Westerns, the hero must take law into his own hands, because the power structure has failed to confront a challenge to society. Masked superheroes operate outside the law to win victories the authorities cannot or will not win. The modern detective hero works outside the police bureaucracy and often outside the law to preserve the spirit of the law, justice. It is only a short cultural distance from these classic American heroes who act outside the power structure in order to save society to American soldiers who are *restrained by corrupt or cowardly politicians and thus not allowed to win the war.*

From the early 1970s to the late 1980s American culture has been reinterpreted to fit the war in Vietnam and those who fought it into this myth—reworked its classic heroes into a "new" version of the warrior and war culture. This new "hero" is the "paramilitary warrior," paramilitary in the sense that the new heroes are rarely members of conventional military or law-enforcement bureaucracies. He is the centre of an emerging paramilitary culture that is actively redefining notions of peace and war to the American public. This culture posits *a mythical interpretation of the Vietnam War* and *a new war* as the path to health for the warrior and regeneration for a society weakened and troubled by mysterious military failure and a world it can no longer control. . . .

■ ■ ■

Hollywood's first wave of Vietnam films began in the late 1970s—*The Deer Hunter* (1978),

Taxi Driver (1976), *Who'll Stop the Rain* (1978) and *Apocalypse Now!* (1979). In each film, a Vietnam veteran returns to war. In *The Deer Hunter* Robert De Niro plays an elite US Army Special Forces soldier who returns to Vietnam to rescue a friend gone native, drug-addicted and insane. His warrior skills enable him to maintain his sanity and survive. In *Taxi Driver,* De Niro plays a Vietnam veteran who cannot create a meaningful life for himself in New York City, and decides to become a warrior again. After failing to assassinate a presidential candidate, he shifts his war towards the pimps who manage a young prostitute he has tried to befriend. *Who'll Stop the Rain* finds Ray Hicks as a veteran who must go to war inside the heroin trade to save a journalist friend he knew in Vietnam who tried to make money importing the drug from Vietnam to the United States but did not have the warrior skills to survive.

In *Apocalypse Now* Martin Sheen plays a drunken, distraught Army captain in the Studies and Observations Group (SOG, the principal co-vert-operations commando organisation in Vietnam) who returns to Vietnam begging a new mission because he can no longer function back in the United States. Sheen's character, Willard, becomes progressively healthier as he moves up-river on his mission to assassinate a renegade colonel who no longer takes orders from higher command.

But these 1970s films demonstrate great ambivalence about the desirability of returning to war. The De Niro character in *The Deer Hunter* brings back his friend's body, not a living man. Although taxi driver Travis Bickle becomes a media hero, his second war does not make him sane. Ray Hicks saves his friend, but is killed in the effort and intelligence agents get the heroin. And Willard kills Colonel Kurtz (played by Marlon Brando) because Kurtz wants to die. His death only frees Willard from his last connections to the military.

In January 1981 Ronald Reagan replaced Jimmy Carter as President. At the same time fifty-one American hostages who had been held prisoner by Iran were released. Interviews with Hollywood directors, Robert K. Brown (publisher of *Soldier of Fortune* magazine) and editors of paper-

back commando novels all confirm that the Iran hostage crisis with its failed "Desert One" rescue mission and the election of President Reagan marked the ascendancy of paramilitary culture.[24]

The transition film appeared in 1983. *Uncommon Valor* introduces an unhappy array of Vietnam veterans. Some are clearly down and out; one is in jail. Those with middle-class jobs and ilies seem a bit bored. At first they resist the call to return to war, but duty to lost comrades beckons. When these men regroup to train for an independent, privately financed mission to rescue their missing comrades held prisoner in Laos, they become mentally and physically healthy warriors again complete with a transcendent purpose in life for which they are willing to die. And most do; the trade-off of rescuers for prisoners is about one to one.

A new war-movie genre soon blossomed. Sylvester Stallone's John Rambo character illustrates this change from ambivalence about the value of a second war to redemption through war. In *First Blood* (1983) Rambo suffers from post-traumatic stress disorder and inadvertently destroys a small Oregon town after being persecuted and then hunted by an arrogant sheriff. Instead of being treated for his affliction, he is sentenced to years of hard labour on a chain gang breaking rocks. In *First Blood II* (1985) Rambo is offered a presidential pardon if he will rescue American prisoners still in Vietnam. His first question to Colonel Trautman is framed around the self-imposed-restraint position: "Do we get to win this time?" Rambo finds the prisoners only to be betrayed and abandoned by the commanding CIA officer. No prisoners are to be brought back because they would embarrass the government. Left on his own, however, he becomes the unrestrained warrior of myth who readily vanquishes Vietnamese who wear Second World War Japanese Army caps and their Russian KGB superiors, who look and sound much like war-movie Nazis. Myth readily substitutes one enemy for another, combining them in ways that make cultural sense: if white Russians really controlled and directed yellow Vietnamese, then US defeat becomes more understandable and belief in white superiority is confirmed.

Rambo illustrates four other vital aspects of paramilitary culture. First, the Vietnamese are not shown as real people from a different culture with different political values. Instead the Vietnamese are portrayed as *criminals*. They retain American prisoners as slave labourers and savagely abuse them. One prisoner is crucified on a bamboo cross. Vietnamese guards sadistically enjoy such abuse; the Communists are *sexually perverted*. As criminal sexual perverts, the Vietnamese do not represent an alternative kind of society, different from American capitalism, but rather they are *outside the boundary of moral conduct of any sort*. Communism is thus shown as a kind of organised criminal hierarchy.

Second, Stallone exemplifies the paramilitary warrior's bodily power. Modern warrior heroes are almost all in superb physical shape, often having extensive martial-arts skills. Neither the classical Western hero with his fast gun draw nor the detective with his reasoning ability nor the soldier leader achieved power from tremendous bodily strength. The new warrior appears as a unified biological and mechanical *weapons system;* there is no separation between body and weapons. Rambo is, as Colonel Trautman calls him, a "pure fighting machine."

Third, Rambo illustrates the paramilitary warrior's inclination to work either alone or in very small groups of brother warriors. American mythology has traditionally portrayed the Western hero warrior operating this way. Warriors are shown as consummate male individualists; to be a warrior is to reach the social position that has the most autonomy. As a mythic warrior, a man expresses his individual potential with his own personal style. Real military organisations are very different; the military is a completely hierarchical institution.

Fourth, the warrior's sexuality often kills his women lovers. When Rambo kisses his female Vietnamese contact, he marks her for death. A warrior's masculinity is confirmed by battle against other men, and his valour is judged by male accomplices or superiors. Sexual relations with women do not confer manhood, and are secondary to more essential relations with fellow warriors.

The principal male enemy whom the paramilitary warrior kills in the final "duel" is often a far more intimate partner to the hero than women lovers.

While many new war movies place their second, redeeming battles in Vietnam, the genre has rapidly expanded to include victories on a worldwide battlefield. *Delta Force* (1986) begins with scenes of a helicopter crashing into a C-130 transport in the Iranian desert. Years later Chuck Norris (who plays a retired commando) is watching television and drinking a Budweiser when the news announces a jet-hijacking by Arab terrorists belonging to the New World Revolution. He rushes to Fort Bragg and rejoins Delta Force and off they go. Norris kills the Arab leader with his rocket-firing motorcycle.

Iron Eagle (1986) opens with an unnamed Middle East country shooting down an American F-16 that has challenged its claim to a 200-mile offshore territorial boundary. The pilot is captured, tried as a criminal and sentenced to hang in three days. Back at their California base, the squadron commander tells the pilot's son that "The White House has our hands tied." Doug (the son) then steals two F-16s with the help of a retired black pilot and successfully rescues his father, shooting down several enemy planes as he goes. To reach the high plateau of mind–body co-ordination needed for this mission he plays hard-beating disco music from a cassette recorder strapped to his thigh.

In *Top Gun* (1986) Tom Cruise's "Maverick" character ranks among the Navy's top 1 per cent of fighter pilots, but he is cocky and unstable, secretly troubled by the legacy of his dead father's mysterious bad reputation. Although he graduates from advanced air-to-air combat school, he is not head gunfighter. But on a subsequent mission he shoots down several MIGs, subordinates his egotism to group safety and emerges a mature man. He then learns that his father was really a Vietnam War hero killed on a secret mission.

By the end of the movie Maverick has overcome his grief at the death of his former navigator, found a father substitute (the senior Top Gun instructor, who was saved by the father on the secret mission), won the respect of his peers, regained the lustful love of a beautiful, brilliant woman, kept his other mistress (his very hot F-14) and become a Top Gun instructor with the task of reproducing his warrior skills among new fledgling top guns. When the movie came out, naval recruiters did quite well. Female students at the University of California at Los Angeles reported that the bars near the Top Gun base near San Diego were the place to go, and that even in Los Angeles strange men began singing to them as a pick-up technique, just like in the movie. This film grossed $175 million in 1986.

Clint Eastwood goes back to war for a *third* time in *Heartbreak Ridge* (1986). As an aging gunnery sergeant approaching retirement he takes command of a sloppy reconnaissance platoon. He inspires the soldiers, ignores a weak intellectual lieutenant who formally commands the platoon, and comes into conflict with the ambitious battalion commander, who has no combat experience but is instead an Annapolis graduate whose expertise resides in management and logistics.

Eastwood leads his platoon to great victory over the Cuban Army during the Grenada invasion by defying the battalion commander's order prohibiting the platoon from capturing a crucial hill. In the process, both a black enlisted man who wanted to become a rock musician and the lieutenant discover their true warrior selves. At the end the sergeant is reconciled with his ex-wife (who always loved him but couldn't stand the strain of waiting while he was at war) and faces retirement secure in the knowledge that he has spiritually reproduced himself. He leaves the Marine Corps with "one, one, and one"—one victory (Grenada), one tie (Korea) and one loss (Vietnam).

The real Grenada invasion came only days after 245 Marines were killed in Beirut; part of the invasion force was *en route* to Lebanon to replace the soldiers garrisoned there. Bernard Coard's regime had offered to co-operate in evacuating all Americans from the island. The medical students whose "rescue" provided the pretext for the invasion weren't secured until late in the second day of the invasion, giving the Grenadans plenty of time to execute them if they so wished. The "military" airport on Grenada was built with assistance from many countries, including the US Agency for International Development. In essence the Reagan administration sought to replace defeat in Lebanon with a public-relations victory in Grenada.

Hollywood redemption of Beirut came a few months after the Grenada film. *Death before Dishonor* (1987) shows Fred Dyer as a Marine Corps sergeant and Brian Keith as a colonel stationed at the US embassy in a Middle East country. International terrorists (white Europeans, dressed in punk fashion) help local Arabs steal US weapons. Sergeant Burns pursues, but the bad guys get away. The black ambassador chastises him, "At no time were your orders to pursue hijackers through the streets endangering civilians." The terrorists then kidnap the colonel (who was friends with the sergeant's father) and a Latino private. Even after the enlisted man's body is dumped in front of the embassy, Ambassador Morgan intones, "You realize this does not change anything." But then the embassy is blown-up by a Beirut-style truck bomb.

Sergeant Burns goes to war, assisted by the Israeli Mossad, and his brother Marines. They storm the terrorist garrison and rescue the colonel. Burns kills the Arab leader, and then chases the European terrorists through the desert, finally crashing his jeep into their truck. Neckbones protrude from the male terrorist, while the female has a .45 crater in her forehead. Burns emerges unhurt.

In television these themes continue, but without the sharp edges. *The A-Team* ran for several years as an elite commando group that was accused by corrupt elements of higher command of killing Vietnamese civilians. Convicted of murder and sent to military prison, they escaped and became a Robin Hood style mercenary force for hire by victims of injustice who were not helped by the legal authorities.

Magnum P. I. is about a Hawaii-based detective who served in Vietnam as a Naval Intelligence officer. Magnum still has contacts with Naval Intelligence (he's in the naval reserves), hangs around with former members of his Vietnam team and one retired British Army Intelligence officer, and has easy access to his buddy's helicopter. Over the years Magnum and his group have rescued dissidents in Kampuchea (Cambodia) from his former Vietnamese Communist enemies, killed both Russian KGB agents and North Vietnamese agents operating in Hawaii, and performed a few jobs for former Navy bosses.

Miami Vice shows two Vietnam veterans who return to war as detectives trying to stop drug-dealers and gun-runners, who have made America itself a *war zone*. "Bad guys" armed with sub-machine guns routinely shoot it out with Crockett and Tubbs. The two detectives' girl friends often die or just disappear; the male warriors remain undomesticated. Crockett and Tubbs often meet defeat because their investigations are stopped by the CIA or other high-level government agencies who need the gun-runners or drug-dealers (and their corporate-banker partners) for covert actions. In this respect *Miami Vice* sometimes presents the most radical analysis of the US government and corporate capitalism found on commercial television.

Moreover, when the Vietnam War is discussed, the conversations focus on American massacres, drug-dealing and high-level government lies. In one 1987 episode, *Miami Vice* even had a North Vietnamese intelligence agent as the hero— he successfully tracked down a political assassin who first worked for the CIA's Phoenix assassination programme in Vietnam and was now killing leftist politicians for a former CIA colleague and his unnamed anti-Communist group. Often, though, the show just puts a hip, luxurious twist on paramilitary culture.

In November 1986 the Crockett character appeared on the cover of *Soldier of Fortune* magazine. *SOF* was started in 1975 by a retired Army Special Forces colonel named Robert Brown. Brown had served in the . . . Vietnam War and was well versed in paramilitary operations.[25] Many of the elite "commando" oriented men . . . such as Army and Marine reconnaissance and navy SEALs (Sea-Air Land), became professional warriors, operating as contract operatives for US intelligence missions, serving in other countries' armies (such as Rhodesia and Nicaragua before their respective revolutions), and working as bodyguards or security experts for corporations and businessmen.

Twenty- to thirty-thousand men served in the commando and reconnaissance units during the Vietnam War. In 1987 around 30,000 US soldiers had been trained and assigned to service in commando, reconnaissance, counter-insurgency and special assault units. Several thousand policemen have volunteered for duty in Special Weapons and Tactics (SWAT) teams across the country. Taking all these together (plus the few hundred real mercenaries), the potential *SOF* community of real warriors totals perhaps 75,000 at most (and that may be way too high). Although this may sound a large number, it is relatively small compared to either the total number of Vietnam veterans (3.5 million men) or the number of American men aged between 18 and 50. Seventy-five thousand is also too small a number to make a mass-market magazine profitable.

But one of *SOF*'s most brilliant features is that it has extended its appeal far beyond the audience of professional warriors. The image of the paramilitary warrior fulfils traditional concepts of masculinity, and in him *SOF* successfully creates a gender ideal for all men—the magazine makes such an identity seem more accessible than movies do. Soldiers and policemen can be warriors, but so can factory workers, clerks, small businessmen, professors and corporate executives. Being a warrior is not an occupation but a male identity.

What characterises the *SOF* warrior? First and foremost, the magazine presents what can be called "cosmopolitan anti-Communism." *SOF* reporters and freelancers travel to many of the world's war zones. Photo essays on Afghan rebels have appeared regularly. *SOF* training-teams frequently travel to Central America. In El Salvador they teach elite shock battalions how to maintain their M-60 machine guns and fire 81mm mortars accurately. In Honduras they assist the Contras—Brown and other *SOF* personnel have been implicated in shipping arms—and *SOF* freelancers accompany them on raids in Nicaragua. Interviews with Contra leaders are a routine feature. Other stories come from travels with South African Army commando groups and Angolan guerrillas (Holden Roberto's UNITA organisation) as they try to destroy the leftist Angolan government and various anti-apartheid guerrilla groups which are categorised as pro-Communist, and therefore the enemy.

SOF also reports on the world's elite commando units—the British Special Air Service and Special Boat Service, Germany's anti-terrorist organisation GS-9, the French Foreign Legion, Israeli paratroopers, and so on. *SOF* thus reads much like *National Geographic* in that both are structured around travelogue narratives with extensive colour photography, except that *National Geographic* looks at Third World cultures and animals, while *SOF* examines small warrior societies and Third World insurgencies and counter-insurgency efforts.

Underlying these world travels to battle-grounds and barracks is the familiar image of the war that could have been won except for self-imposed restraints. Brown founded *SOF* in 1975, the year American efforts in Vietnam finally collapsed. The "I Was There" monthly feature frequently revisits personal combat encounters in Vietnam, while longer articles cover more famous battles such as Khe Sanh in 1968 or survey different military units serving in Vietnam, especially special-operations units. Almost all individual battles end in US victory. Political leaders and the Pentagon are routinely criticised for general US defeat in Vietnam; their lack of resolve in pursuing the war becomes the justification for "independent" or paramilitary warriors who will do what governments are afraid to do.

Another crucial component of being a paramilitary warrior is being an expert on contemporary "weapons families"—the rifles, machine guns, submachine guns, pistols, knives, grenades and anti-tank rocket-launchers carried by both Western and Communist light infantry. Each *SOF* issue covers at least one modern weapon in depth. In this respect it resembles *Consumer's Report*; indeed, some new weapons are taken to Central America for "battlefield testing."

Paramilitary culture calls for extensive consumer purchases. Not only must a paramilitary warrior know about the weapons: he must own them. Semi-automatic assault rifles and carbines begin at around $300 and most cost $500 and upwards. Almost all the world's assault rifles (including Chinese and Yugoslavian manufactured

AK-47s) are now sold in American gun stores and most manufacturers advertise in *SOF.* A back-cover advertisement by the German firm Heckler and Koch shows a commando dressed in black (with black warpaint on his face and a black bandana covering his head) crouched over a log in about three feet of water. There's a big rope on the log and in his hand he holds a HK-91 semi-automatic assault rifle. The caption reads, "When you're determined to survive, you leave nothing to chance." The warrior's survival *requires* that he purchase weapons. . . .

■ ■ ■

Besides weapons, warriors need two-way radios, binoculars, bullet-proof vests, various kinds of "web" gear or "assault vests" to carry all their equipment, and multiple-pistol holsters for hips, shoulders and ankles. New models are marketed each year. All these consumer goods are advertised in *SOF*; one demographic study conducted in the late 1970s found that most *SOF* subscribers spend over $1000 a year on weapons and accessories. Through this consumption the paramilitary warrior can easily reach armament and accessory levels equal to most police SWAT teams and individual infantrymen in Western armies.

At the base of this array of weapons and accoutrements, the paramilitary warrior wears *camouflage uniforms.* "Camouflage" normally means clothing or paint schemes or special devices that help a soldier, vehicle, plane or ship blend into the natural environment so that the person or object's silhouette will be diffused. But, in paramilitary culture, camouflage clothing has the exact opposite function. Camouflage doesn't hide anyone. To pass unnoticed in urban, suburban or rural areas requires dressing as local inhabitants do, in business suits, workman's clothes or casual wear. Wearing olive green or woodland or desert camouflage or SWAT black camouflage indicates that an individual identifies himself as a warrior.

Camouflage clothing also gives men a way to play with costumes, accessories and make-up without appearing effeminate. At a fantasy level, changing clothes means the warrior is no longer bound by the moral code governing civilian actions. To change clothes and put on make-up allows men to fantasise that they have become truly different from the ordinary, law-abiding men they normally are. In the minds of psychotics, this fantasy transition marks a real transition. Once man in San Diego changed into camouflage clothes, took over a McDonald's restaurant and murdered twenty-six people with his Uzi, 12-gauge riot shotgun, and Browning 9mm Hi-Power pistol (favourite paramilitary weapons). A number of similarly dressed and equipped killers have recently been reported in newpapers.

For more "normal" men, wearing camouflage signifies a "key-club" sign of membership of a social–political community of like-minded males who can recognise their common interests and beliefs by their common attire. For example, camouflage fatigues are the required dress at the annual *SOF* conventions in Las Vegas. Here several hundred men attend seminars on how to fight Russian tanks with small arms, hear speeches from famous anti-Communist leaders, and can examine the latest weapons at a huge exposition in the Sahara Hotel and Casino.

Until 1986 the most significant item offered in *SOF* was, literally, "soldiers of fortune." A typical classified ad read: "MERC FOR HIRE: 43, anything, anywhere, work alone, short-term only. Bounty hunting. Will take commission job," followed by a first name and post-office box. A CBS *Sixty Minutes* news investigation in 1986 found that police in twenty states were investigating murders and other serious crimes linked to men hired through *SOF* ads. After CBS announced its findings, *SOF* discontinued taking such ads. The magazine lost two lawsuits for negligence by victims of mercenary assaults and was fined nearly $10 million in damages.[26]

SOF has thus created an incredible combination of real counter-insurgency warfare, mercenaries and military units mixed with traditional American themes of cultural regeneration through violence and a warrior identity for men, ideological anti-Communism, a populist scepticism towards political leaders and consumerism. *SOF* claims that it has around 35,000 subscribers and newsstand sales of another 200,000 or so each month (apparently issues with war-movie covers do the best)....

. . .

Paramilitary culture has provided a deep and broad *legitimation* of the US government's rapid escalation of military forces. If the Vietnam War was lost because of "self-imposed restraints," then future victories require rapid mobilisation. The billions Congress appropriated for the Rapid Deployment Force in part came because it constituted the organisational embodiment of a powerful cultural myth. The US Army's Special Forces, Ranger Battalions, Delta Force and its "secret" equivalents, Navy SEALs, Marine reconnaissance units and Air Force commando squadrons, have all benefited from paramilitary culture's idolisation of warrior heroes operating at the margins of large-scale bureaucracy....

. . .

Paramilitary culture also legitimates *state secrecy.* In novels and films the warrior's actions remain secret from the news media and general public. During the Reagan administration the Freedom of Information Act has been severely reduced in scope; most activities conducted by intelligence agencies are now exempt from the Act. The invasion of Grenada was conducted without the news media present. There was no large-scale public outrage at either the change in the Act or the censorship during the invasion.

Nowhere are the reciprocal relationships between the state and paramilitary culture more visible than in the testimony provided by Marine Lieutenant Colonel Oliver North during the congressional Iran–Contra hearings in July 1987. North proclaimed his right to lie and to deceive Congress as essential to achieve victory against the Sandinista revolution in Nicaragua. Indeed, North perfectly played the paramilitary warrior acting against craven "self-imposed restraints" created by politicians. The popularity he won among the American public as a war hero can be attributed to his embodiment of contemporary myths.

In this way the garrison state and paramilitary culture reinforce one another. Paramilitary culture says that covert operations—meaning real foreign policy—must remain beyond public debate and above the law to achieve success. In turn, the absence of real information on foreign and military policies remains an absolute requirement for successfully propagating myths of extremely powerful heroes fighting and defeating demonic foes.

Yet the myth of regeneration through violence has its limits. *Platoon* (1987) challenged much modern paramilitary mythology; its Vietnam War does not seem at all winnable by unrestrained warriors. Instead it offers a vision of no battlefield victories, massacre of Vietnamese villagers, and deadly moral conflicts among American soldiers. Although the surviving American boy hero vanquishes his foe (another American) and emerges a man, he clearly does not seek another war. He would not "do it all again" if he had to. *Full Metal Jacket* (1987) found no redemption in war, either; the surviving Marines end their day of battle in Hue during the 1968 Tet Offensive with Walt Disney's theme song *Mickey Mouse* on their lips—certainly not an ode to combat glory and transcendent martial experience.

Nor was North's "victory" during the televised Iran–Contra hearings an unequivocal success. Collective fantasies long nourished in American culture became more than a way of legitimating state actions; they formed the assumptions about the world and the political objectives for the Reagan administration's strategic doctrine and operating policies. Other nations and people have not played out their scripted roles in this vision; reality once again intrudes upon fantasy, just as it did in Vietnam with the collapse of war-movie magic. With the Iran–Contra affair, the failure of some of those policies has become public knowledge. Additional congressional investigations, criminal investigations by the Special Prosecuter, lawsuits and news-reporting will increase the domain of public knowledge— and perhaps open the space for a different kind of political and cultural regeneration.

1. A. M. Schlesinger, Jr, *The Bitter Heritage* (Greenwich, Conn.: Fawcett, 1968) pp. 58–9.

2. Colonel Harry Summers, Jr, *On Strategy: A Critical Analysis of the Vietnam War* (Novato, Calif.: Presidio Press, 1982).

3. D. Middleton, "Vietnam and the Military Mind," *New York Times Magazine*, 10 Jan 1982.

4. For an analysis of the US mode of warfare see James William Gibson, *The Perfect War: Technowar in Vietnam* (New York: Atlantic Monthly Press, 1986).

5. *The Pentagon Papers: The Senator Gravel Edition*, vol. 4 (Boston, Mass.: Beacon Press, 1972) p. 427; and Gibson, *The Perfect War*, pp. 93–154.

6. R. L. Samson, *The Economics of Insurgency in the Mekong Delta of Vietnam* (Cambridge, Mass.: Massachusetts Institute of Technology Press, 1970) pp. 54–67.

7. The Public Broadcasting Service's *Frontline* documentary series, 21 June 1983.

8. Taken from Seymour Melman's address to the Socialist Scholars Conference, New York, 1–2 Apr 1983, as cited in Alexander Cockburn and James Ridgway, "Annals of the Age of Reagan," *Village Voice*, 25 Apr 1983.

9. M. T. Klare, *Beyond the Vietnam Syndrome: U. S. Interventionism in the 1980s* (Washington, DC: Institute for Policy Studies, 1981).

10. R. Slotkin, *Regeneration through Violence: The Mythology of the American Frontier, 1600–1860* (Middleton, Conn.: Wesleyan University Press, 1973) p. 7.

11. Ibid.

12. R. Fielding, *The American Newsreel 1911–1967* (Norman, Okla.: University of Oklahoma Press, 1972) p. 30.

13. E. Marri, *The Rise of Theodore Roosevelt* (New York: Coward, McCann and Geoghegan, 1979) p. 613.

14. H. N. Smith, *Virgin Land: The American West as Symbol and Myth* (New York: Vintage Books, 1950) p. 120.

15. K. Brownlow, *The War, the West, and the Wilderness* (New York: Alfred A. Knopf, 1979) p. 32.

16. For accounts of the relationships between Hollywood and the Defense Department, see L. H. Suid, *Guts and Glory: Great American Movies* (Reading, Mass.: Addison-Wesley, 1977); and J. Smith, *Looking Away: Hollywood and Vietnam* (New York: Charles Scribner's Sons, 1978).

17. One significant exception showing Second World War veterans having real difficulty adjusting to civilian life is *The Best Years of our Lives* (1946).

18. R. Kovic, *Born on the Fourth of July* (New York: McGraw-Hill, 1979) pp. 42–3.

19. P. Caputo, *Rumor of War* (New York: Holt, Rinehart and Winston, 1971) p. 14.

20. Quoted in R. J. Lifton, *Home from the War* (New York: Simon and Schuster, 1973) p. 32.

21. C. R. Anderson, *The Grunts* (San Rafael, Calif.: Presidio Press, 1976) p. 100. "Grunts" are infantrymen; "short-timers" are those whose tour of duty has only a short time to run; "newbys" are new arrivals; and "lifers" are regulars.

22. R. Evans and R. D. Novak, *Nixon in the White House: The Frustrations of Power* (New York: Random House, 1971) p. 252.

23. ABC television news, 23 Nov 1969.

24. I have been conducting interviews with the producers of paramilitary culture since September 1985, when I interviewed Robert Brown at the *Soldier of Fortune* convention in Las Vegas, Nevada. The assessment that the Iran hostage crisis strongly influenced the rise of paramilitary culture is one point agreed upon by most cultural producers.

25. For background information on Brown and US mercenaries, see *Covert Action Information Bulletin*, no. 22: "Special: U.S. Links to Mercenaries" (Fall 1984).

26. "Trail of Terror," *Dallas Life Magazine*, Sunday supplement to the *Dallas Morning News*, 6, no. 10 (1987).

Apes and Others

John W. Dower

Despite the kill-or-be-killed nature of the fighting in the Pacific, hundreds of Japanese did become prisoners. Many were ill, wounded, or unconscious when captured. Others were taken by surprise and offered little resistance. Still others took the initiative to surrender, usually at considerable risk. And with few exceptions, their behavior as prisoners confounded initial expectations. The ferocious, fanatic foe suddenly revealed himself to be exceedingly mild and cooperative. Since most had been told they would be killed or tortured if they fell into Allied hands, they expressed gratitude at receiving good treatment. About four out of every five prisoners actually demonstrated "remarkable cooperation," in the words of an internal U.S. report, in such ways as providing military information and offering to assist in trying to persuade other Japanese to surrender.[1]

Presumedly, such behavior should have jarred those on the other side who encountered it, and forced them to rethink their stereotypes of the enemy. To some extent this did happen. Intelligence analysts in Washington, as well as in MacArthur's command after the return to the Philippines, concluded that a serious psychological-warfare campaign directed to the Japanese could expedite surrenders in the field and hasten the end of the war; but such ideas had little impact.[2] The war was so savage and war hates ran so deep that even individuals who encountered the Japanese as prisoners ordinarily found it impossible to change their views. General Blamey's kind of war words were gospel: the Japanese were subhuman.

There may be no better witness to this than the journalist Ernie Pyle, whose down-home style earned him the status of a folk hero among American war correspondents. He was, in American terms, a humanist: he not only gave the names of the soldiers he wrote about, but also the streets on which they lived in the United States and the numbers of their houses. Pyle gained his fame covering the war in Europe, and was transferred to the Pacific in February 1945, three months before Germany surrendered. By this time, his dispatches were carried by almost seven hundred newspapers and reached an estimated fourteen million readers.

What Pyle told this impressive audience, right away, was that the enemy in Asia was different. "In Europe we felt that our enemies, horrible and deadly as they were, were still people," he explained in one of his first reports from the Pacific. "But out here I soon gathered that the Japanese were looked upon as something subhuman and repulsive; the way some people feel about cockroaches or mice." To Pyle himself, this seemed a perfectly appropriate response, for he went on to describe how, soon after arriving, he had seen some Japanese prisoners in a fenced-in enclosure. "They were wrestling and laughing and talking just like normal human beings," he wrote. "And yet they gave me the creeps, and I wanted a mental bath after looking at them."[3]

So commonplace was this attitude that a popular American scientific magazine could publish a short entry in 1945 entitled "Why Americans Hate Japs More than Nazis" without first demonstrating that this was the case. No one questioned such an observation. And although the explanation offered may have been simplistic (the Japanese were more hated because of their greater outward physical differences), the very manner in which the magazine phrased the problem was suggestive in unintended ways. In addition to using the conventionally pejorative "Japs" for Japanese, the article followed the telltale phrasing of the war years by speaking not of the Germans and the Japanese, but of the Nazis and the Japanese. A well-publicized wartime book by a *New York Times* correspondent who had been assigned to both Germany and Japan followed this pattern with a chapter entitled "Nips and Nazis." A poster by the Veterans of Foreign Wars sharpened the distinction even further, in a familiar way, with the warning, "Remember Hitler and the Japs are trying to get us fighting among ourselves." Songwriters caught the same bias in a patriotic song called "There'll Be No Adolf Hitler nor Yellow Japs to Fear."[4]

The implications of perceiving the enemy as "Nazis" on the one hand and "Japs" on the other were enormous, for this left space for the recognition of the "good German," but scant comparable place for "good Japanese." Magazines like *Time* hammered this home even further by frequently referring to "the Jap" rather than "Japs," thereby denying the enemy even the merest semblance of pluralism. Indeed, in wartime jargon, the notion of "good Japanese" came to take on an entirely different meaning than that of "good Germans," as Admiral William F. Halsey emphasized at a news conference early in 1944. "The only good Jap is a Jap who's been dead six months," the commander of the U.S. South Pacific Force declared, and he did not mean just combatants. "When we get to Tokyo, where we're bound to get eventually," Halsey went on, "we'll have a little celebration where Tokyo was." Halsey was improvising on a popular wartime saying, that "the only good Jap is a dead Jap," and his colleagues in the military often endorsed this sentiment in their own fashion. Early in 1943, for example, *Leatherneck,* the Marine monthly, ran a photograph of Japanese corpses on Guadalcanal with an uppercase headline reading "GOOD JAPS" and a caption emphasizing that "GOOD JAPS are dead Japs."[5]

Hollywood movies of the war years practically canonized these contrasting perceptions of the enemy. The closest counterparts to good Germans and bad Germans which they seemed able to muster for Asia were good nationalities (the Chinese, the Filipinos) and bad (the Japanese). That this distinction between the enemy in Asia and the enemy in Europe derived less from the events of the war than from deep-seated racial bias was reflected in the opening months of 1942, when the U.S. government incarcerated Japanese-Americans en masse, while taking no comparable action against residents of German or Italian origin. Indeed, U.S. citizens of Japanese extraction were treated with greater suspicion and severity than German or Italian aliens—despite the fact that the German-American Bund (with an estimated membership of twenty thousand) had agitated on behalf of Hitler in the United States prior to the outbreak of war, and despite the fact that there never was, at Pearl Harbor or later, any evidence of organized subversion among the Japanese community.

In fact, the treatment of Japanese-Americans is a natural starting point for any study of the racial aspects of the war, for it reveals not merely the clearcut racial stigmatization of the Japanese, but also the official endorsement this received.[6] Under Executive Order 9066, signed by President Roosevelt on February 19, 1942, more than 110,000 persons of Japanese ancestry were removed from California, Oregon, and Washington and interned in ten camps in the interior of the United States. The president of the United States, the secretary of war, the U.S. military establishment, the Department of Justice and eventually the Supreme Court, and the U.S. Congress—all actively participated in enacting and upholding this policy. Similar internments were carried out in Canada, Mexico, and Peru. Such official consecration of anti-Japanese racism was profoundly symbolic: if every man, woman, and child of Japanese origin on the western coasts of the Americas was categorically identified by the highest quarters as a potential menace simply because of his or her ethnicity, then the real Japanese enemy abroad could only be perceived as a truly faceless, monolithic, incorrigible, and stupendously formidable foe.

Obviously, "blood told" where the Japanese—but not the Germans or Italians—were concerned, a point clearly articulated by some of the white Americans who supported the relocation of the Japanese. "Blood will tell," declared the mayor of Los Angeles in a public statement urging the government to move against Japanese-Americans on the grounds that they were "unassimilable," and his West Coast counterparts agreed almost to a man; of all the mayors of large cities in the three westernmost states, only one (the mayor of Tacoma, Washington) opposed forced relocation. Secretary of War Henry Stimson, who assumed major responsibility for the decision to go ahead with Executive Order 9066, recorded in his diary for February 10, 1942, that in his estimation second-generation Japanese-Americans were even more dangerous than their immigrant parents. They either had to be removed from the coastal areas as part of a general evacuation, he continued, "or by frankly trying to put them out on the ground that their racial characteristics are such that we cannot understand or trust even the citizen Japanese. This latter is the fact but I am afraid it will make a tremendous hole in our constitutional system to apply it."

Such blood-will-tell racism was encoded in a variety of formulaic images and expressions. The *Los Angeles Times,* for instance, turned to reptilian metaphor: "A viper is nonetheless a viper wherever the egg is hatched—so a Japanese-American, born of Japanese parents, grows up to be a Japanese not an American." In a telephone conversation shortly before the order for evacuation was signed by President Roosevelt, John J. McCloy, the influential assistant secretary of war, agreed with the more prosaic summation of the problem made by Lieutenant General John L. De Witt, commander of the Western Defense Command, to the effect that whereas Germans and Italians could be treated as individuals, "a Jap is a Jap." General De Witt, who administered the evacuation, still found this phrasing felicitous over a year later when called upon to testify before a congressional committee as to why the incarcerated Japanese-Americans, even bona-fide citizens, still could not be allowed to return home. "A Jap's a Jap," he reiterated in public

testimony in April 1943. "You can't change him by giving him a piece of paper." Indeed, in General De Witt's view, the menace posed by the Japanese could only be eliminated by destroying the Japanese as a race. In his testimony of early 1943, the general went on to state frankly that he was not worried about German or Italian nationals, "but the Japs we will be worried about all the time until they are wiped off the face of the map." This was, by then, familiar rhetoric in the nation's capital. A day before the president signed the executive order of February 19, a member of the House of Representatives had declared that the Japanese should be removed "even to the third and fourth generation." "Once a Jap, always a Jap," exclaimed John Rankin of Mississippi. "You can't any more regenerate a Jap than you can reverse the laws of nature."[7]

Another manifestation of this most emotional level of anti-Japanese racism was the routine use of racial slang in the media and official memoranda as well as everyday discourse. "Nip" (from Nippon, the Japanese reading of the country's name) and especially "Jap" were routinely used in the daily press and major weeklies or monthlies such as *Time, Life, Newsweek,* and *Reader's Digest.* "Jap" was also extremely popular in the music world, where the scramble to turn out a memorable war song did not end with the release of tunes such as "The Remember Pearl Harbor March" and "Good-bye Mama, I'm Off to Yokohama." "Mow the Japs Down!" and "We've Got to Do a Job on the Japs, Baby" are fair samples of the wartime songs, although titles with internal rhymes on "Jap" were even more popular. These included "You're a Sap, Mister Jap," "Let's Take a Rap at the Jap," "They're Gonna Be Playing Taps on the Japs," and "We're Gonna Have to Slap the Dirty Little Jap." There was no real counterpart to this where Germany and Italy were concerned. "Nazis" was the common phrase for the German enemy. Cruder epithets for the Germans (heinies, Huns, Jerrys, Krauts) were used sparingly by comparison.[8]

A characteristic feature of this level of anti-Japanese sentiment was the resort to nonhuman or subhuman representation, in which the Japanese were perceived as animals, reptiles, or insects (monkeys, baboons, gorillas, dogs, mice and rats, vipers and rattlesnakes, cockroaches, vermin—or, more indirectly, "the Japanese herd" and the like). The variety of such metaphors was so great that they sometimes seemed casual and almost original. On the contrary, they were well routinized as idioms of everyday discourse, and immensely consequential in their ultimate functions. At the simplest level, they dehumanized the Japanese and enlarged the chasm between "us" and "them" to the point where it was perceived to be virtually unbridgeable. As Pyle matter-of-factly observed, the enemy in Europe "were still people." The Japanese were not, and in good part they were not because they were denied even the ordinary vocabularies of "being human."

For many Japanese-Americans, the verbal stripping of their humanity was accompanied by humiliating treatment that reinforced the impression of being less than human. They were not merely driven from their homes and communities on the West Coast and rounded up like cattle, but actually forced to live in facilities meant for animals for weeks and even months before being moved to their final quarters in the relocation camps. In the state of Washington, two thousand Japanese-Americans were crowded into a single filthy building in the Portland stockyard, where they slept on gunnysacks filled with straw. In California, evacuees were squeezed into stalls in the stables at racetracks such as Santa Anita and Tanforan. At the Santa Anita assembly center, which eventually housed eighty-five hundred Japanese-Americans, only four days elapsed between the removal of the horses and the arrival of the first Japanese-Americans; the only facilities for bathing were the horse showers, and here as elsewhere the stench of manure lingered indefinitely. Other evacuees were initially housed in horse or cattle stalls at various fairgrounds. At the Puyallup assembly center in Washington (which was called Camp Harmony), some were even lodged in converted pigpens. The only redeeming touch of grace in these circumstances lay in the dignity of the victims themselves.[9]

Looking upon the Japanese as animals, or a different species of some sort, was common at official levels in Washington and London before

Pearl Harbor. A year and a half before the outbreak of the war, for instance, Churchill told Roosevelt that he was counting on the president "to keep that Japanese dog quiet in the Pacific." Secretary of War Henry Stimson picked up much the same image in October 1941 when arguing, as he had long done, in support of economic sanctions against Japan. When President Woodrow Wilson took a hard line against the Japanese in 1919, Stimson reminded the U.S. cabinet, they had retreated "like whipped puppies." During the war, "mad dogs" as well as "yellow dogs" were everyday epithets for the Japanese among the Western Allies. An American who spent considerable time in Japan between 1936 and late 1941 wrote a wartime article describing the evolution of one of his Japanese acquaintances from a moderate newsman into a "mad dog" ultranationalist military officer. "Mad dogs," he concluded, "are just insane animals that should be shot."[10]

After his repatriation from Japan in the first half of 1942, former U.S. Ambassador Joseph Grew, whom some Westerners regarded as an oracle on things Japanese, drew equally upon the insect and animal kingdoms in his lectures about the enemy. He never attempted to conceal his personal respect and affection for certain "moderate" members of the cultured upper classes in Japan, but his most often-quoted statements about the Japanese people in general were those which also basically depersonalized them. For instance, Grew described Japan as a bustling hive of bees all servicing the queen (in real life, the emperor), and this image of the busy, buzzing swarm or its grounded counterpart the anthill was also popular with many other Western writers. An American sociologist explained on a wartime radio broadcast sponsored by General Electric that the Japanese were "a closely disciplined and conformist people—a veritable human bee-hive or ant-hill," in sharp contrast to the "independent and individualistic" Chinese. This, he continued, made Japan a "totalitarian" nation long before the word was invented to describe the fascist and Nazi systems. When Japanese ground forces lost the initiative in Southeast Asia and the Pacific, the antlike imagery was evoked in a somewhat different fashion. One reporter described the mid-war battles as a time when "the Japs turned into ants, the more you killed the more that kept coming." General Slim, Great Britain's commander in the epic Burma campaigns, used a similar metaphor in describing how his own forces finally seized the offensive. "We had kicked over the anthill," he wrote in his memoirs; "the ants were running about in confusion. Now was the time to stamp on them."[11]

Former Ambassador Grew also spoke of the Japanese as sheep, easily led, which easily led one awkward publicist for the U.S. Navy to compare the frenzy of obedient Japanese soldiers to "angry sheep." *Yank,* the weekly magazine of the U.S. Army, referred to the "sheep-like subservience" of the Japanese (whom the magazine also called "stupid animal-slaves"), but by and large the sheep metaphor did not become a dominant one for the Japanese (in Churchill's menagerie, as in Stalin's, it was the Germans who were sheep). The more general description of the Japanese as a "herd," or possessing a "herd mentality," however, was routine. With various turns of phrase, the herd was one of the pet images of a group of distinguished Far Eastern experts assembled by Britain's Royal Institute of International Affairs to give advice on enemy Japan at the end of 1944. An Australian war correspondent went further, explaining that Japanese enlisted men not only behaved like, but also looked like, cattle. "Many of the Japanese soldiers I have seen have been primitive oxen-like clods with dulled eyes and foreheads an inch high," he wrote in a 1944 book directed to American readers. "They have stayed at their positions and died simply because they have been told to do so, and they haven't the intelligence to think for themselves."[12]

Other, more random metaphors reinforced the impression of a subhuman enemy. Westerners writing about their personal experiences in Japan, for example, frequently described the Japanese as "hissing," a snakelike impression whether witting or not. As the Japanese extended their overseas imperium, even prior to Pearl Harbor, cartoonists depicted the country as an octopus grasping Asia in its tentacles. In *Know Your Enemy—Japan,* Frank Capra's team enlisted animators from the Walt

Disney studio to present this as a central image, with the tentacles of octopus-Japan reaching out to plunge daggers into the hearts of neighboring lands, and groping toward the United States itself. The bucktoothed Japanese became a standard cartoon figure, prompting comparison to the Looney Tune creation Bugs Bunny; the Warner Brothers studio followed up on this with a short animated cartoon titled *Bugs Bunny Nips the Nips.*

Without question, however, the most common caricature of the Japanese by Westerners, writers and cartoonists alike, was the monkey or ape. Sir Alexander Cadogan, the influential permanent undersecretary of the British Foreign Office, routinely referred to the Japanese in his diary as "beastly little monkeys" and the like even before the war began (or alternatively, in February 1941, as "yellow dwarf slaves"). During the early months of the Japanese conquest of Southeast Asia, Western journalists referred to the "apes in khaki." The simian image had already become so integral to Western thinking by this time that when General Yamashita Tomoyuki's troops made their lightning move down the densely jungled Malay Peninsula to capture Singapore, rumors spread that they had accomplished this breathtaking advance by swinging from tree to tree. In mid-January of 1942, *Punch,* the celebrated British satirical magazine, drew upon the same utterly conventional image in a full-page cartoon entitled "The Monkey Folk" that depicted monkeys swinging through the jungle with helmets on their heads and rifles slung over their shoulders. In much the same way, U.S. Marines in the combat zones made jokes about tossing a grenade into a tree and blasting out "three monkeys—two bucktooths and a real specimen," a witticism that the *New Yorker* carried to its upper-class readership in cartoon form late in 1942 and *Reader's Digest* reproduced for its own huge audience soon after. It portrayed white riflemen lying in firing position in a dense jungle, where the trees were full of monkeys along with several Japanese snipers. "Careful now," one white soldier is saying to another, "—only those in uniform." An American radio broadcaster informed his audience early in the war that it was appropriate to regard the Japanese as monkeys for two reasons: first, the monkey in the zoo imitates his trainer; secondly, "under his fur, he's still a savage little beast."[13]

Among the Allied war leaders, Admiral Halsey was the most notorious for making outrageous and virulently racist remarks about the Japanese enemy in public. Many of his slogans and pronouncements bordered on advocacy of genocide. Although he came under criticism for his intemperate remarks, and was even accused of being drunk in public, Halsey was immensely popular among his men and naturally attracted good press coverage. His favorite phrase for the Japanese was "yellow bastards," and in general he found the color allusion irresistible. Simian metaphors, however, ran a close second in his diatribes. Even in his postwar memoirs, Halsey described the Japanese as "stupid animals" and referred to them as "monkeymen." During the war he spoke of the "yellow monkeys," and in one outburst declared that he was "rarin' to go" on a new naval operation "to get some more Monkey meat." He also told a news conference early in 1945 that he believed the "Chinese proverb" about the origin of the Japanese race, according to which "the Japanese were a product of mating between female apes and the worst Chinese criminals who had been banished from China by a benevolent emperor." These comments were naturally picked up in Japan, as Halsey fully intended them to be, and on occasion prompted lame responses in kind. A Japanese propaganda broadcast, for example, referred to the white Allies as "albino apes." Halsey's well-publicized comment, after the Japanese Navy had been placed on the defensive, that "the Japs are losing their grip, even with their tails," led a zookeeper in Tokyo to announce he was keeping a cage in the monkey house reserved for the admiral.[14]

The variations on the simian theme were endless. Americans learned from Ernie Pyle that Marines in the Marianas had coined the word "Japes," a combination of "Japs" and "apes." A comparable neologism was "monkeynips." As early as February 1942, *Leatherneck* ran an unusually wild comic strip in which an unkempt white soldier—infuriated when a canteen of liquor is shot out of his hands by the "slant-eyed jerks" and "jaundiced baboons"—plunges into the jungle and

emerges with four dead creatures with monkeys' bodies and Japanese faces, tied by their tails and hanging from his shoulders. "They're a bit undersized," he exclaims, "but I got four of 'em!!" A booklet prepared by the U.S. Navy Pacific Command during the final months of the war, in anticipation of the occupation of Japan, related these stereotypes to Japanese atrocities. When Westerners learned of these atrocities, it was explained, they scrapped their picture of the average Japanese "as a comical little person and substituted a blood-soaked beast—half man and half monkey." (The Navy guide, it should be noted, was devoted to repudiating such gross stereotypes.) The Army's *Infantry Journal* took a different tack in warning of the danger of overconfidence that might come from thinking of the enemy as merely "a buck-toothed, near-sighted, pint-sized monkey." (He was better seen, it was suggested, as "a robot-like creature.") Following Japan's capitulation, General Robert Eichelberger, one of MacArthur's key commanders, wrote to his wife that "first, monkeys will come to Manila," in reference to the impending Japanese mission to MacArthur's headquarters to arrange the surrender procedures.[15]

One of the better-known American cartoons of the war years was published in April 1943, after the news of the execution of some of the Doolittle pilots was released. It depicted the Japanese as a slavering gorilla labeled "Murderers of American Flyers"—with the huge pistol of "Civilization" pointing at its head—and can be taken as a concrete illustration of the U.S. Navy's explanation that such animal imagery was directly related to Japanese atrocities. This explanation, however, is too simple. Reports about Japanese atrocities undoubtedly contributed greatly to the Western perception of the Japanese as beasts, but the simian personification existed independently of such associations. This was perhaps the most basic of all metaphors traditionally employed by white supremacists to demean nonwhite peoples. It was more often used in a way that portrayed the colored subject as ridiculous rather than savage. And it was a racist archetype that thoroughly obsessed Westerners, as any survey of the popular graphics of the war soon reveals. Even when one reviews the political cartoons of wartime America and Britain with fore-knowledge of the fondness for apish imagery in depicting the Japanese enemy, the extensiveness of such representation is startling—as is also the fact that the Japanese were portrayed, not just as apelike but as apes plain and simple. While Hitler and the Nazis also occasionally emerged as simians, this was a passing metaphor, a sign of aberration and atavism, and did not carry the explicit racial connotations of the Japanese ape.[16]

The simian image was ubiquitous in the American and British media, appearing in publications both conservative and liberal, popular and highbrow. The *American Legion Magazine*'s contribution to the genre was a cartoon depicting monkeys in a zoo who had posted a sign in their cage reading, "Any similarity between us and the Japs is purely coincidental." *Collier's* featured several full-color covers by the British artist Lawson Wood portraying Japanese airmen as apes, and *Time* ran a cover portrait pertaining to the Dutch East Indies in which a Japanese apeman dangled from a tree in the background. The esteemed antifascist cartoonist David Low, whose work appeared in the *Evening Standard* in London and was widely reproduced, contributed some of the most blunt and memorable graphics of this sort. In July 1941, months before Pearl Harbor, Low produced a cartoon depicting three stalwart white servicemen standing stripped to the waist beneath a palm tree and gazing out into the Pacific; they were identified as the United States, Britain, and the U.S.S.R. Hanging by its tail from the tree was a monkey labeled "Jap," wearing eyeglasses, clutching a dagger, and contemplating which white man to stab in the back. In October, Low portrayed Tōjō's assumption of the premiership with a drawing of a gorilla in admiral's uniform taking command of the Japanese ship of state. Immediately after the outbreak of war, Low presented the Japanese army, navy, and air force as three monkeys on a beach outside Singapore. In March 1942, he returned to the imagery of the previous July to render Japan's grab for power in Asia once again as a monkey suspended by its tail—in this case with an armful of coconuts, precariously reaching for more (representing India and Australia).[17]

The *New York Times* found the latter cartoon so effective that it reproduced it on the front page of its Sunday book-review section, as an illustration for a review of books on Japanese policy. The *Times*'s practice of featuring political cartoons from other newspapers in its Sunday edition provides a convenient source through which to gain an impression of the thoroughly conventional nature of the simian fixation. Thus, in mid-1942, Japanese soldiers in the Aleutians (who died almost to the last man) were depicted as an ape on a springboard. Later that year, the Japanese took the form of a monstrous King Kong figure with a bloody knife. In 1943, they were portrayed squatting in the trees among monkeys, and on a wanted poster in a cartoon entitled "It All Depends on the Neighborhood." In the latter, Hitler was "Public Enemy No. 1" for England and a jug-eared, monkey-faced Japanese was Hitler's counterpart for the Allies in the Pacific. In 1944, as the U.S. Pacific offensive gained momentum, readers were offered a monkey labeled "Japs" with coconuts falling on its head. At the end of 1944, when the bombardment of the Japanese homeland was commencing, the *Times* reproduced a cartoon of a bandaged, bawling ape with horn-rimmed eyeglasses and buckteeth. . . .

■ ■ ■

Obviously, the depiction of groups and individuals by nonhuman forms or symbols is not in itself inherently demeaning. The American eagle and British lion are ample proof to the contrary. The Japanese, on their part, celebrate "Boys' Day"—and "manly" struggle against adversity—with the symbol of a carp leaping against the current (a rather unusual choice by Western standards), and medieval warriors had adopted heraldic emblems depicting wildlife as various as hawks, horses, deer, pigeons, and plovers, as well as butterflies and dragonflies. What we are concerned with here is something different: the attachment of stupid, bestial, even pestilential subhuman caricatures on the enemy, and the manner in which this blocked seeing the foe as rational or even human, and facilitated mass killing. It is, at least for most people, easier to kill animals than fellow humans.

Indeed, it may be easier for many hunters to kill animals by closing their minds to the fact that they are sentient beings that know fear and feel pain. Thus, in a rather rare document, a diary kept by an ordinary American seaman during the entire course of the Pacific War, we find breathless descriptions of what Marines told the sailors when they came on board: "Fighting the Japs is like fighting a wild animal. . . . The Japs take all kinds of chances, they love to die." A profile of the Japanese fighting man in a serviceman's magazine also argued that "he isn't afraid to die. In fact, he seems to like to die." Indeed, this article went on to note that "when they die," it was said that the Japanese enemy "turn over on their backs and smile and face the sun."[18]* By such reasoning, it was almost a favor to kill the Japanese. Beyond this, of course, being beasts, they deserved to die.

This linguistic softening of the killing process was accomplished most often through two general figures of speech: the metaphors of the hunt and of exterminating vermin. The evocation of the hunt appears everywhere in American writing about combat in the Pacific, sometimes with an almost lyric quality, evoking images of the Old West and physical pleasures that have always been part of the picture of the good life in the more rural American consciousness. Advertisers played up this theme. A magazine advertisement for the brewing industry, for example, depicted a hunter and his companions with a fine deer trophy, identified as one of the "little things" (along with beer and ale) that meant a lot to a Marine on leave, and went on to note that "he's been doing a different kind of hunting overseas." An advertisement by a cartridge company carried a headline reading "Now Your Ammunition Is Getting *Bigger* Game," and juxtaposed a painting of a hunter sighting in on a mountain sheep with a scene of ammunition stores on Guadalcanal. An ad for telescopic sights showed a Japanese soldier crouched on his hands and knees, with the cross hairs fixed behind his shoulder. "Rack up another

one," the heading read. Cards for display in automobile windows proclaimed "Open Season for Japs."[19]

"Good luck and good hunting" was a common sendoff for men embarking on a combat mission, as moviegoers learned from the 1944 Hollywood film *Destination Tokyo*. Sometimes the imagery chosen was of a general nature: of Marines descending from the ridges "to hunt out their prey," for example, or simply shooting "animals" or "predatory animals." Sometimes the hunt was violent. General Slim divided the decisive battle of Imphal-Kohima into four stages, the last of which was pursuit—"when the Japanese broke, and, snarling and snapping, were hunted from the field." At another point, Slim recalled that "relentlessly we would hunt them down and when, desperate and rabid, they turned at bay, killed them." The hunt also could be a joke. A satirical article on mopping-up operations on Guadalcanal described the place as a "hunter's paradise . . . teeming with monkey-men." Very frequently, however, the hunt was pastoral, almost lazy, and the quarry small and easy. A cover story in *Life,* showing GIs walking through the jungle with rifles ready, looking for Japanese snipers, explained that "like many of their comrades they were hunting for Japs, just as they used to go after small game in the woods back home." A 1943 book giving a firsthand account of the combat explained that "every time you hit a Jap [with rifle fire] he jumps like a rabbit." The battle of the Philippine Sea in June 1944, in which the Japanese lost three carriers and over 345 aircraft, compared to a loss of seventeen planes on the Allied side, became immortalized as "the great turkey shoot." "Duck hunting" was another popular figure of speech, and naturally brought up references to both dead ducks and sitting ducks. Killing Japanese reminded others of shooting quail. "Tanks are used to flush the Japanese out of the grass," a Pulitzer Prize-winning journalist reported from Guadalcanal, "and when they are flushed, they are shot down like running quail."[20]

*[Footnotes have been renumbered because portions of the original work have been deleted—EDS.]

In its confidential weekly summaries of the social and political climate in the United States (mostly written by the historian Isaiah Berlin), the British embassy in Washington commented in passing at one point on the popular American perception of the Japanese as a "nameless mass of vermin." The observation was accurate, and its implications were clear: vermin must be exterminated. Especially during the last few years of the war, "exterminationist" figures of speech did indeed become a stock way of referring to the killing of Japanese, not only in battle but also in the cities of Japan's home islands. In the steaming combat zones, the Japanese came to be regarded as almost another form of jungle pest. "Well, which would you druther do—exterminate bug-insecks or Japs!?" asked a sergeant in a comic strip in *American Legion Magazine*. A squad mate spraying bugs replied there wasn't much difference, "but slappin' Japs is more satisfyin'!" A more sophisticated series of comic graphics in *Leatherneck* depicted common afflictions suffered by the Marines in the Pacific and concluded with the "Louseous Japanicas," a grotesque insect with slanted eyes and protruding teeth. The first serious outbreak of this pestilence was noted on December 7, 1941, at Honolulu, it was explained, and the Marines had been assigned "the giant task of extermination. Extensive experiments on Guadalcanal, Tarawa, and Saipan have shown that this louse inhabits coral atolls in the South Pacific, particularly pill boxes, palm trees, caves, swamps and jungles. Flamethrowers, mortars, grenades and bayonets have proven to be an effective remedy. But before a complete cure may be effected the origin of the plague, the breeding grounds around the Tokyo area, must be completely annihilated." Other cartoonists picked up the same theme by depicting the Japanese as ants awaiting an application of ant poison, as spiders about to be stepped on, or as "Japanese beetles" being exterminated with the spray gun of American air power.[21]

Another vivid and familiar expression of this exterminationist sentiment involved depiction of the Japanese as rodents, most often trapped or cornered rats. Allied forces picking apart routed Japanese troops were described as being "like terriers onto rats." Reporters spoke of the "beady little eyes" of critically wounded Japanese, and Japanese soldiers pinned down in caves and tunnels on the Pacific atolls were likened to rats caught in their holes. The hero in *The Purple Heart* told his Japanese captors that they were just "cornered rats"; and in March 1945, *The Nation* used exactly the same image to illustrate the categorical difference between the death in battle of a Japanese fighting man and an American on Iwo Jima. A Japanese soldier's death was "the rat's death, defiant in a corner until all fails," *The Nation* explained, while the Marine's death was "a proud man's death, in the open, advancing, for such simple, noble, and old-fashioned reasons as love of comrades and of corps or ambition to set the flag atop bloody Suribachi." One of the most awesome weapons of extermination employed by the Allied forces in their exhausting battles against the last-ditch resistance of the Japanese on the Pacific islands was the flamethrower, which sprayed a long stream of oil burning at a temperature of 2,000° F. In February 1945, when the battle of Iwo Jima was taking place, the *New York Times* ran an illustrated advertisement by a U.S. chemical company showing a GI blasting a path "through stubborn Jap defenses" with a flamethrower. The ad bore the heading "Clearing Out a Rat's Nest."[22]

On Iwo Jima itself (where U.S. casualties were six thousand killed and twenty-five thousand wounded, while the Japanese defense force of twenty thousand was virtually annihilated), many Marines actually went into battle with the legend "Rodent Exterminator" stenciled on their helmets. Like much of the morbid humor of the war, this reflected the fear, fury, and protective black jokes of combat. Something else was also involved, however, for the metaphor of killing rats was not peculiar to the battlefield. It was also part of everyday life on the home front, among civilians who in many cases had never encountered a Japanese man or woman. After Pearl Harbor, many eateries on the West Coast placed signs in their windows reading "This Restaurant Poisons Both Rats and Japs." Right-wing vigilante groups distributed pamphlets with titles like *Slap the Jap Rat,* and placed stickers with the slogan "Remember a

Jap Is a Jap" and the picture of a rat with a Japanese face on the windshields of their automobiles. When concrete plans were broached to evacuate the Japanese-Americans to camps in other states in the interior, or to allow camp inmates to attend nearby educational institutions, the governor of Idaho opposed having any of the evacuees brought into his state and declared that "a good solution to the Jap problem would be to send them all back to Japan, then sink the island. They live like rats, breed like rats and act like rats." If loyal neighbors of Japanese extraction at home could be so summarily categorized as vermin, it is—once again—easy to imagine how such an exterminationist sentiment could be applied not merely to Japanese combat forces in Asia and the Pacific, but to the men, women, and children of the Japanese homeland itself. For a perfect expression of this, we need only attend a patriotic parade in New York City in mid-June of 1942. This mammoth display of martial might and patriotic spirit was the largest parade in the history of New York to that date, and one of its most popular entries was a float called "Tokyo: We Are Coming." As the press described it, this depicted "a big American eagle leading a flight of bombers down on a herd of yellow rats which were trying to escape in all directions." The crowd, it was reported, "loved it."[23]

The scene is worth dwelling on, for at the symbolic level much was captured here: the Manichaean dimension of caricature (the eagle versus the rat); the numerous and undifferentiated pack, devoid not merely of humanness and individuality but even of gender and age; the yellowness of the vermin, as well as their dwarfed size—suggesting not only the "little Japs" but also the yellow hordes of Asia; and also the diminished stature of human targets in the eyes of the bombadier (and in the eyes of the audience on the home front as well). The float was suggestive in another direction also, in that whereas the grand conflict was depicted metaphorically, the technology of the conflict was portrayed realistically: bombers were bombers. Looking back on this expression of grass-roots patriotism, we are reminded that while the expressive forms of race hate remained relatively conventional, a revolution was taking place in military technology and strategy—giving the Allied powers, among other things, the flamethrower, the B-29 Superfortress bomber, napalm, the concept of strategic bombing, the identification of civilian morale as an important and legitimate target in war, the tactical perfection of low-level saturation bombing raids over urban centers, and, finally, nuclear weapons. In the course of the war in Asia, racism, dehumanization, technological change, and exterminationist policies became interlocked in unprecedented ways.

---

1. Foreign Morale Analysis Division, Office of War Information, *The Attitudes of Japanese Prisoners of War: An Overall View* (Report no. 31, December 29; 1945), esp. 15–16; and the same unit's *Wartime Analysis of Japanese Morale* (n.d., but late 1945 or early 1946), esp. 5; U.S. National Archives, R.G. 208, Boxes 443 and 445. The reports of this unit contain many studies of prisoners, and the general findings are summarized by Alexander H. Leighton, former head of the unit, in *Human Relations in a Changing World: Observations on the Use of the Social Sciences* (1949: Dutton); on Japanese prisoners, see 303–4, 321–22.

2. See John W. Dower, *War Without Mercy* (1986: Pantheon Books), chap. 6, especially the concluding section.

3. Ernie Pyle, *Last Chapter* (1945: Henry Holt & Co.), 5. For circulation figures, see Jack Goodman, ed., *While You Were Gone: A Report on Wartime Life in the United States* (1946: Simon & Schuster), 367.

4. *Science Digest* 17.3 (March 1945): 5; Otto Tolischus, *Tokyo Record* (1943: Reynal & Hitchcock), chap. 28; the poster is in the G. William Gahagan papers, Hoover Institution; for the song, see the sheet music illustration in Anthony Rhodes' interesting *Propaganda, The Art of Persuasion: World War II* (1976: Chelsea House), 164.

5. James M. Merrill, *A Sailor's Admiral: A Biography of William F. Halsey* (1976: Crowell), 111; *Leatherneck* 26.2 (February 1943) 12; cf. ibid., 27.2 (February 1944): 10.

6. On the Japanese-American experience and wartime "relocation," see the major studies by Roger Daniels: *The Politics of Prejudice* (1968: Atheneum), *Concentration Camps USA: Japanese Americans and World War II* (1971: Holt, Rinehart & Winston), and *The Decision to Relocate the Japanese Americans* (1975: Lippincott); also Carey McWilliams, *Prejudice: Japanese-Americans—Symbol of Racial Intolerance* (1944: Little, Brown); Audrie Girdner and Anne Loftis, *The Great Betrayal: The Evacuation of the Japanese-Americans During World War II* (1969: Macmillan Co.); Stetson Conn, "The Decision to Evacuate the Japanese from the Pacific Coast (1942)," in Kent Roberts Greenfield, ed., *Command Decisions* (1959: Harcourt, Brace & Co., for the Office of the Chief of Military History, Department of the Army), 88–109;

Stetson Conn, Rose C. Engelman, and Byron Fairchild, *Guarding the United States and Its Outposts* (1964: Office of the Chief of Military History, Department of the Army), 115–49; Eugene V. Rostow, "The Japanese American Cases—A Disaster," *Yale Law Journal* 54.3 (June 1945): 489–533; Commission on Wartime Relocation and Internment of Civilians, *Personal Justice Denied* (December 1982).

7. Cf. Daniels, *Concentration Camps*, 61–62; Daniels, *The Decision to Relocate*, 97; Girdner and Loftis, 17, 24, 101; McWilliams, 116, 251; *Henry L. Stimson Diaries* (Yale University Library microfilm), reel 7: 512 (entry for February 10, 1942).

8. For song titles, see Rhodes, 147, 148, 164; A. Marjorie Taylor, *The Language of World War II*, rev. ed. (1948: H. W. Wilson Co.), 232–38; Colin Shindler, *Hollywood Goes to War: Films and American Society, 1939–1952* (1979: Routledge & Kegan Paul), 35; *Time*, December 29, 1941, 46; Geoffrey Perrett, *Days of Sadness, Years of Triumph: The American People, 1939–1945* (1973: Coward, McCann & Geoghegan), 241.

9. Cf. *Personal Justice Denied*, 139–40; Girdner and Loftis, 151–52.

10. Churchill is quoted in Francis L. Lowenheim et al., eds., *Roosevelt and Churchill: Their Secret Wartime Correspondence* (1975: Saturday Review Press), 95. For Stimson, see Dorothy Borg and Shumpei Okamoto, eds., *Pearl Harbor As History: Japanese-American Relations, 1931–1941* (1973: Columbia University Press), 51; cf. 281. *Leatherneck* 27.7 (June 1944): 63; cf. Daniels, *Concentration Camps*, 32. "Mad dog" was also used in the U.S. Army film *Know Your Enemy—Japan*. For an earlier reference to Orientals in general as "frightened hares," see Stephen Roskill, *Hankey: Man of Secrets, Volume 2, 1919–1931* (1972: William Collins, Sons & Co.), 250–51; cf. also 244.

11. Waldo Heinrichs, *American Ambassador: Joseph C. Grew and the Development of the United States Diplomatic Tradition* (1966: Little, Brown), 370; see also Grew in *United States News*, April 6, 1945, 20. *Science Digest* 12.5 (November 1942): 33–34, and 15.3 (March 1944): 54–56; *Leatherneck* 28.3 (March 1945): 23; William Slim (Field Marshal the Viscount Slim), *Defeat Into Victory* (1961: David McKay Co.), 401. In an interesting guide to Japan prepared by the U.S. Navy when Japan surrendered, the country was described as a "monstrous beehive"; *Guide to Japan* (CINCPAC-CINCPOA Bulletin no. 209–45, September 1, 1945), 65.

12. *Guide to Japan*, 51; Debs Myers et al., eds., *Yank—the GI Story of the War* (1947: Duell, Sloan & Pearce), 148; Winston Churchill, *Triumph and Tragedy* (1953: Houghton Mifflin), 637; Milovan Djilas, *Conversations with Stalin* (1969: Pelican), 79; Chatham House, *Japan In Defeat* (1944: Royal Institute of International Affairs), 8, 71, 119; George H. Johnston, *Pacific Partner* (1944: Duell, Sloan & Pearce), 205.

13. David Dilks, ed., *The Diaries of Sir Alexander Cadogan, 1938–1945* (1971: Cassell & Co.), 353, 358, 392, 416, 445; John Goette, *Japan Fights for Asia* (1943: Harcourt, Brace & Young), 36; William Manchester, *American Caesar: Douglas MacArthur, 1880–1964* (1978: Dell), 264; *Punch*, January 14, 1942; S. E. Smith, *The United States Marine Corps in World War II* (1969: Random House), 247, 252; *New Yorker*, September 12, 1942,

reproduced in *Reader's Digest,* December 1942, 248; Edward Tabor Linenthal, *Changing Images of the Warrior Hero in America: A History of Popular Symbolism* (1982: Edwin Mellen Press), 131.

14. Merrill, 35, 65–66, 73–74, 82–83, 85, 88–89, 106, 111, 142, 202, 209–10, 232, 246; William F. Halsey and Joseph Bryan III, *Admiral Halsey's Story* (1947: McGraw-Hill), 141–42, 206; Foreign Morale Analysis Division, *Japanese Use of American Statements and Acts, Real or Alleged, in Propaganda to Create Fear* (Report no. 21, June 15, 1945), esp. 9; U.S. National Archives, R.G. 208, Box 444.

15. Taylor, 114; Lester V. Berrey and Melvin Van Den Bark, *The American Thesaurus of Slang,* 2nd ed. (1953: Crowell), 385; *Leatherneck* 25.2 (February 1942); *Guide to Japan*, 40; *Infantry Journal*, March 1945, 23–24, and August 1945, 41; Robert Eichelberger, *Dear Miss Em: General Eichelberger's War in the Pacific, 1942–1945*, ed. Jay Luvaas (1972: Greenwood Press), 300, 303.

16. *New York Times,* April 25, 1943.

17. *American Legion Magazine,* October 1942, 56; *Collier's* covers of April 18, 1942, and May 8, 1945; *Time* cover of January 26, 1942; David Low, *Years of Wrath* (1946: Simon & Schuster).

18. James J. Fahey, *Pacific War Diary, 1942–45* (1963: Houghton Mifflin), 45–46; *Leatherneck* 26.1 (January 1943): 45.

19. *American Legion Magazine,* November 1944, 31; *Leatherneck* 26.7 (July 1943): 3; *American Rifleman,* July, August, and September, 1944; cf. ibid., June 1943 and January 1945; McWilliams, 131; *Time*, December 22, 1941, 13.

20. *Time,* November 2, 1942, 30; *Newsweek,* February 7, 1944, 25; *American Rifleman,* January 1945, 47; *Reader's Digest,* January 1945, 88; Slim, 254, 277; *Leatherneck* 26.8 (August 1943): 24–25; *Life,* September 6, 1943, cover, 18, 43; *Science Digest* 12.6 (December 1943), 53; *American Legion Magazine,* November 1942, 55, and August 1943, 20, 48; S. E. Smith, 223, 332, 598. The prize-winning journalist was Ira Wolfert.

21. H.G. Nichols, ed., *Washington Despatches, 1941–1945: Weekly Political Reports from the British Embassy* (1981: University of Chicago), 558 (May 13, 1945); cf. 299 (January 1, 1944). *American Legion Magazine,* October 1944, 52; *Leatherneck* 28.3 (March 1945): 37; Chicago Tribune, *War Cartoons; New York Times,* March 7, 1943.

22. Slim, 392; *Time,* February 15, 1945, 25; Richard Tregaskis, *Guadalcanal Diary* (1942: Random House), 71; *The Nation,* March 3, 1945, 240. Merrill, 138, 210; *New York Times,* February 7, 1945, 36.

23. *Time,* March 19, 1945, 32; Richard Polenberg, *War and Society: The United States, 1941–1945* (1972: Lippincott), 65; McWilliams, 131, 163–64, 237, 241. The parade is reported in the *New York Herald Tribune,* June 14, 1942, 1, 2, which described this as "a grim and bristling war pageant that streamed up Fifth Avenue for eleven hours." A half million people participated, and estimates of the crowd ranged from 2.5 to 5 million. A "Pearl Harbor" float in the same parade "showed a Japanese diplomat smilingly negotiating with Uncle Sam while a Japanese general, urged on by Hitler, prepares to knife Uncle Sam in the back"; cf. Polenberg 135.

Nuclear Language
and How We Learned to Pat the Bomb

Carol Cohn

My close encounter with nuclear strategic analysis started in the summer of 1984. I was one of 48 college teachers attending a summer workshop on nuclear weapons, strategic doctrine, and arms control that was held at a university containing one of the nation's foremost centers of nuclear strategic studies, and that was co-sponsored by another institution. It was taught by some of the most distinguished experts in the field, who have spent decades moving back and forth between academia and governmental positions in Washington. When at the end of the program I was afforded the chance to be a visiting scholar at one of the universities' defense studies center, I jumped at the opportunity.

I spent the next year immersed in the world of defense intellectuals—men (and indeed, they are virtually all men) who, in Thomas Powers's words, "use the concept of deterrence to explain why it is safe to have weapons of a kind and number it is not safe to use." Moving in and out of government, working sometimes as administrative officials or consultants, sometimes in universities and think tanks, they create the theory that underlies U.S. nuclear strategic practice.

My reason for wanting to spend a year among these men was simple, even if the resulting experiences were not. The current nuclear situation is so dangerous and irrational that one is tempted to explain it by positing either insanity or evil in our decision makers. That explanation is, of course, inadequate. My goal was to gain a better under-standing of how sane men of goodwill could think and act in ways that lead to what appear to be extremely irrational and immoral results.

I attended lectures, listened to arguments, conversed with defense analysts, interviewed grad-uate students throughout their training, obsessed by the question, "How *can* they think this way?" But as I learned the language, as I became more and more engaged with their information and their arguments, I found that my own thinking was changing and I had to confront a new question: How can *I* think this way? Thus, my own experience becomes part of the data that I analyze in attempt-ing to understand not only how "they" can think that way, but how any of us can.

This article is the beginning of an analysis of the nature of nuclear strategic thinking, with em-phasis on the role of a specialized language that I call "technostrategic." I have come to believe that this language both reflects and shapes the Ameri-can nuclear strategic project, and that all who are concerned about nuclear weaponry and nuclear war must give careful attention to language—with whom it allows us to communicate and what it allows us to think as well as say.

■

I had previously encountered in my reading the extraordinary language used to discuss nuclear war, but somehow it was different to hear it spoken. What hits first is the elaborate use of abstraction

---

This article is a version extracted from Cohn, "Sex and Death in the Rational World of Defense Intellectuals." *SIGNS* 12(4) (Summer 1987): 687–718 © 1987 by The University of Chicago. All rights reserved.

and euphemism, which allows infinite talk about nuclear holocaust without ever forcing the speaker or enabling the listener to touch the reality of the words.

Anyone who has seen pictures of Hiroshima burn victims, or tried to imagine the pain of hundreds of glass shards blasted into flesh, may at first find it perverse beyond imagination to hear a class of nuclear devices matter-of-factly referred to as "clean bombs." "Clean bombs" are nuclear devices that are largely fusion, rather than fission. They release a somewhat higher proportion of their energy as prompt radiation, but produce less radioactive fallout than fission bombs of the same yield.

"Clean bombs" may provide the perfect metaphor for the language of defense analysts and arms controllers. This language has enormous destructive power, but without the emotional fallout that would result if it were clear one was talking about plans for mass murder, mangled bodies, human suffering. Defense analysts don't talk about incinerating cities: they talk about "countervalue attacks." Human death, in nuclear parlance, is most often referred to as "collateral damage"; for, as one defense analyst said, with just the right touch of irony in his voice and twinkle in his eye, "the Air Force doesn't target people, it targets shoe factories."[1]

Some phrases carry this cleaning up so far as to invert meaning. The MX missile will carry ten warheads, each with the explosive power of 300 to 475 kilotons of TNT: *one* missile the bearer of destruction approximately *250* to *400* times that of the Hiroshima bombing.[2] Ronald Reagan has christened the MX missile "the Peacekeeper." While this renaming was the object of considerable scorn in the community of defense analysts, some of these very same analysts refer to the MX as a "damage limitation weapon."[3]

Such phrases exemplify the astounding chasm between image and reality that characterizes technostrategic language. They also hint at the terrifying way in which the existence of nuclear devices has distorted our perceptions and redefined the world. "Clean bombs" as a phrase tells us that radioactivity is the only "dirty" part of killing people.

It is hard not to feel that one function of this sanitized abstraction is to deny the uncontrolled messiness of the situations one contemplates creating. So that we not only have clean bombs but also "surgically clean strikes": "counterforce" attacks that can purportedly "take out"—that is, accurately destroy—an opponent's weapons or command centers, without causing significant injury to anything else. The image is unspeakably ludicrous when the surgical tool is not a delicately controlled scalpel but a nuclear warhead.

■

Feminists have often suggested that an important aspect of the arms race is phallic worship; that "missile envy," to borrow Helen Caldicott's phrase, is a significant motivating force in the nuclear buildup. I have always found this an uncomfortably reductionist explanation and hoped that observing at the center would yield a more complex analysis. Still, I was curious about the extent to which I might find a sexual subtext in the defense professionals' discourse. I was not prepared for what I found.

I think I had naively imagined that I would need to sneak around and eavesdrop on what men said in unguarded moments, using all my cunning to unearth sexual imagery. I had believed that these men would have cleaned up their acts, or that at least at some point in a long talk about "penetration aids," someone would suddenly look up, slightly embarrassed to be caught in such blatant confirmation of feminist analyses.

I was wrong. There was no evidence that such critiques had ever reached the ears, much less the minds, of these men. American military dependence on nuclear weapons was explained as "irresistible, because you get more bang for the buck." Another lecturer solemnly and scientifically announced, "To disarm is to get rid of all your stuff." A professor's explanation of why the MX missile is to be placed in the silos of the newest Minuteman missiles, instead of replacing the older, less accurate missiles, was "because they're in the nicest hole—you're not going to take the nicest missile you have and put it in a crummy hole." Other lectures were filled with discussion of vertical erector launchers, thrust-to-weight ratios, soft lay downs, deep penetration, and the comparative advantages of protracted versus spasm attacks—or what one military adviser to the National Security Council has called "releasing 70 to 80 percent of our megatonnage in one orgasmic whump."[4]

But if the imagery is transparent, its significance may be less so. I do *not* want to assert that it somehow reveals what defense intellectuals are really talking about, or their motivations; individual motives cannot necessarily be read directly from imagery, which originates in a broader cultural context. The history of the atomic bomb project itself is rife with overt images of competitive male sexuality, as is the discourse of the early nuclear physicists, strategists, and members of the Strategic Air Command.[5] Both the military itself and the arms manufacturers are constantly exploiting the phallic imagery and promise of sexual domination that their weapons so conveniently suggest. Consider the following, from the June 1985 issue of *Air Force Magazine:* Emblazoned in bold letters across the top of a two-page advertisement for the AV-8B Harrier II—"Speak Softly and Carry a Big Stick." The copy below boasts "an exceptional thrust-to-weight ratio," and "vectored thrust capability that makes the . . . unique rapid response possible."

Another vivid source of phallic imagery is to be found in descriptions of nuclear blasts themselves. Here, for example, is one by journalist William Laurence, who was brought by the Army Air Corps to witness the Nagasaki bombing.

> *Then, just when it appeared as though the thing had settled down into a state of permanence, there came shooting out of the top a giant mushroom that increased the size of the pillar to a total of 45,000 feet. The mushroom top was even more alive than the pillar, seething and boiling in a white fury of creamy foam, sizzling upward and then descending earthward, a thousand geysers rolled into one. It kept struggling in an elemental fury, like a creature in the act of breaking the bonds that held it down.*[6]

Given the degree to which it suffuses their world, the fact that defense intellectuals use a lot of sexual imagery is not especially surprising. Nor does it, by itself, constitute grounds for imputing motivation. The interesting issue is not so much the imagery's possible psychodynamic origins as how it functions—its role in making the work world of defense intellectuals feel tenable. Several stories illustrate the complexity.

At one point a group of us took a field trip to the New London Navy base where nuclear submarines are home-ported, and to the General Dynamics Electric Boat yards where a new Trident submarine was being constructed. The high point of the trip was a tour of a nuclear-powered submarine. A few at a time, we descended into the long, dark, sleek tube in which men and a nuclear reactor are encased underwater for months at a time. We squeezed through hatches, along neon-lit passages so narrow that we had to turn and press our backs to the walls for anyone to get by. We passed the cramped racks where men sleep, and the red and white signs warning of radioactive materials. When we finally reached the part of the sub where the missiles are housed, the officer accompanying us turned with a grin and asked if we wanted to stick our hands through a hole to "pat the missile." *Pat the missile?*

The image reappeared the next week, when a lecturer scornfully declared that the only real reason for deploying cruise and Pershing II missiles in Western Europe was "so that our allies can pat them." Some months later, another group of us went to be briefed at NORAD (the North American Aerospace Defense Command). On the way back, the Air National Guard plane we were on went to refuel at Offut Air Force Base, the Strategic Air Command headquarters near Omaha, Nebraska. When word leaked out that our landing would be delayed because the new B-1 bomber was in the area, the plane became charged with a tangible excitement that built as we flew in our holding pattern, people craning their necks to try to catch a glimpse of the B-1 in the skies, and climaxed as we touched down on the runway and hurtled past it. Later, when I returned to the center I encountered a man who, unable to go on the trip, said to me enviously, "I hear you got to pat a B-1."

What is all this patting? Patting is an assertion of intimacy, sexual possession, affectionate domination. The thrill and pleasure of "patting the missile" is the proximity of all that phallic power, the possibility of vicariously appropriating it as one's own. But patting is not only an act of sexual intimacy. It is also what one does to babies, small children, the pet dog. The creatures one pats are small, cute, harmless—not terrifyingly destructive. Pat it, and its lethality disappears.

Much of the sexual imagery I heard was rife with the sort of ambiguity suggested by "patting the missiles." The imagery can be construed as a deadly serious display of the connections between masculine sexuality and the arms race. But at the same time, it can also be heard as a way of minimizing the seriousness of militarist endeavors, of denying their deadly consequences. A former Pentagon target analyst, in telling me why he thought plans for "limited nuclear war" were ridiculous, said, "Look, you gotta understand that it's a pissing contest—you gotta expect them to use everything they've got." This image says, most obviously, that this is about competition for manhood, and thus there is tremendous danger. But at the same time it says that the whole thing is not very serious—it is just what little boys or drunk men do.

■

Sanitized abstraction and sexual imagery, even if disturbing, seemed to fit easily into the masculine world of nuclear war planning. What did not fit was another set of words that evoked images that can only be called domestic.

Nuclear missiles are based in "silos." On a Trident submarine, which carries 24 multiple-warhead nuclear missiles, crew members call the part of the sub where the missiles are lined up in their silos ready for launching "the Christmas tree farm." In the friendly, romantic world of nuclear weaponry, enemies "exchange" warheads; weapons systems can "marry up." "Coupling" is sometimes used to refer to the wiring between mechanisms of warning and response, or to the psychopolitical links between strategic and theater weapons. The patterns in which a MIRVed missile's nuclear warheads land is known as a "footprint." These nuclear explosives are not dropped; a "bus"

"delivers" them. These devices are called "reentry vehicles," or "RVs" for short, a term not only totally removed from the reality of a bomb but also resonant with the image of the recreational vehicles of the ideal family vacation.

These domestic images are more than simply one more way to remove oneself from the grisly reality behind the words; ordinary abstraction is adequate to that task. Calling the pattern in which bombs fall a "footprint" almost seems a willful distorting process, a playful, perverse refusal of accountability—because to be accountable to reality is to be unable to do this work.

The images evoked by these words may also be a way to tame the uncontrollable forces of nuclear destruction. Take the fire-breathing dragon under the bed, the one who threatens to incinerate your family, your town, your planet, and turn it into a pet you can pat. Or domestic imagery may simply serve to make everyone more comfortable with what they're doing. "PAL" (permissive action links) is the carefully constructed, friendly acronym for the electronic system designed to prevent the unauthorized firing of nuclear warheads. The president's annual nuclear weapons stockpile memorandum, which outlines both short- and long-range plans for production of new nuclear weapons, is benignly referred to as "the shopping list." The "cookie cutter" is a phrase used to describe a particular model of nuclear attack.

The imagery that domesticates, that humanizes insentient weapons, may also serve, paradoxically, to make it all right to ignore sentient human beings. Perhaps it is possible to spend one's time dreaming up scenarios for the use of massively destructive technology, and to exclude human beings from that technological world, because that world itself now includes the domestic, the human, the warm and playful—the Christmas trees, the RVs, the things one pats affectionately. It is a world that is in some sense complete in itself; it even includes death and loss. The problem is that all things that get "killed" happen to be weapons, not humans. If one of your warheads "kills" another of your warheads, it is "fratricide." There is much concern about "vulnerability" and "survivability," but it is about the vulnerability and survival of weapons systems, rather than people.

Another set of images suggests men's desire to appropriate from women the power of giving life. At Los Alamos, the atomic bomb was referred to as "Oppenheimer's baby"; at Lawrence Livermore, the hydrogen bomb was "Teller's baby," although those who wanted to disparage Teller's contribution claimed he was not the bomb's father but its mother. In this context, the extraordinary names given to the bombs that reduced Hiroshima and Nagasaki to ash and rubble—"Little Boy" and "Fat Man"—may perhaps become intelligible. These ultimate destroyers were the male progeny of the atomic scientists.

The entire history of the bomb project, in fact, seems permeated with imagery that confounds humanity's overwhelming technological power to destroy nature with the power to create: imagery that converts men's destruction into their rebirth. Laurence wrote of the Trinity test of the first atomic bomb: "One felt as though he had been privileged to witness the Birth of the World." In a 1985 interview, General Bruce K. Holloway, the commander in chief of the Strategic Air Command from 1968 to 1972, described a nuclear war as involving "a big bang, like the start of the universe."

Finally, the last thing one might expect to find in a subculture of hard-nosed realism and hyper-rationality is the repeated invocation of religious imagery. And yet, the first atomic bomb test was called Trinity. Seeing it, Robert Oppenheimer thought of Krishna's words to Arjuna in the *Bhagavad Gita:* "I am become death, destroyer of worlds." Defense intellectuals, when challenged on a particular assumption, will often duck out with a casual, "Now you're talking about matters of theology." Perhaps most astonishing of all, the creators of strategic doctrine actually refer to their community as "the nuclear priesthood." It is hard to decide what is most extraordinary about this: the arrogance of the claim, the tacit admission that they really are creators of dogma; or the extraordinary implicit statement about who, or rather what, has become god.

∎

Although I was startled by the combination of dry abstraction and odd imagery that characterizes the language of defense intellectuals, my attention was quickly focused on decoding and learning to speak it. The first task was training the tongue in the articulation of acronyms.

Several years of reading the literature of nuclear weaponry and strategy had not prepared me for the degree to which acronyms littered all conversations, nor for the way in which they are used. Formerly, I had thought of them mainly as utilitarian. They allow you to write or speak faster. They act as a form of abstraction, removing you from the reality behind the words. They restrict communication to the initiated, leaving the rest both uncomprehending and voiceless in the debate.

But being at the center revealed some additional, unexpected dimensions. First, in speaking and hearing, a lot of these terms are very sexy. A small supersonic rocket "designed to penetrate any Soviet air defense" is called a SRAM (for short-range attack missile). Submarine-launched cruise missiles are referred to as "slick'ems" and ground-launched cruise missiles are "glick'ems." Air-launched cruise missiles are magical "alchems."

Other acronyms serve in different ways. The plane in which the president will supposedly be flying around above a nuclear holocaust, receiving intelligence and issuing commands for where to bomb next, is referred to as "Kneecap" (for NEACP—National Emergency Airborne Command Post). Few believe that the president would really have the time to get into it, or that the communications systems would be working if he were in it—hence the edge of derision. But the very ability to make fun of a concept makes it possible to work with it rather than reject it outright.

In other words, what I learned at the program is that talking about nuclear weapons is fun. The words are quick, clean, light; they trip off the tongue. You can reel off dozens of them in seconds, forgetting about how one might interfere with the next, not to mention with the lives beneath them. Nearly everyone I observed—lecturers, students, hawks, doves, men, and women—took pleasure in using the words; some of us spoke with a self-consciously ironic edge, but the pleasure was there nonetheless. Part of the appeal was the thrill of being able to manipulate an arcane language, the power of entering the secret kingdom. But perhaps more important, learning the language gives a sense of control, a feeling of mastery over technology that is finally not controllable but powerful beyond human comprehension. The longer I stayed, the more conversations I participated in, the less I was frightened of nuclear war.

How can learning to speak a language have such a powerful effect? One answer, discussed earlier, is that the language is abstract and sanitized, never giving access to the images of war. But there is more to it than that. The learning process itself removed me from the reality of nuclear war. My energy was focused on the challenge of decoding acronyms, learning new terms, developing competence in the language—not on the weapons and wars behind the words. By the time I was through, I had learned far more than an alternate, if abstract, set of words. The content of what I could talk about was monumentally different.

Consider the following descriptions, in each of which the subject is the aftermath of a nuclear attack:

> *Everything was black, had vanished into the black dust, was destroyed. Only the flames that were beginning to lick their way up had any color. From the dust that was like a fog, figures began to loom up, black, hairless, faceless. They screamed with voices that were no longer human. Their screams drowned out the groans rising everywhere from the rubble, groans that seemed to rise from the very earth itself.*[7]

> *[You have to have ways to maintain communications in a] nuclear environment, a situation bound to include EMP blackout, brute force damage to systems, a heavy jamming environment, and so on.*[8]

There is no way to describe the phenomena represented in the first with the language of the second. The passages differ not only in the vividness of their words, but in their content: the first describes the effects of a nuclear blast on human beings; the second describes the impact of a nuclear blast on technical systems designed to secure the "command and control" of nuclear weapons. Both of these differences stem from the difference of perspective: the speaker in the first is a victim of nuclear weapons, the speaker in the second is a user. The speaker in the first is using words to try to name and contain the horror of human suffering all around her; the speaker in the second is using words to insure the possibility of launching the next nuclear attack.

Technostrategic language articulates only the perspective of the users of nuclear weapons, not the victims. Speaking the expert language not only offers distance, a feeling of control, and an alternative focus for one's energies; it also offers escape from thinking of oneself as a victim of nuclear war. No matter what one deeply knows or believes about the likelihood of nuclear war, and no matter what sort of terror or despair the knowledge of nuclear war's reality might inspire, the speakers of technostrategic language are allowed, even forced, to escape that awareness, to escape viewing nuclear war from the position of the victim, by virtue of their linguistic stance.

I suspect that much of the reduced anxiety about nuclear war commonly experienced by both new speakers of the language and longtime experts comes from characteristics of the language itself: the distance afforded by its abstraction, the sense of control afforded by mastering it, and the fact that its content and concerns are those of the users rather than the victims. In learning the language, one goes from being the passive, powerless victim to being the competent, wily, powerful purveyor of nuclear threats and nuclear explosive power. The enormous destructive effects of nuclear weapons systems become extensions of the self, rather than threats to it.

∎

It did not take long to learn the language of nuclear war and much of the specialized information it contained. My focus quickly changed from mastering technical information and doctrinal arcana, to an attempt to understand more about how the dogma I was learning was rationalized. Since underlying rationales are rarely discussed in the everyday business of defense planning, I had to start asking more questions. At first, although I was tempted to use my newly acquired proficiency in technostrategic jargon, I vowed to speak English.

What I found, however, was that no matter how well informed my questions were, no matter how complex an understanding they were based upon, if I was speaking English rather than expert jargon, the men responded to me as though I were ignorant or simpleminded, or both. A strong distaste for being patronized and a pragmatic streak made my experiment in English short-lived. I adopted the vocabulary, speaking of "escalation dominance," "preemptive strikes," and one of my favorites, "sub-holocaust engagements." This opened my way into long, elaborate discussions that taught me a lot about technostrategic reasoning and how to manipulate it.

But the better I became at this discourse, the more difficult it became to express my own ideas and values. While the language included things I had never been able to speak about before, it radically excluded others. To pick a bald example: the word "peace" is not a part of this discourse. As close as one can come is "strategic stability," a term that refers to a balance of numbers and types of weapons systems—not the political, social, economic, and psychological conditions that "peace" implies. Moreover, to speak the word is to immediately brand oneself as a soft-headed activist instead of a professional to be taken seriously.

If I was unable to speak my concerns in this language, more disturbing still was that I also began to find it harder even to keep them in my own head. No matter how firm my commitment to staying aware of the bloody reality behind the words, over and over I found that I could not keep human lives as my reference point. I found I could go for days speaking about nuclear weapons, without once thinking about the people who would be incinerated by them.

It is tempting to attribute this problem to the words themselves—the abstractness, the euphemisms, the sanitized, friendly, sexy acronyms. Then one would only need to change the words: get the military planners to say "mass murder" instead of "collateral damage," and their thinking would change. The problem, however, is not simply that defense intellectuals use abstract terminology that removes them from the realities of which they speak. There *is* no reality behind the words. Or, rather, the "reality" they speak of is itself a world

of abstractions. Deterrence theory, and much of strategic doctrine, was invented to hold together abstractly, its validity judged by internal logic. These abstract systems were developed as a way to make it possible to, in Herman Kahn's phrase, "think about the unthinkable"—not as a way to describe or codify relations on the ground.

So the problem with the idea of "limited nuclear war," for example, is not only that it is a travesty to refer to the death and suffering caused by *any* use of nuclear weapons as "limited," or that "limited nuclear war" is an abstraction that obfuscates the human reality beneath any use of nuclear weapons. It is also that limited nuclear war is itself an abstract conceptual system, designed, embodied, and achieved by computer modeling. In this abstract world, hypothetical, calm, rational actors have sufficient information to know exactly what size nuclear weapon the opponent has used against which targets, and adequate command and control to make sure that their response is precisely equilibrated to the attack. No field commander would use the tactical nuclear weapons at his disposal at the height of a losing battle. Our rational actors would have absolute freedom from emotional response to being attacked, from political pressures from the populace. They would act solely on the basis of a perfectly informed mathematical calculus of megatonnage. To refer to limited nuclear war is to enter a system that is de facto abstract and grotesquely removed from reality. The abstractness of the entire conceptual system makes descriptive language utterly beside the point.

This realization helped make sense of my difficulty in staying connected to concrete lives as well as of some of the bizarre and surreal quality of what people said. But there was still a piece missing. How is it possible, for example, to make sense of the following:

> *The strategic stability of regime A is based on the fact that both sides are deprived of any incentive ever to strike first. Since it takes roughly two warheads to destroy one enemy silo, an attacker must expend two of his missiles to destroy one of the enemy's. A first strike disarms the attacker. The aggressor ends up worse off than the aggressed.*[9]

The homeland of "the aggressed" has just been devastated by the explosions of, say, a thousand nuclear bombs, each likely to be at least 10 to 100 times more powerful than the bomb dropped on Hiroshima, and the aggressor, whose homeland is still untouched, "ends up worse off"?

I was only able to make sense of this kind of thinking when I finally asked myself: Who—or what—is the subject? In technostrategic discourse, the reference point is not human beings but the weapons themselves. The aggressor ends up worse off than the aggressed because he has fewer weapons left; any other factors, such as what happened where the weapons landed, are irrelevant to the calculus of gain and loss.

The fact that the subjects of strategic paradigms are weapons has several important implications. First, and perhaps most critically, there is no real way to talk about human death or human societies when you are using a language designed to talk about weapons. Human death simply *is* collateral damage—collateral to the real subject, which is the weapons themselves.

Understanding this also helps explain what was at first so surprising to me: most people who do this work are on the whole nice, even good, men, many with liberal inclinations. While they often identify their motivations as being concern about humans, in their work they enter a language and paradigm that precludes people. Thus, the nature and outcome of their work can utterly contradict their genuine motives for doing it.

In addition, if weapons are the reference point, it becomes in some sense illegitimate to ask the paradigm to reflect human concerns. Questions that break through the numbing language of strategic analysis and raise issues in human terms can be easily dismissed. No one will claim that they are unimportant. But they are inexpert, unprofessional, irrelevant to the business at hand. The discourse among the experts remains hermetically sealed. One can talk about the weapons that are supposed to protect particular peoples and their way of life without actually asking if they are able to do it, or if they are the best way to do it, or whether they may even damage the entities they are supposedly protecting. These are separate questions.

This discourse has become virtually the only response to the question of how to achieve security that is recognized as legitimate. If the discussion of weapons was one competing voice in the discussion, or one that was integrated with others, the fact that the referents of strategic paradigms are only weapons might be of less note. But when we realize that the only language and expertise offered to those interested in pursuing peace refers to nothing but weapons, its limits become staggering. And its entrapping qualities—the way it becomes so hard, once you adopt the language, to stay connected to human concerns—become more comprehensible.

■

Within a few weeks, what had once been remarkable became unnoticeable. As I learned to speak, my perspective changed. I no longer stood outside the impenetrable wall of technostrategic language and once inside, I could no longer see it. I had not only learned to speak a language: I had started to think in it. Its questions became my questions, its concepts shaped my responses to new ideas. Like the White Queen, I began to believe six impossible things before breakfast—not because I consciously believed, for instance, that a "surgically clean counterforce strike" was really possible, but because some elaborate piece of doctrinal reasoning I used was already predicated on the possibility of those strikes as well as on a host of other impossible things.

My grasp on what I knew as reality seemed to slip. I might get very excited, for example, about a new strategic justification for a no-first-use policy and spend time discussing the ways in which its implications for the U.S. force structure in Western Europe were superior to the older version. After a day or two I would suddenly step back, aghast that I was so involved with the *military* justifications for not using nuclear weapons—as though the moral ones were not enough. What I was actually talking about—the mass incineration of a nuclear attack—was no longer in my head.

Or I might hear some proposals that seemed to me infinitely superior to the usual arms control fare. First I would work out how and why these proposals were better and then ways to counter the arguments against them. Then it might dawn on me that even though these two proposals sounded different, they still shared a host of assumptions that I was not willing to make. I would first feel as though I had achieved a new insight. And then all of a sudden, I would realize that these were things I actually knew before I ever entered this community and had since forgotten. I began to feel that I had fallen down the rabbit hole.

■

The language issues do not disappear. The seductions of learning and using it remain great, and as the pleasures deepen, so do the dangers. The activity of trying to out-reason nuclear strategists in their own games gets you thinking inside their rules, tacitly accepting the unspoken assumptions of the paradigms.

Yet, the issues of language have now become somewhat less central to me, and my new questions, while still not precisely the questions of an insider, are questions I could not have had without being inside. Many of them are more practical: Which individuals and institutions are actually responsible for the endless "modernization" and proliferation of nuclear weaponry, and what do they gain from it? What role does technostrategic rationality play in their thinking? What would a reasonable, genuinely defensive policy look like? Others are more philosophical, having to do with the nature of the "realism" claimed for the defense intellectuals' mode of thinking and the grounds upon which it can be shown to be spurious. What would an alternative rationality look like?

My own move away from a focus on the language is quite typical. Other recent entrants into this world have commented that while the cold-blooded, abstract discussions are most striking at first, within a short time you get past them and come to see that the language itself is not the problem.

I think it would be a mistake, however, to dismiss these early impressions. While I believe that the language is not the whole problem, it is a significant component and clue. What it reveals is a whole series of culturally grounded and culturally acceptable mechanisms that make it possible to work in institutions that foster the proliferation of

nuclear weapons, to plan mass incinerations of millions of human beings for a living. Language that is abstract, sanitized, full of euphemisms; language that is sexy and fun to use; paradigms whose referent is weapons; imagery that domesticates and deflates the forces of mass destruction; imagery that reverses sentient and nonsentient matter, that conflates birth and death, destruction and creation—all of these are part of what makes it possible to be radically removed from the reality of what one is talking about, and from the realities one is creating through the discourse.

Close attention to the language itself also reveals a tantalizing basis on which to challenge the legitimacy of the defense intellectuals' dominance of the discourse on nuclear issues. When defense intellectuals are criticized for the cold-blooded inhumanity of the scenarios they plan, their response is to claim the high ground of rationality. They portray those who are radically opposed to the nuclear status quo as irrational, unrealistic, too emotional—"idealistic activists." But if the smooth, shiny surface of their discourse—its abstraction and technical jargon—appears at first to support these claims, a look below the surface does not. Instead we find strong currents of homoerotic excitement, heterosexual domination, the drive toward competence and mastery, the pleasures of membership in an elite and privileged group, of the ultimate importance and meaning of membership in the priesthood. How is it possible to point to the pursuers of these values, these experiences, as paragons of cool-headed objectivity?

While listening to the language reveals the mechanisms of distancing and denial and the emotional currents embodied in this emphatically male discourse, attention to the experience of learning the language reveals something about how thinking can become more abstract, more focused on parts disembedded from their context, more attentive to the survival of weapons than the survival of human beings.

Because this professional language sets the terms for public debate, many who oppose current nuclear policies choose to learn it. Even if they do not believe that the technical information is very important, some believe it is necessary to master the language simply because it is too difficult to attain public legitimacy without it. But learning the language is a transformative process. You are not simply adding new information, new vocabulary, but entering a mode of thinking not only about nuclear weapons but also about military and political power, and about the relationship between human ends and technological means.

The language and the mode of thinking are not neutral containers of information. They were developed by a specific group of men, trained largely in abstract theoretical mathematics and economics, specifically to make it possible to think rationally about the use of nuclear weapons. That the language is not well suited to do anything but make it possible to think about using nuclear weapons should not be surprising.

Those who find the U.S. nuclear policy desperately misguided face a serious quandary. If we refuse to learn the language, we condemn ourselves to being jesters on the sidelines. If we learn and use it, we not only severely limit what we can say but also invite the transformation, the militarization, of our own thinking.

I have no solutions to this dilemma, but I would like to offer a couple of thoughts in an effort to push it a little further—or perhaps even to reformulate its terms. It is important to recognize an assumption implicit in adopting the strategy of learning the language. When we outsiders assume that learning and speaking the language will give us a voice recognized as legitimate and will give

us greater political influence, we assume that the language itself actually articulates the criteria and reasoning strategies upon which nuclear weapons development and deployment decisions are made. This is largely an illusion. I suggest that technostrategic discourse functions more as a gloss, as an ideological patina that hides the actual reasons these decisions are made. Rather than informing and shaping decisions, it far more often legitimizes political outcomes that have occurred for utterly different reasons. If this is true, it raises serious questions about the extent of the political returns we might get from using it, and whether they can ever balance out the potential problems and inherent costs.

I believe that those who seek a more just and peaceful world have a dual task before them—a deconstructive project and a reconstructive project that are intimately linked. Deconstruction requires close attention to, and the dismantling of, technostrategic discourse. The dominant voice of militarized masculinity and decontextualized rationality speaks so loudly in our culture that it will remain difficult for any other voices to be heard until that voice loses some of its power to define what we hear and how we name the world.

The reconstructive task is to create compelling alternative visions of possible futures, to recognize and develop alternative conceptions of rationality, to create rich and imaginative alternative voices—diverse voices whose conversations with each other will invent those futures.

---

1. I must point out that we cannot know whether to take this particular example literally: America's list of nuclear targets is, of course, classified. The defense analyst quoted, however, is a man who has had access to that list for at least two decades. He is also a man whose thinking and speaking is careful and precise, so I think it is reasonable to assume that his statement is not a distortion, that "shoe factories," even if not themselves literally targeted, accurately represent a category of target. Shoe factories would be one among many "military targets" other than weapons systems themselves; they would be military targets because an army needs boots. The likelihood of a nuclear war lasting long enough for foot soldiers to wear out their boots might seem to stretch the limits of credibility, but that is an insufficient reason to assume that they are not nuclear targets. Nuclear targeting and nuclear strategic planning in general frequently suffer from "conventionalization"—the tendency of planners to think in the old, familiar terms of "conventional" warfare rather than fully

assimilating the ways in which nuclear weaponry has changed warfare. In avoiding talking about murder, the defense community has long been ahead of the State Department. It was not until 1984 that the State Department announced it will no longer use the word "killing," much less "murder," in official reports on the status of human rights in allied countries. The new term is "unlawful or arbitrary deprivation of life" (*New York Times*, February 15, 1984, as cited in *Quarterly Review of Doublespeak* 11, no. 1 [October 1984]: 3)

2. "Kiloton" (or kt) is a measure of explosive power, measured by the number of thousands of tons of TNT required to release an equivalent amount of energy. The atomic bomb dropped on Hiroshima is estimated to have been approximately 12 kt. An MX missile is designed to carry up to ten Mk 21 reentry vehicles, each with a W-87 warhead. The yield of W-87 warheads is 300 kt, but they are "upgradable" to 475 kt.

3. Since the MX would theoretically be able to "take out" Soviet land-based ICBMs in a "disarming first strike," the Soviets would have few ICBMs left for a retaliatory attack, and thus damage to the United States theoretically would be limited. However, to consider the damage that could be inflicted on the United States by the remaining ICBMs, not to mention Soviet bombers and submarine-based missiles as "limited" is to act as though words have no meaning.

4. Gen. William Odom, "C³I and Telecommunications at the Policy Level," incidental paper from a seminar, *Command, Control, Communications and Intelligence* (Cambridge, Mass., Harvard University Center for Information Policy Research, Spring 1980), p. 5.

5. See Brian Easlea, *Fathering the Unthinkable: Masculinity, Scientists and the Nuclear Arms Race* (London: Pluto Press, 1983).

6. William L. Laurence, *Dawn Over Zero: The Study of the Atomic Bomb* (London: Museum Press, 1974), pp. 198–99.

7. Hisako Matsubara, *Cranes at Dusk* (Garden City, New York: Dial Press, 1985).

8. Gen. Robert Rosenberg, "The Influence of Policy Making on C³I," speaking at the Harvard seminar, *Command, Control, Communications and Intelligence,* p. 59.

9. Charles Krauthammer, "Will Star Wars Kill Arms Control?" *New Republic* (Jan. 21, 1985), pp. 12–16.

Making Peace with Music

Thomas L. Friedman

To hear Shafik Salman tell it, if the Arab–Israeli conflict could only be put to music it would be settled in no time at all.

Mr. Salman's is probably one of the most famous and beloved Israeli voices in the Arab world today, although few Israeli Jews have ever heard of him.

He is the disk jockey for "From Israel with Love," a popular program on the Arabic service of the Israeli radio. The show is broadcast four times a week for a total of about three hours and offers its Arabic-speaking audience—in Israel, the occupied West Bank and across the Arab world—a diet of "Israeli new wave" music, in which Hebrew words are sung to jazzed-up traditional Arabic melodies.

Joining the Middle East

The popularity of Mr. Salman's show underscores the degree to which Israel is slowly becoming a Middle Eastern country, in music and in many other ways.

Although this may not change anything politically, at least in the short run, the facts that Israeli singers are adapting Arabic melodies or that someone may be humming a Hebraized Arabic song on the streets of Damascus suggests that the future may not be all bleak. Despite the curtain of conflict separating Arabs and Israelis, a certain cultural mixing is taking place on an uncontrolled popular level.

Each month Mr. Salman, a Jew born in an Arab country that he prefers not to identify, receives about 900 letters from Arab listeners writing from places like Mecca, Cairo and Damascus, as well as Mr. Salman's own backyard in Israel. Most of the letters ask him either to dedicate Arabic-style Hebrew songs to friends or relatives in their Arab countries, play their favorite Israeli new wave tune, interview their favorite Israeli singer or send them pictures and tapes of Israeli pop stars, all of which he does.

'Never Thought for a Second'

"Six years ago I just started playing a few Hebrew songs with short Arabic translations, but I never thought for a second that I would get the response I did," said Mr. Salman, who caresses his listeners through the studio microphone in a flowing, honey-like Arabic while flipping Hebrew albums on and off the turntables.

"The first letter came from an Arab girl in Hebron who wrote five pages why she is just crazy about Tzvika Pik," he said, referring to an Israeli singer who sings in Hebrew in the eastern Arab style. "These eastern songs, the new style that is sung today by many Israeli singers, that is what attracts them."

Primarily because of Mr. Salman's show, the black market for cassettes of Israeli new wave songs has blossomed in the Arab world—so much so that an Egyptian opposition newspaper, Sawt al-Shaab, published an article on July 2, 1985, by Wafa Ahmad, a journalist, in which she complained that the popularity of Israeli songs had reached such proportions among Egyptian youths that it "weakens the standing of the Egyptian nation."

A Letter from Syria

In his cramped office, Mr. Salman is surrounded by an avalanche of letters and postcards spilling out of every drawer, closet and cardboard box. Most are written by listeners in the Arab world who mailed their notes to a special post office box in Geneva, from which they were forwarded to Israel.

"Here, here, read this one from some Syrian girls," he said, handing a visitor a letter from a fistful he had scooped out of a drawer:

Dear Shafik Salman:

We follow all of your programs. I record each show and I now have 250 tapes. We cannot give you our names because we know that many here listen to you, including President Assad's bodyguards. There is a singer who captures with his voice everyone

I know, including my father. If the birds in heaven heard him, they would stop singing. He is Moshe Eliyahu. I hope you will interview him. We send greetings of peace.

The Syrian Roses
March 14, 1986

Many writers are bold enough to sign their own names and have them read out over the Israeli Arabic radio.

A Request for Friends

Jamila from Marrakesh, Morocco, wrote that she and her friends "love Israeli songs" and would appreciate it if Mr. Salman would play "Mabruk ya-Hatan" and dedicate it to her friends "Jamila, Fadiya and Suad in Amman." The song title itself is a mixture of Hebrew and Arabic, meaning "Congratulations to the Groom."

Tahsin wrote from Mecca, Saudi Arabia: "I have listened to your program more than once and am pleased with what you present. I hope you will regard me as your friend."

Fuad, from Kuwait, wrote that "this is the first time I have listened to Hebrew songs, and I find them very pretty."

"I listened to the song by Chaim Moshe, 'Love Story,' and it is so beautiful I want to hear it again," he wrote.

The Israeli new wave musicians began to achieve prominence in the late 1970's, as Sephardic Jews—those of Middle Eastern origin—were becoming the majority of Israel's population.

When they immigrated, these Sephardic Jews brought with them the echo of Arabic music in their ears, said Edmond Sehayek, the director of the Arabic service, and some of their singers began to translate into Hebrew the Arab songs they had learned in their youth, or from their parents. One such song was "Laila," or "Night," by Farid al-Atrash of Egypt, which was turned into a Hebrew hit by the Israeli singer Ruby Chen.

In addition to translating the Arabic songs into Hebrew, many Israeli new wave singers added more electronic instrumentation and a faster beat and reduced the length and repetitions of the Arabic originals. Others simply integrated Arabic musical motifs into their songs.

At first, the Israeli radio Hebrew service refused to play what some Israelis were calling "bastardized music." But when the Hebrew radio disk jockeys discovered that many of their listeners were shutting off their radios and listening instead to this Hebrew–Arabic blend on cassettes, they felt forced to put it on the air.

A Controversial Move

One day Mr. Salman, who was a studio technician, suggested that the Arabic service, which played only Arabic music, also broadcast a few hours of this new style.

"It was very controversial," Mr Sehayek said. "We are an Arabic radio and we did not want our listeners to be insulted by playing Arabic melodies with Hebrew words. What made us finally go ahead was when we discovered that Arabs in the Old City of Jerusalem were listening to this new wave music on their cassettes."

Two of Mr. Salman's favorite letters came from young women in Damascus. One arrived in April 1985, from two women, 18 and 19 years old, who asked that Mr. Salman convey their regards to the Israeli new wave singers Shimi Tavori, Yardena Arazi, Danny Shoshan and many others.

"We want to invite them to Syria when peace comes," the letter said, "so that they can sing for us here—Allah willing." Before ending their letter the Syrians asked, "What is the feeling of the Israeli singers, or even you, when Syrians write to you?"

At the top of another letter, sent in October 1984, a young Syrian woman managed to write in crude Hebrew letters, possibly copied from an old synagogue or cemetery in her town, the Hebrew words "shalom uvraha," meaning "hello and welcome."

"If the Syrian people requested, do you think Israeli singers would come sing for them personally, without the Syrian ruling family stopping it?" the young woman wrote. "I am trying to learn Hebrew so I will know what they say in their beautiful songs. I ask God that an agreement will be reached between our two countries so that we will be able to see you."

PART FOUR

Inequality

The relationship between war and inequality has long been debated within the peace movement. Pacifists and socialists have argued that the concentration of wealth and power in society is a major cause of war because historically, powerful elites have seen wars as opportunities to expand their economic might, through foreign conquest of countries with their markets and natural resources and/or through profiting off weapons contracts. At the same time, in many wars the ruling elite has not had to send many of *their* sons off to war but has been able to secure military forces manned largely by the poor and middle classes. Elites may also promote war to maintain their political power. War can deflect popular unrest with the class hierarchy and undermine foreign revolutionary regimes whose success might inspire political changes at home. Given this war-promoting social structure, many radicals have contended that domestic social reforms that give more power to subordinate classes and races are necessary to achieve peace.

On the other hand, most academics in international relations and experts in the foreign service think that war results from competition and inequality among nations and that domestic social structures are relatively unimportant. The key to peace, for these "internationalists," is to improve relations between governing elites of the great powers and to promote arms control and international law (see Howlett and Zeitzer, in this volume). Peace thus becomes an agreement among powerful elites to follow international law.

The selections in Part Four explore aspects of this debate on the relationships between hierarchical social structures and war. David Fabbro's "Equality in Peaceful Societies" discusses seven peaceful societies in which property, power, and respect are fairly equally distributed. Men and women are relatively equal in these societies, an important finding congruent with other work showing that societies in which men have a great deal of power over women have high rates of warfare.[1] In these more egalitarian societies, the ideal man is not a warrior. Men are instead expected to respond to violence with flight or trickery. Although these small, mostly nonindustrial societies are very different from the United States, they suggest many hypotheses about how we can promote peace by creating more democratic relationships.

The next two articles debate the question, Would the United States be more peaceful if it became socialist and there was more economic and political equality? Yes, answers Thomas Weisskopf in "Inequality and Imperialism": The capitalist elite of the United States supports war because it increases their profits and their political power. In addition, the emphasis on competition under capitalism increases the public's disposition to dominate and rule over countries. In "Socialism Is Not the Solution," Robert Tucker responds with an argument that socialism is irrelevant to promoting peace. Competition among nations, not classes, is the cause of war, he maintains, and a shift to socialism in the United States would not change people's desire for domination.

In the final article, an analysis of the social class and ethnicity of soldiers in Vietnam, James William Gibson describes how members of the poor, working class, and especially the minorities among them, were drafted for military service and were used by the military in Vietnam.

---

1. See Peggy Reeves Sanday, *Female Power and Male Dominance* (New York: Cambridge University Press, 1981).

Equality in Peaceful Societies

David Fabbro

Introduction

The majority of work in peace research has been directed toward gaining an understanding of the sources and dynamics of direct and structural violence. Elaboration of the social preconditions of peace has all too often been neglected, viewed as an abstraction and/or utopia, or been of a purely theoretical nature. This paper is an attempt to arrest this underdevelopment by directing attention toward a number of concrete examples of peaceful societies.

Criteria of Peace

There are a number of levels or intensities of peace which members of a society may experience. In ascending order of comprehensiveness these would include:

1. The society has no wars fought on its territory;

2. The society is not involved in any external wars;

3. There are no civil wars or internal collective violence;

4. There is no standing military–police organisation;

5. There is little or no interpersonal physical violence;

6. There is little or no structural violence;

7. The society has the capacity to undergo change peacefully; and

8. There is opportunity for idiosyncratic development.

An example of a study using criterion 1 is provided by Melko (1973); this work is interesting as it is one of the few attempts to study peace, but it is disappointing because of its reliance on a behavioural definition of peace. Because no consideration is given as to the justice of such peace it becomes a study of stable empires and states rather than an analysis of social structures and organisations which minimise both direct and structural violence. The seven societies considered in this paper fulfil criteria 1 to 5. The societies selected represent the first seven to meet these criteria from a collection of possible societies drawn from various works which make reference to societies lacking in warfare or other forms of violence (Benedict 1935; Davie 1929; Fromm 1973; Mead 1961; Otterbein 1970; Sipes 1973).

In terms of their social structure many of these societies correspond to the first level of development in Fried's (1967) schema of political evolution: egalitarian band society. That is, they generally lack formal patterns of ranking and stratification, place no restriction on the number of people capable of exercising power or occupying positions of prestige, and have economies where exchange is based on generalised reciprocity (Fried 1967:28–35). As such it can be argued that

Reprinted from David Fabbro, "Peaceful Societies: An Introduction," *Journal of Peace Research* 15 (1978):67–83, by permission of Norwegian University Press, Oslo.

these societies do not experience certain types of structural violence.

The similarities between the societies examined cannot simply be attributed to the occupation of a common ecological niche (Service 1966:3). Neither can their similarity be solely attributed to a common mode of production— hunting and gathering—as at least two of the sample have an agricultural base.

External Factors

Before considering the internal characteristics of these societies it is necessary to consider possible external influences upon them. For example, Sipes (1973) rejected several societies from one of these samples because their peacefulness appeared to be based on the presence of stronger and more aggressive neighbours. Although all these societies are bounded by more complex and powerful neighbours it would be misleading to assume that this is the sole reason for their peacefulness. In relation to external war it should be noted that all but one of these societies lack some of the major structural prerequisites for engaging in it: a coercive hierarchy and leadership, and a surplus to support a nonproductive military organization. Admittedly warfare is only one form of externally directed physical violence and less organised forms such as feuding and raiding are possible at this level of social organisation (Fried 1967:99–101). Indeed the Siriono, for example, at one time engaged in acts of violence against white colonisers. But external stimuli capable of eliciting violent responses from a society raise issues of a different, although related, order than those to which this preliminary paper is directed.

Internal Factors

A number of questions have been developed in order to demonstrate various aspects of these societies, and, where sources allow, to extract the same type of information for each society.

General

1. In what type of natural habitat does the society reside?
2. How is subsistence gained?
3. What is the prevailing ideology–cosmology– world view of the society? What are the core or paramount norms which act as the basis of regulation in social intercourse?
4. On what basis is the society integrated?

Direct Violence

5. What are the major characteristics of the child socialisation process?
6. Does physical violence exist? If so, what forms does it take?
7. What conflict resolution processes exist? Are they institutionalised or informal?

Structural Violence

8. Is there any division of labour and if so does it lead to specialisation?
9. Are there any forms of socially coercive organisations which are capable of gaining compliance on the basis of power?
10. Are there any forms of hierarchy? If so are they exclusive or restrictive?
11. Who participates in decisionmaking concerning the society as a whole? Is such participation direct or mediated?
12. Who exercises social control?
13. What forms does social control take?
14. Are there any forms of discrimination which militate against an equal distribution of self-respect between individuals?

The Societies

The Semai of Malaya

(1) The Semai Senoi live in western Malaya and are subdivided into eastern and western groups.

Their habitat is a mixture of lowland tropical rain forest and mountain ridges. (2) The Semai gain their subsistence by hunting, trapping, fishing, and some swidden—slash and burn—agriculture. Some gathering of wild food consisting mainly of fruit is also carried out. They also have domesticated animals such as hens, ducks, and goats.

(3) The religious system of the Semai is complex but does not give rise to any religious leaders or elite. Central to social organisation and the regulation of interpersonal relations is the concept of *punan*. Implicit in *punan* is the idea that making someone unhappy, especially by frustrating desires, increases the probability of that person suffering physical injury. The notion of *punan* pervades their whole lifestyle and influences matters such as child rearing and sexual relations.

(4) The band is the largest form of social organisation; each one being composed of a number of nuclear families. In the west the predominant settlement pattern is a cluster of small houses which together form a homestead. The houses of the western Semai generally have between five and twenty-four inhabitants while the eastern Semai live communally in long houses which may have as many as fifty residents.

(5) Semai children enjoy a considerable amount of freedom in their behaviour. If a child does not wish to engage in some activity parents do not force it to do so; such action would be *punan*. Generally children learn through voluntary imitative play. When children misbehave, adults invoke the threat of evil spirits or the occurrence of certain evil happenings to gain compliance with their wishes. Where physical punishment is used it consists of a pinch on the cheek or a tap on the hand. All child rearing practices are geared toward the personal internalisation of norms of conduct. This is especially so with children who display aggressive behavior. In such cases the Semai deliberately do not punish such behaviour physically and so personal experience of violence is very limited. Moreover it is very difficult for children to rebel against their parents because adults do not object if a child does not wish to do something.

(6) Physical violence is more or less unknown in Semai society. Apparently between 1956 and 1967 a number of cases of murder and attempted murder occurred but this appears to have arisen because of the political turbulence in Malaya in general at this time. Also the Semai apparently abandoned the very old or sick during times of scarcity but this was done reluctantly. According to Dentan (1968:59) violence appears to terrify the Semai who meet force with passivity or flight.

(7) Conflict resolution processes do exist in Semai society but they are not particularly formalised. In a dispute one party usually suffers (that is, is taken to suffer) *punan*. The victim has two courses of action available. The *punan* may be endured or the offender may be asked for compensation. Generally the offender pays it. In a dispute where both parties feel in the right they may appeal to a respected elder; but, should one of the parties think the judgement unjust it can be ignored. Disputants who become angry manifest such feelings by avoiding the other party. Generally, most quarrels are conceived of by the participants as being a personal matter.

(8) There is some division of labour in Semai society but mainly in relation to hunting which is a male activity. Men, women, and children help to clear the forest for agriculture. Men and women too old to hunt supplement the diet by fishing. Domestic activities such as basket weaving or carrying water are performed by women. Both men and women plant crops but only women harvest the rice. Both sexes cook and winnow grain. There does not appear to be any specialisation of labour in Semai society; even the headman must gain his own subsistence.

(9 and 10) There is no specifically political organisation within Semai bands. All elders are accorded respect on two grounds. Firstly, they have the largest amount of experience and as such are valuable sources of information. Secondly, most young people and young married couples move frequently between homesteads. Thus it is the elders who provide continuity and stability within each homestead. The foremost male elder is regarded as the headman of the group. As with all

other elders, however, young people may ignore his advice. The headman keeps the peace—when disputes cannot be solved by the parties directly involved—by conciliation rather than coercion. If the headman is to function efficiently he must be respected; one who is not respected will find people turning to another elder for advice. People only recognise the headman's authority in specific situations: in the mediation of a dispute, as a group representative in external matters, and in the west, in deciding upon the selection and apportionment of land. The position of headman appears to be held by males only.

(11 and 12) Theoretically all adults participate in decisionmaking and social control. Women are not formally prevented from being influential within the group but in general they apparently feel embarrassed about participating in discussions about matters of general concern. In practice a few women are influential in discussions but the majority appear to abstain. Both social control and decisionmaking are implemented through the medium of public opinion. Usually it is the older men who have the greatest influence on public opinion but paradoxically such elders are often regarded with suspicion by the rest of the group and so their authority is probably less than would appear at first sight. Another person who has a major influence on public opinion is the one who enjoys popularity. Such popularity accrues to an individual who shares what can be afforded without appearing to calculate the cost of such generosity. (13) The main sanction is embarrassment; when public opinion goes against an individual that individual is "embarrassed" (Dentan 1968:69). Sanctions other than public opinion do not appear to exist. Strong internalised norms of behaviour combined with the influence of public opinion appear to make deviance very uncommon.

(14) Self-respect appears to be fairly evenly distributed among the Semai. Children have great freedom of action and can if they wish ignore adult instructions. Men and women seem to enjoy equal sexual license with divorce and separation as frequent occurrences. It should be noted, however, that there appear to be informal barriers which prevent women from fully participating in group decisionmaking and neither do women hold the position of headman.

The Siriono of Eastern Bolivia

(1) The Siriono live in the tropical rain forest centred on eastern Bolivia. (2) They are seminomadic aborigines who practice some swidden agriculture but are primarily hunter-gatherers. (3) The kinship system is based on the matrilineal extended family. A band—the highest level of social integration—is composed of a number of nuclear families who all occupy a communal hut. Each family has an area in the hut where the parents' hammocks are hung. (4) Sorcery is more or less unknown to the Siriono. Reciprocity does exist between families but it is generally forced; and, there is a general reluctance to share food which has not been produced cooperatively.

(5) It is usually females who look after children although both parents spend a lot of time playing with their children. Holmberg characterises child rearing practices as: "informal, random and haphazard" (1966:203). Reward and punishment techniques are used but there is little or no physical punishment. Apparently Siriono mothers almost always cry after they have been angry with their children. Both sexes are taught early to contribute to the family economy. From about eight years of age boys accompany their fathers when hunting, while girls help with household tasks. (6) Physical violence does occur among the Siriono but fighting with weapons and clubs is rare. Males seldom express direct aggression against other males. Neither do males beat their wives but there are apparently quarrels among women, frequently culminating in fighting with digging sticks. At one stage the Siriono engaged in violence against white colonisers although it did not continue for long and did not become an institutionalised feature of Siriono society. (7) Various conflict resolution processes exist but usually disputes are settled by those who start them. An exception to this general rule arises at drinking feasts—a regular feature of social life—when quarrels are settled by wrestling

matches. Any other type of fighting is frowned upon and is usually stopped by nonparticipant men and women. There are no formal agencies of social control and the chief does not interfere in disputes. The final form of conflict resolution is fission. In this instance one of the parties to the conflict will leave the band temporarily or permanently and join another group or alternatively a number of families may leave a band and establish a new one.

(8) The Siriono do practice division of labour to a small extent. Hunting is a male occupation whereas food gathering and horticulture are joint pursuits. There is no occupational specialisation, and there are no nonproductive sectors in the society. Even the chief must provide for himself. (9 and 10) Leadership which exists among the Siriono is based solely on the personal qualities of the incumbent. It appears, however, to be held by males only. (11) Participation in decisionmaking does not appear to arise because there are very few collective enterprises requiring decisions. Husband and wife or wives appear, in the given situation, equal in prestige even if this is only indicated by the fact that women start quarrels as frequently as do men. (12) Social control appears to be based on individual action toward the offender; calling for satisfaction by reference to group norms rather than group action against the offender. "Justice is an informal and private matter. . . . Generally speaking it would seem that the maintenance of law and order rests largely on the principle of reciprocity (however forced), the fear of the supernatural, sanctions and retaliation, and the desire for public approval" (Holmberg 1966:153).

(13) Norms of behaviour appear to be flexible as evidenced by the lack of recognition in the culture of sexual offences or theft. (14) Self-respect appears to be fairly evenly distributed. Individuals may ignore the advice of a chief if they wish. Sexism does exist as shown by the informal exclusion of women from the leadership position. Females do, however, have sexual license and hold their own drinking feasts and dances. Holmberg does not offer any evidence that women are subservient to their husbands or men in general.

The Mbuti Pygmies of the Ituri Forest

(1) The pygmies live in the equatorial forest belt of central Africa. (2) The Mbuti are hunter-gatherers with the emphasis on hunting. Some bands use nets for trapping game while others rely on individual hunting with bows and arrows. (3) Their myth system is in one sense very pragmatic. According to Barrington Moore, "they have made for themselves no oppressive taboos and have about as light hearted an attitude toward their own social regulation as it is possible to have and still maintain the degree of social cohesion necessary for their particular form of society" (1972:18). They have a great feeling of identification with the forest. It is viewed as the benevolent provider of life, all good things, and the protector from the malevolence of nonforest peoples. Rituals associated with birth, puberty, sickness, and death all symbolically express the identification between forest and pygmy which is also expressed in interpersonal relations through cooperation and mutual aid.

(4) Mbuti bands are composed of several nuclear families. Their kinship system is relatively undeveloped. The extended family is the largest blood-tie group, but the Mbuti use kinship terms to relate to both blood relatives and friends. (5) Babies are breast-fed for between eighteen months and three years. Once a child has been weaned he or she may demand and expect to be disciplined by any adult. From an early age children are encouraged to imitate adult activities. By the age of six both girls and boys contribute to the general economy by helping with camp chores. From nine years of age onwards children participate in hunting in bands which use nets. At this age the form of punishment changes; ridicule replacing physical punishment. "The whole process of child training is characterized by informality and by emphasis on the child's responsibilities to the band as a whole" (Turnbull 1965:306).

(6) Mbuti bands do not appear to experience much interpersonal violence. Fighting does take place between husbands and wives. The violence which does occur has a peculiar property which mitigates lethality.

The human body is in a sense, boru. . . . It is a term seldom used, but the concept affords a firm basis for a code of respect for the body, abuse or mutilation of which may drive away the pepo causing death. Thus physical violence as a means of settling a dispute is abhorred as sacrilege. A sound thrashing is perfectly in order, but any violence that produces blood causes an opening through which pepo *may escape. (Turnbull 1966:250)*

(7) Various conflict resolution processes exist. The most common form is third-party intervention. Young married couples, older married couples, or elders may intervene depending on the nature of the dispute. If any one of these mediators fails then the band as a whole may take part in mediation. Individuals may also mediate in a dispute. One major form of this is intervention by the "clown." The clown is often unmarried but entitled to respect because of prowess in a skill and also because he possesses a certain amount of impartiality. Generally he mediates through the voice of ridicule or he may be singled out by the parties to the dispute as the source of their difference which he accepts without letting it get him down. Should reconciliation at the band level fail it may split into two sections or a family may join another band.

(8) Some division of labour exists in Mbuti society but it is not well defined and does not lead to specialisation. Men, women, and children all participate in the hunt in bands using nets. In archer bands, men hunt without the aid of women and children. All individuals help with the gathering of vegetable foods. There are no unproductive people in Mbuti bands. (9) Political organisation is not differentiated from general social life. The only distinction which the Mbuti make is in respect to their dealings with the Negro cultivators who live in villages on the edges of the forest. (10 and 11) It is only in relation to the village that leadership exists. One particular individual who is a past master at trickery but who is willing to appear subservient to the villagers acts as leader in the exchange relationship. In the village the other pygmies refer to him as the leader but on return-

ing to the forest his leadership ceases. Life in the forest does not produce leadership although older people and those who are considered foremost—by virtue of their prowess—in a particular activity have influence in the band in general. Almost every adult has the right to express himself in almost any activity. It is interesting to note that even in the Negro villages during a crisis all members of the band present participate in decisionmaking even where villagers have poisoned a pygmy to bring about the desired results of sorcery. In this situation the leader does not make the decision to return to the forest, neither does the victim or the immediate family; the whole band does. The reaction of the pygmies to this threat provides an insight into their general outlook: "The pygmy attitude is ambivalent: they do not believe in supernatural powers of this order . . . their reaction is not one of fear, even when their fellows dies, nor is it coloured by the desire for revenge, nor even of anger or hatred" (Turnbull 1965:304).

(12) All members of a band ultimately exercise social control through the medium of public opinion. (13) The major form of sanction related to norm breaking is ridicule and the appeal to the need for mutual cooperation. (14) It would seem that self-respect is fairly evenly distributed between members of Mbuti bands. Women have an equal voice with men in all major decisions. The early encouragement of children to contribute to the general economy probably militates against the effect of feeling inadequate in an adult world. There is, however, one major drawback: marriages are arranged by parents. To offset this constraint the Mbuti practice divorce which does not appear to cause much dislocation in the lives of the individual or of the band.

The Kung Bushmen of the Kalahari Desert

(1) The Kung live in the Kalahari desert of southern Africa. The desert has a mean average height of 3,000 feet above sea level. It is covered in windblown sand to a depth of three to four hundred feet. There are some water holes and a variety of drought-resistant plants, plus numbers of small and large game. (2) The Kung are hunter-gatherers.

They have few material artifacts, the main ones being bows and arrows and digging sticks. (3) The kinship system is of a patrilineal extended family type. When the old father dies, however, that particular extended family ceases to exist; dependents who are left are usually supported by close blood relatives. A band is composed of a number of nuclear families who usually have some blood tie.

(4) The Kung myth system is comparatively well developed. There are two gods, a greater and a lesser one. Neither god is inherently good or evil. The greater god created the world, animals, plants, women, and then men. The Kung pray spontaneously and, in part, it reflects the major preoccupations of life: hunger, sickness, and death. The great god, however, gave healing powers to medicine men who exist solely to cure people and do not engage in witchcraft or sorcery. Social norms that are emphasized are the institutionalised patterns of sharing and their determined striving for cooperation and harmony.

(5) Kung parents are protective, gentle, and permissive in their child training. Parents do not make demands on children to help with work, Marshall maintains, because there are few household tasks to perform because of their low level of technology (1965:264). Lee, on the other hand, maintains that few demands are made on children to contribute to the general economy because a modest work effort by adults produces enough food to support all the members of a band (1968a:39). Children are always kept within sight of adults because of the dangers arising from predators and becoming lost in a featureless landscape. Children are, however, encouraged to imitate adult activities. Marshall sums up child development: "They usually fall in with group life and do what is expected of them *without* uncertainty, frustration, or fear; and expression of resistance or hostility toward their parents, the group, or each other are very much the exception" (1965:264).

(6) Physical violence appears to be rare in Kung society. According to Thomas, the Bushmen deplore bravery and in their legends the heroes are the animals which survive through trickery and deception rather than force (1969:32). The Kung do practice infanticide occasionally and it generally occurs when a woman is already nursing one child. (7) Conflict or wrongdoing is usually judged and controlled through public opinion which is usually expressed through conversation. Occasionally an individual may try to obtain revenge personally. Such individual reprisal is ostracised by the band; it is the band as a whole which mediates and controls conflict. The headman is not a formalised judge of the people in a band. Neither can he punish a wrongdoer.

(8) Division of labour exists mainly along age and sex lines and does not, with the exception of medicine men, give rise to specialisation. The major division occurs over hunting, which is a male activity. Although women gather four-fifths of the food requirement it is the men who are accorded esteem for the production of the remaining fifth in the form of meat. This situation has arisen, according to Lee, because hunting is a less predictable activity than gathering (1968a:40).

(9) There does not appear to be any dividing line between political, social, or religious life. (10) Leadership does exist in Kung bands. Usually it is an inherited position which passes from father to son. But in certain circumstances people may turn away from a headman because another may be more suited. The areas of leadership are, however, circumscribed. The headman personifies the rights of a band over a given geographical area but does not own the land in a private individual capacity. Every family has an inalienable right to the resources on the land. (11) The headman's authority extends only to the coordination of the band's movement in relation to the use of resources. Apart from the decision to move the camp it is individuals who decide on various questions. There is strong informal pressure on men to go and hunt, but it is the individual who decides with whom and where to hunt. Within hunting groups there is no leadership. (12) All the adult members of a band exercise social control, which is usually done through the medium of public opinion. (13) Norms appear to be fairly rigid in Kung society. The very ethos of mutual dependency appears to forestall much norm breaking. (14) Self-respect seems to be fairly evenly distributed. Divorce is a characteristic feature of marital life

although adultery is severely condemned. Sexism does exist in several forms: whereas a man may have more than one wife, women only take one husband at a time. Neither do females appear to hold leadership positions or receive acknowledgement commensurate to the amount of food which they provide.

The Copper Eskimo of Northern Canada

(1) The area which the Copper Eskimo inhabit is part of the arctic tundra. The subsoil is permanently frozen, being covered with snow during the winter months. Temperatures range from $-47°F$ to $+70°F$ in August. (2) Seals and caribou were the most abundant game animals which provided not only meat but also skins for clothing and equipment. Migratory game birds, musk oxen, squirrels, foxes, some brown bears, and salmon, lake trout, and tom cod also supplemented the diet.

(3) The Copper Eskimo conceive of the world as a flat, unbroken expanse of land and sea. Above this real world, supported at its four corners by wooden pillars is another flat level abounding in animals. Above this is another level for the sun, moon, and stars, which are semispiritual beings— the sun being a woman, the moon a man, and the stars either animal or human spirits before they ascended into the sky (Jeness 1922: 179). The world of human existence is partly composed of spirits which may be benign or malevolent. All people have a soul—*nappan*—which is conceived of as the vital life force. The Copper Eskimo practice propitiation of these spirits by offering food and drink. Many phenomena and unusual events are attributed to the intervention of spirits. Such an outlook means the Copper Eskimo is "a true Epicurean, holding that life is a short and uncertain thing at the best, and that the wise man will grasp at what pleasures he can in his course without stopping to ponder over those things that do not directly affect his immediate welfare" (Jeness 1922:229). Relationships between individuals are based on the idea that in theory all the members of a group—a composition of a number of nuclear families—are free and equal. The Copper Eskimo are intolerant of restraint upon individual behav-

iour. Such values mean that their society is a tolerant one. Only individual acts which have a direct effect upon the community as a whole are evaluated in terms of being morally good or bad. The foremost virtues of Copper Eskimo society are: peacefulness, good name, courage, energy, patience and endurance, charity toward both the young and the old, and loyal cooperation. Fair dealing and truthfulness are of secondary importance only while sexual relations are hardly considered as coming within the scope of group consideration. (4) Bands are composed of a number of nuclear families which usually have some blood ties. The composition of a band changes over time.

(5) Children are suckled for three to four years and sometimes for as long as five. Rarely is the child away from its parents during this stage and the mother usually carries it with her wherever she goes. Copper Eskimo children display a certain amount of deference to adults but such behaviour does not imply passivity. Children usually address adults as their equals and will join in any conversation that is taking place and do not hesitate to interrupt and correct their parents (Jeness 1922:169). In general parents do not use corporal punishment in child rearing although "a child may receive a thump with a fist or a blow from the snow duster in the passion of the moment when it will often try to retaliate" (Jeness 1922:169). Usually, however, the shame of public disapproval is sufficient to control a child's behaviour. From the age when children start to move about on their own until puberty they are left without adult interference to a great extent.

(6) Various forms of physical violence have been documented around the Copper Eskimo. They practice infanticide for material and social reasons—both the parents of a newborn child must wish to bring it up, otherwise the child is abandoned. Some physical punishment is used in child rearing but it is not consistently used as part of an established practice. Homicide does occur and Rasmussen (1932:17) intimates that it is quite frequent, a point reinforced by Palmer (1965:322). Physical violence also occurs among marriage partners although men appear to use it more frequently. Much of the violence appears to be

spontaneous rather than premeditated. (7) Conflict resolution processes in Copper Eskimo bands are generally informal and take place at the interpersonal level. Only in rare instances will the band as a whole engage in joint action against an individual, leading to that person's exclusion from the group. The only remedy for minor offences such as theft or the abduction of a wife is for the individual to extract personally compensation or vengeance. It is fairly common for murderers to go unpunished but where they are punished it is always a close relative of the deceased who is responsible for retribution. This situation does not, however, lead to a hereditary vendetta system.

(8) Division of labour occurs mainly along age and sex lines. Heavier work and hunting tend to devolve on males while women are responsible for all the domestic tasks. Some younger women do, however, hunt. In the caribou drives all the band participates either in the killing or the beating. Specialisation appears to extend only to shamanism and even here individual shamans have to provide the bulk of their own material needs. (9 and 10) There appear to be no socially coercive organisations basing their compliance on power in Copper Eskimo bands. Similarly there is no hierarchy. Certain individuals may have influence but it is restricted in application and declines with old age. (11) All adults appear to participate directly in general group discussions; women apparently being as vociferous as men in the dance house and on caribou drives. (12 and 13) Only in extreme cases where an individual's behaviour becomes a threat to the group as a whole will collective action ensue; in all other situations people mind their own business even to the extent of quietly standing by and witnessing a robbery or a murder (Jeness 1922:235).

(14) It appears that all men have a relatively equal amount of self-respect as do women between themselves. While, according to Jeness, "marriage involves no subjection on the part of the woman" (1922;162), he mentions cases where wives are beaten by their husbands for failing to perform, in the husbands' opinion, their tasks sufficiently quickly. But in general women participate as freely as do men in various aspects of social life. Shamanism, for example, is open to women as well as men.

The Hutterites of North America

(1) The Hutterites live in North America in both the United States and Canada in temperate grassland areas. (2) They maintain themselves by mixed agricultural production. The surplus which they produce is sold and used to buy in various types of equipment and clothing and to establish new colonies. (3 and 4) Hutterites are extremely religious in a Western sense. Their religious belief system is the basis of their whole material culture. Absolute authority resides in a supernatural being—God—who created everything. It is thought that human nature has a natural carnal tendency which can only be overcome by continued submission to God's will through communal living. "Self-surrender, not self-development is the divine order" (Hostetler and Huntington 1967:15). Natural carnality is overcome by teaching children the divine discipline, and until they are capable of self-control, obedience to elders. Male dominance in the culture is reflected in the creation of the universe. The male is thus the religious example and women are required to be submissive and obedient to men.

(5) The socialisation of children cannot be characterised in terms other than authoritarian. The premise of child development is that they are expected to behave badly because they have not yet learned to cope with their carnal desires. Part of the punishment for misdemeanour is the instilling of the need to try harder in the future. This does not mean that there is no physical punishment, the reverse is in fact prevalent. "Punishment is usually physical, arbitrary, and inconsistent, and, from the child's point of view, often unpredictable" (Hostetler and Huntington 1967:61). Much of the child's life is spent in hands other than those of its parents: with babysitters, adults in general, the kindergarten, the German school, and the English school. Children do not take their meals with adults—who eat communally—but are fed at home.

(6) The only physical violence in Hutterite communities occurs—apart from the disciplining of children by adults—between the children. This plays an important role in the socialisation of the children as Hostetler and Huntington point out.

> *Much of the children's play is physically rigorous and often rough. . . . They fight hard, quickly and quietly. They vie with one another, showing no physical fear of jumping off high places or pushing one another in front of the tractor. Adults generally ignore the children's dangerous games. . . . The free play of school children reinforces community values: the children learn to ignore physical discomfort and fear of injury and to minimise the importance of the body; the changing play groups teach the unpleasantness of being excluded (1967:72–73).*

(7) Given that a Hutterite colony is structured hierarchically, conflict resolution processes tend to be a set of decisions handed down from above. The preacher often has the task of smoothing over differences. The executive council also adjudicates in interpersonal disputes. Some potential conflict situations are structured in a random fashion as for example when a colony divides to create a new one. Who stays and who goes is done by selection from a hat. (8) There is a definite division of labour on age and sex lines. Women work predominantly in the communal kitchen and look after the hens and geese. During the busy harvesting period they also help in the fields. Men work solely with the larger animals and the land. In the kitchen and in the fields there is a hierarchy; and with the men there is also specialisation of labour. (9) It appears that Hutterites do not differentiate political and social activities and forms. Their distinction is between worldly (material) existence and spiritual life.

(10) Only baptised males are eligible for departmental positions such as cattleman, pigman, or shoemaker. Between five and seven of the baptised men are elected to form an executive council. These men hold the key colony positions including first and second preacher, householder, and field manager. The executive makes decisions concerning colony life. The preacher holds the highest leadership position but his actions are subject to review by the council. The preacher has no formal training and is elected by lot from nominations of his own colony. He does not gain full power until after several years of proven leadership; he can be removed should his conduct meet with general disapproval. (11) All baptised males of a colony exercise social control, although it is often delegated to the preacher or executive for more minor breaches of norms. (12) Similarly all baptised males participate in decisionmaking on major policies and determine who will hold the leadership positions. (13) Norms of behaviour are very rigid. This is offset to an extent by the propensity of the Hutterites to forgive individuals for misdemeanours, even where the individual has left the colony to live in the world outside. The deciding factor in forgiveness appears to be repentance on the part of the individual concerned.

(14) The distribution of self-respect appears to be highly skewed. The Hutterite ideology creates its own feudal structure. God is at the top, then men who preside over women, who together control children, all of whom dominate nature. As was seen above, child training is authoritarian and punishment can be arbitrary. Women do not participate in deciding colony affairs either by voting or by holding leadership positions. Sexism exists in a blatant form where women are believed to be intellectually and physically inferior to men and, whereas men reflect some of God's glory, women have weakness (Hostetler and Huntington 1967:30). This has given rise to male and female subcultures. While men attempt to avoid confrontation with the colony's power structure, women often complain because they have little to lose. The net result is a condition where a woman "often projects her annoyance and mildly dislikes men as a group" (Hostetler and Huntington 1967:30).

The Islanders of Tristan da Cunha

(1) They inhabit the island of Tristan da Cunha which is located in the South Atlantic Ocean. It includes two smaller islands within reach of rowing boat. It has a mild wet windy climate. (2) The economy of Tristan has taken three distinct forms

since its initial colonisation in the early nineteenth century. During the nineteenth century it was based primarily on barter with passing ships, fresh vegetables and meat being traded for items which the islanders could not produce themselves. From about 1915 to 1940, with the end of sailing ships, Tristan was almost totally isolated from the outside world. In this period a subsistence economy developed based on fishing, farming, gathering, and earlier hunting. Gradually after 1945 a money economy was introduced via a South African fishing company and later by various public works instituted by the British government. The islanders have always been dependent on the outside for items such as rope, canvas, wood, flour, sugar, salt, tea, and coffee. While at one stage the introduction of a money economy appeared to threaten the core values of the community, the islanders have managed to adopt it to their own ends. "The islanders refused to become 'chained to the labour market.' They refused to give up their subsistence economy with its network of reciprocal relations and its independence. These were values that they would not sacrifice for all the affluence and prosperity" (Munch 1971: 306–307).

(3) The islanders have many bilateral kinship ties with neither the male or female line taking precedence. This gives rise to many self-selective labour exchange relationships. The founding ethos of the community was based on the principles of equality, communal ownership, cooperation, and freedom from government control. These founding values are still the predominant ones on the island although communal ownership no longer exists.

(4) Most of the inhabitants are Christians but this does not appear to have a great effect on social organisation (Munch 1964:371; Munch 1971:136—for two different examples). (5) Child-rearing practices on the island have a peculiar nature.

> *The importance attached to the avoidance of open violent display of aggressive feeling among Tristan people is well seen in the ways in which children are taught. . . . Paradoxically it is through threats or acts of physical punishment that children are inculcated with the importance of non-violent behaviour (Loudon 1970:307).*

Parents go to great lengths to remove what they characterise as willful behaviour in children. One of the basic aims in child rearing is to instill patience so that immediate gratification of desires is not expected. To gain this end parents will tease and provoke children into displays of willful behaviour and then physically punish it. There is a graded use of physical punishment which tends to increase in severity with increasing age of the child.

(6) Apart from the physical punishment of children the only other physical violence on Tristan occurs between husband and wife. Furthermore there is no theft, misdemeanor, or disturbances. (7) When some conflicts have arisen on the island individuals have intervened. On only one occasion did an outsider act in this capacity: in 1908 when an Anglican clergyman intervened in a dispute which was not purely internal to the island (Munch 1971:80–81). In fact many of the disputes which arose during the nineteenth century occurred between existing inhabitants and newcomers—generally from shipwrecks. Among the islanders themselves there is little need for third-party intervention and there are even norms militating against it because esteem is accorded to the person who minds his own business and leaves others to do as they please (Munch 1970:1302). Public opinion takes a distinct form on Tristan which Loudon has termed "public teasing," which basically is making jokes at another's expense. Although Loudon identifies this as one of the legitimated forms of hostility, it is interesting to note the issues over which it arises. "Characteristics and tendencies particularly liable to expose people to public ridicule are what may be termed cowardice, laziness, stupidity, and credulity, but above all boastfulness and self importance and over-readiness to push oneself forward" (Loudon 1970:315)[1]—that is, basically all those aspects of personal behaviour which the ethos of the community would define as normatively bad. It is interesting to note the sexism in this situation; women are neither the butt of such teasing nor do they participate in it.

(8) In principle every household is economically self-sufficient. The islanders do, however, cooperate on various tasks. There are those tasks such as crewing a boat which demand cooperation

and others such as berry picking to reduce the tedium. All cooperation is reciprocal. Division of labour exists on age and sex lines but does not appear to lead to occupational specialisation.

(9) Political organisation only exists on Tristan insofar as it has relations with the outside world. Internally there is no leadership or organisation based on power. A person may influence others by example rather than dictum (Munch 1970:1303). There is evidence that political organisations have been formed on two occasions. The first occurred in Britain after evacuation because of volcanic activity. Initially it was a spontaneous outburst against a bureaucrat from Whitehall who maintained that they might not be able to return to Tristan. A petition was then sent to the government and when no reply was forthcoming the islanders held a public meeting. Even in this case they had received encouragement and moral support from outsiders (Munch 1964:374). The second time was after the return to Tristan when all those men working on the new dock spontaneously walked out—under threat of dismissal—in order to travel to Nightingale Island to collect guano.

(10) As was mentioned previously there is no universally recognized hierarchy on Tristan. Church authorities often tried to establish some form of authority but it was usually short-lived and always ignored where possible (Munch 1964:371). (11) Munch also mentions two cases when individuals from within the community attempted to establish themselves as leaders. The islanders spontaneously thwarted these two attempts by simply ignoring the self-styled leaders: "They had received the most severe denunciation this atomistic and pacific community would hand out to anybody: they were ignored, isolated, denied a status in the community, not by communal decree but simply as a consequence of the withdrawal of individual reciprocal relationships" (Munch 1974:256).

(12 and 13) Social control exists only insofar as all the inhabitants of Tristan abide by the norms of the founding charter. The main sanction of social control rests with the withdrawal of individual reciprocal relations. (14) Only tentative comments can be made on the distribution of self-respect. One would expect there to be equality between

men as all have similar tasks to perform with similar resources. Munch does mention one of the more "prominent" families in relation to the meeting in England. Women and children may suffer in this respect. They do not participate in fishing expeditions and women cook for men even during cooperative ventures such as the thatching of a house.

Discussion

The attributes selected for examination in these societies are presented in summary form in Table 1. Although there are differences between these groups a number of patterns emerge from this preliminary sample. It is, however, necessary to consider some other aspects of these societies in order to gain some insight into their internal dynamics.

All of these groups are essentially small, local, face-to-face communities, although some of them exist within a larger cultural milieu—there are, for example, some 40,000 Mbuti Pygmies. The small size of all these societies is a major contributory factor in their open and basically egalitarian decisionmaking and social control processes.

The five traditional groups all experience a changing composition in their membership in the short term. This "flux" derives in part from seasonal–ecological variables and in certain cases from need for collective activity to maintain boundary distinctions (Turnbull 1968a:135).[2] But conflicts within these groups are also partly responsible for personnel changes, fission being used as a dissociative conflict resolution form. The changing composition of these traditional societies is partly responsible for the lack of lineal leadership. To maintain such a system of control would not only be difficult given the large geographical area which these groups cover but in certain circumstances it would stand in the way of "economic" necessity in terms of the production and distribution of food (Fried 1967:106).

The traditional groups produce little or no surplus. As such, material inequality between individuals on a long-term basis is impossible. As a corollary, leadership remains on the level of per-

TABLE 1 Common factors of peaceful societies

Groups / Items	Semai	Siriono	Mbuti	Kung	Copper Eskimo	Hutterites	Tristan
1 Habitat	Tropical rain forest	Tropical rain forest	Tropical rain forest	Hot desert	Arctic tundra	Temperate grassland	Temperate grassland
2 Subsistence	Hunting-gathering, swiddening	Hunting-gathering, swiddening	Hunting-gathering	Hunting-gathering	Hunting, some gathering	Mixed agriculture	Mixed-subsistence agriculture
3 Cosmology	Ideational*	Ideational	Ideational	Ideational	Ideational	Ideational	Idealistic
4 Integration	Kinship and interest	Kinship and interest	Kinship and interest	Kinship and interest	Kinship and interest	Interest and kinship	Interest and kinship
5 Socialisation	Permissive	Permissive	Permissive	Permissive	Permissive	Authoritarian	Authoritarian
6 Physical violence	Little, lethal	Little, non-lethal	Little, non-lethal	Little, lethal	Some, lethal	Some, non-lethal	Some, non-lethal
7 Conflict resolution	Individual and group	Individual, some group	Individual and group	Individual and group	Individual, some group	Group	Individual
8 Division of labour	Yes	Yes	Yes	Yes	Yes	Yes specialisation	Yes
9 Coercive organization	No	No	No	No	No	Perhaps	No
10 Hierarchy	Yes, non-restrictive for males	No	No	Yes, non-restrictive for males	No	Yes, non-restrictive for males	No
11 Decision	All adults	All adults	All adults	All adults	All adults	All male adults	All adults
12 Social control	All	All	All	All	All	All male adults	All adults
13 Forms of social control	Usually psychic	Usually psychic	Usually psychic	Usually psychic	Psychic and physical	Psychic	Psychic
14 Discrimination	Yes	Yes	Yes	Yes	Yes	Yes	Yes

*Used in Sorokin's (1962: 55–102, Vol. I) sense.

sonal authority rather than coercive power because there is no surplus to appropriate and
utilise. According to Fried (1967:117), however, the
first step in the establishment of power-based
leadership is the creation of a centre for the
redistribution of material surplus for the benefit
of the society as a whole (as per the Mountain
Arapesh, Mead 1961:34) rather than an appropri-
ation centre for personal–sectional advancement.
What these groups do produce, however, is distributed equitably. In this context the cases of
Tristan da Cunha and the Hutterites are of importance. Although the domestic mode of production
on Tristan undoubtedly keeps the surplus small,
the more specialised techniques employed by the
Hutterites create a larger one and yet no great
material inequality exists within them. The Hutterites in fact hold their surplus collectively and
use it for the benefit of the group as a whole. It
is interesting to note that both of these groups
were "created"; they were established in the historical past with specific social structures designed to achieve definite goals.

The differences in child-rearing practices
between the traditional and created societies are
open to a number of possible—and contradictory—explanations. Firstly, it could be argued that
the latent "violence" of the created societies—the
existence of surplus which does not produce
material inequality—manifests itself in their authoritarian child rearing methods. Alternatively,
their violent socialisation ways are a product of
their historical background. Their respective conceptions of human nature—natural carnality or
willful behaviour—are only a reflection of their
Western European Christian origin which emphasises control rather than development and as such
directly influences the way they rear their children.
Another possible explanation derives from their
mode of subsistence. Both Tristan da Cunha and
the Hutterites have sedentary farming lifestyles
which are incompatible with independent adven-

turous personalities which permissive child socialisation processes tend to create.

Fortunately this sample of peaceful societies
is not solely composed of hunting-gathering
groups. If it were so composed then the absence
of large structural inequalities might simply be
attributed to this particular level of sociocultural
development. The cases of Tristan da Cunha and
the Hutterites demonstrate that it is possible for a
society to produce a surplus and still retain a fairly
egalitarian social structure which is not maintained
by the use or threat of physical violence.

Conclusion

Any points derived from this small sample of
peaceful societies must necessarily be tentative.
The attributes of the groups considered, however,
do not point toward a basic incompatibility between social justice or equality on the one hand
and an absence of physical violence on the other.
The very idea that the presence of one is the
"price" paid for the absence of the other may
simply be a manifestation of Western—although
now becoming global—culture and its concomitant hierarchical world view.

Much more work is needed on the study of
peaceful patterns of social organisation in terms
of increasing the sample and perhaps more importantly of locating groups where there is sufficient
information for longitudinal studies. Also, compar-
isons with societies which are physically violent
but have basically similar social structures would
possibly aid in identifying factors critical in the
production of peace. This area of study has links
with various other approaches, in particular the
study of futures (e.g., Targ 1971; Weiss 1975). This
type of information would not only provide insights
into how various groups have "achieved" a relatively peaceful lifestyle but also, and perhaps more
importantly, would demonstrate that peace is not a
utopian and by implication unobtainable goal.

The groundwork for this chapter was carried out while I was an
undergraduate in the School for Independent Studies, University
of Lancaster 1974–1975. Many thanks go to my supervisor of that
time, David Osterberg. My thanks also go to my current supervisor
Paul Smoker whose comments encouraged me to rework parts of
the original. Also for various personal friends whose support has
encouraged me to stay with the original idea.

1. A number of authors of works used here (Dentan 1968; Loudon
1970; Chance 1966; Hostetler and Huntington 1967) display a

common tendency to use some form of neo-Freudian drive reduction model of human aggression. Thus, even these peaceful societies, according to this approach, have violence ready to break out. Such a theory of course does little to explain the variance in the distribution of violence between egalitarian band societies and nation-states for example. When dealing with such macro categories of social organisation, hierarchy and compulsive organisation appear to account for a more significant amount of the variance.

2. Contrary to the argument maintaining some form of instinctual disposition to possess land as a part of human inheritance these least complex of societies are not generally territorial in the sense of maintaining an exclusive monopoly over an area of land. Other groups may come and go, and in times of shortage an incumbent band may share the food and water resources with another less fortunate group (Fried 1967:94–98; Lee and Devore 1968a:12).

References

Balicki, A. 1968. "The Netsilik Eskimos: Adaptive Processes." Pp. 78–82, in *Man the Hunter,* edited by Lee and Devore. Chicago: Aldine.

Benedict, R. 1935. *Patterns of Culture.* London: Routledge & Kegan Paul.

Broch, T., and J. Galtung. 1966. "Belligerence among the Primitives." *Jnl. Peace Research* 3:33–45.

Chance, N. A. 1966. *The Eskimo of North Alaska.* New York: Holt, Rinehart & Winston.

Coon, C. S. 1972. *The Hunting Peoples.* London: Cape.

Davie, M. R. 1929. *The Evolution of War: A Study of Its Role in Early Societies.* Port Washington, New York: Kennikat Press, 1968.

Dentan, R. K. 1968. *The Semai: A Non-Violent People of Malaya.* New York: Holt, Rinehart & Winston.

Dole, G. E., and R. L. Carneiro (eds.). 1960. *Essays in the Science of Culture: In Honour of Leslie A. White.* New York: T. Y. Crowell.

Forde, D. C. 1963. *Habitat, Economy and Society: A Geographical Introduction to Ethnology.* New York: Dutton & Co.

Fourie, L. 1960. "The Bushmen of South-West Africa." Pp. 87–95 in *Cultures and Societies of Africa,* edited by S. and P. Ottenberg. New York: Random House.

Fried, M. H. 1967. *The Evolution of Political Society: An Essay in Political Anthropology.* New York: Random House.

Friedl, E. 1975. *Women and Men: An Anthropologist's View.* New York: Holt, Rinehart & Winston.

Fromm, E. 1973. *The Anatomy of Human Destructiveness.* New York: Holt, Rinehart & Winston.

Galtung, J. 1969. "Violence, Peace and Peace Research." *Jnl. Peace Research* 6:167–191.

Gardner, P. M. 1968. "Discussion: Primate Behaviour and the Evolution of Aggression." Pp. 338–344, in *Man the Hunter,* edited by Lee and Devore.

Gjessing, G. 1967. "Ecology and Peace Research." *Jnl. Peace Research* 4:125–139.

Godlier, M. 1975. "Modes of Production, Kinship, and Demographic Structures." Pp. 3–27, in *Marxist Analyses and Social Anthropology,* edited by M. Bloch. London: Malaby Press.

Holmberg, A. R. 1966. *Nomads of the Longbow: The Siriono of Eastern Bolivia.* Natural History Press.

Honigman, J. J. 1968. "Interpersonal Relations in Atomistic Communities." *Human Organisation* 27:220–229.

Hostetler, J. A. 1974. *Hutterite Society.* Baltimore and London: The Johns Hopkins University Press.

————, and G. E. Huntington. 1967. *The Hutterites of North America.* New York: Holt, Rinehart & Winston.

Jeness, D. 1922. *The Life of the Copper Eskimo.* Report of the Canadian Arctic Expedition 1913–1918, Vol. XIIa. Ottawa: F. A. Acland.

————. 1946. *Material Culture of the Copper Eskimo.* Report of the Canadian Arctic Expedition 1913–1918, Vol. 16. Ottawa: E. Clouter.

Lee, R. B. 1968a. "What Hunters Do for a Living: Or How to Make Out on Scarce Resources." Pp. 30–48, in *Man the Hunter,* edited by Lee and Devore.

————. 1968b. "Discussion: Predation and Warfare." Pp. 157–158, in *Man the Hunter,* edited by Lee and Devore.

————, and I. Devore (eds.). 1968. *Man the Hunter.* Chicago: Aldine.

————, and I. Devore. 1968a. "Problems in the Study of Hunter-Gatherers." Pp. 3–12, in *Man the Hunter,* edited by Lee and Devore.

Lenski, G. 1966. *Power and Privilege: An Essay in the Theory of Social Stratification.* New York: McGraw Hill.

Loudon, J. B. 1970. "Teasing and Socialisation on Tristan da Cunha." Pp. 293–331, in *Socialisation: The Approach from Anthropology,* edited by P. Mayer. London: Tavistock.

Marshall, L. 1965. "The Kung Bushmen of the Kalahari Desert." Pp. 241–278, in *Peoples of Africa,* edited by J. L. Gibbs. New York: Holt, Rinehart & Winston.

Mead, M. 1961. *Cooperation and Conflict among Primitive Peoples.* Boston: Beacon Press.

————. 1972. *Culture and Commitment: A Study of the Generation Gap.* London: Panther Books Ltd.

————. 1973. "Warfare Is Only an Invention Not a Biological Necessity." Pp. 112–118, in *Peace & War,* edited by C. R. Beitz and T. Herman. San Francisco: Freeman & Co. Institute Press.

Moore, B., Jr. 1972. *Reflections on the Causes of Human Misery and upon Certain Proposals to Eliminate Them.* London: Allen Lane, The Penguin Press.

Munch, P. A. 1964. "Culture and Superculture in a Displaced Community: Tristan da Cunha." *Ethnology* 3:369–376.

————. 1970. "Economic Development and Conflicting Values: A Social Experiment in Tristan da Cunha." *American Anthropologist* 72: 1300–1318.

————. 1971. *Crisis in Utopia: The Ordeal of Tristan da Cunha.* New York: T. Y. Crowell.

————. 1974. "Anarchy and Anomie in an Anarchistic Community." *Man* 9:243–261.

Otterbein, K. F. 1970. *The Evolution of War: A Cross-Cultural Study.* Human Relations Area Files Press.

Palmer, S. 1965. "Murder and Suicide in Forty Non-Literate Societies." *Jnl. Criminal Law, Criminology, and Police Science.* 56:320–324.

Rasmussen, K. 1932. *Intellectual Culture of the Copper Eskimo.* Report of the Fifth Thule Expedition to Arctic North America, Vol. IX. Copenhagen:

Gyldendalske Boghandel, Nordisk Forlag.

Sahlins, M. 1974. *Stone-Age Economics.* London: Tavistock.

Schapera, I. 1930. *The Khoisan Peoples of South Africa: Bushmen and Hottentots.* London: Routledge & Kegan Paul, 1965.

Service, E. R. 1966. *The Hunters.* Englewood Cliffs, N.J.: Prentice-Hall.

Sipes, R. G. 1973. "War, Sports and Aggression: An Empirical Test of Two Rival Theories." *American Anthropologist* 75:64–86.

Sorokin, P. 1962. *Social and Cultural Dynamics.* 4 vols. New York: Bedminster Press.

Sweet, L. E. 1973. "Culture and Aggressive Action." Pp. 325–344, in *Aggression & Evolution,* edited by C. M. Otten. Lexington, Mass.: Xerox College Publishing.

Targ, H. R. 1971. "Social Science and a New Social Order." *Jnl. Peace Research* 8:207–220.

Thomas, E. 1969. *The Harmless People.* Penguin.

Turnbull, C. M. 1965. "The Mbuti Pygmies of the Congo." Pp. 279–318, in *Peoples of Africa,* edited by J. L. Gibbs. New York: Holt, Rinehart & Winston.

————. 1966. *Wayward Servants: The Two Worlds of the African Pygmy.* London: Eyre & Spottiswoode.

————. 1968a. "The Importance of Flux in Two Hunting Societies." Pp. 132–137, in *Man the Hunter,* edited by Lee and Devore.

————. 1968b. "Discussion: Resolving Conflicts by Fission." P. 156, in *Man the Hunter,* edited by Lee and Devore.

————. 1968c. "Discussion: Primate Behaviour and Human Aggression." Pp. 338–343, in *Man the Hunter,* edited by Lee and Devore.

Watanabe, H. 1968. "Subsistence and Ecology among Northern Food Gatherers." Pp. 69–77 in *Man the Hunter,* edited by Lee and Devore.

Weiss, T. G. 1975. "The Tradition of Philosophical Anarchism and Future Directions in World Policy." *Jnl. Peace Research* 12:1–17.

Wright, Q. 1964. *A Study of War.* Chicago: University of Chicago Press (abridged ed.).

DOES SOCIAL INEQUALITY ENCOURAGE WAR?

Inequality and Imperialism: Is Socialism the Solution?

Thomas E. Weisskopf

Introduction

"Would a Socialist America pursue a foreign policy fundamentally different from the foreign policy pursued by a Capitalist America?" asks Robert W. Tucker in a critical analysis of the views of the American "radical left."[1] His answer to this rhetorical question is a resounding "no."[2] In this essay I shall seek to demonstrate that the appropriate answer is "yes."

Almost a decade of overt war in Indochina; military interventions in Greece, Iran, Lebanon, the Congo, Cuba, the Dominican Republic, Colombia, Guatemala, Panama, Bolivia, China, Korea and Thailand; military missions throughout most of the "free world"; and American economic dominance of countless Third World countries have combined to impress upon all but the most recalcitrant observer the truth in the assertion that in the postwar period the United States has been a formidably imperialist power. Indeed, a brief review of American history points to a pattern of imperialist behavior that goes back long before the

postwar period to the very beginning of the federal republic.[3] That the United States is now and has long been an imperialist power is a proposition that is no longer subject to serious debate. Very much a matter of dispute, however, are the sources of American imperialism.

For Tucker and most of his "orthodox" colleagues, American imperialism is attributable primarily to the international competition that results from the existence of a system of geographically distinct societies claiming independent political sovereignty.[4] The internal socio-economic organization of a society has very little to do with its propensity for imperialist behavior. A putative Socialist America would have just as imperialist a foreign policy as does the existing Capitalist America.

For the "radical left" (and for this author in particular), American imperialism results to a significant extent from the fact that the United States is a capitalist society.[5] Radical theorists argue that the internal socio-economic organization of a society does make a great deal of difference, and

Reprinted by permission of the publisher, from *Testing Theories of Economic Imperialism* by Steven J. Rosen & James R. Kurth (Lexington, MA: Lexington Books, D.C. Heath and Co. © 1974 D.C. Heath & Company).
The author is particularly grateful to Sam Bowles, Noam Chomsky, Arthur MacEwan, and Harry Magdoff, who, among other friends, provided helpful criticism of two earlier versions of this chapter.

that the replacement of Capitalist America by a Socialist America would significantly reduce the extent of American imperialism.

To argue the radical case,[6] I begin by defining clearly what I mean by the term "imperialism" and by listing as comprehensively as possible various potential motivations for imperialism. In the next section I define the terms "capitalism" and "socialism" and examine some of the significant differences between the two types of social systems. I then go on to consider the extent to which potential motivations for imperialism depend upon whether a society is capitalist or socialist. Finally I conclude in the last section that the radical view of American imperialism is indeed a valid one, and I proceed to examine some of the implications of that conclusion.

Alternative Motivations for Imperialism

The word "imperialism" is notoriously imprecise. So many writers have used it in so many different ways and for so many different purposes that it is incumbent upon anyone intending to discuss the subject to define quite clearly what is to be understood by the term.[7]

In this essay I will use the term imperialism in a non-Marxist sense[8] according to the following definition: imperialism is activity on the part of a national government that involves the use of power (or the threat of its use) to establish or maintain a relationship of domination or control over the government or (some of) the people of another nation or territory over which the imperialist government has no traditional claim to sovereignty. This definition deliberately focuses attention on the activity of government agencies rather than private organizations, thereby ignoring an important but separable component of American imperialism.[9] Included among the imperialist activities of government agencies are not only the most obvious instances of territorial annexation and military occupation but also any use of military, economic, or diplomatic power to establish, maintain, or expand spheres of control over foreigners.

In short, imperialism is defined here essentially as an expansionary foreign policy.[10]

Every imperialist activity involves some expenditure of energy and resources by the imperialist government. The expenditure may be trivial—as in the case of diplomatic pressure—or it may be very substantial—as in the case of military intervention. If such expenditure is undertaken by a government, it must be done with the expectation that some kind of benefits will result from it. Accordingly, one can distinguish alternative motivations for imperialism according to the alternative kinds of interests that might be promoted by imperialist activity.

In analyzing alternative interests in imperialism, I will distinguish carefully between a "national interest" and a "class interest." I will say that there is a national interest in an imperialist activity when the activity is expected to benefit the imperialist nation as a whole, in the sense that the aggregate benefits to citizens of the imperialist nation are expected to exceed the aggregate costs. I will say that there is a class interest in an imperialist activity when it is expected to result in net benefits for a particular class of people from among the citizens of the imperialist nation. If there is a national interest in an imperialist activity, there is bound to be also at least one class interest, although there may be other classes for whom the anticipated net benefits are negative. On the other hand, if there is a class interest in an imperialist activity, there may or may not also be a national interest. In the following pages I will review as comprehensively as possible the major national and class interests in imperialism that have been suggested explicitly or implicitly by both radical and orthodox theorists. In so doing, I will attempt to determine which of these interests could conceivably motivate imperialist activity by the government of a modern industrialized society such as the United States.

A major national interest in imperialism that is always cited and most strongly emphasized by orthodox theorists is to enhance *national security*.[11] It is argued that every nation has a collective interest in defending its territory against possible attack by other nations that may be or may become hostile and aggressive. Nations that are sufficiently powerful to engage in imperialist activity will find that efforts to control other nations can contribute significantly to national security by improving the military posture of the imperialist nation vis-à-vis its actual or potential enemies. Although there is good reason to suspect that national security considerations are often invoked to justify an imperialist policy motivated by other concerns, there is no reason to doubt that a modern nation state does have an interest in national security that can independently motivate imperialist activity.

A second possible national interest in imperialism is one that is suggested in the work of many radical theorists: to maintain *macro-economic prosperity*—that is; to avoid economic crises that threaten the viability of the whole economy.[12] A variety of different arguments have been advanced to explain how the pursuit of an imperialist foreign policy can help to maintain the prosperity of an economy. The arguments are usually presented in the context of capitalist economies, although some of them may conceivably apply to non-capitalist economies as well. In the following paragraphs I shall discuss alternative lines of reasoning that have been developed to link imperialism with macro-economic prosperity.

The first line of reasoning is derived from the classical theory of underconsumption and associated with the work of Hobson, Luxemburg, and—apparently erroneously—Lenin.[13] Although various writers have expressed the basic argument in different ways, it can be summarized in a consistent and logically valid form as follows: (1) there is a chronic tendency in a capitalist economy for aggregate demand to be insufficient to absorb all of the output that is produced; (2) there is consequently a continual need to find new outlets for surplus production in order to avoid an economic crisis; (3) foreign countries and territories represent important potential markets for the domestic surplus; and (4) an imperialist foreign policy provides access to these markets for the imperialist country. . . .

■ ■ ■

A variant of this line of reasoning can be formulated by extending the work of modern Marxists on the problem of surplus absorption in a capitalist economy.[14] This variant begins with the same premise of underconsumption or insufficient aggregate demand. However the solution to the problem is attributed not to net capital exports but to military expenditures. In this case, a motivation for imperialism arises from the need to legitimize such expenditures: an interventionist foreign policy creates a climate in which it is easy to justify the maintenance of a large military establishment and high levels of military spending.

Apart from arguments linking imperialism to macro-economic prosperity via the need to maintain a high level of aggregate demand, there is an alternative line of reasoning that focuses directly on a need to maintain access to foreign economies. . . . [Access to foreign economies is necessary in order to assure profitable investments abroad, and to obtain imported raw materials—EDS.]*

■ ■ ■

The desire to maintain macro-economic prosperity and avoid major crises is not the only possible national economic interest in imperialism. Most writers would agree that imperialism may be motivated on national economic grounds simply in order to increase the *aggregate economic gains* accruing to the imperialist nation from its economic relations with other nations. The conditions under which private or public enterprises in one nation enter into trade or investment activities with or in other nations are obviously susceptible to the exercise of power. To the extent that one nation can exercise some degree of control over another, there are a variety of ways in which it can secure greater economic gains for its nationals than would be possible under a relationship of equality. The imperialist nation can use its power to improve the terms of trade and thereby lower the effective

---

*[Exporting domestic commodities may also be necessary—EDS.]

price of various imported commodities; it can enlarge export markets and increase the country's export earnings; it can secure more favorable conditions for its investors and thereby increase their repatriated profits; and in general it can open up new trade and investment opportunities in areas, which for whatever reasons might otherwise not be receptive to economic intercourse. In all such cases there are of course particular classes of people who have the most to gain from imperialism, and there are others who may have something to lose. But there is always a potential national interest—in addition to a class interest—so long as the overall benefits realized by citizens of the imperialist nation exceed the associated costs.

A fourth kind of national interest in imperialism that has been suggested by some writers is based on a generalized *missionary spirit*.[15*] It is argued that the people of a nation can be so imbued with a belief in the desirability of their own institutions and values that they feel morally justified—indeed morally obliged—to extend their system to other parts of the world, even where this requires the use of power to impose the system on recalcitrant foreigners. The gains arising from imperialism of this kind are neither military-strategic nor economic; they are psychic gains involving a sense of satisfaction derived from promoting (what is perceived to be) a better world.

It is certainly true that many governments have sought to represent their imperialist activity as being in the best interest of the people upon whom it is practiced. As in the case of alleged national security interests, one suspects that this kind of argument often serves merely as a legitimizing cover for other interests with less widespread acceptability. But it is nonetheless plausible to suggest that popular belief in the "civilizing mission" of one's country can act as an independent stimulus to imperialist activity.

A final possible national interest in imperialism resembles the missionary spirit in that it involves psychic rather than military-strategic or economic gains: this arises simply from a general-

ized *urge to dominate*. Proponents of this view often contend that there *is inherent in human nature an aggressive instinct that applies both on an individual and a group or national level*.[16] People derive satisfaction from domination—from being "number one." Hence nations that can develop and apply the power to dominate other nations will be inclined to do so if only to satisfy the atavistic urge among their people to achieve a position of supremacy over others. Whether or not one considers the urge to dominate a natural human instinct, one can argue that in certain historical periods, it can help to motivate imperialist activity.

Among possible class interests in imperialism one can identify first the interest of the dominant classes of any unequal society in promoting their own *social legitimacy*.[17] There are several ways in which imperialist actions might serve to legitimate the dominance of some classes over others within a nation. By generating or accentuating antagonisms between the nation and other nations on an international level, imperialism can deflect attention and concern away from internal conflicts between dominant and subordinate classes and rally all people behind the leadership of the dominant classes. By maintaining or extending the geographic spread of institutions and values characteristic of the imperialist nation and by limiting the spread of alternative institutions and values, imperialism can discourage the notion that there are any real alternatives to the existing system with its particular class relations. Indeed a national "missionary spirit," as well as excessive concern over "national security," may actually result from the efforts of dominant classes to promote their own social legitimacy on an ideological plane.

A second possible class interest in imperialism may arise from the desire of civilian or military government bureaucracies for *organizational expansion*.[18] Members of virtually any organization have something to gain from an expansion in the volume of activity for which the organization is responsible: it leads to more promotions, more

---

*[Footnotes have been renumbered because portions of the original reading have been deleted—Eds.]

prestige, more power, if not more pay. This general phenomenon is no less true of the civilian and military agencies of government that are directly involved in imperialist activity. Such agencies will have a natural inclination to favor the expansion of imperialism wherever it is at issue.

One last major class interest in imperialism, most frequently stressed by radical writers, arises from opportunities for particular firms, agencies, or classes to increase their *particular economic gains* from international economic relations. Such opportunities are as varied as the opportunities cited earlier for increasing the aggregate economic gains from international economic relations, the only difference being that in this case there may be losses to other groups within the society that outweigh the gains from imperialism. Improving terms of trade, widening export markets, providing privileged access to raw materials, securing better conditions for investors, opening up new areas for trade and investment—any and all of these—can lead to economic gains for particular firms, agencies, or classes. They will therefore be motivated to press for imperialist acts to achieve such results, whether or not the net benefits to the nation as a whole are positive.

The economic interest of private enterprise in imperialist activity is much greater than might appear from current figures on foreign economic involvement. Not only do those firms that have invested abroad, that export to foreign markets, or that import from foreign sources stand to gain by having governmental power exercised on their behalf to help shape the terms and conditions of foreign economic relations, but private firms without any past involvement in foreign economic relations may nonetheless look forward to future opportunities made possible by imperialist actions that help to preserve or to extend the areas open to private enterprise. And even those firms that never trade or invest abroad stand to gain to the extent that imperialism promotes an increasing internationalization of the division of labor, for this places the relatively scarce labor supply of an industrial economy in increasing competition with the relatively abundant labor supply of less industrialized foreign economies.[19]

When there is a national interest in an imperialist activity, there is a *prima facie* motivation for the government to undertake it. The government will refrain from the imperialist activity only if there is a particular class (or combination of classes) that anticipates net losses and also has sufficiently disproportionate power to prevent the government from undertaking the activity, even though the anticipated net gains to other classes in the society exceed the anticipated net losses to the losing classes. But such circumstances are unlikely to arise no matter what the distribution of power in a society. For in the unlikely event that potential losers from an imperialist activity actually have more power than the potential gainers and are prepared to exercise that power, the gainers will be in a position to compensate the losers for their losses while still maintaining some net gains. Hence one would not expect any national government to refrain from imperialism when a national interest is really at stake.

When there is no national interest in a potential imperialist activity, there may nonetheless be a motivation for the government to undertake it if (1) there is a particular class (or combination of classes) with an interest in the activity *and* (2) the power of the interested class(es) is sufficiently disproportionate to induce the government to undertake the activity even though other classes stand to lose more than the particular class(es) stand to gain by it. These class interests in imperialism can but need not necessarily motivate a government to undertake imperialist activity. The extent to which they will do so depends upon the distribution of power among various classes in the society in question.

Capitalism and Socialism

Like "imperialism," "capitalism" and "socialism" are words that mean many different things to many different people; hence it is important to define clearly how I intend to use the terms. I shall begin by juxtaposing definitions for capitalism and socialism and then go on to analyze some important distinctions between the two.

Capitalism is a form of socio-economic organization (or a "mode of production," to use the Marxist term) that is characterized by *all* of the following conditions.[20]

1. *Private ownership of the means of production.* Most of the productive assets of the society are owned by private individuals; private owners of any asset have a special (if not exclusive) claim on any income generated by the asset and on decision-making with respect to the use of the asset.

2. *Proletarianization of the work force.* Most of the population has virtually no source of income other than that resulting from the sale of its labor services in a labor market. It follows that income generated by productive assets (as well as the ownership of such assets) is concentrated among a small proportion of the population.

3. *Hierarchical control of the production process.* Productive activity is carried out by units of enterprise in which decision-making is the prerogative of (at most) a few top owners and managers, while the great majority of workers have no involvement in the decision-making process.

4. *Individual material gain incentives.* Work is motivated primarily by the prospect of material rewards in the form of higher income for the individual worker.

Socialism I shall define as a form of socio-economic organization characterized by four sharply contrasting conditions.[21]

1. *Public ownership of the means of production.* Most of the productive assets of the society are owned by public agencies accountable to the society as a whole, so that everyone shares in income generated by such assets and in the control of decisions with respect to their use.

2. *Emancipation of the proletariat.* Every member of the society is guaranteed an adequate level of living (given the overall economic constraints and cultural norms of the society), and no person receives a substantial amount of income from privately owned productive assets.

3. *Participatory control of the production process.* All persons working in an enterprise participate in the process of decision-making (within the constraints set by the accountability of the enterprise to the society as a whole).

4. *Collective and/or non-material gain incentives.* Work is motivated primarily by (a) the prospect of material gains for one's whole community or one's whole society rather than for oneself alone; and/or (b) the prospect of non-material gains for oneself (e.g., honor or esteem from one's peers, or satisfaction from the work activity itself).

There can be no doubt that the four conditions associated with my definition of capitalism are satisfied in many parts of the contemporary world, notably in the United States, Canada, Western Europe, Japan, Australia, and New Zealand. It is much more difficult to find any contemporary examples of countries displaying the conditions by which I have characterized socialism. In many of the contemporary countries conventionally labeled "socialist," the means of production are predominantly under public ownership, each person is assured a modest level of living, and no person receives a large amount of income from privately owned productive assets. But even where productive assets are under public ownership and not the source of large private income flows, it is rarely the case that everyone shares in the control of decisions with respect to the use of those assets. Moreover, few "socialist" countries show much evidence of participatory control of the production process or the use of collective and/or non-material gain incentives. In these latter respects, China is probably the country that has progressed furthest toward socialism,[22] but even China is only partially socialist in the sense in which I have defined the term.

The fact that there are no contemporary examples of a fully socialist society makes it difficult to test empirically the hypothesis that a socialist society is significantly less imperialist than a capitalist society. But it remains possible at a theoretical level to reach some relevant conclusions. To develop the argument, I turn now to consider some important consequences of the different conditions defining capitalist and socialist modes of production.

The viability of any social system requires that there be a prevailing set of institutionalized values that encourage patterns of behavior consistent with the smooth functioning of the system.[23] These values are an essential complement to the basic socio-economic institutions that define the system. In the case of capitalism, the successful operation of individual material gain incentives requires that people behave as "homo economicus," the economically rational man.[24] Homo economicus strives for individual gain; he seeks to maximize his money income in order to satisfy his wants; he is concerned about the extrinsic rewards for his productive activity rather than the intrinsic quality of the activity itself. Such behavior must be sustained by a set of values that emphasize the importance of the individual rather than the larger community, that urge competition rather than cooperation, and that stress the primacy of material goods and services (purchasable with money income) for satisfying human needs and promoting human welfare. These capitalist values place a tremendous premium on increasing the supply of marketable goods and services available to the society, while other conceivable social goals—that is, greater equity, development of more meaningful and less fragmented communities, improvement of the quality of the work experience, greater diversification of economic activity at an individual, local or national level—are viewed as subordinate to the primary goal of economic growth.

In the case of socialism a very different set of institutionalized values would be essential to the functioning of the system. For collective incentives to replace individual incentives, the socialist value system would have to emphasize the importance of the community rather than the individual and to urge cooperation rather than competition. The social goal of greater equity would be much more important than under capitalism (and the goal of economic growth would be correspond-

ingly less important) because of the need to sustain a sense of common participation by everyone in both the responsibilities and the privileges of membership in the society. For non-material gains to replace material gains, the socialist value system would have to de-emphasize the significance of money income and the consumption of material goods and services while emphasizing the rewards deriving from the esteem of one's peers and from the intrinsic process of work itself. Such an emphasis would also tend to devalue the goal of economic growth in relation to other social goals such as the development of more meaningful communities, improvement in the quality of work, and diversification of economic activity.

Apart from the significant differences in the value systems associated with the capitalist and the socialist modes of production, there are important differences in both the process and the outcome of income distribution. Private ownership of the means of production and reliance on individual material gain incentives imply that in a capitalist society income distribution is linked directly to the process of production.[25] Property income and labor income are distributed to the owners of productive assets and the sellers of labor essentially according to the market-valued contribution of their assets and their labor to the output of goods and services. Income distribution is therefore not a matter for political determination by the society as a whole; instead, it emerges largely from the process whereby the market mechanism allocates resources to production. This process of income distribution is bound to create great inequalities of income. Not only does the small proportion of the population that owns most of the means of production receive the lion's share of property income, but also labor income is very unequally distributed because of the need to allocate and motivate work through differential economic rewards. Hence, a capitalist society is inherently an economically unequal society.

In a socialist society, by contrast, the process of income distribution is largely divorced from the process of production. Productive assets are mainly under public ownership and the disposition of any income generated by the assets is a matter for political decision-making. And to the extent that work is motivated by collective and/or non-material incentives, the income accruing to workers need not bear any relationship to the quantity or quality of labor provided by the worker. As a result, income can and must be distributed under socialism by a consciously political mechanism. Given the guarantee of a basic level of living for everyone, the absence of large private claims to income generated by productive assets, and the greater importance of equity to the functioning of the system, the outcome of the process of income distribution in a socialist society is bound to be much more equal than in a capitalist society.

A final important distinction between capitalist and socialist societies stems from differences both in the outcomes of the process of income distribution and in the nature of control of productive enterprises. Under capitalism, a high degree of economic inequality results from the process of income distribution and a high degree of social inequality results from the hierarchical control of productive activity. Economic and social inequality (which are bound to be highly correlated) imply political inequality. A society that is predicated upon significant economic and social differentials is a society in which there cannot be genuine democracy, in the sense of equal participation in political decision-making by those affected by the decisions. So long as some people have much greater access to economic resources than others, they can have much greater influence on political decision-making;[26] and so long as the structure of decision-making at the workplace is highly authoritarian, one cannot expect the structure of decision-making at the community or national level to be egalitarian.[27] Thus capitalism is fundamentally incompatible with democracy.

Under socialism there is much less economic and social inequality than under capitalism. Both income and the control of productive activity at the enterprise level are shared more equally. It follows that socialist societies can and will be more democratic than capitalist societies at all levels of decision-making.

The Socio-Economic Roots of Imperialism

We may now return to the question posed at the beginning of this essay and consider whether a Socialist America would be significantly less imperialist than a Capitalist America. In the following pages I will examine each of the motivations for imperialism identified in the previous section as potentially relevant to a modern industrialized society in order to determine if and how their significance depends on whether the society is capitalist or socialist. I will first consider the relative strength of national and class interests in imperialism under capitalism and socialism, and I will then turn to differences in the distribution of *power* that affect the extent to which class interests in imperialism are translated into government policy.

Among national interests in imperialism the first potentially relevant one is the interest in *national security*. To the extent that this interest is not merely an ideological cover for other interests, it is one that arises as a result of potential external threats to a nation. The existence and strength of such threats depend upon the disposition of foreign powers towards the nation in question. Whatever the character of the nation's internal socio-economic organization, there is always a possibility that foreign powers will prove hostile. So long as the world is divided into nation-states without an accepted and respected superior authority to maintain world peace, each individual nation-state will have some justifiable concern about its national security. Hence the national security interest in imperialism is one that would not seem to be dependent in any significant sense on whether a society is capitalist or socialist.

The second national interest in imperialism discussed previously is the interest in maintaining *macro-economic prosperity*. Among various theories explaining how imperialism could serve such an interest, only one has been identified as plausible for a modern industrial economy: that imperialism may be important in ensuring regular and dependable access to foreign sources of key raw materials. . . .

∎ ∎ ∎

Obviously a socialist society might sometimes have an interest in imperialist activity designed to secure access to foreign sources of raw materials. But the frequency and the strength of such an interest would be considerably higher in a capitalist society by virtue of its emphasis on economic growth and its inherent economic inequality.

A national interest in *aggregate economic gains* like a national interest in macro-economic prosperity could serve to motivate imperialist activity both in capitalist and in socialist societies. But again there are good reasons to believe that such an interest would be particularly forceful under capitalism. First of all, the emphasis placed on the desirability of increasing the available supply of goods and services in a capitalist society puts a great premium on the ability of a government to promote economic growth. In a society where there is such pressure to "deliver the goods," the government will be more highly motivated to seek out and exploit opportunities for economic gain through imperialism than it would in a socialist society where other social goals were relatively more important.

Secondly, the opportunities for aggregate economic gain through imperialism are likely to be considerably more extensive for a capitalist than for a socialist society. This is because capitalism encourages a high degree of economic specialization in order to reap the economic gains made possible by a wider international division of labor. Socialist values put less emphasis on such economic gains and more emphasis on alternative goals that involve deliberate diversification rather than specialization of economic activities. Hence a capitalist economy is likely to become more heavily involved in international trade and investment than a socialist economy with the same resource base. As a result there will be many more situations in which a capitalist government can use its power to

affect the terms of international economic relations in favor of its national economy.

The existence of a *national missionary spirit* that motivates imperialism requires that two conditions be satisfied. On the one hand, there must be a strong belief by the people of a society that their own way of life is a superior one. On the other hand, there must be a belief in the acceptability of imposing a way of life on others through the use of dominant power. The first of these conditions cannot be identified more strongly with one form of socio-economic organization than another. For good or bad reasons, people in both capitalist and socialist societies may well come to believe in the superiority of their own system. But whether people will find desirable the use of power to spread a system depends upon the extent to which concern about outcomes overrides concern about the processes whereby those outcomes are achieved. The more highly the values of a society stress genuine democracy—participation in decision-making by those affected by the decisions— the less acceptable will be the imposition of a system on others no matter how "good" for them it may appear to be. Hence the more truly democratic the form of socio-economic organization, the less will be the interest in imperialism based on a *missionary spirit*. And because capitalism precludes true democracy, a capitalist society will be more susceptible to undertake missionary imperialism than a socialist society that is inherently more democratic.

The *urge to dominate* as a source of imperialism is often described as an innate human drive, an element of human nature impervious to the social environment. Yet it seems quite unreasonable to insist that the form of socio-economic organization and the values that complement it have no influence on the attitude of people towards one another. Instead, one would expect rather different attitudes to emerge from (1) a society that stresses the importance of the individual and competition among individuals and (2) a society that stresses the importance of the community and cooperation among its members. The more competitive a society, the more an individual is likely to have an interest in dominating others, and the more the society as a whole may have an interest in dominating other societies. Without question, capitalism is a highly competitive form of social organization, and the urge to dominate is therefore more likely to motivate imperialism in a capitalist society than in a much less competitive socialist society.

The potentially relevant categories of class interest in imperialism identified in section II are associated with the promotion of social legitimacy, organizational expansion, and particular economic gains. A class interest in promoting *social legitimacy* through imperialism becomes significant whenever dominant classes in a society have reason to be concerned about the acceptance of their dominance by the rest of the people. As a very unequal form of socio-economic organization, capitalism obviously generates some dominant classes, and these classes have a potentially greater concern about their social legitimacy than would any identifiable class in a more equal socialist society. But while its basic economic institutions imply profound inequalities, the value system associated with capitalism—with its emphasis on the right (and obligation) of individuals to compete with one another in striving for personal advancement—suggests an ideal of free and fair competition. As people within a capitalist society come to recognize how unfree and unfair the competition often is (because of the inequality inherent in the underlying institutions), they are unlikely to accept the domination of the dominant classes. Thus, under capitalism, a contradiction between the socio-economic base and certain aspects of the ideological superstructure will further intensify the interest of dominant classes in providing some kind of legitimacy for their dominance. No comparable class interest in using imperialism for legitimizing purposes would arise in a socialist society.

A class interest in promoting *organizational expansion* through imperialism would not appear to be significantly more likely under either capitalism or socialism. On the one hand, a socialist system necessarily involves greater use of public

administrative organizations than does a capitalist system that relies more heavily on the market mechanism to motivate work and allocate resources. On the other hand, to the extent that the capitalist system of private enterprise limits the role of government organizations in domestic affairs, civilian and military agencies would be all the more enthusiastic about satisfying their growth imperative abroad. In any event, the differences in the demands placed upon public organizations under capitalism and under socialism have been declining over time as the viability of capitalism in a modern industrialized society has become increasingly dependent on involvement by the state in domestic economic and social affairs.[28]

Class interests in *particular economic gains* can be shown to be much more strongly associated with capitalism than with socialism; indeed, such class interests most probably account for a substantial share of the imperialist activity undertaken by capitalist governments. This is not only because of the importance attached to strictly economic objectives in a capitalist society. Nor is it due simply to the fact that under capitalism most of the means of production are privately rather than publicly owned. There is a more fundamental reason why in a capitalist society particular groups should seek to promote imperialism as a means for realizing particular economic gains. This reason has to do with the manner in which income is distributed under capitalism.

To see this, one must recognize that an imperialist activity motivated by a class interest in economic gain involves in effect an anticipated redistribution of economic benefits from the rest of the population to the particular interested class. This redistribution does not involve any direct transfer, but it results indirectly from (1) taxing (or otherwise burdening) the society as a whole for the cost of the activity and (2) benefiting the particular class by bringing about changes in the international economic situation that increase its income-earning opportunities.

It is precisely the *indirect* character of the redistribution that makes it attractive to particular classes in a capitalist society, for under capitalism income is supposed to be distributed to individuals in accordance with their market-valued contribution to production. The only legitimate source of income is the production process itself, as mediated by the market mechanism. . . .

* * *

It remains now to consider whether the distribution of power differs systematically as between capitalist and socialist societies in such a way as to result in differential motivations for the government to undertake imperialist activities that serve class interests but no national interest. As a general rule, it is clear that there can be no class-based motivation for imperialism in a genuine democracy. For if everyone in a society participated equally in the political process, the government could not undertake imperialist activities whose anticipated costs to the society as a whole were greater than the anticipated benefits to a particular class. Since socialism is far more conducive to genuine democracy than capitalism, one would expect that any possible class interest in imperialism would be far less likely to motivate imperialist activity in a socialist society than in a capitalist society. To prove the point, however, it is necessary to show that the more unequal distribution of power in a capitalist society favors those classes that stand to gain rather than to lose from imperialism.

Among the classes most likely to lose from imperialism are the taxpaying citizens and firms who ultimately bear the financial burden of imperialism; the soldiers who suffer injury or death in cases of military action; consumers who pay higher prices when the monopolistic position of multinational corporations is protected; workers who lose their jobs because a firm shifts its operations to a more profitable foreign location; businesses that find themselves at a competitive disadvantage because a rival firm secures a privileged position abroad; and so forth. It is quite evident that such possible losers from imperialism have little political strength in a capitalist society. The taxpaying public is a large, amorphous body that is difficult to mobilize politically; soldiers are drawn dispro-

portionately from the poorest and weakest strata of society; consumers, workers and businesses who lose from imperialist activity tend to be isolated and organizationally weak.

On the other hand, the classes that are likely to gain from imperialism tend to be among the most powerful in a capitalist society. The dominant classes with an interest in promoting their own social legitimacy have by definition a dominant position and correspondingly disproportionate power to shape government policy. The civilian and military bureaucracies interested in organizational expansion are close to the levers of power in government. And the capitalist class with its interest in particular economic gains is disproportionately strong in both economic and political terms. Moreover, within the capitalist class, the firms most directly involved in foreign economic operations are typically among the most powerful. For example, in the United States 9 of the largest 10 and at least 18 of the largest 25 corporations (ranked by sales) in 1965 were significantly involved in foreign operations.[29] These 18 corporations alone accounted for almost 20 percent of the total sales and almost 30 percent of the after-tax profits of all American industrial corporations. Hence even when there are conflicts of interest within the capitalist class over particular imperialist activities, the balance of power often tilts in favor of the pro-imperialists.

An important factor that enhances the effective power of the beneficiaries of imperialism is that the gains from an imperialist action tend to be large for the immediate beneficiaries while the losses tend to be spread widely and therefore thinly over the much larger number of losers. Under such circumstances, the gainers are always better motivated and better situated to mobilize themselves as an effective political force. It is not necessary that the beneficiaries of imperialism dominate all policy-making in order that the government be induced to undertake imperialist activities that serve particular class interests; it is only necessary that the beneficiaries exercise disproportionate influence in the sphere of foreign policy, which they can more easily do if the losers have less at stake and hence less interest in foreign policy decisions than the beneficiaries.

In sum, the balance of power is likely to tilt in favor of class-based imperialism in a capitalist society unless the aggregate costs of a given activity become so high as to weigh heavily and obviously on large segments of the population, or unless the activity involves a sharp conflict of interest among powerful classes themselves. Such situations do arise from time to time and they set limits on the extent to which—or the manner in which—a capitalist government is motivated to pursue imperialist policies. The recent history of American imperialism in Indochina is a good case in point. But it is clear that before such a point is reached there is a much greater scope for class-based imperialism under capitalism than under socialism.

Conclusions

The previous discussion leaves no doubt that a capitalist society is significantly more likely to generate imperialist activity than a socialist society. Most of the potential sources of imperialism in a modern industrialized society owe their existence or their strength to characteristics of capitalism, which are either absent or much less significant under socialism. The only relevant source of imperialism that appears to be quite unrelated to the internal socio-economic organization of a society is the one based upon a national interest in national security. Not surprisingly, this is the source that is given the greatest (if not the sole) attention by orthodox theorists. But every other relevant source of imperialism based upon a national interest, as well as every source based upon a class interest, is clearly more forceful in a capitalist than in a socialist society. The radical view of imperialism is thus confirmed.

The analysis of the relationship between capitalism and imperialism in this paper suggests certain directions for anti-imperialist movements in capitalist countries such as the United States. By identifying the specific characteristics of capitalism that contribute most significantly to imperialism,

one can gain some understanding of the kinds of reforms that might help to limit the extent of imperialist activity under capitalism and the kinds of radical changes in basic institutions that would be necessary to develop an alternative and much less imperialist society.

Within the context of a capitalist society, the motivations for the government to undertake imperialist activity may be lessened to the extent (1) that the primacy of economic gain as a social objective can be diminished, (2) that the distribution of income can be made a more explicitly political issue, and (3) that income inequality can be reduced and democracy can be made more effective. Progress in these directions depends largely upon the ability of the disenchanted groups and the dominated classes in capitalist society to organize themselves and develop a stronger political force with which to oppose the power of the dominant classes who have the most to gain from the *status quo*. There is some hopeful evidence that the war in Indochina has served to galvanize more effective opposition to American imperialism in particular and to the oppressive aspects of American capitalism in general.

But one must recognize that the very nature of capitalist society places significant limits on the extent to which political reform movements can expect to curtail imperialism under capitalism. So long as the basic institutions of American society remain capitalist, economic gain will remain an important goal, inequality will persist, and genuine democracy will be unattainable. The kinds of institutional changes necessary to make substantial progress in eliminating the imperialist urges of a capitalist society would involve the development of a radically different form of socio-economic organization in which (1) economic activity would be motivated by an incentive system that did not rely primarily on the prospect of individual economic gain in competition with other individuals; (2) income and wealth would be shared in an egalitarian manner; (3) control over the process of production would be exercised by all those involved and the distinction between owner and worker would disappear. For an egalitarian society in which economic activity was based upon collective rather than individual incentives and cooperative rather than competitive behavior would encourage a set of institutionalized values in which social goals other than economic gain were paramount and would facilitate the functioning of a truly effective democracy. In short, the best way to contain imperialism is to build socialism.

The lack of a contemporary example of a fully socialist society has led many critics of the radical view to argue that such a society is an unachievable utopia. Until the allegedly inachievable is achieved, there may be no way to convince

the hardened skeptic—or the determined opponent—about its feasibility. But the great variety of historical examples of socio-economic organization, and the extent to which some contemporary "socialist" countries have progressed from capitalist toward socialist institutions and values, suggests that socialism can be a real possibility. Utopian as such a system may appear to some observers, it represents the kind of long-run goal toward which an anti-imperialist movement must be directed if it is to achieve any significant and lasting progress.

---

1. The quote is from Tucker (1971), p. 138.

2. The negative answer is not stated explicitly, but it is clearly implied in the discussion in Tucker (1971), p. 138.

3. See, for example, the historical accounts of American imperialism in Zevin (1972), pp. 321–333; in Magdoff (1970); and in Williams (1969).

4. Thus Cohen (1973) states that "the real tap-root of imperialism" is "the anarchic organization of the international system of states.... The logic of dominion derives directly from the existence of competing national sovereignties"; and Tucker (1971), p. 73, asks: "Why may we not say simply that the interests of states expand roughly with their power and that America has been no exception to this experience?"

5. It would be impossible to list the names of all radical writers on the subject of American imperialism. For a representative sample of recent radical work, see Magdoff (1969), Kolko (1969), MacEwan (1972), and many of the essays reprinted in Fann and Hodges (1971).

6. There are of course many different varieties of radical theories of imperialism; the radical argument I develop in this paper is a personal one not necessarily shared by other radical theorists.

7. For useful discussions of the problems involved in defining imperialism, see Zevin (1972), pp. 316–321, and Cohen (1973), Chapter 1.

8. For Marxists "imperialism" represents a stage of capitalism associated with the growth of monopolistic firms in the industrialized capitalist nations and the spread of the capitalist mode of production across national borders into previously non-capitalist areas; see, for example, Lenin's definition of imperialism as the "monopoly stage of capitalism" on pp. 88–89 of the 1939 edition of Lenin (1917). For the purposes of this essay, imperialism must be defined in terms that are independent of any particular form of socio-economic organization.

9. By focusing attention on government activity, I am ignoring the variety of means by which private firms or organizations use their own power *directly* to affect conditions abroad. But I do take account of the way in which they do this *indirectly* through their influence on government; see the discussion of motivations for imperialism based on class interests in particular economic gains in the second and fourth sections of this chapter.

10. My definition of imperialism is not equivalent simply to intervention abroad, for it excludes instances of economic or military aid to foreign friends and allies who do not entail any relationship of domination and control.

11. See, for example, Tucker (1971), especially pp. 55–82, and Cohen (1973), Chapter 7.

12. The desire to maintain macro-economic prosperity is often presented by radical theorists in the context of a capitalist society as a class-based rather than a national motivation for imperialism. The reasoning is that only the dominant classes have a real interest in maintaining prosperity because it is primarily they who benefit from the existing economic system, while most of the people would be better off under another system that might replace a crisis-stricken capitalism. But this long-run outcome is problematic: in the short run everyone stands to lose if the economy is in crisis. Thus there is at least a short-run national interest—and possibly also a long-run national interest—in maintaining economic prosperity. This kind of national interest is quite distinct from the kind of class interest discussed later in which the short-run and the long-run benefits accrue only to particular classes.

13. See Hobson (1902), Luxemburg (1913), and Lenin (1917). Although some writers—e.g. Alavi (1964)—associate Lenin with an underconsumption/surplus-capital theory of imperialism, drawing mainly on Lenin (1917), Chapter 4, Harry Magdoff has stressed to me that this is a misrepresentation of Lenin's overall approach to imperialism.

14. Baran and Sweezy (1966), Chapter 7, and Reich and Finkelhor (1970) have developed the argument that military expenditures are an important source of surplus absorption in the American capitalist economy. Although these authors do not suggest that imperialism is necessary in order to sustain such expenditures, Baran and Sweezy do stress the strong compatibility of militarism and imperialism.

15. The notion of a missionary spirit as one among several sources of American imperialism is implicit in the work of Williams (1969), and it is suggested explicity by Zevin (1972), pp. 357–360.

16. The view that imperialism results from an atavistic human urge to dominate is most prominently associated with Schumpeter (1919), but it is also stated by Landes (1961).

17. Social legitimacy as a class-based source of American imperialism is proposed by MacEwan (1972), especially pp. 49–51.

18. Emphasis on the military bureaucracy as a source of American imperialism is common among contemporary "liberals"; see, for example, Bosch (1968) and Melman (1970).

19. This point follows from the neoclassical theory of international trade and was first emphasized in a classic article by Stolper and Samuelson (1941).

20. For a similar characterization of the capitalist mode of production, see Edwards, Reich, and Weisskopf (1972), introduction to Chapter 3.

21. This definition of socialism is closer to the Marxist notion of pure communism than to either the conventional or the Marxist usage of the word socialism.

22. For evidence of the extent to which China has moved toward the socialist model, see Gurley (1971) and Riskin (1973).

23. This proposition has been elaborated in the work of Gintis (1972), who combines elements of Marxian and Parsonian theories of the structure of social systems.

24. See Edwards, Reich, and Weisskopf (1972), introduction to Chapter 3, as well as Gintis (1972) for discussion of this point.

25. The process and the outcome of income distribution in a capitalist society is analyzed in greater detail by Weisskopf (1972a).

26. Miliband (1969), Chapters 6 and 7, describes many of the means by which economically powerful classes are able to have a vastly disproportionate influence on political decision-making even in a formally "democratic" society.

27. That democracy at the workplace is a prerequisite for democracy in other spheres of life is emphasized by Pateman (1970).

28. For an illuminating analysis of the growing role of the state in modern capitalist societies, see O'Connor (1970).

29. The figures cited in this paragraph are documented in Weisskopf (1972c), Table 10-E.

References

Alavi, Hamza. 1964. "Imperialism: Old and New." *Socialist Register 1964.* New York: Monthly Review Press.

Baran, Paul and Paul Sweezy. 1966. *Monopoly Capital.* New York: Monthly Review Press.

Bosch, Juan. 1968. *Pentagonism: A Substitute for Imperialism.* New York: Grove Press.

Brown, Lester R. 1972. *World Without Borders.* New York: Random House.

Cohen, Benjamin J. 1973. *The Question of Imperialism.* New York: Basic Books.

Dean, Heather. 1971. "Scarce Resources: The Dynamics of American Imperialism," in *Readings in U.S. Imperialism,* edited by Fann and Hodges. Boston: Porter Sargent.

Edwards, Richard C., Michael Reich, and Thomas E. Weisskopf. 1972. *The Capitalist System.* Englewood Cliffs, N.J.: Prentice-Hall.

Fann, K. T. and D. C. Hodges (eds.). 1971. *Readings in U.S. Imperialism.* Boston: Porter Sargent.

Gintis, Herbert. 1972. "A Radical Analysis of Welfare Economics and Individual Development." *Quarterly Journal of Economics* (4): November.

Gurley, John. 1971. "Maoist Economic Development." *Monthly Review* (9): February.

Hilferding, Rudolf. 1910. *Das Finanzkapital.* Vienna.

Hobson, J. A. 1967. *Imperialism: A Study.* Ann Arbor: University of Michigan Press. First published in 1902.

Hymer, Stephen. 1972. "United States Investment Abroad," in *Direct Foreign Investment in Asia and the Pacific,* edited by Peter Drysdale. Canberra: Australian National University Press.

Julien, Claude. 1971. *The American Empire.* Boston: Beacon Press.

Kolko, Gabriel. 1969. *The Roots of American Foreign Policy.* Boston: Beacon Press.

Landes, David S. 1961. "Some Thoughts on the Nature of Economic Imperialism." *The Journal of Economic History* (4): December.

Lenin, V. I. 1939. *Imperialism: The Highest Stage of Capitalism.* New York: International Publishers. First published in 1917.

Luxemburg, Rosa. 1951. *The Accumulation of Capital.* London: Routledge. First published in 1913.

MacEwan, Arthur. 1972. "Capitalist Expansion, Ideology and Intervention." *Review of Radical Political Economics* (1): Spring.

Magdoff, Harry. 1969. *The Age of Imperialism.* New York: Monthly Review Press.

——————. 1970. "Militarism and Imperialism." *Monthly Review* (9): February.

Melman, Seymour. 1970. *Pentagon Capitalism: The Political Economy of War.* New York: McGraw-Hill.

Miliband, Ralph. 1969. *The State in Capitalist Society.* New York: Basic Books.

Miller, S. M., Roy Bennett, and Cyril Alapatt. 1970. "Does the U.S. Economy Require Imperialism?" *Social Policy* (3): September/October.

O'Connor, James. 1970. "The Fiscal Crisis of the State." *Socialist Revolution* (1–2): January/February–March/April.

O'Connor, James. 1971. "The Meaning of Economic Imperialism," in *Readings in U.S. Imperialism,* edited by K. T. Fann and D. C. Hodges. Boston: Porter Sargent.

Pateman, Carole. 1970. *Participation and Democratic Theory.* Cambridge, England: Cambridge University Press.

Reich, Michael and David Finkelhor. 1970. "The Military Industrial Complex: No Way Out," in *Up Against the American Myth,* edited by Christoffel, Finkelhor and Gilbarg. New York: Holt, Rinehart & Winston.

Riskin, Carl. 1973. "Maoism And Motivation: Work Incentives in China." *Bulletin of Concerned Asian Scholars* (1): July.

Russett, Bruce M. et al. 1964. *World Handbook of Political and Social Indicators.* New Haven: Yale University Press.

Schumpeter, Joseph. 1955. *Imperialism.* New York: Meridian Books. First published in 1919.

Shonfield, Andrew. 1965. *Modern Capitalism.* London: Oxford University Press.

Stolper, Wolfgang F. and Paul A. Samuelson. 1941.

"Protection and Real Wages." *Review of Economic Studies* (1): November.

Tucker, Robert W. 1971. *The Radical Left and American Foreign Policy.* Baltimore: Johns Hopkins Press.

Weisskopf, Thomas E. 1972a. "Capitalism and Inequality," Section 3.7 in Edwards, Reich, and Weisskopf, *The Capitalist System.* Englewood Cliffs, N.J.: Prentice-Hall.

————. 1972b. "The Problem of Surplus Absorption in a Capitalist Society," Section 9.1 in Edwards, Reich, and Weisskopf, *The Capitalist System.* Englewood Cliffs, N.J.: Prentice-Hall.

————. 1972c. "United States Foreign Private Investment: An Empirical Survey," Section 10.3 in Edwards, Reich, and Weisskopf, *The Capitalist System.* Englewood Cliffs, N.J.: Prentice-Hall.

Williams, William A. 1969. *The Roots of the Modern American Empire.* New York: Vintage Books.

Zevin, Robert. 1972. "An Interpretation of American Imperialism." *Journal of Economic History,* (1): March.

Socialism Is Not the Solution

Robert W. Tucker

Would a Socialist America pursue a foreign policy fundamentally different from the foreign policy pursued by a Capitalist America? Would it no longer seek to influence the course of development of other peoples? Would it abandon its hegemonial position along with the advantages this position has conferred? Would it provide a generous measure of assistance to developing nations while neither seeking nor expecting any tangible advantages in return?

Whether explicitly or implicitly, a radical critique answers these questions affirmatively. Whatever the differences otherwise separating them, the belief that a Socialist America would pursue a fundamentally different foreign policy is common to all radical critics. The pervasiveness of this belief is in itself significant. That it is held with equal fervor by those who nevertheless stress the independent force of conviction in the determination of policy must remain inexplicable, unless conviction is seen as not only having grown out of but as continuing to reflect the socio-economic structure of society.

What may we say of the radical belief? Clearly, a Socialist America would in some respects behave differently from a Capitalist America. It would no longer seek to insure the triumph of liberal-capitalist values. But a radical critique cannot be content with telling us what no one would care to dispute. What many would dispute is the contention that such an America would no longer attempt to control its environment, that it would no longer attempt to fashion some sort of greater order, and that it would no longer entertain imperial relationships with other and weaker states. That these relationships would be undertaken for ostensibly different reasons cannot preclude the prospect that they would still be characterized by inequality and by some form of coercion.

It is not enough, then, to content oneself with saying that a Socialist America would no longer pursue Capitalist ways. For unless the "ways" of capitalism are equated with the ways collectives have displayed from time immemorial, we might be expected to retain interests that have little to do with capitalism but a great deal to do with the pretensions great powers have almost invariably manifested. If history is to prove at all relevant in this regard, there is no apparent reason to assume that the new America would refrain from identifying the collective self with something larger than the self. If this is so, the nation's security and well-being would still be identified with a world that remained receptive to American institutions and interests. No doubt, a Socialist America would define those institutions and interests in a manner different from the definition of a Capitalist America. But this difference cannot be taken to mean that we would refrain from attempting to influence the course of development of other peoples. The possibility—or, rather, the probability—must be entertained that there would still be revolutions, even radical revolutions, the nature and international consequences of which we might oppose. Nor is there any assurance that our opposition would appear less oppressive to others simply because it was no longer motivated by the desire

to safeguard private investments or needed sources of raw materials.

That American policy would no longer be concerned with maintaining an environment receptive to the investment of capital follows by definition. Would the same lack of concern be manifested toward safeguarding present sources of raw materials, particularly if they are as critical to the economy as the radicals contend? Radical critics make a great deal of the political and psychological necessity of a Capitalist America to preserve access to needed sources of raw materials. Why is it assumed that this is a "necessity" unique to capitalism? Is it unreasonable to assume that a Socialist America might also wish to preserve similar access? It may of course be argued that a Socialist America would not consume the quantities of raw materials a Capitalist America consumes and that for those raw materials it still needed to import it would pay a "just" price. But this argument is one that proceeds by definition, that is, by defining how a truly socialist society would act, rather than by experience.

Let us assume, however, that a Socialist America would not identify its security and well-being with a world that remained receptive to American institutions and interests. Let us assume that the new society would have no incentive to find its fulfillment in foreign policy. Given a physical security that is no longer dependent upon what transpires outside the North American continent, the triumph of socialism would signal, on this assumption, the disappearance of any remaining need to find our security and well-being in the greater than physical sense dependent upon events occurring beyond our frontiers. In these circumstances, it may then be argued, America's economic and political frontiers could at last become coextensive with its territorial frontiers and the compulsion, whether institutional or psychological, to expand and to control our environment would atrophy and, indeed, disappear.

In these same circumstances, however, what would prevent us from disinteresting ourselves in the rest of the world, and particularly in the developing states? Why should it matter to us whether the impoverished remain impoverished, if their fate carries no consequences for our own well being?[1]* On the other hand, if it is argued that our fate is inextricably tied to the fate of the developing states, then even a Socialist America would continue to have a compelling incentive to influence its environment. Then even a Socialist America would not refrain, because it could not safely refrain, from identifying the collective self with something larger than the self. That identification has been a principal source of what justice men have been capable of showing in their collective relations. In a world of unequals, it has also been the source of an interest that has readily assumed imperial dimensions.

The world of a Socialist America would still be a world marked by great inequalities. It would still be a world of the strong and the weak, the rich and the poor. If injustice springs from such inequalities, what are the grounds for believing the new society would act justly toward the weak? It is, after all, not only Capitalist states that have sought to take advantage of their strength when dealing with poor and weak states. The record of the Soviet Union's relations with the underdeveloped states scarcely bears out a reluctance to draw such advantages as it can from its position of strength. It may of course be argued that this only proves that the Soviet Union is not a truly Socialist state. It may also be argued that the Soviet Union's behavior indicates that the real source of injustice and exploitation today stems from the fact that the world is divided into rich and poor states. The latter argument is a striking departure from Marxism or its Leninist adaptation, but it is still not enough of a departure. It is not only the division of humanity into the rich and the poor that gives rise to the various forms of unequal relationships the radical equates with imperialism. It is also the division of humanity into discrete collectives. If advanced states, whether Capitalist or Socialist, may behave similarly in many respects toward backward states, it is not simply because they are advanced but because collectives have very little

sense of obligation to others. That is why we have no persuasive grounds for assuming that a society which acts justly at home will also act justly abroad.

Why do radicals either neglect or dismiss these altogether commonplace considerations? In part, the answer must be found in the view that the world as we know it today is America's special creation. "The elimination of American hegemony," one radical declares, "is the essential precondition for the emergence of a nation and a world in which mass hunger, suppression, and war are no longer the inevitable and continuous characteristics of modern civilization."[2] In this view, it is the hegemony of a Capitalist America that perpetuates mass hunger in India, suppression in the Soviet Union and China, and conflict between Israel and Egypt, India and Pakistan, and China and the Soviet Union. What a hegemonic Capitalist America has created, a truly Socialist America may destroy.

This extreme version of America's all-encompassing power for maintaining the evil that presently exists in the world is not shared by all radical critics. Some acknowledge that the world of a Socialist America, however humane and democratic this socialism, would still be a world of conflict, if only for the reason that it would still be a world divided into sovereign states. They might well argue that a Socialist America would alleviate hunger in India to a degree a Capitalist America is either unwilling or incapable of doing, but they do not insist that a Socialist America would form the essential precondition for resolving the present differences between China and the Soviet Union. (If this conflict holds out dangers to a Capitalist America, there is no apparent reason for believing it would not hold out dangers to a Socialist America. Moreover, if it is once conceded that a Capitalist America is not responsible for the Sino-Soviet conflict, and the aspirations that conflict reveals, it must also be conceded that there is little reason for believing that a Socialist America would moderate either Soviet or Chinese aspirations generally. If anything, we must expect that the kind of America

---

*[Footnotes have been renumbered from the original work because this reading has been excerpted from a larger body of work—EDS.]

the radicals look forward to would cause Soviet and Chinese behavior to become much less moderate than it is today.)

Even so, there is no essential disagreement among radicals on the manner in which the new society would behave. If this vision is immune to the considerations we have earlier raised, it is because the radical is not concerned with men as they have been but with men as they might and presumably will be once they have been emancipated from the existing social order. It is only a view which assumes the past to be irrelevant in projecting the future that can entertain the expectation of a Socialist America's providing a generous measure of assistance to poor states for no other reason than the desire to alleviate suffering. What a Capitalist society is presently incapable of doing for its own, a Socialist society will do not only for its own but for others as well. The radical belief in the foreign policy of a Socialist America ultimately rests on the assertion—a tautology—that if men are transformed they will then behave differently. If we believe that a "humane and democratic" socialism will lead to the transformation of men, to a new beginning in history, then it indeed follows that America would behave toward the world in the manner radicals confidently expect. But this is to resolve the problem of how a Socialist America would behave by defining the problem away.

---

1. The response may of course be made that even if we assume a Socialist America would be indifferent to the fate of the impoverished this would still be infinitely preferable to the repressive "concern" of an imperialist America, that between a real neglect and a repressive concern the former must appear quite benign. This response, which is not only made by radicals, cannot be easily dismissed, however much it may exaggerate America's responsibility for the plight of impoverished peoples. Even so, it leaves open the question raised above. At least, it leaves open this question unless we assume that in a truly Socialist society men's sense of sympathy would, at long last, know no boundaries.

2. Gabriel Kolko, *The Roots of American Foreign Policy*, p. 87.

Class and the Draft in Vietnam*

James William Gibson

In reflecting upon World War II, military leaders had concluded that scientific and technological progress had been threatened by having too many college-educated men serving in combat (and dying) in comparison to the total college-educated pool. Therefore, when Selective Service was renewed in 1948, college attendance constituted a draft exemption. Selective Service established a whole array of exemptions to "channel" American men toward higher education and occupations that

---

Reprinted by permission of the author.

*Excerpt from Chapter 6 of *The Perfect War: Technowar in Vietnam* (New York: Atlantic Monthly Press, 1986), pp. 214–219.

the military thought would contribute to the national defense. A 1965 Selective Service policy statement explained the theory:

> *While the best known purpose of Selective Service is to procure manpower for the armed forces, a variety of related processes takes place outside delivery of manpower to the active armed forces. Many of these may be put under the heading of "channeling manpower." Many young men would not have pursued a higher education if there had not been a program of student deferments. Many young scientists, engineers, tool and die makers, and other possessors of scarce skills would not remain in their jobs in the defense effort if it were not for a program of occupational deferment. Even though the salary of a teacher has historically been meager, many young men remain in that job seeking the reward of deferment. The process of channeling manpower by deferment is entitled to much credit for the large amount of graduate students in technical fields and for the fact that there is not a greater shortage of teachers, engineers, and other scientists working in activities which are essential to the national defense.[1]**

College deferments lasted until 1973, when the Selective Service System instituted a lottery method for determining who was going to be drafted. Graduate school deferments lasted until 1968. Thus college-educated men were able to minimize their exposure to the draft, as well as pursue legal means of securing an exemption through conscientious objector status, or physical or psychiatric exemption. Social science research has shown a strong relationship between a man's parental class position and the educational level he achieves. The higher the class position and the higher the income and education of his parents, then the greater the chances are of a young man's

finishing high school and college. Sons of the upper-middle class did not enter the military and go to Vietnam in the same proportions as did the sons of the working class. Lawrence M. Baskir and William A. Strauss have conducted the most extensive study relating a man's family background and education to his chances of fighting in Technowar [see Table 1—Eds.].

Note that an individual from a low-income family has over twice the likelihood of serving in a combat capacity than does a man from a high-income family. Another study found that of the hundreds of thousands of men drafted in 1965–1966, only 2 percent were college graduates![2] Once in the military, army records show, an enlisted man with a college degree had only a 42 percent chance of going to Vietnam, while high school graduates had a 64 percent chance and high school dropouts faced 70 percent odds.[3] At each level of the filtering process leading toward the point of war production—the ground forces—progressively fewer men with college educations serve. Those who were from the lower levels of the social stratification system served in the most dangerous jobs (ground troops). And they died in those jobs. Sociologist Maurice Zeitlin and his associates found that nearly 29 percent of all men from Wisconsin who died in

TABLE 1   Likelihood of Vietnam-era service

	Military Service	*Vietnam Service*	*Combat Service*
Low-Income	40%	19%	15%
Middle-Income	30%	12%	7%
High-Income	24%	9%	7%
High School Dropout	42%	18%	14%
High School Graduate	45%	21%	17%
College Graduate	23%	12%	9%

Source: Lawrence M. Baskir and William A. Strauss, *Chance and Circumstance* (New York: Alfred A. Knopf, 1978), p. 9.

---

*[Footnotes have been renumbered because this material has been excerpted from a larger body of work—Eds.]

Vietnam were from poor families, while only 15 percent of men in high school came from poor families. Therefore, they died in *twice* their proportion of men their age.[4]

Only 2.4 percent of the Wisconsin casualties were black men, but Wisconsin is an unusually "white" state, with only 1.8 percent of all males between five and eighteen being black. Taking the United States as a whole, black men died in greater numbers than their proportion of the population. Twenty-four percent of army deaths in Vietnam in 1965 were black men's deaths. The next year the figure declined to 16 percent, and by 1968 black casualties from all military services totaled 13 percent.[5] A Department of Defense campaign to reduce the disproportionate presence of blacks in combat units apparently had some effects. Originally the army had made a special effort to draft minorities. The Armed Forces Qualification Tests given to all prospective volunteers and draftees classified people in one of five mental categories according to test scores. People scoring in categories I–III were automatically taken, while those scoring in Category V were automatically rejected. During peacetime, military recruiters tried to limit the number of men inducted with Category IV scores, but once the ground war started in 1965 these standards were lessened. The military was encouraged to drop its standards by civilian officials in Lyndon Johnson's administration. Political scientist Daniel Patrick Moynihan chaired the Task Force on Manpower Conservation in 1964 and found that the military rejected around 600,000 men each year who were school dropouts. Moynihan published a study on black family structure the next year, 1965. He was disheartened by the "disorganized and matrifocal family life" in black communities. Suddenly he saw how the military could get the men it needed and how blacks could become real men for the first time.

> There is another special quality about military service for Negro men: It is an utterly masculine world. Given the strains of the disorganized and matrifocal family life in which so many Negro youth come of age, the Armed Forces are a dramatic and desperately needed change; a world away from women, a world run by strong men of unquestioned authority, where discipline, if harsh, is nonetheless orderly and predictable, and where rewards, if limited, are granted on the basis of performance. The theme of a current Army recruiting message states it as clearly as can be. "In the U.S. Army you get to know what it means to feel like a man."[6]

Moynihan wrote this extraordinarily paternalistic encomium when he was an assistant secretary of labor.

Military life also took these newly made black men off welfare and gave them job skills and the means for upward mobility:

> Military service is disruptive in some respects. For those comparatively few who are killed or wounded in combat, or otherwise, the personal sacrifice is inestimable. But, on balance, service in the Armed Forces over the past quarter century has worked greatly to the advantage of those involved. The training and experience of military duty is unique; the advantages that have generally followed in the form of GI Bill mortgage guarantees, federal life insurance, Civil Service preference, veterans' hospitals and veterans' pensions are singular, to say the least.[7]

To help more black men receive the fruits of military life, a special remedial education program was set up for Category IV recruits; 40 percent of all blacks scored in Category IV. Secretary of Defense Robert McNamara called it Project 100,000. The "subterranean poor . . . have not had the opportunity to earn their fair share of this nation's abundance, but they can be given an opportunity to return to civilian life with skills and aptitudes which for them and their families will reverse the downward spiral of decay." The war-managers would produce highly productive men, men with earning capacities "*two or three times what it would have been had there been no such program.*"[8]

Recruitment standards changed; 240,000 Category IV test-scorers officially entered the military under the program's auspices from 1966 to 1968. Additional Category IV recruits entered the military but were not registered with the program. Some troops received remedial instruction in reading and some were placed in special training programs to get them through basic and advanced schools. But mostly these men, 40 percent of whom were black, took assignments in the combat arms (infantry, armor, artillery) and half of those in the army and marines went to Vietnam.[9] The great welfare program was a hoax; Technowar needed an ever-increasing labor supply at the point of production. Standards were changed so that those at the bottom of the racial and economic system of power could fight and die in Vietnam.

However deficient in test scores, many members of what Douglas Glasgow terms "the black underclass" understood completely where they were and why they were there.[10] David Cortright's investigations in *Soldiers in Revolt* found that "of all the troops in Vietnam, the most rebellious were the blacks. As was the case throughout the armed forces, black GIs in Vietnam were militant leaders of the GI resistance, posing great problems for American commanders."[11] War-managers attempted to contain black rebellion by sending them to military prisons. Prisons in Vietnam became locales for massive revolts. On August 16, 1968, marine inmates at the Danang brig (prison) rioted and seized control of the central compound for twenty hours. Full control over the prison was not obtained for several days. Two weeks later the massive army prison at Long Binh, holding 710 prisoners (in an area designed for 502), erupted. Fighting between military police and inmates protesting the living conditions went on for several hours. Later, a work strike was conducted by approximately 200 black inmates, and a smaller group maintained control of one prison section for nearly a month. Cortright describes how black nationalism manifested itself in these actions: "During the occupation, the militants reportedly simulated African dress and customs and transformed their tiny holding into a kind of liberated African state."[12]

The list of racial epithets applied to black soldiers by many white troops was longer than the list for Vietnamese. Besides the old favorites, "coon," "nigger," and "spade," there were "reindeer," "Mau Mau," "jig," "spook," "brownie," and "warrior." Even without slander, the message came through. David Parks, author of *G.I. Diary*, said he heard the call: "The FO [forward observer]'s job is one of the hairiest in the mortar platoon. He's on more patrols because an FO is required to be with the patrolling squad at all times, and there are only three FOs to cover sixteen squads. The odds are against him. Sgt. Paulson hand picks the men for this job. So far he's picked only Negroes and Puerto Ricans. I think he is trying to tell us something."[13] Stanley Goff heard the news from his friend Piper:

> At that particular time, most of the whites depended on the brothers to fight. That's how it got to be. And he [Piper] and every brother knew that, too. His thing was, "Don't let them use you all the way to the grave." And that was what they were really doing. He told us, "The government is sending us over here. When we get here, we're doing the most fighting." Piper was trying to make us see how they were using us. Here we were doing all the fighting out of proportion to our number. Anyway, that's what he was preaching. That was his lesson. He was enabling us to understand the system as he saw it and to realize that all the money that was being poured into the Nam could have been used to clean up the ghetto. He was politically oriented and just a hell of a guy.[14]

Drafted from the underclass and sent to die as grunts in combat units, the black men's audacious revolt was punished by their white commanders. According to the National Association for the Advancement of Colored People, black soldiers received 45 percent of all "less-than-honorable discharges issued in the Vietnam era."[15] A bad discharge rating is a stigma that lasts for a lifetime—a way of keeping someone at the socioeconomic bottom.

Other minorities, particularly Hispanics, also served and died in Vietnam in larger proportions than their ethnic and racial groups are represented in the United States. Ralph Guzman studied Hispanic deaths in Vietnam as a percentage of total deaths suffered by men from the southwestern states of California, Arizona, New Mexico, Colorado, and Texas. From 1961 through March 1969, casualties with Spanish surnames comprised around 19 percent of the total killed in Vietnam from southwestern states. This figure is significantly higher than the U.S. Bureau of the Census figures of 11.8

percent total Hispanic population of the Southwest and 13.8 percent of all males from seventeen to thirty-six.[16] Neither stories from ground troops nor academic studies indicate whether Chicano soldiers participated in the revolt against Technowar. But their high death rate again makes clear how Selective Service and the military division of labor reproduced the stratification system.

1. "Channeling" was one of ten documents in an orientation kit for local draft boards published by Selective Service in July 1965. See Waterhouse and Wizzard, *Turning the Guns Around*, p. 204.

2. Lawrence M. Baskir and William A. Strauss, *Chance and Circumstance: The Draft, the War and the Vietnam Generation* (New York: Alfred A. Knopf, 1978), p. 9.

3. Ibid., p. 10.

4. Maurice Zeitlin, Kenneth Lutterman, and James Russell, "Death in Vietnam: Class, Poverty, and the Risks of War," in *The Politics and Society Reader*, edited by Ira Katznelson et al. (New York: David McKay, 1971), pp. 55–57.

5. Baskir and Strauss, *Chance and Circumstance*, p. 8.

6. Daniel Patrick Moynihan, "The Negro Family: The Case for National Action," *The Moynihan Report and the Politics of Controversy* (Cambridge, Mass.: Massachusetts Institute of Technology Press, 1967), p. 42.

7. Ibid., p. 47.

8. Baskir and Strauss, *Chance and Circumstance*, p. 126.

9. Douglas G. Glasgow, *The Black Underclass: Poverty, Unemployment, and Entrapment of Ghetto Youth* (New York: Vintage Books, 1980).

10. For accounts of what happened to category IV soldiers see Paul Starr, *The Discarded Army: Veterans after Vietnam* (New York: Charter House, 1973). pp. 192–193; Cortright, *Soldiers in Revolt*, pp. 194–195; Baskir and Strauss, *Chance and Circumstance*, pp. 128-129.

11. David Cortright, *Soldiers in Revolt: The American Military Today* (Garden City, N.Y.: Anchor Press/Doubleday, 1975, p. 46.

12. Ibid., p. 40–41.

13. David Parks, *G.I. Diary* (New York: Harper and Row, 1968), p. 86.

14. Stanley Goff and Robert Sanders with Clark Smith, *Brothers: Black Soldiers in the Nam* (Novato, CA: Presidio Press, 1982), p. 30.

15. Baskir and Strauss, *Chance and Circumstance*, p. 139.

16. Ralph Guzman, "Mexican Casualties in Vietnam," *La Raza*, 1 (1971), 12.

PART FIVE

Political Economy of the Armaments Industry

The contemporary military-industrial complex in the United States has its origins in World War II. During World War II the United States government radically changed the American economy from a relatively decentralized structure in which 250,000 companies produced 70 percent of the nation's manufactured goods and the largest 100 manufacturing companies produced only 30 percent, to a highly centralized economy in which the largest 100 manufacturers produced 70 percent of all products.[1] This centralization was accomplished by the formation of the military-industrial complex. Government officials granted hundreds of billions of dollars worth of defense contracts to relatively few large companies. Government administrators thought that only the largest firms had the managerial expertise and the truly "scientific" production lines to produce the huge quantities of airplanes, ships, weapons, uniforms, medicines, and other supplies needed for warfare on a global scale. Thus the large-scale corporation came to dominate the economy through war production for the government.

During World War II American military leaders developed a keen appreciation for the contributions of science and industry to modern warfare;

they thought American technological superiority and the ability to mass-produce these superior weapons were largely responsible for victory. In 1946 General Dwight D. Eisenhower, chairman of the Joint Chiefs of Staff, wrote a memo to his fellow generals and admirals entitled "Scientific and Technological Resources as Military Assets." Eisenhower wanted the military to sustain its close working relationships with universities and industry in the post-World War II era. The memo is thus one of the foundation documents establishing a permanent military-industrial complex as a basic structure of American politics and economics in both war and peace. However, after Eisenhower served his two terms as president, he warned the American people in his 1960, "Farewell Address to the Nation," that the growing powers of the military-industrial complex could become a threat to world peace.

In Part Five, Eisenhower's original memo and his later critique introduce the political economy of the armaments industry. Then, in "The Weapons System," Mary Kaldor analyzes how armaments have changed into progressively more complex and expensive "weapons systems" that often do not work. Other readings discuss whether weapons help our economy. Conventional wisdom has held that such spending has been beneficial, but in recent years several researchers have argued that military spending has hurt American capitalism. In "The Economics of War and Peace," Alexander Cockburn and James Ridgeway introduce Seymour Melman's analysis of how the rate of military spending in the post-World War II era has grown to the point where the United States can not afford to rebuild the infrastructure of roads, bridges, and schools that supports American industry. Lloyd Dumas and Suzanne Gordon contend that converting defense companies to civilian production is a feasible solution to U.S. economic problems and a way to achieve peace. Gordon Adams presents a rejoinder to this contention.

---

1. John Morton Blum, *V was for Victory: Politics and American Culture during World War II* (New York: Harcourt Brace Jovanovich, 1976) 123.

Scientific and Technological Resources as Military Assets

General Dwight D. Eisenhower

The following is the full text of a memorandum by General Eisenhower written in 1946, when he was Chief of Staff of the United States Army. The memorandum, which advocates a close relationship between the Army and civilian scientists, industry, and universities, became an influential policy guide. By 1961, Eisenhower, who was then President, warned the nation of the dangers of the military-industrial complex. This document is from the Henry L. Stimson Papers in the Sterling Library of Yale University—EDS.

Memorandum for Directors and Chiefs of War Department General and Special Staff Divisions and Bureaus and the Commanding Generals of the Major Commands:

The recent conflict has demonstrated more convincingly than ever before the strength our nation can best derive from the integration of all of our national resources in time of war. It is of the utmost importance that the lessons of this experience be not forgotten in the peacetime planning and training of the Army. The future security of the nation demands that all those civilian resources which by conversion or redirection constitute our main support in time of emergency be associated closely with the activities of the Army in time of peace.

The lessons of the last war are clear. The military effort required for victory threw upon the Army an unprecedented range of responsibilities, many of which were effectively discharged only through the invaluable assistance supplied by our cumulative resources in the natural and social sciences and the talents and experience furnished by management and labor. The armed forces could not have won the war alone. Scientists and business men contributed techniques and weapons which enabled us to outwit and overwhelm the enemy. Their understanding of the Army's needs made possible the highest degree of cooperation. This pattern of integration must be translated into a peacetime counterpart which will not merely familiarize the Army with the progress made in science and industry, but draw into our planning for national security all the civilian resources which can contribute to the defense of the country.

Success in this enterprise depends to a large degree on the cooperation which the nation as a whole is willing to contribute. However, the Army as one of the main agencies responsible for the defense of the nation has the duty to take the initiative in promoting closer relation between civilian and military interests. It must establish definite policies and administrative leadership which will make possible even greater contributions from science, technology, and management than during the last war.

In order to ensure the full use of our national resources in case of emergency, the following general policies will be put into effect:

(1) *The Army must have civilian assistance in military planning as well as for the production of weapons.* Effective long-range military planning can be done only in the light of predicted developments in science and technology. As further

scientific achievements accelerate the tempo and expand the area of our operations, this interrelationship will become of even greater importance. In the past we have often deprived ourselves of vital help by limiting our use of scientific and technological resources to contracts for equipment. More often than not we can find much of the talent we need for comprehensive planning in industry or universities. Proper employment of this talent requires that the civilian agency shall have the benefit of our estimates of future military problems and shall work closely with Plans and the Research and Development authorities. A most effective procedure is the letting of contracts for aid in planning. The use of such a procedure will greatly enhance the validity of our planning as well as ensure sounder strategic equipment programs.

(2) *Scientists and industrialists must be given the greatest possible freedom to carry out their research.* The fullest utilization by the Army of the civilian resources of the nation cannot be procured merely by prescribing the military characteristics and requirements of certain types of equipment. Scientists and industrialists are more likely to make new and unsuspected contributions to the development of the Army if detailed directions are held to a minimum. The solicitation of assistance under these conditions would not only make available to the army talents and experience otherwise beyond our reach, but also establish mutual confidence between ourselves and civilians. It would familiarize them with our fundamental problems and strengthen greatly the foundation upon which our national security depends.

(3) *The possibility of utilizing some of our industrial and technological resources as organic parts of our military structure in time of emergency should be carefully examined.* The degree of cooperation with science and industry achieved during the recent war should by no means be considered the ultimate. There appears little reason for duplicating within the Army an outside organization which by its experience is better qualified than we are to carry out some of our tasks. The advantages to our nation in economy and to the Army in efficiency are compelling reasons for this procedure.

(4) *Within the Army we must separate responsibility for research and development from the functions of procurement, purchase, storage and distribution.* Our experience during the war and the experience of industry in time of peace indicate the need for such a policy. The inevitable gap between the scientist or technologist and the user can be bridged, as during the last war, by field experimentation with equipment still in the developmental stage. For example, restricted-visibility operations with the aid of radar, such as blind bombing and control of tactical air, were made possible largely by bringing together technologists who knew the potentialities of the equipment and field commanders familiar with combat conditions and needs. Future cooperation of this type requires that research and development groups have authority to procure experimental items for similar tests.

(5) *Officers of all arms and services must become fully aware of the advantages which the Army can derive from the close integration of civilian talent with military plans and developments.* This end cannot be achieved merely by sending officers to universities for professional training. It is true that the Army's need for officers well trained in the natural and social sciences requires a thorough program of advanced study for selected military personnel, but in addition we must supply inducements which will encourage these men in the continued practical application of scientific and technological thought to military problems. A premium must be placed on professional attainments in the natural and social sciences as well as other branches of military science. Officers in each arm and service must familiarize themselves as much as possible with progress and plans made in other branches. Only then can the Army obtain the administrative and operative talents essential to its task and mutual understanding by the arms and services of their respective problems.

In general, the more we can achieve the objectives indicated above with respect to the cultivation, support and direct use of outside resources, the more energy will we have left to devote to strictly military problems for which there are no outside facilities or which for special security reasons can only be handled by the military. In fact, it is our responsibility deliberately to examine all outside resources as to adequacy, diversity, and geographical distribution and to ensure their full utilization as factors of security. It is our job to take the initiative to promote the development of new resources, if our national security indicates the need. It is our duty to support broad research programs in educational institutions, in industry, and in whatever field might be of importance to the Army. Close integration of military and civilian resources will not only directly benefit the Army, but indirectly contribute to the nation's security, as civilians are prepared for their role in an emergency by the experience gained in time of peace. The association of military and civilians in educational institutions and industry will level barriers, engender mutual understanding, and lead to the cultivation of friendships invaluable for future cooperation. The realization of our objectives places upon us, the military, the challenge to make our professional officers the equals in knowledge and training of civilians in

similar fields and make our professional environment as inviting as those outside.

In the interest of cultivating to the utmost the integration of civilian and military resources and of securing the most effective unified direction of our research and development activities, this responsibility is being consolidated in a separate section on the highest War Department level. The Director of this section will be directly supported by one or more civilians, thus ensuring full confidence of both the military and the civilian in this undertaking. By the rotation of civilian specialists in this capacity we should have the benefit of broad guidance and should be able to furnish science and industry with a firsthand understanding of our problems and objectives. By developing the general policies outlined above under the leadership of the Director of Research and Development the Army will demonstrate the value it places upon science and technology and further the integration of civilian and military resources.

Signed by General Eisenhower
on April 27, 1946.

President Eisenhower's Farewell to the Nation*

President Dwight D. Eisenhower

My fellow Americans: Three days from now, after half a century in the service of our country, I shall lay down the responsibilities of office as, in traditional and solemn ceremony, the authority of the Presidency is vested in my successor.

This evening I come to you with a message of leavetaking and farewell and to share a few final thoughts with you, my countrymen.

Like every other citizen, I wish the new President and all who will labor with him God-

*Delivered to the Nation by television and radio on Jan. 17 (White House press release).
SOURCE: U.S. Department of State, *Bulletin*, Vol. 44, Feb. 6, 1961.

speed. I pray that the coming years will be blessed with peace and prosperity for all.

Our people expect their President and the Congress to find essential agreement on issues of great moment, the wise resolution of which will better shape the future of the Nation.

My own relations with the Congress, which began on a remote and tenuous basis, when long ago a member of the Senate appointed me to West Point, have since ranged to the intimate during the war and immediate postwar period and, finally, to the mutually interdependent during these past 8 years.

In this final relationship the Congress and the administration have, on most vital issues, cooperated well to serve the national good rather than mere partisanship and so have assured that the business of the Nation should go forward. So my official relationship with the Congress ends in a feeling on my part of gratitude that we have been able to do so much together.

II

We now stand 10 years past the midpoint of a century that has witnessed four major wars among great nations. Three of these involved our own country. Despite these holocausts, America is today the strongest, the most influential, and most productive nation in the world. Understandably proud of this preeminence, we yet realize that America's leadership and prestige depend not merely upon our unmatched material progress, riches, and military strength but on how we use our power in the interests of world peace and human betterment.

III

Throughout America's adventure in free government our basic purposes have been to keep the peace, to foster progress in human achievement, and to enhance liberty, dignity, and integrity among people and among nations. To strive for less would be unworthy of a free and religious people. Any failure traceable to arrogance or our lack of comprehension or readiness to sacrifice would inflict upon us grievous hurt both at home and abroad.

Progress toward these noble goals is persistently threatened by the conflict now engulfing the world. It commands our whole attention, absorbs our very beings. We face a hostile ideology— global in scope, atheistic in character, ruthless in purpose, and insidious in method. Unhappily the danger it poses promises to be of indefinite duration. To meet it successfully there is called for not so much the emotional and transitory sacrifices of crisis but rather those which enable us to carry forward steadily, surely and without complaint the burdens of a prolonged and complex struggle—with liberty the stake. Only thus shall we remain, despite every provocation, on our charted course toward permanent peace and human betterment.

Crises there will continue to be. In meeting them, whether foreign or domestic, great or small, there is a recurring temptation to feel that some spectacular and costly action could become the miraculous solution to all current difficulties. A huge increase in newer elements of our defense, development of unrealistic programs to cure every ill in agriculture, a dramatic expansion in basic and applied research—these and many other possibilities, each possibly promising in itself, may be suggested as the only way to the road we wish to travel.

But each proposal must be weighed in the light of a broader consideration: the need to maintain balance in and among national programs—balance between the private and the public economy, balance between cost and hoped-for advantage, balance between the clearly necessary and the comfortably desirable, balance between our essential requirements as a nation and the duties imposed by the Nation upon the individual, balance between actions of the moment and the national welfare of the future. Good judgment seeks balance and progress; lack of it eventually finds imbalance and frustration.

The record of many decades stands as proof that our people and their Government have, in the main, understood these truths and have responded to them well in the face of stress and threat. But threats, new in kind or degree, constantly arise. I mention two only.

IV

A vital element in keeping the peace is our Military Establishment. Our arms must be mighty, ready for instant action, so that no potential aggressor may be tempted to risk his own destruction.

Our military organization today bears little relation to that known by any of my predecessors in peacetime, or indeed by the fighting men of World War II and Korea.

Until the latest of our world conflicts, the United States had no armaments industry. American makers of plowshares could, with time and as required, make swords as well. But now we can no longer risk emergency improvisation of national defense; we have been compelled to create a permanent armaments industry of vast proportions. Added to this, 3½ million men and women are directly engaged in the Defense Establishment. We annually spend on military security more than the net income of all United States corporations.

This conjunction of an immense Military Establishment and a large arms industry is new in the American experience. The total influence—economic, political, even spiritual—is felt in every city, every statehouse, every office of the Federal Government. We recognize the imperative need for this development. yet we must not fail to comprehend its grave implications. Our toil, resources, and livelihood are all involved; so is the very structure of our society.

In the councils of government we must guard against the acquisitions of unwarranted influence whether sought or unsought, by the military-industrial complex. The potential for the disastrous rise of misplaced power exists and will persist.

We must never let the weight of this combination endanger our liberties or democratic processes. We should take nothing for granted. Only an alert and knowledgeable citizenry can compel the proper meshing of the huge industrial and military machinery of defense with our peaceful methods and goals so that security and liberty may prosper together.

Akin to and largely responsible for the sweeping changes in our industrial-military posture has been the technological revolution during recent decades. In this revolution research has become central; it also becomes more formalized, complex, and costly. A steadily increasing share is conducted for, by, or at the direction of the Federal Government.

Today the solitary inventor, tinkering in his shop, has been overshadowed by task forces of scientists in laboratories and testing fields. In the same fashion the free university, historically the fountainhead of free ideas and scientific discovery, has experienced a revolution in the conduct of research. Partly because of the huge costs involved, a Government contract becomes virtually a substitute for intellectual curiosity. For every old blackboard there are now hundreds of new electronic computers.

The prospect of domination of the Nation's scholars by Federal employment, project allocations, and the power of money is ever present and is gravely to be regarded.

Yet, in holding scientific research and discovery in respect, as we should, we must also be alert to the equal and opposite danger that public policy could itself become the captive of a scientific technological elite.

It is the task of statesmanship to mold, to balance, and to integrate these and other forces, new and old, within the principles of our democratic system—ever aiming toward the supreme goals of our free society.

V

Another factor in maintaining balance involves the element of time. As we peer into society's future, we—you and I, and our Government—must avoid the impulse to live only for today, plundering for our own ease and convenience the precious resources of tomorrow. We cannot mortgage the material assets of our grandchildren without risking the loss also of their political and spiritual heritage. We want democracy to survive for all generations to come, not to become the insolvent phantom of tomorrow.

VI

Down the long lane of the history yet to be written, America knows that this world of ours, ever growing smaller, must avoid becoming a community of dreadful fear and hate and be, instead, a proud confederation of mutual trust and respect.

Such a confederation must be one of equals. The weakest must come to the conference table with the same confidence as do we, protected as we are by our moral, economic, and military strength. That table, though scarred by many past frustrations, cannot be abandoned for the certain agony of the battlefield.

Disarmament, with mutual honor and confidence, is a continuing imperative. Together we must learn how to compose differences, not with arms but with intellect and decent purpose. Because this need is so sharp and apparent I confess that I lay down my official responsibilities in this field with a definite sense of disappointment. As one who has witnessed the horror and the lingering sadness of war, as one who knows that another war could utterly destroy this civilization which has been so slowly and painfully built over thousands of years, I wish I could say tonight that a lasting peace is in sight.

Happily I can say that war has been avoided. Steady progress toward our ultimate goal has been made. But so much remains to be done. As a private citizen I shall never cease to do what little I can to help the world advance along that road.

VII

So, in this my last good night to you as your President, I thank you for the many opportunities you have given me for public service in war and peace. I trust that in that service you find some things worthy; as for the rest of it, I know you will find ways to improve performance in the future.

You and I, my fellow citizens, need to be strong in our faith that all nations, under God, will reach the goal of peace with justice. May we be ever unswerving in devotion to principle, confident but humble with power, diligent in pursuit of the Nation's great goals.

To all the peoples of the world, I once more give expression to America's prayerful and continuing aspiration:

We pray that peoples of all faith, all races, all nations, may have their great human needs satisfied; that those now denied opportunity shall come to enjoy it to the full; that all who yearn for freedom may experience its spiritual blessings; that those who have freedom will understand, also, its heavy responsibilities; that all who are insensitive to the needs of others will learn charity; that the scourges of poverty, disease, and ignorance will be made to disappear from the earth; and that, in the goodness of time, all peoples will come to live together in a peace guaranteed by the binding force of mutual respect and love.

The Weapons System

Mary Kaldor

It has become commonplace to compare the command of an army with the management of a large corporation. But there is one essential difference. It is easier to persuade men to work than to kill or to risk getting killed. The basis of persuasion in the armed forces has varied according to time and place. It has involved such things as personal loyalty, the appeal to ideas like patriotism and democracy, and discipline. Yet is it probably true to say that in modern society the persuasive techniques used by military officers have more nearly come to resemble the techniques adopted in industry. Except during the Vietnam War, when, as we shall see, the inadequacies of military persuasion were acutely revealed, the output of the armed forces, the business of killing has become more remote, and the production of armed forces, the organisations of men and machines, has become more and more of an industrial undertaking.

Morris Janowitz, in his seminal book *The Professional Soldier,* which was published in 1960, described "the shift from authoritarian domination to greater reliance on manipulation, persuasion and group consensus."[1] And he ascribed this shift to modern technology:

> *The technology of warfare is so complex that the coordination of a complex group of specialists cannot be guaranteed simply by authoritarian discipline. Members of a military group recognize their greater mutual dependence on the technical proficiency of the team members, rather than on the formal authority structure.*[2]

In industry the embodiment of technology is the machine, and much has been written about the domination of man by machine in the twentieth century. The military equivalent of the machine is the weapons system. The weapons system combines a weapons platform: ship, aircraft or tank; a weapon: gun, missile, or torpedo; and the means of command and communication. The concept of the weapons system emerged in the late nineteenth century with the Anglo-German naval arms race and came to fruition in World War II as the aircraft and the tank came of age, although the term was not used until the 1950s. It was associated, as we shall see, with the entry of capitalist industry into the arms market; shipbuilding and heavy engineering in Britain in the 1880s, aircraft and automobiles in the 1940s.

As the term is used in this book, the "weapons system" is more than just a military classification of hardware. It is a classification of people as well. The weapons system implies the existence of an entire supporting cast—scientists to invent the weapons, workers to build them, soldiers to use them, and technicians to repair them. Indeed, the concept was developed by the U.S. Air Force in the 1950s as a tool of management, in order to organize this ever-growing cast. The institutions and language of "systems" however, served eventually to conceal the relationship between government and industry, which underlies the very concept of the weapons system.

In most Western countries, the procurement of armaments, what one might call the fixed capital of warfare, accounts for about half the military budget. Moreover, the procurement budget is dominated by a few major weapon systems. In the United States, for example, the Trident submarine and the new nuclear-powered aircraft carrier, together with their missiles and aircraft, account for about 60 percent of the naval procurement budget. The latest Air Force fighters, F-15 and F-16, account for more than 40 percent of the Air Force procurement budget, while the XM-1 battle tank accounts for a major share of the Army budget. The same is true in Western Europe. In Britain, the Multi Role Combat Aircraft (MRCA) Tornado accounts for around 40 percent of the Royal Air Force budget; the three anti-submarine warfare cruisers, with their associated escort and support ships, probably account for a fifth to a quarter of the British naval procurement budget.

The major weapons system defines, by and large, the lines of command in modern armed forces. Navies, for example, are organized by ship, with groups of ships organized hierarchically into task forces. At the apex of the U.S. surface navy is the aircraft carrier, requiring destroyers and a submarine or two for protection, aircraft to fly from its deck, and supply ships of various kinds. The bomber and the battle tank have a similar role in the Air Force and Army. The Air Force is divided into bomber, fighter, and transport commands. The Army is made up of armour, artillery, parachute, and infantry units. But the armoured units are, to quote Colonel Vernon Pizer, "the mailed fist that strikes hard, fast and deep,"[3] the core of the combined arms team. The House Armed Services Committee of the U.S. Congress recently reasserted its belief that "the tank is—and will continue to be—the heart of land warfare."[4] The independence of individual services or military units is achieved through independent strategies associated with particular weapons systems. This would explain why strategic bombing is so central to the U.S. Air Force or why the British Navy remains committed to an oceangoing role associated with carriers, long after the abandonment of overseas commitments.

The growing capital intensity of warfare is also reflected in the composition of skills. The direct labour of war, which includes infantrymen,

tank crews, artillerymen, fighter and bomber crewmen, fighting ships' personnel, who actually do the fighting, has declined dramatically as a proportion of total military manpower. It is known as the declining "teeth to tail" ratio.

> *In all the [U.S.] services fewer than one out of every six persons in uniform—360,000 out of 2,200,000—currently serve in a combat specialty. By way of historical comparison, better than nine of every ten persons serving in the Union forces during the American Civil War had combat specialties.*[5]

The lone fighter pilot, who was the heroic individual of World War II, was in fact part of a team that serviced, operated, and maintained his aeroplane; a team which today has grown to seventy people. The tendency to substitute "the firepower and mobility of improved war machines for manpower"[6] is also reflected in what is known as "grade creep," the increase in middle-level officers—the white-collar military technicians—so that the traditional pyramid shape of the military hierarchy has come to look like a diamond.

The role of the individual is thus defined in relation to the weapons system, and the lower his position in the hierarchy, the more specialised is his job. At the base of any modern military organization is the small group of about ten to thirty enlisted men, identified by occupation (e.g., a division of ship's cooks) or by function (e.g., a gun crew). Modern military sociologists argue that the individual thinks of himself as a member of a specific skill group rather than of a social class and that his motivation is based on technical pride in his work. There is a powerful ideology of team spirit in the well-integrated, technically efficient military unit, which, combined with modern awe for technology, is supposed to supplement, if not supplant, traditional techniques of command and control. According to Morris Janowitz, this is symbolised in the uniform of the soldier. In the past, smart uniforms were an expression of the military idea of honour. Today, the occupational uniform of both the U.S. Army and U.S. Air Force is the fatigue suit.

The uniform which obscures the differences between ranks similarly obliterates the difference between the military and the industrial. It is a persistent expression of the thought that military men are not only representative men, but representative of the technical contemporary society rather than of a previous historical period.[7]

The link between the military and the industrial is not only an idea, it is materialised in the weapons system. Like the machine, the weapons system is both an object of use and an object of production. The military capabilities of a particular weapons system, which define its role in a particular military unit, reflect the manufacturing capabilities of a particular defence company. Thus, there are parallels, which have become closer over time, between military organisation and industrial structure.

The design, development, and production of weapons systems is, by and large, undertaken by a handful of companies known as prime contractors. With a few significant exceptions, to be discussed in a later chapter, the prime contractors are generally the manufacturers of weapons platforms—aircraft, shipbuilding, automobile, or engineering companies.* They assemble the complete weapons system, subcontracting subsystems, like gun or missile, the engine and the electronics and components, and so create an interdependent network of big and small companies. The prime contractors are generally among the largest industrial companies. Since World War II, between forty and fifty companies have regularly appeared both on *Fortune's* list of the top one hundred United States companies and on the Pentagon's list of the one hundred companies receiving the highest prime contract awards. The stability of the primes has been widely noted. Since the war, firms have disappeared through merger or, in Europe, through nationalisation, but there have been virtually no closures and virtually no new entrants.

Each of the primes specialises in types of weapons systems. Boeing, General Dynamics, and Rockwell are bomber enterprises. Grumman and Vought make fighters for the Navy; McDonnell Douglas and General Dynamics make fighters for the Air Force; Lockheed makes heavy air transports as well as submarine-based missiles. Chrysler and General Motors are the prime contractors for battle tanks. Dassault in France, MBB in Germany and British Aerospace in Britain make combat aircraft. Fokker in Holland makes transport aircraft. Westland, in Britain, like Sikorsky (now a division of United Technologies), Bell, or Boeing Vertol in America, or Sud Aviation (now Aerospatiale) in France, are the manufacturers of helicopters. Electric Boat, now owned by General Dynamics, has made submarines since the 1890s, when it was purchased by the British company Vickers. Today Electric Boat is building the Trident submarine, the projected system for the American underwater nuclear forces in the 1980s. Newport News makes aircraft carriers. And so on.

Each of these companies represents a manufacturing experience, a particular combination of plant, equipment, and people, a specific mix of skills and techniques, an hierarchical organisation of people, of relationships with customers (the military units) and suppliers (the subcontractors). The president of Newport News, when justifying financial claims on the government to a congressional committee, explained:

What we have built at Newport News is a unique ship-manufacturing complex—the only one in the United States that has the facilities, equipment and human resources to build, repair, overhaul and refuel the full range of Navy vessels and the only one now building nuclear-powered surface ships. Newport News is truly a national asset.[8]

Literally thousands of subcontractors are dependent on the primes. Some are very large and

---

*In Europe tanks are made by engineering companies rather than by automobile companies.

are prime contractors themselves. These would include the engine companies like Rolls Royce, Pratt and Whitney (now United Technologies), and General Electric, or the electronic companies like Texas Instruments, Raytheon, Westinghouse in the United States, or Ferranti and Marconi-Elliot in Britain. There are also many small suppliers; some are established by the primes to produce a particular component. The small subcontractors are not at all stable. Their composition varies along with technology, and in the lean years it is they who go bankrupt.

Very often, prime contractors and their families of subcontractors dominate a region, so that the economic impact of producing a weapons system may be very great. Boeing is the biggest company in the state of Washington. Several aircraft companies—Lockheed, Rockwell, Douglas, for example—are located in Southern California. McDonnell dominates manufacturing in St. Louis, while Bath Ironworks, which makes destroyers, is the most important employer in Maine. Hundreds and thousands of people may work on a single contract. At Electric Boat in Groton, Connecticut, 31,000 people are estimated to work on the Trident submarine. And this does not include the people employed by subcontractors or the ripple effect on the producers of consumer goods purchased by the people employed or the capital goods acquired by the contractors. At Rockwell, 13,000 people were working on the B-1 bomber project when it was cancelled in 1977, and about 40,000 people were said to have been employed by Rockwell's subcontractors throughout the nation. Had the B-1 bomber gone into production, many thousands more would have been employed. In the 1960s, it was estimated that, although military contracts account directly for only 8 percent of California's employment, the total impact including indirect employment by subcontractors and indirect employment among producers of consumer and capital goods was 40 percent.[9] And if we also take into account the fact that many small firms which produce both military and civil goods are dependent on the military market to ensure their survival, then it is evident that the defence industry is deeply embedded in the economy as a whole.

The weapons system is subject to a technological dynamic characteristic of its industrial environment. As the social structure of industry and the armed forces converge, the competition which epitomizes private industrial enterprise pervades the various institutions which make up the organisation of defense. The National Security Industrial Association, an organisation of American defence contractors, reports:

> Within DoD [the U.S. Department of Defense] itself, competition is a very active force. This is reflected in DoD's drive to stay ahead of our potential enemies by fielding weapons which incorporate the latest possible technology; in DoD's relationships with other governmental departments; in the efforts of the military services to protect and expand their respective roles and missions and to obtain a larger share of the defense budget; in the relationship between the military services and the Office of the Secretary of Defense; and in the competition among the branches, commands, arsenals, yards, centers, and laboratories of the military services.
>
> For industry, competition is keen because the overall total of defense business is seldom adequate to support the available capacity of even the hard-core defense contractors, thus forcing the companies into a continuous life-and-death struggle to obtain defense contracts. Defense programs often are of gigantic magnitude, which results in competition more intensely concentrated than is typically encountered in the commercial marketplace.[10]

The consequence of this competition is rapid technical change, in which every component part of successive weapons systems is pushed up to and beyond the "state of the art." It is the fantastic space-age dimensions of much modern weaponry which so awes the soldier and the civilian observer. And yet the direction of technical change, it can be argued, is confined within limits that are defined by the persistence of military and industrial institutions. The stability of prime contractors and their customers has helped to preserve traditions about the kind of military equipment that is considered appropriate. Indeed, the very sophistication and complexity of hardware may be a sign of conservatism and narrow perspective. In peacetime, in the absence of external necessity imposed by war, decisions about what constitutes technical advance are necessarily subjective. They tend to be taken by people who make and use the weapons systems, whose ideas are necessarily shaped by institutional experience and interest in survival. "We have," writes John Downey, an eminent British soldier,

> *a situation in which the nature of present strategy (deterrence) precludes the acid test of war, while complexity invalidates the rough and ready evaluations of public opinion.*[11]

The consequence is that

> *the system is almost completely introverted, concentrating on the perpetual perfection of itself against some future day of judgement. The dynamic tensions, commonly regarded as necessary in all systems, must also be generated internally and can only come from debate between vigorous minds. But although the system strives hard to recruit able people, it chooses and trains them in its own image.*[12]

Morris Janowitz makes much the same point when he emphasises the routinisation of innovation in the military establishment, with the consequence that

> *traditional thinking has more often than not led to trend thinking, to a concern with gradually perfecting technical instruments, rather than strategic re-evaluation of weapons systems. This orientation in itself is a form, though a modified one, of technological conservatism whether the problem is missiles or manpower, planning toward the future tends to be a perfection of trends*

> *rather than an imaginative emphasis on revolutionary development.*[13]

This is what we mean by baroque technology. "Baroque" technical change consists largely of improvements to a given set of "performance characteristics." Submarines are faster, quieter, bigger, and have longer ranges. Aircraft have greater speed, more powerful thrust, and bigger payloads. All weapons systems have more destructive weapons, particularly missiles, and greatly improved capabilities for communication, navigation, detection, identification, and weapon guidance. Even the development of nuclear weapons can be regarded as an extension of strategic bombing. While the basic technology of the delivery system has not changed much, such marginal improvements have often entailed the use of very advanced technology; e.g., radical electronics innovations such as microprocessors or nuclear power for submarines, and this has greatly increased the complexity of the weapons system as a whole.

Any "improvement" to a particular performance characteristic tends to beget others, and any "improvement" to a particular weapons system as a whole tends to infect whole families of weapons systems. Witness this description of the carrier:

> *To achieve greater air capability . . . the individual naval aircraft and the ships' complement have grown in size and complexity. . . .*
>
> *These trends have caused growth in the carrier itself, because of the need for more aviation fuel, more hangar-deck space, greater strength and size of the landing deck to support the heavier aircraft with higher landing speeds and so forth. As all parts of the design move together, the carrier, its power plant, its auxiliary services, and its crew have all grown. . . .*[14]

Baroque technical change may also lead to versatility, the development of multipurpose weapons systems. Competition tends to promote institutional expansion. Military branches, services, and commands poach the roles of others; corporations imitate the capabilities of competitors. The Army emphasises the development of amphibious and airborne missions. The Navy clings to the ability to fly aircraft and land Marines. The Air Force, in order to retain its organisational autonomy through its bombing role, insists that fighter aircraft be able to strike deep into enemy territory. Prime contractors tend to diversify into a wider range of defence products. Lockheed, Litton, and General Dynamics, aerospace companies, have purchased shipyards. North American Aviation merged with Rockwell, the company which makes axles for army trucks. The Ford Motor Company has acquired an aerospace subsidiary. At the same time, the growing cost of individual weapons systems has tended to result in a decline in their number and variety so that military units have had to share the same systems and contractors have learned to collaborate in development and production.

The consequence is the all-rounded weapons system: the number of "performance characteristics" specified for a weapons system is increased. The different characteristics that were formerly specified for several individual systems are now combined into one. The F-111, which was to have been the main combat aircraft of the American Air Force and Navy during the 1970s, was expected by Tactical Air Command to have to take off from short and rough landing strips and to fly the Atlantic non-stop,

> to travel extremely long distances, carrying a load of nuclear weapons and fly at treetop level . . . engage in aerial combat at high altitudes and at speeds in excess of 1,700 miles per hour . . . [and to have] a large ordnance carrying capacity.[15]

These were the characteristics which defined the Air Force missions of interdiction, air superiority, and ground support. In addition, the Navy wanted a plane for fleet air defence. For this, the plane had to be able to circle "a fleet of ships at high altitudes for long periods . . . [and] to locate and destroy up to twenty miles away any enemy aircraft approach-

ing the fleet."[16] It turned out to be very difficult to make one plane which could do all these things well, and in the end, the Navy version was cancelled.

The British cruiser *Invincible* and its sister ships *Indefatigable* and *Ark Royal* are expected to combine roles of command, control, and coordination of British and NATO maritime forces, the deployment of anti-submarine warfare aircraft, and the capacity to carry one thousand commando troops—tasks which were formerly carried out by several different ships. The European Multi Role Combat Aircraft, which is jointly developed and produced by Britain, Germany, and Italy, has been described as the "egg-laying, wool-producing, milk-giving sow."[17] Britain wants MRCA for long-range strike and strategic air defence (against bombers). Germany wants MRCA for close air support. Italy wants MRCA for air superiority (against fighters). As we shall see in a later chapter, these requirements are not easy to reconcile; MRCA has ended up primarily as an expensive low-level bomber for nuclear strike.

These features of baroque technical change—trend improvement and multiplication of roles—are designed to preserve the military-industrial structure. But technical change demands organisational change. What occurs is a kind of regroupment for survival. More and more men are required to produce and operate a particular type of weapons system, increasing the size of military and industrial teams, as well as the degree of individual specialisation. As the variety of weapons systems declines, the tactics of different military missions, and even the broader land, sea, and air strategies, are more closely integrated. The number of prime contractors for each type of weapons system falls and the interdependence of companies is increased through mergers, collaboration, and an interlocking set of contractual relationships. The smaller subcontractors become more fragmented and more specialised; duplicate suppliers for particular components are squeezed out, while the total number of components increases. Essentially, these changes mean greater hierarchy and less individual autonomy; a narrowing of the apex of the pyramid in both military and industrial spheres. Transnational projects like MRCA or the Anglo-French Jaguar, or even the American and German attempt to achieve "commonality" in tank design, represent the development of multinational forms of military and industrial organisation.

The consequence of this elaborate combination of conservatism and technical dynamism is what economists call "diminishing returns": more and more effort is expended for smaller improvements in military effectiveness. As military and industrial teams grow bigger and more hierarchical, the relationship of the individual to the whole is at once narrower and more remote; the inability to see beyond the design of a component, the repair of a part, or the wrath of an immediate superior may impair the ability to consider the industrial technology or the military mission in its entirety. Conflict and compromise are increasingly built into the design of weapons systems as formerly competing users and producers join in a single project. A former Litton employee describes the problems that were encountered when two hundred people were assigned the task of preparing a proposal for the series production of Spruance class destroyers for the Navy:

Scarce top engineering talent was siphoned into management roles, from which positions they had little time to actually work on, or even think about, the actual problem. Instead, they became embroiled in jurisdictional fights and empire-building. If a job got behind, the group involved automatically claimed it didn't have enough people. More people were supplied, and management problems compounded.

Efforts at communication took up much of the time. This was aggravated by the fact that group managers sometimes withheld information if this was judged to be in the individual group's parochial interest.... Thus a technical mistake ... could proceed for some time without being noticed....

Finally, a group this size presents severe problems in motivating the people who actually do the work to operate in accordance with the goal of the overall project. The people who actually did the work were so far removed from the corporate reward system that their own goal became minimizing the risk that their individual subsystem be judged infeasible.... The result was consistent overdesign and conservatism. The lowest level would design an individual system element with plenty of margin, his boss would throw in another margin just to make sure, and so on.[18]

The problem was compounded by the size of the Navy evaluation team:

Litton realized that whatever the merits of its basic concept, unless the proposal defined such subsystems as, say, the galley in great detail, whoever was evaluating the galley part of the proposal would give the proposal low marks. Since there were many such subsystems, a disproportionate amount of Litton's effort was devoted to routine subsystem design.[19]

Similar problems have been recounted for the design of other systems. On the F-111, for example, Graham Allison, in a summary of a study by Robert Coulam, describes how the contractor and the Air Force organised their engineering teams "in parallel fashion with horizontal communications quite strong between counterpart contractor and Air Force civilian engineers." This greatly hampered the ability to make technical trade-offs.

If results at one level of design indicated the need to trade among higher order objectives, the whole elaborate hierarchy of specification detail—detail which coordinated the engineering efforts of thousands of contractors and government officials—stood in the way.... Even relatively minor reformulations would require the concurrence of layer upon layer of contractor and government authorities.[20]

The outcome of this contradictory process, in which technology is simultaneously promoted and restrained, is gross, elaborate, and very expensive hardware. The Trident programme will cost the American taxpayer over $30 billion (in 1980 prices). The latest nuclear-powered aircraft carrier, the subject of controversy between Congress and President Carter, will cost, together with its associated ships and aircraft, more than $60 billion. An Air Force F-15 fighter costs $19 million; the Navy F-14 costs $22 million. The Air Force F-16 and Navy F-18, which were originally designed as cheap, lightweight fighters, are currently estimated to cost $11 million and $18 million respectively. These costs are several times greater than the cost of World War II predecessors, even when inflation is taken into account. One well-known estimate suggests that if current trends continue, the U.S. Air Force will be able to afford only one plane in 2020.[21] Bombers cost two hundred times as much as they did in World War II. Fighters cost one hundred times or more than they did in World War II. Aircraft carriers are twenty times as expensive and battle tanks are fifteen times as expensive as in World War II. A Gato class submarine cost $5,500 per ton in World War II, compared with $1.6 million per ton for the Trident submarine.[22]

These costs primarily reflect amazing sophistication and technical complexity. And complexity means thousands and thousands of parts, each part a servicing and logistical problem. The F-4, for example, the predecessor to F-14 and F-15, required 70,000 spare parts. In Vietnam, despite the most extensive logistical operation ever mounted, there were always shortages. All military aircraft are much less reliable than commercial aircraft. They break down more often; they require more maintenance, more repairs, more spares, and more fuel. Tanks are much less reliable than tractors, and warships are much less reliable than merchant ships. As weapons systems become complex, particularly as they incorporate more electronic equipment, reliability declines and operational costs increase at an exponential rate (despite the increased reliability of solid-state devices and improved automated maintenance). According to Captain O'Rourke, a U.S. Navy officer:

Expensive airplanes are complex airplanes, and complex airplanes, over the past ten to fifteen years, have been the bane of our existence. The costs of keeping a stable of these complex machines in fighting trim is astronomical—in terms of people. Our maintenance and support people have repeatedly fallen behind the heavy demands which these complex, sophisticated systems have made. The Navy supply system, bound up in red tape of its own space age bureaucratic computerdom, has rarely been able to stay apace with the ever-increasing demands for high cost, one-of-a-kind spare parts for the sophisticated systems.[23]

Complex weapons systems are also complex to operate. And yet training hours, combat exercises, and firing practice are reduced because of high operating cost as well as the risk of an expensive accident. And families of weapons systems are increasingly dependent on complex systems of communication which are also costly to operate and maintain.

Nor is it at all clear that cost and complexity are justified by increased performance. First of all, measurable improvements in performance characteristics are rarely proportionate to the increase in costs. In particular, all-roundedness, as we have seen, tends to *reduce* the efficiency of any one role. Second, improvements in the accuracy and lethality of munitions have greatly increased the vulnerability of all weapons systems and their associated communication and support systems. As a result, many of the performance characteristics so dear to the services and contractors have become irrelevant in modern warfare. The classic examples are aircraft speed, which reduces the accuracy of pinpoint bombing, and speed of surface vessels, which cannot reduce vulnerability to aircraft and submarines. A recent Pentagon exercise, known as Air Missile Intercept Evaluation, demonstrated that numbers were more important than sophistication in air warfare. In close engagements, F-5s, F-14s, and F-15s consistently destroyed one another. Major General Frederick C. Blesse (USAF ret'd), who observed the exercise, explained: "it doesn't make much difference how fast your airplane is or how high it will fly. Once you get inside your enemy's missile envelope, you're not likely to escape."[24] The more sophisticated aircraft, F-14 and F-15, imposed great strain on the pilots, who were unable to make use of the many theoretical capabilities of the planes.

The Trident, perhaps, is the best example, because most people would think that nuclear-firing missile submarines represent just about the best that modern military technology has to offer. The Trident submarine is huge. It is 560 feet long, longer than the Washington Monument, and six inches too deep to get out of the Thames Channel in Connecticut from its building site to the sea. It is faster than its predecessors, the Polaris/Poseidon submarines. It carries more missiles with a longer range. It has a natural circulation nuclear reactor which is significantly quieter at normal patrol speeds. Its size and its large complement of missiles, however, may actually increase its vulnerability, since it will be easier to detect than its predecessors. Its top underwater speed (25 knots) is still significantly lower than that of attack submarines (30 knots), and in any case, it is so noisy at top speed that it would have to go slowly to escape detection. The increased missile range is of dubious advantage since, for the foreseeable future, Soviet anti-submarine warfare forces cannot detect submarines within the operating area of the current Poseidon submarine.

Similar criticisms can be made of the main systems now under development in the United States: the XM-1 Main Battle Tank, the new MX intercontinental missile, the new class of Air Force and Navy fighters, the cruise missile carriers, and the latest aircraft carriers. William W. Kaufman, an adviser to James Schlesinger when he was Secretary of Defense, said of the aircraft carrier that

> *no more costly method of keeping a limited number of airplanes at a forward base has ever been devised by the mind of man. The Navy cannot define circumstances in which these very expensive sorties will make a significant difference in a situation where we care.*[25]

It is equally difficult to explain why some of the European systems like MRCA or Invincible will be better than their predecessors.

In short, the weapons system, in perfecting itself along the lines projected by users and producers, seems to have overreached itself. It has become big, costly, elaborate, and less and less functional. It serves a certain social purpose, in creating an ever more complicated set of connections between soldiers, sailors, officers, managers, designers, workers, and bureaucrats. And it retains a certain grandeur, a certain ability to instill social awe, that is often to be found in the baroque, whether art, architecture, or technology—a grandeur that may portend degeneration.

---

1. New York: Free Press, 1960, p. 8.

2. Ibid., p. 41.

3. Vernon Pizer (Lt. Colonel, U.S.A. Ret.), *The U.S. Army* (New York: Praeger, 1967), p. 39.

4. Quoted in Jonathan E. Medalia and A. A. Tinajero, "XM-1 Main Battle Tank Program," *Issue Brief* Number IB 75052, Washington, D.C.: Library of Congress, Congressional Research Service, July 1975, updated May 1978.

5. William D. White, U.S. *Tactical Air Power: Missions, Forces and Costs* (Washington, D.C.: The Brookings Institution, 1974), p. 5.

6. Ibid.

7. Janowitz, op. cit., p. 230.

8. *U.S. Congressional Record,* 95th Cong., 1st Sess., CXXIII, Part 8, p. 9269, March 28, 1977.

9. Charles M. Tiebout, "The Regional Impact of Defense Expenditures: Its Measurement and Problems of Adjustment," in Roger E. Bolton, *Defense and Disarmament: The Economics of Transition* (Englewood Cliffs, N.J.: Prentice-Hall, 1966).

10. Quoted in J. R. Fox, *Arming America: How the U.S. Buys Weapons* (Cambridge, Mass.: Harvard University, 1974), pp. 100–1.

11. *Management in the Armed Forces: An Anatomy of the Military Profession* (London: McGraw-Hill, 1977), p. 195.

12. Ibid., p. 198.

13. Op.cit., pp. 27–28.

14. Seymour J. Deitchman, *New Technologies and Military Power: General Purpose Forces for the 1980s and Beyond* (Boulder, Colo.: Westview Press, 1979), p. 107.

15. Robert J. Art, *The TFX Decision: NcNamara and the Military* (Boston: Little, Brown & Co., 1968), p. 15.

16. Ibid., p. 25.

17. Ulrich Albrecht, et al., "Das ender des MRCA?" in Studien-gruppe Militärpolitik, *Ein Anti-Weisbuch Materialien für eine Alternative Militärpolitik* (Hamburg: Rowohlt, 1974), author's translation, p. 83.

18. J. W. Devanney in "The DX Competition," *U.S. Naval Institute Proceedings* (August 1975), pp. 25–26.

19. Ibid.

20. "The F-111," in *Commission on the Organization of the Government for the Conduct of Foreign Policy* (Murphy Commission) (Washington, D.C., June 1975), *Volume 4, Appendix K: Adequacy of Current Organization: Defense and Arms Control,* pp. 131–2.

21. Norman R. Augustine, "One Plane, One Tank, One Ship: Trend for the Future," *Defense Management Journal* (April 1975).

22. Aerospace Systems Analysis, McDonnell Douglas Astronautics Corp., *Cost of War Index* (Santa Monica, Calif.: September 1968).

23. "Two Views on Navy Fighters," *Armed Forces Journal* (November 1974).

24. Quoted in Jo. L. Husbands, "The Long Long Pipeline. Arms Sales and Technological Dependence," unpublished, Center for Defense Information, Washington, D.C., 1978.

25. Quoted in John Wicklein, "The Oldest Establishment Permanent Floating Anachronism in the Sea," *Washington Monthly* (February 1970).

The Economics of War and Peace: Is War the Only Way to Save U.S. Capitalism?

Alexander Cockburn • James Ridgeway
From an Original Speech by Seymour Melman

In the 1930s the left used to argue that capitalism led to war and that therefore the way to end war would be to end capitalism. Intellectuals such as Lewis Mumford argued, with a wealth of illustration, that war, in preparation and execution, had always been at the cutting edge of capitalism and was indeed its motive force in productive innovation and development.

In fact war "saved" American capitalism from the continuing slump of the late 1930s, and the slump following World War II was itself brought to an end by the Korean War boom.

In the 1970s a rather different gloss was put on the economic consequences of war and of military spending. The financing of the Vietnam War, it was claimed, fueled the inflationary spiral that continues—alternating with savage deflation—until today. So nowadays there is not too much talk about ending capitalism, and liberals and even many leftists have taken to arguing that the way to save capitalism is to end war—or at least diminish military spending—to "sensible" levels. Once they said "war is bad." Now "war is bad for the economy."

Many of the groups currently battling Reagan's defense budget buildup argue that a genuinely "peace-based" U.S. capitalist economy would produce greater prosperity than the war-based economy the country has now. This is the position of Jobs with Peace, a group actively campaigning among grassroots labor. . . .

• • •

The role of war-spending in the economy has been a vital and highly vexed topic since the late 1940s, when the idea of "military Keynesianism"—war-or-war-related spending to stimulate the economy—was discussed by Harry Truman's military and economic advisers, notably Leon Keyserling. Today one of the best-known exponents of the supposedly baneful relationship between military spending and the performance and prospects of U.S. capitalism is professor Seymour Melman of Columbia, author of such books as *The Permanent War Economy* and the forthcoming *Profits Without Production.*

At the Socialist Scholars Conference held at Cooper Union on April 1 and 2, Melman spoke at a panel on "The State and the Economy." On the same panel were Paul Sweezy, Representative John Convers, Robert Lekachman, and Anthony Mazzocchi. Space restrictions do not permit us to reproduce more than the bulk of Melman's address here. We do so because it graphically expresses one view: that U.S. capitalism might be saved and indeed enhanced—at least in terms of provision of employment and satisfactory goods and services to the citizenry—if it is "converted" from a war to a peace footing.

But what if it can't be saved? What if there is no salvation for U.S. capitalism beyond the purviews of war-spending? This is a side of the argument one hears less of today than in the 1930s. . . .

The Social Contract
Has Been Broken

Melman: For a century, a sustaining characteristic of a radical critique of American capitalism has been coupled with the understanding that the managers of industry were competent to organize work, were competent, within the limits of their calculations of profit, to see to the production of goods that were technically acceptable and economically acceptable in the marketplace.

That classic assumption is no longer valid. . . . Until recently, the managers of U.S. industry were the world's best organizers of industrial work. That was the basis for their profits and for their claim to large personal incomes. Since a community must produce in order to live, and since a core task of a community is to organize people to work, the managers, within the constraints of their profit-making concerns, performed a vital function. The decision-power and personal wealth accorded to managers was one side of a historic exchange of a social contract. In return for these privileges, management was expected by working people and community to organize work.

That social contract was threatened by the Great Depression, and was restored as a legitimation for management only when a new contingent of *state* managers was introduced to share in the decision power over the industrial economy. Thereafter, management's economists, informed by the theories of Keynes, hoped that a new public-sector military economy would help to stabilize the functioning of the management's decision processes, extending to the private sector as well.

But the successful pursuit of profits and power by both private and state managers also resulted in a major *unintended* effect: a process of economic and technological depletion of the means of production itself was set in motion, causing major contraction of opportunities for productive life. Management's social contract with working people and community has been broken. The evidence of that break now pours forth in the daily papers, the weekly newsmagazines, and in an array of books dealing with depletion of interest.

Collapse of Competence

Since the mid-1960s, the production competence of many U.S. industries has obviously been deteriorating. By 1980, a fifth of the steel used in the U.S. was supplied from abroad. A fourth of the new machine tools, a third of the new automobiles, were no longer produced by American workers in American factories. A visit to almost any hi-fi or camera store in an American city will confirm that only a minor part of the sophisticated products offered for sale are made in the U.S. The domestic production of these and many other capital and consumer goods has been replaced increasingly by products of Western Europe and Japan. Managers in those countries, sometimes using exported U.S. capital, have learned how to do what U.S. managers did for a century, 1865–1965: namely, to compensate for high and still rising wages by rapid improvements in productivity.

The collapse of the production competence of U.S. managers has many components. The components that deal with short-term profit-taking . . . the attention to exporting capital the better to make a profit, all these matters have been addressed in what is now a widening literature. What is characteristically *not* addressed is the role that managerialism, and especially that of the state, has played in accelerating the decline in production competence. We should do nothing less now than pay attention to the fact that Karl Marx's greatest work was called *Capital*. And use that as a hint to pay attention to capital and its use today. By capital I mean production resources. The money expression we'll call finance capital. In the United States from 1951 to the present year, the finance capital allotted to the military functions in this society has exceeded, every year, the net profits of *all* corporations. That means that the state and one branch of it has become the principal controller of finance capital. It is crucial to understand that a modern military budget is a capital fund, where by capital we mean, as in an ordinary enterprise, fixed and working capital. (Fixed: land, labor, and buildings. Working capital: the money value of raw materials, power, purchase components, and all the work of all the classes of people needed to set the enterprise in motion.)

It is crucial to appreciate the magnitude of the military use of capital in relation to civilian use of capital, year by year. The last data available to us are for 1979, as compiled in United Nations reports, and they show us that for every $100 of domestic fixed capital formation, and that means civilian new capital formation, we have used (in 1979) $33 worth of capital separately for the military. By domestic fixed capital formation I mean the money value of all new civilian capital items: streets, sewers, subways, factory buildings, schools, all manner of facilities of a civilian sort appreciated as fixed capital.

That ratio of 33 to 100 in the United States is important to compare to a comparable ratio of 20

to 100 in West Germany, and 3.7 to 100 in Japan. A regrettable paucity of data for the Soviet Union makes it difficult to make a comparable analysis. However, I have prepared an estimate for the Soviet Union which I will stand by until that government announces its proper, official data, and that is, for 1979, 66 per 100. What is of great import for the United States is to appreciate the course that is being followed by the federal government with the evident approval of most of the country.

The military budgets are prepared for five years ahead—five-year plans for military budgets are as American as apple pie—so we *know* the military budget plan for 1988, and we estimate the fixed capital for the military formation civilian by extrapolating the pattern of performance during the 1970s. With those estimated data, I reckon that by 1988 the U.S. will be allotting $87 in fixed and working capital for the military for every $100 of new civilian capital formation. My judgment is that in the course of attaining that level of use of capital for the military, the industrial system of the United States and the infrastructure of American society will be driven to conditions of deterioration so severe as to render it problematic whether it's possible to plan, let alone execute, a return of ordinary workaday production competence. . . .

Decay of Productivity

It is crucial to understand that in the long history of industrial capital, the interior mechanism—what economists call the microeconomy—has operated by a pattern of cost-minimizing. And that meant that managements, the better to maximize profit, would try to offset cost increases of whatever sort. The consequences, for the whole system, of this procedure, especially in the machinery-producing industries, were of crucial importance. For as the producers of machinery offset *their* cost increases, the prices of their profits—machinery used in the rest of the system—did not rise in price as much as the wages of labor, so that for a century, 1865–1965, U.S. management confronted a steady incentive to install and use machinery in place of manual work. A derived effect of that was of course the growth of productivity at what seemed to be an inexorable steady rate. That process has come to a halt. For by 1965 and after, the microeconomy of U.S. industrial firms was transformed. . . .

In parallel, for the rest of manufacturing firms, there was a shift away from cost-minimizing to cost pass-along; that is to say, management proceeded to adopt a pattern of passing cost increases along to price rather than striving to offset them by their internal methods. . . .

During the period 1971 to 1978 in Japan, average hourly earnings rose 177 per cent, but machine-tool prices only rose 51 per cent. That's exactly the way it used to look in the United States, and so what has happened internally in Japan is nothing more or less than the classic pattern that was once characteristic of U.S. industrial management, operating vigorously in that country. In West Germany, wages increased in 1971–1978 by 72 per cent, and machine-tool prices by 59 per cent. Still a margin favoring further mechanization of work. In the United States, while wages in that period also rose 72 per cent, machine-tool prices rose 85 per cent. The consequence is precisely what one would expect. That is, the stock of metal-working and metal machinery in the United States became the coldest stock of any industrialized country.

It is well to appreciate the meaning of the vast capital fund that has been given over to the military, for the military prop, I remind you, is one which has a money price, and is therefore considered, in every economics textbook, as an economic prop. But if you shift your understanding of economic prop to use value, and give attention to usefulness of consumption, or usefulness for further production, then the military product is clearly exempt from those characteristics.

Insatiable Military

It is therefore of enormous importance that the United States expended on its military budgets from 1946 to 1981 $2001 billion, and that the budget planned, and the budgets executed from 1961 to 1988, will amount to $2089 billion. One need make no adjustments for purchasing powers of money to appreciate that these are colossal magnitudes of resources. The more so as we understand these to be capital resources in character. . . .

In a word, the cumulative military budgets 1946–1968 equaled more than 90 per cent of the assessed money value of reproducible national wealth, which means the money value of everything man-made on the surface of the United States, excluding the money value assigned to the land.

Another way of understanding this is of course to appreciate that this intensive abuse of capital for this type of nonproductive function, as I have defined it, has the necessary consequence of extracting not only prime physical but also prime hands and brains from economically useful work. Hence the private and the state managers of American economy are embarked on a course of policy and practice that promises the further industrial economic decay of this society.

Another way of appreciating the magnitude of what is at stake is to understand the estimates that have been prepared of what it might take to repair the damage that has been wrought. Thus a conservative newsweekly, *U.S. News & World Report,* ventured the estimate that to repair the infrastructure of the United States—that is, not to bring it up to first-class quality but to have subways that run on time, waterworks that function, sewage-treatment systems that really operate, and housing that shelters competently—would require an outlay of about $2500 billion. I've estimated that a repair for the damage now wrought in the industrial manufacturing system itself requires an outlay of not less than $2000 billion—so altogether, $4500 billion.

Appreciate that if this were to be contemplated, and that if the task were to be performed in about 20 years, then the arithmetic tells you immediately that we're talking about the wielding of fresh capital-productive resources on the order of magnitude averaging $225 billion a year. There is no place in the American economy for obtaining such a collection of capital resources other than from what is now utilized in the military economy.

The grand-scale character of this tradeoff is absolutely clear: the continuance of the military economy, especially together with the rest of the private industry, promises the industrial deterioration of the U.S. on a massive scale. Accordingly, the suggestions that I have been able to render from this analysis go to the following:

- In place of managerialism, workplace democracy, at all levels.
- In place of centralism, decentralized planning, decentralized control.
- In place of the arms race, attention to a serious, coherent process whereby the entire arms race may be reversed, not simply acting to oppose one or another weapons system.

I'm pleased to tell you, as a co-chairman of SANE, that you can reasonably expect to hear from us a few months hence about a 1983 version of a comprehensive plan for arms race reversal, bringing up to date the last proposal ever made of that sort by the U.S. government, which was in 1962.

Secondly, you can expect us to give renewed emphasis to the idea of converting from a military to a civilian economy, and to call attention to the importance of the legislation that has been placed in the hopper of the House of Representatives by Ted Weiss, that being an economic-conversion bill, which is indispensable for acquiring the resources and for carrying out part of the arms race reversal, which is indispensable for all the rest. . . .

We confront an array of issues *really without precedent.* I remind you that in the Great Depression of the 1930s, there was never a *suspicion* as to the technical, economic competence of U.S. industrial production. That is *precisely* what is at issue today. And the management process—private and state managerial—that has caused this to come to pass must be dealt with at the root.

Economic Conversion: An Exchange

Lloyd J. Dumas ▪ *Suzanne Gordon*

This article and the next debate the usefulness of "economic conversion"—converting firms from military to civilian production, so that military spending can be reduced without creating unemployment and economic decline. First, Lloyd Dumas and Suzanne Gordon attack Gordon Adams's argument against economic conversion. They maintain that converting to civilian production can play a crucial role in promoting peace and strengthening the economy, if it is accompanied by retraining managers and engineers, and other changes. Gordon Adams then replies that economic conversion does not work in the real world—EDS.

Economic conversion has a crucial role in both the revitalization of U.S. industrial competitiveness and the rebuilding of the nation's security. Gordon Adams's attack on conversion and its proponents

(*Bulletin,* February 1986) is based on a combination of factual error, poor economic arguments, fundamental misconceptions, and disturbing distortions of the analysis, goals, and strategies of economic conversion advocates. Because of the potential of the conversion approach, and because such a careless and flawed attack does not contribute to a useful or meaningful debate on the relative merits or weaknesses of this or any other strategy, we feel compelled to respond.

Adams's main argument against conversion is that after many serious, substantial, and sincere attempts, conversion has simply never worked. In his words, "Nearly 25 years of analysis, organizing, and legislative effort aimed at local conversion and national legislation . . . have borne little fruit," and so "economic conversion has come to a dead end." Conversion as it has been advocated is an "impossible, utopian" strategy. Adams's implication that conversion has been aggressively lobbied for, actively organized around, and effectively promoted by a substantial group of activists and legislators is his first major distortion.

Over its 20-year history, conversion has *not* been a major priority of any large group of social or political activists, trade unionists, or legislators. No mass peace movement or any other mass movement for social change has made conversion a central focus of its activities. Peace groups have not lobbied aggressively for conversion legislation. Only a few unions—the International Association of Machinists most prominent among them in recent years—have championed conversion, either by local campaigns or national legislative initiatives. (Fortunately, this situation seems to be changing, and more unions are considering the conversion approach.) It is no surprise, then, that such legislative efforts as have been attempted and the small number of conversion campaigns that have been initiated have not gone further.

Even were conversion supported by a vigorous and well-organized lobby, it would not be easy to promote. Conversion attacks the idea that the employment levels and general economic well-being of workers and communities currently dependent on military spending can be assured only by a continued flow of military money. No one who understands the dynamic of fundamental political change would be astonished to learn that a strategy which deprives defense contractors of a politically powerful argument for increased military spending and against contract cancellations might not be enthusiastically supported by politicians, managers of military-oriented firms, and workers dependent on the military. But more to the point, conversion is seen as a fundamental challenge to management's important prerogatives—the ability to shut down operations whenever and wherever it desires and to produce whatever it wants, whenever, wherever, and however it wants. That also has made it less than popular with the managers of military industry.

Conversion on a massive scale has not "worked," has not swept the land; but then neither have peace and disarmament, economic justice, racial and sexual equality—or attempts, like those Adams himself has been involved in, to cut the military budget. Does that mean we should abandon any or all of these? Hardly. It is fortunate that those who, in the past, advocated such major social, political, and economic changes as an end to the divine right of kings, the abolition of slavery, women's suffrage—and more recently civil rights and environmental awareness—did not take such a short-term view of the struggle. Positive social change can come quickly, but only a dilettante would be surprised if it did not.

Rather than placing the conversion movement in an accurate historical and political context, Adams presents his own version, citing several examples of "failures":

■ The Trident Conversion Campaign, a small group of dedicated and committed, but poorly funded, activists in Connecticut did not, during their relatively brief existence, successfully stop the multibillion dollar Trident nuclear submarine program—one of the largest and most central weapons programs in the nuclear forces.

■ The "strong effort" in the early 1980s to organize alternative use planning to take up slack capacity at the Douglas Aircraft plant in Long Beach, California has been largely pushed aside by new military contracts. This "strong effort," primarily animated by one activist with the cooperation of one local trade union official and one economic specialist from the state of California, was backed by a budget that would not purchase even a few of those now infamous Air Force coffee pots. Further, the proximate goal of the project was to utilize some idle plant capacity and call back some laid-off workers, not to convert the whole facility and its workforce to civilian-oriented production as Adams implies. That this project even reached the stage of serious discussion with managers at the plant is a testament to the power of the constructive alternative approach that is central to the conversion strategy.

■ Adams's discussion of conversion legislation is hopelessly muddled. Senator Christopher Dodd did not introduce a defense dependency bill in the late 1970s. At that time Dodd and Connecticut Congressman Stewart McKinney introduced amendments (including small pieces of ideas contained in a comprehensive conversion planning bill) to the Economic Development Administration (EDA) bill. The bill, with these amendments attached, was passed by the House of Representatives. The version passed by the Senate did not contain comparable conversion-related amendments, and a fierce debate ensued in conference committee where the bill finally died. So while it is true that "no part of this act was ever passed by Congress," the conversion-related amendments did pass successfully through one House of Congress, an important step forward.

Beyond this, the current Defense Economic Adjustment Act (DEAA) proposal (also referred to as the Weiss bill, HR229) is essentially the same as the McGovern-Mathias bill introduced in the late 1970s. The bill, however, is completely different from the legislation earlier proposed by United Auto Workers President Walter Reuther. Reuther could not, of course, have supported the conversion planning approach represented by the Mc-Govern–Marthias–Weiss bill, as Adams implies, because that strikingly different approach was not developed until 1977, and Walter Reuther was killed in a plane crash in 1970.[1]

■ Congressman Ron Dellums's amendment to the 1985 defense bill did not seek to create an Office of Economic Conversion in the Pentagon,

but only called for a feasibility study. The study was carried out by the Department of Defense itself which, not surprisingly, did not favor the idea.

■ No conversion proponent we know has cited the Lucas Plan in the United Kingdom as an example of successful conversion, contrary to Adams's claim. The Lucas Aerospace management never allowed the plan to be implemented, despite the fact that some British management-oriented periodicals praised the trade unionists who drew it up for the quality of their work in suggesting more than 150 civilian-oriented products that could have replaced the military products of the aerospace company. But for years the mere existence of the plan gave the trade unionists who developed it the political leverage to prevent any of the hundreds of layoffs the company kept threatening. Because there was no thoroughgoing implementation of the plan, no one could argue that it represents a successful conversion effort. It did, however, demonstrate that the workforces of military-industrial firms are capable of playing a positive and creative role in the search for civilian-oriented alternative products.[2]

Moreover, key conversion activists have taken jobs with such municipal agencies as the Greater London Council and Enterprise Board and the Sheffield City Council, where they use their insights about community-worker involvement in planning for alternative, socially useful production in Great Britain. In these positions they have worked to create development programs to fight structural unemployment—with enough success so that Prime Minister Thatcher has moved to abolish the kind of metropolitan councils in which they are employed. The Lucas Plan has also been imitated in Italy, West Germany, and Sweden. Thus Adams's statement that it "is now scarcely discussed, even by the trade union movement" is certainly untrue if what he meant is that the Lucas Plan model is considered a dead letter. In fact, there is little doubt that this kind of creative initiative has played an important role in moving the British Labour Party itself to a much stronger position in opposition to the ever-expanding arms race.

■ Adams's examples of the repeated failures of military-oriented firms (like Rohr Corporation and

Grumman Aerospace) at commercial ventures are correct. But none represents an attempt at conversion. These firms simply tried to make civilian products in essentially the same way that they manufactured their more customary military products. But, among other things, differences in cost sensitivity between the world of military production, where extraordinary cost overruns are normal, and the world of civilian commercial industry, where excessive costs are a sure road to bankruptcy, virtually guarantee failure. Economic conversion, as its proponents have always argued, requires the thoroughgoing retraining and reorientation of managers, engineers, and scientists (along with other changes) to allow them successfully to negotiate the transition between these very different worlds. Thus these examples reinforce, rather than refute, the argument for real economic conversion.

■

Adams alleges that "many of the most vociferous advocates of economic conversion are not primarily concerned about the health of the U.S. economy." Instead, they manipulate the issue so they can pursue a peace strategy. Indeed, many conversion advocates are unapologetic and proud disarmament advocates. They are justifiably concerned that high military budgets and current military policies threaten the very survival of the world. Yet we know of no serious conversion proponent who is not also deeply concerned about the health and strength of the economy, and the economic well-being of both local communities and the nation as a whole. This concern is central to the argument that military production facilities should not be shut down and their workforces laid off, but should be converted instead to production activities that strengthen rather than drain the economy.

No conversion proponent that we can think of would argue, as Adams insists they do, that the arms race is generated by military workers and defense-dependent communities and would thus collapse if conversion plans were initiated in every arms factory. Conversion advocates are well-aware that international relations, foreign policy consid-

erations, and other external and internal factors drive the arms race. What we do argue, however, is that military contractors mobilize their workforces and unions representing military workers to support and legitimate high military budgets and to protect particular weapons systems when they are under congressional attack. Providing concrete plans for civilian-oriented work to replace military-oriented, should contracts be lost, is crucial to undercutting the enormous political leverage that the threat of job loss gives to those who want to keep the arms race going. In that sense, conversion planning has a crucial role in moving decisions on the production of any given weapons system out of the arena of competition for job and money flow to certain congressional districts, and into the arena of legitimate security needs.

As for the credibility and economic credentials of conversion advocates, so cavalierly dismissed by Adams, many of those thinkers and researchers who have done pioneering work in the field hold doctorates in economics and industrial economics. Some are at the highest levels of the labor movement, while others have made their mark in business and industry. We must protest, however, against Adams's implication that only "experts" are qualified to comment on economic, political, and social matters. The essence of conversion is the belief that workers and community residents are highly qualified to discuss what products and services they need, and are qualified to help in the design and development of those products. They may not be certified experts, but their tacit skills and knowledge of their own needs certainly enable them to participate in the kind of democratic decision-making processes that conversion embodies.

Central to Adams's attack on conversion is his attack on criticism of the military economy that is often used by opponents of military spending. Although he presents little evidence to refute this criticism, he is dismissive, even condescending, toward the argument that military spending is economically damaging. His allegation that such spending is relatively neutral in economic terms represents, however, a profound misunderstanding of the economic damage argument.

The essence of the argument that military spending is economically burdensome is that it drains critical productive resources out of the rest of the economy. When continued at high levels, over long periods, this drain undermines the efficiency of industries that produce goods and services for the civilian sector. The decades-long diversion, for example, of more than 30 percent of the nation's scientists and engineers to military research and development has dramatically slowed the rate of making cost-saving improvements in American production techniques. This is very significant. Historically, the development of cost-saving inventions has been a major force in U.S. economic growth, allowing wages to rise while prices were held stable. Thus, the purchasing power—and therefore the standard of living—of the average American rose as well. Simultaneously, low-priced, high-quality goods "made in the USA" were extremely attractive to customers here and abroad.

■

The military drain of the past 40 years has limited American industry's ability to offset cost increases. And the high price of American-made goods has caused the loss of markets here and abroad. The result: industrial decline, unemployment, and a lower standard of living for many Americans.

Adams says that proponents of the military damage argument believe that military spending leads to high inflation. Yet, he states, "The past five years have demonstrated that high rates of military spending and lowered rates of inflation can coincide." In fact, the average annual rate of inflation for the first five years of the 1980s was 7.5 percent—higher than during any half-decade between 1950 and 1974, and only 0.6 percent lower than the 1975–1979 peak average of 8.1 percent. In fact, the average annual inflation rate over the 25 years between 1950 and 1974 was only about 3 percent.[3]

Moreover, the economic damage argument does not state that high military spending must lead to inflation, but rather that it has led to the reduced ability of industry to offset costs. Thus, when wage increases and other input cost in-

creases occur, they are passed on in the form of higher prices. The last five years have seen both lower oil prices and wage concessions forced from U.S. workers; when costs are falling, the loss of cost-offsetting ability obviously does not force prices up. There is no evidence, however, that the ability of U.S. industry to cope with higher wages or other costs has improved at all over those five years.

A further point is that wage give-backs are equivalent to inflation in terms of impact on a worker's standard of living. There is little difference to workers if wages are stable and prices are rising at a rate of 10 percent, or if wages fall by 10 percent and there is no inflation. In fact, over the first half of the 1980s purchasing power earned per hour in the nonfarm business sector rose a total of only 0.1 percent. Wages and salaries in 1984 actually bought less than they did nearly a decade earlier in 1976.[4]

Adams is also wrong when he states: "It is simply not true that more defense spending means a loss of jobs, or fewer jobs in the economy." In the long term he is most certainly wrong, since military spending has played a key role in generating widespread job loss, not gain. Even in the short term, the preponderance of empirical evidence on this point, from studies of private research groups to those of the U.S. Department of Labor, contradict this contention.

The well-known "spin-off" argument in support of the idea that development of military technology does not seriously harm the rest of the economy is another of Adams's erroneous offerings. He writes: "Investments in defense technology, it is argued, mean that some other form of technology is slighted. . . . This makes no sense." Yet Simon Ramo, formerly chief scientist of the U.S. ICBM program, chairman of the President's Committee on Science and Technology, and co-founder of TRW, Inc., a company with heavy military involvement, writes: "In the past thirty years had the total dollars we spent on military R&D been expended instead in those areas of science and technology promising the most economic progress, we probably would be today [1980] where we are going to find ourselves arriving technologically in the year

2000."[5] One need only compare the rate of civilian technological development in industrialized nations heavily involved in military research (the Soviet Union, Great Britain, and the United States) with that in countries involved in relatively little military research (Japan and West Germany) to see that spinoff does not compensate for this drain.

■

Military spending at high levels for long periods is very much at the heart of what is wrong with the U.S. economy. Clearly, military spending has not brought about all of America's economic and political ills. But it has gone a long way toward creating the conditions that have undermined the ability of domestic producers to compete for world markets.[6]

Even if military spending proved to be good for the nation's economy, we would not favor continued high levels of military spending or the policies it protects. But our profound commitment to peace, disarmament, and economic justice does not alter the objective fact that military spending is not economically neutral; it is, instead, a critical economic disadvantage.

Adams also distorts the organizing aspects of the conversion proponents' argument, questioning the strategy because it makes "defense workers" a primary organizing target. To take on the "toughest target" first, he feels, does not make good organizing sense. (We might say the same of taking on Congress, yet no one seems reluctant to jump into that fray.) This is a serious misstatement of the intent of the conversion strategy, one which supports the prevalent assumption that politics is a zero sum game played by competing single-issue groups. And unfortunately, many accept the idea that integrating conversion as *one* component of their strategy means that they are being asked to drop "their" issue to work on "your" issue.

Conversion certainly has a local component, and conversion advocates would encourage— whenever and wherever realistically possible— defense workers and defense-dependent communities to begin conversion campaigns in their factories; but it is ludicrous to imagine that conversion advocates are asking peace activists to race to

their local military contractor and relentlessly patrol the factory gates. We caution those who target military factories against the kind of "peace witness" approach that all too frequently, and needlessly, alienates military workers. We counsel peace activists to consider alternatives if the workers inside that factory are not willing to discuss conversion.

Furthermore, conversion is not simply an escape route for the "statistically white, 48-year-old, highly skilled, highly employable male workers in the defense sector," as Adams implies. It is a strategy basic to rebuilding the U.S. economy for the benefit of the nation's workforce and population as a whole. While we agree that we must reorder the nation's economic priorities, no alternative industrial policy can succeed unless we greatly lessen the military burden on the economy.

Because scientific, technical, engineering, managerial, and, to a lesser extent, production personnel employed in military industries are acclimated to that peculiar, cost-insensitive world, they must undergo a specific retraining and reorientation to the very different world of civilian industry in order to accomplish the transition smoothly. That is why conversion is essential in any strategy to redirect the U.S. economy.

"Conversion," according to Adams, "seems to threaten jobs because the program supported by conversion advocates offers no visible alternatives to defense jobs." Not only is this complete nonsense; it also makes one wonder if Adams has any idea of what conversion is. The central proposition of economic conversion is precisely to develop "visible alternatives to defense jobs."

On one point, we do at least partly agree with the spirit of one of Adams's recommendations. Conversion advocates should be willing to get involved on the local level with community efforts at economic planning in general. This could be useful experience for dealing with the special problems of defense-dependent communities.

We welcome the opportunity to discuss the issues involved in efforts to create peace and justice in our society and in our world. Democratic debate and collective empowerment are, after all, the guiding principles of the conversion strategy. The moment one advocates conversion, one must ask: "Conversion to what?" This initiates a crucial discussion about what should be produced, what goods and services are needed, what technologies should be used in production of these goods, who should decide what to produce and be involved in

planning, production, and distribution. Such steps help to empower people who have been taught that they are incapable of planning for their own future, and lead to their direct involvement in the activities and decision-making processes that govern their lives.

1. Lloyd J. Dumas worked with the McGovern and Weiss offices as one of the principal designers of the Defense Economic Adjustment Act.

2. For further details see "The Lucas Aerospace Corporate Plan for Transition to Socially Useful Production," by the Lucas Aerospace Combine Shop Stewards Committee in L. J. Dumas, ed., *The Political Economy of Arms Reduction* (Boulder, Colo.: Westview Press for the American Association for the Advancement of Science, 1982), pp. 127–44.

3. Average of year-to-year changes in the consumer price index for all items, from *Economic Report of the President* (Feb. 1985), table B-56, p. 296.

4. Ibid., table B-41, p. 279.

5. Simon Ramo, *America's Technology Slip* (New York: Wiley and Sons, 1980), p. 251.

6. See L. J. Dumas, *The Overburdened Economy: Uncovering the Causes of Chronic Unemployment, Inflation and National Decline* (Berkeley: University of California Press, 1986).

A Rejoinder

Gordon Adams

I welcome the comments of Lloyd J. Dumas and Suzanne Gordon . . . who have been involved in conversion efforts for a number of years. The dialogue is important; on it will depend the future effectiveness of efforts to implement a better vision of the U.S. economic future than the one we have lived with since 1981. The terms Dumas and Gordon apply to my views—such as "condescending," "complete nonsense"—are, however, regrettable, and I will not respond in kind.

My point is simple: We need a vision and a policy for economic change that works in the real world; conversion does not provide it. Repeated efforts to create and implement a vision around alternative uses of defense plants have burned out a generation of organizers, and have failed.

Dumas and Gordon explicitly acknowledge this failure in the United States, using my examples

of the Trident and Douglas efforts. Invited last year by the Department of Defense to provide examples of successful conversion in this country, its advocates provided none at all.

Instead of shooting the messenger, we should ask why conversion has not become a "major priority." New conversion advocates should not be sent out to organize without reflection. Certainly we have much to learn from Europe, though not the lessons noted by Dumas and Gordon. The Lucas plan was *not* implemented—a key test of success—and a worker role in product development and company management was vehemently rejected; Lucas remains an arms producer. The lesson: the Labour Party was not prepared for or financially able to tackle the problem of economic transition in Britain. The Party still needs a better, more persuasive, economic revitalization strategy than the sordid Thatcher record. Defense plants can be dealt with only in this broader framework. The Greater London Council's conversion task force, which failed long before the Council itself was abolished, encountered the reality that London's scattered defense industry is a source of jobs in an economy of high unemployment. In sum, the task force could neither promise nor deliver a credible alternative.

More broadly, Europe has much to offer, but the narrow conversion focus of Dumas and Gordon misses it. The tradition of a strong local and central government role in economic planning and adjustment is more deeply rooted in Europe. The coal and steel community carried out a far-reaching transition in the failing European steel industry on much better terms than has our own. Whole new industries and jobs have been created in Germany, Italy, and France as part of public industrial policy. When any industry fails in Sweden, the government has general planning mechanisms we lack.

If we are serious about the fate of workers and local economies and are not simply pushing ideology in disguise, then we must broaden our framework and begin to put into place the institutions and resources which far transcend the alternative uses of a defense plant.

■

The effectiveness of a broader approach also requires a coherent economic analysis. While Dumas and Gordon . . . deny they believe that military spending is the core U.S. economic problem, they offer no other explanation and point repeatedly to military spending as the culprit.

It won't wash. In 1960 defense spending was 9.7 percent of U.S. gross national product (GNP); in 1985 it was 6.4 percent, even after the five-year Reagan buildup. Although it is at unprecedentedly high peacetime levels, military spending is consuming a smaller share of our economic resources than it did 25 years ago. . . .

• • •

Dumas and Gordon argue that by a mysterious process of osmosis (the mechanism is never explained), "this [military] resource drain undermines the efficiency of industries" in the com-

mercial sector. Even if the military economy is inefficient and U.S. productivity has failed to grow (neither of these assertions is universally true . . .), how are these problems linked? Most companies are not defense plants. How do they catch the disease? How do we explain away the efficient ones?

High rates of defense research and development do not explain the problem. The federal government's share of total U.S. (public and private) investment in research and development has actually declined from 64 percent in the 1960s to roughly 47 percent today. Although it may have some impact, military research and development is not eating up or "diverting" our economic resources from the private sector in a zero-sum game; the economy continues to grow, as does private sector research and development.

Economies ebb and flow for a wide range of reasons: different pricing structures, wage structures, international market shifts, currency values, the age of their industrial plants, and rates of investment. Dollars spent on the military are only one of those ingredients and, I would argue, not the most powerful one.

Inflation is a good example. Dumas [and] Gordon . . . argue that inflation rates are related to military spending. They offer no explanation and ignore some crucial issues: Vietnam War spending surely played an inflationary role, but almost any large increase in government spending, uncompensated by taxes, would have done the same. Oil prices drove up inflation in the 1970s, while military spending fell. Today inflation rates are nearing those of the 1950s, despite high rates of military spending; a recession (cushioned by the military dollar in Connecticut) and lower oil prices were important factors.

■

We would all surely prefer to make other economic choices, would not throw workers and communities on the ash heap when we were finished with an industry, and would want meaningful job programs for the unemployed. This is a larger question than alternate uses of a defense plant; it involves choices. But how do we make choices for the U.S. economy, locally and nationally? What kinds of choices would we make: What positive visions do we have for the economy? If Dumas and Gordon want to ask this question, I join them. . . .

Once we turn away from weak models and narrow targets and put the pieces of a wider vision and policy together, we need to work for it locally and nationally. The broader message has a bigger audience, one that includes, but does not especially target, defense workers and their communities.

Success is, in my view, the litmus test for politics; Dumas and Gordon, however, seem not to agree with this. Continual losses necessitate rethinking the problem. . . . The road out of failure and frustration lies in taking the broader issues of economic policy, economic adjustment, and investment policy seriously. It also lies in abandoning the chimera of successfully convincing the workers, management, and community around a defense plant that defense spending is the source of their economic ills and that they "could" be done something different, although they cannot carry it out locally and local conversion efforts cannot deliver either the resources or the jobs. Jobs don't grow out of hopes, not even out of the definition of "visible alternatives to defense jobs." They grow out of broad coalitions, politically astute organizing, and the judicious use of resources.

■

Defense-related organizing efforts that have made some small progress—examples exist in Minnesota, Los Angeles, even Connecticut—have begun to recognize that conversion organizing is "burnout city" for well-intended peace activists. They have moved toward a broader effort, which requires hard work and taking the political process seriously. It also means taking the economic issue seriously, not simply using larger adjustment issues as "useful experience" for dealing with defense-dependent communities, as Dumas and Gordon propose. Let us not drag peace activists down the road of an unconvincing economic analysis and a losing tactic, to leave them stranded, empty-handed, in front of a working defense plant or a shipyard that has been closed down because the local and state governments lack the tools, will, or resources to deal with the problem.

Those who want a better economy should address that goal and work with those who share it or could provide the resources for its achievement: unions, planners, plant-closing coalitions, budget priorities groups, members of Congress, investors. They should work within the broader framework toward a public policy which helps Americans diversify their local economies and survive transitions with less pain. In that framework, defense workers and communities can only be better off and more secure about the future.

PART SIX

Education and Scientific Research

Education and research contribute to both war and peace. University education contributes to war, according to some observers, by training students to be detached and "objective," instead of empathic and morally committed. And most classes teach students to ask limited questions within specialized fields instead of challenging the goals and structures of our society. Students sitting passively in lecture classes are being trained to obey government and military authorities. Education in grade school and high school also teaches obedience and nationalism.

On the other hand, the detached, look-at-both-sides-of-the-issue style of thinking taught in universities undermines passionate nationalism and probably encourages a skeptical attitude toward the "glories" of war and the superiority of the American way of life. University students were major participants in the peace movement in the 1960s and other eras, and a minority of faculty members have produced peace-oriented courses and research that challenges nationalism and the military-industrial complex (such as most of the articles in this book). To understand the mixed impact of education, it would be helpful to reflect on our experiences as students and teachers and on how these experiences have shaped us into productive members of war systems and peace systems.

The links between university research and the war system are more obvious. The Department of Defense provides money and defines problems for many researchers, and the university provides plans for more lethal weapons and students trained for the military-industrial complex. In academic fields like computer science and math, 50 percent of all federal funding comes from the Department of Defense. And of the 600,000 U.S. scientists and engineers inside and outside universities, about one third work on military-related projects and one ninth work on nuclear weapons, according to Anne Roark's article in this section.

But some research, such as Carl Sagan's studies of nuclear winter, challenges the arms race, and many scientists have contributed their knowledge and prestige to the peace movement. One of the best sources of information on promoting peace is the *Bulletin of the Atomic Scientists,* published by the Union of Concerned Scientists.

Roy Preiswerk opens Part Six with a scathing criticism of teaching and research in the social sciences. Most studies are dehumanized and irrelevant to human problems, he charges, because they are too detached and specialized, and they pretend to be value free when in fact they support the status quo. The other two papers, "How Well They Meant" by Martin J. Sherwin and "'Star Wars' Politicizing Science in U.S." by Anne Roark, consider the role of physical scientists. In 1945, physicists participated in the decision to use the atomic bomb against Japanese civilians. The most influential scientists argued that the bomb should be used because that would promote peace: The Russians' fear of our horrible weapon would deter them from starting a war. Others predicted that using the bomb would destroy trust and thereby increase the chances of nuclear war. Today, physical scientists are debating their involvement in producing weapons. Research on Star Wars is becoming the largest source of funding in many fields, but some scientists are organizing a boycott of Star Wars research.

Could We Study International Relations as if People Mattered?

Roy Preiswerk

When we study international relations we are often quite remote from social reality. This sounds provocative, but it is necessary regularly to re-examine the nature and purpose of our work in a rapidly changing world.

There are enough studies to demonstrate how many things have gone wrong with the development of mankind. Some say we are on a dangerous path. I would go one step farther and submit that mankind's development has taken a pathological direction. Perhaps just one example would suffice to illustrate the point. According to the 1976 Yearbook of the Stockholm International Peace Research Institute, the nuclear equipment of the world now amounts to 50,000 megatons, which is about 15 tons for each one of us and 60 tons for each inhabitant of a NATO or Warsaw Pact country. Between 1945 and 1975, the world has spent 7,000 billion dollars on military expenditure. No other species in nature, no species of the category of animals which the French call *bêtes* (synonymous with stupid) has ever invested such a proportion of its resources in means of mutual destruction while so many of the same species are dying of hunger every minute. During the same period only 200 billion dollars, or 3 percent of the above amount, were spent on development aid.

We will not present an inventory of all aspects of mankind's madness. What we must ask ourselves is whether anything can be done to make the social sciences in general and the study of international relations in particular less irrelevant to the solution of the most acute contemporary social problems.

I. Social Science in General: Four Reminders

We now come to a brief series of generalizations which may sound unfair to those social scientists who occasionally reflect on professional ethics and who sincerely try to tackle fundamentals. What follows is valid if, as I think is the case, it is applicable to at least 51 percent of social science research.

1. Social Science Is Dehumanized

The dehumanization of social sciences is parallel to the dehumanization of social life, particularly in the industrial societies. K. William Kapp epitomizes this in one sentence: "Neither in science nor in society are the concrete human beings and their interests at the centre of interest."[1] Let us make it clear that we are not speaking of the concern with the individual in the sense that this term has assumed in Western individualistic societies. The concern is with people, with the human being as a social being.

Social science in general takes little interest in the lives of human beings when it deals with

First published by Graduate Institute of International Studies, *International Relations in a Changing World,* Geneva, 1977. Reprinted by permission of the publisher.

institutions, processes, or events as if people were molecules which do not matter as such, but are noticed to the extent that they function as members of institutions, heroes or victims of processes and participants in events. The average social scientist treats people as objects, as sources of information, and he uses more and more technological hardware to achieve highly specialized and often esoteric results. Actually this kind of professional ethics (the more specialization the better) runs parallel to the interest of the ruling power (the more specialization, the weirder the language becomes for the layman, consequently no one can use the specialists' findings to question the established system). Thus, the consumers of social science are not people, but other social scientists (who admittedly are also people, but in very small numbers), governments or corporations. The question remains open for the moment, what these other social scientists or institutions do with the knowledge obtained.

We submit that many social scientists become alienated from their own societies, or from the societies they study, largely because of dominant thinking about what are supposed to be serious academic standards and research methods.

This may be a good occasion to point out that Western scientists could here and now learn something from other civilizations. Joseph Needham, a biochemist and embryologist, who came into close contact with engineering and medicine, says: "Of one thing I feel certain, namely that China will not produce those types of utterly inhuman scientists and engineers who know little, and care less, about the needs and desires of the average man and woman."[2]

2. Fragmented Social Sciences Can Be Useless or Counterproductive

The dehumanization of the social sciences is partly the result of their fragmentation. Fragmentation prevents an understanding of what man is all about. To narrow the sphere of observation is considered a sign of seriousness in academic circles. Specialization is necessary, but leads to abuses if there is

no awareness of the ideological and ethical presuppositions of knowledge.[3] In a different form, Alfred Sauvy highlights this when he says: "Science has indeed succeeded in making men live longer and worse."[4]

Fragmented social sciences can be useless, because they only provide information on minute issues, because other researchers often cannot build on the findings of their colleagues and because the degree of comparability across classes, nations, and cultures is low. It is simply absurd to invent a *homo œconomicus,* a *homo psychologicus,* or a *homo sociologicus* and then refuse to relate these analytical abstractions to the totality of the real human beings.

Quite a few social scientists find themselves at peace with their conscience when they say things such as: "The arms race is none of my business, I'm dealing with human rights." Or: "I'm specializing in balance-of-payments problems, I can't find the time to look into income inequalities." Or worse still: "It's for the economists to solve the problem of hunger, I'm looking at political systems in the Third World." Tom Lehrer, former Harvard professor in mathematics, who became a rather cynical songwriter, once imagined an interview with Wernher von Braun, in the course of which he speculated about the moral implications of building rockets which were generously sprinkled over the British population during World War II. The answer was this: "Once the rockets are up, who cares where they come down—that's not my department, says Wernher von Braun."

Fragmented social sciences can be counterproductive because they make us lose sight of mankind's development, they blur the pathological direction of that development and prevent an understanding of real forces at work. They also make it easier for technocrats and autocrats to manipulate society with knowledge which has the blessing of so-called scientists.

Fragmentation, incidentally, is not only a problem within the social sciences. It is becoming increasingly difficult to separate the social and the natural sciences. Some of the most disturbing questions today are: What are the social and psychological consequences of the continuing exploitation of nature? What type of energy produc-

In many societies, those who agree with the tion corresponds to a social structure we desire? What kind of socio-psychological problems arise from the means of self-destruction that the physicists are providing us with? How far will the chemical manipulation of peoples' minds go? The significance of these questions is dawning upon an increasing number of natural scientists, ecologists and physicists in particular.

3. If Presumed to Be Separate from Ethics and Ideology, Social Science Can Be Irrelevant or Dangerous

Science, at this stage of our development, probably creates as many problems as it solves. In fact, many "scientists" spend their time denying that our present development *is* pathological. Others specialize in setting up some kind of coherent interpretation which makes this very pathology look acceptable.

Science can be useful, but it is not sufficient. If scientists say that X thousands of people die of hunger every day, or that nuclear weapons can exterminate mankind X times, is that enough? Such information is useful and necessary, but if nobody has the courage to draw a conclusion other than that "mankind" is synonymous with "madness," then we might as well dispense with scientists. More people must come forward, even if they are—in a derogatory sense—termed "ideologues," to say that hunger is scandalous (therefore we must redistribute wealth) and that preparing an "overkill" is simply idiotic (therefore we must stop the race towards mutual annihilation). The "ideologues" are thus a disturbing factor: they express anxiety which others want to ignore, they ask for change which implies an effort and a commitment that others are reluctant to accept.

In fact, it is false to oppose science to ideology. There is no science without ideology. Whoever refuses to admit this elementary truth is either naive or completely unaware of his implicit ideological position. In some cases, however, he is a shrewd calculator who manages to hide his ideology behind some esoteric vocabulary or math-

ematical formula. Science is in the midst of politics. established power and values stand a good chance of being considered as scientists, while those who disagree and demand social change are easily discredited by the label of "ideologues."[5]

The present dilemma does not arise from the fact that we have insufficient knowledge about social problems. It stems from the fact that self-styled "neutral" scientists do not know who will do what with their findings. To discover something and let public or private power structures use that knowledge in unethical ways is a totally irresponsible attitude on behalf of scientists.

One contribution we can all make immediately is to claim less often that what we are asserting has "scientific" value. Today, we are in a phase of the development of the sciences which is largely determined by positivistic standards. This is a school of thought which is particularly limited in finding instruments to deal with human problems.

The value-neutrality of science is a stubborn myth. Let us take one example. It is being stated over and over again that the functioning of the market system is a process which is linked with no particular ideology. This statement is false in four respects: ideologically, culturally, ecologically, and ethically. The market is a place where the purchasing power of those who have money, rather than the essential needs of *all* people, determines the distribution of goods. The products available on the market are an expression of the income inequalities within the population. The satisfaction of demand is not the same thing as the satisfaction of needs. In almost every Third World country, you can buy egg shampoo to wash your hair with, while a large proportion of the population cannot afford to buy eggs to eat. In poor societies, the market system guarantees access of the privileged few to luxury goods. In rich societies, the market system can be seen as a way to fight simultaneously capitalist monopolies and excessive State interference in private spheres. All of this has something to do with *ideology*. with choices made by human beings concerning who gets what, when, how, where and why. There is no law of nature saying that there must be a market. The distribution of goods can be organized in various ways.

Western economists and anthropologists have noticed that there are societies without a market system. This has usually been considered, in the ethnocentric tradition, as a sign of backwardness. But the introduction of trade based on a monetary economy has led to much confusion, to the dislocation of entire societies, to the destruction of distributive systems which made it possible, in many parts of the world, to assure the survival of every member of a group. The market system is the product of a specific type of *culture*. Once again, it is not a law of nature.

The market system puts a price on everything, but the very low-priced factor of production is nature; probably because it cannot scream, publish pamphlets, or organize a trade union. The fact that the resources of nature, particularly the sun, air and water, to some extent have no price at all, has led to the most disastrous abuses with which economic theory has acquainted us under the powerful umbrella of "science." The market system, in reality, is not value-free in terms of *ecology* either.[6]

There is a dreadful concept in economics which is called the "labour market." In fact, we are talking here about the price of human beings, although not exactly in the same terms as the slave traders were able to do. The labour market is an inhuman concept, because it means pricing the value of people according to their (more or less accidentally acquired) qualifications and to the circumstances prevailing at a particular time and place. It is also an irrational concept when one thinks that the demand on this particular "market" must always be met, just to satisfy the needs of production, whether it be for food or for arms. The market concept, consequently, is not neutral in *ethical* terms either.

This is just one example, among many thousands we could find in the so-called social "sciences," of intellectual constructs based on either naivety or dishonesty. Let us, then, proceed to think what social science, and the study of international relations in particular, could be if we stopped talking about what may seriously be regarded as scientific and instead started to think realistically about the world we are living in.

Realism is a big word, particularly when it makes claims to "scientific" evidence. It is used widely to discredit those who find something wrong with the present international system. The kind of realism we are propagating today may result in widespread famine, growing inequalities, and World War III (which, incidentally, will destroy the supermonsters and leave a number of peripheral and "primitive" peoples quite undisturbed, nuclear fall-out notwithstanding). If we accept the arms race, poverty, racism, and other charming attributes of the present system, we are being "realistic." There is something weird about a human mind capable of producing the contemptuous assertion that those who denounce these phenomena are idealists, ideologues, or dreamers. The term "realism" should be given a new meaning: not to conform with what is happening, but to be able to see what our present options mean, what could result from them, and what changes we have to envisage, drastic as they may be.

The antinomy of science versus ideology and ethics is beautifully abolished by the physicist Victor Weisskopf, when he says: "Human existence depends upon compassion, and curiosity leading to knowledge, but *curiosity and knowledge without compassion is inhuman,* and compassion without curiosity-and-knowledge is ineffectual."[7]

4. Social Science Often Creates Obstacles to Knowledge

It may sound absurd that the official knowledge-producers in society may actually turn out to be the knowledge-hiders. But the problem is a real one. Let us take two examples. In *development economics,* we have accumulated tons of learned writings over the past thirty years. Two approaches are dominant: a more theoretical one, which usually extrapolates from the experience of industrial societies to formulate proposals concerning growth, productivity, and other marvels. There is also a more pragmatic approach, defended by those who descend on some Third World village and use their "common sense," telling the natives what they have to do about irrigation, fertilizers, and other down-to-earth matters. Both approaches have led to visible or measurable signs of "success" (buildings, plantations, growth rates, etc.), but have failed in two ways: first, they cannot free themselves of the idea that their own society is superior to all others and their "science" the only possible source of any conceivable change. Today it is becoming clear that different civilizations move in different directions and that the social sciences offered by industrial societies have not discovered much to explain the diversity of developing processes. Second, the social sciences were unable to warn us that the development strategies adopted after 1945 would lead to a deterioration of living conditions in many parts of the world. The large majority of development economists obscured our vision for three decades, pretending that the world was "progressing." In 1977, we find more hunger, misery, and unemployment than thirty years ago. Those who were the first to say this publicly were rarely academics, and when they were, as in the case of Gunnar Myrdal or René Dumont, for example, they were frowned upon by most of their colleagues, unable to cope with so much unorthodoxy. But can we be taken seriously when we produce splendid studies on balance-of-payments adjustments, Special Drawing Rights, transfers of technology, capital accumulation and growth rates, only to realize at the end, that every day more human beings in the poor countries see their living conditions deteriorate while in rich countries profound feelings of alienation from our way of life are spreading rapidly?

Another example is that of *history*. Our libraries are stacked with "World History" books. A recent study of thirty school textbooks from eight different countries reveals enormous distortions in our knowledge of other civilizations.[8] Anyone who really takes the trouble to examine these distortions must agree with the statement that some ways of systematizing knowledge under the label of "objective science" constitute a veritable obstacle to knowledge. But the striking element in the situation is the exclusion of human beings. All these thousands of pages concentrate on invasions, catastrophes, royal weddings, "discoveries," and various other events, mostly sad ones. Except for a few heroes (Christopher Columbus or Winston

Churchill), villains (Ghengiz Khan or Adolf Hitler), hero-villains (King Chaka, Cortez, or Pizarro) and distinguished aristocrats (all the kings of France, for instance, even the most feeble-minded), there is no reference to the fact that history ought to have something to do with people. We are quite often treated to the most gruesome details about ever more sophisticated techniques which heroic warriors have been using on every occasion to slice each other up. However, there is not a word about how the common man throughout these thousands of years went through his daily life, struggled for the survival of his family, or suffered within his natural and social environments.[9]

These are brief illustrations, but there is enough evidence that similar distortions of knowledge through science are widespread.[10]

II. International Relations in Particular: Four Examples

Our purpose is to reach constructive proposals as quickly as possible. Therefore this section will be extremely brief and go no further than pointing out a few of the difficulties we face when studying international relations.

1. The State-Centric Approach

"The objective of International Relations is to study relations among States." How many times have we been given this simplistic definition of the scope of our field of study? Of course, the definition represents a pragmatic and realistic view; after all, the State alone holds military and police power and is entitled to sovereignty. But this definition is unacceptable for two reasons: it limits the scope of investigation (States related to States) and presents almost as a law of nature what is merely a man-made system (problem pertaining to epistemology). It also covers up an elaborate network of power relationships which are often based on extreme inequalities and injustices (problem pertaining to ethics and ideology).

Contemporary international law consolidates a system based on the supremacy of the State. In recent years it was said that the state-system is being eroded by various forces. Some analysts see three such forces: international organizations, transnational corporations, and liberation movements. In our view none of these are eroding forces; on the contrary, international organizations are based on the state-system and contribute to its consolidation. It is extremely difficult to give power to an inter-state agency dealing directly with people without passing through governments. The only important exceptions are the European Communities and the European Commission on Human Rights.[11] Transnational corporations are, it is true, more powerful and richer than many States. The annual turnover of the largest corporations is greater than the Gross National Product of a majority of States in the Third World. In comparison to these states, the corporation can indeed be considered as an eroding factor. But at the same time, they are strengthening the power of their home base and are thus contributing to growing inequalities within a state-based international system.[12] Finally, liberation movements may indeed question the legitimacy of a particular State, be it a colonial power or a State made up of different ethnic groups. But they only aim at the creation of new States which will become parties to the already established international system. If the Bretons, the Basques, the Occitans, the Alsatians, and the Corsicans all manage a revolution against France, one and indivisible as the Constitution says, setting up five more nation-states, and taking their seats at the United Nations, they will merely contribute to the consolidation of a state-based international system.

The state-based international system raises the crucial question of the way people are represented at the world level. We argue that dominant elites, not populations, are in fact represented. Behind the walls of sovereignty and non-interference in domestic affairs, ruling elites are protected and left quite free to practice domestic colonization, to advance the interests of a small minority and to resort to almost any method of repression. The New International Economic Order, adopted at the United Nations on 1 May 1974, and so

vigorously defended by Third World diplomats, illustrates this eloquently. Only States can act, no State can be questioned about its domestic situation. And what the "representatives" of the Third World are asking for, is to obtain the means to consolidate *their* power: more money, more technology, in short, more of what we have seen in the past, despite obvious failures, when we look at the situation of the majority of the people. Critics of this approach in rich countries are now accused of a new paternalism towards Third World leaders. It is convenient for conservative elements in rich countries to say what the progressives were saying twenty years ago: do not interfere with the choices made by the newly independent countries. When, in 1975, the question was raised in Switzerland whether technical co-operation should be initiated between people rather than governments, one prominent businessman replied: "Poverty of the masses is a matter lying within the domestic jurisdiction of a country." The implication of this argument is that we are to be concerned with famine, malnutrition, disease, and other evils which, in various ways, affect at least half of the world's population only when *governments* allow us to do so. But how many of these governments have been looking seriously into such questions? 1977 is not 1947, when aid programmes were launched, or 1960, when many of us hoped that independence would lead to a better life for the populations of the former African colonies. If those who, today, are deeply concerned about the deteriorating situation must be labelled "paternalists," then let them be proud of it.

It is true that we now have a lot of those "soft states" that Gunnar Myrdal has been talking about when it comes to questions of administrative inefficiency in the field of economic development. But most of these same States are also becoming "tough states" through militarization and improvements in their capacity to suppress any forces contesting the rights of privileged minorities to continue to ignore the basic needs of the people. It is true then, for all of these reasons, that the State is here to stay for some time, but students of international relations should not merely acknowledge this fact:

they should start trying to imagine an alternative system which eliminates the inhuman aspects of a state-based international system.

2. Fragmentation and Isolation

It is quite obvious, and needs no undue elaboration, that the study of international relations reproduces the fragmentation of the social sciences in general. It remains multidisciplinary, a juxtaposition of separate disciplines jealously guarding their precarious identity. Sometimes it claims to be interdisciplinary, an objective which it usually fails to attain. It is never transdisciplinary.

Isolation results from arbitrary decisions on what is included or excluded from the study of international relations. There is no reason, advanced by either God, Thucydides, or contemporary epistemologists for legal, economic, or historical aspects of international relations to be given priority, while social psychology or political anthropology are left out. Furthermore, there is no valid argument why the natural sciences should not be part of the study of international relations. Why not call upon ecologists, nutritionists, or nuclear physicists to teach international relations?

3. On Hiding Values

There is an enormous fraud in contemporary science which allows the credibility of the "scientist" to increase at the same rate as he manages to hide his value judgements, personal preferences, and political attitudes. The technical term for this is positivism. The non-technical word for it is dishonesty. Somehow, although we "internationalists" are outside of the spectrum of established academic disciplines, we have not overcome this problem, because we do not realize that a good portion of positivistic epistemology leads us right into intellectual dishonesty. Dishonesty in a very small way, perhaps. If we do not announce our ideology, we are probably more acceptable in the society. Also, we probably do not know to what extent our academic upbringing has brainwashed us into the positivistic mould.

4. On Forgetting Basic Human Needs

In Freudian terms it is called scotomization, more simply it means disregarding what deeply disturbs us. It could be inequality, poverty, torture, unemployment or the arms race. What is really expected of us? That we describe in depth the process taking place in diplomatic gatherings and the deliberations of some international court which has no power to change anything whatsoever in the international power game? Or are we to think of the fact that what human beings need is food, fresh air and water, habitat, and a few other essential things? If international relations is to remain a relevant discipline, these problems will have to be given top priority. Otherwise we may soon be associated with stamp collectors, mountain climbers, or numismatists as far as our impact on society is concerned.

Two dangers of immense significance are involved in forgetting about basic human needs. One is to indulge in retrospection while neglecting contemporary and future worlds. This is unacceptable from a merely cognitive point of view. The other is that of sacrificing half of this generation, condemning them to a state of underprivileged existence, and putting an enormous burden on future generations. The preoccupation with basic needs has a totality to it: today's inequalities are linked with tomorrow's injustices: the exploitation of man by man runs parallel to the domination exerted by man over nature.

III. Alternative Thinking: Epistemology and Methodology

If we have a grain of optimism left, we must agree with E. Boulding that "ways can be found to transform the whole international system into something less costly economically and less outrageous morally."[13]

Before indicating areas of research which should be given priority, some remarks on epistemology and methodology are necessary. This is very simple: the question has to be asked again *who* studies *what, why, how,* and *for whom*? In other words: who are the producers of knowledge (researcher, observer), what is the object of their research (observed reality), what are the motives, the ideology, the value system behind the research, which method is applied, and who is the consumer of knowledge, the public to which the producer addresses himself?

1. What Has Been Done?

More than a decade ago, a growing group of social scientists started to look for what T. Kuhn would call a new "paradigm."[14] Peace research, world society studies, world order studies, world future studies all have attempted to overcome the "stato-cracy" approach and widen the spectrum of inquiry. From the narrow perspective of interstate relations, they have moved to intergroup, inter-societal or intercultural relations, taking into consideration the role of units left outside of the classical study of international relations mainly because such units have no status as recognized actors under present international law.

The most important contribution of the new approaches is not to have widened the scope of levels and units of analysis. It lies in the qualitative transformation of the researchers' motivations. Let us take the example of hunger. It is no longer sufficient to be descriptive (how many people are dying every day), nor to be explanatory (what are the causes of hunger), or even predictive (how many people will die of hunger by the year 2000). What is required is an explicit ideology, which in this case means an extension into the normative domain (what kind of world do we want to live in) with prescriptive substance (how are we going to prevent increasing hunger).

At present, a very fundamental change is occurring in the new approaches to the study of contemporary and future world problems. So far, various groups have been trying to establish new schools of thought in the hope that they might be recognized as giving *the* answer to the inadequacy of classical international relations studies. Now we notice a movement towards the convergence of these approaches. A first example: peace research and world order studies converge when the following methodology is proposed; first, state values, second, analyse forecasts, third, devise a design, fourth, clear up contradictions and incompatibilities, fifth, propose transitional strategies.[15] Another example: peace research and development studies find a common objective when development ceases to be seen as a "problem" afflicting poor countries and becomes a process taking place in all countries with important connections being revealed between the poverty of the former and the affluence of the latter.[16] If a complete convergence between peace studies, development studies, and future studies can be achieved, we will have a formidable coalition to confront the classical study of international relations. We will then have teams of people working simultaneously for the elimination of war, poverty, social injustice, ecological imbalance, and mass alienation. In positive terms, they will produce ideas for the achievement of peace, economic well-being, social justice, ecological stability, and participation, in all parts of the world, both for present and future generations.[17]

2. What Should Happen

What the social sciences can do to contribute to the goals just stated depends on the willingness to recognize a few fundamental principles of an epistemological and methodological nature.

(a) *The Acceptance of Utopian Thinking.* "A map of the world that does not include Utopia is not worth even glancing at ...," says Lewis Mumford.[18] But Mumford also reminds us of an important differentiation which Sir Thomas More makes regarding the etymology of the word. Outopia is "no place," it is a vain dream of a land never to exist. Eutopia is "the good place." It arises out of a real environment and is part of an effort to reshape man's condition according to some ideal standards. It is about Eutopia that we are talking. This is not to be confused with an idealistic view of history. Even if infrastructures or productive forces are decisive in man's history, human integration of knowledge, says: "Inasmuch as we thought and inventiveness going beyond existing structures also have something to do with the shaping of history. Those Marxists who have not forgotten about dialectics (there are a few who have) would agree with this.

Utopias, incidentally, are not simply mental constructs aimed at bringing about a better world. A lot of what is considered "realistic" thinking about mankind's present development, contained in many forecasts, is utopian. The most widespread utopia, using the word in the negative connotation which most "realists" tend to give to it, is that exponential economic growth must and *can* continue.

(b) *The Integration of Knowledge*. As long as knowledge remains fragmented, as we have said before, it contributes to the dehumanization of society. Specialization in one particular discipline is necessary, but not sufficient. Many scientists have managed to break out of the narrow field of study which the university has defined for them. The demand for "generalists" is increasing in national governments, business enterprises, and international organizations. This is an indication that to be even a perfect specialist will be increasingly considered as valid in academic circles alone, while people and institutions of public interest will develop a different view.

The integration of knowledge has at least these four fundamental facets: transdisciplinary concepts (e.g., structure or culture used in all disciplines), structural isomorphisms (the same hypotheses tested in all disciplines), globalism (the interrelations of problems in different parts of the world made evident), and totality (the interrelations of problems attributed to different disciplines made explicit).

Two remarks are necessary about the integration of knowledge. The first is that all those, and they are a vast majority in the academic world, who adhere to the cult of specialization, get off too lightly when they call the generalists dilettantes. Modesty obviously has to be the prime quality of the generalist. K. William Kapp, an economist who has written one of the path-breaking works on the

proceed to elaborate the tentative conceptual frameworks of man and culture, we are dealing with concepts and findings of disciplines outside our narrow specialty. This was unavoidable and no one is more aware of the hazards of such an enterprise than the author."[19]

The second remark has to do with a more profound dilemma. Transdisciplinarity is more than interdisciplinarity; it has to be achieved within the conceptual work of a researcher instead of merely bringing together specialists of various disciplines who politely listen to each other without budging from their original positions. A good number of so-called interdisciplinary exercises taking place today actually reinforce specialization, each person involved finding it necessary to draw more precise lines between "his" field and that of the others.[20]

(c) *The Humanization of Knowledge*. Social Scientists have to rediscover that their prime task is to put the human being and his essential needs back into the centre of attention. As we have pointed out earlier, the dehumanization of social science is parallel to the dehumanization of society.[21] So we are facing one of these famous chicken-and-egg questions again. Do we have to wait for society to change in order to change science? In my view, it is in the true nature of dialectic thinking, and not an expression of philosophical idealism, to affirm that scientists can modify their behaviour as social actors and begin to help changing the society. Social change has never been the exclusive result of anonymous forces. The dissident thought of social analysts also makes its impact. One clear example is the profound transformation of development objectives at the present time, as compared to the first two United Nations Development Decades. Certainly, those who began to put basic needs into the centre of the debate were inspired by a deteriorating situation among the poorest segments of the world's population. Someone however had to come along, not only to see this phenomenon occur, but to represent a value system within which such a situation is intolerable. It is the combination of an objective situation with a subjective (personal, ideological, affective, etc.) valuation that leads to action for social change.

Humanization is, of course, closely interrelated with the other aspects of a new social science epistemology. It means being value-oriented and transdisciplinary. The Japanese economist Shigeto Tsuru expresses it in this way for his discipline:

> *Economists are called upon to extend their inquiry in two directions; (1) to be prepared to make normative judgements, and (2) to widen the scope of their enquiry to encompass what were once regarded as externalities. The former task required specifying the processes through which a normative judgement can be derived from social consensus, and the latter task implies replacing the idea of economics as being a closed equilibrium system with that of it being an open-ended discipline having symbiotic contact with neighboring disciplines.*[22]

Another economist, Kurt Dopfer, goes a little further than "symbiotic contact" when he claims that a holistic approach has to take the place of interdisciplinarity. His hope is that a study of economics which covers ecology will contribute to human well being.[23] The interesting point here is that taking a much broader view, thereby arriving at a considerable degree of abstraction, including such methods as systems analysis, may bring us closer to an understanding of basic human needs. Paradoxical as it may sound, the humanization of science will not be achieved through the simplification of problems, the repudiation of such basically inhuman gadgets as the computer, or a return to non-scientific approaches. Empirical data-gathering, conceptualization, and theorizing on a very large scale are still necessary.

(d) *Responsibility of the Scientist.* The three preceding points inevitably lead to a more general one in the field of the professional ethics of the knowledge producer. Once we accept the demand for the humanization of knowledge, we have to admit two further principles: social science must be committed to the reduction of social inequalities in today's world and must concern itself with

the well-being of future generations. In abstract terms these are the principles of equity and intertemporal distribution. They are not new in peace research or future studies. They have found their way into development thinking through, among other things, the Cocoyoc Declaration.[24] Unfortunately they are neglected in positivistic social science.

A third type of responsibility, which has not been underlined as much as the other two, is the one that the social scientist ought to have with regard to the natural sciences. It is truly surprising how little attention is paid to the socio-cultural consequences of food technology, genetic manipulation or nuclear energy. In a broader definition of the field of international relations, such questions are a matter of concern simply because they are not confined to particular territories. The influence exerted by some States on others in the field of science and technology is enormous. It affects relations between industrial States, but probably has more profound implications in relations between industrial and non-industrial societies.

The responsibility of the scientist with regard to equity, intertemporal distribution, and natural sciences can only be achieved if he is prepared to examine the value of utopias (or to create some), and to contribute to the integration and humanization of knowledge.

(e) *Respect for the Diversity of Intellectual Styles.* A new social science epistemology has to take into account cultural diversity and the diversity of modes of thinking that goes with it. International relations studies are deeply affected by the lack of concern with this very problem.[25] Whether we analyse negotiations, conflicts, or decolonization, we will always be handicapped if we disregard the significance of cultural diversity.

Unfortunately there is no encyclopedia of intellectual styles. Probably it is beyond the capacity of any living human being to produce such a source of information, because no one has been brought up with the idea that this is a worthwhile exercise to undertake.[26] A modest beginning would be to examine the ways in which Western societies, with the enormous military and economic power they exert over the world, "grasp" non-Western worlds. The study of international relations would greatly benefit from it in this polycentric, multicultural world. Just to give a hint: Western thought is deeply anthropocentric (man is outside and above nature), dichotomous (good and bad, body and soul, civilized and savage, etc.), unilinear (progress from here to eternity), and compartmentalized (fragmentation and hyper-specialization as discussed above). To be aware of this and to know that these structures of knowledge might be different in other societies is absolutely indispensable.

These are just a few dimensions of a new epistemology for social science, and consequently for the study of international relations. What we also have to reflect upon are the concrete research areas which ought to be given priority in the future....

■   ■   ■

Conclusion

The purpose of this inquiry has been to propose constructive avenues for international relations

research. New fields must be explored and new methods applied. Merely descriptive, or even explanatory and predictive approaches will only describe, explain, and predict mankind's pathological development without any chance of contributing to change.

One condition for this is that people should not simply be considered as objects of knowledge but as knowledge-producers. Let us conclude therefore with this statement by Johan Galtung: A less exploitative system of knowledge production implies that we are not content with doing "research on people, but together with people, not to act as a stimulus and registrar of responses, but to enter dialectically in a dialogue with the 'researched.' In that case, they would, in fact, no longer be researched people but be part of a team, of an effort to explore some aspect of the social condition of humankind together."[27]*

With this in mind, we can begin to hope that the scope and methods of the study of international relations will expand to include a preoccupation with basic human needs more so than in the past.

The title of this chapter is obviously inspired by E. F. Schumacher's book *Small Is Beautiful: A Study of Economics as if People Mattered.* London, Sphere Books, 1974. The author is particularly grateful for comments on a first draft of Part I to Johan Galtung, Ekkehart Müller-Rappard, Peter O'Brien, Denis de Rougemont, Rolf Steppacher, Albert Tevoedjre, Monica Wemegah, and especially Noa Zanolli.

1. K. W. Kapp, "Zum Problem der Enthumanisierung der 'Reinen Theorie' und des gesellschaftlichen Realität, *Kyklos,* vol. 20, 1967, p. 329 (hereafter K. W. Kapp, "Zum Problem").

2. J. Needham, "History and Human Values: A Chinese Perspective for World Science and Technology," *The Centennial Review,* vol. 20, 1976, p. 27.

3. E. F. Schumacher, *Small Is Beautiful,* p. 76.

4. A. Sauvy, *La fin des riches,* Paris, Calmann-Lévy, 1975, p. 19.

5. See also J. Habermas, *La technique et la science comme "idéologie,"* Paris, Gallimard, 1973.

6. More precisely, what is meant is that air or sunshine are not calculated in terms of monetary costs, but of course the use and abuse of air or water resources present a problem of social costs. See K. W. Kapp, *The Social Costs of Private Enterprise,* Cambridge, Mass., Harvard University Press, 1950. We must remember also that public enterprise may create similar social costs, a

fact that representatives of East European countries have sometimes attempted to deny at the Stockholm Conference on the Environment.

7. V. F. Weisskopf, *Physics in the Twentieth Century: Selected Essays,* Cambridge, Mass., Harvard University Press, 1972, p. 364. Italics added.

8. R. Preiswerk and D. Perrot, *Ethnocentrism and History: Africa, Asia and Indian America in Western Textbooks.* New York: Lagos NOK Publishers, 1978.

9. There are, of course, other approaches. See UNESCO, *Histoire du développement culturel et scientifique de l'humanité,* Paris, Laffont, 1967, 9 vols.

10. See, for instance, F. S. C. Northrop and H. Livingstone, *Cross-Cultural Understanding: Epistemology in Anthropology,* New York, Harper and Row, 1964. Also the interesting debate between M. Herskovits and F. Knight, in M. Herskovits, *Economic Anthropology,* 2nd ed., New York, Norton, 1960, appendix. For similar problems in intercultural psychology, see R. Preiswerk, "Jean Piaget et l'étude des relations interculturelles," in G. Busino (ed.), *Les sciences sociales avec et aprés Jean Piaget.* Geneva, Droz, 1976.

11. We will subsequently present a more balanced picture as far as the role of international organizations is concerned, particularly with regard to the ILO, WHO, and FAO. See Part IV.

---

*[Footnotes have been renumbered because portions of the original reading have been deleted—Eds.]

12. The converse is sometimes true, as R. J. Barnet and R. E. Muller show in *The Global Reach: The Power of the Multinational Corporations,* New York, Simon and Schuster, 1974.

13. Quoted by M. Banks, "The Relationship between the Study of International Relations, Peace Research and Strategic Studies," paper presented to UNESCO Advisory Meeting of Experts on UNESCO's Role in Developing Research on Peace Problems, Paris, July 1969, pp. 5–6.

14. T. S. Kuhn, *The Structure of Scientific Revolutions, Chicago,* University of Chicago Press, 1970.

15. M. S. Soroos, "A Methodological Overview of the Process of Designing Alternative Future Worlds," in L. R. Beres and H. R. Targ (ed.), *Planning Alternative Futures,* New York, Praeger, 1975, pp. 3–27.

16. For instance, Hessische Stiftung für Friedens und Konfliktforschung, *Friedensanalysen,* Schwerpunkt Unterentwicklung, Frankfurt, Suhrkamp, 1976.

17. See the contribution of Saul Mendlovitz in the volume edited by Beres and Targ quoted in note 15.

18. L. Mumford, *The Story of Utopias,* New York, Viking Press, 1962 (1st ed. 1922).

19. K. W. Kapp, *Toward a Science of Man in Society,* The Hague, Nijhoff, 1961, pp. ix–x.

20. See J. Piaget, *Epistémologie des sciences de l'homme,* Paris, Gallimard, 1976, and the article on Piaget mentioned in note 10, p. 207.

21. See K. W. Kapp, "Zum Problem."

22. S. Tsuru, "Towards a New Political Economy," in K. Dopfer (ed.), *Economics in the Future,* London, Macmillan, 1976, p. 112.

23. *Ibid.,* p. 9.

24. Published in *Development Dialogue,* no. 2, 1974, pp. 88–96.

25. R. Preiswerk, "The Place of Inter-Cultural Relations in the Study of International Relations," *The Yearbook of World Affairs,* London, 1978.

26. There are, of course, quite a few attempts. See, for instance, F. S. C. Northrop, *The Meeting of East and West,* New York, Macmillan, 1946. This book is stimulating but also to be read sceptically because its marked dichotomy between East and West. See also J. Galtung, *Deductive Thinking and Intellectual Style: An Essay on Teutonic Intellectual Style,* Oslo, Chair in Conflict and Peace Research, 1976, no. 2.

27. J. Galtung, "Is Peaceful Research Possible? On the Methodology of Peace Research," in *Peace: Research, Education, Action,* Copenhagen, Christian Ejlers, 1975. p. 273.

How Well They Meant

Martin J. Sherwin

"History is a very important thing," I. I. Rabi told his audience of physicists at Los Alamos on the fortieth anniversary of that facility's founding, "because by perusal of history you see the greatness and the folly of humanity." And so it was with the Manhattan Project to which many of the finest minds in American physics dedicated themselves. Their first objective was "to save Western civilization" from fascism by building an atomic bomb ahead of the Germans; their second objective was "to save Western civilization" from the atomic bomb itself, by devising formulas to prevent a nuclear arms race.[1]

As Rabi and others are painfully aware, the ironies associated with those rescue efforts are numerous. But one that has gone almost unnoticed is particularly poignant: all of the ideas currently associated with nuclear weapons derive from those originally conceived by scientists during the war for the purpose of preventing a nuclear arms race afterward. Appropriately, the title of Rabi's 1983 Los Alamos speech was: "How Well We Meant."

The Strategic Arms Limitation Talks (SALT) were presaged by Niels Bohr and James Conant in 1944, and then officially proposed in 1946, in the State Department's Acheson-Lilienthal Report, the earliest nuclear arms control proposal. Nuclear intimidation, the psychological premise of nuclear containment, was anticipated in 1945 at the atomic bomb targeting committee meetings in Los Alamos. Limited nuclear war—an idea popularized in 1958 by Henry Kissinger's *Nuclear Weapons and American Foreign Policy,* and then adopted in 1980 as Presidential Directive-59 by the Carter Administration—was discussed during the war as an integral part of plans for international control. Deterrence and even the "warning shot" strategy, if not the terms themselves, were implicit in the decisions that led to the destruction of Hiroshima and Nagasaki.

The concept of the atomic bomb as the final arbiter of war was recognized in 1939 with the publication of the discovery of nuclear fission. Every scientist familiar with the physics of this phenomenon understood that in theory a weapon of extraordinary power might be fashioned if the technical requirements could be mastered. To this end scientists enlisted the president's support; they formed committees to study the possibility of an atomic bomb; they lobbied the military; and they conducted experiments. But it was not until the summer of 1941, two-and-a-half years after fission was discovered in Germany, that scientists in England thought of a way to harness the theory to practical technology. In the fall of 1941 an Anglo–American scientific partnership was initiated. Its goal was to beat the Germans in a race for the atomic bomb.

The delay literally terrified the scientists associated with the bomb project. Aware of the weapon's potential and their own desultory start, they reasoned that the Anglo–American effort lagged behind Germany's, perhaps by as much as two-and-a-half years. In their minds the atomic bomb was the *ultimate weapon*; if the Germans developed it first, the Allied cause was lost. Arthur Compton, director of the atomic energy project at the University of Chicago, was so distressed at the slow rate of progress that, in June 1942, he urged a program for researching and developing "countermeasures" against a German atomic bomb. In July J. Robert Oppenheimer wrote despairingly that the war could be lost before answers to the

immediate problems under consideration could be found. "What Is Wrong with Us?" was the heading Leo Szilard chose for a memorandum in September criticizing the rate of progress.[2]

Despite the concern expressed at a high-level meeting at the White House in October 1941, the actual development of the bomb had not yet started at the beginning of 1943; and only limited progress had been made in constructing the many necessary facilities. General Leslie Groves was not appointed to head the project until September 17, 1942. The site for the uranium separation plant at Oak Ridge, Tennessee, was acquired only two days later. The land on which the bomb laboratory would be constructed outside Los Alamos, New Mexico, was not even purchased by the government until November; and it was December 1942 before Oppenheimer was appointed director. Enrico Fermi's critical experiment, the first controlled nuclear chain reaction, was completed that same month at the University of Chicago.

Thus, four years after fission was discovered, scientists were not confident that the United States was closing the lead the Germans were assumed to have. A feeling of desperate urgency grew with each passing month, and with it the conviction that once developed, the bomb would be a decisive factor in the war—a conviction that permeated the entire chain of command. Vannevar Bush and James Conant, the science administrators who oversaw the Manhattan Project, kept President Roosevelt informed of both their colleagues' progress and their fears.

The implications of Bush's ability to communicate directly with the president can hardly be exaggerated. Roosevelt came to accept the scientists' view that the Allies were involved in a two-front war. Not only were there hard enemies on the fields of battle, but in German laboratories there were enemies who posed an even greater danger: scientists who might be first to develop a weapon that could alter the course of the war. This view of the bomb assured that its importance would not be underestimated by policy-makers. Indeed, it assured that its value would be exaggerated, and that those responsible for the military security of the United States after the war would view it, as Secretary of War Henry L. Stimson did at the Potsdam Conference, as a "badly needed equalizer," as a panacea for any real or imagined deficiencies of U.S. power.[3]

The atomic scientists' view that the bomb could win the war for Germany was easily converted by policy-makers to the idea that it could expedite the winning of the war for the United States. By the spring of 1944 the bomb's successful development appeared likely, but the timing of its completion remained uncertain. January 1945 was a possibility, but a later date—perhaps the summer of that year—appeared more probable.

■

Under the circumstances there is an irony in the decision to target Japan. Whatever other reasons may have contributed to that still incompletely understood decision, one element was the fear that an atomic attack on Germany might under certain conditions increase the possibility of a retaliatory attack in kind. This embryonic form of nuclear deterrence was expressed early. The May 5, 1943 minutes of a military policy committee meeting note that in a discussion of use of the first bomb "the general view appeared to be that its best point of use would be on a Japanese fleet concentration in the Harbor of Truk. General Styer suggested Tokio [sic], but it was pointed out that the bomb should be used where, if it failed to go off, it would land in water of sufficient depth to prevent easy salvage." The minutes went on to say: "The Japanese were selected as they would not be so apt to secure knowledge from it as would the Germans."[4]

Two years later, in the spring of 1945, with the Germans on the verge of defeat, confidence replaced caution and urban centers replaced military targets. While this shift in atomic bomb targets parallels an earlier shift in conventional bombing strategy, it also marks a new appreciation of the atomic bomb as a weapon of psychological intimidation. It was not expected that the destruction and havoc that two atomic bombs might wreak would suddenly break the back of Japan's war machine; but it was hoped that such attacks would shock the Japanese government into discontinuing their hopeless struggle. The selection of targets reflected this intention.

Guided by instructions from Groves, a target committee, composed of Manhattan Project scientists and ordnance specialists, studied the available options and developed criteria for their selection. The report of the committee's second and third meetings, held in Oppenheimer's office at Los Alamos in May 1945, suggests a major concern with the weapon's psychological impact. The minutes record the committee's view that any small, strictly military target should be located in a much larger area subject to blast damage "to avoid undue risks of the weapon being lost due to bad placing of the bomb." The members of the committee agreed, too, that the psychological impression the bomb made was not just a matter of wartime interest. "Two aspects of this," the report states, "are 1) obtaining the greatest psychological effect against Japan and 2) making the initial use sufficiently spectacular *for the importance of the weapon to be internationally recognized* [emphasis added] when publicity on it is released."[5]

The Target Committee's concern that the full implications of the bomb be recognized internationally reflected a pervasive anxiety among those scientists who had begun to worry about the bomb's role in the postwar world. As an instrument of peace based on the international control of atomic energy, or as an instrument of diplomacy to be used in postwar negotiations, the influence of the weapon depended upon a general recognition that pre-atomic age calculations had to give way to new realities. If the Japanese did not accept this view, the war might continue; if the Soviets ignored it, the peace would be lost. In this sense the bomb became its own message, and within the context of the war the scientists who participated in the decision to bomb Japan were consumed by a single objective—to transmit in the most dramatic fashion possible the message that the new age required new forms of international organization.

Leo Szilard, who had composed Einstein's famous letter to Roosevelt warning of the military implications of the discovery of fission, was the first to suggest a resolution to the problem of the bomb in the postwar world. Writing to Bush in January 1944, he referred to the potential development of a bomb of even greater power (the hydrogen bomb), and commented that "this weapon will be so powerful that there can be no peace if it is simultaneously in the possession of any two powers unless these two powers are bound by an indissoluble political union." Some type of international control scheme had to be created, he argued, "if necessary by force," to prevent a war that would recreate the dark ages, or worse.[6]

■

This was not the last time a scientist would suggest the use of military force to achieve security against nuclear uncertainty. The overwhelming sense of hopelessness before the developing of an unprecedented power created an urge to seek assurance against that power being turned upon its inventors. Bound to their task by fear of German progress, and terrified by the consequences of their own success, men of sensibility, culture, and peace were driven to recommend policies that they would find abhorrent in other circumstances.

Like Kurt Vonnegut's Trafalmadorians in *Slaughterhouse Five,* the scientists could see into the future: a postwar nuclear arms race leading to circumstances that literally could bring about the end of the world. But no one with power to prevent such a catastrophe seemed to recognize that this problem existed. As they worked desperately to build the bomb, scientists who were alert to these issues grasped at schemes to keep its potential destructive force under control.

The first serious attempt to meet this challenge was offered by Niels Bohr, who escaped to England from Nazi-occupied Denmark in September 1943. "Officially and secretly he came to help the technical enterprise," Oppenheimer noted, but "most secretly of all . . . he came to advance his case and his cause." In the broadest sense, Bohr's cause was to ensure that atomic energy "is used to the benefit of all humanity and does not become a menace to civilization." More specifically, he warned that "quite apart from the question of how soon the weapon will be ready for use and what role it may play in the present war," some agreement had to be reached with the Soviet Union about the future control of atomic energy before the bomb was developed.[7]

Bohr's ideas on the international control of atomic energy remain significant today beyond any

actual effect they might have had on Anglo–American policy. Arguing for a unilateral initiative, he insisted that the time to prepare for security in the nuclear age was before the bomb's development overwhelmed the possibility of international cooperation. If the bomb was born in secret in the United States, it would be conceived in secret by the Soviets. The only hope for avoiding a nuclear arms race after the war was to create an international-control arrangement before the war ended and before the bomb was tested. A nuclear arsenal was simply too big, in every sense, to be placed on any negotiating table; a weapon in the process of becoming was not.

As a scientist, Bohr apprehended the significance of the new weapon even before it was developed, and he had no doubt that Soviet scientists would also understand its profound implications for the postwar world. He was also certain that they would convey these implications to Stalin, just as scientists in the United States and Great Britain had explained them to Roosevelt and Churchill. Thus the diplomatic problem, as Bohr analyzed it, was not the need to convince Stalin that the atomic bomb was an unprecedented weapon that threatened the life of the world, but the need to assure the Soviet leader that he had nothing to fear from the circumstances of its development.

Roosevelt and Churchill shared neither Bohr's assumptions nor his vision, and perhaps it is too much to expect that they could. Harnessed to the yoke of war, without a scientist's intuitive understanding of the long-range implications of a weapon that did not yet exist, they accepted the bomb as it had been presented to them—as an ultimate weapon. "The suggestion that the world should be informed regarding [the atomic bomb], with a view to an international agreement regarding its control and use, is not accepted," they agreed in September 1944. "The matter should continue to be regarded as of the utmost secrecy."[8]

It was not only Bohr who tried to shed light on the dark shadow the bomb cast across the future. Scientists of a more politically conventional turn of mind, once alerted to the problem, turned to unconventional ideas. James Conant favored "the calculated risk," and to achieve a fair chance of success he was inclined "to talk in terms of concrete and limited objectives." Yet as early as May 1944, as James Hershberg has shown, Conant confronted the problem of the atomic bomb in the postwar world and came to the conclusion that limited objectives were dangerously inadequate. In the long run, he wrote to Bush, "the only hope for humanity is an international commission on atomic energy with free access to all information and right of inspection."[9]

In a memorandum entitled "Some Thoughts on International Control of Atomic Energy," Conant peered into the future and discerned only two alternatives: an atomic arms race and "in the next war destruction of civilization," or "a scheme to remove atomic energy from the field of conflict."[10] To achieve the second alternative Conant proposed 14 points. An association of nations specifically committed to control atomic energy had to be formed, and an international commission on atomic energy, which would include Britain, the United States, the Soviet Union, and perhaps six other nations, had to control all atomic energy work.

The commission would license, finance, and control all research and development work, and all results would be published. Agents of the commission would police the system by frequent inspections of all laboratories, factories, or other relevant facilities, and even if two countries were at war, the inspectors would have the right of entry. The commission was to have its own international air force and an army of 10,000 men to prevent the seizure of supplies. If any nation refused to permit inspections, or interfered with the commission in any other important way, its actions would be "considered an act of war."

But, Conant asked, "what happens if a nation refuses entry of agents to factories etc. or disobeys [the] edicts of [the] commission?" His answer was "war," declared by the other members of the international organization who might, if the commission approved, *use atomic bombs* to bring the renegade nation to heel. This idea of a limited nuclear war to prevent a general conflagration was even extended to the "use of bombs by arsenal guards," if the United States, Canada, or Britain tried to seize the commission's atomic arsenal, which Conant had located in Canada.

By recommending the use of a limited number of atomic bombs to prevent a general nuclear war, Conant succumbed to the temptation that lies across the path of all nuclear arms control efforts. If the desire to rid the world of the potential danger of nuclear war stems from a fear of their destructive potential, then why not use that threat in the service of international security?

Conant believed not only that the bomb was an ideal weapon to shock Japan's leaders into surrender, but that its use was necessary to impress upon the world in general, and on the Soviet government in particular, his vision of the destruction that it could inflict. Assuming "that in another war atomic bombs will be used," he recommended to Stimson that in the present war "the bomb *must be used*" for that was "the only way to awaken the world to the necessity of abolishing war altogether. No technical demonstration . . . could take the place of the actual use with its horrible results." Nor was Conant the only scientist to hold this view. "If the bomb were not used in the present war," Arthur Compton wrote to Stimson in June 1945, "the world would have no adequate warning as to what was to be expected if war should break out again,"[11]

■

A group of scientists at the University of Chicago reasoned quite differently, their analysis flowing from alternative assumptions formulated during the closing months of the war. Far removed from political pressures, and from considerations associated with the policy-making process, they broadcast a prescient warning to a deaf audience: the indiscriminate military use of the atomic bomb would undermine the possibility of achieving the international control of atomic energy.[12]

Early in June 1945, under the chairmanship of the distinguished emigre physicist James Franck, they assembled as the Committee on the Social and Political Implications of the Atomic Bomb. Their central concern was "the conditions under which international control is most probable," and their basic assumption is that the "manner in which this new weapon is introduced to the world will determine in large part the future course of events." They too saw the path from atomic bombs to superbombs with limitless destructive power.

They too described the uncertain security that an attempt at monopoly would bring. And they too outlined methods of international control that might be feasible.

Their primary purpose, however, was less to enumerate the dangers of the atomic age than to recommend policies that might circumvent those dangers. The central argument of the report was that a surprise atomic attack against Japan was inadvisable—whether one was optimistic or pessimistic about the possibility of international control. "If we consider international agreement on total prevention of nuclear warfare as the paramount objective, and believe that it can be achieved," they argued, "this kind of introduction [surprise attack] of atomic weapons to the world may easily destroy all our chances of success. Russia, and even allied countries which bear less mistrust of our ways and intentions, as well as neutral countries may be deeply shocked."

They argued against dropping the bomb on a populated area to show its capacity for terror and annihilation. "It may be very difficult to persuade the world that a nation which was capable of secretly preparing and suddenly releasing a weapon as indiscriminate as the [German] rocket bomb and a million times more destructive, is to be trusted in its proclaimed desire to have such weapons abolished by international agreement."

The report also made the converse case for not using the atomic bomb, even "if one takes the pessimistic point of view and discounts the possibility of an effective international control over nuclear weapons at the present time . . . early use of nuclear bombs against Japan becomes even more doubtful—quite independently of any humanitarian considerations. If an international agreement is not concluded immediately after the first use," they reasoned, exhibiting Bohr's sense of timing that was elsewhere lacking, "this will mean a flying start toward an unlimited armaments race. If this race is inevitable, we have every reason to delay its beginning as long as possible in order to increase our head start still further."

The members of the Franck Committee shared a basic assumption with those who had a sanguine view of the results that would flow from using the bomb: an atomic attack against Japan would "shock" the Soviets as well as the Japanese. But their reasoning about the effect of such a shock was very different. Conant, Compton, Truman, Stimson, and Secretary of State James Byrnes shared the view that an undeveloped weapon was not a very useful bargaining counter, a concept that is all too familiar today. They believed that an actual combat demonstration would make a far greater impression on those who needed to be convinced to end the war, and on those who needed to be persuaded that postwar international control of the atomic bomb was in their long-range interest. It was this quest to make an *impression*—the psychological impact of a single bomb dropped from a lone aircraft causing damage equal to that caused by thousands of bombs dropped from hundreds of aircraft—that was the basis for the decisions that led to Hiroshima.

The Franck Committee, however, drew the diametrically opposite conclusion: the more awesome the bomb's demonstrated power, the more likely an arms race. The most important demonstration needed was some means of conveying to Moscow a U.S. commitment not to use the bomb, a commitment that might instill in the Soviets a measure of confidence that the Anglo–American monopoly would not be turned on them, a commitment that might persuade them that the objective of U.S. policy was the neutralization of the atomic bomb. Szilard made this point to Oppenheimer when they saw each other in Washington in June. "Don't you think," Oppenheimer rejoined, "if we tell the Russians what we intend to do and then use the bomb in Japan, the Russians will understand it?" "They'll understand it only too well," was Szilard's prescient reply.[13]

■

In a sense more complex than originally stated, P. M. S. Blackett's charge "that the dropping of the atomic bombs was not so much the last military act of the second World War, as the first major operation of the cold *diplomatic* war with Russia," contains an essential truth.[14] The scientists and policy-makers who promoted the international control of atomic energy and supported the use of the bomb against Japan never expected that good relations with the Soviet Union would be possible if diplomatic efforts to achieve a nuclear arms control pact were not successful. They never thought that achieving such an agreement would be easy, nor that tough negotiations and a measure of intimidation should be avoided. Hiroshima and Nagasaki were part of that diplomatic strategy. So were the postwar tests at Bikini, held in the summer of 1946, at the same time that Bernard Baruch was presenting the U.S. plan for the international control of atomic energy to the United Nations.

Following a line of reasoning that President Truman stated in January—that "unless Russia is faced with an iron fist and strong language another war is in the making"[15]—Conant believed that atomic diplomacy would serve a useful purpose in bringing about security from atomic war. Speaking at an off-the-record dinner sponsored by the Council on Foreign Relations in New York on April 12, 1946, Truman responded to a question about the relationship between the Bikini tests and the upcoming United Nations Organization's international control conference: "The Russians," he stated, "are more rather than less likely to come to an effective agreement for the control of atomic energy if we keep our strength and continue to produce bombs."[16]

Atomic testing was not the only arrow in Conant's atomic diplomacy quiver; history also had a role. The atomic bombings of Japan were supported by the majority of Americans, but in the aftermath of the war Conant discerned a "spreading accusation that it was entirely unnecessary to use the atomic bomb at all," particularly among those whom he described to Stimson as "verbal minded citizens not so generally influential as they were influential among the coming generations of whom they might be teachers or educators."[17] To combat that view he urged Stimson to write an article on "the decision to drop the bomb," which subsequently appeared under that title in the February 1947 issue of *Harper's* magazine.

If "the propaganda against the use of the atomic bomb had been allowed to grow unchecked," Conant wrote to Stimson after reading a prepublication version of the article, "the strength of our military position by virtue of having the bomb would have been correspondingly weakened," and the chances for international control undermined.[18] "Humanitarian considerations" that led citizens to oppose the strengthening of the U.S. atomic arsenal, in Conant's opinion, were likely to subvert the common effort to achieve an international atomic energy agreement. "I am firmly convinced," he told Stimson, "that the Russians will eventually agree to the American proposals for the establishment of an atomic energy authority of world-wide scope, *provided* they are convinced that we would have the bomb in quantity and would use it without hesitation in another war."[19]

That Conant and those who supported this view were wrong is less a criticism of their logic than of their fundamental assumptions about the nature of the forces underlying the atomic arms race. If the Americans viewed the bomb as an effective instrument of diplomacy, and as a weapon to be used "without hesitation in another war," the Soviets could hardly be expected to take a loftier view. Scientific greatness gave way to political folly with the view that the atomic bomb could be used to fashion a solution to its own existence. It is a folly that we continue to live with today. And, to paraphrase Rabi, how well we mean.

1. I. I. Rabi, "How Well We Meant," transcript of Rabi's 1983 talk, Los Alamos National Laboratory Archives (no date).

2. Arthur Compton to Henry Wallace, June 23, 1942, F. D. Roosevelt, President's Secretary's File, Vannevar Bush folder, Roosevelt Library, Hyde Park, N.Y.; Robert Oppenheimer to John Manley, July 14, 1942, Oppenheimer Papers, Box 49, Library of Congress; Martin J. Sherwin, *A World Destroyed* (New York: Vintage Books, 1977), p. 47; Richard G. Hewlett and Oscar B. Anderson, Jr., *The New World, 1939/1946: A History of the United States Atomic Energy Commission, I* (University Park, Pa.: Pennsylvania State University Press, 1962), p. 179.

3. Henry L. Stimson and McGeorge Bundy, *On Active Service in Peace and War* (New York: Harpers, 1947), p. 617.

4. "Policy Meeting, 5/5/43," p. 2, Record Group 77, Manhattan Engineering District Records, Top Secret, folder 23A, National Archives.

5. Derry and Ramsey to Groves, May 12, 1945, MED–TS, Box 3, Target Committee Meetings, folder 5D.2.

6. Szilard to Bush, Jan. 14, 1944, in Gertrude Weiss Szilard and Spencer R. Weart, eds., *Leo Szilard: His Version of the Facts* (Cambridge, Mass.: MIT Press, 1978), p. 163.

7. J. Robert Oppenheimer, "Niels Bohr and Atomic Weapons," *The New York Review of Books,* 3 (Dec. 17, 1966), p. 7. Bohr memorandum, May 8, 1945, Oppenheimer Papers, box 34, Library of Congress; Bohr to Roosevelt, July 3, 1944, Oppenheimer Papers, box 34, LC.

8. Hyde Park Aide-Memoire, Sept. 18, 1944, President's Map Room papers, Naval Aide's File, box 172-General folder, Franklin Delano Roosevelt Library, reprinted in Sherwin, *A World Destroyed,* p. 284.

9. "The Tough-Minded Idealist," Sept. 23, 1946, *Harvard Alumni Bulletin* 49, no. 2 (Oct. 12, 1946), quoted in James G. Hershberg, *Ends Versus Means: James B. Conant and American Atomic Policy, 1939-47* (unpublished senior thesis, Harvard College, 1982), pp. 208–9. See also marginal comment by Conant on a memorandum, Bush to Conant, April 17, 1944, entitled "Shurcliff's memo on Post-War Policies," Atomic Energy Commission Historical Document no. 180, Department of Energy Archives, Energy Research Collection.

10. James Conant, memo dated May 4, 1944, Bush–Conant files, box 9, folder 97, Office of Scientific Research and Development, S-1 Section files, National Archives; reprinted in Hershberg, *Ends Versus Means,* pp. 189–90.

11. James Conant to Grenville Clark, Nov. 8, 1945, Bush Papers, box 27, Conant folder, LC; Henry Stimson to Raymond Swing, quoting Conant, Feb. 4, 1947, Stimson Papers, Swing folder, Sterling Memorial Library, Yale University; Arthur Holly Compton,

Atomic Quest: A Personal Narrative (New York: Oxford University Press, 1956), pp. 239–40.

12. The Franck Report is reproduced in Alice Kimball Smith, *A Peril and A Hope: The Atomic Scientists' Movement, 1945–1947* (Chicago: University of Chicago Press, 1965), Appendix B, pp. 560–72.

13. Leo Szilard, "Reminiscences," edited by Gertrude Weiss Szilard and Kathleen R. Winsor, in Donald Fleming and Bernard Bailyn, eds., *The Intellectual Migration: Europe and America, 1930–1960* (Cambridge, Mass.: Harvard University Press, 1969), p. 128.

14. P. M. S. Blackett, *Fear, War and the Bomb: Military and Political Consequences of Atomic Energy* (New York: Whittlesey House, 1948), p. 139.

15. Harry S. Truman, *Memoirs: Year of Decisions* (Garden City, N.Y.: Doubleday, 1955), pp. 551–52.

16. James Conant, "International Controls of Atomic Energy," April 12, 1946; *Records of Meetings,* vol. XII, July 1945–June 1947, Council on Foreign Relations Archives, New York, quoted in Hershberg, *Ends Versus Means,* p. 157.

17. Stimson to Felix Frankfurter, quoting Conant, Dec. 12, 1946, Stimson Papers, box 154, folder 14.

18. Conant to McGeorge Bundy, Nov. 30, 1946, Stimson Papers, box 154m folder 11.

19. Conant to Stimson, Jan. 22, 1947, Stimson papers, box 154, folder 18.

"Star Wars" Politicizing Science in U.S.
Military Influence Stirs Campus Debate

Anne C. Roark

James R. Melcher surely would not fit anyone's image of an anti-war protester.

The 50-year-old professor has spent the bulk of his professional life in what is politically the most conservative of scientific disciplines—electrical engineering. For 25 years he has been at the Massachusetts Institute of Technology, the nation's biggest defense contractor among universities.

During the 1960s, he was a critic not of the Vietnam War but of the war protesters. Today, as director of a major laboratory at MIT, he is clearly part of America's scientific establishment.

But lately, Melcher has become something of a campus agitator. He has joined about 8,000 other American scientists in protesting President Reagan's Strategic Defense Initiative, popularly known as "Star Wars," and he is making his views known in a wide variety of rallies, seminars and other public forums.

Initially, when the protest began more than two years ago, scientists opposed "Star Wars" largely on technical grounds: A protective "shield" of the kind the President envisioned to keep the country safe from nuclear attack was simply a scientific impossibility, the experts argued.

Later, political objections emerged as well. Last fall, for example, after the Reykjavik summit between President Reagan and Soviet leader Mikhail S. Gorbachev, scientists were as vocal as politicians in expressing alarm that the prospect of halting the nuclear arms race was being jeopardized by Reagan's insistence on moving forward with a strategic defense plan.

More recently, however, many members of the nation's research establishment have gone beyond questioning technical and political aspects of just the Strategic Defense Initiative. Perhaps more significant, says William D. Carey, executive director of the American Assn. for the Advancement of Science, is that scientists have begun to reconsider "the entire scope and thrust of America's research enterprise."

Though more restrained and certainly lacking the violence of the political troubles that erupted on campuses during the Vietnam era, the protest of the 1980s is no less significant, Carey said, because of what the scientists themselves believe is at stake: the future of American research.

"There probably has never been so much concern . . . such widespread protest" about any subject affecting American science, said Daniel J. Kevles, a historian of science at Caltech who is writing a book on the history of military spending since World War II.

No matter what becomes of "Star Wars"— whether the American public supports it or rejects it, whether it succeeds or fails—it has already had one undeniable spin-off, Kevles said: the politicizing of American science to an extent that has not occurred since the years immediately after World War II, in response to the dropping of the atomic bomb on Hiroshima and Nagasaki.

The protest is far from one-sided. On some campuses, a counter-protest has begun to emerge among strong advocates of military research. Although fewer in number and less organized than the critics of the defense buildup, the pro-military scientists are expressing support for the nation's growing defense budget not only on the grounds that it will improve national security but because, they say, it will ultimately benefit science as well.

Money Accepted

"Although they are quite well organized and have been quite vocal . . . it would be a mistake to think that these are the views of all American scientists," said John Kwapisz, director of the Center for Peace and Freedom, a pro-military foundation set up in Washington a little more than a year ago.

To counter the impression that all U.S. scientists oppose the recent thrust of military spending, Kwapisz's center recently spawned an ad hoc university group of about 100 scientists called the Science and Engineering Committee for a Secure World.

In reaction to the statements and activities of the anti-"Star Wars" forces, a number of high-ranking government federal officials have also spoken out harshly, accusing university scientists of having abandoned their objectivity as researchers and their loyalty as citizens. The "Star Wars" supporters also note that many researchers, while critical of the government's programs, are not hesitant about accepting its money.

Certainly there are plenty of takers for "Star Wars" research grants and contracts. According to Maj. David Rigby, a spokesman at the Pentagon for the SDI project, the Defense Department received more than 3,000 unsolicited proposals for basic research last year—10 times the number it could support—and most of them were from university professors.

Much of the debate over "Star Wars" and defense research in general has centered on university campuses. In one regard, this is to be expected because universities have often been at the center of major intellectual and political upheavals. But in other ways, the universities' involvement in the current debate over military spending is surprising.

For one thing, scientists, at least in many disciplines, are among the most conservative of academicians, according to several surveys of American professors.

The military, furthermore, appears at first glance to have relatively little direct impact on campuses. According to government budget documents, the Department of Defense now accounts for only about 17% of all federal spending for campus research.

Yet what troubles many university scientists is that the defense budget is one of the few sources of funds, federal or otherwise, that is still growing significantly.

While defense funds to universities rose nearly 14% last year, funds from all other federal agencies combined are estimated by the American Assn. for the Advancement of Science to have grown by less than 1%. And while defense-financed campus research was just $930 million last year, that was up 89% from 1980 and was double the 1975 level, the Council for Economic Priorities said in a report last year entitled "Pentagon Invades Academia."

What's more, the report said, the Defense Department's 17% share of federal campus research masks an almost total dependence by some academic disciplines on defense grants and contracts. More than 50% of all federally financed university research in mathematics and computer science now comes from the Pentagon. In electrical engineering, the Pentagon's share of university research is now 56.9% and in astronautical engineering it is 81%

"We are now facing the prospect that defense research in general and 'Star Wars' in particular will be the largest source of federal funds likely to be available for at least a decade to come," said John P. Holdren, professor of energy and resources at UC Berkeley and former chairman of the Federation of American Scientists.

"Since universities do the bulk of the country's basic research . . . and train the majority of American scientists . . . , we have to ask what that

will mean for our universities and the country as a whole," Holdren said.

It is more than just the size of military support that disturbs American scientists. It is, MIT's Melcher said, the extent to which the military is both directly and indirectly dictating the nation's research agenda that is so troubling.

"Shift in Thinking"

In a recent telephone interview from his laboratory in Cambridge, Melcher contended that a basic "shift in thinking" has occurred in American science in the past few years. Increasingly, he said, the best academic scientists and the best American industries are turning away from research and manufacturing of civilian goods such as airplanes and automobiles, where money is tight and market competition is stiff, and toward military hardware, where research money is plentiful and profits are assured.

Melcher said he is well aware of companies' obligations to seek maximum investment returns for stockholders. He is also sympathetic with his university colleagues, many of whom believe they would not receive support for their research were it not for potential military applications.

But citing example after example of what he believes are questionable government and business practices that affect his own laboratory and those of his colleagues, he has come to believe that the nation's priorities are now misguided—headed in a direction no one ever really intended.

Slowly but surely, Melcher has begun to make his views known—and not only to his immediate colleagues. He is taking part in conferences, and has helped organize lectures and other gatherings on the subject of military research.

And last spring, he joined 6,500 university scientists and scientific educators in signing a pledge, organized by professors and students at the University of Illinois and Cornell University, to boycott the "Star Wars" program. A similar petition calling on Congress to curb funding for the strategic defense program was also circulated last spring and signed by 1,600 industrial and government researchers and scientists, some of whom would be directly affected by the very cuts they were demanding.

Impressive List

Together, the two groups account for just a small fraction of the nation's scientific work force—perhaps 1%, according to critics. Yet by almost any measure, the list of signers is an impressive one. Half of the science and engineering faculty in each of more than 100 research departments pledged to accept no more "Star Wars" money. In the 20 top-ranked departments, including Harvard, Berkeley and Stanford, more than 50% of the combined faculties said they would not participate in the program, Among them were 15 Nobel laureates.

Strong protests have also been lodged in recent months by members of the National Academy of Sciences, the elite organization whose members are generally regarded as the nation's brightest and most productive researchers. A poll of academy members whose disciplines were deemed relevant to the SDI found that only 9.8% of the respondents supported or strongly supported the program, while nearly 70% opposed or strongly opposed it.

The protest has taken other forms as well.

A dozen or more new scientific societies, specifically focusing on the priorities and ethics of American science, have been established largely in response to the military's growing share of the total federal research budget. Uneasiness about the military's role in science also has even been evident in the older and more traditional scientific organizations.

Perhaps the most dramatic illustration of that concern has come from the 10,000-member Institute of Electrical and Electronics Engineers. In a recent poll of that conservative scientific organization, one-third of the members surveyed said they considered assignment to non-military work a key factor when changing jobs.

Students Not Informed

As with most campus protests, students have been at the center of the activity, organizing the petition drives, setting up conferences and handing out information. But, for the most part, the foot soldiers of this protest have not been angry undergraduates or the campus activists involved in protests against South African apartheid or American intervention in Central America. They have been research fellows and graduate students in the sciences, working toward doctorates in such fields as physics and engineering.

Lisbeth Gronlund, for example, is one of the organizers of the nation-wide campus boycott. She is a physics Ph.D. candidate at Cornell University who got involved in the movement because of a sense of frustration about her own career options.

Graduate students, she said in an interview from her laboratory on campus, simply are not informed about the real purposes of the research on which they work in university laboratories. Nor, she said, do they understand the kind of careers that are likely to be available once they finish school.

The odds are, she said, that most of the next generation of scientists will find openings only in military-related work. And that is also true, she said, for scientists who stay in academe.

"I've cut into my [research] considerably this year by getting involved in this protest," Gronlund said. "But in a way I have to look at it as a short-term investment in a really long-term problem."

"A Guide for Young Scientists and Engineers," prepared by a group at the Institute for Theoretical Physics at UC Santa Barbara, reports that one-third of the 600,000 working scientists and engineers in the United States are now employed in military-related projects. Of those 200,000, at least one third—almost 70,000—work on nuclear weapons projects, the report estimated. Although no one knows for certain what the impact will be if military research keeps growing at its current rate, it will surely employ "tens of thousands of new graduates over the next five years," the study said.

Few of these researchers will have the luxury of doing what a handful of established scientists have done in recent years—that is, voluntarily leave their posts on weapons projects to take up positions in non-military programs.

Growing Misgivings

One such researcher is physicist Thomas Grissom, who two years ago left his job at Sandia National Laboratory in Albuquerque, where he had been working to develop neutron generators. For almost 15 years, Grissom said, he was so engrossed in his research that he almost forgot its purpose—to trigger nuclear weapons. Eventually his misgivings about the threat of nuclear war grew so large that he took a dramatic pay cut and went to Evergreen State College in Olympia, Wash., an institution known far better for its innovative teaching programs than for its scientific discoveries.

Perhaps the most celebrated case of a scientist leaving military research involves the man who invented the laser that helped launch "Star Wars." In what is generally seen as a severe blow to the strategic defense program, Peter Hagelstein just this winter left Lawrence Livermore National Laboratory for MIT, saying that he wanted to leave weapons work for research that "will benefit mankind." His only connection with Livermore now is as a consultant and only on what he insists will be unclassified, non-military projects.

For many, the only alternative to doing weapons-related research may be to leave science altogether, but even those who are sympathetic with the protest contend that this is a dangerous view for scientists to take.

Caltech President Marvin L. Goldberger likens the attitude of many young scientists today to the women of ancient Greece in Aristophanes' comedy, "Lysistrata." Like the wives of Athens and Sparta who refused to make love to their husbands until the men stopped making war, so many scientists "want to stop making science until politicians agree to use research only for peaceful, productive purposes."

"This is a very naive and idealistic point of view," Goldberger said. "Even if scientists stopped working right now on military things, we'd still be in a hell of a mess. We'd still have 50,000 nuclear weapons. . . . The idea that nirvana would happen is silly."

Still, many university scientists contend their institutions are facing some very real concerns that should not be overlooked by either policy-makers or taxpayers.

One of the universities' most pressing issues has to do with the method by which the Pentagon hands out its research money.

Peer-Review Process

Since the end of World War II, the standard method for deciding who will get government grants has been the peer-review process, in which non-government scientists examine the research proposals of their own colleagues and decide on their scientific merit. Although it is not a foolproof system and is periodically accused of having biases, it is an approach that most American scientists believe has been extremely successful.

For the "Star Wars" program, however, Pentagon officials acknowledge that they have begun to circumvent the peer review process in their awards of grants and contracts. The change is necessary, they say, because the old method has tended to favor elite universities that have always captured the bulk of government support for scientific research. The peer review process, the officials say, has failed to provide enough money to scientists with good ideas who are outside the "establishment" and is too conservative and cumbersome for a program such as "Star Wars," which demands dramatic new approaches to highly technical military problems.

"Look at the list of who is getting most of the 'Star Wars' money," noted one university president, "and you will see it is not the . . . Harvards and Berkeleys. Sure they are getting some. But an awful lot is going to institutions whose reputations are built on their agricultural extension programs and their basketball teams, not their contribution to high-caliber science."

Doing away with peer review and adopting the Pentagon's new approach, added MIT's Melcher, means that research is being judged on the basis of military applicability rather than pure scientific merit.

For universities, that is particularly troublesome, because the whole raison d'etre of a university is to support the free flow of ideas whose ultimate usefulness often cannot be predicted.

Short-Term Emphasis

Indeed, said Franklin A. Long, a noted chemist at Cornell, military research in general and "Star Wars" in particular are antithetical to a university's basic purpose for two fundamental reasons: In the first place, the Pentagon emphasizes short-term applied projects that have immediate military payoffs. It also requires, for reasons of national security, that much of its research be done in secret.

"Universities do [and in my judgment should] restrict themselves to research programs which are either for basic research or for long-range applied research," Long wrote in a recent article in the Bulletin of Atomic Scientists. "The central reason for university research is its coupling with advanced training of students, and the teaching process is by its very nature one in which deadlines and time-urgent demands characteristic of development programs do not fit well."

"Equally important," he said, "is that the teaching process demands open, uninhibited communication. Students and teachers must talk freely with each other; they cannot be bound by a hidden agenda or restrictions imposed from outside."

The Defense Department, although it has had little to say about its growing emphasis on applied research, has tried to allay fears about secrecy by promising not to retroactively classify any university research project.

University researchers, however, continue to be wary. Their concerns, they say, have been borne out in at least one case in which a researcher at a university-administered government lab—Andrew M. Sessler, former director of Lawrence Berkeley Laboratory—not only had his research on lasers classified but also had the project taken away from him altogether. Details of the situation have never been made public because of the government's classification restrictions, but it is generally suspected that the action against Sessler may have come at least partly as a result of his public criticism of SDI.

"The truth is that many faculty members are quite concerned, but for various reasons—fear of reprisals, a sense that [the military] may be their only source of funding—many have opted to remain silent or at least to say less than they might have," said MIT physicist Vera Kistiakowsky.

Many remember the government's quick retaliation to university-organized anti-military protests during the Vietnam War. In 1971, President Richard M. Nixon refused to give any National Medals of Science. In 1973, not long after his reelection victory, he announced the abolition of the White House's Science Advisory Committee and the government's main research policy body, the Office of Science and Technology.

Nixon also added the names of scientists and university presidents to his famous "enemies list." And according to high-level sources within the Nixon Administration, the President even tried to cut off funds to MIT because its president at the time had spoken out against the White House's defense policies.

But it is more than just concern about reprisals that is keeping scientists from speaking out. According to MIT's Melcher, it is accompanied by a fear of not being taken seriously any longer as a scientist.

Many, for example, point to the experience of Charles Schwartz, an outspoken advocate of the peace movement on the Berkeley campus for many years. Although Schwartz has long been a highly regarded physicist, his activities outside the laboratory have made him an object of scorn in some quarters.

"You can imagine the reaction when he announced [at a meeting last spring of the American Physical Society] that he would not teach most regular physics classes after this year because he no longer wanted to train the physicists and engineers who will become the front-line soldiers in developing new weapons systems," one longtime Berkeley professor recalled. "People just said, 'Oh there goes Charlie again.' No one hears what he's saying any longer. And that's too bad. It really is."

Knowing this kind of reaction at other universities, Melcher is inclined to tread softly at MIT. "You have to ask yourself: Can you walk up and down the halls and still have people's respect? After all, some of us are saying things that make people very, very uncomfortable."

Nonetheless, Melcher concluded, "Every institution is being tested right now. I am determined that MIT will not flunk."

"However you look at it, this is tricky business," said one president of another prestigious research university, who asked not to be quoted by name. "Let me give you just one example.... Look, if the truth be known, I'm sitting on a half-million dollar grant application made by some of my faculty to the 'Star Wars' program. Now, I don't like this program and I don't like the whole thrust of the military budget today, but just because these are my views does not mean I have the right to jeopardize someone else's grant proposal."

PART SEVEN

The Peace Movement

The peace movement—organized groups of citizens working against the arms race, the draft, and war—has been part of our society since colonial times. The strength of this movement has waxed and waned, and the movement has not established a lasting peace. But the peace movement in recent decades has had some important successes: The 1963 nuclear test ban treaty, the winding down of the Vietnam War in the early 1970s, and the 1988 disarmament agreements between the United States and Russia all followed major upsurges of activities by the peace movement.

Achieving peace in the future will in large part be dependent on the regeneration of the peace movement because much of the political system and the military-industrial-academic complex are devoted to permanent war mobilization in the name of deterrence. Studying the strengths and weaknesses of past movements will contribute to more effective movements in the future. Traditionally, history has been described in terms of wars and the "blank" spaces between wars. By learning the history of peace, peace making will become a more concrete activity instead of a vague ideal or a blank space between wars.

In a survey of the peace movement in the United States since World War I, Charles Howlett and Glen Zeitzer describe its long-term vitality. A large coalition of peace groups worked for disarmament in the 1920s and 1930s, and in 1938 the House of Representatives almost passed the Ludlow amendment, which would have required a national referendum (public vote) to permit U.S. involvement in any foreign war. In the 1960s the movement against the Vietnam War created the largest and broadest coalition of peace activists—a vast network of pacifists and internationalists, members of the New Left, hippies and businesspersons that at times mobilized over 1 million people in simultaneous demonstrations across the country.

Robert Cooney and Helen Michalowski describe the peace movement in the late 1960s, especially the involvement of pacifists committed to nonviolent actions such as demonstrations, draft card burnings, and other protests. The government and military responded to this growing antiwar movement by creating a huge intelligence apparatus for surveillance, most of it illegally infringing on people's constitutional rights to free speech, free press, and free assembly, as J. Frank Donner documents.

During the 1970s the peace movement in the United States was relatively small and inactive, but it blossomed again in the early 1980s, this time as a movement to "freeze" all nuclear weapons testing as a first step to halt the arms race and eventually eliminate the weapons. Earl and Roger Molander, major participants in the 1980s antinuclear movement, use their "stage" theory of how a successful movement must develop to explain the rise and fall of the proposal for a nuclear freeze.

Part of the 1980s movement was the growth of peace organizations within professional and religious groups. The "Statement of the International Physicians for the Prevention of Nuclear War" provides an example. Although these professional bodies have made great contributions, their success points to the continuing challenge facing the peace movement to form broader coalitions beyond its normal core of middle-class, white activists.

The final articles turn to the international scene and different peace movements' strategies for reaching peace. Jason Salzman presents an account of the successful movement in New Zealand to forbid ships and planes carrying nuclear weapons to land or dock there, creating what the movement calls a "nuclear-free zone." The United States government adamantly opposed this movement and tried to stop it, but failed. In the next reading, Rudolf Bahro describes how in Europe, especially in West Germany, "Green" political parties are trying to unite the peace, feminist, and ecology movements in an international effort to oppose industrial society with its concomitant forms of social domination as found in both communist and capitalist countries, and to work for achieving a new relationship with the environment. In the last reading, Pam Solo, Ted Sasson, and Rob Leavitt present the "Principles of Common Security," a peace movement program based on the strategy that "no nation can ensure its own security at the expense of another, or put another way, the security of one cannot be rooted in the insecurity of another."

THE HISTORY OF
THE PEACE MOVEMENT

The History of the American Peace Movement

Charles F. Howlett ▪ *Glen Zeitzer*

Approaches to the Peace Movement

Historians have always noted the importance of armed conflict in United States history, yet opposition to war has hardly been mentioned in public schools or even in colleges and universities.[1] Despite the omission of such material in the standard histories of our national past, war opposition, or peace activism, has a history, and peace advocates and organizations deserve historical recognition.[2] To neglect this important aspect of American life is to cheat the dissenters of their historical roots. To rob them of their attachment to one of the fundamental principles upon which this nation was built—individual liberalism—is also a gross injustice.[3] Even though violence and wars permeate much of our heritage, there exists a solid tradition of nonviolent antiwar activity as well as an abundance of pacifist arguments.

The peace movement in America has occupied a major part of our reform tradition, absorbing along the way innumerable individuals and organizations. Historically, it has been characterized by five approaches.[4] Many peace seekers have limited their commitment to specific antiwar actions, opposing American involvement in various wars for any number of reasons; the vast majority of this group have not been pacifists. Others have upheld the banner of internationalism, maintaining that

peace would be secured with the institutionalization of organizations established for the prevention and settlement of disputes among nations.[5] Some peace seekers have subscribed to various pacifist ethics on the grounds that peace is based on ongoing human relationships, which precludes resorting to violence. Numerous peace seekers have pursued peace through antimilitarism, believing that the existence of large standing armies poses a threat to individual liberty and constitutional democracy as well as to peace. Others have connected peace action with their own allied interests, such as capitalism, civil rights, feminism, anarchism, anti-imperialism, and socialism.[6]

Despite their diversity, peace seekers have generally operated throughout American history along two parallel lines of action. First, for reasons of principle, they have denounced war as a form of collective behavior that corrupts social order, Judeo-Christian ethics, and human welfare and justice. Second, they have worked from that principle to establish alternative means of resolving human conflicts and to develop forms of group harmony so that peace might persist as an ongoing social dynamic. Over the course of the American experience, peace workers and organizations have tried either to form ideal communities for the larger society to emulate, or to engage in reform efforts intended to replace those political policies, social institutions, or cultural patterns that have prevented the triumph of lasting peace. Peace activists and their representative organizations have sought positively to make peace, and not simply to oppose war.

Because peace workers have envisioned peace as something more than the absence of war, it has been difficult to compare the success of the peace movement with that of other social movements. In most cases historians have found it troublesome to comprehend the diversity of views, activities, and approaches associated with the peace movement. How can one characterize the movement?

First, as historian Charles Chatfield reminds us in *Peace Movements in America* (1972), it is evident that each peace effort must be defined with respect to the specific issues and choices that engendered it. Opposition to America's earliest wars was confined within the boundaries of contemporaneous issues that traditionally have not been connected with peace action. Much of the activity labeled peace work has been a reaction to concrete problems facing society as a whole, such as the late nineteenth-century arms race and imperialism, the Great War, the rise of totalitarianism in the 1930s, and the contemporary threat of nuclear destruction. War and injustice have presented unique challenges to each generation of peace seekers; indeed, peace leaders in every era have differed among themselves in assessing massive social crises. Thus, the response of each antiwar movement has been distinctive with regard to policy issues as well as to the kind of society within which it operated. Clearly, peace movements are conditioned by the very crises to which they react.[7]

Second, peace efforts must be comprehended in light of the political processes in operation during their times. A peace effort is composed of at least its workers. The membership of each group is bonded by a distinct viewpoint (e.g., pacifism, world court, international government), together with either social characteristics (e.g., Christianity, socialism, feminism) or functional programs (e.g., dramatizing issues, lobbying, educating). All of these groups enlist some members who are interested only tangentially and only at the point of some particular issue. In this fashion, an antiwar constituency may attract groups with inconsistent interests, much as opposition to World War I aligned socialists with some moderate liberals, as the position of strict neutrality in the 1930s captured both isolationists and pacifists, and as condemnation of the Vietnam War joined New Left radicals and conservative business leaders, as well as cold war political warriors. Significantly, the peace movement, bonded by alternative strategies to global harmony, has been noted for its ability to form coalitions that vie with prowar groups or with the government for public support in the political realm.

Finally, peace efforts must be understood in relation to their values and assumptions. The very word *peace*, for instance, has become the subject of searching analysis—even the Marine Corps today inappropriately labels itself the "Peacekeepers." Historians and activists alike are trying to replace peace's negative connotation as the absence of war with a more positive, constructive concept. Both "peace" and "internationalism," unfortunately, have become "a counterpane for all sorts of idealistic bedfellows."[8] They have become synonyms for the "higher good" to which we might aspire; but they do not always express the conceptions of reality upon which our values rest. It is ironic that peace, which has a longer historic permanence than war, is considered the ideal, while war remains solidly planted on the landscape of reality.

It is obvious that approaches to peace are many and varied, yet there exists a certain consistency to the peace movement's life. It has been described best by Lawrence S. Wittner. According to Wittner, the peace effort has resembled an onion, with the absolutists at the center and the less committed forming the outside layers. At times of popular enthusiasm for war the less committed outside layers peel off, leaving the pacifist core; in times of strong aversion to militarism new layers appear, and the onion grows in size. This structural fluidity accounts both for the peace movement's repeated weakness in times of international tension and for its peculiar resiliency. How has the onion grown and shrunk throughout the history of the United States?[9] . . .

. . .

The Modern American Peace Movement

In August 1914 war engulfed many of the world peace movements. American peace leaders reacted predictably at first, expressing shock, abhorrence, and dismay. But as the outstanding peace advocates from all classes came to the defense of one warring power or another, the established peace societies wavered or actually supported the Allied cause. . . . Impatient pacifists formed new organizations in opposition to American involvement. Eventually, the peace movement was restructured between those who supported the war and those who adamantly opposed it.[10]

In April 1917, when the United States finally entered World War I, the differences within the peace movement became even more prominent. On the one hand, there were internationalists who supported the war, ever hopeful that a democratized and reformed postwar world order would develop from the war. . . . They believed in the ability of a people to change conditions and achieve a stable world order, based on cooperation rather than force, through the establishment of world agencies. In supporting the war, these advocates of peace did not abandon their international vision. Instead, they attributed to the war the very values for which they had worked previously: the search for international equity, law, and order. On the other hand, a contingent of pacifists withdrew to fight the only enemy they knew: war. From their opposition would emerge new pacifist organizations such as the Women's International League for Peace and Freedom, the American Friends Service Committee, the War Resisters League, and the American branch of the Fellowship of Reconciliation. Led by noted pacifists A. J. Muste, John Nevin Sayre, Norman Thomas, and Jane Addams, these organizations proved more receptive to socialist analysis of the nature of capitalism's failings and

more radical, though not violent, in their prescriptions for its overhaul and displacement. Lasting peace, from their perspective, was contingent upon domestic social reform.[11]

From these two approaches emerged, as DeBenedetti so brilliantly explains in *Origins of the Modern American Peace Movement, 1915–1929* (1978), the modern American peace movement. This was a movement that understood that peace required social reform as well as social order. Leaders of the new movement, whether pacifist or internationalist, understood justice as the amelioration of social wrongs and not simply the adjudication of courts; they viewed nationalism in terms of cultural diversity rather than as some form of Anglo-Saxon exclusivity; they saw war as a byproduct of militarism, nationalism, and imperialism and not merely as an irrational outburst of mass ignorance; and they sought a reformed and democratized international system by which responsible policymakers would manage peace through applied social justice and world agencies. Although the modern American peace movement contained all the ingredients of a pacifist persuasion, internationalists nonetheless recognized the virtue of viewing peace as a social process. In their eyes, as in those of their pacifist counterparts, peace was "an ongoing process of reconciling peoples by means of democratic structures developed through self-conscious human planning."[12]

The modern American peace movement and its alignments created by World War I characterized peace forces until the mid-1950s, when a new coalition of pacifists and internationalists developed with an apparent thaw in the cold war. Organizationally, from the Great War through World War II, the modern American peace movement continued to develop from the separate experiences of pacifist opposition to the war and internationalist support for it. Neither wing formed a unified whole, even though both wings were in agreement on the social processes of peace. Both peace persuasions were led by a generation of well-educated people who were influenced by progressivism, social gospel Christianity, pragmatism, and a social mode of social analysis, and who were deeply affected by their own personal confrontation with war. Both represented a loose and shifting coalition, sometimes cooperating with one another and sometimes conflicting. Although there would be no coalition between pacifists and internationalists per se, both wings recognized the need to work together. Thus, in the immediate postwar years, despite occasional friction and divergent paths to peace, both peace factions supported the common goal of cooperation to abolish the problem of international violence. An understanding had been reached on the end, if not the means.

Accordingly, at the conclusion of World War I the modern American peace movement was composed of two distinct ideological wings: internationalist and pacifist. The internationalist wing, composed of organizations such as the Carnegie Endowment for International Peace, the World Peace Foundation, and the League of Nations Association, believed that peace required international cooperation. These groups felt that peace could be achieved through international mechanisms based upon the voluntary cooperation of nation-states. For them the principle of national autonomy remained intact. Support for war was acceptable in the name of national security. The pacifist wing, which consisted of the Women's International League for Peace and Freedom, the National Council for Prevention of War, the Committee on Militarism in Education, the War Resisters League, the Fellowship of Reconciliation, and others, favored antimilitarism, complete disarmament, and the need to rid the world of the "war spirit." The pacifists' objective was to eliminate war altogether, not merely to prevent it; domestic reform was their primary vehicle. They approached the peace problem from a transnational perspective. They viewed peace as a process based on individual and group cooperation sustained through common values and institutional and cultural mores. Opposition to all forms of organized violence was a must. Because of national disillusion over the Great War and skillful organization, the pacifist wing, albeit small, exerted a profound influence on American public opinion.[13]

The war generated considerable, if not ideo-

logically united, opposition. In a rather limited way the war was attacked by antiwar socialist laborites, who established the People's Council of America for Democracy and Peace as a means for countering the American Federation of Labor's patriotic group known as the American Alliance for Labor and Democracy. Tentatively organized on May 30, 1917 in New York City and officially established in September of that year amid turmoil, public denunciation, and armed repression, this coalition of radicals, labor leaders, and bohemian intellectuals insisted that the workers despised war, recognized it as a conspiracy against their fundamental interests, and from the very nature of their economic position of deprivation sought brotherhood and cooperation with workers in other parts of the world.

These socialists and members of the Industrial Workers of the World (the majority of which were not members of any organized peace group) who refused to serve in World War I were also active in reform movements to improve society. In their opinion, a decent future required, in fact demanded, a basic change in values and political power. Socialist ideals, they believed, would inevitably lead to a perfect or at least greatly improved society. Among other things, socialism would lead to the abolition of war, which they viewed, perhaps narrowly, as an aspect of capitalism and imperialism. As representatives of the international working class, they could not sanction a war against their fellow workers in other nations. Ernest L. Meyer, a noted political resister during the war, wrote in his classic memoir *"Hey! Yellowbacks"* (1930) the following observation: "There are times when the individual must withdraw himself from the state, if he feels his deepest convictions of right and wrong invaded. This is one of those times. I cannot aid in the destruction of life when I feel that no happiness is gained by it, or no honest cause advanced."[14]

Opposition during World War I, moreover, took the form of both individual and organized resistance. Approximately 4000 conscientious objectors were recorded, most of whom went into noncombatant military service; 500 were court-martialed and imprisoned, 17 sentenced to death but never executed, and 142 given life terms but released by 1921.[15] World War I prisoners of conscience best known today included civil libertarian Roger Baldwin and socialist leader Eugene V. Debs. Jailed twice for war opposition and in prison during the presidential election of 1920, Debs received nearly a million votes as the Socialist candidate. . . .

. . .

Even though there did not exist a homogeneous American search for peace between 1919 and 1941, there was an extraordinarily active peace movement. Peace reformers and war resisters struggled to realize their cause through the League of Nations, the World Court, arbitration treaties, disarmament agreements, the Kellogg–Briand Pact of 1928 (also known as the Pact of Paris), and stable economic arrangements.[16] The peace movement expressed a sense of urgency in the wake of the destructiveness of modern technological war. The potential for human loss and suffering had never been so great.

The movement, however, was marked by ideological differences that deserve mention. For example, some internationalists in the League of Nations Non-Partisan Association (later renamed the League of Nations Association in 1929) pushed for United States leadership in the collective maintenance of global peace; they placed their highest hopes on the creation of a permanent world order in the League of Nations and its associated agencies. The league represented a unique laboratory for experimentation in human and institutional cooperation, while at the same time amplifying America's voice in European affairs. Others in the Foreign Policy Association favored democratic diplomacy and international economic reconstruction. Pacifists in the Women's International League for Peace and Freedom and the Fellowship of Reconciliation promoted transnational nonviolent action in defense of justice, while those in the War Resisters League pledged absolute opposition to the war system. Numerous individuals from both the internationalist and pacifist wings nevertheless supported the Outlawry of War scheme (a proposal

optimistically perceived in the public mind as something much more than it was), which called for the de-legalization of the war system and the establishment of a court, modeled after the United States Supreme Court, to settle disputes without resorting to sanctions (formalized in the Kellogg–Briand Pact), as well as the Committee on Militarism in Education, which vigorously opposed the War Department's Reserve Officers Training Program on college campuses. Despite somewhat obvious differences in approach and strategy, all of these organizations were convinced that either industrial peoples would have peace or they would perish.[17]

Peace groups, moreover, were mildly successful in influencing the government to initiate disarmament schemes. This was especially true in the 1920s, when the United States government convened a conference in Washington in 1921 to discuss curbing an emerging naval arms race among the victorious Allies. The resulting agreement established fixed ratios and tonnage limits for the capital ships of the leading naval powers and a freeze on naval fortifications and bases in the western Pacific. Four years later a protocol, the result of U.S. initiative, was signed at Geneva, prohibiting the use of poison gas and bacteriological weapons in war. Though these disarmament agreements did little to halt the general arms race, peace groups were delighted. The agreements gave them an additional opportunity to drive home the point that the designing, testing, building, and maintaining of military hardware was quite costly, and unless acquired from the outside, under a military aid program, the money must be raised by some form of public or corporate taxation. Those in the peace movement maintained that lower taxes would always be preferable to the public.

Organized peacemaking after World War I also provided the impetus for a vast expansion of peace education activities. . . .

. . .

School textbook revision became a notable by-product of the peace crusade, since nationalism was widely blamed as a cause of the Great War and excessively nationalistic tendencies in education were seen as important contributing factors. At Columbia University, for example, John Dewey argued for "a curriculum in history, geography and literature which will make it more difficult for the flames of hatred and suspicion to sweep over this country in the future, which indeed will make this impossible, because when children's minds are in the formative period we shall have fixed in them through the medium of the schools, feelings of respect and friendliness for the other nations and peoples of the world."[18] In line with Dewey's call for "transnational patriotism," the Association for Peace Education published a report in 1924 on the impact of curriculum materials related to war and peace, based on a quantitative and qualitative content analysis of typical school histories used in the United States.[19]

Although there were decidedly ideological differences among peace workers in the twenties, the peace movement itself remained relatively stable and active. One of the earmarks of the peace movement throughout this decade was the cooperative working relationship that existed among peace workers from all quarters. Organized peace-making struck a harmonious balance due to the public reaction against the Great War. It was common to regard the war as a mistake, an attitude that was strengthened by revisionist histories and popular novels. In 1926 Harry Elmer Barnes published his *Genesis of the World War,* an attack on the widely accepted idea of unquestioned German responsibility for the conflict. Two years later *Origins of the World War* by Sidney B. Fay left little doubt that the official Allied propaganda did not square, at many points, with a critical analysis of primary sources. Even America's literary giants expressed disappointment in their works, including Willa Cather in *One of Ours* (1922), John Dos Passos in *Three Soldiers* (1921), and Ernest Hemingway in *A Farewell to Arms* (1929). The popular disillusionment with Wilsonian idealism, as reflected in the writings of revisionist historians and popular novelists, strengthened antiwar sentiments and enabled peace workers with divergent view-

points to work together in advancing global harmony.

Throughout the first half of the 1930s peace workers continued their harmonious relationship in the crusade against war. The pangs of a world-wide depression, Japanese military expansion in the Far East, and the rise of fascist power in Western Europe caused peace advocates to work even harder for the prevention of another world war. Pacifists and antiwar activists circulated throughout the country a modified version of the British Oxford Pledge against participation in war. Schools held peace essay contests and featured peace speakers. In 1935, sixty thousand college and university students engaged in a nationwide strike against war.[20] The Women's Peace Union undertook a campaign to make war unconstitutional, and much energy went into support for Senator Lynn J. Frazier's efforts to gain congressional support for a constitutional amendment to that effect. The Ludlow amendment, which required a national referendum on involvement in any foreign war, was narrowly defeated in the House of Representatives on January 10, 1938. . . .

• • •

Coinciding with the organized peace movement's efforts to avoid another war was a powerful isolationist sentiment. According to Manfred Jonas's *Isolationism in America, 1935–1941* (1966), isolation was an old habit, rooted in American tradition. Geography, economics, politics, and patriotism contributed to this feeling. Like Thomas Jefferson, most Americans saw the Old World as corrupt, quarrelsome, and autocratic—the antithesis of democratic America. Thus . . . disillusionment over the results of the 1914–18 conflict turned Americans inward. The overselling of the war, the pernicious propaganda, the war debts, the role of munitions makers, and the Versailles treaty created a strong isolationist impulse. . . .

• • •

Although the organized peace movement, despite its anti-interventionist position, was by no means "isolationist," it did try unsuccessfully to cooperate with isolationists in their common struggle to keep America out of war. Of all the peace groups, the National Council for Prevention of War (NCPW) strayed furthest down the isolationist path. . . .

. . .

As Lawrence S. Wittner's *Rebels Against War* (1969) shows, the organized peace movement underwent a disastrous split in 1935, when the obvious collapse of the League of Nations and heightened European militarism created fears of another great war. The NCPW and the Women's International League for Peace and Freedom, as well as other staunchly pacifist groups, realized their inability to prevent war in Europe and directed their attention to isolating America from that war. Internationalist elements, including the Carnegie Endowment, the Church Peace Union, the World Alliance for International Friendship through the Churches, the Catholic Association for International Peace, and the League of Nations Association, gradually shifted to doctrines of collective security. In the heated neutrality debates, the former groups supported the maintenance of mandatory neutrality, while the latter worked for the modification of the neutrality provisions and, eventually, for their repeal.[21]

By the late 1930s peace leaders attempted to form a new coalition. An Emergency Peace Campaign (EPC) was established, which sought to promote international economic justice and keep America neutral in case of war. An extensive peace campaign was initiated in which study conferences and lecture tours were conducted in nearly two hundred cities and throughout almost every state. Although it propagated programs favorable to traditional internationalists, the EPC's vigorous campaign on behalf of neutralism divided the peace movement's fragile coalition. In the years just prior to Pearl Harbor, pacifists themselves divided their attention between cooperative political activity with neutralist groups and turning inward to prepare for the coming war. After 1940, therefore, Japanese imperialism and Nazi militarism further quieted the peace movement.[22]

Individual opposition to conscription remained strong, however, and characterized much of the peace activism that took place during the Second World War. In fact, during World War II well over 49,000 Americans were conscientious objectors: 25,000 received noncombatant status, 1,950 did alternative service work in Civilian Public Service (CPS) camps, and a total of 12,662 draft violators were imprisoned. Some (perhaps most) of those in prison were there mainly because they had been unable to meet the requirements for conscientious objector status under the narrow provision of the Selective Service Act of 1940. Still, many were objectors not only to war but also to conscription. Refusing to register for the draft, they charged that conscription was incompatible with human freedom.

As the war proceeded, the ranks swelled within the CPS camps. Initially, the major pacifist groups had cooperated in the establishment of an alternative service program for objectors, convinced that it was the best that could be salvaged under the circumstances and that CPS camps would render a humanitarian service in a world at war. Yet increasingly, military control, inconsequential work projects, and a sense of futility led many in the camps to the belief that they had betrayed their basic principles. Walkouts began in 1942. Soon the trickle of illegal walkouts broadened into a steady stream, while inside the camps objectors began campaigns of nonviolent resistance, which spread from coast to coast.[23]

Upon their arrival in prison, according to Mulford Q. Sibley and Philip E. Jacob in *Conscription of Conscience: The American State and the Conscientious Objector, 1940–1947* (1952), CPS resisters joined their counterparts in organizing an unprecedented revolt behind bars. Fasts, strikes, and programs of total noncooperation cropped up in the federal penitentiaries at Danbury, Connecticut; Springfield, Missouri; Lewisburg, Pennsylvania; and others. After a 135-day strike shattered Danbury's system of racially segregated dining halls, objectors moved on to new programs of resistance. In early 1946 the prison was picketed outside and in by hundreds of sign-carrying pacifists demanding amnesty for all selective service violators and war resisters. Some pacifists even refused parole, rejecting release from prison on any terms except absolute freedom.[24]

During World War II pacifists generally accepted their status as a dissenting minority isolated from public view by virtue of their own convictions. Unfortunately, their wartime isolation extended far into the cold war era. Unable to acquiesce to the policies of military containment, nuclear deterrence, or calculated limited warfare, and incapable of sharing the anticommunist ideology of the nation, even though most of them had few illusions of Soviet goodwill, pacifists still found themselves in the role of a minority with little access to the public. Although they would challenge the terms of the cold war, they were almost without means to affect policymaking decisions.

The Cold War Era

Between 1941 and 1961 the preeminence of national security concerns, coupled with heightening East–West tensions symbolized by the cold war, led most Americans to view peace seeking as a subversive endeavor. Even atomic scientists, fearing global annihilation, and internationalists, supporting the creation of the United Nations, identified their world view with American national interest and military–political capacity. Convinced that the Soviet Union threatened not only the status quo but also the operation of U.N. security arrangements, internationalists became cold warriors. Historians studying this particular period, like Lawrence Wittner, Charles Chatfield, Justus Doenecke, and Charles DeBenedetti, have pointed out that the cold war dramatized the continuity of the internationalist wing of the American peace movement.

There was continuity also in the pacifist wing. During the post-World War II period the peace movement broadened its concerns and became involved with a variety of direct-action projects. These activities branded peace workers subversives. The appearance of the Peacemaker movement in 1948 influenced this trend toward direct action. Peacemakers involved some of the more

activist leaders, and although the movement was never highly organized, it encouraged absolute resistance to the draft and refusal to pay any taxes for war. Peacemakers caused the more traditional organizations to reevaluate their programs, and the result was more direct action throughout the peace movement.[25]

The emergence of direct action was further exemplified by the tax resistance efforts of pacifist A. J. Muste. "They who profit by violence," he once said, "though it be indirectly, unwillingly, and only in small measure, will always be under suspicion and rightly so of seeking to protect their profits, of being selfishly motivated, if they address pious exhortations to those who suffer by that violence."[26] Peace action was also enhanced by the establishment in 1947 of the United World Federalists, a pressure group dedicated to moving the United States toward leadership in ensuring "world peace through world law," and by the formation of the National Committee for a SANE Nuclear Policy in the 1950s. SANE brought together internationalists like Norman Cousins and scientists like Linus Pauling, who were opposed to mounting nuclear weapons systems and the dangers of fallout from bomb tests.[27]

Significantly, for the first time since the mid-1930s pacifists and internationalists were operating in tandem to alter foreign policy, and sporadic attempts were made to formalize a coherent coalition opposed to the development of nuclear weapons. But the results of the Korean War and a surge of right-wing nationalism, magnified by the fear of worldwide communism and intensified at home by the "accusatory fallout" of McCarthyism, shoved the peace movement hopelessly to the defensive. Within this climate, the movement tumbled to the lowest point of its twentieth-century influence.

Nevertheless, by 1957 the call for a ban on the A-bomb led to the creation of a committee known as Non-violent Action Against Nuclear Weapons (NVA), which two years later changed its name to the Committee for Non-violent Action (CNVA); it was intitiated by peace activist Lawrence Scott. Its first project, a prayer and conscience vigil with attempted entry into the Nevada A-test proving grounds, was the first antinuclear demonstration to be conducted at a nuclear test site. The next year NVA undertook a far more ambitious project, the protest voyage of the *Golden Rule*. This ketch, with four Quakers aboard, attempted to sail into the restricted area of the Pacific where the Atomic Energy Commission was conducting hydrogen bomb tests. Although the *Golden Rule* was stopped in Hawaii and its crew sentenced to sixty days in jail, the *Phoenix,* with the family of Earle Reynolds and a Japanese mate aboard, carried on the protest. Reynolds was not arrested until well inside the forbidden zone, and his trial, aided by the supportive activities of NVA, gained worldwide attention.[28]

By 1960 a permanent Committee for Nonviolent Action had been formed, with A. J. Muste as national chair and George Willoughby as executive committee chair. While SANE provided leadership for traditional peace advocates of the internationalist persuasion, CNVA served as the base for radical pacifists to organize and implement their nonviolent efforts on behalf of peace and justice. Militant nonviolent action, a new approach for the pacifist wing, became CNVA's most effective tactic. Educational activities designed to inform and to persuade were replaced by obstructionist tactics designed to confront and to coerce. Confrontational tactics against nuclear weapons production (e.g., the intercontinental ballistic missile base at Cheyenne, Wyoming; the Meade Intercontinental Ballistic Missile Base near Omaha, Nebraska; and the Polaris submarine base at New London, Connecticut) popularized CNVA's direct action techniques.

How much effect all of this activity, together with the protests of such groups as SANE and CNVA, had upon the signing of a partial nuclear test ban treaty in 1963 can never be accurately estimated. There is no doubt, however, "that CNVA and those who acted under its influence brought home to the United States the danger of nuclear testing and confronted the American public with the moral imperative of speaking truth to power."[29]

By the early sixties concern for domestic change, symbolized by the civil rights movement, captured the attention of the peace movement. In their commitment to social change, pacifists found an expanding base of political activity contingent upon the exploration of nonviolent action and the need for social redemption. Some pacifists, like Bayard Rustin and George Houser of the Fellowship of Reconciliation (FOR), had been involved in the civil rights struggle before; in 1943 they had helped establish the Congress of Racial Equity (CORE) in Chicago. Now, spearheaded by Dr. Martin Luther King's Southern Christian Leadership Conference (in 1964 King was awarded the Nobel Prize for Peace), pacifists from FOR and CORE provided leadership and support in the wake of civil rights sit-ins. Students, in particular, joined the civil rights movement early in the 1960s and quickly adapted to nonviolent action techniques. In the late 1960s, as the Vietnam War intensified, these civil rights activists aligned themselves with the antiwar movement.

Significantly, the civil rights movement of this period turned the peace movement toward an emphasis on fundamental social change, inevitable when the masses, rather than solitary intellectuals, become involved in action. The black protest movement signified a new direction involving nonviolent action; it represented a shift from public accommodation to acquisition of the twin levers of power in American society: the vote and the job. Equally important in the modern civil rights struggle, nonviolence was referred to both as a "tactic" and as a "way of life." Such a position developed because these activists were outnumbered and outgunned, and because their refusal to retaliate when attacked won them necessary sympathizers. In terms of political strategy, civil rights nonviolent action ultimately became nonviolent revolution.

The drive against atmospheric nuclear testing, moreover, brought to the peace movement new organizations such as the Student Peace Union (1959) and Turn Toward Peace (1961). Many who joined these organizations were socialists and radical college students without pacifist beliefs who were dissatisfied with the current state of American foreign policy. Driven by a combination of feminists, students, and intellectuals including Harvard sociologist David Reisman and cultural critic Lewis Mumford, the peace movement made promising strides until expanding United States involvement in Vietnam forced peace advocates into antiwar activism and diverted their attention from the arms race and social injustice.

The Vietnam Era

Antiwar opposition to the conflict in Southeast Asia stemmed from Washington's unyielding pursuance of the Vietnam War. The antiwar movement gained considerable momentum in February 1965, after American bombing of North Vietnam and Johnson's order to land marines at Da Nang the following month. Johnson's plans for major troop increases during the intervening months quickly set off a shockwave of opposition that covered the political spectrum from respectable conservative leaders to New Left radicals.

The war in Vietnam produced a wide variety of resistance activities, including teach-ins on college campuses; the largest peace march in American history in Washington on November 15, 1969; and a mass, nonviolent attempt to shut down the machinery of government in Washington in May 1971. The war also produced an antiwar coalition that included congressional critics like Eugene McCarthy, Wayne Morse, and William J. Fulbright, as well as New Left radicals who organized the Students for Democratic Society (SDS) in 1965. In late 1967 disillusioned war veterans returning from the Far East established the Vietnam Veterans Against the War. This group forced middle-class Americans to face the possibility that Washington's commitment to global stability through military deterrence was illusory; it also dramatized the erosion of morale and effectiveness within the armed forces.

Opposition to the war was marked by the convergence of numerous peace coalitions. The first demonstration against the war took place in early 1963. It was organized by the War Resisters League (WRL) and involved only a few dozen people. Two years later the first draft card burnings took place, and the demonstrations were no longer limited to handfuls of peace workers but had grown from hundreds, to thousands, and then to tens of thousands of people. The range of those involved broke across ideological lines that had divided Americans for decades. In the vast crowds of protest marches one could find priests, nuns, Communist party functionaries, Trotskyites, socialists, anarchists, religious pacifists, and conservative Republicans. A new coalition developed that included not only pacifists and internationalists, the traditional vanguard of the peace movement, but also thousands of Americans in no way connected to the organized peace movement.

The first antiwar coalition was the Fifth Avenue Vietnam Peace Parade Committee, headed by Muste and sparked by Norma Becker, a WRL member. Later coalitions changed names as they formed and dissolved, but at all times represented an almost full political spectrum of Americans who, shocked by America's Vietnam policy, put aside profound differences with one another to join in protest. The ideological divisiveness, which traditionally had kept pacifists and internationalists at arm's length during wartime, was put aside in favor of a unified movement to end American military involvement in Southeast Asia. The Vietnam War energized the peace movement as no other war had done in the nation's history.[30]

Significantly, the student antiwar movement that formed around the Vietnam War displayed some important departures from previous antiwar student activism. It was prompted by neither internationalist nor pacifist sentiments, although its critique of American society contained many of their combined objectives. For example, the movement that emerged was not as dependent on "parent groups," such as the Communist and Socialist parties or the Fellowship of Reconciliation, as were earlier movements. A new group of young "anti-war, anti-heroes" like Tom Hayden and Abbie Hoffman led the movement as part of an incipient revolt against the older generation. The war became a vehicle for criticizing the society their parents had built. The sixties marked the era of "obstructive demonstration" and a new tactical approach of "violence for violence" to counter warmaking attempts. Finally, the Vietnam War, unlike previous wars, did not weaken student protest, but invigorated it. The antiwar movement among students in the 1960s had more significant political impact than had any of the earlier movements.[31]

The student antiwar movement of the Vietnam era represented a marked departure from the respectability of passive nonresistance. The idea that students might become the "radical agency of change" represented the SDS's modus operandi. The SDS's opposition to the war was embodied by its wide-ranging critique of American society—a critique of racial injustice, the danger of nuclear war, the failure to develop peaceful nuclear energy, the cold war, reflexive anticommunism, the maldistribution of wealth, the meaninglessness of work, the political apathy of students, the exhaustion of liberal and socialist thinking, and the isolation of the individual from power. The SDS called for a radically changed social order, for a "participatory democracy" in which individuals could take part in making decisions that affected their own lives. Throughout the war the SDS represented student radicalism and advocated violent acts in opposition to America's war machine. Though opposed to war in principle, their violent tactics were not appreciated by mainstream American peace groups. Traditional pacifist concerns—a commitment to principled nonviolence for meaningful social change and a condemnation of all wars and violence as destroyers of physical and spiritual life—were subsumed by the radical students' search for a common cause upon which to build a mass movement on behalf of social reform. Many veteran peace activists therefore expressed displeasure with student antiwar violence.

Less violent and certainly much more acceptable to pacifists was the tax resistance movement. Tax resistance became a popular tool used by pacifists to oppose the war. In 1966 the federal telephone tax was raised, and in a rare moment of candor, the federal government admitted that the additional money would be used to help subsidize the war. The Peacemakers, War Resisters League, CNVA, and other peace groups urged nonpayment of this tax. The discomfort of the IRS with the burgeoning movement grew, and as the government's reprisals became more frequent, the need for legal information within the tax resistance community became manifest. In 1969, therefore, War Tax Resistance was formed. Under the leadership of Robert and Angela Calvert, it devoted itself to all the aspects and ramifications of conscientious tax refusal.

While tax refusal grew in popularity, opposition to the draft increased dramatically. The rate of conscientious objection was four times as large as during World War II, and levels of draft evasion violations and exile to Canada or into the domestic underground reached record heights. Though many more men volunteered for military service or accepted the draft unwillingly, unprecedented personal antiwar decisions became more and more commonplace. In November 1969, however, the Nixon administration created the draft lottery system. This system succeeded where nothing had before in separating the twin issues of opposition to the draft and opposition to the war. Almost all young Americans were by this point against the draft and were rapidly filling the ranks of peace groups. The masterstroke of the new system was the limiting of all men—students and nonstudents alike—to one year of draft vulnerability after their nineteenth birthdays. If a high lottery number were drawn, the chance of being drafted decreased significantly. Consequently, with more than one-half of all students instantly freed from the possibility of going to Vietnam, the antiwar movement lost its most immediately compelling issue.

After 1965 the first concern of peace-minded Americans had been to reverse the nation's war policy in Southeast Asia. The expanding peace movement of the early sixties had shifted its focus from international problems to the domestic sources of American foreign policy. Specific emphasis had been directed at antimilitarism and anti-imperialism. A narrowing of goals became evident as the peace movement was less able to meet issues such as the arms race, nuclear proliferation, and poverty. In many respects the Vietnam War paralyzed the peace movement's cosmopolitan approach to internationalism.

After the Vietnam War ended in the early 1970s, the American peace movement again turned to the demand for nuclear and conventional disarmament. The oppressive nature of the arms race was confronted, and links were made between a huge military budget and the shameful neglect of such human needs as education, health care, and housing for the poor. The most important peace demonstration of the postwar seventies was the

Continental Walk for Disarmament and Social Justice, which started at Ukiah, California on January 1, 1976 and ended with a rally in Washington, D.C. in October of the same year.

Present-Day Peace Activism

Although many veteran observers have characterized the immediate post-Vietnam peace movement as apathetic, the label is inappropriate for the 1980s. Activists have been engaged in a variety of projects on many different levels. There has been an ambitious campaign to stop production of the costly B-1 bomber and deployment of MX missiles; a sustained campaign to halt the Trident missile project; growing demonstrations to protest the proliferation of nuclear weapons; work to prevent reinstatement of the draft and counseling on the newly imposed government registration for eighteen-year-olds; and efforts to expose and eliminate the institutionalized sexism and racism in American society.

Perhaps the most significant development within the peace movement since the Vietnam War has been effectiveness in lobbying for legislation and in influencing election campaigns. The movement's most telling political effectiveness so far has been in waging a campaign for a freeze to the nuclear arms race. On June 12, 1982 nearly a million people gathered in New York City to protest the nuclear arms race (this was the largest political demonstration in American history). This protest initiated the Nuclear Freeze Campaign. The Freeze calls on the United States and the Soviet Union to adopt a mutual ban on the testing, production, and deployment of nuclear weapons. It has been endorsed officially by 12 state legislatures, 321 city councils, 10 national labor unions, numerous ranking clergy of all faiths, and the U.N. General Assembly. In November 1982 the Freeze appeared on state ballots across the nation, thus representing the largest referendum on any issue in American history. Sixty percent of those voting supported the Freeze issue in spite of the Reagan administration's vociferous opposition. In May of 1983, moreover, the House of Representatives passed a Freeze resolution by nearly a 2-to-1 vote.

At the present time, peace activism is most noticeable in the classroom. The outpouring of public concern about nuclear war has led to numerous efforts by educators to provide citizens with opportunities to learn more about the threat of nuclear war and how to reduce it. Conceptual efforts for the study of nuclear weapons are being developed. High on the list of priorities are the following: assessment of the technical and political potential for the annihilation of life on this planet; understanding of the scale of weaponry being produced, combined with historical knowledge about the destructiveness of past nonnuclear wars (demonstrating the tremendous quantitative and qualitative differences between conventional and nuclear weapons); identification of the ethical and economic consequences of national security as defined in military terms; knowledge of the origins and rationale of the deterrence theory; clarification of the theoretical, practical, and political differences between arms control and disarmament; concern for the global scope of the problem of arms control; and development and dissemination of information on a broader range of alternative policy options from "ban the bomb" to "peace through strength." In back of all this remains the responsibility of socially concerned educators to teach students *how* to think about nuclear issues, not *what* to think.

At the forefront of educational peace activism has been the Educators for Social Responsibility, a national organization formed in 1981 to educate teachers of all grade levels, school administrators, and parents about strategies for reducing the threat of nuclear war. The recently established Student/ Teacher Organization to Prevent Nuclear War (STOP) represents a national network of high school students and teachers who develop curricular materials about the arms race and nuclear war; its primary contribution is the development of extracurricular activities, presentations, and projects in schools, churches, and communities. In addition, the United Campuses to Prevent Nuclear War, established in 1981, has been involved in cosponsoring national education programs, canvassing incumbent and aspiring congressional candidates on voting records and positions with respect to nuclear weapons, collecting and distributing syllabi of courses on the arms race, and publishing a newsletter. These organizations, along with more traditional peace bodies like the World Policy Institute, the Federation of American Scientists, and the Union of Concerned Scientists, have been instrumental in expanding the nuclear war education movement so that creative analysis of possible solutions to the problem will be stimulated and nourished.[32]

Is there a vibrant peace movement in America today? Yes, but it is modest in size and limited in effectiveness. During periods of peace, excitement is generated only when talk of military buildup echoes from the portals of the White House. It is then that peace activists suddenly take to the streets in protest. In the past, when war has been declared, the number of peace advocates has diminished. The political power of peace activism has been dramatically curtailed. Why has the peace movement been unable to mount a sustained political force against the warmaking powers of the national government?

Indeed, the essential point is that peace movements, historically, follow a pattern of enthusiasm and growth, impasse and apathy, and a general decline into political ineffectiveness. It is in times of danger and stress, before a country is caught up in a war that concentrates all its energies, that peace activism exerts its greatest attraction and peace advocates their best efforts. Still, the greatest problem for the American peace movement is its relationship not with the internationalists but with the pacifists—those whose moral and individual judgments mitigate against effective political action on a mass basis. The failure of the peace movement, even when it is of significant proportions to create a "politics of pacifism," rests with the pacifists' inability to transform their individual judgments into collective action. Perhaps David McReynolds, a former editor of *Liberation,* said it best: "What is required by pacifism and what cannot be given up is the ability of people to make individual judgments. But that also mitigates against its becoming an effective political force."[33]

Whatever the case may be, the peace movement, from a social viewpoint, exerts its greatest appeal among middle-class women, clergymen, educators, and those business people who possess a combination of advanced education, leisure time, and a reform Christian conscience; a broader appeal is urgently needed among the less educated, working-class population if the next war is to be averted. Intellectually, the peace movement appeals to religious liberals, political leftists, and cultural dissidents. Geographically, its centers of strength are found in the large metropolitan areas of the Northeast, the Midwest, and along the West Coast. Practically, however, the organized peace movement, if it is to be truly united, must succeed in penetrating the dense layers of American society. It remains on the fringes of society, awaiting the next threat to civilization in order to gain new recruits.[34]

1. This sad omission has been duly noted in Larry Gara, *War Resistance in Historical Perspective* (New York, 1980). One historian who has made an effort to correct this oversight is Merle Curti. His popular textbook, *The Rise of the American Nation* (New York, 1978), deemphasizes the patriotic glory of war and gives due credit to leading pacifists and peace organizations. See also Charles F. Howlett, "A Historian's Concern for World Peace: Merle Curti," *Peace Research,* XII (January 1980): 15–22.

2. Gara, *War Resistance in Historical Perspective,* 3–4.

3. Arthur A. Ekirch, Jr., *The Decline of American Liberalism,* rev. ed. (New York, 1967), gives proper account of the historical roots of American liberalism and its "decline" in the face of the rise of the "Garrison State" during the twentieth century. See also Mulford Q. Sibley, "Anonymity, Dissent, and Individual Integrity in America," *Annals of the American Academy of Political and Social Sciences,* 378 (July 1968): 45–57.

4. An excellent overview of the various approaches to peace is Charles DeBenedetti, *The Peace Reform in American History* (Bloomington, 1980).

5. Basically, there are two kinds of internationalists: polity and community. Polity internationalists are in favor of organized mechanisms for the prevention of war. Community internationalists

have argued for a more organic world consciousness, proposing economic and social changes such as disallowance of trade advantages, international regulation of the world's food supply, international control of the arms industry, and establishment of international health and education programs. For a comprehensive discussion of internationalism, consult the introduction to Warren F. Kuehl, ed., *Biographical Dictionary of Internationalists* (Westport, Ct., 1983).

6. One of the major problems with peace history analysis lies in the diversity of views related to nomenclature.

7. Consult the superb introduction written by Charles Chatfield, ed., *Peace Movements in America* (New York, 1973), xxvi–xxviii.

8. Ibid., xxvii.

9. Lawrence S. Wittner, *Rebels Against War: The American Peace Movement, 1941–1960* (New York, 1969), vii.

10. Blanche Wiesen Cook, "Democracy in Wartime: Antimilitarism in England and the United States, 1914–1918," in Chatfield, ed., *Peace Movements in America*, 39–56.

11. Charles DeBenedetti, "Alternative Strategies in the American Peace Movement in the 1920s," in Chatfield, ed., *Peace Movements in America*, 57–58. See also H. C. Peterson and Gilbert Fite, *Opponents of War, 1917–18* (Madison, Wis., 1957); Betty L. Barton, "The Fellowship of Reconciliation: Pacifism, Labor and Social Welfare, 1915–1960" (PhD diss., Florida State University, 1974). It is also worth mentioning that criticisms of capitalism found their way into the teachings of Brookwood Labor College in the twenties and thirties. At Brookwood there existed a concerted effort to gain organized labor's support for opposition to all wars and reformation of the existing economic system. The chairman of the faculty was a leading pacifist, A. J. Muste. For a brief account on this perspective, see Charles F. Howlett, "Brookwood Labor College and Worker Commitment to Social Reform," *Mid-America*, 61 (January 1979): 47–66.

12. Charles DeBenedetti, *Origins of the Modern American Peace Movement, 1915–1929* (Millwood, N.Y., 1978), passim, and *The Peace Reform in American History*, 106.

13. Robert H. Ferrell, "The American Peace Movement," in Alexander DeConde, ed., *Isolation and Security* (Durham, N.C., 1957).

14. Ernest L. Meyer, *"Hey! Yellowbacks!" The War Diary of a Conscientious Objector* (New York, 1930), 94–95. His work became a basic source book for some World War II objectors.

15. Ann Davidson, "Resistance to World War I,: in Larry Gara, ed., *To Secure Peace and Liberty: Creative Non-Violence in the American Past* (New York, 1976). 82–83.

16. DeBenedetti, "Alternative Strategies in the American Peace Movement in the 1920s," 70–80.

17. Charles Chatfield, *For Peace and Justice: Pacifism in America, 1914–1941* (Knoxville, 1971), is the most definitive work on the subject during this period.

18. Quoted in Charles F. Howlett, "The Pragmatist as Pacifist: John Dewey's Views on Peace Education," *Teachers College Record*, 83, no. 3 (Spring 1983): 441.

19. Mary Alice Matthews, *History Teaching and School Text-Books in Relation to International Understanding: Select List of Books, Pamphlets, and Periodical Articles* (Washington, D.C., 1931).

20. Ralph S. Brax, *The First Student Movement: Student Activism in the United States in the 1930s* (Port Washington, N.Y., 1981), 90–96. See also Eileen Eagan, *Class, Culture and the Classroom: The Student Peace Movement in the 1930s* (Philadelphia, 1982).

21. Wittner, *Rebels Against War*, chap. 1.

22. Justus D. Doenecke, "Non-intervention of the Left: 'The Keep America Out of War Congress,' 1938–41," *Journal of Contemporary History*, XII (April 1977): 221–31.

23. Arthur A. Ekirch, Jr., "CPS and Slavery," *Pacifica Views*, II, no. 12 (25 August 1944): 1, 4.

24. Mulford Q. Sibley and Philip E. Jacob, *Conscription of Conscience: The American State and the Conscientious Objector, 1940–1947* (New York, 1952), passim.

25. Glen Zeitzer, "The American Peace Movement During the Second World War" (PhD diss., Bryn Mawr College, 1978), passim; Wittner, *Rebels Against War*, chaps. 2 and 3; Charles DeBenedetti, "The American Peace Movement and the National Security State, 1941–1971," *World Affairs*, 141 (Fall 1978): 118–29.

26. Quoted in Nat Hentoff, ed., *The Essays of A. J. Muste* (New York, 1967), 52–53. See also Jo Ann O. Robinson, *Abraham Went Out: A Biography of A. J. Muste* (Philadelphia, 1982).

27. Milton S. Katz, "Peace, Politics and Protest: SANE and the American Peace Movement, 1957–1972" (PhD diss., St. Louis University, 1973), passim.

28. Gara, ed., *To Secure Peace and Liberty*, 108–109.

29. Barbara Reynolds, "Non-Violent Action Against Nuclear Weapons," in Gara, ed., *To Secure Peace and Liberty*, 112–13.

30. Two noted peace historians, Larry Wittner and Charles DeBenedetti, are currently writing accounts of the post-World War II peace movement. Wittner has recently revised and expanded his *Rebels Against War*. See Lawrence S. Wittner, *Rebels Against War: The American Peace Movement, 1933–1983* (Philadelphia, 1984).

31. Peterson, "Student Organizations and the Anti-War Movement in America, 1900-1960," 129–31.

32. Consult Erik Markhusen, "Education About Nuclear War," *Educational Perspectives*, XXI (Fall 1982): 32–36.

33. Quoted in James Finn, *Protest: Pacifism and Politics* (New York, 1967), 499.

34. In a letter to one of the authors. Merle Curti reflected on the dilemma of peace research in history. It is a revealing letter, which states in part: ". . . To neglect American glorification of war heroes and generally enthusiastic acceptance of wars once we were engaged in them, poses a problem which I [did not meet] clearly and cogently. In other words, my own sympathy with pacifism made me insufficiently critical of its limitation in [the] face [of] probably much stronger emotional thrusts and the existing realities in the power structure. This doesn't mean at all that I think it wasn't important for historians to work on the peace movement, only that it should be set more in the context of what opposed it, with more emphasis on that, than I managed to do. Still, someone had to make a beginning. . . . " Merle Curti to Charles F. Howlett, 8 April 1982.

PEACE MOVEMENTS OF THE SIXTIES

The Power of the People
Active Nonviolence

Edited by Robert Cooney ▪ *Helen Michalowski*
From an Original Text by Marty Jezer

The Year Of Vietnam

1965 was, as the *CNVA Bulletin* declared, "The Year of Vietnam." [CNVA, the Committee for Nonviolent Action, formed in 1958, was a pacifist group dedicated to direct action and civil disobedience— EDS.] Picketing and sit-downs across the country marked the announcement of the first US bombing of North Vietnam on February 7. These continued throughout the month and much effort was expended gathering signatures for a new appeal, the Declaration of Conscience, circulated by radical pacifist groups, urging civil disobedience. The Peacemakers group in Cincinnati organized a "No Tax for War in Vietnam Committee" calling for tax resistance. In December 1969 a separate group—War Tax Resistance, coordinated by Bob Calvert—was established and at one time included some 200 local tax resistance centers across the country.

On March 16, 1965, Alice Herz, an 82-year-old widow who had fled Nazism, left a note saying, "I choose the illuminating death of a Buddhist to protest against a great country trying to wipe out a small country for no reason," and set herself afire at a busy Detroit intersection. She died ten days later. On November 2 Norman Morrison,

secretary of a Friends Meeting, burned himself to death in front of the Pentagon, and later was honored by the North Vietnamese. One week later Roger La Porte, a young volunteer for the Catholic Worker movement in New York, immolated himself in front of the United Nations.

The first national demonstration against the war was organized by the Students for a Democratic Society on April 17, a March on Washington to end the war in Vietnam. This demonstration was controversial because SDS refused to prohibit Communists from taking part. At first, radical pacifists protested this policy, but they eventually came around to support it and the non-exclusionary policy became a part of the Vietnam protest movement. This represented a deliberate and constructive break with the anti-communist past. The SDS March gave the anti-war movement its first national publicity and led to bitter attacks on it from the Johnson administration and all segments of the press.

On June 16, officials of the Pentagon, confronted with a CNVA-organized civil disobedience demonstration, turned the steps of the Pentagon over to the pacifists for a "speak-out," with talks by Muste, Bill Davidon, Gordon Christiansen and others. The idea of a "speak-out" derived from the

Reprinted by permission of New Society Publishers, 4527 Springfield Ave., Philadelphia, PA 19143.

"teach-ins," round-the-clock meetings on Vietnam that, beginning at Ann Arbor in March, swept the college campuses for the duration of the school year, and made students aware of the facts about Vietnam for the first time.

The Assembly of Unrepresented People, August 6 to 9, brought the civil rights and peace movements together for the largest civil disobedience demonstration ever held in Washington up to that time. Eric Weinberger, a CNVA activist and CORE field worker, and Robert Parris Moses of SNCC were the coordinators. [CORE, the Congress of Racial Equality, and SNCC, the Student Nonviolent Coordinating Committee, were major civil rights organizations.—Eds.] A march from the Washington Monument to the Capitol ended with a sit-down in which 350 people were arrested.

At the same time, students from Berkeley and other Bay Area schools attempted to stop trains arriving at Oakland with soldiers destined for Vietnam. This demonstration was organized by the Vietnam Day Committee (VDC), a coalition in which pacifists played an important part. The VDC also staged a march to the Oakland Army Terminal that was broken up by Oakland city police and Hells Angels. It was this march that led Allen Ginsberg to write a poem entitled "How to Make A March/Spectacle" that urged, among other suggestions

> Masses of flowers—a visual spectacle—especially concentrated in the front lines. Can be used to set up barricades, to present to Hells Angels, Police, politicians, and press and spectators whenever needed or at parade's end. Masses of marchers can be asked to bring their own flowers. Front lines should be organized and provided with flowers in advance.

The Assembly of Unrepresented People also produced the National Coordinating Committee to End the War in Vietnam which planned demonstrations for October 15 and 16, 1965, called the Days of International Protest. This led to the formation in New York of the Fifth Avenue Peace Parade Committee, a unique coalition of all groups op-posing the Vietnam War, including liberals, pacifists, Communists, and the new and old left. What made such a broad based coalition possible was the personality of A. J. Muste. While few of the groups had ever agreed, worked with or much less trusted one another, they were all united in their respect for A. J. Under his leadership, a walk down Fifth Avenue with over 50,000 participants was achieved and an organizational model for future and nationwide mobilizations created.

Draft Card Burnings

The highpoint of the first International Days of Protest occurred on October 15 at a small demonstration at the Whitehall Street Induction Center in New York City, organized by radical pacifists and attended by about 500 people. One of the speakers, David Miller, a Catholic Worker, decided to burn his draft card instead of giving a speech. The act received enormous publicity, for Miller's was the first draft card burning following a Congressional law, enacted earlier in the summer, making destruction of a draft card a felony equal in seriousness to draft refusal.

Draft card burning had been a traditional way pacifists protested against the draft. The draft card burnings in 1947 have been related earlier. In May 1964, 12 men burned their draft cards in New York City to protest conscription. A few weeks before the Assembly of Unrepresented People, there was another draft card burning in New York which was reported in the national media and caused the patriots in Washington to rush a bill through Congress making it illegal.

On November 6, again in New York City, A. J. Muste presided over a carefully organized draft card burning in which Dave McReynolds, Marc-Paul Edelman, Tom Cornell, Jim Wilson and Roy Lisker took part. The following month, at a SANE rally in Washington, D.C., SDS President Carl Oglesby delivered a speech entitled "Let Us Shape the Future" which called the war in Vietnam a product of "corporate liberalism," and emphasized that the war was not an aberration as liberals thought, but a basic result of American policy at home and abroad.

Local Pacifist Groups

Up to this point there were few local pacifist action groups in the country. CNVA-West was active in the Bay Area and there was a core group of Boston activists—Dave Reed, John Phillips, John Benson, and Dave O'Brien—that existed briefly during the winter of '65 and '66 before going out of existence after a wave of draft card burnings and induction refusals. There was also New England CNVA which, like the Boston chapter, was now concerned mainly with draft resistance.

About this time Maris Cakars and Gwen Reyes, with help from the WRL and CNVA, formed the N.Y. Workshop In Nonviolence which produced *WIN* magazine as one of its major projects. [WRL, the War Resisters League, was founded in 1923 and originally supported conscientious objectors to the draft—EDS.] Many of the people connected with *WIN* were new to pacifism and saw themselves more in the bohemian-beat setting, then going through a rejuvenation on New York's Lower East Side, than in the pacifist tradition. Many poets and artists, some in the beat generation and some not, were already involved with radical pacifism: Jackson MacLow, Allen Ginsberg, Tuli Kupferberg, Ed Sanders, and the General Strike for Peace people centered around Julian Beck and Judith Malina of The Living Theater. In the West there was the pacifist Anarchist Circle in San Francisco with poets Kenneth Rexroth, Robert Duncan, Philip Lamatia, and William Everson (Brother Antoninus) as members.

What *WIN* was most attracted to, however, was the gentle and playful commitment of the Dutch Provos, the Diggers in San Francisco and the pioneer spokesmen for psychedelics. Dissatisfied with the negative connotations of a peace movement that was *anti*-war and in favor of *non*-violence, *WIN* tried to bring a positive joy to peace demonstrations, to make them celebrations of a new and different kind of life. The result was the launching of a 10-foot canvas yellow submarine, inspired by the Beatles and Polaris Action, which was marched through the streets of Manhattan with flowers, balloons and music. The Yellow Submarine demonstration was indicative of a new mood in the nation, a new way of living.

Beginning of a Counter-Culture

Pacifists had long urged people to stop working in war industries and to disassociate themselves from the war-making government. Many young people now came to view the whole society as being part of a war culture and simply dropped out of it; they became non-cooperators with the American way of life which had produced Vietnam. This movement was apolitical in intent but in effect it was a decisive political rejection of militarism and the state. Because it was opposed to violence and addressed itself to life style rather than abstruse rhetoric, radical pacifists found they could relate to it easily. The *WIN* group in New York, Jim Hayes and friends in New England, the people around WRL-West in San Francisco and a newly formed anarchist-oriented WRL chapter in Los Angeles began addressing themselves to the drop-out community in an attempt to give the new life style political content. The time was ripe for this kind of transformation and, as a result, the peace movement became more than a movement against the war in Vietnam and made changes reaching deeply into the most basic ways that Americans saw themselves and structured their lives.

Making Protest Visible

This change came gradually, beginning in 1966, peaking in the euphoria of the summer of love of 1967 and crashing with the reality of the Chicago demonstrations of 1968. And the war continued. In the spring of 1966 CNVA sent Muste, Lyttle, Barbara Deming, Karl Meyer, Sherry Thurber and Bill Davidon to Saigon. They met with anti-war Buddhist and Catholic leaders and then picketed the

US embassy with placards denouncing the war for which they were deported. Meanwhile, Vietnamese translated and circulated their message illegally throughout South Vietnam.

Street demonstrations were frequent during 1966. The slightest provocation was enough to bring people into the streets to picket a dinner addressed by Secretary of State Dean Rusk, to block traffic in protest of renewed bombing of North Vietnam, to block military recruiters on campus, to sit-in at the Dow Chemical offices protesting its manufacture of napalm, to distribute anti-draft leaflets in the early morning hours at induction centers urging young men to refuse to be drafted and offering advice on how to stay out—there was a demonstration for every occasion. The main purpose of these demonstrations was to make the anti-war movement visible to the American public and to make the media, which was over-whelmingly in support of the war and opposed to criticism of government policy, acknowledge that an opposition did exist, that it had facts, that it was vocal and could disrupt the status quo if provoked far enough.

Apparently, President Johnson got the message. According to David Halberstam, Pentagon officials advised the President in 1966 that their computers forecast victory if he would authorize the bombing of Hanoi and Haiphong. Johnson refused to allow this escalation. He told the military to ask their computers "how long it will take five hundred thousand angry Americans to climb that White House wall out there and lynch their President." The voice of the peace movement was now being heard.

The Resistance

Radical pacifists had always insisted that "wars would cease when men refused to fight." Thus, much of their energy went into organizing draft resistance activities. Throughout the early years of the Vietnam conflict there were numerous in-stances of men refusing to be inducted or even to register for the draft. Peacemakers published a list of noncooperators which grew in length each

month and many activists connected with CNVA burned draft cards or refused induction, but none of these efforts was organized as mass actions.

The first mass anti-draft action took place April 15, 1967, at what was until then the largest peace demonstration in American history, a rally at the Sheeps Meadow in New York's Central Park followed by a walk to the UN with hundreds of thousands of participants. The morning of the march, 175 men burned their draft cards in a joint effort organized by Bruce Dancis and five other Cornell students. After the march, the draft card burners met to organize themselves in a mutual support organization. Non-draftable friends also met and organized support groups that eventually came together as Resist—Support-in-Action.

About the same time, David Harris, Dennis Sweeney, Lenny Heller, Richard Ian Harrison and Steve Hamilton, all of them activists in the Bay Area and Palo Alto, began talking up the idea of The Resistance. They would choose a specific day for young men to gather all across the country and publicly declare their independence by returning their draft cards to the government. The Resistance operated in decentralized local offices throughout the nation. The first turn-in took place on October 3, 1967, and more than 1500 men returned their cards. A second turn-in on December 4 brought forward about 475 new resisters and on April 3, 1968, another 630 began their noncooperation with the draft.

In 1967 CNVA, realizing that its nonviolent direct action tactics and civil disobedience campaigns were being used by everyone, dissolved itself into the WRL. The Resistance then became the cutting edge of the movement, with people willing to put their bodies on the line to confront the government on principle and as directly as possible. The implicit threat of The Resistance was that going to jail was no longer thought cowardly. If an escalated war would enlarge the draft calls, thousands of young men would not go. *The Pentagon Papers* later revealed that this indeed did limit the government's involvement in the land war. But The Resistance, though it might have prevented enlargement of the war, failed to bring it to an end. Draft calls never reached that total size and The

Resistance never succeeded in reaching those large numbers of men, many of whom never discovered the varying alternatives, legal and illegal, to military service.

Confronting the Warmakers

Noncooperation with the draft was only one facet of The Resistance. In Philadelphia and throughout the country, GI coffee houses were set up, military bases were leafletted and entered, and deserters were given refuge while legal aid was arranged or they were aided in getting out of the country. As important were attempts to apply the spirit of resistance to actions in the streets. The crucial action, and probably the most memorable one, was billed as a "confrontation with the warmakers" and took place at the Pentagon October 21 and 22, 1967. Thousands of people marched on the building and, when it was blocked off by soldiers, sat down at their feet for an impromptu teach-in that lasted all Saturday night and on into Sunday night. Hundreds of people were arrested, and many were beaten by U.S. marshals who tried to break the morale of the demonstrators by riotous brutality. People brought away different memories. Some remembered the community created among strangers on the steps of the Pentagon, the sharing of food, the refusal to fight back or break ranks in the face of government aggression; others remembered best the feeling of oneness with the soldiers and came away with the idea that soldiers were not the enemy, despite their uniforms, and that they shared many of the movement's values and beliefs and should be approached as brothers. Still others, chafing at the failure to get through the military lines and invade the Pentagon, considered the whole thing a failure and blamed it on the nonviolent tactics.

A second crucial action occurred in the Bay Area the week of the Pentagon confrontation. Stop The Draft Week was structured to close down the Oakland Induction Center. On Monday a pacifist sit-in shut down the Center for three hours and caused 123 arrests. Tuesday was not under a nonviolent discipline and the demonstrators got roughed up by the police. Friday they returned for another encounter, with mobile tactics: avoiding static confrontation with the police, but remaining in the streets one step ahead of them and disrupting traffic and the pattern of everyday business. The demonstrators managed to tie up the Center and much of the city of Oakland. Roy Kepler commented:

> *Eight or ten thousand people on Friday, milling through the streets and blocking intersections in a mix of "self-defense" and "militant" styles, were little more successful than the 123 of Monday in terms of the amount of time that they prevented access to the Induction Center. But has anyone asked himself what might have been possible Monday (or any other day of the week) if instead of 123 people there had been 500 or 1000 or more people ready to undertake disciplined nonviolent action backed up by the readiness both to absorb any violence on the part of the police and to accept arrest and imprisonment?*

But most activists preferred the excitement of skirmishes with the police. Radical pacifists were left with the option of entering into coalitions in an effort to bring a nonviolent spirit into the confrontations or of going back to small disciplined demonstrations as in the CNVA days. To many this seemed irrelevant at a time when the movement had grown from a group of dedicated individuals to a movement of millions of people with varying politics and levels of commitment.

For much of 1968 the pacifist movement coexisted with the movement at large, participating in the street actions that climaxed in August 1968 at the Democratic National Convention. By then the tide had swung partially towards violence, peaking with the futility of the Weathermen actions and terrorist bombings. Partly in reaction to this, mass rallies and marches, organized by various Mobilization committees headed by Dave Dellinger, Muste's successor as coalition leader, were organized to keep visible, broad-based public pressure on Washington. On November 15, 1969, more than half a million people came to Washington for the biggest anti-war demonstration in U.S. history. Local Peace Centers were also set up throughout the country to organize people to work for an immediate end to the war. Nonviolent groups like Clergy and Laity Concerned and the Syracuse Peace Council in New York, and local chapters of WILPF, AFSC, and other pacifist groups across the nation continued to educate and demonstrate with each new development in the war.

GI Resistance

The Pentagon demonstration of 1967 brought the attention of the movement to the growing number of GI resisters against the war. All during the war, pacifist and other anti-war groups were counseling GI resisters and occasionally helping them find refuge in Canada and elsewhere. In doing this, people regularly sheltered AWOL soldiers and provided for their safety much as abolitionists had established an Underground Railroad for runaway slaves during the Civil War. There were an estimated 80–100,000 military deserters and draft evaders, mostly in Canada, but also in Sweden, France, and most other West European countries, in many of which they had been granted legal asylum.

Beginning in 1966, the War Resisters' International, of which the WRL is an American section, began a campaign to encourage GIs to resist the military. Until 1967, individual cases of GI resistance, such as Dr. Howard Levy and the Fort Hood 3, who were the first soldiers to refuse to serve in Vietnam, attracted attention because of their uniqueness. After 1967 a growing GI movement was organized with civilian support that encouraged and supported resistance to the military by men in uniform. This movement, represented best by Vietnam Veterans Against the War and the hundreds of uniformed men in prison was a powerful part of the anti-war movement.

Opposition Spreads

In the 1970s the anti-war movement as a whole was badly fractured into violent and nonviolent factions as well as into assorted sectarian political groups. None was able to command the enthusiasm of large numbers of activists as SDS had been able to do before 1969. Part of this, as we now know, was due to the disruptive tactics of the FBI's Cointelpro (Counterintelligence Program) focused on the New Left and the anti-war movement. Nevertheless, the Peoples Coalition for Peace and Justice (successor to the various Mobilization Committees) was able to mobilize scores of thousands of demonstrators for peaceful rallies. The most impressive took place in May 1970 when over 100,000 people came to the capital on a week's notice to protest the invasion of Cambodia and the murder of four students at Kent State University, Ohio, by National Guardsmen, and the police shootout at the black Jackson State College, Miss., where two students were killed. . . .

• • •

Ending the War

On January 20, 1973, thousands of demonstrators converged on Washington to protest Richard Nixon's inauguration and the Christmas attempt to terrorize North Vietnam into submission with 36,000 tons of bombs. When the Paris Peace Agreements were concluded, most Americans felt relieved that the Vietnam War, finally, was over. They were unaware that, in effect, the war would continue for over two more years, with Vietnamese casualties mounting progressively. It was to be a war-by-proxy, conducted by the U.S. through its puppet government in South Vietnam under the leadership of Nguyen Van Thieu.

The total of Thieu's political prisoners had mounted to about 200,000 and, despite the Paris Agreements, he refused to release them. Freeing these political prisoners became the focus of protest in the U.S. The symbol became replicas of the notorious tiger cages, manufactured in the U.S. and used for holding prisoners in South Vietnam.

The first such demonstration, two days of international protest, took place February 28 to March 1, 1973 under the sponsorship of the Emergency Project for Saigon Civilian Prisoners. Thereafter, tiger cage demonstrations took place frequently in many American cities. When Thieu came to Washington in April, he was "greeted" with a tiger cage and placards asking: "Why Do You Violate the Truce?" Throughout the summer of 1974, a tiger cage was mounted on the Capitol steps and protestors came from all parts of the country to leaflet, fast and vigil there.

Linking the Watergate scandal to the war-by-proxy in Southeast Asia, some 2,500 demonstrators, with placards focusing on the Cambodia bombing, marched from the Watergate Hotel to the White House in mid-June 1973. Ten months later, on April 27, 1974, some 10,000 people marched down Pennsylvania Avenue demanding Nixon's impeachment. On the fourth of July, Washington was also the scene of the first sizeable demonstration demanding universal and unconditional amnesty for all Vietnam war resisters.

By early fall, Watergate exposures and popular pressure forced Nixon to resign, but foreign policy in general, and Southeast Asia policy in particular, remained unchanged. On January 25 to 27, 1975, over 1,500 anti-war activists from across the U.S., and a number of prominent peace people from abroad, came to Washington for an Assembly to Save the Peace Agreements, climaxed by a candlelight march to the White House. It was two years since the signing of the Paris Agreements, but still there was no peace in Southeast Asia.

Peace finally came in April 1975, but not as a consequence of the Paris Agreements. Despite massive U.S. support, the war effort in South Vietnam and Cambodia became totally demoralized and collapsed. On May 11 at the Sheep's Meadow of New York's Central Park, some 80,000 people turned out to celebrate the end of the war. On a big banner across the speakers' platform, on placards and on white balloons was painted the slogan "The War Is Over!" It was a joyous celebration, with music and a minimum of speeches. Joan Baez, Pete Seeger, Richie Havens, Phil Ochs and Odetta were among the singers.

The idea that "wars will end when men refuse to fight" always seemed utopian. But never before had resistance to war been so widespread, committed and effective as against U.S. involvement in Southeast Asia. Men and women in and out of uniform and numbering in the tens and hundreds of thousands took risks and interrupted the routine of their lives to say "No" to war. Even more important, growing numbers took to searching for ways of living that could minimize violence in their own lives and militarism in public life.

In the years since World War I, radical pacifism had become a political and cultural force in American life. No longer an isolated and individualistic attitude towards war, it had become a way of life for many, a way of life which included continued work against militarism and injustice and towards a more peaceful and healthy world.

Surveillance of Peace Movements

Frank J. Donner

The Institutional Setting

By the late sixties the intelligence units of the armed forces had become, next to the FBI, the most important single component in the domestic intelligence community. As in the case of the CIA, the latter-day bloating of military surveillance of political expression and activity in this country must be seen, in part as yet another flowering of the liberal quest for benign, presidentially sponsored forms of repression, and in part simply as a "natural" response.

In every modern state, the military has played an important role in the development of institutions to monitor civilian politics. Even when these surveillance functions pass from military into civilian hands, the influence of military attitudes, assumptions, and practices continues to be felt. But here we are concerned not with the residual influence of the Army on civilian intelligence practices, but rather with a huge intelligence system operated by the Army itself without civilian authorization or control. . . .

• • •

Military Intelligence Structures

The civil rights disturbances and demonstrations of the early sixties prompted a limited number of troop commitments and modest Army intelligence activity of a preparatory nature in anticipation of possible troop deployments to selected trouble spots. But as the disorders spread and criticism of the Vietnam War intensified, the earlier restraints were abandoned. By the end of the decade a huge intelligence structure had emerged, which planned, programmed, processed, interpreted, stored, and disseminated civilian-focused intelligence. Its intelligence function, mission, and product are generically described as CONUS INTEL or simply CONUS, an acronym for Continental United States Intelligence. During the period of its greatest activity this apparatus functioned through a hydra-headed bureaucracy, consisting of the U.S. Intelligence Command (USAINTC), the Continental Army Command (CONARC), the Counter-Intelligence Analysis Branch[1]* (CIAB) attached to the office of Chief of Staff of Intelligence (OACSI), and the Directorate of Civil Disturbance and Planning (DCDPO), renamed in 1970 the Directorate of Military Support (DOMS).

USAINTC, organized in 1965 and headquartered at Fort Holabird, Maryland, served as the principal instrument of CONUS intelligence. By the late sixties it boasted a nationwide network of some 1500 agents, stationed in over 300 posts scattered throughout the country and organized into seven Military Intelligence Groups (MIG), substructured into regional field and resident offices. The MIGs were responsible for Special Investigations (personnel investigations) and CONUS intelligence, functions that overlapped operationally as the decade progressed. The surveillance of both civilian and military dissidents engaged in anti-war activities involving military personnel was entrusted to a special USAINTC program, Resistance in the Army (RITA). Surveillance operations were primarily the responsibility of the field and resident offices, while the group and regional offices were largely involved in command, review, and administrative functions, and also served as custodians of the more important files. . . .

• • •

An outstanding aspect of both the USAINTC and the CONARC systems was their extraordinarily comprehensive and sophisticated communication grids—teletypes, hotlines, tie-ins with law enforcement telephones and radio transmissions, and electronic links to virtually all collection posts in the country. According to the Ervin Committee Report, "In some cities, these lines extended to every precinct station and were manned at both ends by Army agents."[2] The sophisticated communication equipment—videotape equipment (mobile and stationary), citizen band broadcast interceptors, miniaturized transmitters with hidden throat mikes—reflected the Army's doomsday assumption that only a lightning-fast response would hold off the holocaust. The spate of raw information from the field ultimately emptied into elaborate file systems at Forts Holabird and Monroe. The core Fort Holabird USAINTC collection was stored at the fort's repository, the United States Army Investigative Records Repository (USAIRR), comprising about 8 million dossiers, developed by USAINTC. This central collection was augmented by a number of satellite compilations dealing with civilian political activity, comprising two computer systems, two noncomputerized collections, and a library of documents, photographs, and videotapes. Of the two noncomputerized files, one was the so-called subversives file, which had been in long-term use as a search file in security clearance investigations and for background material on civilians and organizations suspected of sabotage, espionage, and related offenses. Based on inputs from all sources, this collection included dossiers on elected officials (congressmen and governors) and organizations such as the Friends, the NAACP, and indeed all political groups over the entire left-liberal spectrum, each with a specially assigned dossier number.[3] . . .

• • •

Operational Patterns

All intelligence operations in the political sphere outrun their asserted purposes. Nowhere is this more true than in the case of military intelligence. The formal justifications—preparation for emergency troop call-outs and the monitoring of threats to the military function itself—serve as little more than pretexts. The scope and intensity of the field operations of the Army's intelligence personnel established all too clearly that, as in the case of the Bureau's surveillance system, they were at root forms of aggression against legitimate political expression. The limitations on the use of the military in civilian life discussed above barred open, direct actions to suppress protest activities, but still left available intelligence as a weapon, a means of projecting a hostile military presence into dissenting political activity. To be sure, discretion would seem to have been required—some attempt to maintain a low profile, to tread carefully in the political arena, to observe targeting restraints, and to respect the constitutional protections of the individual targets. But caution fell prey to the ideological hostility released by the eruptions of the sixties. If the collection plans summarized in the previous section were intended as a curb, it is not apparent from the field operations.

The assassination of Dr. Martin Luther King, Jr., led in April 1968 to a nationwide military intelligence mobilization, which monitored the King funeral, the urban riots in the wake of the assassination, the Poor People's March, and the subsequent Resurrection City encampment in Washington. Atlanta agents were assigned to monitor the funeral procession in unmarked cars and instructed to report back every fifteen minutes by "hotline" to Fort Holabird with instructions from their commanding officer, Major General William Blakefield, to "beat the AP" in their reporting, and to surveil everyone who attended the funeral, including such dignitaries as the Vice-President of the United States.[4] When the March began a month later at King's gravesite, agents in unmarked cars recorded the license plates of those who visited the grave. Coretta Scott King, the slain leader's wife, predicted to those who were about to start on the trek to Washington that her slain husband's "dream" ("I have a dream") would come true. When an agent reported her words back to his field office he was told to go "find out what dream she is referring to."[5] The March itself, as well as the encampment, were heavily infiltrated by Army agents who spied on infiltrators planted by civilian units. The demonstration was also closely monitored by law enforcement agencies; there was no prospect of a breakdown of local peacekeeping efforts that might justify military involvement. The Army's informers were, as they subsequently recounted it, alternately bewildered and amused at the kinds of information they were instructed to report.*

Both the 1968 national political conventions were placed under military intelligence surveillance.[6] The August Miami Convention was monitored by ASA electronic technicians as well as by military agents based at Fort McNair, Georgia, in plain clothes.[7] The security coordinator for the Miami Beach Police Department explained: "The Army intelligence as well as Navy intelligence had rather complete files on people who might be trouble-prone, and they also had contact with Washington and other parts of the country where they could get immediate information on any of these individuals, should that be necessary. The Army circulated in the area with concealed walkie talkies which enabled them to maintain communication with agents who had penetrated the target groups. They had other sophisticated devices as well and many of them were put to use." About sixty agents attached to at least four separate intelligence units monitored the Democratic Convention in Chicago. Operatives infiltrated the protesting groups and also invaded the convention floor without the knowledge of party functionaries. Reports transmitted from the surveillance units

back to OPS IV at Fort Holabird were in turn relayed to the newly launched Directorate of Civil Disturbance Planning and Operations (DCDPO), which was also receiving hourly reports from three employees of the CIAB—not supposed to be an operational unit at all. The Army's intelligence coverage of public events peaked with the presidential inauguration in January 1969, which was covered by no less than 107 agents from MIG units all over the country. About eight of them were assigned to undercover work throughout the District of Columbia and nearby suburbs. Informers were planted in groups considered potential sources of disruption.[8]

The field personnel—especially in the more remote areas—were structured into an identifiable intelligence community, which not only exchanged information occasionally but met together on a regular basis. For example, in Region II of the IIIth Military Intelligence Group (Greensboro and Winston-Salem, North Carolina), regular area intelligence meetings were held. These were attended by members of the FBI, the North Carolina State Bureau of Investigation, local police from nearby police departments and remoter municipalities as well, and sometimes university security officers from Lake Forest University. We encounter frequent examples of joint patrols, seemingly for law enforcement purposes (a clear violation of the Posse Comitatus Act), and even joint undercover operations.[9] The operatives exchanged information about their targets with law enforcement and campus security personnel, and even kept "contact files" on other members of the intelligence community. The field operations were built around a countersubversive axis. A Winston-Salem agent recalled: "We were trained to be paranoid. On the day we graduated from training, the Commanding Officer told us that the Communists already had dossiers and pictures of each one of us."[10] . . .

---

*At one point they were told to observe whether the mule teams leading the caravan were being abused. Said one agent, "It was a very strong requirement of the Army to know the exact number of mules and the exact number of horses at all times." A black officer assigned to infiltrate the Resurrection City campsite "was requested to get information on the sanitation facilities, the depth of the mud when it rained . . . and information of that nature"—*Ervin Hearings* (1971), pp. 253, 1469, 1471.

The number one target in the military surveillance repertory was the university campus. Every intelligence unit in the country monitored college-level institutions in its area, and in some instances even high schools. The extensive coverage reflected the role of the campus in the antiwar movement, as well as draft resistance; it was extraordinarily intensive because of the ease with which young operatives could pose as students and the readiness of most college administrators to cooperate with field offices. In at least one instance an agent penetrated a New York University course in black studies, recorded the contents of lectures and discussions, and identified the students. But other areas were not slighted. In the Winston-Salem unit, for example, agents had standing orders to follow "any suspicious black man, learn his identity and find out what he was up to."[11] And the scope was matched by the thoroughness of the surveillance. In testimony before the Ervin Committee, Texas State Representative Curtis M. Graves said that he had learned that the data collected about the targets in the Houston area included "how many teeth they had extracted, how many times they complained about back injury, surgery records...."[12]

In addition to monitoring local branches of national groups—such as the Black Panthers, the SDS, the Friends, the Women's Strike for Peace—the regional and field offices spied on local ad hoc groups, meetings, and demonstrations. Agents monitored or infiltrated such targets as:

an anti-war meeting in a Washington, D.C., Episcopal church

demonstrations by a welfare mothers' organization in Milwaukee, Wisconsin

a procession of black Olympic stars

a conference of dissenting priests in the Washington, D.C., diocese protesting Archbishop Boyle's position on birth control

a Halloween party for elementary school-children in Washington, D.C., suspected of harboring a local dissident

a demonstration of welfare recipients in New York City

a meeting of a sanitation workers' union in Atlanta, Georgia

a Fayetteville, North Carolina, church group

a Southern Christian Leadership Conference Upward Bound—an OEO project

an anti-war vigil in the chapel of Colorado State University

the members of the congregation of the Unitarian Church in Houston, Texas, and of another in Monterey, California

a Godfrey Cambridge concert held in Washington, D.C.[13]

The chartered bus trip to an anti-war demonstration became a military intelligence specialty. Intelligence agents worked with the bus companies to obtain all available information about the sponsor and passengers, and mingled with the passengers en route to a protest site. The November 1969 March on the Pentagon was the most heavily infiltrated of these pilgrimages. MIG agents who traveled from New York with the demonstrators encountered so many other operatives in Washington that they were unable to report back as instructed because the phones were tied up by their colleagues from other areas under similar instructions.[14] An earlier Washington demonstration was similarly saturated by surveillants: "Agents took pains to dress and look like hippies, and when the pictures they took were developed, it turned out that New York agents snapped New Jersey agents...." Obstructive tactics were sometimes used to delay departure or—by substituting an agent for the regular driver—arrival; agents were also permitted to replace drivers in order to monitor the passengers.

The MIG regions were stocked with high-grade surveillance gear: communications equipment, tape recorders, cameras with a variety of lenses, binoculars, lock-picking kits, lie detectors, and interview rooms with two-way mirrors.[15] The larger units in urban centers boasted special command headquarters, emergency rooms, communications equipment and hotlines housed in an "operations center" mirroring on a smaller scale the OPS IV and Pentagon facilities. Despite the

Army's paper constraints on covert methods, the records show that they were routinely used. Agents were issued "Leroy Kits," which enabled them to forge such identification as drivers' licenses and registration certificates. The most common kind of deception was of the shallow variety, such as posing as a peace protester with a hidden transmitter or a camera. Agents frequently used a media cover, equipped with bogus credentials as reporters or photographers.[16] As we have seen, the campus was often targeted by such imposters, as well as by infiltrators from Army units and civilians under military direction. An agent of the II6th MIG who infiltrated a Washington, D.C., Yippie commune in 1969 was authorized to use marijuana and liquor as a cover.[17] This same unit ran two informers who worked for two months undercover in the New Mobilization Committee, an anti-war group, and a third in a GI organizing program held at a Washington area school. The range of infiltration is indicated by the following statement by an operative:

> To gather. . . information, the II6th routinely assigned some twenty of its men as full-time undercover agents to infiltrate political groups and observe politically active persons. . . . Some of these groups have grown beards and long hair to pass as students on local college campuses. In addition, other members posed as members of the working

press to obtain pictures of those involved in political activities; concealed tape recorders were also commonly used to record speeches and conversations at political events.

Though not with the scope and intensity of the COINTELPROS, the Army did conduct aggressive intelligence. The Fort Holabird CONUS intelligence system included an "offensive operations function." Enough evidence of "dirty tricks" has emerged to justify the conclusion that they were part of a deliberate program.*. . .

. . .

Evidence of aggressive intelligence includes arranging for the delivery of unordered fried chicken to the home of a Chicago professor where an anti-war meeting was in progress; posing as a bus driver, collecting bus tickets of departing demonstrators and directing them to a nonexistent bus—a "disinformation" tactic widely practiced in Washington area demonstrations; heckling speakers in order to cause disruptions; and removing notices of rallies and demonstrations from school bulletin boards. The II3th also played an active role in the 1968 national surveillance programs already mentioned, including the identification of members of the Chicago contingent of the Poor People's March; vehicular surveillance of leaders and coverage of the National Democratic Convention.† Under a variety of covers, personnel attached

---

*The report of the Ervin Committee indicates that various MI groups conducted offensive operations against targets such as anti-war and student groups. Further information about these operations was withheld through the Pentagon's refusal to declassify the relevant records.
†According to a semi-official account of the surveillance (Ervin Hearings [1971], pp. 1481–1482):

a. Around-the-clock coverage was provided by two shifts. Operations center was located in the existing Evanston, Illinois, unit. Direct communications were established to Fort Holabird, Maryland; Fifth US Army; and Fourth US Army. Direct lines were connected between the FBI and Chicago police to the Evanston office.
b. Concept of coverage consisted of two-man agent teams at focal points, particularly at those selected and manned by Chicago police.
c. Departure of normal coverage by liaison consisted of:
   (1) Roving teams, on foot, equipped with handi-talkie radios, to report on incidents.
   (2) Vehicle roving teams, also radio equipped, dispatched as required. One such team also had still photo cameras.
   (3) Stationary observers at sites manned by Chicago police. Two such places were the Hilton Hotel and a tower near the convention hall.
   (4) One team equipped with a TV camera for recording video tape.

to the II3th infiltrated a number of organizations and rallies organized to protest the Democratic National Convention, including a Lincoln Park rally addressed by Panther leader Bobby Seale, a sunrise meeting conducted by poet Allen Ginsberg ("other than singing and meditation, the meeting was uneventful"), and a Grant Park meeting addressed by pacifist Staughton Lynd, then a professor at Roosevelt University.[18] . . .

• • •

The Ultimate Reckoning—Exposé and Cover-up

The cult of secrecy, the protective cloak of national security, the classification system, the pledge of the individual agent not to disclose what he has learned in the course of his duties ("the debriefing oath")—all provide a protective shelter for intelligence abuses.[19] In the case of military intelligence, the doors and windows were opened wider than those of other intelligence systems as the result of a scouring probe conducted over a four-year period by the Ervin Committee. . . .

• • •

When the Defense Department civilian leadership began to probe, the high intelligence brass denied the existence of computers and computer records altogether. The mere possibility of a cutback in computer-processing capability terrified Fort Holabird's career officers.* When orders finally came down to destroy or curb Fort Holabird's file collection, they were obeyed—but not before the files had been duplicated. The custodial personnel were made to feel that ingenuity in circumventing file destruction orders would ultimately be rewarded by promotion. One clerk quoted in the Ervin Testimony recalled: "The tendency was to keep the information while obeying the order. . . . The order didn't say destroy the information, just destroy the Compendium." This gloss made it possible to transfer both volumes of the Compendium to microfilm before destroying it physically.

The field resources were viewed by the intelligence command as its trump card and it was at the field level that the worst sabotage took place. When attempts were made to implement new, more restrained policies through a council composed of high civilian defense officials, field compliance inspection visits were frequently evaded by crafty ploys reminiscent of Gogol's Inspector General.[20] Intelligence field commanders assured their cadres that the regional files would remain intact and that surveillance operations would continue unchanged. Other forms of field deception consisted of restructuring the intelligence collection process so that when CONUS intelligence sections were liquidated as ordered, the same work was transferred to the section engaged in personnel security investigations. A blunter procedure was simply to juggle files: personality files were merged into organizational files; anti-war surveillance files were relabeled RITA files, even though the subject groups had nothing to do with proselytizing military personnel. In the same way, file collections were secretly transferred to nonfederal units or stored in the homes of agents and officers.

The skirmishes of the Army's intelligence headquarters and field personnel to nullify and circumvent attempts by the civilian leadership to curb intelligence abuses, the token palliatives of the leadership itself, the persistent attempt to appease critics without surrendering ground un-

*In the words of a former agent: "The lieutenant colonels and the full colonels at Fort Holabird pride themselves on their ability to retrieve information really quickly. If Colonel or General So-and-So out in Oregon wants to know about so-and-so real quick, then they can get this file out real quick and read it to him over the phone and the general is just snowed. This is the mentality, to try to snow the next rank up so that the next time it's your turn to be promoted they'll look at you favorably. So when you get down to the middle- and lower-ranking officers, that's where they begin to think, 'Well, good heavens, you know, if we destroy this, we might not be able to answer requests and then that's going to put me in a bad light. So we'll remove it and it will look like it was never there, or as if it were destroyed, but we'll just put it in another place, so we'll still be able to retrieve it.' "

necessarily, the promulgation of vaguely worded guidelines—all finally ended in December 1970. A directive was issued setting down guidelines that were entirely new in the sense that, instead of dealing with isolated abuses in piecemeal fashion, they structurally confined the Army's civilian intelligence program within appropriate legal and functional limits. This was achieved simply by liquidating CONUS intelligence and confining its targets to conduct that threatens a legitimate palpable Army interest. The work of liquidation and reform was later (on March 1, 1974) completed by a Defense Department directive covering all of the services. While retaining the potential for abuse,* the new provisions unquestionably pointed military intelligence in a new direction. For the first time, responsibility for the conduct of domestic surveillance was lodged by a positive directive in the civilian Secretary of Defense. To complete the dismantling process, on June 1, 1971, the Army issued an implementing directive, which among other things dissolved the role of CIAD. Under the new dispensation, it was left all dressed up in an analytic capability with nowhere to go. CIAD was authorized to receive from civilian agencies "early warning intelligence" about civil disturbance situations that might, in the future, overtax local law enforcement resources, to be supplemented by public media data. But the agency was specifically forbidden to use the latter source either to collect "background information about the beliefs of civilians or the nature of civilian organizations" or to develop files about such individuals or organizations.

Fixing the Blame

Although there are ambiguities in the record, it is fair to conclude that CONUS INTEL was the creation of Army intelligence and that it simply continued

toutes proportions gardées in the upheavals of the sixties the tactics with which it had historically confronted domestic unrest.[21] The role of Johnson administration officials in this development parallels the domestic CIA build-up. That there was pressure from the White House and the Attorney General's office for an accelerated flow of information dealing with the urban riots and their causes is incontestable: the hope persisted that somehow the Army with its superior resources would come up with the desperately sought prize— a means of predicting riots. But the Johnson administration cannot escape responsibility for encouraging the Army to enter barred areas, for failing to ensure civilian control of any kind, and finally, for a refusal to recognize that, however well intentioned, its quest for forecast intelligence would be ideologized and implemented by illegal methods.[22] To be sure, the civilian leadership of the Defense Department, the White House, and the Attorney General's office were left in the dark about the military intelligence colossus. But it is fair to conclude that they preferred it that way. When the Nixon administration took over, "intelligence" wholly replaced "information" (recall the IDIU's transformation) as the key objective. In 1969, Justice and Defense agreed on an Interdepartmental Action Plan (IAP) to share responsibility for civil disturbance intelligence. The plan—a phase in the groping of the Nixon administration for an integrated intelligence structure and hierarchy—assigned the IDIU an evaluative role and rather cloudily left the Army with a collection responsibility. The civilian Defense Department leadership did argue for turning collection over to the Bureau in accordance with the Delimitations Agreement. But by this time it was too late. The Bureau preferred safer passage, and the entrenched intelligence brass viewed such a move as a death sentence. Most important, the Nixon civilian high command, whose knowledge of the scope

---

*Possibly the most serious defect in the new directive is that the Defense Secretary was given carte blanche to authorize the most questionable form of surveillance (undercover penetration) without the specific findings required in more routine monitoring that "there is a distinct threat of a civil disturbance exceeding the law enforcement capabilities of state and local authorities."

and style of the collection effort is incontestable, felt that it was vital to its offensive, commenced in the spring of 1969, against domestic dissent. And by that time the Army was also irreversibly committed: in April 1969 USAINTC promulgated its collection plan, even more comprehensive than its predecessors. As an Army intelligence functionary tersely summarized the situation in the spring of 1969: "We created addicts for this stuff all over the Government."[23]

But the armed services were perhaps more addicted to "this stuff" than any other government agency. And nothing shows this more than their involvement in developing the Huston Plan* in the summer of 1970 and their subsequent participation in the IEC, at the very time when responsible military and civilian leaders were—by directive, assurances in legal proceedings, and public statements—insisting that civilian intelligence collection had ended. It is doubtful whether addiction to "this stuff" can be cured, short of the severe criminal sanctions that Congress has rejected. The Army as a whole is congenitally vulnerable to shifting winds, and stateside civilian intelligence would seem to exercise a far more precarious hold than other peacetime Army functions. Yet it has maintained unbroken continuity for over half a century. Its survival formula is simple enough: when democratic values are in the ascendant, the intelligence system retires to the shadows to hibernate, so to speak, until social unrest changes the weather—an extension on an institutional scale of a flexibility required in day-to-day intelligence operations. But intelligence professionals regard such a retreat as merely tactical, a temporary setback that confirms the strength of the subversive enemy. The need to avoid destructive confrontations with powerful civilian critics also explains the evasions, the resort to tokenism, and the pseudo-contrition of the "sorry about that" variety all regularly invoked when the demands for an accounting grow strong.

Continuity is assured in a variety of ways, not the least of which is an old-boy network of former agents. As we have seen, after World War I many displaced intelligence officers and agents found similar work either with the government or with private groups. When, after World War II, intelligence became a negotiable skill, former Army practitioners of the art either found private intelligence-related employment or were encouraged to hole up in other intelligence agencies. A similar process is already at work to provide shelter for displaced post-Vietnam intelligence personnel.

These agents form the core of the nativist countersubversive constituency, providing it with literature and file information. Such materials are in steady demand in the countersubversive marketplaces of the nation. It is this sense that countersubversive files will have future value and indeed ultimately serve as a showdown resource that explains the tenacity and evasiveness of the Army's response to civilian cleansing efforts. And it would be folly to take comfort from official directives ordering the destruction of civilian file collections. Given current reproduction technology, the duplication of these collections is a certainty. If history is a guide, copies of the Army collections have been secretly retained by intelligence agents and added to other file holdings on federal, state, and local levels. In addition, again judging from the past, the Army files have surely been acquired by private agencies to augment collections originally built through the same process of clandestine acquisition. Nor, in considering the Army's survival prospects in the domestic civilian intelligence arena, can we ignore its technological "capability" (including computerized data encoding to thwart access by outsiders), its financial resources and spaces on intelligence manning charts for long-established military specialties (MOS).[24] After all, "intelligence" in a battle context is a normal military function, served by specialists and the most advanced equipment. Why, for example, should the sensors developed in Vietnam be mothballed when they could be used to monitor domestic civilian politics?[25] It should be recalled that the Army's cognitive passions also embrace—

---

*[For increased, illegal surveillance of civilians—EDS.]

clumsily, to be sure— the social sciences: information theory, behavior analysis, social indicators. What other domestic intelligence agency, from the FBI to the lowly red squads, is so richly qualified for the task of ferreting out dissent? In the light of both recent and more remote history, how can self-regulation alone create the assurance of protection against future abuse?

---

1. The branch is now a "Detachment."

2. *Report*, p. 48.

3. A partial listing of these organizations "of intelligence interest" and their corresponding dossier numbers appears in the USAINTC Information Collection Plan (ICP)—*Report*, pp. 129–130.

4. NBC, "First Tuesday," Dec. 1, 1970. A transcript of the telecast is reproduced in CR, Dec. 10, 1970, pp. S19937–19942.

5. NYT, Jan. 18, 1971.

6. The most detailed account of the military spying at the 1968 conventions is given by investigative reporter Jared Stout, "Military Agents Used at 1968 Conventions," Washington *Star,* Dec. 2, 1970, reprinted in CR, Dec. 2, 1970, pp. S19198–20000. See also Stout, "Big Brother Pentagon—Keeping Tabs on Civilians," *Nation,* Dec. 28, 1970.

7. A spokesman for the Secret Service, which was authorized by Congress to draw aid from the Army in protecting presidential candidates after the assassination of Robert Kennedy, denied having asked for the ASA. However, a former Secret Serviceman who covered the convention said he had been told the ASA was present "to help the Secret Service protect against the use of electronic surveillance against candidates." When ASA's role was uncovered in December 1970, both Ramsey Clark and Clark Clifford (at the time of the conventions Attorney General and Secretary of Defense, respectively) denied knowledge of the ASA role in Chicago. However, two years later, *New York Times* investigative reporter Seymour Hersh reported that he had obtained government documents implicating Clark in the decision to allow the ASA to eavesdrop not only in Chicago but in Miami at the Republican Convention. Hersh also reported he had seen a memo showing that the ASA was authorized by Army Chief of Staff William Westmoreland to institute eavesdropping of the Republican Convention and the Huey Newton trial. The agency had apparently been assigned by Westmoreland's predecessor as Chief of Staff, General Harold K. Johnson, to surveil the 1967 March on the Pentagon, the April 1968 riots in Washington, and the Poor People's March. A secret Army analysis of these activities concluded, according to Hersh, that approval was obtained for these activities from civilian authorities—Seymour Hersh, "Files Disclose More Army Snooping Under Johnson," NYT, Dec. 1, 1972, and Jared Stout, "Military's Spying on Civilians at '68 Conventions Revealed," Pittsburgh Press, Dec. 1, 1970.

8. *Ervin Hearings* (1971), p. 440.

9. Ibid., pp. 1468–1469.

10. Ibid., p. 1488.

11. Ibid., p. 148.

12. Ibid., p. 337.

13. Ibid., pp. 285, 286, 289, 291, 1457, 1486, 1488, 1499.

14. Ibid., pp. 219, 291, 1460.

15. Ibid., p. 1475.

16. Ibid., pp. 1465–1466.

17. Ibid., p. 280.

18. *Westmoreland*, p. 1062.

19. The agents who testified or wrote statements for use by the Ervin Committee had taken debriefing oaths but insisted that none of the material they disclosed was properly classified in the first place.

20. Assistant Defense Secretary Froehlke himself was deceived on his field inspection tours. For example, the video viewer used by 113th MIG, Region I, usually prominently displayed in the office, was locked up in a vault until Froehlke and his inspection team came through and, on their departure, brought out on display again—*Ervin Hearings* (1971), p. 490.

21. The view of the brass on the responsibility for the Army's spy program is put forth in a *New York Times* article by Major General Thomas A. Lane, "A Right To Intelligence," Lane said that "the tasks were undertaken reluctantly, only on the direct orders of the President and his civilian Cabinet officers." But as in the case of similar justifications, he did not explain why the civil disturbance mission required the objectionable intelligence program. He added that claims of military invasions of the civilian sphere seemed contrived "in an era when President Johnson could boast that 'not a chicken shed in North Vietnam was bombed' without his permission." The kernel of his argument appears to have been that, since all other phases of the war were under civilian control, the intelligence effort must also have been a civilian initiative. Lane also hinted that former Attorney General Ramsey Clark could support his charges. For reasons that have never been adequately explained, Justice Department officials in the Johnson and Nixon administrations who were mentioned in connection with the military spying issue were never invited to testify before the Ervin Committee. See "Who's The Snoop-in-Chief? Nobody Is Saying," NYT, March 14, 1971, and "Spying on Long-Hairs and Other Dangerous Types," NYT, March 4, 1972.

22. "Johnson and Clark Linked to Surveillance Planning; Ex-Attorney General Disputes Files on His Role in White House Talk and Changes of Memorandums," NYT, April 17, 1971; "Files Disclose More Army Snooping Under Johnson," NYT, Sept. 1, 1972. These and related charges were leaked by Nixon's civilian officials and the Pentagon in a planned campaign with a dual objective; to transfer blame for the Army's excesses to civilians and at the same time to relieve the Nixon Administration of responsibility. See especially the testimony of Nixon's Defense Secretary Melvin R. Laird, Hearings on the Department of Defense Appropriations for 1972 (March 4, 1971), p. 215.

23. "Army Spied on 18,000 Civilians in 2-Year Operation," NYT, Jan. 18, 1971.

24. Exclusive of tactical intelligence in Vietnam combat operations and of the intelligence activities of the CIA and State Department, the armed services in fiscal year 1970 spent $2.9 billion on intelligence collection and related functions, foreign and domestic. In testimony in March 1970, Assistant Defense Secretary Froehlke indicated that these figures for fiscal year 1971 would be reduced by about $100 million, to $2.8 billion—"Intelligence Costs for Military in '70 Put at $2.9 Billion," NYT, May 20, 1970. The resulting cutback in jobs led to a protest by Army intelligence agents that they were being forced out of undercover work in direct violation of contracts they signed when they enlisted. The men complained at a mass meeting that they had volunteered to

serve for four years as opposed to the normal enlistee's three-year tour in combat. The Army replied that the fine print showed they were guaranteed only an "initial assignment" with the ASA. See UPI story, June 19, 1971, "Army Security Men Protest Cutback."

25. The electronic devices—sensors, laser beams, computers, relay and read-out capabilities—which came into use in the Vietnam War form an awesome arsenal readily adapted to peacetime surveillance uses. Among the newly developed sensor devices already in use are more than 250 night observation and other types of sensors called, generically, Surveillance, Target Acquisition, and Night Observation (STANO). The STANO items include a searchlight undetectable by the enemy, and chemical and biological "people-sniffing" equipment. Other systems transmit information through "seismic intrusion detectors" signaling the movements of enemy forces.

THE NEW PEACE MOVEMENT TODAY

The Anti-Nuclear War Movement of the 1980s

Earl A. Molander • Roger C. Molander

In 1981, a movement against nuclear weapons and the threat of nuclear war emerged in the United States. This paper offers an explanation for the rise and decline of that movement, using as a basic framework a theoretical model for the evolution of social movements generally.

An Overview

In 1981, the first year of the Reagan administration, a series of events catalyzed the formation of a broad-based peace movement not seen since the last years of the Vietnam War. The rapid increase in U.S. defense spending, the increasingly strident anti-Soviet rhetoric, and half-hearted initiatives in arms control led to a resurgence of the peace movement, focused on nuclear weapons. The developing European disarmament movement, pub-

lication of Jonathan Schell's *The Fate of the Earth* (1982), and successful Freeze initiatives in New England were preludes to a nationwide movement focused on a range of peace and nuclear arms control issues.

At the center of the movement was the nuclear weapons Freeze campaign and its call for a particular policy change: "an immediate bilateral verifiable freeze on the testing, deployment, and production of nuclear weapons." Around this flagship were such organizations as the Physicians for Social Responsibility, Educators for Social Responsibility, and Ground Zero, with the latter two focusing their educational efforts in schools and community groups. Other national organizations developed in response to specific nuclear war-related policies and programs, such as the M-X missile, increases in the defense budget, and, eventually, the Strategic Defense Initiative or "Star Wars" program.

Reprinted by permission of the author.

In the first two years of the Reagan administration, more than two dozen new national anti-nuclear war/pro-arms control peace groups were activated. Many were long-standing peace groups that had become moribund but were revived by the new public climate of anti-nuclear war sentiment, e.g., SANE and the American Friends Service Committee. In other cases, established organizations and institutions like Common Cause and the Union of Concerned Scientists (UCS) redirected their focus from other social issues (Common Cause) and nuclear power (UCS) to nuclear weapons and arms control. Although a majority of these groups would eventually work cooperatively or at least in parallel with the national Freeze campaign, they were divided significantly on the appropriate goals, strategy, and tactics for themselves individually and for the movement as a whole.

Theoretical Framework: The Evolution of Social Movements

To explain the rise and decline of the anti-nuclear war movement, this paper uses a theoretical framework developed by the authors (Molander and Molander 1987). This "threshold" model explains social movement evolution in terms of multi-path and multi-stage movement development, with key thresholds between movement stages (Figure 1). The model attempts to reconcile the debate between two major theories about how social movements develop: resource mobilization theory and classical collective behavior theory (Killian 1984; McAdam 1982; McCarthy and Zald 1977; Morris 1981).

Stage 1. Premovement: Strains in the System

The premovement conditions that ultimately led to the anti-nuclear war movement are shown in Figure 1. As the figure emphasizes, there were multiple factors involved in the external environment, and internally in the expert community and among policy makers. There were specific strains in the

system, arising from the failure of the ratification of SALT II. The consensus on Mutual Assured Destruction (MAD) as the principal deterrent to nuclear war was coming unraveled, and the solutions under consideration, such as developing a limited nuclear war fighting capability and civil defense, were not receiving broad-based support in the expert community, the political system, or the mass public.

Threshold 1: The Movement Reaches a Critical Mass

The strains in the social system reached a critical mass with the election of Ronald Reagan to the presidency in November 1980. The Reagan election was accompanied by the success of a number of local Freeze initiatives, and his assumption of office saw the departure of a generally pro-arms control group of policy experts from the executive branch. Within a few months of taking office, President Reagan set forth major initiatives to expand defense spending and declared his open hostility to and distrust of the Soviet Union, including the Soviet's perspective and record on arms control. As a result of these developments, in early 1981 a number of new social movement organizations (SMOs) were formed at the national level, and there was a quantum jump in the number of inquiries from the local level to these national organizations, especially the newly formed national Freeze campaign.

As social movement entrepreneurs (individuals who started new SMOs or revived older ones) began to emerge at the local and national levels, the becalmed anti-nuclear war movement of the 1960s began to come back to life. These entrepreneurs came from inside and outside the system; e.g., the leadership of the Freeze was from the pacifist community, and the founder of Ground Zero, Dr. Roger Molander, was a former arms control expert who had served on the National Security Council staff under Nixon, Ford, and Carter. In the face of the fading consensus on MAD, the movement saw an opening for major new initiatives in reducing, if not eliminating, nuclear weapons levels around the globe. Simultaneously,

FIGURE 1   Stages in a social movement

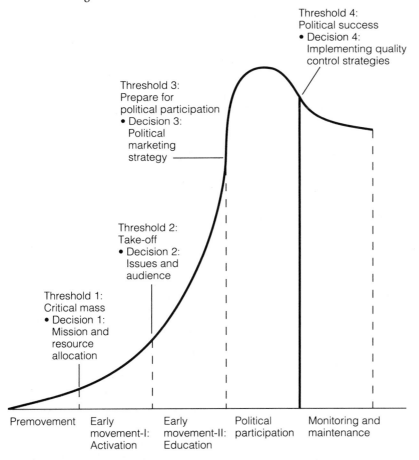

Threshold 4:
Political success
• Decision 4:
  Implementing quality
  control strategies

Threshold 3:
Prepare for
political participation
• Decision 3:
  Political
  marketing
  strategy

Threshold 2:
Take-off
• Decision 2:
  Issues and
  audience

Threshold 1:
Critical mass
• Decision 1:
  Mission and
  resource
  allocation

Premovement   Early   Early   Political   Monitoring and
              movement-I: movement-II: participation   maintenance
              Activation   Education

Stage 1. Premovement Stage: Strains Form Movement Elements
The social system experiences strains, which, if unanswered, foster the spontaneous formation of essential elements for a social movement that can challenge the equilibrium of the system and the consensus that underlies it.

Threshold 1. Critical Mass: Movement entrepreneurs drive a wedge into gaps opening in the prevailing equilibrium.

Stage 2. Early Movement-I: Activation
Emphasis is on agitation and awareness building where the primary goal is to dramatize the core movement concerns and bring them to the awareness of the general public and especially prospective movement members.

Threshold 2. Take-Off: Funders, national media, politicians, and other institutions endow the movement with legitimacy and lend their support. For a time, growth will now be self-sustaining.

Stage 3. Early Movement-II: Expanding the Circle and Education
Movement organizations must persuade movement adherents that the technical issues that may seem beyond their grasp are in fact accessible, and then persuade adherents to learn about these issues so they can articulate their concerns in ways understandable to political decision makers and policy analysts.

Threshold 3. Preparing for Political Participation: Entrepreneurs endeavor to turn the energy of the movement away from movement building actions and toward the political process, focusing on development of political endorsements and other power resources.

Stage 4. Political Participation

Social movement organizations engage the political process as advocates for particular policy positions. They exhort their members to exercise their personal sphere of influence through lobbying on policy questions and participating in the electoral process.

Threshold 4. Staying Power: Political Success or Failure: Having had its first trial by fire in the political process, (a) if defeated, the movement must labor to reestablish its lost momentum, keep movement adherents on board, and prevent "freefall" of the movement past the previous stage 3 back to stage 1 or 2; (b) if successful, movement organizations must be partially transformed to lobbying institutions that work to secure and protect this and subsequent victories at the same time as it mobilizes adherents for the next political contest.

Stage 5. Defeat: Regroup, reassess, and rebuild

The social movement, having survived the defeat, must now decide on the causes for failure and choose whether to return to movement building, hopefully still at the education stage, or how, when and where to reengage the political process.

or

Stage 5. Success. Monitoring/Maintenance

The social movement seeks to reassure reticent officials and other policy makers of the legitimacy and safety of policy changes along lines articulated by the movement, and monitor policy evolution in an effort to keep it from falling back to previous forms.

movement leaders began to assess the receptivity of essential networks—specifically the Congress, experts, and the national media—to a grassroots anti-nuclear war movement. Although the response was lukewarm in all three institutions, there was enough positive feedback for the SMOs to move forward to the early movement-building stage. (In the first half of 1981, only one major story was carried in the national media predicting a resurgence of the anti-nuclear war movement, a *New York Times* magazine story by Wade Greene, who worked as an advisor to part of the liberal funding community.)

The failure to carefully analyze the openness of the Congress to an anti-nuclear war movement at this stage would later prove to be a fatal error for the movement. The door to Congress was partially open at this time, but never really opened any further. Only in the media and the expert community did the doors open widely later on.

Stage 2. Early Movement: Activation Occurs

In the early stage of this new movement, there was plenty of room for organizations to pursue their own agendas with relatively little duplication of effort or conflict. Tentative efforts in the fall of 1981 to unite the movement were unsuccessful. The principal initial task was to broaden the audience and deepen public awareness of the state of the

threat posed by nuclear weapons—the threat of nuclear war. Because there had been no large-scale organized public opposition to nuclear weapons in many years—most particularly in the years immediately preceding President Reagan's election—the groups found themselves working relatively untilled ground. The threat posed by nuclear war and nuclear weapons was painted with a broad brush in this early stage, as were individual issues that arose, such as the Freeze or eliminating the M-X mobile ICBM. Where disagreements did occur within and between SMOs, there was little pressure for resolution, so these issues went unresolved.

Although the movement was expanding rapidly in terms of numbers of people and organizations involved, it had not yet achieved legitimacy as a movement in the media or in Washington, D.C. Despite the best effort of UCS, Ground Zero, Physicians for Social Responsibility and others, the anti-nuclear war movement was still a political sideshow. However, this changed abruptly in the first half of 1982.

Threshold 2. Take-Off: Legitimation of the Movement as a Movement

The anti-nuclear movement reached the take-off stage early in 1982. Among the critical events in that period was the publication of Jonathan Schell's *Fate of the Earth*. Schell's reputation among fellow journalists had been established by his early reporting on the Vietnam war. His declaration that the nuclear peril was *the* "fate of the earth" issue in a series of *New Yorker* articles that later were collected in the book of the same name opened the floodgates of media coverage on the issue. Within two months, *Time* and *Newsweek* carried major cover stories on the issue, and by April it was the focus of other national print and broadcast media as well.

More than any other organization, Ground Zero was positioned to take advantage of these developments. It had set out in the spring of 1981 to put on an "Earth Day-like" event on nuclear war in mid-April 1982, and by early 1982 it had the national headquarters staff and a skeleton national organization on which a national event could be constructed. As the "only game in town" in the spring of 1982, Ground Zero found it easy to persuade other local and national anti-nuclear war organizations to channel their spring activities into the Ground Zero Week framework.

Despite the breadth of the Ground Zero Week event—week-long activities in over 1,000 U.S. cities—and the extensive coverage it received in the national media, elected officials still were reticent about the political viability and policy virtues of the arms control message it contained. Although somewhat more active, the experts community was still not pressing hard on policy makers to change established policy. However, thousands of new movement adherents joined anti-nuclear war SMOs and otherwise offered support for the movement.

Although some funders had been giving assistance to anti-nuclear war groups for over a year, including the New World Foundation and the Rockefeller Family Fund, it was not until after the nationwide week of educational activity sponsored by Ground Zero that the more conservative end of the liberal funding community joined in to support the movement.

Stage 3. "Expanding the Circle" and Problems with Education

Thanks to broad media coverage of the nuclear war issue and the active promotional efforts of local peace groups, especially those associated with the Freeze campaign, by the fall of 1982 the movement was rapidly expanding its membership into the middle ground of society, encompassing groups and individuals who historically had not been involved in anti-war activities or other liberal causes.

The first major problems began to occur within the movement as the anti-nuclear war SMOs sought to move citizens rapidly through an education phase toward political participation, most particularly on the Freeze issue. (Virtually all anti-nuclear SMOs claim to be non-partisan educational organizations, in part to protect their non-profit status with the Internal Revenue Service, but only a very few take the idea of education seriously.) At this point, some groups (including some elements within the flagship national Freeze campaign) argued for a more protracted and thorough education phase. They identified three priorities for the movement:

1. Intelligent and persuasive *arguments* for a broad variety of changes in policy that could be articulated to elected officials in one-way communication;

2. *Responses* to the countermovement arguments being made with increasing effectiveness by the Reagan administration and traditional conservatives.

3. *Education to strengthen the commitment of movement adherents* for what was anticipated to be a lengthy battle, i.e., "staying power."

It was clear to many movement leaders that it was unlikely that the experts community was going to spontaneously and radically argue for alteration of the course of U.S. nuclear policy as it had been practiced in the United States for over two decades. Moreover, the state, in the form of the Reagan administration and Republican majority in the Senate, was strongly committed to policies that ran directly counter to the movement.

Because of the passion in the Freeze movement, the elegant simplicity of the Freeze proposal, and the general inclination of Americans to favor action over learning, those who argued for a longer education phase lost, and the stage was either bypassed or given only token attention as the movement pushed forward. As a result, at both the national and local levels, organizations and individuals with widely divergent "Nuclear IQs" battled constantly on issues of strategy and tactics on the Freeze resolution as well as other issues. At the same time, they were competing for (1) funds and time from individuals, (2) institutional financial support, (3) media coverage, and (4) the designation of leadership of the movement. Such differences were not in themselves fatal to the movement. However, the failure to resolve these differences exacerbated the problems when the movement was carried too rapidly into the political participation phase. Then it became apparent that movement adherents were not sufficiently educated or committed on key issues to sustain the movement when it "bounced off" the policy-making system.

Threshold 3. Preparation for Political Participation

Although there were a number of other concerns of the anti-nuclear war movement, eventually the proposal for a "bilateral nuclear weapons freeze" emerged as the movement centerpiece and focus. The national Freeze campaign was doing everything it could to prepare its members emotionally and organizationally for participation in the political process, but there was only a limited effort made to educate them to the possible counterarguments they would encounter from members of Congress and their staffs and from Freeze opponents. Even more important, little groundwork was being done within the political system itself. Thus, the Freeze proposal was pressed on the Congress prematurely—before the members of Congress had a chance to work through the possible ramifications of such a proposal for national security and how these ramifications would be viewed by constituents back home in their districts.

The experts were moving forward more rapidly, with many well-known arms control figures, including former SALT negotiators and luminaries such as Robert McNamara and McGeorge

Bundy, giving cautious endorsement to the Freeze proposal. However, the administration remained strongly opposed to the Freeze proposal itself, countering that (1) despite its demand for a "bilateral" nuclear weapons Freeze, it was implicitly unilateral, (2) it tied the hands of the administration in strategic security matters and arms control negotiations, and (3) it fell short of the administration's own goal of cutting, not freezing, nuclear weapons levels, arguments that played well with grassroots constituents and the Congress.

Stage 4. Premature Entry into Political Participation

Deprived of the necessary educational preparation that would have enabled them to be more effective in conflict with an administration and Congress that resisted their views, movement adherents and those elements of the state they had captured (principally the Democratic side in the Congress and the 1984 Democratic presidential ticket) proved unable to respond adequately on key policy questions (e.g., verification) raised by their detractors. Movement adherents were also poorly prepared to respond to the uncertainties and queries posed by open and uncommitted policy makers and ordinary citizens concerned about war and peace issues.

With the movement's headlong drive toward political engagement in Congress, movement adherents lost the battle to win over uncommitted citizens and policy makers. In frustration with the complexities of technical issues, many movement advocates had no alternative but to focus all their energies on the highly touted but ill-fated Freeze resolution, or the impregnable but highly visible fortress of the Reagan defense budget. They had no effective response to the oft-asked "What About the Russians?" question, or queries about verification and Soviet cheating on past treaties. Unable to achieve their grand goals or even their modest ones, unschooled in the Clausewitzian order of political battle, and uncertain as to how long and difficult the battle was sure to be, many movement adherents quit the battlefield to return to their homes and inactivity or to less technical and more accessible local issues.

The result was the movement was able to have only a limited impact on any of the major policy issues to which it gave primary attention: (1) the Freeze resolution that passed the House and failed in the Senate was a diluted version of what had been sought, and it was seen by the media and most political observers as a major loss for the movement; (2) the M-X missile was built, albeit to date only for silo, not mobile, deployment; (3) the defense budget approved by the Congress rose dramatically from 1982 to 1986; and (4) the budget for the president's SDI program was reduced but still grew dramatically during this period. Arms talks in Geneva were revived, and there was some indication that this was in response to grassroots pressures from the country's anti-nuclear war movement. However, little progress was made before the October 1986 summit in Iceland.

Threshold 4. Movement Collapse in the Face of Political Failure

With the failure of the Congressional Freeze resolution, the anti-nuclear war movement went into a tailspin. In its rejection of the Freeze resolution, the movement perceived the Congress as sending a message to the movement and its grassroots adherents not unlike that of the previous two decades—leave the business of national security to us—you just do not understand it well enough to participate in the serious decision making.

There was a feeble attempt to revive the movement with a Freeze Voter '84 campaign in the 1984 Congressional elections, but it had only isolated success. As a result, the movement became fractionated, and individual SMOs shrunk to 1/10 their former size in terms of budgets and numbers of active local members.

In this period, two new movements developed to draw adherents and funding away from the anti-nuclear war movement—the citizen diplomacy movement, which sought to build bridges

between the U.S. and Soviet people at the grassroots, and Central America. Across the country, local chapters of ESR, PSR, Ground Zero, and random peace groups turned their attention to one or the other of these issues.

Stage 5. A Movement Becalmed: Failure in the Maintenance Stage

When the media declared that the Freeze movement had failed, and there appeared to be little success in holding back the continued Reagan defense expansion in the face of indifferent approaches to arms control with the Soviet Union, from 1985 onward the anti-nuclear war movement became becalmed. Many of the more policy-oriented SMOs such as the Federation of American Scientists and Union of Concerned Scientists turned their attention exclusively to the president's Strategic Defense Initiative (SDI) or "Star Wars" proposal.

Ground Zero closed its Washington, D.C. office and moved its operations, which now consisted largely of supplying educational materials to schools, to Portland, Oregon. Educators for Social Responsibility and the Freeze campaign saw most of their local organizations fold or shrink dramatically. Local movement adherents turned their attention briefly to Star Wars and the Nuclear Test Ban Treaty, but the majority moved on to other issues. Only the Center for Defense Information among the major organizations continued to have a major public education program, although that program did not have a major outreach component.

Nuclear arms control was a non-issue in the 1986 elections, and in 1987 two of the largest organizations in the movement—the Freeze and SANE—merged. Meanwhile, *Nuclear Times,* the most widely circulated movement journal, despite its best cheerleading efforts, carried the tone of an exhausted movement. Although the skeleton of the movement remained in place, and despite the merger, by the end of 1987 it was far weaker than it had been at any time since 1981.

Conclusions

The principal conclusion from applying threshold theory to the anti-nuclear war movement is that a successful movement must sequentially pass through the stages of agitation/activation, education, and political participation. The role of timing as the movement "moves" between the various stages of evolution is important, and the evolution of the movement needs to be coordinated with changes in perspective within the expert community. Our study also highlights the critical importance of the "education" stage (which is absent from the classical model of movement evolution), especially where there is a significant informational or technical component to policy.

In addition to passing through these stages, the social movement must "capture" a credible segment of the media, the experts community, and the state, and it must establish its legitimacy with these organizations. Some commitment from a segment of all these organizations must be sustained through the *monitoring/maintenance* stage, to the point where it can be "left to the experts" and the people in the social movement energy can rest or go elsewhere.

Good relations with different organizations are critical in different stages of the movement's development. Good relations with segments of the media are especially important in the *activation* stage, where they are the best communications "medium" for the message that "the status quo is getting out of hand," and other essential promotional functions.

The "experts community" or "priesthood" (both publicly recognized and accepted experts and anonymous experts inside the community) plays important roles in three stages of movement development. In the *education* stage, their role, at a minimum, is to translate key concepts and technical issues into lay terms and to "draw the circle wider." They must look at legitimate alternative policy options, assuring lay persons that they *can* know as much (and sometimes more) as the president and those senators know when they make decisions. Second, in the *political participation and engagement* stage, experts can reassure

reticent elected officials and other policy makers of the legitimacy and safety of policy changes along lines articulated by the movement. Finally, in the *monitoring/maintenance* stage, experts can support the commitment of the men and women of the state to sustaining policy changes.

The movement also must establish good relations with parts of the state, in particular with elected officials or high-ranking administrators in significant positions of authority. State authorities are especially important in the *political participation and engagement stage,* where they can form the core of risk-taking advocates of new policy initiatives. In the *monitoring/maintenance* stage, they can "set the sails" of policy and monitor policy evolution, to keep it from falling back to previous forms, or sound the alert as unanticipated threats to achieving policy objectives emerge.

Our study also identifies some of the reasons for the failure of movements that depend on experts and education. First, the requirement for an education stage in expert-dependent social movements leads to SMO specialization that can create intramovement competition, not cooperation. Specialization can also foster premature political participation and engagement, which may doom the movement.

Second, the experts' support of the movement may be weak. National anti-nuclear war groups were able to capture a segment of the expert community, but these experts were unable to share the peace groups' enthusiasm for the centerpiece of the movement—the formal Nuclear Weapons Freeze resolution. As a result, the experts went their own way, without the active support of the movement—and vice versa. However, it is worth noting that many experts were energized to reexamine both the underlying assumptions of existing policy, such as the theory of deterrence, and the basic policies themselves.

Another cause of the failure of peace movements that are dependent on experts and education is that local anti-nuclear war groups prefer touting a cause to organizing an educational program. They are unaccustomed to conducting educational programs, are unfamiliar with the structure and details of policy debates, and are highly dependent on national organizations to establish agendas. These factors make the local peace groups highly susceptible to premature political involvement, and inadequate attention is given to education and learning. On the positive side, local anti-nuclear war groups are able to cooperate somewhat more among each other than national peace groups. But to date, they still cooperate far less than would be necessary to expand the circle of people currently involved to the point where the movement could achieve its goals.

References

Barkan, Steven E. 1979. "Strategic, Tactical and Organizational Dilemmas of the Protest Movement Against Nuclear Power." *Social Problems* 27 (Oct.): 19–37.

Blumer, Herbert. 1969. "Social Movements," in Barry McLaughlin, ed., *Studies in Social Movements,* New York: The Free Press.

Clark, Peter B. and James Q. Wilson. 1961. "Incentive Systems: A Theory of Organizations." *Administrative Science Quarterly* 6 (Sept.): 219–66.

Edney, Julian J. 1980. "The Commons Problem: Alternative Perspectives." *American Psychologist* 35 (February): 131–50.

Freeman, Jo. 1979. "Resource Mobilization and Strategy," in Zald and McCarthy: 167–89.

Freeman, Jo, ed. 1983. *Social Movements in the Sixties and Seventies.* New York: Longman.

Gamson, William. 1982. *The Strategy of Social Protest.* Homewood, IL: Dorsey.

Gamson, William, B. Fireman, and S. Rytina. 1982. *Encounters with Unjust Authority.* Homewood, IL: Dorsey.

Gerlach, L. and V. Hine. 1970. *People, Power, Change.* New York: Bobbs-Merrill.

Herzberg, Frederick, B. Mauser, and B. Snydeman. 1959. *The Motivation to Work.* New York: Wiley.

Jenkins, J. Craig. 1983. "Resource Mobilization Theory and the Study of Social Movements." *American Review of Sociology* 9: 527–53.

Killian, Lewis M. 1984. "Organization, Rationality and Spontaneity in the Civil Rights Movement." *American Sociological Review* 49: 770–83.

Lang, Kurt and Gladys Engel Lang. 1961. *Collective Dynamics.* New York: Thomas Y. Crowell.

Maslow, Abraham. 1982. "A Theory of Human Needs." *Psychological Review* 80: 545–70.

McAdam, Doug. 1982. *Political Process and the Development of Black Insurgency, 1930–1970.* Chicago: University of Chicago Press.

McCarthy, John and Mayer N. Zald. 1977. "Resource Mobilization and Social Movements." *American Journal of Sociology* 82: 1212–41.

Moe, Terry M. 1981. "Toward a Broader View of Interest Groups." *Journal of Politics* 43: 531–43.

Molander, Earl A. 1980. *Responsive Capitalism.* New York: McGraw-Hill.

Molander, Earl A. 1987. "An Equilibrium Theory to Explain Development of the Anti-Nuclear Movement of the 1980s." Accepted for presentation at annual meetings of the American Sociological Association, Chicago, IL, August 17–21.

Molander, Earl A. and Roger C. Molander. 1987. "Social Movement Builiding in Expert-Dependent Issue Areas." Paper accepted for presentation at the annual meetings of the American Political Science Association, Chicago, IL, September 4.

Molander, Earl A. and Theo Brown. 1987. "The Risks of Capitalist-Style Entrepreneurship in Citizen Diplomacy: A Case Study." Paper accepted for presentation at the annual meetings of the International Society of Political Psychology, San Francisco, CA, July 4–6.

Morris, Aldon. 1981. "Black Southern Student Sit-In Movement: an Analysis of Internal Organization." *American Sociological Review* 46: 744–67.

Olson, Mancur. 1968. *The Logic of Collective Action.* New York: Schocken.

Rogers, M. 1974. "Instrumental and Infraresources." *American Journal of Sociology* 79: 1418–33.

Tilly, Charles. 1978. *From Mobilization to Revolution.* Reading, MA: Addison-Wesley.

Turner, Ralph H. and Lewis M. Killian. 1972. *Collective Behavior.* Englewood Cliffs, NJ: Prentice-Hall.

Walker, Jack L. 1983. "The Origin and Maintenance of Interest Groups in America." *American Political Science Review* 77: 390–406.

Zald, Mayer N. and Roberta Ash. 1966. "Social Movement Organizations: Growth, Decay and Change." *Social Forces* 44: 327–41.

Zald, Mayer N. and John D. McCarthy. 1979. *The Dynamics of Social Movements.* Cambridge, MA: Winthrop.

Statement of the International Physicians for the Prevention of Nuclear War

It is difficult for us, as physicians, to describe adequately the human suffering that would ensue a nuclear war. Hundreds of thousands would suffer third-degree burns, multiple crushing injuries and fractures, hemorrhage, secondary infection, and combinations of all of these. When we contemplate disasters, we often assume that abundant medical resources and personnel will be available. But contemporary nuclear war would inevitably destroy hospitals and other medical facilities, kill and disable most medical personnel, and prevent surviving physicians from coming to the aid of the injured because of widespread radiation dangers. The hundreds of thousands of burned and otherwise wounded people would not have any medical care as we now conceive of it: no morphine for pain, no intravenous fluids, no emergency surgery, no antibiotics, no dressings, no skilled nursing, and little or no food or water. The survivors will envy the dead.

It is known from the Japanese experience that in the immediate aftermath of an explosion, and for many months thereafter, the survivors suffer not only from their physical injuries—radiation sickness, burns, and other trauma—but also from profound psychological shock caused by their exposure to such overwhelming destruction and mass death. The problem is social as well as individual. The social fabric upon which human existence depends would be irreparably damaged.

Those who did not perish during the initial attack would face serious—even lifelong—dangers. Many exposed persons would be at increased risk, throughout the remainder of their lives, of leukemia and a variety of malignant tumors. The risk is emotional as well as physical. Tens of thousands would live with the fear of developing cancer or of transmitting genetic defects, for they would understand that nuclear weapons, unlike conventional weapons, have memories—long, radioactive memories. Children are known to be particularly susceptible to most of these effects. Exposure of fetuses would result in the birth of children with small head size, mental retardation, and impaired growth and development. Many exposed persons would develop radiation cataracts and chromosomal aberrations. . . .

Nuclear war would be the ultimate human and environmental disaster. The immediate and long-term destruction of human life and health would be on an unprecedented scale, threatening the very survival of civilization.

The threat of its occurrence is at a dangerous level and is steadily increasing. But even in the absence of nuclear war, invaluable and limited resources are being diverted unproductively to the nuclear arms race, leaving essential human, social, medical, and economic needs unmet.

For these reasons, physicians in all countries must work toward the prevention of nuclear war and for the elimination of all nuclear weapons. Physicians can play a particularly effective role because they are dedicated to the prevention of illness, care of the sick and protection of human life; they have special knowledge of the problems of medical response in nuclear war; they can work together with their colleagues without regard to national boundaries; and they are educators who have the opportunity to inform themselves, their colleagues in the health professions, and the general public.

What Physicians Can Do to Prevent Nuclear War

- Review available information on the medical implications of nuclear weapons, nuclear war and related subjects.

- Provide information by lectures, publications and other means to the medical and related professions and to the public on the subject of nuclear war.

- Bring to the attention of all concerned with public policy the medical implications of nuclear weapons.

- Seek the cooperation of the medical and related professions in all countries for these aims.

- Develop a resource center for education on the dangers of nuclear weapons and nuclear war.

- Encourage studies of the psychological obstacles created by the unprecedented destructive power of nuclear weapons which prevent realistic appraisal of their dangers.

- Initiate discussion of development of an international law banning the use of nuclear weapons similar to the laws which outlaw the use of chemical and biological weapons.

- Encourage the formation in all countries of groups of physicians and committees within established medical societies to pursue the aims of education and information on the medical effects of nuclear weapons.

- Establish an international organization to coordinate the activities of the various national medical groups working for the prevention of nuclear war.

Kiwis Just Say "No!"

Jason Salzman

When David Lange became prime minister of New Zealand in 1984, the Labour Party leader kept a campaign promise: He declared the nation a nuclear-free zone.

Not long afterward, the Reagan administration asked Lange for permission to dock a nuclear-capable warship, the USS *Buchanan,* in Auckland harbor. Lange asked for assurances that the *Buchanan* would not be carrying nuclear weapons. Reagan refused to reassure him. So, early in 1985, Lange announced that the warship would not be allowed to visit New Zealand. The prime minister added, however, that he would welcome a vessel he knew not to be nuclear-armed or nuclear-powered.

And so the trouble began. By adhering to a long-held policy of not divulging, even to close allies, which U.S. ships carry nuclear weapons, the Reagan administration collided with New Zealand. The small South Pacific nation, with 3.2 million people and 70 million sheep, suddenly became a leader in the growing international movement against the nuclear arms race.

Stunned by the country's bold antinuclear stand, Reagan halted all military exercises and most intelligence-sharing with New Zealand. Then, in August 1986, after Lange refused to change his position, the U.S. terminated the ANZUS alliance, a 35-year-old mutual defense pact among New Zealand, the U.S., and Australia. Secretary of State George Shultz said that by banning nuclear ships from its ports New Zealand had "walked off the job," and therefore the U.S. would no longer consider itself obligated to defend its old ally.

Lange maintains that ANZUS is a conventional, not a nuclear, defense pact; thus, New Zealand's nuclear-ship ban has not violated the treaty. He asks why two democratic nations cannot tolerate differences of opinion and emphasizes that his country's stand is anti-nuclear, not anti-American.

"New Zealand does not ask, nor do we expect, to be defended by nuclear weapons," the 44-year-old Lange has said. "We would never ask an ally to defend us by annihilating the planet."

The hostility toward and rejection of nuclear weapons by the United States' allies has been labeled a "nuclear allergy" by the Reagan administration. In a variation on the domino theory, the administration argues that if the U.S. allows New Zealand to ban nuclear weapons, other U.S. allies with strong grassroots anti-nuclear movements—Japan, Australia, Britain, West Germany—would be more likely to reject them as well. "It would be a tragedy for freedom and Western values for the policy of New Zealand to spread," Shultz said when ANZUS was disbanded.

Lange is portrayed abroad as the prime mover behind his country's acute case of nuclear allergy. But a persistent and well-organized grassroots anti-nuclear movement has been gaining momentum in New Zealand over the past 10 years, a motivating element in Lange's decision to confront the United States.

According to Deputy Prime Minister Geoff Palmer, New Zealanders are particularly sensitive to the danger of nuclear war, a legacy of the nuclear testing that has been conducted in the South Pacific since World War II. More than 200 nuclear explosions have shaken the area, and Palmer says that the testing has fomented anti-nuclear sentiments.

New Zealanders worry in particular about France's testing program at Mururoa Atoll in French Polynesia, northeast of New Zealand. France has exploded 110 nuclear weapons there since 1966, and plans to continue its testing (which was conducted above ground until 1974) indefinitely. In 1973, New Zealand protested the French tests by dispatching a naval frigate to Mururoa to monitor the explosions.

When the vessel returned from its mission, an Anglican priest and anti-nuclear activist named George Armstrong reasoned that if the government could send ships to protest French nuclear tests at Mururoa, the people of New Zealand could use boats to protest the visits of nuclear warships to Auckland, the nation's largest port.

Beginning in 1976, Armstrong and hundreds of other protesters on yachts, motorboats, and surfboards circled British and U.S. warships as they entered Auckland harbor. Calling themselves "Peace Squadrons," these seaborne protesters have provided an uncomfortable greeting for the nuclear ships that have visited Auckland since then.

"The Pacific Ocean has a special importance to us," says Armstrong. "The waters of the Pacific carry images of peace and health. One of the most ghastly things any government can do is bring nuclear warships here."

Pictures of small, colorful boats resisting gray or black submarines and cruisers spread across New Zealand. Inspired, activists began protesting warship visits at other ports.

■

From 1982 to 1984, record numbers of people filled New Zealand's streets to protest the arrival of nuclear ships. The largest of these demonstrations occurred when the USS *Texas* came to New Zealand during Hiroshima week in 1983. Some 30,000 people (the equivalent of more than 2.2 million in the U.S.) marched in Auckland.

Meanwhile, the anti-nuclear movement entered another arena. In 1981 a number of peace groups—led by the New Zealand Nuclear Free Zone Committee, based in Christchurch—began a campaign to persuade city and county councils to proclaim their districts nuclear free. The goal was to establish as many nuclear-free zones as possible by the 1984 elections. As the anti-nuclear movement swelled, many local councils that had at first rejected the resolutions reversed themselves. The Auckland Regional Council, for example, passed a nuclear-free-zone resolution in 1983 by a vote of 22 to 10. The same council had rejected an identical resolution a year earlier by 23 to 9.

"Such was the magnitude of public opinion that if councillors did not endorse the nuclear-free-zone concept, they were likely to be in trouble in the elections," says Wallace Rowling, New Zealand's ambassador to the United States. Today, 72 percent of all New Zealanders live in locally declared nuclear-free zones, the largest percentage of any nation in the world.

Responding to grassroots pressure from an array of constituencies, New Zealand's Labour Party pledged to declare the entire country a nuclear-free zone if elected. Four smaller parties made the same promise. Only the governing National Party, which had been in power for eight years, said it would allow nuclear ships to continue visiting.

■

Labour politicians say that their 17-seat victory in the 1984 election (the country has a 95-seat unicameral parliament) resulted both from Lange's commitment to the nuclear-free policy and from his promises to bolster the nation's sagging economy. Former Prime Minister Robert Muldoon acknowledges that his National Party's nuclear policy "might have played some part" in Labour's victory, but adds that voters were also "tired of me as prime minister" and were looking for new solutions to economic problems.

New Zealand's anti-nuclear stand is a signal to grassroots organizers overseas that governments can be made to respond to public pressure, according to Larry Ross, director of the free-zone committee. "Significant numbers of people in the

United States and Europe, majorities in some cases, support anti-nuclear initiatives," he says. "New Zealand is the first country in the Western Alliance where people's anti-nuclear sentiments are reflected in government policy. I think others will follow our lead."

Ross recognizes, however, that New Zealand's organizers have had it easier than their counterparts overseas: Theirs is a country with a small population, without major military bases or a defense industry. But Ross says that New Zealand's nuclear-free stand is particularly significant because his country and America have so much in common, including language, democratic traditions, and colonial history. "New Zealand is a friend telling the United States to take another look at its nuclear policies," says Ross. "Because we are so much like you, Reagan cannot categorize New Zealand as he does other anti-nuclear countries."

The Reagan administration's harsh and unexpected response to their nuclear-free policy has left some New Zealanders shaken. By disbanding ANZUS, Reagan has forced New Zealanders to choose between their alliance with the U.S. and the nuclear-ship ban. Polls show that about 70 percent of the population want both, and there is an even split of opinion as to which should be sacrificed.

Those who favor a return to ANZUS, with port visits by nuclear ships, argue that New Zealand needs U.S. protection and can do more to help prevent nuclear war by remaining within the Western Alliance. "Looking at it in hard reality, we can't defend ourselves," says Terry O'Cain, director of the Plains Club, one of a number of pro-ANZUS groups that has formed recently. "If the Soviets see that we're part of an alliance with the United States, they won't dare invade. Now we are isolated from our Western allies, and we have absolutely no influence over their actions. We've thrown away any chance we had to help stop the nuclear arms race."

The National Party has promised to reverse Lange's nuclear policy if it wins the next election, scheduled to take place by October. "We've lost friends around the world thanks to this government's policy," says Muldoon. "The people of New Zealand want a government that will restore their reputation."

But Canterbury University sociologist Kevin Clements, who recently completed a study of New Zealanders' attitudes on defense and security issues, says that the nuclear-ship ban is a manifestation of the country's emerging Pacific identity. "New Zealanders don't want to be America's poodle any longer," he says. "National will not be able to defeat Labour unless it changes its nuclear policies."

"If we lose our ship ban, the international peace movement will take a step backward," says Kate Boanas of the New Zealand Foundation for Peace Studies. "Our work here has succeeded because we've thought globally and acted locally. Now we hope people will act where they are to help us." Accordingly, anti-nuclear groups are asking people overseas to show their support by buying New Zealand products (kiwifruit, lamb, apples, Steinlager beer, orange roughy fish, Corbans wine) to boost the economy and to alleviate fears that the anti-nuclear policy will hurt trade.

As in the U.S., the anti-nuclear movement in New Zealand is connected to a strong environmental ethic. Ambassador Rowling feels that appreciation of his country's natural splendor contributes to the citizenry's aversion to nuclear weapons. "The fact that we live in one of the most beautiful countries in the world gives us a greater determination to say, 'Well, we've been blessed in this sense—therefore we should fight even harder to preserve what we have and share it with others.'"*

*[The Labour government of Prime Minister David Lange won a second three-year term in the election of August 15, 1987—Eds.]

Eco-Pacifism vs. Industrial Society: A New Approach for the Peace Movement

Rudolf Bahro

The New Sounding-Board

Edward Thompson argues that the dominant tendency of the present epoch is exterminism—an impulse towards mass destruction, annihilation and extinction that is generated by our industrial civilization and radiates outwards from it to threaten the whole world.[1] This is a view that I share. Thompson's thesis, in fact, has implications that go far beyond his rejection of the very different definition of our epoch given by Lenin: imperialism as the highest stage of capitalism. For his case radically puts into question that traditional historical optimism for which the very essence of the human species points towards socialism, and not to barbarism, let alone a premature self-destruction.

The basic issue here is whether the course of human evolution has not taken a wrong turn; and it must be conceded that the perspective which has governed the Left up till now does not allow this question to be posed unflinchingly enough. If history is a process with certain immanent laws, and we believe it is, it cannot be accidental that our civilization should generate a tendency towards the self-destruction of its subject as a defining trait of its most recent stage. Rather, such an impulse must have long been inscribed in human nature (conceived as the "ensemble of social relations").

The first precondition for the arms race is, of course, modern industry as such. Exterminism is rooted in the very foundations of this system and its innermost driving forces. Exterminism does not just find expression in nuclear weapons and power stations; it is the quintessence of the whole complex of tools and machines operative on humanity and the planet. Those particular elements within it that bear a different stamp—elements which Illich calls "convivial"—have so far been subordinate to the exterminist principle. Our collective practices break up and destroy natural conditions, degrade energy potentials, suffocate the Earth's surface and isolate human beings from spontaneous energy cycles. The result is inevitably a distortion of both body and mind, whose consequences range from cancer to crime.

It is plain that this impulse to self-destruction is rooted in European industrial capitalism, at least as far as its current acute form is concerned. From 1750 onwards, all the familiar curves of "growth" and pressure on resources start to show the ever more precipitous ascent that heralds a collapse. But the phenomenon has its origins further back than capitalism, and it persists on the other side of capitalism as well. European society had long been preadapted for its capitalist constitution: all its antecedent historical trends, from antiquity onwards, contributed to this outcome. There is a good deal of evidence that the "Fall" took place

In Edward P. Thompson, et al., eds. "Exterminism and the Cold War," *New Left Review,* London. Distributed by Schocken Books, NY 1982.

already with the transition from female-centered societies of gatherers and hunters to patriarchal societies of agriculture and cities (paralleled by nomadism). This transition occurred at so many more or less independent points in time and space that it must necessarily be seen as a historical law—that is, as unavoidably inscribed in the endowment of our species.

In this sense, therefore, our starting-point should not be a *superficial* critique of (contemporary) political economy, but a more *fundamental* critique of human nature itself. This does not mean we should cease to concern ourselves with economics, simply seeking the source of evil in ourselves, in defiance of the whole legacy of the Enlightenment. The impending catastrophe is evidently linked to that social dynamic which has made all written history a history of class struggle[2] and caused the process of human development so far to hurtle forward in limitless material expansion and acceleration.

If this is so, then so long as we continue to see class struggle as the key to the contemporary crisis, we will only remain trapped in the very circle out of which it is imperative to break. Even the goal of socialism shares the same limitation in a decisive respect: it sets our sights on a classless *industrial* society,[3] without stopping to criticize the origins and consequences of industrialism. Traditional socialist analysis has fixed its focal point "too high," in a "base" which is not yet the base—in other words, in "relations of production" instead of "forces of production." Marxism was precisely conceived from the standpoint of the proletariat as the second *industrial* class. In the common field of struggle of *both* contemporary classes, therefore, it seeks only to abolish the deforming processes of exploitation and domination. Almost invariably, we have attacked only the *capitalist* form of our societies, scarcely ever the *industrial* system of capitalism. Since we were unable to do away with capitalism, this neglect has now caught up with us. The "gathering determinism of the exterminist process"[4] is evident enough. With or without a complete explanation of it, we must now orient ourselves to a practical critique of the industrial system and its military spearhead.

Unexpectedly, as it were, red flags are now a minority in demonstrations against nuclear power stations that challenge the very basis on which the traditional labour movement emerged. Wage-labour stands accused not just because it is "abstract" and "alienated," but because its results are in large measure simply deadly. The abolition of at least half the work now performed in the industrialized countries must take unquestioned precedence over the demand for full employment within the industrial system. The same applies to education as to work: education for the industrial system is quite rightly rejected by more and more young people.

No contemporary movement that seeks anything less than a transformation of the entire system, right down to its material and cultural foundations, that attacks only the military programmes, and weapons technologies which exterminism relentlessly and inexorably produces, can achieve anything more than minor modifications or variations of this perverted production. The whole question of human emancipation has taken a new form. The insight that the impulse to obliteration, to the self-extinction of humanity, lies in the very foundations of our industrial civilization and pervades every structure of its economy, science and technology, its political apparatus and its sociology and psychology, is today of such immediate importance that the socialist perspective takes second place, and in any case must be redefined.

Our whole social organism is riddled by the disease of militarism; and just as it seems that cancer can only be cured at the level of the organism as a whole, so we cannot hope to root out militarism, which now consumes resources in the region of £200,000 million per year and transforms these into murderous waste products, without a similarly holistic therapy. "The ultimate dysfunction of humanity: self-destruct"[5] can only be prevented by a movement that goes beyond reactive defence—a movement that actively seeks to live a different life, and to release hitherto obstructed and untapped potentialities of the human species. The concept of exterminism tells us why the peace movement has found an unprecedented new sounding-board in the ecology movement. The connection between the two was not immediately apparent from the start to all of those involved. Those political ecologists who early advocated an integration of the two currents can themselves testify how difficult it often is to link specific campaigns to more far-reaching horizons. Now, however, their labours are bearing fruit, above all because the facts themselves are being forced on people's awareness. Whenever I have spoken on the ecological crisis in recent months, it has been a matter of course that the discussion has moved on to the problems of foreign policy and peace.

The new peace movement is based right from the start on the premise that exterminism is simply the rank outgrowth of a parasite attacking and consuming the tree from root to crown. I too did not at first understand why the ecology movement started by attacking not nuclear weapons, but nuclear power stations and even establishments less harmful than these. I have since come to see the essential condition for its breadth and strength, and above all its potential for victory, in its growth from the bottom upwards. Peace can only thrive in a mental soil quite different from the culture of domination. The humus first needs to form. The abolition of both nuclear weapons and nuclear power is a far stronger demand than the "ban the bomb" slogan of the late 1950s and 1960s, not just because of the addition, but because the new slogan aims deeper. It strikes right at the fundamental exterminist axiom of our misdirected civilization, which is aggressive in its innermost being, based on the principles of expansion and explosion. This response will be all the more effective, the more clearly nuclear power itself is seen as only the most prominent outgrowth of the tumour, which could go on poisoning our social life even if the button is never pressed to unleash the missiles, as in our (I hope) most pessimistic fears.

Even where the ecological movement has not yet found a comprehensive expression, it provides the explanation for the increased strength of the peace movement. In Denmark and Holland the fusion of the two is unmistakeable. It is surreptitiously present even in Britain, although there the close linkage of nuclear disarmament with the more traditional social policies of the Labour Left, a strength in the short run, still impedes its wider extension. I am personally convinced that the potential for a politics of peace on the part of the entire social-democratic, socialist and Eurocommunist left in Western Europe depends on a fundamental modernization of its general strategy.

If these socialist forces do not abandon their traditional union with capitalist industrialism and achieve a radical change in the concept of well-being inherent in it, they will be unable to put up an effective resistance either to the ecological crisis or to the arms race. Such a break with the industrial system is, moreover, a precondition for a settlement with the peoples of the Third and Fourth Worlds. Without "industrial disarmament"—that is, an absolute reduction in global demand for raw materials and energy, and a corresponding technological transformation—it will be possible neither to attain a genuine military disarmament nor to restore the ability of the South to provide itself with adequate means of subsistence. The voracity of our giant machinery cannot do without rapid deployment forces and neocolonial production branches. That is why it reproduces a majority consensus for these as a matter of course. There is no way of avoiding this fatality. We have to embark on a psychological revolution that starts with ourselves, and liberates our politics from the aggressive model of reactive class antagonism that only reinforces and accelerates exterminism.

It goes without saying that an understanding of this connection is not an "entrance condition" for joining the new peace movement, but rather an argument for its prospects. Those opponents of war and armaments who are not yet convinced ecologists can conclude from their own experience that a single-issue peace movement will very probably remain stuck in its tracks. But borne forward by the ecology movement, which is something quite other than a single-issue campaign—it in-

cludes, among other things, the women's movement—but represents rather the beginning of a
general awakening to that new phase of our evolution which alone can promise us any future, it
has a far greater chance of success, as an alliance
of all life-preserving and emancipatory forces.
There is, of course, no guarantee of success, but
so far the attempt is still afloat.

The protection of life is a fundamental principle of infinite scope. Thus the struggle against
war and the arms race is a natural consequence of
an ecological orientation, an organic development
of its basic stance. Here should be the general soil
and sounding-board of the peace movement. The
rescue of the planet and our species requires the
systemic dismantlement of all structures that
threaten life. This principle includes within it the
core of the traditional goals of socialism, even if
the form of these is certainly changed.

Survival, in any case, will mean a very
different way of life. If everything goes on as it
does today, there will indeed be a Third World
War, as the most extreme consequence of the
everyday war against Earth and humanity that is
inseparable from the capitalist industrial system.
We have to generate the mental preparation for a
change in the totality of this system. That will
involve agreement on means and aims, in a common project capable of subordinating the opposing
special interests of all those engaged in it to their
own fundamental and long-run interests.

■ ■ ■

Away With the Blocs!

. . . The present *increase* in East–West tension has
arisen not primarily from the competition between
the two blocs, but rather from contradictions within
the two systems. Hostile depictions of the other
side are nurtured in order to suppress resistance
at home. The arms race is in this sense also a
strategy for the maintenance of power on either

side. Anyone who rejects the consensus of "security
through strength" thus disturbs the basic legitimation of the system of domination. It is very
instructive, again, that Thompson's description of
the complex of interests that underlie the nuclear
arms race in the West coincides entirely with the
findings of Klaus Traube's study of the West German nuclear energy lobby.[6*] The mechanisms involved here are thus quite "normal" ones. Similar
conclusions are likely for the Eastern bloc and the
Soviet Union. Thompson's argument sits perfectly
well with my own analysis of the "anatomy of
actually existing socialism" in *The Alternative in
Eastern Europe.* The capitalist profit motive is only
one specific form in which interests of domination
come to prevail. Certain apologists for the Soviet
Union argue as if no other ruling class but the
bourgeoisie had ever been marked by militarism.

But whatever the internal forces that profit
from the bipolar confrontation between the two
blocs, and have an interest in its reproduction, the
confrontation itself is the precondition for any
profit made out of it and any career that is built on
it. In a society without an external enemy it is
impossible for anyone to make a living out of
weapons production or to seek personal affirmation in the fame of war. This is in itself a trivial
observation, but what it suggests is that confrontation and competition must themselves be abolished if the arms race is to come to an end.

Since the arms race has now reached a
technological level which threatens the mutual
extermination of those states and peoples caught
up in it, there is no other solution but to do away
with bloc confrontation. In previous history, all
such complexes of power as those presently facing
each other in Europe and across the Atlantic have
led to war. This time, another way must be found.
But we cannot hope to find it if we are not prepared
to tailor all our actions to this necessity.

We socialists must understand, above all else,
that the fracture dividing the world, Europe and
Germany into two systems no longer represents
any kind of positive perspective, that it no longer

*[Footnotes have been renumbered because portions of the original work have been deleted—EDS.]

shows any trace of a boundary between revolution and counter-revolution, socialism and anti-socialism, world proletariat and world bourgeoisie—in so far as this ever was the case, at least in a favourable interpretation. This fracture is rather the immediate obstacle to the most radical revolution that humanity has ever needed: its rapid transition to a different basic pattern of civilization, at a time when the present pattern has put the further advance of the human species into question, over the last 200 years.

Further scrutiny only confirms that the confrontation of blocs in the Northern hemisphere, which has generated the arms race, is indeed the number-one world problem—the *general* barrier that prevents a solution of all remaining problems, by both absorbing and perverting the energies and forces needed to resolve them. Unless it is overcome, it will be possible neither to solve the basic social question facing humanity, the tendency towards absolute impoverishment of more than half of its members, nor to restore the balance between civilization and nature.

Of course, each of the two blocs has its own conception as to how their confrontation can be overcome. Somewhat simplified, the Western version is to make the East "capitalist" once again, the Eastern version to make the West "socialist." Both of these concepts are preeminently designed to lead people astray. Neither, in fact, means anything more than an attempt to redeem the evil system on the other side by reshaping it in the image of one's own good system.[7] On occasion it will be conceded that one's own system is not without its faults, and that the other system cannot be compared with it in every particular, but the effect of such provisos is actually to reinforce the principle behind these projections, rather than to dispense with them. In Germany, for instance, we have a whole industry of "system comparison," in which many social scientists are stubbornly engaged.

The first commandment, in coming to grips with the actual reality of the two systems, is to abandon the idea that the other system can be cured or even improved by applying the standards of one's own idealized system. For some socialists in the West, unfortunately, this commandment must be for the time being reversed: to abandon the idea that one's own system can be cured or even improved by applying the standards of the other idealized system. There is *nothing* we can learn or adopt from the *system* over there. The same applies to those on the other side too.

Those who claim a dialectical heritage, in particular, should stop resorting to the idea of a distinction between good and bad elements, as if some kind of organ transplant were possible, for example of an educational or medical system. (In general, the supposed superiorities of the other side are mythological.) Those too weak emotionally to do without a strong homeland far away should at least understand rationally that the trap it represents undermines their entire socialist commitment. The peace movement can only be made up of those ready to break with the justificatory ideologies of *both* blocs.

The network of peace organizations in West Germany still bears the marks of its Cold War origins. There cannot but be problems in integrating the ecology movement and the peace movement, so long as the latter even indirectly sees the Soviet Union as the head of the forces of peace. These problems only increase when this allegiance is concealed, as it would have no influence if it were openly admitted. A new approach for the peace movement based on independence from both blocs requires that we bypass its traditional structures, whatever new forms of organization may be adopted.

I deliberately use the word "structures" here, to refer to traditional organizational connections. We must certainly offer access to individuals, even if they have been involved in these structures and identified with them for a long time. But there is a necessary process of education. Is it not an indisputable experience that if any peace initiative—indeed any initiative in general—favours the interests and intentions of one superpower, no matter how indirectly or even unconsciously for the individuals concerned, it ends up integrated into the logic of exterminism? This applies equally, of course, to any "loyalty to the Atlantic Alliance." Fixation on the "peace-loving Soviet Union" can only damage the mobilization of our people against the arms race, and thus in the last instance even injures the false purpose that underlies it.

Conversely, a negative fixation on only one side also leads into an impasse, as in the case of protest against American aggression in Vietnam, or Soviet aggression in Afghanistan. In particular, we would only follow the logic of deterrence and contribute to the spread of conflict were we to oppose the image of the Soviet Union as the enemy—which the West deploys in its preparations for war—with a similar image of the United States as the enemy. There is no point even in depicting particular representatives of exterminist policies as the enemy; to do so only mystifies the real dangers.

Neither anti-Sovietism nor anti-Americanism! Freedom from both blocs! Thompson notes, as we experience for ourselves every day, that *refusal* of the blocs and their logic is either vehemently attacked as neutralism and pacifism, or scoffed at as an illusion. Neutralism and conscientious objection, however, for all the risks they involve, still remain arrested in a stance of negation, so long as we do not manage to transform such attitudes into a growing political movement that can overthrow the present political and psychological balance of forces. Freedom from blocs, on the other hand, is a positive idea. It clears a space for exploring the possibilities that escape from the logic of blocs might offer.

If the competition for power between the two industrial systems is to be overcome without war, then we must seek a different way for their integration, their convergence, the construction of an order embracing both. The demand for Europe "from Portugal to Poland" to be free from military blocs is thus only an anticipation in foreign policy of a movement for a Third Road that still awaits closer definition. If both systems are simply two sides of the same coin, and their pernicious interaction is no more than the most acute expression of the general crisis of civilization, it follows that any future we may hope for depends on continuing processes of *internal* transformation in both East and West. There is no better home for these than

the ecology movement, in the broadest sense, which by its very nature is not fixated on images or relations of friend and foe.

A different way of life means the restoration of inward and outward balance with nature, the protection of life in every respect, the securing of human rights for the most elementary provision of food, clothing, housing, education, work and leisure, through to guarantees of personal freedom and political participation as indispensable needs of human dignity. This is a programme rising above the conflict of the superpowers and the blocs crystallized around them. Just for that reason it can cross their frontiers without using means of subversion and psychological warfare. It would be the bearer of that new internationalism for which Thompson calls, an attitude and a practice which can be termed alike truly human, planetary, or ecumenical: the sense of each of these terms is becoming increasingly identical.

If the weaker Eastern side in the ideological battle can find no other response than to attribute a practice of this kind to the opposite bloc, it will risk losing its last remaining scrap of credibility vis-à-vis its own population. The suppression of political liberties in the Eastern bloc even damages the inadequate level of official efforts for disarmament and detente. From the standpoint of the interests of humanity it is an ancillary function of exterminism, whatever the external and internal causes that originally generated it. It stifles those energies the peoples of Eastern Europe need for the necessary transformation of their own conditions, which they cannot undertake so long as they do not even enjoy political democracy. The stubborn defamation in the East of projects for reform as "anti-socialist" is the mirror image of the slanderous use that reactionary forces in the West make of the word "communist."

The psychological war between two systems that mutually condition, reinforce and stabilize each another, a war with its rituals of boast and threat, intimidation and adventure, embellishment and vilification, not least of self-deception even when the facts are known—this is the conspiracy that the new peace movement must defeat. However familiar it may be, the peace movement today has a quite new prospect of success, arising from the ground of the ecology movement and aiming not simply at an equal distance from the two superpowers but at an unconditional independence from them. . . .

• • •

For a Nationwide Debate on Security

To summarize the arguments of the last two sections:

1. The idea that the civilization of the industrialized North can be preserved through a balance of terror between the superpowers or military blocs—an idea which underlay detente policies in the 1960s and 1970s—has completely broken down.

2. The logic of contemporary weapons development has led to the perspective of a "limited nuclear war" on our continent.

3. The Eastern bloc countries now exhibit a visibly advanced stage of internal destabilization. The nerves of the bankrupt polit-bureaucracy in this region are wearing thin, and this can lead them to a risky resort to their cudgels. The state of its empire, however, makes any massive invasion of Western Europe impossible, whatever view is taken of Soviet appetite for one. Russian missiles may come, especially if attracted by American ones, but the Russians themselves will not.

Given these three conditions, the entire security policy of Western Europe falls to the ground. All decisions taken since the 1950s must be rethought anew. What is needed now is a comprehensive debate to produce a new definition of our security interests.

The conclusion that directly forces itself upon us is that Europe, including our German homeland, *must not* be armed with nuclear mis-

siles designed to reach the territory of the other superpower, as this only attracts the evil of total destruction. The stationing of these missiles must be prevented at all costs.

Europe, including our German homeland, *cannot* be defended by so-called tactical or battlefield nuclear weapons, as this would mean the certain annihilation of the civilian life to be defended, rather than its protection.

Europe *does not need* nuclear weapons, since there is no real threat of a conventional war of conquest.

What nuclear armaments mean for tomorrow, moreover, is that we are preparing not just for mutual mass murder with the Eastern bloc, but with the entire non-Western world as well. The new security debate must widen out to explore alternative directions for our economy and society in general, if we are not to be set on a collision course with the vital interests of other peoples, as well as with the Earth and its biosphere.

Life depends far more on decisions in this field than it does on such pressing short-run problems as prices, rents and jobs—issues that often crowd in to such an extent that they absorb all public attention and energy. There can scarcely be a single person in this country who would not be *fundamentally* interested in his own and our security, once a civilly conducted debate got under way and the institutions that are supposed to represent society and its subdivisions politically were compelled to do their duty.

Psychological motivation is the key to a new security policy. The promotion of a debate over it falls within the terms not only of the formal constitution of West Germany, but also of its actual constitution—for all the criticism that may be made of it. Neither the mass media nor the political parties, neither parliament nor courts, neither private and public sectors of the economy, nor federal and local government at all levels, are immune to popular influence. The proof can be found in the effect of protests against nuclear power stations, against new international airports, against the consequences of property speculation in the cities. If a popular movement against a new airport can cut right across party divisions, why cannot a similar movement against the military establishment, in favour of conscientious objection of all kinds? It is just that resistance has not yet reached the necessary level of intensity, and above all the necessary ubiquity.

The effect of such a campaign will be all the greater, the more the sweet force of reason prevails in our methods. Peace with nature, peace among nations and individuals, are values and goals unattainable through violence. (I do not of course question the right of both individuals and whole peoples to defend themselves against murderous terror, as recently in Nicaragua, and now in El Salvador.) Happily, it seems to have become accepted on almost all sides that actions should not be directed against the life of political or administrative opponents. It should also be similarly accepted that violence against material objects generally fails in its purpose, unless this purpose is precisely to vent aggression. There will always be someone who has to break a window, or a few people who cannot keep from overturning a car. The problem begins when a strategy is made out of this, and intellectual justifications are produced, instead of addressing those involved as in the recitative from Beethoven's 9th Symphony: "Oh friends, not these tones, but more joyful ones." It is still open to debate whether it might not help things now and again to give a signal by an act of destruction. But this can always be done in a demonstrably non-aggressive and communicative fashion. In that case, symbols will serve equally well. A calculated and fundamental opposition to the status quo can always convey its message to women and men in such a way that not only are the indifferent neutralized or converted, but even the adversary is troubled. As for the mega-machine, anyone who understands what it is made of knows that it cannot be seriously challenged by blowing up a pylon carrying electricity from a nuclear power station, and that it is only exercised and strengthened if people put on helmets and throw Molotov cocktails against it.

I do not rule out—unfortunately no one can rule out—that the great machine might prove so immune to popular influence that the only way to avert general disaster would be outright civil war. But then this would be no act of liberation, simply the penultimate catastrophe. We have not even attempted a fraction of the possibilities that lie between our present concern and that extreme situation. Much depends on the intellectual and moral quality of the pressure we bring to bear on the established institutions. Such pressure will appear pointless only so long as we forget that for all their alienated character these are still staffed by human beings. If we fetishize the apparatuses by lumping together the whole administration and all who perform its functions as the "enemy," then matters will pursue their present destructive course.

Is it still too easily forgotten, or at least not sufficiently heeded, that the proper "target" of our attack is the consciousness of those on the other side. If we make this our explicit aim, then we maximize our chance of influencing those who are undecided, those who waver between listening to us and listening to the enemy. Goliath must be hit on his forehead, the place which his armour doesn't cover. That is the proper way to practise the necessary "love of the enemy." We should even avoid needlessly antagonizing someone like Franz Josef Strauss, but rather work towards a position where we can invite him, listen to him and debate with him without personal abuse. We need to do this in every town and every village in the country.

Exterminism does not divide society into social classes of the traditional kind. Certainly, classes still retain their influence, but exterminism rather divides society into servants (active and passive) and opponents (or victims) of the megamachine. The decisive demarcation is which of these roles predominates in each particular individual. We shall not be saved, therefore, by a small and sham-radical protest movement which is sometimes itself destructive, often still echoes the great machine and drives the majority over to the other side by the anxiety it inspires, but rather by a politics which aims at the divide between the two souls that exist in each person's breast, and seeks to release their energies by widening it.

There is no possibility of defeating exterminism except in the minds of the exterminists. Please don't laugh: there are far more people in the governing cliques than the handful of self-proclaimed "hawks." Not the least of these, moreover, are those ambitious physicists given charge of various murderous projects. Certain "fighters for peace," on the other hand, themselves belong among the exterminists—those not prepared to see the beam in their own eye, the crimes of those good, brave battalions with which they identify. We should never forget how much we are ourselves still trapped in the worship of idols, both with and without realizing it.

At the risk of labouring the point: we shall only defeat exterminism if we can make inroads into its own elites, far beyond the periodic "treason" of a few individuals. Is there really only ever one General Bastian?* Without a scission in the elites, we shall fail to stay the spontaneous march of the mega-machine. What other way is there, given that we shall find it hard to get near the death-dealing buttons ourselves and switch them off?

To preempt misunderstanding: what I have in mind is totally different from the tactic of paper petitions to governments and parliaments, which feed the fatal illusion that we can do our duty by delegating our responsibilities to institutions which are by their very nature incapable of bearing them. The former British diplomat Ronald Higgins, in his excellent popular book *The Seventh Enemy,* has shown very accurately that nothing can be expected of those in government, where all kinds of special interests, no matter how sinister, exert greater real pressure than the long-run vital interests of the great majority that are now jeopardized by the impending catastrophe.

Campaigns such as those around the Berlin housing squats, the Frankfurt and Munich II airports, as well as the Brokdorf nuclear power plant, show *in nuce* the only way in which the great machine can be forced to something like an adequate response—that is, by actions of such scale that the interest in question is brought to the

head of the agenda for the sake of the system's own stability. It is only thus that the more alert and conscientious elements within the apparatuses will find any opportunity of expressing their sensibility, normally blocked by everyday political routines and the pressures of special interest groups.

In short, transactions are possible with the state and its institutions without absorption or recuperation, if there exists a genuinely autonomous movement in the country, which is not a reflection of its governing structures. The problem is how to promote such a non-violent popular uprising directed at the minds of its opponents. The spread of information and understanding, forms of communication that transcend existing barriers and fears of contact, are the most important services we can provide our society and ourselves. . . .

. . .

Some Points on Steps and Methods

Finally, how could we proceed, how must we proceed—assuming that we are more or less in agreement over both our goal and the political and psychological preconditions for achieving it? The latter, as we have seen, must include: readiness for action "at the face," a break with the logic of blocs, rejection of foe imagery, an attempt to communicate even with the adversary, a search for allies in the apparatus, including its central instances, and commitment to change in the framework of legality, including change in the orientation of the institutions themselves.

First and foremost, we must realize how far our possibilities depend on ourselves, on changing ourselves for the task in hand, on a new adaptation to it as our goal and means, on our positive action. For it *is* possible to prevent the deployment of Euro-strategic nuclear missiles in our country. It *is* possible to achieve the withdrawal of those "tactical" nuclear weapons that are already in place. It

---

*[General Bastian was a German general who joined the peace movement—EDS.]

is possible to establish an independent Western Europe, with a particular type of freedom from the blocs. It *is* possible, in this European context, to alter the whole position of this partial German state in world politics, and thus put the national question in a new perspective. It *is* possible to influence the development of the other German state in a constructive, unarrogant and unchauvinistic way, without the intention of remodelling things there according to the fashion here.

Second, we must acquaint ourselves in an all-round way with the fundamental structures of military and industrial exterminism. This great subject, which includes also the hunger and poverty of the South, should have a particular claim on our time. Each one of us must be in a position to provide concrete refutations of those who manipulate public opinion, to expose their tricks and enlighten those whom they seek to manipulate.

Third, what we learn in this way must be propagated in every conceivable way: that is, it must be transformed into well-drafted addresses to people. The mass media are the crucial nerve center here, for us as for others. In this respect, especially, we have to break out of the ghetto of the left. No local paper is too small or too reactionary for our intervention. Nor can we afford to ignore the Springer press itself, unless we want to cripple our own capacity for communication; we may often need to expose and rebut it, but we can also make selective use of it—even this branch of the media is not impervious! The current international danger and the failure of official security policy is all too apparent. There is no journalist, of whatever stripe, who cannot and must not be morally forced to rethink his opinions on the subjects that concern us. Many of them indeed want to be forced to "get something in." Articles or readers' letters can still have an effect even if they are not published. The need is to find a way of expressing ourselves that cannot be sidestepped.

Fourth, we must organize debates, preferably in manageable groups rather than large halls, where representatives of the other side are actually present. In such debates, the mechanisms of anxiety and projection described by Horst Eberhard Richter should not just be repressed, but actually worked through. Given the new situation, it is possible to bring the argument to a head and redirect people's anxiety. When it comes to the crunch, it is not just the launching-ramps that are targets for incoming missiles; so are all other military establishments, as well as every significant factory and traffic intersection, and our own nuclear defences would carve empty holes for the other side's tanks to advance through. So long as the majority of the population still believe in security through armaments, there can be no political breakthrough.

Fifth, we have to tear away the curtain of talk about balanced disarmament, troop reduction, arms limitation and arms control. Berta von Suttner once wrote that the delegates of the great powers at the Hague disarmament conference of 1899 seemed to her like a meeting of shoemakers convened to decide on the abolition of shoes. We must ceaselessly repeat what everyone already knows: these people just talk past one another, and cooperate in driving one another on. Treaties simply channel the arms race. The only way forward is for the people of each country to force through major steps of unilateral disarmament, of a kind that the peoples on the other side cannot fail to see and to appreciate.

Sixth, we should be quite serious, and quite expert too, in spreading the idea of an alternative defence policy, which has already been developed in its basic elements (for example by Afheldt, Ebert, Mechtersheimer, Vilmar) and is the only viable strategy:

- *non-nuclear:* without long-range nuclear missiles, which only attract destruction, and without self-destructive tactical nuclear weapons for the domestic "battlefield";

- *unambiguously defensive:* without any capabilities aimed at the territory of the opponent; but a massive frontier defence with the most modern non-nuclear armour, aircraft and possibly also non-nuclear missiles;

- *decentralized territorial defence:* scattered across the whole country, not concentrated into large units presenting large targets; specialized forces with light armour and anti-aircraft weapons;

- *social defence:* that is, in combination with territorial defence, non-military forms of popular resistance deployed at the right time, as well as technical sabotage designed to make any occupation problematic in advance;
- *civil defence:* important also as a psychological compensation for the renunciation of retaliation in kind against an enemy attack.

The essential difference between such a policy and the existing strategy of deterrence (through retaliation from an already destroyed territory) can be summed up in the concept of "restraining" the adversary. Just as is the case with energy supply, the two options—nuclear and non-nuclear—are not both possible simultaneously. The population must decide on which they want to spend the immense tax resources involved.

Seventh (last but not least): even this alternative defence concept, still governed by the "reality principle," does not escape the exterminist framework. For a definitive break out of this vicious circle we need a more radical model of behaviour, which I would like to call *eco-pacifism.* Not only must we maintain the demand for general and complete disarmament; this must be supplemented by a programme for the industrial dismantling of our Northern civilization, or rather a constructive re-mantling of it. This should be both our own choice, and the basis of a widening effort to bring about a change of thinking among the majority of the population.

Politically, this means standing for an alternative defence policy; morally, however, it means rising to that higher reason and trust visible in the declaration distributed by certain Protestant circles: "I am prepared to live without the protection of armaments. I intend to support a policy for our state that seeks peace politically and not by weapons."

We should take on the task of distributing the declaration in millions of copies, engaging in personal discussion with every single child, woman and man without exception. The questions and answers that are important in this connection should be composed in the style of a catechism. Everyone who helps distribute the declaration must have at their disposal arguments that take into account the mental barriers, prejudices, hostilities that the division of Europe and the manipulation of both blocs has created. It is impossible to think of any better starting-point for a debate on the entire complex of problems discussed in this essay than by challenging people in this way to make a thought-out existential decision by individually signing their name on a sheet of paper.

It may be that we find ourselves here at a point of unconditional agreement with the message of Christ. It is in this precise sense that I adhere to this declaration, convinced that there was never a moment in history when the words of the Sermon on the Mount were more pertinent or pressing: "Blessed are the gentle in spirit; for they shall inherit the Earth."

---

1. Edward Thompson, "Notes on Exterminism, the Last Stage of Civilization." The present essay is written as a "supplement" to Thompson's article, in the sense that I endorse Thompson's arguments and aim to extend them, though not necessarily in a way with which he would agree. But I can literally say that I agree with every one of Thompson's points. If he says that he "do[es] not claim to have discovered a new 'exterminist' mode of production," I would only add that he has provided the concept for the prevailing tendency in which the "two imperial formations" converge. The question then arises: what is the ultimate basis of this tendency, if not the prevailing presence of the one and only industrialism which has so far existed? It is scarcely very meaningful to say that industry is deformed by certain well-known class interests, given that these are evidently dependent subfunctions of an apparently spontaneous "progress," and the stimuli on which this "progress" seems to thrive. We must accordingly consider, far more radically than in the past, not how these "historical laws" can be as it were obediently fulfilled, but rather how they can be broken.

2. "Manifesto of the Communist Party," *The Revolutions of 1848,* Penguin/NLR, Harmondsworth 1973, p. 67 and note.

3. Wolfgang Sternstein, for example, draws attention to this in *Marx, Lenin, Mao. Darstellung und Kritik der marxistischen Industriegesellschaft,* Frankfurt 1980.

4. Thompson, see above, p. 27.

5. Ibid., p. 14.

6. Klaus Traube, *Frankfurter Rundschau,* 4–5 December 1980.

7. Horst Eberhard Richter, "Und ist es Wahnsinn, hat es doch Methode," *Kritik* 26, 1980.

Outlining the Future:
Principles of Common Security

Pam Solo · Ted Sasson · Rob Leavitt

The next several years offer tremendous opportunity for the peace movement to take the lead in redefining the terms of the US security debate. In so doing, the movement can put forward policy proposals to end the arms race, restructure US–Soviet relations, reduce military spending, and create a US foreign policy dedicated to peacemaking and global problem-solving. In order to turn such proposals into policy, however, the movement must first articulate a powerful and persuasive new paradigm that moves beyond the logic of the Cold War.

Following the path breaking work of the Palme Commission and many other groups and individuals, a new "beyond the Cold War" paradigm of Common Security has begun to take shape. Under the framework of Common Security we are able to present a series of principles to guide US peace movement thinking and action in the years ahead:

> *The fundamental principle of Common Security is that no nation can ensure its own security at the expense of another, or, put another way, the security of one cannot be rooted in the insecurity of another. Common Security necessitates real steps toward nuclear and conventional disarmament, economic and social development, and active conflict resolution.*

Advocates of Common Security arrive at this position out of a common sense recognition about the limits of military force in the nuclear age, and out of a growing recognition that economic and environmental threats to global security can no longer be relegated to secondary status.

The following principles and actions derive from this guiding concept of Common Security.

1. All nations and peoples have a right to security—security from the threat of war and nuclear devastation, from infringements on national sovereignty, from poverty and despair, and from politically repressive governments.

2. In the nuclear age, national security cannot be achieved through unilateral action. Because there is no possible defense against nuclear attack, military power and nuclear weapons cannot make a nation fundamentally secure.

3. True security derives not from military forces but from economic prosperity and justice, vibrant social and cultural life and freedoms, the broadest affirmation of human, civil, and political rights, and full ecological integrity. Massive spending for military forces drains societies of needed financial, technical, and human resources.

4. Military force is not a legitimate instrument for resolving disputes among nations or promoting national interests. Restraint should characterize the underlying tenor of all international relations, not only in recognition of all nations' rights to security but also in recognition of the unparalleled danger of escalation from military confrontation to nuclear destruction. National military forces, to the extent they are necessary, must be confined to strictly defensive, non-threatening postures.

5. US policy toward the Soviet Union must reject exaggerated and dangerous confrontation and instead promote mutual cooperation, trade, cultural interaction, problem-solving, and peacemaking.

6. US allies are autonomous and should take primary responsibility for defining and acting upon their own security needs.

7. US relations with nations of the Third World must rest upon respect for different paths of political and economic development, and support for global efforts to transcend pervasive poverty, repression and environmental degradation throughout the Third World.

Local conflicts in the Third World must not be used as theaters of East–West confrontation, and strict standards of military non-intervention must apply.

8. International security leadership and direction must derive more and more from transnational institutions devoted to conflict resolution, peacekeeping, verification and monitoring of military forces and agreements, problem-solving research, and development of international standards of economic, social, and political rights.

These principles are not an exact guide to peace. Potential contradictions appear, such as the demands for self-determination and autonomy of nations and demands for stricter international standards of political, social, and economic rights. They also affirm the right for nations to defend themselves, while promoting a strong anti-military bias. Current military policies, of course, are always justified as "strictly defensive." Corrupted language surrounding today's debates on security is itself a deep problem in formulating a set of morally and politically appropriate principles to help guide a new peace politics.

PART EIGHT

Modern Military Strategies

"Strategy" refers to the basic theory of how a government uses military force to achieve its political objectives. Strategic theories always contain within them a social theory about how power is organized in society. A strategic theory tries to take advantage of the strengths of its "side" and the weaknesses of both the opposing society and its military. Sometimes the social dimensions of warfare are made explicit in strategic theory, and sometimes they are unstated assumptions. Nationalist and communist revolutionary forces fighting colonial powers for national independence have made the most conscious incorporation of social theory into strategic theory.

In his essay, "Our Strategy for Guerrilla War," Nguyen Van Thieu, a Vietnamese revolutionary leader, demonstrates how the communist forces valued the political mobilization of the populace as a crucial component of their strategy. In contrast, American military leaders formed a strategy for Vietnam based on the strength of their industry and technology. In "Strategy of Warfare in Vietnam: War as a Production Process," James William Gibson shows that the Vietnam War was conceptualized as a high-technology production process in which the officer corps were managers, the enlisted men were workers, and the product was enemy deaths—the famous body count. Sarah

Miles, in "The Real War: Low-Intensity Conflict in Central America," describes a change in U.S. military strategy in response to the defeat in Vietnam: the development of "low-intensity war" for fighting revolutionary insurgencies in the Third World without introducing large numbers of American combat troops.

The second section, "Nuclear Deterrence Versus Defense," moves to the question of nuclear war strategy. In their essay, "Victory is Possible," Colin Gray and Keith Payne argue that the United States can win a nuclear war against the Soviet Union and should therefore consider nuclear war as a viable strategic option. Michael Howard criticizes their analysis in his rejoinder, "On Fighting a Nuclear War."

J. David Singer, in "Military Preparedness, National Security and the Lessons of History," and Richard Lebow, in "Deterrence Reconsidered," examine the argument that preparing to fight nuclear war "deters" nuclear war from ever occurring. Deterrence theory says that the United States must be able to totally destroy an enemy society with nuclear weapons to prevent or "deter" a nuclear attack on the United States. This argument has been the principal U.S. rationale for building larger numbers of nuclear weapons and increasing their technological sophistication. Singer's study focuses on the historical relationships between preparing for war and the outbreak of war. He concludes that high levels of expenditures for armaments help lead to war. Lebow studies the psychological dynamics of preparing for war as a way to secure peace.

Randall Forsberg, in "Confining the Military to Defense," offers an alternative to the armaments race and deterrence, namely a different military strategy and organizational structure for purely defensive purposes. Such a military could stop an attack but could not threaten to destroy another society. Thus no foreign government could possibly view the U.S. military as preparing for a nuclear attack. They would not need their own strategic nuclear weapons to "deter" the United States. In this way the tremendous fear and resulting arms race that is currently built into the strategy and practice of deterrence could perhaps be overcome, so creating a path toward peace.

The concluding essay by Gene Sharp, "Civilian-Based Defence," explores the possibility of training civilians to stop an enemy power's occupation of their country by making the society ungovernable and economically unproductive. In Sharp's view, this defensive strategy would have a great advantage for maintaining peace, because it would not appear to another country as a potentially threatening offensive system of war technology.

GUERRILLA AND CONVENTIONAL WARFARE

Our Strategy for Guerrilla War

Nguyen Van Thieu

Nguyen Van Thieu lived in the maquis for sixteen years during the two wars in Vietnam. As an N.L.F. leader, he was in charge of the relationship between the towns and the countryside in the early 1960s and was a member of the N.L.F.'s central comittee.*

As far as we are concerned, revolutionary war is the people's war. In other words, the role played by the population is not just important: it is fundamental.

In 1954–1959, the Diem regime controlled the towns and even the countryside—or was at least trying to. It had firm social backing within the towns and had managed to attract the support of many religious sects. With the help of landlords and their agents, it strived to control the villages. But it made one fatal error. During the resistance against the French, nearly one million hectares had been distributed to the peasantry; the regime took these lands back. It began by doing away with everything the revolution had brought the peasants, simply because those gains had been the work of the Vietminh. But the peasants that had been given the land put up strong resistance, in some cases

even assassinating the landlords that repossessed the fields. The class struggle was very acute; peasants knew their interests were being violated, and they nursed a lasting hatred for the Diem regime.

In order to control the villages, the Diem regime relied on the Ac-on, its most cruel agents. Six to twelve were assigned to each village. Each village was divided into groups of households that were kept under regular surveillance. A board was posted in front of each house, displaying the name, sex, and age of everybody who lived there. Sometimes the Ac-on ran checks at night. Any member of the household who was absent when they came was expected to produce a good explanation. The Ac-on were in fact more effective than the French administration and the old notables had ever been. No stranger could pass through without being reported.

After 1954 and the Geneva Accords, those of our revolutionary cadres who came from peasant backgrounds returned to work as peasants. The village is our basic unit. Most villages have about 2,500 to 5,000 inhabitants and are divided up into little hamlets. If they are not picked up by the

From *Partisans,* special "Vietnam" edition (Paris: Librairie François Maspero), 1968. © 1982 The Regents of the University of California. Reprinted by permission.

*[The National Liberation Front (N.L.F.) organized both political and military revolutionary war in South Vietnam from 1954–1975. It was led by the Communist Party, but included non-party members in its activities—EDS.]

forces of repression, our cadres influence the population through the daily contacts established when working.

Life was becoming much harder for the peasantry now that Diem had repossessed their lands. The cadres' task was to make the best use of the discontent created by the regime. For example, they might say, "What has the Diem regime ever done for us apart from taking our lands and increasing the cost of tenancy?" All our political propaganda was based on the peasants' everyday personal interests and on the general feeling of discontent, most pronounced among the very poor. *We absolutely had to have cadres who knew and understood the peasantry.* Fortunately about 85 percent or our cadres are of peasant origin.

We did not stress that we were fighting for freedom—that would come later. The overthrow of the regime was presented as a matter of immediate and direct personal interest. Big words are just so much hot air. What matters most is land. The first task is to liquidate the notables, the Ac-on, and the landlords. If the peasants are discontented, then their discontent can be elevated into positive hatred of the regime, and then they will join the struggle for a better life.

Not all our revolutionary cadres were based in villages. Many lived in the jungle, in the mountains, or in deserted areas. With nightfall, these cadres would try to enter the village—their own village—to maintain contacts. Generally the revolutionary cadres would stick to their village, where they knew the people and the lay of the land, where they had relatives. Some cadres lived like this for years, hiding out during the day, emerging only at night. A few even lost their eyesight as a result of never seeing daylight. Life was hard under Diem. Everybody realized that conditions were unbearable, that something had to be done if we did not want death to be our only hope of respite.

Political struggles began to break out. The peasants would outline their grievances to the council of notables, but the usual result was more repression. Bit by bit the peasants began to realize that the only way out was to take up arms and that they alone could change things. The fewer conditions you as revolutionaries impose, the more the

peasants will be able to act as conscious agents. Of course everything depends on the prevailing conditions, and you will no doubt have to rely largely on your own experience.

The main task is to make people aware of the need for armed struggle. Weapons can always be found. The insurrection began in 1959, in the Mekong delta, with hunting rifles. No munitions were en route from the North. The core of the peasant question is that it cannot be hurried. If the peasants do not understand the situation, it is dangerous and often useless for us to make a move by ourselves. The peasants themselves raised the issue of armed struggle in 1959.

In the Mekong delta, the first objective was to break the regime's stranglehold by liquidating the Ac-on. They were judged in open court. Once the villages had been liberated, we were able to intensify our propaganda effort.

Naturally the repressive forces usually reacted quickly and appeared on the scene in strength. The peasants would tell them, "Well-armed people come in the middle of the night and liquidated so-and-so. They told us not to leave the village and forced us to destroy the strategic hamlet's entire defensive system. They also hid things under those trees over there and warned us to keep away." Diem's men would not believe the last part of the story. Some would go to investigate and be blown to bits by mines. Another important propaganda effort is trying to convince the enemy's troops to desert. Some may be persuaded; others may simply become frightened as our strength increases.

To return to the problem of implanting yourself in the population; the main thing is to *stick to a village.* From 1954 to 1959 we lost many peasant cadres because Diem's men were well entrenched. But we held on, sometimes under very tough conditions. Sympathetic peasants dug holes to hide people in. The Ac-on had metal spikes to find such hideaways, and often they did discover people. But the cadres managed to maintain their contacts with the peasantry and were often able to hold little meetings with seven or eight reliable people at night to discuss the local situation and divide up tasks. Each cadre had at least three hideouts in the village. The villagers themselves elected struggle committees composed of the most active and conscious peasants—those the others trusted.

One difficult but essential point is to ensure that the struggle becomes generalized rather than confined to only one region. There must be coordination and mutual aid between regions if we are not to be easily beaten, and this must in turn fit into a coherent overall plan that articulates to the greatest possible extent action in the village, the district, the province, the regions, and the country. Without patience you cannot make a revolution. Cadres who work at the village level must be stubborn and cautious at the same time. They also have to be highly mobile, since the enemy is constantly trying to find them. Peasant sympathizers will keep them supplied with rice, salt, and sometimes fish, which can be carried away to an underground hideout where the cadres will eat, sleep, and wait for nightfall, when they can begin to act. Sometimes the surveillance will relax such that sympathizers can put one of our people up for a while. In any case the peasants look after our cadres, providing them with shelters in several houses, in gardens, sometimes in wells. But the life is very hard; being a revolutionary is no simple matter. The peasant question is the most difficult and complex of all, but if it can be resolved then victory is sure; you can no longer be beaten. But just because the conditions are favorable does not mean you can simply grab a rifle and go out to tell the peasants that everything is going to change.

Since December 20, 1960, the Front has been leading the struggle, but it was the peasants that initiated it.

The problems of establishing yourself in the community are complex and various. You must study and know the local peasant mentality very well, especially anything concerning divisions within the peasantry. I do not mean only the land problem. In Africa there is the tribal problem. In Asia, for the most part, there are religious problems. Here, in Vietnam, religious sects account for 50 percent of the population. There are about 4,000,000 Buddhists, 1,800,000 Catholics, 1,000,000

Hoa-Hoa, and 1,000,000 Caodaists. And a great variety of problems arise in mobilizing these people.

We also have underpopulated areas, a fact which is all too often forgotten. Outside the Mekong delta, especially in the mountains, the population density is low and settlements are thinly scattered. Communication between people who live there is not easy to establish, but it is vital to do so. In addition to different religions, there are also various customs. In the Camau plain for example, where the peasants live in considerable isolation, their universe is restricted to their little plot of land, their family, and a few neighbors. The question is how to put these people in contact with other peasants. The cadres begin by bringing news of relatives who live elsewhere, perhaps 30 miles away, and leave having gathered news for the distant relatives. They go back and forth in this way for a while, and links gradually become established. It is a difficult process and requires patience, but it is very important. Gradually the peasants realize that they can move about, and, thanks to the cadres, they begin to see beyond their little plot of land. Then they start venturing out themselves, and the resulting increase in the number of travelers makes it easier for our cadres to go unnoticed. Of course all this is impossible if one lacks peasant cadres.

The peasant struggle naturally must be coordinated with the workers' struggle. The struggles are not separate; on the contrary, they are common and share a common goal. They must be fused into a single movement. The secret of the N.L.F. is simple: the Front has united the peasant problem, the workers' problem, the problem of the religious sects, and the problem of the national minorities.

This last point is very important. One thing I regretted about the O.L.A.S. conference* was the absence of any Indian elements, even though Indians form the majority in many Latin American countries. Here, in Hanoi, there are five of us on the committee, and one is a comrade from the national minorities.

---

*Held in Havana in 1967.

To become accepted by the national minorities, our cadres have not only learned the language; they have pierced their ears or filed their teeth if that is the custom of the minority in question. They have lived like the minority, and that can be very hard. You must be patient, because these people are initially very suspicious of anyone from outside their own ethnic group. It is a delicate but decisive issue: obviously the ultimate aim is for cadres to come from the national minority itself. The reason we have been able to fight battles in which we had to commit up to an entire division is that our policy of forming alliances with the national minorities has been very successful: in the South, the minorities participate in the struggle.

I must admit that it is a very difficult task. You must study the language, the customs, and the mentality in order to win their trust; it is not easily won, but, once you have been accepted, you can rely on them absolutely. The Americans, like the French and the Japanese before them, have sought to divide us. But we have managed to establish ourselves. There are nationalities among whom we have been working five or even ten years in order to convince them to fight alongside us. If you want to make a revolution, you have to be prepared to make sacrifices and wage a long-term struggle.

The next phase is to articulate the town and the countryside. In our country, the working class has only recently emerged. Workers still have peasant relatives; their families still live in the villages. They go back there from time to time, and we use this movement between town and country to reinforce political links. Certain actions can be coordinated. For instance, when the enemy bombs and kills people all over the countryside, the peasants bring the bodies to the towns to put pressure on the regime and to show what is happening to the people; the workers support these demonstrations by going on strike. Correspondingly, the peasants support the workers when they strike. The coordination is complex, but it produces results.

We are not trying to lead isolated struggles of the population but to coordinate all forms of the revolutionary struggle—that is, the people's war—to overthrow the regime by cutting it off from all its bases, be they passive or active.

Naturally, one may trigger the armed struggle before the political tasks are complete, but political work must follow the armed struggle very closely. The armed struggle helps break the regime's grip and opens the way for propaganda and political work. But political work is always necessary. Without it, there can be no victory.

If we did no political work, the peasants would not support us and we would probably be isolated. The enemy is always militarily stronger at first. When the enemy comes, you have to move and repression ensues, for which the peasants blame you, since you created the conditions that attracted the repression. You must explain the situation, and that demands political work. Our political cadres have remained, sticking desperately to their village despite the repression, in order to continue their political work, organize the population, and train more cadres in the village. We believe study and knowledge of the region in which one is establishing oneself to be quite fundamental. Areas exist where the regime and the landowners exert severe pressure and where the population is discontented yet does not know how to go about changing things. If the cadres understand how to establish themselves, they can create favorable conditions for political work and armed struggle. Every revolutionary movement needs to carry out this kind of painstaking study, because in the beginning what really matters is knowing how to create the most favorable conditions for the initiation and intensification of armed struggle.

You should never impose conditions on the peasantry; they must be helped to understand for themselves why armed struggle is necessary: they are already aware of their own interests. Above all, you should help elevate their political consciousness and their level of organization. We will never have more weapons, more tanks, more planes than the Americans. The real problem of revolutionary war is not primarily military. It is political. The secret of our success is that we strive to mobilize the people, resolve the peasant question, coordinate the town-countryside struggle, resolve the problem of the national minorities and religious sects, and elevate the level of organization and political consciousness. That is why we can stand up to the most powerful imperialism in the world.

Strategy of Warfare in Vietnam:
War as a Production Process

James William Gibson

At the height of the war, the army had only over 100 battalions in Vietnam, while there were close to 2,500 lieutenant colonels in the pool competing for those 100 to 130 battalions. At the next level up, the ratio of applicants to positions became worse. By the early 1970s the army only had seventy-five or so brigade-equivalent commands in Vietnam for colonels, while 2,000 of the 6,000 colonels in the army were serious competitors for these jobs. For those relative few who survived the cut-off between colonel and general, the structure did not open any farther. In the early 1970s around 200 major generals (two star) were in competition for thirteen division commander positions.

Given the large number of managers in competition for relatively few jobs, competition became intense, particularly at the key structural level, command of the infantry maneuver battalion. Battalion commanders had only a six-month tour of duty to begin with—as opposed to the normal tour of one year in Vietnam for enlisted men. If they didn't produce high body counts immediately, they were threatened with replacement. According to Professor Francis West of the Naval War College, a battalion commander "had a 30 to 50 percent chance of being relieved of command because [of failure]. If you were a division commander, however, you had less than a 5 percent chance of being relieved of command, given your resources."[1]* A division commander could "play" with the numbers, rearrange them to signify productivity. But

to signify his own success, a division commander demanded that his battalion and brigade officers follow the "rules" and produce a high body count. Threats to battalion commanders became very explicit. In *The Lionheads,* a fictional account of General Ewell's 9th Infantry Division, Josiah Bunting describes Ewell's treatment of the brigade commander with the lowest body count:

> *IV Corps [Mekong Delta] below the River is lousy with VC. The MRB gets mortared two nights out of three. Your body-count is a standing joke. Tell you what; Robinson, you have one week to produce. . . .*
>
> *Colonel Robinson knows—it is as simple as this—that he will be relieved unless he achieves a good body-count based on a major contact, and though he hates Lemming [Ewell] he knows the General can ruin him, can keep him from being a general, can keep him from riding through Persepolis, can make it difficult for him to keep paying his son's tuition at Cornell, can keep him from commanding a division himself some day, can vindicate his own wife's hatred for what he has been doing with his professional life, can make him a retired colonel selling fire insurance, with a Legion of Merit in his buttonhole. Can ruin him. The prospect is discomforting even to George Robinson.*[2]

Excerpt from James William Gibson, *The Perfect War: Technowar in Vietnam* (New York: The Atlantic Monthly Press, 1986). Reprinted by permission of the author.
*[Footnotes have been renumbered because portions of the original work have been deleted—Eds.]

On the other hand, if "Robinson" and the other middle-management officers used their troops as the human "bait" called for in Technowar strategy, then many rewards were available. Simply flying in their command and control helicopters above effective anti-aircraft range became a way of earning prestigious medals. Cincinnatus notes that by February 1971 (close to the end of the major U.S. ground war) the army had given out 1,273,987 awards for bravery. Around 800,000 of these awards were Air Medals, emblems previously given out only to those who served in an extraordinary way as a member of an aircraft crew. But in Vietnam Air Medals were distributed simply for flying a set number of missions in a "war zone." One chaplain described how officers manipulated criteria for receiving the award:

> *Think of Air Medals. A guy goes up for a five-minute flight in a perfectly peaceful area, and that counted toward an Air Medal. He does everything he can so he can get up in the air and get another Air Medal. It was easy and it was cheap. It was the kind of war-type mentality in Vietnam where some acted as if it was a play war—but elsewhere people were dying.[3]*

• • •

. . . Few ground troops were deceived by such fabrications and false awards. One soldier found his whole battalion trapped in a vertically walled canyon: "Everybody was pretty scared, except for the battalion commander, who was in his chopper."[4] Another trooper comments on the banality of medals: "Medals are a farce. Our Colonel got an Air Medal, which is a pretty impressive medal. He got an Air Medal for flying over a fire fight. Well, we were in it. He was up so high you could hardly see the helicopter."[5] Those soldiers who became wounded on search-and-destroy missions to fulfill their commanders' needs for high body counts give particularly bitter testimony. A man who lost his foot says:

> *It's one thing to be in Nam huntin' Charlie and another to be there in some air-conditioned trailer. A lot of them guys don't have*

to sweat none. They fly around in them command choppers once in a while and then they go back to Saigon or somewhere and live it up. Nobody give a shit what happened to us grunts. I mean they just didn't really care. Just so everything looked okay and none of the wheels chewed anybody's ass— that was all that mattered to 'em. I mean they kept givin' you all that fucking bullshit about helpin' the fucking gooks ain't gonna do nothin'. The main thing was that the wheels look good. Shit, I lost my foot going into a fuckin' village that the sergeant kept trying to tell the captain was just one big fuckin' booby trap. But the captain, he was new, and the battalion commander wanted the village checked and we had to go chargin' in there so the captain wouldn't look bad. Now I ain't got no foot, mister, and what for? I'll tell you why, because the Army don't give a shit about guys like me. . . . I wish I'd gone AWOL.[6] . . .

• • •

Command pressure for determining productivity included ordering body counting missions either in the midst of combat operations or in the immediate aftermath when the battlefield was still a highly dangerous place. So many soldiers were either killed or wounded on body counting missions that the Department of the Army included an extensive account of incidents as a way of warning officers in its pamphlet *Vietnam Primer: Lessons Learned* (1967).

> Item. *A U.S. rifle company in a good defensive position atop a ridge is taking a steady toll of an NVA force attacking up hill. The skipper sends a four-man patrol to police weapons and count bodies. Three men return bearing the fourth, who was wounded before the job was well started. Another patrol is sent. The same thing happens. The skipper says, "Oh, to hell with it!"* Item. *In Operation Nathan Hale three men working through a banana grove were hit by sniper fire. They were counting bodies.* Item. *In Operation Paul Revere IV a much-admired line sergeant was*

killed, and two other enlisted men were wounded, and a lieutenant barely escaped ambush, when the four together were "tidying up" the field. They ran into a stay-behind party planted in a thicket on the morning after the fight.[7]

The authors, retired General S. L. A. Marshall and Colonel David Hacksworth, said nothing about the production model of war and the war-managers' competition for promotion. Instead, their recommendations placed responsibility on lieutenants and captains—the "small unit commanders"—to defy their superiors: "If he believes that a present, but unmeasured danger forbids body counting or that a more urgent military object should come first, he need only have the courage of his own convictions in coming to that decision. No one may rightly press him to trade bodies for lives."[8] Yet the war-managers continued to do just that. Years later, one anonymous general confided in a survey of army generals who served in Vietnam: "I shudder to think how many of our soldiers were killed on a body-counting mission—what a waste."[9]

Technowar thus suffered from severe internal contradictions in its big-unit search-and-destroy operations. United States military officers conceived of themselves as business managers rather than combat leaders. Enlisted men were seen as a kind of migrant labor force of only marginal importance. They were marginal in that artillery, jet fighter-bombers, and helicopter gunships were officially responsible for producing enemy deaths, while infantry and armored cavalry became the "fixing force." Enlisted men were also marginal in that with the shift to the production model of war and the managerial officer corps, senior and middle-level officers became fixated on their individual career advancements with little attention given to troop welfare. Traditional military social bonds between troops and their commanders deteriorated. Soldiers instead became "costs of production" for Technowar as a whole while virtually "free" to any given war-manager. Casualties could be replaced by increasing Selective Service or draft quotas each month. Draftees as a percentage of those killed in Vietnam rose

each year: 1965, 16 percent; 1966, 21 percent; 1967, 34 percent; 1969, 40 percent. These figures are for the U.S. military on the whole. Taking the army separately finds 62 percent of 1969 battle deaths and 70 percent of 1970 battle deaths from draftee ranks.[10] But regardless of whether an enlisted man was drafted, or joined because of draft pressures, or joined out of genuine desire, he was still conceptualized as a small production cost in a vast war machine run by management for management.

This abstract technological and production-oriented approach permeated all phases of war. For example, the concept of producing mass enemy deaths through high-technology, capital-intensive weapons assumed an empty, transparent kind of battlefield—as if comparing U.S. and NVA weapons systems on paper—and finding U.S. weapons could saturate an area more quickly. But in the real world, nature existed in its concrete, raw form. Rainy weather, for instance, grounded U.S. planes and helicopters. Thomas Bird describes what happened to the 1st Air Cavalry Division during the 1965–1966 Ia Drang Valley battle:

> *The joke of Ia Drang Valley is, If you can't bring a chopper in to give air support, what good is it? If they can't fly because it's too humid or because the weight they are carrying won't let them get off the ground or they'll burn up too much ammo to go out and resupply and get back to base camp, what good is it? Then you're down on the enemy's level and they are masters there.*[11]

Another soldier describes his unit's shock when they discovered the unit that ambushed them was dug into a mountain valley to keep U.S. jets away:

> *Like valleys where you're pinned down. A lot of times we've had jets come in over the top of us, when it was hard to hit them any other way. They couldn't come across because of the mountains and stuff. They release the bombs right over our heads. And you can see the bombs. They'd be going towards us. And we're saying, "Ooh, fucking things just don't drop." But they like carried on the*

momentum of the speed they're going. They go in front of you. They blow up. That takes a lot of skill on an estimate. And a lot of fucking luck. The gooks choose this type of thing because they know that our jets can't come into a valley this way and make it. Because there's a mountain there and they can't get up. So they set up their defenses so they can shoot down the planes as they're coming in.[12]

Psychiatrist Charles J. Levy heard this story from a patient. Levy classified it as an example of "inverted warfare," the sense in which American common sense on how the world operates was reversed or inverted in Vietnam. The jet aircraft represents America's mastery of scientific principles concerning how nature works. To see the aircraft's efficacy vanquished by the *technologically* primitive technique of burrowing into a mountain inverts the normal Technowar order. Levy says: "The rationale for much of American technology had been the conquest of nature. But in Vietnam, the VC/NVA used nature for the conquest of technology."[13]

By far the most important Vietnamese use of nature was their use of the *earth.* Vietnamese villagers and Vietcong cadres and NVA troops all built thousands of miles of elaborate tunnels inside the south. The more sophisticated tunnel networks stretched from the northern supply routes along the Ho Chi Minh Trail in Cambodia to the very outskirts of Saigon. Hundreds, if not thousands, of more locally oriented tunnels hid Vietcong troops and supplies from U.S. search-and-destroy operations, artillery barrages, and air strikes. The Vietcong's tunnel system totally confounded American commanders.

General Fred Weyland, commander of the 25th Infantry Division, selected Cu Chi as headquarters for his division in 1966. As the general explains his choice, "I selected Cu Chi as an area that was well away from the populated center of Saigon, to act as a sort of lightning rod for the enemy. We picked the specific area because of the topography. It was the one place that was above the water table, where we could put trucks and

tanks without having them sink out of sight during the monsoon season.[14]

Unfortunately for the general, the very topography sufficient to support Technowar was also sufficient for a vast tunnel system. One American adversary, Captain Nguyen Thanh Linh, describes how U.S. forces responded to their first encounter with attack from Vietcong hidden in the earth: "They were so bewildered, they did not hide or take defensive positions. They did not know where the bullets had come from. We kept on shooting. . . . although their fellows kept falling down, they kept on advancing. They should have retreated. They called for artillery. When the first shells landed we simply went into the communications tunnels and went on to another place. The Americans continued advancing, but we'd gone." In recalling all his battles, Linh says of the tunnels, "They are something very Vietnamese and one must understand what the relationship is between the Vietnamese peasant and the earth, *his earth.* Without that, then everything here is without real meaning."[15]

Unable to see outside Technowar, warmanagers often attempted to destroy "raw nature" with its mountains and forests and places to hide. They tried to create a physical terrain equivalent to the abstract, mathematical space of 1,000 meter by 1,000 meter grid squares necessary for jets and artillery to find orientation. Technowar attempted to defoliate Vietnam with herbicides as a way of reorganizing nature to meet its needs, rather than to see the contradiction of its project. Another of Ronald Glasser's patients told him what happened:

Let me tell you about the defoliation program. It didn't work. No, I mean it. It ain't done a damn thing it was supposed to do. I'll give 'em there are a lot of dead people out there because of it, but not theirs—ours. The whole idea was to prevent ambushes, to clear the area. Some idiot somewhere sold somebody the idea that if the gooks couldn't hide, then they couldn't ambush you, and they bought the idea, I mean really bought it. The trouble with the whole thing is that the VC and NVA use guns in their ambushes instead of bows and arrows. Nobody mentioned that. They don't have to be sitting on top of you to pull off an ambush. An AK-47 round is effective up to 1,500 meters and accurate up to 600. So we'll hit an area, like along a busy road, billions of gallons of the stuff, and pretty soon there's nothing except for some dead bushes for fifty or even 300 meters on both sides of where the road or track used to be. So the gooks will start shooting at you from 300 meters away instead of only five, only now you're the one that ain't got no place to hide. Ever try running 100 meters or 200? It takes time, and they're firing at you the whole way. And I mean the whole way.[16]

Note how intended protection created a larger killing zone. In theory, defoliated territory was perfect for helicopter observation by war-managers and quick marshaling of planes and artillery. But at ground level soldiers had to run out of the barren zone to survive. Unable to produce the desired number of enemy deaths because the Technowar apparatus was so visible to a hostile population, the war-managers sought a solution by applying more force, more technology. Technowar must produce victory: debit can be transformed into credit by increasing war production. Contradictions become compounded. The foreign Other repeatedly took the "bait" while the traps backfired. Senior officers got medals and the troops got killed.

Thus far, analysis of search-and-destroy has concerned only how the production model of war with its split between management and labor, suffered from structural contradictions that both mitigated American technological superiority against actual enemy combatants and rendered ground troops expendable. However, there are several other important dimensions of ground Technowar that must be explored to understand this complex system of power and knowledge. First, the production system with its precise reports of how many bodies were found on operations created the *appearance* of highly rational, scientific warfare. Body counts, weapons/kill ratios, charts of patrols conducted, helicopter and jet plane missions flown, and artillery rounds fired— all the indices of war production created at various command levels—presented Vietnam as a war managed by rational men basing their decisions on scientific knowledge. Statistics helped make war-managers appear legitimate to the American public.

The appearance of a science-governed war in turn helped make Vietnam seem like a lawful war. Rational men do not engage in systematic slaughter but fight real enemies—the foreign Other invading from without, trying to "take over" the sovereign state of South Vietnam. The representation of Technowar as a law-governed war was enhanced by command's proliferation of numerous and lengthy regulations determining conditions under which American forces could bomb, shell, and otherwise engage the enemy. Yet these rules had little truth in practice. War-manager pressures for high body counts led to both systematic falsification of battle reports, routine violation of the rules of engagement and regulations covering treatment of prisoners, and systematic slaughter of Vietnamese noncombatants. The production model of war simultaneously destroyed both its own troops and the Vietnamese people, but it could not produce victory. Instead, as the war progressed, the increasing death and destruction, together with the accumulating "layers" of official lies throughout the chain of command, created conditions for Technowar's decay and collapse through internal contradictions.

The simplest aspect of false reporting concerns the many cases when troops and commanders invented enemy body counts out of thin air. Lieutenant William Calley says that one day his battalion commander threatened to relieve him from command of his platoon unless he became more productive. In response, Calley ordered his sergeant to have the platoon open fire on the surrounding jungle. Artillery fire was called in to repel the pseudo-attack. And when the "mock little firefight" was over, "I called in a body count: three and a combat loss of some compasses. It was near inventory time and I had lost those compasses somehow."[17]

One of Cincinnatus's informants has a similar story at company level. "I know one unit that lost 18 men killed in an ambush and reported 131 enemy body count. I was on the ground at the tail end of the battle and I saw five enemy bodies. I doubt if there were any more."[18] Moving up the chain of command, Captain Greg Howard describes the pressures his division commander put on his battalion commander in late 1968. Captain Howard is testifying before Congressman Ronald Dellums's unofficial hearings on war crimes in Vietnam:

> *Our 3rd Battalion, 22nd Infantry, had not been getting the body count that the other battalions in the division had, and General Williamson told that battalion commander, Lieutenant Colonel Carmichael, that he had better start* producing *or we would get a battalion commander in that battalion that could produce. Colonel Carmichael got the message loud and clear.*
>
> *Approximately two weeks later his fire base was attacked.* He called in that night a body count of 312 and he had taken one wounded. *We flew out the next morning, I flew with General Williamson the next morning. We landed and counted the bodies around the perimeter of that base camp, and there were 30-plus North Vietnamese bodies and a few wounded prisoners.*
>
> *General Williamson questioned him a bit further, and said I understood you have 312 body count and I see 30-plus here, where are the other bodies? Colonel Carmichael then gave a vague statement of, well I had an ambush patrol in a particular location on the map and they saw 100 Viet Cong moving across an open field that night in preparation for attack and we called in a lot of artillery fire out there, and we counted those 100.*
>
> *He gave instances like that which amounted to 312. It was obvious to everybody that that was a lie. But General Williamson had put so much pressure on the colonel to* produce *the body count, the man had no choice. He is forty-five years old and he probably has two kids to send to college, and General Williamson, recognizing that he had placed this pressure on the battalion commander, accepted this lie.*[19]

Both the colonel and the general meet their production quotas in terms of reporting high body counts. Both become eligible for rewards. Indeed, in some stories, fabricating enemy body counts becomes an activity one party conducts to "reward" another party for doing something. General Williamson's acceptance of the lie is a tacit reward for Colonel Carmichael's submission to his will. In other cases body counts appear as compensations, as imaginary credits to take the place of real-life debits. As Lieutenant Calley says, "I knew damn well, *Weber's dead. A boy in the second platoon has no legs anymore. A boy in the third platoon—* I had to do it. I wrote in the after-action report [concerning a U.S. artillery barrage that hit no one], 'VC body count six.' "[20]

At higher command levels the numbers just got larger. In one incident, an assistant division commander ordered a high enemy body count for a company that had taken heavy casualties so "we can tell the survivors they did well."[21]

Beyond simple fabrications of body counts come inferential counting rules, rules that a unit followed as "standard operating procedure" but that were not part of official doctrine. An inferential counting rule is a rule that a company uses to infer numbers of enemy dead according to some found object or sign—an enemy weapon, a blood trail, a dismembered body part, or other mark of enemy presence. Inferential counting rules tended to maximize enemy body count. Severed limbs signified a whole body for counting purposes. One senior officer upset with the body count heard a lower-level field officer tell "of an experience where he almost had to get in a fist fight with an ARVN adviser over an arm, to see who would get credit for the body, because they were sorting out pieces. . . . It just made him sick to the stomach that he was put in such a position that a body was so important to the next higher headquarters or to the division, that he had to go down and argue over pieces of a body to get credit for it."[22]

In another case Martin Russ, author of *Happy Hunting Ground,* describes the problems one captain faced counting body parts and estimating deaths:

> *Later he [the colonel] told Bizelle he wanted to see all the bodies he reported. Bizelle looked shamefaced and said he actually found only parts of bodies. "But there's a long trail of blood," he added. "And you can see where they stacked them before taking them up the mountain."*
>
> *"You've no idea how many?"*
>
> *"I didn't measure the density of the gore, no sir, if that's what you mean."*
>
> *Suggins said, "There's hands and feet and hunks of meat all over, but the main housing groups [body trunks] are just gone."*[23]

The captain estimated fifty dead from the severed limbs his unit found. Missing bodies created a real problem. Enemy units dragged their fallen comrades from the field when possible, and friends and relatives likewise buried civilian casualties. Encountering Vietnamese graves while on operations was consequently a common occurrence for many U.S. units. Such encounters gave rise to another counting rule—counting graves as part of a unit's body count even if they were newly arrived in the area—counting them *twice.* One of Glasser's patients said, "He'd heard about units of the 101st [Airborne—elite unit] burying their kills on the way in and digging them up again to be recounted on the way out."[24] Captain Michael O'Mera, of the 25th Infantry Division, says units often doubled their bodies and graves as a rule of thumb: "Another way, you come across the graves and you call in the number of graves you find. If you come across dead bodies, you count dead bodies. You resweep the area, recount the numbers, *double it,* and call it on in."[25] ...

• • •

Captain O'Mera gives an example of fabricating body counts involving ground radars and the blips of light showing up on the screens:

> *We would reference reports constantly and it was usually a Second Brigade policy that I know, they would detect 20 to 25 persons, perhaps it could have been trees moving—it could never be substantiated—and 20 to 25 persons stationary, no less.*
>
> *Artillery was fired and the brigade would report 12 body count.* It was practice for them to take half the number on the radar screen and count it as a body count. *The next day when troops would sweep the area there would be nothing there. Yet this was accepted and it was good, because the pressure was on and this is what they had to do. This was the only way they could come up with it.*[26]

Journalist Dale Minor found the same kind of extrapolation being done in units he visited: "When the battle is over and reporting time has come, a probable 'kill figure' is extrapolated from the estimated density of enemy troops hit by a known or approximate number of artillery and mortar rounds, bombs and rockets."[27] To make the body count even more imaginary, such extrapolations were often conducted by every military unit participating in a particular battle. A pacification official once complained that in his province, "Whenever several agencies combined in a single operation, it appears to be common practice for each to claim 100% of the results."[28]

These fabrications and inferential counting rules are not simply a deviation of Technowar, something that could be reformed leaving the system intact. Maximizing productivity—and therefore *reporting* high body counts—was essential both for individual commanders and for Technowar as a whole. To the war-managers, the deployment of this massive apparatus of plans, helicopters, artillery, and troops without a "product" became an *unthinkable* contradiction. The fetishism of advanced war technology where the mere appearance of Technowar will help persuade the NVA and the NLF "that they cannot win" in practice persuaded the war-managers that they could not lose: *the bodies must be out there, somewhere.* The visible presence of the superior war-production apparatus created a conceptual "wall" in which all contrary data from the real world became transformed into information that affirmed Technowar as successful even as it failed.

1. W. Scott Thompson and Donaldson D. Frizzell, eds., *The Lessons of Vietnam* (New York: Crane, Russak, 1977), pp. 81–82.

2. Josiah Bunting, *The Lionheads* (New York: George Braziller, 1972), p. 49.

3. Cincinnatus, *Self-Destruction: The Disintegration and Decay of the United States Army during the Vietnam Era* (New York: W. W. Norton), p. 162.

4. Fred Halstead, *GIs Speak Out against the War: The Case of the Fort Jackson Eight* (New York: Pathfinders Press, 1970), p. 67.

5. Mark Lane, *Conversations with Americans* (New York: Simon and Schuster, 1970), p. 181.

6. Edward L. King, *The Death of the Army: A Pre-Mortem* (New York: Saturday Review Press, 1972), pp. 28–29.

7. S. L. A. Marshall and Lieutenant Colonel David Hacksworth, *Vietnam Primer: Lessons Learned* (Washington, D.C.: Department of the Army, 1967; Sims, Arkansas: Lancer Militaria, 1984), p. 48.

8. Ibid., p. 49.

9. Douglas Kinnard, *The War Managers* (Hanover, Mass.: University Press of New England, 1977), p. 75.

10. Gloria Emerson, *Winners and Losers: Battles, Retreats, Gains, Losses and Ruins from a Long War* (New York: Random House, 1978), pp. 254–255.

11. Al Santoli, *Everything We Had: An Oral History of the Vietnam War by Thirty-three American Soldiers Who Fought It* (New York: Random House, 1981), p. 43.

12. Charles J. Levy. *Spoils of War* (Boston: Houghton Mifflin, 1974), p. ix.

13. Ibid., p. 70.

14. Tom Mangold and John Penycate, *The Tunnels of Cu Chi: The Untold Story of Vietnam* (New York: Random House, 1985), p. 137.

15. Ibid., pp. 50, 66–67.

16. Ronald Glasser, *365 Days* (New York: George Braziller, 1971), p. 129.

17. John Sack, *Lieutenant Calley: His Own Story* (New York: Viking Press, 1974), p. 56.

18. Cincinnatus, *Self-Destruction*, p. 81.

19. Citizens Commission of Inquiry, ed., *The Dellums Committee Hearings on War Crimes in Vietnam: An Inquiry into Command Responsibility in Southeast Asia* (New York: Vintage Books, 1972), pp. 62–63.

20. Sack, *Lieutenant Calley,*, p. 56.

21. Cincinnatus, *Self-Destruction*, p. 81.

22. Ibid., pp. 79–80.

23. Martin Russ, *Happy Hunting Ground* (New York: Atheneum, 1968), p. 83.

24. Glasser, *365 Days*, p. 34.

25. Citizens Commission of Inquiry, *Dellums Committee Hearings*, p. 72.

26. Ibid.

27. Dale Minor, *The Information War* (New York: Hawthorn Books, 1970), p. 47.

28. Guenter Lewy, *America in Vietnam* (New York: Oxford University Press, 1978), p. 80.

The Real War: Low-Intensity Conflict in Central America

Sarah Miles

> *If we ever reach the point of shooting it out with conventional Red Army formations, we already will have lost. What we are talking about here is the real war.*
>
> John Michael Kelly, Deputy Assistant Secretary, U.S. Air Force

> *The U.S. logistical liability in South East Asia was compounded by a major military mistake: determined dedication to a doctrine of strategic defense and tactical offense. The U.S. played poker. The foe played go.*
>
> Lewis B. Tambs, U.S. Ambassador to Costa Rica

Kelly's "real war" is happening today in various parts of the Third World. It is unconventional, undeclared and probably permanent. "Dirty little wars," as they unfold in Central America, the Philippines or Angola, are among its current manifestations. This is a different kind of warfare, which U.S. military strategists call "low-intensity conflict." But though the United States is deadly serious about winning this war, its real nature, as well as its origins, remains largely invisible to the U.S. public.

Washington's ability to control events in Central America, by force and/or by other means, is still perceived as crucial to the projection of U.S. power worldwide, and for U.S. strategists, the current war there has become the most important

laboratory for testing advanced models of low-intensity conflict. The countries of Central America and the Caribbean have always been central to U.S. ideas of empire; historically, Washington has used force in the region to meet any challenge to continued domination of its "backyard." The war that the United States is fighting in Central America today indicates that old-fashioned military force is not enough to defeat a new generation of revolutionary movements. But if the United States can dominate Central America by using low-intensity strategies, the region could become a model for a world that is never really "at peace" again.

Low-intensity conflict requires a radical departure from conventional military thinking. Its name comes from its place on the "intensity spectrum" of warfare which ascends from civil disorders, through classical wars, to nuclear holocaust. The traditional military defines low-intensity conflicts as those which require less resources, less manpower and cause fewer casualties than conventional war. But low-intensity conflict is not simply a scaled-down version of a conventional war. It is not less of the same thing, nor just a preliminary stage to "real" conflict.

"This kind of conflict is more accurately described as revolutionary and counterrevolutionary warfare," explains Col. John Waghelstein, currently commander of the Army's Seventh Special Forces. He warns that the term "low-intensity" is misleading, as it describes the level of violence

---

strictly from a military viewpoint. In fact, Waghel-stein argues, this type of conflict involves "political, economic, and pyschological warfare, with the military being a distant fourth in many cases." In perhaps the most candid definition given by a U.S. official, Waghelstein declares that low-intensity conflict "is total war at the grassroots level."[1]

■

As a conceptual framework, rather than just a new set of tactics, the idea requires far more emphasis on non-military instruments of power and persuasion. "Low-intensity conflict is neither simple nor short-term," write U.S. Army Majors Donald Morelli and Michael Ferguson. "It is a complex, multilevel, and multidimensional problem which has its roots in change.... The initiative rests with those who can influence or exploit the process of change."[2] A strategic study commissioned by the Pentagon concluded that there is no such thing as victory by force of arms in a low-intensity conflict. Victory is such a context, the study suggests, can be better measured by "avoidance of certain outcomes, or by attitudinal changes in a target group."[3]

Fundamental to this view is the understanding that military intervention is not enough to win in low-intensity situations and may, in fact, be counterproductive. "This does not imply," warn Morelli and Ferguson, "that we are incapable of conducting tactical operations in the low-intensity arena; ... the direct assistance of the United States may be required, and planning for that eventuality must be continuous and thorough.... However, if we must commit U.S. forces to combat in a low-intensity situation, we have lost the strategic initiative."[4]

Although the United States has been fighting low-intensity wars in the Third World, under different names, for decades, the total concept, enlarged and redefined, is finally catching on within the military itself, where "low-intensity conflict" is a term currently in vogue. The doctrine is gaining ground as a strategic framework for rethinking the nature of conflict in the Third World. In part, this is because of real changes taking place in the world; in part, it is because an assortment of powerful figures in the United States believes it to be the correct strategy to deal with those changes.

U.S. low-intensity conflict doctrine has evolved as a response to the growing challenge of popular movements in the Third World, which Defense Secretary Caspar Weinberger calls "the most immediate threat to free world security for the rest of the century."[5] It assumes that revolutions are not purely military events. As U.S. Army Secretary John Marsh explains, "The roots of insurgencies are not military in origin, nor will they be military in resolution."[6]

Proponents of low-intensity conflict call for rethinking traditional tactics. Instead of relying on conventional armies to deal with unconventional and revolutionary conflicts, they advocate "total war" on a variety of fronts—economic, social, political and psychological. The former head of the Defense Intelligence Agency, Lt. Gen. Samuel Wilson, bluntly sums up the attitude of low-intensity conflict advocates:

> There is little likelihood of a strategic nuclear confrontation with the Soviets. It is almost as unlikely that Soviet Warsaw Pact forces will come tearing through the Fulda Gap in a conventional thrust. We live today with conflict of a different sort ... and we had better get on with the ballgame.[7]

■

To a large extent, the reading of the Central American crisis by the U.S. public, and the political response from opponents of the war, grew from the belief that the region was potentially "another Vietnam." Many assumed that the U.S. buildup was the prelude to troop landings in El Salvador or a full-scale invasion of Nicaragua. They foresaw another war in which "our boys" would fight and die, with the United States becoming bogged down in a quagmire before eventually destroying the region or being forced into an ignominious withdrawal.

As the war in Central America becomes more difficult to understand in conventional terms, it seems that the public and the policymakers may have drawn two entirely different sets of conclusions from Vietnam. The lessons of Vietnam have informed the thinking of the U.S. national security establishment, and helped to bring about profound changes in their approach to military intervention.

Fears of "another Vietnam" in Central America stem from a failure to understand some of the key twists and turns in US military strategy that took place during that war, and the important—if hidden—strategic debate that underlay them. Contrary to conventional wisdom, there was no single "hawk" view on Vietnam: the hawks took at least two key positions, which emerged during the earliest days of the war and have remained ever since. While the two camps may have coincided in some of their tactical recommendations, their strategic conceptions are quite different.

In the first view, war is essentially a *military* confrontation, a battle between two armies. Its goals are to capture and hold territory, and eventually to annihilate the enemy's main force units through air, sea and ground operations using superior force and firepower.

In the second view, war is fundamentally a *political* confrontation between two social systems ("democracy" and "communism"). Rather than simply destroying the largest number of enemy troops, it targets the civilian population with a combination of military force, economic pressure, psychological warfare and other means, and attempts to destroy the enemy's political and social structures. This approach, labeled "counterinsurgency" in Vietnam, tends to be tactically flexible: it may use conventional military operations and/or guerrilla tactics. In this kind of war, winning means ensuring that the civilian population will accept a political and social alternative to the enemy's system.

■

Throughout the Vietnam War, these two hawk perspectives remained in conflict. CIA specialists who had served during the Kennedy era of counterinsurgency and special operations experts who had practiced unconventional warfare in Korea lined up against traditional Army officers and Pentagon bureaucrats. Within the services, the Green Berets and the Marines more often took a counterinsurgency approach, while regular U.S. Army units tended to engage in conventional combat. Civilian agencies like AID and the CIA preferred "political warfare," while the military in general took the conventional approach of maximum firepower to devastating lengths.

In a 1983 article on Marine "security assistance" and pacification operations, military historian John Hoyt Williams wrote:

> *While Army and Saigon command continued to be obsessed with the numbers game, search-and-destroy missions, bombing and large-unit sweeps, the Marines kept stubbornly experimenting with local, small-unit tactics. . . . they lived in the hamlets, cooperated with the peasants, offered free medical and dental services, helped build schools and created a grassroots gendarmerie. In return, the villagers were to supply intelligence and finger VC cadre in their midst. The Marine operations were successful because they de-escalated the war and guerrilla'd the guerrillas . . . recognizing that the Vietnamese peasant, rather than the Viet Cong, was the genuine goal of the war.*[8]

Under largely civilian direction, U.S. and South Vietnamese military units, the CIA, AID and the United States Information Agency (USIA) were combined into CORDS (Civilian Operations and Revolutionary Development Support) to carry out similar programs: agricultural development, police training, psychological warfare, paramilitary operations by small units and economic assistance to Vietnamese refugees and villages. CORDS operations took a comprehensive "carrot and stick" approach, ranging from "humanitarian relief" projects to the notorious Phoenix program, which identified and assassinated over 20,000 suspected Viet Cong cadre in 1969 with the help of "turned" guerrillas and local informers.

Meanwhile, neighboring Thailand and Laos saw similar attempts to build an infrastructure for the U.S. regional strategy, combining military operations with wide-ranging development programs to restructure local societies along lines that would benefit U.S. interests. Reflecting on the gamut of programs he had supervised in Indochina, former CIA Chief of Station Douglas Blaufarb noted:

> *All of this was done under the formal rubric of refugee emergency assistance and resettlement, and of rural development, in order to conform to AID categories of approved activity. In actual fact, it constituted the civilian front of an unconventional war which could not have been prosecuted without the aid program.*[9]

■

The new generation of counterinsurgency experts offered a number of basic arguments about strategy. These were:

1. Pacification, or the "hearts and minds" approach, correctly targets *population,* not territory, as the strategic objective.

2. Military escalation is often counterproductive; overkill can win battles but lose wars. As former Vietnamese Marshal Nguyen Cao Ky admitted bitterly, "You cannot use a steamroller against a shadow."[10]

3. Counterinsurgency fails where it does not take indigenous culture and history into account; successful operations need solid intelligence about local political, cultural, social and economic conditions.

4. Counterrevolution can only succeed if it is combined with "nation-building"—the construction of an alternative social system. Nation-building combines "internal defense" (protection against insurgents) with economic assistance, in order to create a strong security apparatus, a manageable political community and stable national institutions.

5. The United States cannot act alone; in fact, using U.S. combat troops is likely to significantly decrease the chance of victory. It is ultimately the role of local forces to win their own population. The United States should, however, train and "clean up" client forces so that abuses and corruption do not alienate

the population from the nation-building; and it should control and direct the non-military aspects of the war.

6. The United States needs regional strategies to deal with regional conflicts. It must deny the enemy political and military sanctuary in neighboring theaters, while "going to the source" of the regional conflict. It cannot allow itself to become bogged down in fighting on one subsidiary front while the enemy fights on several—an argument shared by analysts of conventional warfare.

7. The U.S. military establishment must overcome its own prejudices against unconventional, "unmilitary" warfare; it must achieve greater coordination among the branches of the service as well as with civilian intelligence, aid and development agencies.

8. This kind of warfare must seek to win the support of the U.S. population, as well as the foreign target population.

■

Yet even as the science of political warfare developed, men like Gen. Maxwell Taylor, Chairman of the Joint Chiefs of Staff, complained about "all this cloud of dust" from advocates of counterinsurgency who claimed to have a new model for warfare. Army commanders denounced Secretary of Defense Robert McNamara and his "Washington whiz kids" for "ignoring time-vindicated principles of military strategy," and for allowing civilian agencies to plan military programs. "I'll be damned," said one senior officer, "if I permit the United States Army, its institutions, its doctrine and its traditions to be destroyed just to win this lousy war."[11]

This kind of opposition from conventionally minded strategists pushed aside the arguments of the advocates of counterinsurgency and nation-building. The new doctrine was never implemented comprehensively in Vietnam; it remained in the realm of small-scale incomplete experiments. One of its supporters, U.S. Army Lt. Col. James A. Taylor, later wrote,

There are those who contend that this kind of effort did not work in Vietnam, and will not work elsewhere. The concept actually worked quite well in Vietnam. But is was not seen that way by those who were so busy with quantifiable activities that they failed to notice who controlled the countryside when the sun went down.[12]

It was those in the Pentagon busy with "quantifiable activities" who held the upper hand in the Vietnam War. Under Gen. William Westmoreland, they stepped up the military's traditional reliance on heavy units, massive firepower, high technology and airpower. And like Westmoreland, they argued, "It takes the full strength of a tiger to kill a rabbit."

The United States lost that war, and a defeated U.S. military rushed to assign blame: the press lost the war, the public lost the war, the politicians lost the war, the South Vietnamese lost the war. Military officials who had killed a million Asians, and turned half the Vietnamese countryside into scorched moonscape, even claimed they had lost because they were "not allowed to fight."

In the sweeping revisions of history that followed, the general consensus was that "counterinsurgency didn't work" and was now irrelevant. It would take the next wave of Third World revolutionary movements, together with the rebirth of the U.S. Right, for the real lessons of Vietnam to be studied seriously.

■

The 1970s brought a new generation of revolutions in the Third World, and their impact was sweeping. In Zimbabwe and Nicaragua, indigenous revolutionary movements took power; in the former Portuguese territories of Africa, colonial rule crumbled; and in Iran, a different kind of radical nationalism swept away the Shah. The developed world began to take the concerns of the non-aligned nations seriously, and the axis of conflict, worldwide, began to shift from East–West to North–South.

U.S. strategy proved temporarily inadequate against such change. Certainly, attempts at controlling the Third World never ceased, and many of the elements of low-intensity conflict were adopted during the 1970s, albeit in a piecemeal fashion. Under Nixon, Washington decided to keep its own forces at home, supplying "friendly" regimes with the wherewithal to police their own countries, and limiting actual counterrevolutionary operations to the CIA. Under Carter, the Trilateralists attempted to implement "nation-building" and economic measures that coopted the language of social reform. But a coherent long-term strategy was absent.

After Vietnam, the military establishment had largely gone back to preparing for orthodox conflict in Europe and for nuclear war. Special Forces units were dismantled, counterinsurgency training declined precipitously, and the political conception of war was dismissed as a preoccupation of civilians who had betrayed the Army. By the time of the Carter presidency, growing revelations of "dirty tricks" had even led to declining support for the CIA's paramilitary capability and the dismissal of hundreds of the agency's covert action experts.

During the 1970s most of the national security establishment assumed that the U.S. "backyard"—the Caribbean, Central and South America—was under control. U.S. assistance had engineered the death of "Che" Guevara in Bolivia in 1967 and destroyed the *foco* theory of guerrilla warfare. In Guatemala and Nicaragua, small local guerrilla forces met with serious reverses in 1967–1968. Modest counterinsurgency and security assistance programs extended to repressive governments kept the lid on popular movements elsewhere, and with the help of the CIA, Allende's experiment in democratic socialism in Chile was over. Cuba, seen as the source of all revolutionary movements in Latin America, was generally assumed to be effectively "contained." U.S. Southern Command (SOUTHCOM) had no overall strategy; a country-by-country, haphazard array of old programs seemed enough to keep its domain quiet.

But the Sandinista triumph in Nicaragua in 1979 sounded alarm bells in Washington. For the Right, unprepared for "another Cuba" so close to home, it was a frightening new development. Coming just four months after Maurice Bishop's equally unexpected seizure of power in Grenada, the Sandinista revolution—an explosion of indigenous nationalism—signaled that the U.S. strategy for counterrevolution was in need of a thorough overhaul. Col. John Waghelstein commented,

> *The triumph of the Sandinistas in Nicaragua, the insurgency of El Salvador and Cuba's renewed efforts in the Caribbean Basin have conspired to force the Army to re-evaluate its priorities—and, like St. Paul on the road to Damascus, many have become converts and begun to reassess our capability.*[13]

■

Within the United States, the Right was in open rebellion. "After the disasters of the loss of Vietnam and the collapse of the Nixon presidency," charged Ray S. Cline, a right-wing policy adviser and former Deputy Director of the CIA, "the U.S. began to drift almost aimlessly in its strategic thinking."[14] Dissident officials of the Nixon–Ford era like Fred Ikle had joined with Jeane Kirkpatrick and other neoconservative Democrats to form the Committee on the Present Danger and other think tanks and policy groups. Dozens of military and intelligence experts dissatisfied with the direction of U.S. national security policy flocked to older entities such as Georgetown University's Center for Strategic and International Studies (CSIS) and the National Strategy Information Center (NSIC). "We have done nothing but try to forget what we should have learned from our defeat," wrote one right-wing analyst.[15] Bitter and determined, they began to study war some more.

Spearheaded by members of the intelligence community, the conservatives launched an all-out assault on the strategy of accommodation with the Soviet Union and its Third World "proxies." In its place, they called for a resumption of Cold War principles, but with a contemporary twist. Their

perspective was not one of simple old-style militarism, and they had no objection to counterinsurgency as such. Rather, the Right lobbied against what it saw as an insufficiently anti-communist perspective by the Trilateralists and the Carter Administration, which it blamed for the "loss" of a number of Third World countries.

The conservatives read an ominous trend in "Kremlin support for so-called wars of national liberation."[16] U.S. national security, they argued, required not only a major buildup of conventional and nuclear forces, but the development of a new capability and an effective strategy for fighting revolutionary forces in the Third World.

The military itself was a relatively minor player in this emerging policy debate, although its reassessment of the Vietnam War did take on growing significance. The best-known critic of the United States' performance in Vietnam, Col. Harry Summers, called for a return to the fundamental principles of warfare in his book *On Strategy*. Summers charged that the U.S. military bureaucracy itself was responsible for the defeat in Vietnam. The internal bickering, failure to set and agree on goals and lack of unity of command that had marred its performance in Vietnam now left the United States "dangerously unprepared" to fight future Third World conflicts.[17]

Though Summers explicitly rejected counterinsurgency as a U.S. Army mission, some of his criticisms fit the agenda of the resurgent Right. Vietnam-era "political warfare" hawks, in particular, identified with Summers' insistence on subordinating military means to political goals, and agreed that U.S. troops could not substitute for local forces engaged in counterinsurgency and nation-building. They counted on Summers' prestige at the Pentagon, where he was admired as a radical conservative, to give credibility to proposals for structural changes in the national security apparatus.

The low-intensity advocates neither expected nor wanted the Pentagon to abandon its NATO commitments or to scrap existing nuclear and conventional weapons programs. But hoping to gain some turf—probably in a Third World arena of lower priority—they lobbied incessantly for a new capability against "terrorism" and insurgency, fronts on which they claimed the United States was losing ground to communist forces. In promoting low-intensity conflict, they were practicing their own form of insurgency against the conventional military establishment: in the words of one advocate of the new approach, they were "using special operations on the system to make the system work."[18]

■

Today, the proponents of low-intensity conflict are enjoying a political climate in which their ideas can flourish. Even so, the doctrine is still an emerging one, and though it has made major advances, it has not been entirely accepted at the theoretical level—much less effectively implemented on the ground. Lewis Tambs, currently U.S. Ambassador to Costa Rica, complains that victory by means of low-intensity principles depends on winning "three battles—in the field, in the media, and in Washington within the Administration."[19] Low-intensity conflict advocates still have some way to go on each front.

Bureaucratic inertia is the first obstacle. Like most large institutions, the Pentagon is not eager to embrace sudden change. Within the defense establishment, there is a bias against the disruption of the traditional patterns of command, career development and procurement implied by a major doctrinal shift. The regular military has always resented "special" or elite forces separate from the other services, yet has resisted the introduction of "unconventional" perspectives within its own ranks. For civilian agencies such as the CIA, the State Department and AID, coordinating operations among rival bureaucracies, and with the Pentagon, remains a major problem. On the ground, meanwhile, local forces trained for decades in conventional military science, and local leaders with their own national agendas, are often resistant to further *yanqui* interference.

Even before engaging the enemy in the Third World, then, the advocates of low-intensity conflict must convince the Pentagon bureaucracy, civilian officials and other government agencies of their case. They must win over key decision-makers—both political and military—in the security establishments of their foreign allies. And, increasingly, they must complement this internal debate and diplomacy with a full-scale effort to rally the U.S. public behind the policy.

■

Low-intensity conflict is a radical concept partly because it calls for changes within the system itself. It means integrating military science with all other aspects of government policy, and implies new levels of inter-agency coordination. It involves securing the agreement of third parties—countries that include Israel, Taiwan and South Korea—to act as reliable suppliers of hardware and training. And the new doctrine, as it has evolved since Vietnam, means enlisting the resources and ideological convictions of the private sector to aid the efforts of government.

Low-intensity conflict is also radical, however, in the comprehensiveness of its approach. It draws on a wide-ranging study of the different elements of conflict, few of which are strictly military. Researchers at think tanks and universities attempt to analyze and mimic the politico–military structures of revolutionary movements; others study the "backwards" tactics of guerrilla warfare, which invert traditional military rules of engagement, or delve into anthropology and social psychology; others still, like Britain's Brig. Gen. Frank Kitson, dwell on the British and French colonial experiences, and propose sophisticated police states as the means for preventing insurgencies.[20]

The low-intensity conflict strategists have analyzed earlier U.S. experiments with unconventional warfare behind enemy lines, such as the work of the Office of Strategic Services—forerunner of the CIA—during World War II. They have reassessed nation-building projects such as the Alliance for Progress, and evaluated new economic assistance programs in terms of their potential contribution to internal security. Edward Lansdale, the legendary counterinsurgency expert whose exploits in the Kennedy era have made him a hero to a new generation of low-intensity hawks, recalls his experiences with psychological warfare and covert operations in the Philippines and South East Asia and predicts, "I think they're going to listen to us this time."[21]

■

The most visible manifestation of this new interest in low-intensity conflict has been the promotion of "special operations forces" (SOF), a concept that builds on the counterinsurgency capability of the U.S. Army Special Forces, Navy SEALS and irregular units of the other services. Since 1981, old units have been revitalized and expanded by at least a third; special operations forces now number 14,900—or 32,000 including reserves.[22] They have an important role to play in training, combat support and "special operations" in a low-intensity context. Both the Army Civil Affairs and Psychological Operations battalions, based at Fort Bragg, North Carolina (home of the John F. Kennedy Special Warfare Center), played a vital part in the invasion of Grenada and the post-invasion "pacification" of the Grenadian population. Army Special Forces Mobile Training Teams (MTTs) are currently assigned to El Salvador, Honduras, Belize and Costa Rica. The 55 SOF advisers in El Salvador are involved in most phases of the counterinsurgency war, and a battalion of Green Berets is permanently stationed at Fort Gulick in Panama.

This visible growth in SOF strength does not, however, suggest that elite U.S. commando units would take the lead in fighting a Central American war. Rather, they are conceived of as one element in a strategy of flexible response to a complex, multidimensional conflict situation. Though some doubts about their usefulness may linger in more conventional quarters of the Pentagon, the special operations forces have become a convenient handle for addressing the issue of how the United States should build a low-intensity capability.

Another proposal, to develop a "light infantry," is a compromise program with something for everyone: it is a further avenue for the creation of new combat units and training programs, and for initiating research and development on counter-revolutionary warfare. Like the SOF, the "light infantry" concept offers low-intensity conflict advocates a new field for experimentation without threatening entrenched services, and a way of enlisting Pentagon support for low-intensity conflict. It also conveniently dovetails with the concerns of congressional proponents of "military reform."

While the military builds its unconventional warfare capability, the intelligence community has undergone a parallel expansion. The CIA has rehired hundreds of covert action experts lost during the Carter years, and strengthened its position within the national security establishment, recovering prestige as well as influence. It has also developed a virtual army of its own, a secret and unconventional force of soldiers and guerrilla warfare specialists. This vast expansion of the CIA's paramilitary assets, together with resources supplied by friendly third countries, has allowed it to expand into areas that go far beyond traditional intelligence-gathering or limited tactical operations. The United States is now able to take the strategic initiative in low-intensity conflicts, and launch offensive guerrilla operations against established governments—the mining of Nicaragua's harbors being only the most striking example.

■

All these elements have now been combined into a new instrument for re-establishing U.S. political control in the Third World. The 1980s have seen the birth of the so-called Reagan Doctrine, which proclaims a "global offensive against communism at the fringes of the Soviet Empire."[23] This doctrine, outlined by the President and by Secretary of State George Shultz in 1984, places "Soviet imperialism" squarely behind instability and what the Administration calls "terrorism" in the Third World. Rather than directly attack the Soviet Union in Eastern Europe, the doctrine singles out alleged embodiments of the Soviet/terrorist threat, such as Nicaragua, Angola, Kampuchea and Afghanistan, as targets for "rollback" by the United States. As Elliott Abrams, Assistant Secretary of State for Inter-

American Affairs, explains, "We all believe that it would be morally justifiable to invade Poland for the same reasons that it was morally justifiable to invade Grenada. But it would be crazy to do it."[24]

At the same time, the Reagan Doctrine provides a more subtle rationale for continued low-intensity intervention in the Third World. On the premise that the Soviet Union has initiated a global plan for low-intensity war in the developing world, the doctrine has the potential to convert conflicts in such places as the Philippines, Haiti or Southern Africa into anti-communist and anti-terrorist showdowns. The Reagan Administration, facing a real decline in U.S. hegemony over a changing world, is determined to reassert itself by "projecting U.S. power" overseas, and stands ready to take direct control over a number of countries in crisis, both in Latin America and elsewhere in the Third World. Washington will block existing or potential models of independent development, and impose substitute models of its own—though these may not necessarily resemble the old autocracies blindly backed in the past.

The Reagan Doctrine attempts to blend older, often conflicting, approaches to Third World revolutionary movements into a new, integrated whole. Earlier administrations and their security advisers promoted differing interpretations of the origins of revolution. Some thought the causes were internal, lying in social and economic inequalities, poverty, lack of education and the absence of democratic political structures. Others insisted the causes were external, rooted in world communism and Soviet—or Soviet/Cuban—agitation.

Under President John F. Kennedy, the United States made its first stab at dealing with both aspects, combining the reforms of the Alliance for Progress with aggressive anti-communism on the military front. The counterinsurgency specialists of the Kennedy era argued for aid to civilians as well as for the development of the Green Berets to be "our own guerrilla force." But these solutions lacked any consistent ideological framework, and proved unable to cement the institutional support that is needed for multi-agency programs to work effectively.

■

The synthesis offered by the Reagan Administration begins, in a sense, where the Kennedy experiment left off, but with new urgency and coherence. It reiterates that revolution has both internal and external causes, and in the emerging doctrine of low-intensity conflict, it claims to have found a methodology that can deal with both. Regardless of its eventual success on the ground, the new doctrine does at least have the potential, in the present political climate, to become a truly bipartisan framework for approaching conflict in the Third World.

The Reagan Doctrine, while admittedly drawing on the experiments of the past, is qualitatively different from its predecessors. Reagan's innovation is to provide open backing for paramilitary insurgents or "freedom fighters" against a series of established Third World governments while simultaneously waging counterinsurgency campaigns against left-wing guerrilla movements. This gives "political" warfare an entirely new dimension. In Reagan Administration parlance, this is "revolutionary democracy," an ideological struggle designed to prove that the United States is capable of exporting counterrevolution, and that it has not only the means, but also the will and the moral and legal right to do so.[25]

In the right-wing political climate of 1986, there is more support than ever for restructuring parts of the U.S. military to conduct these unconventional forms of warfare, and for expanding the "Army" to include new institutional players from outside the Pentagon. But lobbying is not enough: the proponents of low-intensity conflict need to demonstrate the success of their theory on the ground. Each country in Central America—Panama, El Salvador, Nicaragua, Honduras, Costa Rica and Guatemala—as well as Cuba and the other island nations of the Caribbean—is a laboratory for what Col. Waghelstein calls "total war at the grassroots level." And the outcome of these experiments in the Caribbean Basin will determine, to a large extent, the lasting impact of low-intensity conflict doctrine on U.S. strategy.

1. Jeff Stein, "An Interview with Robert E. White, Former U.S. Ambassador to El Salvador," *The Progressive* (September 1981), p. 22.

2. *Newsweek,* October 26, 1981.

3. Morton Kondracke, "Enders' End," *The New Republic,* June 27, 1983.

4. Lt. Com. Frank Aker, "The Third World War and Central America: U.S. Strategic and Security Considerations in the Caribbean Basin," Military Policy Symposium, U.S. Army War College (November 1982), p. 9.

5. Lt. Col. David L. Caldon, USMC, "The Role of Security Assistance in the Irregular Conflict Ongoing in the Caribbean Basin Today: Prevention—Deterrence—Counteraction," *Journal of International Security Assistance* (Spring 1983), p. 31.

6. George Tanham, discussant, "Organizational Strategy and Low-Intensity Conflicts," in *Special Operations in U.S. Strategy,* p. 294.

7. Morelli and Ferguson, "Low-Intensity Conflict: An Operational Perspective," p. 7.

8. Bernard Fall, *Street Without Joy* (Harrisburg, PA: Stackpole Books, 1963), p. 356.

9. Dr. Sam C. Sarkesian, "Low-Intensity Conflict: Concepts, Principles and Policy Guidelines," *Air University Review* (January–February 1985), p. 5.

10. *The New York Times,* June 26, 1985.

11. "Approaching a New Stage of the War," *Envío* (Managua, Nicaragua: Instituto Histórico Centroamericano, December 1984).

12. Morelli and Ferguson, "Low-Intensity Conflict: An Operational Perspective," p. 11.

13. *The Miami Herald,* October 24, 1983.

14. "The Wartime Economy," *Envío,* October 1984.

15. Lt. Gen. Gordon Sumner (Ret.), "Negotiating with Marxists in Central America," address to International Security Council Forum, Washington, DC, March 21, 1985.

16. The author is indebted for this phrase to the Instituto Histórico Centroamericano. See *Envío,* December 1984.

17. "FM 95-1A Guerrilla War Manual," special supplement to *Soldier of Fortune* (February 1985). The manual was also published as *Psychological Operations in Guerrilla Warfare* (New York: Vintage Books, 1985) with essays by Joanne Omang and Aryeh Neier. Translations here are from *Soldier of Fortune.*

18. David Kamowitz, "Low-Intensity Warfare in One Region: Nicaragua's Segovias" (unpublished ms., July 1985).

19. Al Zamierowski, interview with Adolfo Calero on Radio Liberty, Dallas, TX, September 11, 1985.

20. Interview with *Comandante* Luís Carrión, in "La Voz de América Latina Frente al Terrorismo," *Envío* (August 1985).

21. Robert Asprey, *War in the Shadows* (New York: Doubleday & Co., 1975), Vol. II, p. 1129.

22. See "Duarte: Prisoner of War," *Report on the Americas,* Vol. XX, no. 1 (January–March 1986).

23. Clarence Lusane, "Israeli Arms in Central America," *Covert Action Information Bulletin* (Winter 1984).

24. For a discussion of these developments, see José Rodolfo Castro Orellana, "El plan de contrainsurgencia norteamericano para El Salvador y los cambios en las fuerzas armadas gubernamentales" (Managua, Nicaragua: Coordinadora Regional de Investigaciones Económicas y Sociales, CRIES: August 1985).

25. Col. John Waghelstein, talk at American Enterprise Institute, Washington, DC, January 16, 1985.

NUCLEAR DETERRENCE VS. DEFENSE

Victory Is Possible

Colin S. Gray ▪ *Keith Payne*

Nuclear war is possible. But unlike Armageddon, the apocalyptic war prophesied to end history, nuclear war can have a wide range of possible outcomes. Many commentators and senior U.S. government officials consider it a nonsurvivable event. The popularity of this view in Washington has such a pervasive and malign effect upon American defense planning that it is rapidly becoming a self-fulfilling prophecy for the United States.

Recognition that war at any level can be won or lost, and that the distinction between winning and losing would not be trivial, is essential for intelligent defense planning. Moreover, nuclear war can occur regardless of the quality of U.S. military posture and the content of American strategic theory. If it does, deterrence, crisis management, and escalation control might play a negligible role. Through an inability to communicate or through Soviet disinterest in receiving and acting upon American messages, the United States might not even have the option to surrender and thus might have to fight the war as best it can. Furthermore, the West needs to devise ways in which it can employ strategic nuclear forces coercively, while minimizing the potentially paralyzing impact of self-deterrence.

If American nuclear power is to support U.S. foreign policy objectives, the United States must possess the ability to wage nuclear war rationally. This requirement is inherent in the geography of East–West relations, in the persisting deficiencies in Western conventional and theater nuclear forces, and in the distinction between the objectives of a revolutionary and status quo power.

U.S. strategic planning should exploit Soviet fears insofar as is feasible from the Soviet perspective; take full account of likely Soviet responses and the willingness of Americans to accept those responses; and provide for the protection of American territory. Such planning would enhance the prospect for effective deterrence and survival during a war. Only recently has U.S. nuclear targeting policy been based on careful study of the Soviet Union as a distinct political culture, but the U.S. defense community continues to resist many of the policy implications of Soviet responses to U.S. weapons programs. In addition, the U.S. government simply does not recognize the validity of attempting to relate its freedom of offensive nuclear action and the credibility of its offense nuclear threat to the protection of American territory.

Critics of such strategic planning are vulnerable in two crucial respects: They do not, and cannot, offer policy prescriptions that will insure that the United States is never confronted with the stark choice between fighting a nuclear war or surrendering, and they do not offer a concept of deterrence that meets the extended responsibilities of the U.S. strategic nuclear forces. No matter how elegant the deterrence theory, a question that

Reprinted with permission from *Foreign Policy* 39 (Summer 1980), pp. 14–27. Copyright © 1980 by Carnegie Endowment for International Peace.

cannot be avoided is what happens if deterrence mechanisms fail? Theorists whose concept of deterrence is limited to massive retaliation after Soviet attack would have nothing of interest to say to a president facing conventional defeat in the Persian Gulf or in Western Europe. Their strategic environment exists only in peacetime. They can recommend very limited, symbolic options but have no theory of how a large-scale Soviet response is to be deterred.

Because many believe that homeland defense will lead to a steeper arms race and destabilize the strategic balance, the U.S. defense community has endorsed a posture that maximizes the prospect for self-deterrence. Yet the credibility of the extended U.S. deterrent depends on the Soviet belief that a U.S. president would risk nuclear escalation on behalf of foreign commitments.

In the late 1960s the United States endorsed the concept of strategic parity without thinking through what that would mean for the credibility of America's nuclear umbrella. A condition of parity or essential equivalence is incompatible with extended deterrent duties because of the self-deterrence inherent in such a strategic context. However, the practical implications of parity may be less dire in some areas of U.S. vital interest. Western Europe, for example, is so important an American interest that Soviet leaders could be more impressed by the character and duration of the U.S. commitment than by the details of the strategic balance.

A Threat to Commit Suicide

Ironically, it is commonplace to assert that war-survival theories affront the crucial test of political and moral acceptability. Surely no one can be comfortable with the claim that a strategy that would kill millions of Soviet citizens and would invite a strategic response that could kill tens of millions of U.S. citizens would be politically and morally acceptable. However, it is worth recalling the six guidelines for the use of force provided by the "just war" doctrine of the Catholic Church: Force can be used in a just cause; with a right

intent; with a reasonable chance of success; in order that, if successful, its use offers a better future than would have been the case had it not been employed; to a degree proportional to the goals sought, or to the evil combated; and with the determination to spare noncombatants, when there is a reasonable chance of doing so.

These guidelines carry a message for U.S. policy. Specifically, as long as nuclear threat is a part of the U.S. diplomatic arsenal and provided that threat reflects real operational intentions—it is not a total bluff—U.S. defense planners are obliged to think through the probable course of a nuclear war. They must also have at least some idea of the intended relationship between force applied and the likelihood that political goals will be achieved—that is, a strategy.

Current American strategic policy is not compatible with at least three of the six just-war guidelines. The policy contains no definition of success aside from denying victory to the enemy, no promise that the successful use of nuclear power would insure a better future than surrender, and no sense of proportion because central war strategy in operational terms is not guided by political goals. In short, U.S. nuclear strategy is immoral.

Those who believe that a central nuclear war cannot be waged for political purposes because the destruction inflicted and suffered would dwarf the importance of any political goals can construct a coherent and logical policy position. They argue that nuclear war will be the end of history for the states involved, and that a threat to initiate nuclear war is a threat to commit suicide and thus lacks credibility. However, they acknowledge that nuclear weapons cannot be abolished. They maintain that even incredible threats may deter, provided the affront in question is sufficiently serious, because miscalculation by an adversary could have terminal consequences; because genuinely irrational behavior is always possible; and because the conflict could become uncontrollable.

In the 1970s the U.S. defense community rejected this theory of deterrence. Successive strategic targeting reviews appeared to move U.S.

policy further and further from the declaratory doctrine of mutual assured destruction adopted by former Secretary of Defense Robert S. McNamara. Yet U.S. defense planners have not thoroughly studied the problems of nuclear war nor thought through the meaning of strategy in relation to nuclear war. The U.S. defense community has always tended to regard strategic nuclear war not as war but as a holocaust. Former Secretary of Defense James R. Schlesinger apparently adopted limited nuclear options (LNOs)—strikes employing anywhere from a handful to several dozen warheads—as a compromise between the optimists of the minimum deterrence school and the pessimists of the so-called war-fighting persuasion. By definition, LNOs apply only to the initial stages of a war. But what happens once LNOs have been exhausted? If the Soviets retaliated after U.S. LNOs, the United States would face the dilemma of escalating further or conciliating.

Deterrence may fail to be restored during war for several reasons: The enemy may not grant, in operational practice, the concept of intrawar deterrence and simply wage the war as it is able; and command, control, and communications may be degraded so rapidly that strategic decisions are precluded and both sides execute their war plans. Somewhat belatedly, the U.S. defense community has come to understand that flexibility in targeting and LNOs do not constitute a strategy and cannot compensate for inadequate strategic nuclear forces.

LNOs are the tactics of the strong, not of a country entering a period of strategic inferiority, as the United States is now. LNOs would be operationally viable only if the United States had a plausible theory of how it could control and dominate later escalation.

The fundamental inadequacy of flexible targeting, as presented in the 1970s, is that it neglected to take proper account of the fact that the United States would be initiating a process of competitive escalation that it had no basis for assuming could be concluded on satisfactory terms. Flexible targeting was an adjunct to plans that had no persuasive vision of how the application of force would promote the attainment of political objectives.

War Aims

U.S. strategic targeting doctrine must have a unity of political purpose from the first to the last strikes. Strategic flexibility, unless wedded to a plausible theory of how to win a war or at least insure an acceptable end to a war, does not offer the United States an adequate bargaining position before or during a conflict and is an invitation to defeat. Small, preplanned strikes can only be of use if the United States enjoys strategic superiority—the ability to wage a nuclear war at any level of violence with a reasonable prospect of defeating the Soviet Union and of recovering sufficiently to insure a satisfactory postwar world order.

However, the U.S. government does not yet appear ready to plan seriously for the actual conduct of nuclear war should deterrence fail, in spite of the fact that such a policy should strengthen deterrence. Assured-destruction reasoning is proclaimed officially to be insufficient in itself as a strategic doctrine. However, a Soviet assured-destruction capability continues to exist as a result of the enduring official U.S. disinterest in strategic defense, with potentially paralyzing implications for the United States. No matter how well designed and articulated, targeting plans that allow an enemy to inflict in retaliation whatever damage it wishes on American society are likely to prove unusable.

Four interdependent areas of strategic policy—strategy, weapons development and procurement, arms control, and defense doctrine—are currently treated separately. Theoretically, strategy should determine the evolution of the other three areas. In practice, it never has. Most of what has been portrayed as war-fighting strategy is nothing of the kind. Instead, it is an extension of the American theory of deterrence into war itself. To advocate LNOs and targeting flexibility and selectivity is not the same as to advocate a war-fighting, war-survival strategy.

Strategists do not find the idea of nuclear war fighting attractive. Instead, they believe that an ability to wage and survive war is vital for the effectiveness of deterrence; there can be no such thing as an adequate deterrent posture unrelated to probable wartime effectiveness; victory or defeat in nuclear war is possible, and such a war may have to be waged to that point; and, the clearer the vision of successful war termination, the more likely war can be waged intelligently at earlier stages.

There should be no misunderstanding the fact that the primary interest of U.S. strategy is deterrence. However, American strategic forces do not exist solely for the purpose of deterring a Soviet nuclear threat or attack against the United States itself. Instead, they are intended to support U.S. foreign policy, as reflected, for example, in the commitment to preserve Western Europe against aggression. Such a function requires American strategic forces that would enable a president to initiate strategic nuclear use for coercive, though politically defensive, purposes.

U.S. strategy, typically, has proceeded from the bottom up. Such targeting does not involve any conception of the war as a whole, nor of how the war might be concluded on favorable terms. The U.S. defense community cannot plan intelligently for lower levels of combat, unless it has an acceptable idea of where they might lead.

Most analyses of flexible targeting options assume virtually perfect stability at the highest levels of conflict. Advocates of flexible targeting assert that a U.S. LNO would signal the beginning of an escalation process that the Soviets would wish to avoid in light of the American threat to Soviet urban-industrial areas. Yet it seems inconsistent to argue that the U.S. threat of assured destruction would deter the Soviets from engaging in escalation following an LNO but that U.S. leaders could initiate the process despite the Soviet threat. What could be the basis of such relative U.S. resolve and Soviet vacillation in the face of strategic parity or Soviet superiority?

Moreover, the desired deterrent effect would ably depend upon the Soviet analysis of the entire nuclear campaign. In other words, Soviet leaders would be less impressed by American willingness to launch an LNO than they would be by a plausible American victory strategy. Such a theory would have to envisage the demise of the Soviet state. The United States should plan to defeat the Soviet Union and to do so at a cost that would not prohibit U.S. recovery. Washington should identify war aims that in the last resort would contemplate the destruction of Soviet political authority and the emergence of a postwar world order compatible with Western values.

The most frightening threat to the Soviet Union would be the destruction or serious impairment of its political system. Thus, the United States should be able to destroy key leadership cadres, their means of communication, and some of the instruments of domestic control. The USSR, with its gross overcentralization of authority, epitomized by its vast bureaucracy in Moscow, should be highly vulnerable to such an attack. The Soviet Union might cease to function if its security agency, the KGB, were severely crippled. If the Moscow bureaucracy could be eliminated, damaged, or isolated, the USSR might disintegrate into anarchy, hence the extensive civil defense preparations intended to insure the survival of the Soviet leadership. Judicious U.S. targeting and weapon procurement policies might be able to deny the USSR the assurance of political survival.

Once the defeat of the Soviet state is established as a war aim, defense professionals should attempt to identify an optimum targeting plan for the accomplishment of that goal. For example, Soviet political control of its territory in Central Asia and in the Far East could be weakened by discriminate nuclear targeting. The same applies to Transcaucasia and Eastern Europe.

The Ultimate Penalty

Despite a succession of U.S. targeting reviews, Soviet leaders, looking to the mid-1980s, may well anticipate the ability to wage World War III successfully. The continuing trend in the East–West military balance allows Soviet military planners to design a theory of military victory that is not implausible and that may stir hopes among Soviet political leaders that they might reap many of the rewards of military success even without having to fight. The Soviets may anticipate that U.S. self-deterrence could discourage Washington from punishing Soviet society. Even if the United States were to launch a large-scale second strike against Soviet military and economic targets, the resulting damage should be bearable to the Soviet Union given the stakes of the conflict and the fact that the Soviets would control regions abroad that could contribute to its recovery.

In the late 1960s the United States identified the destruction of 20–25 per cent of the population and 50–75 per cent of industrial capacity as the ultimate penalty it had to be able to inflict on the USSR. In the 1970s the United States shifted its attention to the Soviet recovery economy. The Soviet theory of victory depends on the requirement that the Soviet Union survive and recover rapidly from a nuclear conflict. However, the U.S. government does not completely understand the details of the Soviet recovery economy, and the concept has lost popularity as a result. Highly complex modeling of the Soviet economy cannot disguise the fact that the available evidence is too rudimentary to permit any confidence in the analysis. With an inadequate data base it should require little imagination to foresee how difficult it is to determine targeting priorities in relation to the importance of different economic targets for recovery.

Schlesinger's advocacy of essential equivalence called for a U.S. ability to match military damage for military damage. But American strategic development since the early 1970s has not been sufficient to maintain the American end of that balance. Because the U.S. defense community has refused to recognize the importance of the possibility that a nuclear war could be won or lost, it has neglected to think beyond a punitive sequence of targeting options.

American nuclear strategy is not intended to defeat the Soviet Union or insure the survival of the United States in any carefully calculated manner. Instead, it is intended to insure that the Soviet Union is punished increasingly severely. American targeting philosophy today is only a superficial improvement over that prevalent in the late 1960s, primarily because U.S. defense planners do not consider anticipated damage to the United States to be relevant to the integrity of their offensive war

plans. The strategic case for ballistic missile defense and civil defense has not been considered on its merits for a decade.

In the late 1970s the United States targeted a range of Soviet economic entities that were important either to war-supporting industry or to economic recovery. The rationale for this targeting scheme was, and remains, fragile. War-supporting industry is important only for a war of considerable duration or for a period of postwar defense mobilization. Moreover, although recovery from war is an integral part of a Soviet theory of victory, it is less important than the achievement of military success. If the USSR is able to win the war, it should have sufficient military force in reserve to compel the surviving world economy to contribute to Soviet recovery. Thus, the current trend is to move away from targeting the recovery economy.

To date, the U.S. government has declined to transcend what amounts to a deterrance-through-punishment approach to strategic war planning. Moreover, the strategic targeting reviews of the 1970s did not address the question of self-deterrence adequately. The United States has no ballistic missile defense and effectively no civil defense, while U.S. air defense is capable of guarding American air space only in peacetime. The Pentagon has sought to compensate for a lack of relative military muscle through more imaginative strategic targeting. Review after review has attempted to identify more effective ways in which the USSR could be hurt. Schlesinger above all sought essential equivalence through a more flexible set of targeting options without calling for extensive new U.S. strategic capabilities. Indeed, he went to some pains to separate the question of targeting design from procurement issues.

The United States should identify nuclear targeting options that could help restore deterrence, yet would destroy the Soviet state and enhance the likelihood of U.S. survival if fully implemented. The first priority of such a targeting scheme would be Soviet military power of all kinds, and the second would be the political, military, and economic control structure of the USSR. Successful strikes against military and political control targets would reduce the Soviet ability to project military power abroad and to sustain political authority at home. However, it would not be in the interest of the United States actually to implement an offensive nuclear strategy no matter how frightening in Soviet perspective, if the U.S. homeland were totally naked to Soviet retaliation.

Striking the USSR should entail targeting the relocation bunkers of the top political and bureaucratic leadership, including those of the KGB; key communication centers of the Communist party, the military, and the government; and many of the economic, political, and military records. Even limited destruction of some of these targets and substantial isolation of many of the key personnel who survive could have revolutionary consequences for the country.

The Armageddon Syndrome

The strategic questions that remain incompletely answered are in some ways more difficult than the practical problems of targeting the political control structure. Is it sensible to destroy the government of the enemy, thus eliminating the option of negotiating an end to the war? In the unlikely event that the United States identifies all the key relocation bunkers for the central political leadership, who would then conduct the Soviet war effort and to what ends? Since after a large-scale counter-control strike the surviving Soviet leadership would have little else to fear, could this targeting option be anything other than a threat?

The U.S. defense community today believes that the political control structure of the USSR is among the most important targets for U.S. strategic forces. However, just how important such targeting might be for deterrence or damage limitation has not been determined. Current American understanding of exactly how the control structure functions is less than perfect. But that is a technical matter that can in principle be solved through more research. The issue of whether the Soviet control structure should actually be struck is more problematic.

Strategists cannot offer painless conflicts or guarantee that their preferred posture and doctrine promise a greatly superior deterrence posture to current American schemes. But, they can claim that an intelligent U.S. offensive strategy, wedded to homeland defenses, should reduce U.S. casualties to approximately 20 million, which should render U.S. strategic threats more credible. If the United States developed the targeting plans and procured the weapons necessary to hold the Soviet political, bureaucratic, and military leadership at risk, that should serve as the functional equivalent in Soviet perspective of the assured-destruction effect of the late 1960s. However, the U.S. targeting community has not determined how it would organize this targeting option.

A combination of counterforce offensive targeting, civil defense, and ballistic missile and air defense should hold U.S. casualties down to a level compatible with national survival and recovery. The actual number would depend on several factors, some of which the United States could control (the level of U.S. homeland defenses); some of which it could influence (the weight and character of the Soviet attack); and some of which might evade anybody's ability to control or influence (for example, the weather). What can be assured is a choice between a defense program that insures the survival of the vast majority of Americans with relative confidence and one that deliberately permits the Soviet Union to wreak whatever level of damage it chooses.

No matter how grave the Soviet offense, a U.S. president cannot credibly threaten and should not launch a strategic nuclear strike if expected U.S. casualties are likely to involve 100 million or more American citizens. There is a difference between a doctrine that can offer little rational guidance should deterrence fail and a doctrine that a president might employ responsibly for identified political purposes. Existing evidence on the probable consequences of nuclear exchanges suggests that there should be a role for strategy in nuclear war. To ignore the possibility that strategy can be applied to nuclear war is to insure by choice a nuclear apocalypse if deterrence fails. The current U.S. deterrence posture is fundamentally flawed because it does not provide for the protection of American territory.

Nuclear war is unlikely to be an essentially meaningless, terminal event. Instead it is likely to be waged to coerce the Soviet Union to give up some recent gain. Thus, a president must have the ability not merely to end a war, but to end it favorably. The United States would need to be able to persuade desperate and determined Soviet leaders that it has the capability, and the determination, to wage nuclear war at ever higher levels of violence until an acceptable outcome is achieved. For deterrence to function during a war each side would have to calculate whether an improved outcome is possible through further escalation.

An adequate U.S. deterrent posture is one that denies the Soviet Union any plausible hope of success at any level of strategic conflict; offers a likely prospect for Soviet defeat; and offers a reasonable chance of limiting damage to the United States. Such a deterrence posture is often criticized as contributing to the arms race and causing strategic instability, because it would stimulate new Soviet deployments. However, during the 1970s the Soviet Union showed that its weapon development and deployment decisions are not dictated by American actions. Western understand-

ing of what determines Soviet defense procurement is less than perfect, but it is now obvious that Soviet weapon decisions cannot be explained with reference to any simple action–reaction model of arms-race dynamics. In addition, highly survivable U.S. strategic forces should insure strategic stability by denying the Soviets an attractive first-strike target set.

An Armageddon syndrome lurks behind most concepts of nuclear strategy. It amounts either to the belief that because the United States could lose as many as 20 million people, it should not save the 80 million or more who otherwise would be at risk, or to a disbelief in the serious possibility that 200 million Americans could survive a nuclear war.

There is little satisfaction in advocating an operational nuclear doctrine that could result in the deaths of 20 million or more people in an unconstrained nuclear war. However, as long as the United States relies on nuclear threats to deter an increasingly powerful Soviet Union, it is inconceivable that the U.S. defense community can continue to divorce its thinking on deterrence from its planning for the efficient conduct of war and defense of the country. Prudence in the latter should enhance the former.

On Fighting a Nuclear War

Michael E. Howard

Thirty-five years have passed since Bernard Brodie, in the first book that he or indeed anyone else had written about nuclear war, set down these words:

> The first and most vital step in any American security program for the age of atomic bombs is to take measures to guarantee to ourselves in case of attack the possibility of retaliation in kind. The writer in making this statement is not for the moment concerned about who will win the next war in which atomic bombs have been used. Thus far the chief purpose of our military establishment has been to win wars. From now on its chief purpose must be to avert them. It can have almost no other useful purpose.[1]

For most of those thirty-five years, the truth of this revolutionary doctrine was accepted in the Western world as self-evident, and our whole military posture became based on the concept of deterrence that Brodie had defined so presciently and so soon. The fear of nuclear war *as such* was considered sufficient deterrent against the initiation of large-scale violence on the scale of the Second World War, and the policy of the United States, its allies, and perhaps also its adversaries was to create a strategic framework that made it not only certain that a nuclear attack would provoke a nuclear response, but likely that an attack with conventional weapons would do so as well. It was agreed almost without a dissenting voice that nuclear wars were "unwinnable." A nuclear exchange on any scale would cause damage of a kind that would make a mockery of the whole concept of "victory."

When Brodie died, that consensus was beginning to disintegrate. In the last article he published, on "The Development of Nuclear Strategy," he reprinted the passage and defended it. While accepting the changes that had occurred both in weapons technology and in the structure of the military balance over the past thirty years, he saw no reason to alter his view. It was necessary to develop and to deploy nuclear weapons in order to deter their use by others. Such weapons, he believed, might perhaps be utilizable on a limited scale in the European theater. But as instruments of policy, as strategic tools in a general war, they could have no utility. Nuclear war was unfightable, unwinnable.

Was he wrong? Let me offer my own answer to that question.

Bernard Brodie's belief that a nuclear war could not be "won" did not of course mean that he did not hold strong views about the optimal deployment and targeting of nuclear weapons, a matter on which his opinion was greatly valued by successive Chiefs of the Air Staff. The maintenance of a credible capacity for nuclear retaliation, and its structuring so as to create maximum political and psychological effect, was a problem with which he concerned himself deeply throughout his career. But if deterrence failed and these weapons had in fact to be used, what then? What should the political objective of the war be, and how would

Reprinted from *International Security,* Vol. 5, No. 4 by permission of The MIT Press, Cambridge, MA. © 1981 by the President and Fellows of Harvard College and the Massachusetts Institute of Technology.

nuclear devastation help to attain it? How and with whom was a peace to be negotiated? Above all, in what shape would the United States be, after suffering substantial nuclear devastation herself, to negotiate any peace?

Brodie could have asked further questions, and no doubt did. What would be the relations between the Soviet Union and the United States after such a war? What would their position be in an international community that could hardly have emerged intact from a nuclear battle on so global a scale? In what way could the post-nuclear world environment be seen as an improvement on the pre-war situation and one which it was worth enduring—and inflicting—such unimaginable suffering in order to attain? It is not surprising that, in his 1978 article, Brodie should have defined "the main war goal upon the beginning of a strategic nuclear exchange" as being "to terminate it as quickly as possible and with the least amount of damage possible—on both sides."

This phrase was taken up a year later by one of Brodie's keenest critics, Mr. Colin Gray, who countered: "Of course the best prospect of all for minimizing (prompt) damage lies in surrendering pre-emptively. If Bernard Brodie's advice were accepted, the West would be totally at the mercy of a Soviet Union, which viewed war in a rather more traditional perspective."[2] By the time that article appeared, Bernard Brodie had died, but I can well imagine his sardonic response: "Would the Soviet Union or anyone else view *anything* in a 'traditional perspective' *after* a nuclear exchange?"

Colin Gray's question does however go to the heart of the problem that has led many people in the United States to reject the conventional wisdom of Brodie's position as no longer relevant in a new and harsher age. Today, there is widespread doubt that a posture of nuclear deterrence, however structured, will be enough to prevent a Soviet Union that accepts nuclear war as an instrument of policy and has built up a formidable nuclear arsenal from thinking the unthinkable, from not only initiating but fighting through a nuclear conflict in the expectation of victory, whether the United States wishes to do so or not. And if such a conflict is forced upon the United

States, how can she conduct it effectively unless she also has a positive objective to guide her strategy, other than the mass annihilation of Soviet civilians? Should she not also regard nuclear war "in a rather more traditional perspective"?

The controversy over this question will be familiar to every reader of foreign policy and military affairs. But it is worthwhile to at least briefly review it, in an effort to clarify current perceptions on the matter.

Let me make it clear from the outset that on the fundamental issue of nuclear war-fighting, I side with Bernard Brodie rather than with his critics. As I understand it, the criticism of the deterrent posture arises from two linked sources. The first is the development of missile technology; the growing accuracy of guidance systems, the miniaturization of warheads, the increasing capability of target acquisition processes, the whole astounding panoply of scientific development in which the United States has, to my knowledge, in every instance taken the lead, with the Soviet Union, at great cost to its economy, keeping up as best it can. Incidentally, I find it curious that a scientific community that was so anguished over its moral responsibility for the development of the first crude nuclear bombs should have ceased to trouble itself over its continuing involvement with weapons systems whose lethality and effectiveness make the weapons that destroyed Hiroshima and Nagasaki look like clumsy toys. Be that as it may, it is the continuous inventiveness of the scientific community, and I am afraid primarily the Western scientific community, that has made the pursuit of a stable nuclear balance, of mutually assured *deterrence* (which seems to me the correct explication of that much abused acronym MAD) seem to be the chase for an *ignis fatuus,* a will o' the wisp.

The second ground for criticizing the original concept of deterrence is the widespread belief that the Soviet Union does not share it, and never has shared it. The absence from Soviet text-books of any distinction between a "deterrent" and a "war-fighting" capability; the reiterated statements that nuclear weapons cannot be exempted from the Clausewitzian imperative that military forces have no rationale save as instruments of state policy; the confident Marxist–Leninist predictions of socialism ultimately prevailing over the capitalist adversary whatever weapons systems or policies he might adopt: does this not make it clear that American attempts to indoctrinate the Soviet Union in strategic concepts quite alien to their ideology and culture have failed? And this perception of the Soviet Union as a society prepared to coolly contemplate the prospect of fighting a nuclear war as an instrument of policy is enhanced by a worst-case analysis of its capacity to do so; its first-strike capacity against U.S. land-based ICBMs; its much discussed civil defense program to reduce its own casualties to an "acceptable" level; and a historical experience of suffering which, according to some authorities, enables their leaders to contemplate without flinching the prospect of frightful damage and casualties running into scores of millions if it enables them to achieve their global objectives.

Now in dealing with those who hold this view of the Soviet Union I am conscious, only too often, that I am arguing with people whose attitude, like that of committed pacifists, is rooted in a visceral conviction beyond the reach of any discourse that I can command. It was a realization that was borne in on me by their deployment of two arguments in particular. The first was that since the Soviet Union had suffered some twenty million dead in the Second World War, they might equally contemplate further comparable losses in pursuit of a political objective sufficiently grandiose to warrant such a sacrifice. Now the United States has never suffered such losses and I hope that it never will. But it is a matter of historical record to what shifts and maneuvers Stalin was reduced in his attempt to *avoid* having to fight that war; and speaking as a representative of a people who sustained nearly a million war dead between 1914 and 1918, I suggest that the record also shows that readiness to risk heavy losses in another war does not necessarily increase in direct ratio with the sacrifices one endured in the last.

The second argument that I encountered with even greater astonishment was that which maintained that Soviet civil defense measures provided incontrovertible evidence of Soviet intentions to launch a first strike. These arguments were all the more curious in that they were advanced almost simultaneously, and often from the same sources, as the very well-reasoned advocacy of a United States civil defense program of an almost identical kind; a program adopted by President Kennedy's Administration and abandoned only in face of the kind of popular and Congressional resistance with which the Soviet leadership does not have to contend. The difference between the development of civil defense in the two countries thus tells one rather more about their respective political structures than about their strategic intentions. Until recently indeed it would not have occurred to anyone outside a tiny group of strategic analysts in this country that civil defense preparations were anything except prudent and proper precautions for a remote but horribly finite possibility. Unfortunately their view is now more widely spread; and those of us in Europe who have been urging the advisability of taking even minimal precautions for civil defense now find ourselves accused by true believers on the left, as the Russians are accused by true believers on the right, of planning to precipitate the very catastrophe against which we seek to insure.

The debate about Soviet intentions has been conducted by people so far more expert than myself that I shall not seek to add to it beyond underlining and reinforcing Bernard Brodie's gently understated comment on those who see the build-up of Soviet forces over the past two decades as incontrovertible proof of their aggressive intentions:

> *Where the Committee on the Present Danger in one of its brochures speaks of "the brutal momentum of the massive Soviet strategic arms build-up—a build-up without precedent in history," it is speaking of something which no student of the American strategic arms build-up in the sixties could possibly consider unprecedented.*[3]

In fact one of the oldest "lessons of history" is that the armaments of an adversary always seem "brutal" and threatening; adjectives that appear tendentious and absurd when applied to one's own.

The sad conclusion that I draw from this debate is that no amount of argument or evidence to the contrary will convince a large number of sincere, well-informed, highly intelligent and now very influential people that the Soviet Union is not an implacably aggressive power quite prepared to use nuclear weapons as an instrument of its policy. My own firmly-held belief, however, is that the leadership of the Soviet Union, and any successors they may have within the immediately foreseeable future, are cautious and rather fearful men, increasingly worried about their almost insoluble internal problems, increasingly aware of their isolation in a world in which the growth of Marxian socialism does little to enhance their political power, deeply torn between gratification at the problems which beset the capitalist world economy and alarm at the difficulties which those problems are creating within their own empire; above all conscious of the inadequacy of the simplistic doctrines of Marxism–Leninism on which they were nurtured to explain a world far more complex and diverse than either Marx or Lenin ever conceived. Their *Staatspolitik,* that complex web of interests, perceptions and ideals which Clausewitz believed should determine the use of military power, thus gives them no clearer guidance as to how to use their armed forces than ours gives to us.

The evidence for this view of Soviet intentions seems to me at least as conclusive as that for the beliefs of, for example, the Committee on the Present Danger, who will no doubt consider me to be as visceral, emotive and irrational in my beliefs as I have found all too many of their publications. I would only say, in defense of my own views, first that they take rather more account of the complexities of the historic, political and economic problems of the Soviet Union than do theirs; and secondly, for what it is worth, that they correspond more closely with those held by most of the Europeans among whom I move than do those of the Committee on the Present Danger. Naturally in Europe as elsewhere there is a diversity of views, and there can be few more enthusiastic supporters of Mr. Paul Nitze than my own Prime Minister. Nonetheless, I have found in Europe a far more relaxed attitude towards the Russians than I have ever encountered in the United States; because,

paradoxically, we are not more frightened of them than are Americans, but rather less. I think we find it easier to see them as real people, with real, and alarming, problems of their own: people of whom we must be constantly wary and whose military power and propensity to use it when they perceive they can safely do so is certainly formidable; but with whom it is possible to do business, in every sense of the word, and certainly not as people who have any interest in, or intention of, deliberately unleashing a nuclear war as an instrument of policy.

And here again I should like to underline, if possible with even greater emphasis, what Bernard Brodie had to say about the Soviet dedication to Clausewitz's theory of the relationship of war to policy, if only as an act of personal homage to both Brodie and Clausewitz. Clausewitz was a subtle, profound and versatile thinker, and his teaching about the relationship between war and policy was only one of the many insights he provided into the whole phenomenon of war. "War," he wrote, "is only a branch of political activity; it is in no sense autonomous . . . [It] cannot be divorced from political life—and whenever this occurs in our thinking about war, the many links that connect the two elements are destroyed, and we are left with something that is pointless and devoid of sense."[4]

Insofar as the Russians believe this and hammer it into the heads of successive generations of soldiers and politicians, we should admire and imitate them. When they castigate us for ignoring it and for discussing nuclear war, as we almost invariably do, *in vacuo,* they are absolutely right, and we should be grateful for their criticism. When I read the flood of scenarios in strategic journals about first-strike capabilities, counterforce or countervailing strategies, flexible response, escalation dominance and the rest of the postulates of nuclear theology, I ask myself in bewilderment: this war they are describing, *what is it about?* The defense of Western Europe? Access to the Gulf? The protection of Japan? If so, why is this goal not mentioned, and why is the strategy not related to the progress of the conflict in these regions? But if it is not related to this kind of specific object, what are we talking about? Has not the bulk of American thinking been exactly what Clausewitz described—something that, because it is divorced from any political context, is "pointless and devoid of sense"?

When I made these comments in a now much quoted article in *Foreign Affairs,* I was gratified but slightly alarmed by the response. I certainly did not expect my arguments to be cited in support of the thesis that a nuclear war is fightable and winnable, and that we should base our strategy on that assumption; and I am grateful for this opportunity to distance myself from that school of thought and explain why I do so.

I do not deny that Soviet theoreticians attempt to fit nuclear weapons into their Clausewitzean framework, and maintain that, should nuclear war occur, nuclear weapons should be used in order to forward the overall goals of policy and ensure a victory for the armed forces of the Soviet Union. But one only has to state the opposite of this doctrine to accept that it is in theory unexceptionable, and that it would be difficult for them to say anything else. The ideological and bureaucratic framework within which this Soviet teaching has evolved has been convincingly described in recent articles by such experts as Ambassador Raymond Garthoff and Mr. Benjamin Lambeth,[5] and I find convincing the formulation propounded by the latter:

> [The Russians] approach their strategic planning with the thoroughly traditional conviction that despite the revolutionary advances in destructive power brought about by modern weapons and delivery systems, the threat of nuclear war persists as a fundamental feature of the international system and obliges the Soviet Union to take every practical measure to prepare for its eventuality. . . . They appear persuaded that in the nuclear age no less than before, the most reliable way to prevent war is to maintain the appropriate wherewithal to fight and win it should it occur.

Logical as this doctrine may appear, and no doubt necessary for the maintenance both of ideological consistency and of military morale in the Soviet Union, the West's response, it seems to me, should *not* be to imitate it but to make it clear to the Russians, within their own Clausewitzean framework, that it simply will not work: that there is no way in which the use of strategic nuclear weapons could be a rational instrument of State policy, for them or for anyone else.

This view commands a satisfying wide consensus—or did until recently. Mr. Paul Nitze himself, in his famous plea for a maximalist U.S. defense posture, emphasized that the object of the measures he proposed "would not be to give the United States a war-fighting capability: it would be to deny to the Soviet Union the possibility of a successful war-fighting capability";[6] and another leading thinker of the maximalist school, Mr. Colin Gray, also accepts that "one of the essential tasks of the American defense community is to help ensure that in moments of crisis the Soviet general staff cannot brief the Politburo with a plausible theory of military victory."[7] But Mr. Gray believes that another task of the defense community is to brief the White House with a plausible theory of military victory, and that is surely a very different matter.

Mr. Gray is a Clausewitzean and believes that U.S. strategy should be geared to a positive political object. "Washington" he suggests, "should identify war aims that in the last resort would contemplate the destruction of Soviet political authority and the emergence of a post-war world order compatible with Western values."[8] For this it would be necessary to destroy, not the peoples of the Soviet Union in genocidal attacks on cities, but the apparatus of the Soviet state. The principal assets of the latter, he identifies as "the political control structure of the highly centralized Communist Party of the Soviet Union and government bureaucracy; the transmission belts of communication from the center to the regions; the instruments of central official coercion (the KGB and armed forces); and the reputation of the Soviet state in the eyes of its citizens. . . . The entire Soviet political and economic system," he writes, "is critically dependent upon central direction from Moscow. If the brain of the Soviet system were destroyed, degraded, or at minimum isolated . . . what happens to the cohesion, or pace of recovery, of the whole?"[9]

Now about this scenario there are several things to be said, and I am only sorry that Bernard Brodie is not still around to say them. The first problem is one that Mr. Gray quite frankly admits himself. "Is it sensible," he asks, "to destroy the government of the enemy, thus eliminating the option of negotiating an end to the war?"[10] The answer is no, it is not; unless we believe that out of the midst of this holocaust an alternative organized government would somehow emerge, capable, in spite of the destruction of all internal communications networks, of taking over the affairs of State. The alternative is, presumably, the conquest, occupation, and the re-education of the Soviet peoples in "Western values"—an interesting but ambitious project which might be said to require further study.

Secondly, it is quite unrealistic to assume that such strikes against centers of government and communications could be carried out without massive casualties, numbering scores of millions, among the peoples we would be attempting to "liberate." And if historical experience is any guide at all, such sufferings, inflicted by an alien power, serve only to strengthen social cohesion and make support for the regime, however unpopular it might be, a question literally of physical survival. We now know that the strategic bombardment of Germany only intensified the control exercised by the Nazi regime over that unhappy nation. The sufferings inflicted on the Russian peoples during the Second World War—those twenty million casualties which, we are asked to believe, only whetted their appetite for starting a Third—not only strengthened Stalin's tyranny; it went far to legitimize it. The prospect of any regime in the least compatible with what Mr. Gray calls "Western values" emerging from a blood-bath on yet more horrific scale is, to put it mildly, pretty remote.

Finally, what would be going on here while the strategic strike forces of the United States were conducting their carefully calibrated and controlled nuclear war? I shall leave out of account the problems of command and control, of maintaining fine-tuning and selective targeting under the kind

of nuclear retaliation that is to be expected during such an attack. This is the famous "C³I factor" addressed in President Carter's recent Directive No. 59, and some of the United States' finest technologists are no doubt working on the problem. Even if they do come up with plausible solutions, however, nobody can possibly tell whether in practice they will work; and for strategic planners to prepare to fight a nuclear war on the firm assumption that they would work would be criminally irresponsible. Nor do I address the question, more interesting to the allies than perhaps it is to the superpowers, of what would be happening in Western Europe during such an exchange. Dr. Kissinger, in that very curious speech he delivered in Brussels in September 1979, informed his audience that "the secret dream of every European was . . . if there had to be a nuclear war, to have it conducted over their heads by the strategic forces of the United States and the Soviet Union."[11] In fact I have yet to meet an intelligent European who thinks that anything of the kind would be possible, or that Western Europe would under any circumstances be omitted from the Soviet targeting plan. Few of us believe that there would be much left of our highly urbanized, economically tightly integrated and desperately vulnerable societies after even the most controlled and limited strategic nuclear exchange.

But it is the implications for the United States itself that I want to consider. Mr. Gray and his colleagues admit that there is a problem here, but they assert that "strategists can claim that an intelligent United States offensive strategy, wedded to homeland defenses, should reduce U.S. casualties to approximately 20 million, which should render U.S. strategic threats more credible."[12] Well, perhaps they can claim it, in the same way that Glendower could claim, in Shakespeare's *Henry IV,* that he could "call spirits from out the vasty deep"; they should be asked in return though, "but will they come when you do call for them?" How valid is such a claim—especially since a Soviet leadership in its death-throes would have no possible incentive, even if it had the C³I capability, to limit the damage to twenty million or to any other figure?

But even if it *is* valid, and granted that 20 million is a preferable figure to 180 million, it is not clear to me that Mr. Gray has thought through all the implications of his suggestion. Those twenty million *immediate* casualties—and we leave out those dying later from residual radiation—are only the visible tip of an iceberg of destruction and suffering of literally incalculable size. Most readers will be familiar with the very careful and sober report by the Congressional Office of Technology Assessment on "The Effects of Nuclear War,"[13] which came to the conclusion that

> The effects of nuclear war that cannot be calculated are at least as important as those for which calculations are attempted. Moreover even these limited calculations are subject to very large uncertainties. . . . This is particularly true for indirect effects such as deaths resulting from injuries and the unavailability of medical care, or for economic damage resulting from disruption and disorganization rather than direct destruction.

As for a small or "limited" attack, the impact of this, points out the Report, would be "enormous . . . [and] the uncertainties are such that no government could predict with any confidence what the results . . . would be, even if there was no further escalation." Certainly the situation in which the survivors of a nuclear attack would find themselves would be unprecedented.

> Natural resources would be destroyed; surviving equipment would be designed to use materials and skills that might no longer exist; and indeed some regions might be almost uninhabitable. Furthermore, pre-war patterns of behavior would surely change, though in unpredictable ways.

As for the outcome of the conflict in which these sufferings were incurred, I can only quote from a memorandum that Bernard Brodie wrote for Rand over twenty years ago but which has lost none of its relevance;[14]

> Whether the survivors be many or few, in the midst of a land scarred and ruined beyond all present comprehension, they should not be expected to show much concern for the further pursuit of political–military objectives.

Under such circumstances, the prime concern of everyone, American, Russian, European—to say nothing of the rest of the world, which is always left out of these scenarios—would be simply to survive, and in an unimagineably hostile environment. As to what would become of "Western values" in such a world, your guess is as good as mine. It is my own belief that the political, cultural and ideological distinctions that separate the West from the Soviet Union today would be seen, in comparison with the literally inconceivable contrasts between *any* pre-atomic and *any* post-atomic society, as almost insignificant. Indeed I am afraid that the United States would probably emerge from a nuclear war with a regime which, in its inescapable authoritarianism, looked much more like that which governs the Soviet Union today than that of the Soviet Union would in any way resemble the government of the United States; and this would almost certainly be the case in Western Europe.

Admittedly, this is all guesswork. But what is absolutely clear is that to engage in nuclear war, to attempt to use strategic nuclear weapons for "war-fighting" would be to enter the realm of the unknown and the unknowable, and what little we do know about it is appalling. Those who believe otherwise, whether they do so, like the Soviet writers, because of the constraints imposed by their ideology and cultural traditions, or, as do some Americans, out of technological hubris, are likely to be proved equally and dreadfully wrong; as wrong as those European strategists who in 1914 promised their political masters decisive victory before Christmas.

I take issue with Mr. Colin Gray in particular not because I do not admire his work, but simply because he has had the courage to make explicit certain views that are now circulating widely in some circles in the United States and which, unless publicly and firmly countered, might become influential, with catastrophic consequences. I also believe that if a thinker as intelligent as Mr. Gray is unable to provide nuclear strategy with a positive political object, no one else is likely to succeed any better. But this does not mean that Clausewitz's theory has to be abandoned, and that nuclear weapons can serve no political purpose. Clausewitz accepted that strategy might have a *negative object* and pointed out that, historically, this had more often than not been the case. This negative object he defined as being to make clear to the other side "the improbability of victory... [and] its unacceptable cost."[15] In a word, deterrence; or to reiterate Mr. Gray's own admirable words, to "ensure that in moments of acute crisis the Soviet general staff cannot brief the Politburo with a plausible theory of military victory."

This takes us back to where we began, to Bernard Brodie's warning that: "The first and most vital step in any American security program ... is to take measures to guarantee to ourselves in case of attack the possibility of retaliation in kind." In principle nothing has changed since then, even though in practice the problem has become enormously more difficult. In particular, Bernard's phrase "in kind" has acquired a significance that he could not possibly have anticipated. With the diversification of nuclear delivery systems, deterrence becomes an ever more complex business; and prudent account has to be taken of the contingency that deterrence might fail, so as to provide feasible alternatives between holocaust and surrender. But the object of such "intra-war deterrence" would still be, as Mr. Brodie put it, "to terminate the strategic exchange as quickly as possible, with the least amount of damage possible—on both sides"; in the interests not just of the United States but of mankind as a whole. Can one doubt that in 1914, rational European statesmen would have cut their losses and made peace at the end of the year if they had not been driven on by popular pressures and delusive expectations of victory? Or that if they had done so, the world would be a rather better place than it is today?

What about Bernard Brodie's other pronouncement, that "thus far the chief purpose of our military establishment has been to win wars.

From now on its chief purpose must be to avert them"; does this remain valid? Well yes, it does; but with respect to Bernard's shade, there is nothing new about this. It has always been the role of military establishments in peacetime to dissuade their opponents from using force as an instrument of policy—even if needs be of *defensive* policy—by making it clear that any such action on their part would be counter-productive; either because they would *lose* in such a war, or because they could gain victory only at an unacceptably high cost. That still seems to me to be true. And it also seems to me to be true that such a deterrent posture lacks conviction if one does not have the evident capacity to fight such a war—in particular, to defend the territory which our opponent may wish to occupy.

This is where a "war-fighting capability" comes in; a capability, not to fight through a war to an impossible, mutually destructive "victory"— and let us remember Clausewitz's epigram "in strategy there is no such thing as victory"—but to set on victory for our opponent a price that he cannot possibly afford to pay. And for this we must have the evident will and readiness to defend ourselves and one another: something that can only be made clear by the presence or availability of armed forces capable of fighting for territory; adequately armed, adequately trained, adequately supported and, in our market economies, adequately *paid*.

This is the war-fighting capability that acts as the true deterrent to aggression, and the only one that is convertible into political influence. There is as little reason to suppose that Soviet nuclear superiority will give them political advantages in the 1980s as that American nuclear superiority lent weight to the foreign policy of the United States in the 1960s. The neighbors of the Soviet Union are primarily impressed by the war-fighting capacity of her *conventional* forces, and the rest of the world by her growing capacity to project that force beyond her frontiers. Within Europe, the "theater nuclear balance" concerns only a tiny group of specialists. The presence and fighting capability of the United States army and air forces are seen as [conventional forces] the real, and highly effective deterrent against

Soviet attack. I have expressed elsewhere my regret that the British Government should have decided to spend five billion pounds out of our very restricted defense budget on a strategic nuclear strike force, which can only be at the expense of the conventional forces we can contribute to the Alliance. And however much the new administration of the United States may feel it necessary to spend on new strategic nuclear weapons systems to match or overmatch those of the Soviet Union, the effect on America's influence within the international community is likely to be negligible if it is not matched by a comparable and evident capability to defend American interests on the oceans and on the ground with forces capable of *fighting.*

For the best part of a century the peoples of industrial societies have been applying technological expertise and industrial power, initially to assist but increasingly to replace the traditional military skills and virtues on which they formerly relied for the protection of their political integrity.

As a result they have been able to attain their objects in war only at the cost of enormous and increasingly disproportionate destruction. With the advent of nuclear weapons, the disproportion becomes insensate. It is politically so much easier, so much less of a social strain, to produce nuclear missiles rather than trained, effective military manpower and to believe that a valid trade-off has somehow been made between the two. It has not. And the more deeply we become committed to this belief, on both sides of the Atlantic, the greater will be the danger that we are trying to avoid: on the one hand the impossibility of defending the specific areas and interests that are seriously threatened by a potential adversary, and, on the other, the possibility that, in a lethal mixture of hubris and despair, we might one day feel ourselves compelled to initiate a nuclear war. Such a war might or might not achieve its object; but I doubt whether the survivors on either side would very greatly care.

1. Bernard Brodie (ed.), *The Absolute Weapon* (New York: Harcourt Brace, 1946) p. 76.
2. Colin Gray, "Nuclear Strategy and the Case for a Theory of Victory," *International Security*, Vol. 4, No. 1 (Summer 1979), pp. 54–87.
3. Bernard Brodie, "Development of Nuclear Strategy," *International Security*, Vol. 2, No. 4 (Spring 1978), pp. 65–83.
4. Carl von Clausewitz, *On War*, Book VIII, Chapter 6B, "War Is an Instrument of Policy" (Princeton, N.J.: Princeton University Press, 1976).
5. Raymond L. Garthoff, "Mutual Deterrence and Strategic Arms Limitation in Soviet Policy," *International Security*, Vol. 3, No. 1 (Summer 1978) pp. 112–147; and Benjamin Lambeth, "The Political Potential of Soviet Equivalence," *International Security*, Vol. 4, No. 2 (Fall 1979), pp. 22–39.
6. Paul Nitze, "Deterring Our Deterrent," *Foreign Policy*, Number 25 (Winter 1976–7).
7. Colin Gray, "Nuclear Strategy: the Case for a Theory of Victory." *International Security*, Vol. 4, No. 1 (Summer 1979), pp. 54–87.
8. Colin Gray and Keith Payne, "Victory is Possible," *Foreign Policy*, Number 39 (Summer 1980).
9. Gray, *Nuclear Strategy, loc. cit.*
10. Gray, "Victory is Possible", *loc. cit.*
11. *Survival*, November–December 1979, p. 266.
12. Gray and Payne, *loc. cit.*
13. U.S., Congress, Office of Technology Assessment, "The Effects of Nuclear War," 1979.
14. "Implications of Nuclear Weapons on Total War." Rand Memorandum, p. 1118, July 1957.
15. Clausewitz, *op. cit.*, Book I, Chapter 2, "Purpose and Means in War."

Military Preparedness, National Security, and the Lessons of History

J. David Singer

Introduction

The literature of international politics is replete with many self-evident propositions and one among them has seemed particularly incontrovertible. I refer to the idea that in a system that is so ungoverned and so unconstrained by legal and moral norms, the nations have little choice but to maintain high levels of military preparedness. Given the absence of effective global institutions and the presence of dissatisfied nations, revolutionary factions, and bloodthirsty leaders, those who neglect their defenses are thought to be courting disaster. As the Roman Vegetius is said to have put it: if you want peace be prepared for war. There is no doubt that most governments since the inception of the post-Westphalia international system have followed this dictum, and there is no more popular pastime than to recall the fate of those who failed to man the ramparts and keep their powder dry.

Yet in every period of international tension there have been the nay-sayers, those who doubted the accuracy of the *para bellum* doctrine. Some did so on grounds of morality, often opposing *any* level of national preparedness, and others did so more on grounds of prudence, concerned that excessive armaments might be too dangerous and too costly. Despite the charges of naivté, or even of treason, levelled against them, despite the economic retribution or political ostracism they suffered, and despite the steady drumbeat of militaristic propaganda, these small bands of doves and owls are always with us. In the Western world today, however, the nay-sayers are no longer a small band of utopians. They are joined (and not only in the West) by large numbers of people whom we'd expect to find in the ranks of the "strong defense" majorities: businessmen, housewives, factory workers, university professors, former diplomats, retired military officers, and even leaders of the established churches. Whether advocates of a more modest level of armaments, a more prudent military doctrine, or outright renunciation of all weapons and armed forces, these people cannot all be reacting out of cowardice, self-hate, naiveté, or lack of patriotism. Despite such intimations from the political establishment, there may be something to their scepticism about the efficacy of military preparedness.

To be sure, the pro-preparedness forces often argue with many of the anti-preparedness arguments. Many concur that military spending is often inflationary, detrimental to economic development at home and abroad, and that large stocks of arms and soldiers are corrosive of freedom, harmful to the environment, and even subversive of morality. But there the consensus ends. We have no choice! What are we to do? We cannot trust the——— ! Only determination and preparedness can protect us from the enemy! Weakness invites aggression!

In B. Huldt (ed.) *Swedish Yearbook of International Affairs* (Stockholm: Utrikespolitiska Institutet), pp. 236–256. Reprinted by permission of Utrikespolitiska Institutet and the author.

In these centuries-old debates, there is, of course, frequent recourse to what "history teaches." From all sides, the historical grab-bag is ransacked for those cases that seem to support one or the other particular viewpoint. Often the same episode is used by rival groups to justify radically different positions, and it is no problem to assemble historical anecdotes that support virtually any stance on the preparedness issue. And the same holds even across national and ideological boundaries, with "Munich" invoked as eagerly in the Kremlin as in Whitehall, and the Trojan horse recalled with as much fervour in Istanbul as in Athens.

With so much at stake, it is remarkable how cavalierly we invoke the "lessons of history," how uncritically we treat analogies from cases that may bear only the faintest resemblance to one another, and how gullibly we accept generalizations that rest on a small and unrepresentative "sample" of the past. This is particularly striking when we see how much better evidence is demanded when the stakes are embarrassingly low. For example, the typical family would examine the results of gasoline economy tests before purchasing a new auto, a television advertiser would insist on seeing the popularity indicators of the competing shows for recent years, and a political office-seeker would urge that his managers check out ways in which his constituency has responded to different strategies in the past before beginning the election campaign. Even a restaurant diner would consult the Guide Michelin for the experience of previous connoisseurs, and an American college student would peruse the scores given to various professors before signing up for the next term's courses. In all of these relatively minor decisions, we tend to ask for systematic historical evidence as to the likely consequences of our choice, but when it comes to national security we fall back on speculation and anecdote. Despite the obvious self-interest of the advocates of given policies, and their alarmingly poor track records, we rarely ask them for the historical evidence on which their positions rest. (When we do, we usually find them to be poor historians indeed. Examining over a dozen historical generalizations found in the Nixon-Kissinger "State of the World" reports, we found slightly more than half to be inconsistent with the historical evidence; see Singer and Small 1974.) Without suggesting that the historical record is our *only* legitimate ground for choosing among national security policies, it would certainly seem to be one of the more reliable ones available. What might we demand of a historically based argument in favor of a given set of policies?

The Requirements for Historical Evidence

To begin, the relevant geographical–temporal domain must be specified, and second, *all* relevant cases from that domain must be examined. Third, the cases or situations must be compared with one another in a rigorous fashion, and in terms of characteristics that are both precisely defined and clearly germane to the case at hand. To illustrate, when the American foreign secretary Dean Rusk asserted that the "lessons of Munich" were equally applicable to the Indochina confrontation in 1967, journalists, congressmen, and citizens should have posed the following questions: "Along which dimensions were these two cases similar? How similar? Along which dimensions were they different? How different? How many cases of this type do we find since, let us say, the Congress of Vienna? In which cases were which policies pursued? Which cases turned out which way? In sum, Mr. Secretary, please tell us about Fashoda, Agadir, Constantinople, and Sarajevo, as well as about the one case that you happen to like!"

This same principle would seem to apply to the question of military preparedness: under which circumstances are various levels of preparedness most successful in enhancing a nation's security? Could it be more complicated than it appears to both the over-armers and to the under-armers? More specifically, can a nation jeopardize its security by over-arming as well as by under-arming? Obviously, no two situations are perfectly identical, but neither are any two situations totally different. Nations differ, but have many characteristics in common. Military strategies differ, but rest upon remarkably similar premises. Historical periods are marked by change, but also by an impressive degree of continuity. Thus, despite the variation across time, place, and circumstance, and the degree of interpreting historical lessons *too* literally, it would be irresponsible *not* to turn to the historical record for policy guidance.

As already suggested, we cannot expect to learn much from history if we merely use the past as a grab-bag from which we select the cases that support our views of the moment, while putting back into the bag those cases that contradict these prejudices. Only a well-defined total population of cases, or a carefully and explicitly drawn sample of that population, can serve as a legitimate basis for generalization; a biased or distorted population or sample of cases will inevitably give us distorted results.

But that is not the only requirement for discovering the lessons of history. A second requirement is that each of the phenomena about which we seek to generalize must be converted into very clear verbal forms (that is, a variable) and thence into unambiguous quantitative forms that can serve as an indicator of the variable. This is achieved by "operationalizing" the variable, on the basis of one or the other processes of quantification. The most obvious type of quantification is that of *measurement:* height in centimeters, temperature in degrees, earthquake severity in the logarithmic Richter scale units, velocity in kilometers per hour; many physical phenomena are operationally quantified by measuring them against a scientifically accepted scale. Less obvious, but equally familiar, is quantification by *enumeration:* the percentage of women in a parliamentary body, the number of bottles in a case of wine, the fraction of the work force that is unemployed, the number of tanks in an armoured division; many physical and social phenomena are operationally quantified by enumeration, or counting.

However, accurate counting requires unambiguous classification, and that is easier when it comes to women, bottles, workers, or tanks than when it comes to less easily defined phenomena like crises, manic-depressives, small businesses,

political radicals, great musicians, effective teachers, or economic depressions. The criteria for inclusion and exclusion of our cases in or out of these categories are often not sufficiently clear and operational, and even if they are, there may well be some disagreement over the classification criteria or "coding rules." Thus, when it comes to events or conditions that are not ordinarily treated as quantifiable—such as national security or military preparedness, as in this particular study—we need first to articulate our coding rules. If most of the specialists in a given area of competence agree on these coding rules and how to apply them, so much the better. That seldom happens at the beginning, and it often takes years or decades before they come to general agreement on how to identify a genius, a delinquent, and a typhoon, or how to measure the hardness of a steel alloy, the viscosity of a liquid, the permeability of a membrane, the severity of a war, the culpability of a criminal's accomplice, the duration of a business cycle, etc. Eventually, however, certain conventions emerge, and general agreement is reached on the procedures for inclusion–exclusion and measurement, permitting us to produce scientifically useful sets of data. Hence in the field of international politics today, we find a rather clear consensus of how to identify sovereign states, major powers, military disputes, civil wars, and international wars, and on how to measure national capabilities, diplomatic importance, the severity and magnitude of a war, etc. This is, unfortunately, not yet true of some of the concepts and variables that are used in the study at hand, but that need not be a source of paralysis; most of those listed above were also ignored or regarded sceptically when they were originally devised and applied.

There is, finally, a third major requirement to be satisfied if we are to learn from history. We must not only operationalize our concepts and examine all of the relevant cases; we must also statistically analyze the resulting sets of data in such fashion that our expectations or preferences do not pre-determine the results of the investigation. Our analyses must not be allowed to "load the dice" in favor of, or against, a given theoretical position, and we must look not only at those patterns that point in the hypothesized direction, but also at those that point in other directions as well. In the same vein, our statistics must tell us how probable it is that the observed patterns could have occurred by chance alone, so as to distinguish between historical accident and randomness on the one hand and robust empirical findings on the other.

With these methodological considerations out of the way, let me turn now to the specific question at hand: since the Congress of Vienna, what has been the relationship between the levels of military preparedness of nations and their success in achieving a basic degree of national security? Have higher levels been most consistently correlated with more security? Lower levels? Or, is there no historical connection between preparedness and security? In the study reported here, we hypothesize—as do most practitioners and a good many scholars—that the relationship is a positive one, with greater preparedness associated with greater security. Let us turn now to the measurement of our key variables.

Measuring National Security

Given the breadth and elusiveness of a concept like national security, it might seem overly ambitious to propose that we measure it. This is certainly true if we mean to capture its *entire* meaning in operational terms, but scientists rarely attempt this in any discipline. Rather, we try to capture one or more of the most central and salient characteristics or dimensions of the variable or concept, or alternatively, to find some more easily observed phenomenon that reflects the changing magnitude of the central concept, in the form of a proxy, surrogate, or trace.

Following this line of reasoning, one can readily appreciate that—at a minimum—a fairly secure nation would be one that was able to come close to meeting these aspirations:

1. minimize the frequency of involvement in militarized dispute; but

2. prevail over the adversary if such disputes cannot be avoided;

3. minimize the frequency of involvement in wars; but

4. emerge on the victorious side if such wars cannot be avoided.

Surely these are the basic and most salient elements of the security of a nation in the modern international system, and we will be asking here whether nations that have been high on military preparedness since 1816 are also the nations that have scored high on these four criteria for security. How do we operationalize them? Given the space limitations, we can only summarize the coding rules here, and for full details see Singer and Small, *Wages of War,* 1972 or Small and Singer, *Resort to Arms,* 1982; Gochman and Maoz, "Militarized International Disputes" in *Journal of Conflict Resolution,* December 1984; and Maoz, *Paths to War* (1982).

Very briefly, a militarized dispute is a confrontation between two or more sovereign nations in which at least one of them does one of the following: (1) uses military force short of war, as in the sinking of a ship, bombardment of a town, military raid across a border, the imposition of a blockade, etc.; (2) deploys or re-deploys existing military forces, such as movement of troops, sending aircraft aloft, putting ships to sea, etc., in situations other than regular peace-time maneuvres; (3) mobilizes potential forces, such as calling up reserve units, distributing weapons to active duty units, etc., or (4) issues an explicit threat to use military force. Any such move converts a milder type of international dispute, of which there are perhaps a few hundred per decade (and they have yet to be identified and counted) in the international system, into a militarized, brink-of-war situation, of which there has been an average of about 60 per decade since 1816. The ability to stay out of these dangerous confrontations is certainly one objective of a national security policy.

But if a government drifts into, or knowingly chooses to get into such a dispute, it is certainly desirable to prevail: to "have its way" to a greater extent than its adversary. Admittedly, it is far simpler to identify the existence of these disputes than to identify which side came out on the prevailing side, but we have developed, tested, and applied a number of criteria that seem to stand up under scrutiny, and these are carefully spelled out in Maoz *Paths to War* (1982). Basically, our coders examine several treatments of each dispute, written in different periods by historians of different nationalities, and they are given specific standards by which they judge the magnitude of gains and losses experienced by the protagonists, with particular attention to the discrepancy between intentions and achievements as they entered into the dispute.

A third intention of national security policy is the ability to stay out of war, which is to say, prevent military disputes from going over the brink of war without, of course, having to capitulate or make most of the concessions. If a nation *must* go to war, with the tremendous costs involved, in order to protect its interests, there is little question that its level of security is rather low. The fourth and final intention, as noted, is that if a nation cannot prevent being dragged or pushed into war, it must at least come out on the victorious side. When a nation gets into militarized disputes, cannot prevail, ends up in war, and loses, one can hardly classify it as secure. Here we will examine each nation's track record on these four criteria from the Napoleonic period to the present.

Measuring Military Preparedness

Turning from our outcome variable—national security in its most elementary forms—to the predictor variable—military preparedness—the problem of measurement is somewhat more direct. Here, we will use two different indicators, one of which reflects the basic material and military capabilities of the nation year by year, and the other of which is the military allocation ratio. By the former, we mean the industrial and military might of the nation, and by the latter we mean the extent to which it allocates its industrial resources to the acquisition of military hardware and to mobilized military forces.

As to the basic capabilities dimensions, there are two categories, one of which is industrial and the other is military. To measure the *industrial* capabilities of each nation, we have gathered the

historical figures that reflect, year by year, both its iron and steel production and its energy consumption. Although the importance of these two sets of industrial capabilities will vary from period to period and region to region, they seem to capture the basic ingredients of an effective military machine for most of the world during the years since the Congress of Vienna; if not quite sufficient, they are undoubtedly necessary, to use the standard distinction.

For the *military* capabilities themselves, we use the two familiar dimensions of military expenditures (converted to a standard currency and modified to account for the fluctuations in purchasing power across time and nations) and armed forces size (in terms of active duty, uniformed personnel). Again, these may not be the most perfect indicators, given that expenditures can be converted into war-fighting hardware with varying efficiency, and that some armies and navies can be quite superior to others of the same size and having the same equipment. But most specialists concur that they seem to capture military capabilities as well as any other indicators, given the range of nations and periods that we embrace.

Shifting from basic capabilities to allocation ratios, we merely ask what fraction of its industrial and demographic resources each nation assigns to military preparedness in order to capture the idea of determination and effort. Even a nation with vastly superior wealth, population, and productive facilities will be relatively weak vis-a-vis those with a smaller resource base but higher allocation ratios. We calculate first the percentage of the total population that is on active duty in the armed forces each year, and that is a relatively straightforward piece of arithmetic. But to get at the ratio for military expenditures, one cannot divide that figure by tons of steel or kilowatt-hours of energy; thus we first convert each of these figures into each individual nation's percentage share of all the nations' totals of iron and steel produced, energy consumed, and money spent in each year. From that, it becomes a simple matter of dividing each nation's percentage share of system-wide military expenditures by its share of iron and steel and energy each year. And since the most valid indicator of a nation's industrial base is the *combination* of both iron–steel production and energy consumption, we use the *average* of these two percentages as the denomination in our ratio.

Testing the Hypotheses

It is now appropriate to turn to the results of the investigation, given the procedures and indicators that have been described. To what extent *does* military preparedness help to keep nations out of armed conflict—at least, those whose leaders want to avoid it—and if unable to avoid such conflict, help them to prevail in disputes and to win in war? In as much as it is essential to test the hypotheses that reflect the belief that preparedness enhances security in several different ways, we divide this section into four distinct parts. First, we examine the efficacy of military and industrial capabilities in reducing the frequency of involvement in militarized disputes and in wars. Second, we shift from capabilities to allocation ratios to ascertain how well they do in reducing involvement in disputes and wars. Third, we examine the efficacy of capabilities in ensuring success in disputes and in wars. And fourth, we return to allocation ratios and their efficacy in providing military success in disputes and wars. Worth noting is that all of the results reported here are based on the major powers only, to make the presentation less complicated, but the findings are essentially the same for minor powers as well.

Involvement in Armed Conflict

Looking first at national capabilities and involvement, we find a very clear pattern: on both the military and the industrial dimensions for the period since 1816, those major powers that rank high on these are also the ones that rank high on the frequency of their involvement in disputes and wars. If we look at each nation-year score (such as France/1911 or Russia/1933) on military capabilities, and compare that to the involvement in disputes the following year, we find that the nation-years with the higher capability scores are fol-

lowed by the nation-years (same nation, next year) with the higher frequency of dispute involvement, and conversely, the lower the capability score, the lower the dispute frequency. Similarly, those nation-years that score high on industrial capability are those that are usually followed by higher frequency of dispute involvement, while the lower ones are typically followed by lower dispute scores.

Our findings are clearly summarized in Table 1, where we group the major power nation-years according to the nation's percentage share of either the military or the industrial capabilities of all the major powers that year, counting the number that fell into the low, medium, and high categories. For each of those three groups of nation-years, we calculate the percentage of them that were followed by involvement in militarized dispute. Thus, of the 397 nation-years characterized by low capability scores (less than a 14% share of the total group of nations that year), only 7% were followed by disputes, and of the 370 medium ones (from 14% to 28% share) a slightly higher 10% were followed by disputes; but of the 141 with high military capabilities (over 28%) a very much higher 17% were followed by dispute involvements. For the industrial rankings, we find a similar but somewhat weaker pattern; being near the top of the list industrially is dangerous, but not quite as dangerous as being near the top of the list in military capabilities.

Turning from the nations' shares of absolute capabilities to the way in which they allocate industrial capabilities to the military, we find a somewhat more ambiguous pattern. As Table 2 shows, the *low* allocation nation-years are indeed followed by low frequencies of dispute, but this is almost as true for the *high* allocation nation-years as well. Here we find that the most dangerous state of affairs is for a major power to be among the *medium* allocators for any given year; using either of our two indicators of allocation ratios, we see that the medium scoring cases experience a 31% and a 33% frequency of dispute involvement. The message seems to be that too much internal compromise on military allocation gets the "worst of both worlds": armed enough to be provocative to its neighbors, but not armed enough to restrain

TABLE 1   Involvement in military disputes and capability

Capability		Number of Nation-Years with a Given Capability	Percent of Nation-Years Followed by International Dispute
Military	Low	397	07
	Medium	370	10
	High	141	17
Industrial	Low	635	07
	Medium	118	09
	High	155	14
Demographic	Low	383	07
	Medium	395	09
	High	130	19

TABLE 2   Involvement in military disputes and allocation of resources to military

Resource Allocation		Number of Nation-Years with Given Allocation	Percent of Nation-Years Followed by International Dispute
Military expenditure relative to industrial capacity	Low	234	06
	Medium	93	31
	High	550	06
Military expenditure relative to steel production	Low	246	07
	Medium	89	33
	High	533	08
Military personnel relative to population	Low	234	12
	Medium	344	13
	High	259	04

them; perhaps the "golden mean" is not adequate for the anarchical norms of international politics.

We turn next from involvement in *militarized disputes* to involvement in *war* itself; do high capabilities or high allocation ratios do any better in helping the major powers stay out of war than they do in keeping them away from the brink of war? Given the mixed success of high preparedness in deterring the escalation of mild disputes to the more serious, militarized level, might we expect any better from the conventional wisdom, once we are on the brink of war? In a preliminary study some years ago, Bremer (1980) examined the war-proneness of nations as a function of their overall military-industrial-demographic capabilities from 1816 to 1976 in a straightforward fashion. He ranked the top 50 nations each year by their capabilities and by their war involvement in the several years following, and found the remarkable

high rank-order correlation coefficients of .74 in the 19th century and .65 in the 20th century.

Our more recent results, using the more restricted indicators described earlier in this paper, strongly confirm those earlier ones, with the higher capability nation-years followed by the highest percentage of war involvement, and the lower scoring ones associated with the lowest war frequency. Finally, the same pattern appears to hold for allocation ratios: the nation-years with the high expenditure and personnel ratios are followed by years with the higher frequencies of war, and the lower ones are followed by lower frequencies of war.

Success in Armed Conflict

As we noted earlier, there are at least two sets of criteria by which national security might be estimated. The first is the ability to steer clear of militarized disputes and of all-out wars, and we have seen how ineffective military preparedness has been on this score over the past century and a half. The second, of course, is the ability to prevail in such disputes and wars if they cannot be avoided. Do higher capabilities and preparedness ratios do any better on this dimension?

To test our hypotheses here, we use a slightly different procedure, again restricting the analysis to disputes and wars in which there was at least one major power on each side. Above, we wanted to be able to evaluate a nation's success in avoiding disputes and wars in terms of *all* those with whom it *would* become involved, but once that involvement does occur, it is vis-a-vis a specific other nation. Hence, this set of analyses proceeds by comparing the nation's capabilities and allocations with those of its specific adversary, rather than to all the nations under examination.

What are the lessons of history in this particular question? First, it turns out that superiority in the military sector is indeed associated with a nation "having its way" in a militarized dispute. But our findings show that this association is a *negative* one: a *weaker* nation prevails in 39% of the cases and the stronger prevails only 21% of the time when military expenditure is the capability indicator, and the figures are nearly the same (39% and 27%) when military personnel is the indicator. (The figures do not add up to 100% because in many cases both sides are approximately equal, and in some cases—a stand-off—neither side prevails.) But if we shift from the military to the industrial criterion, we find that strength *does* matter, and in the expected direction. Hence the superior nation in terms of energy consumption prevails in 29% of the cases, compared to only a 19% success rate for the weaker adversary. And if the iron and steel indicator is used, superiority offers a 39% success rate, compared to 20% for the inferior side. In sum, *industrial* superiority is an asset in these brink-of-war disputes, but *military* superiority is a liability.

Turning now to allocation ratios, the unexpected pattern is even more pronounced. Using military expenditure shares divided by overall industrial capability shares (energy and iron/steel), we find that the under-allocators prevail twice as often (36% to 18%) as the over-allocators. For those readers with a statistical bent, such a pattern would be expected to occur by chance alone once in a thousand times. Not quite as dramatic, but pointing in the same direction is the military personnel-to-total population indicator: the under-allocator prevails in 44% of the cases, while the over-allocator does so in only 30% of the cases. Again, many times the adversaries are allocating at about the same rate, and there are also a good many stand-offs in which neither side prevailed. As a matter of fact, if we used a more demanding indicator of success, and included both a defeat *and a tie* or stand-off as "failure to prevail," the evidence against high allocation ratios would be even more pronounced. Those nations that put excessive amounts of their industrial and demographic resources into the military have consistently done very badly in their efforts to face down and intimidate a rival.

Finally, we turn to *war* itself, and here we find some modest vindications of the "peace through strength" doctrine. As to capabilities, the major powers with the "big battalions" (i.e., larger armed forces) emerge victorious 64% of the time, while those with smaller forces win their wars 47% of the time. Military expenditures—for hardware and infra-structure, as well as personnel—are also quite valuable, with the higher scoring side winning 57% of the time and the lower spenders winning only 36% of the time. (These figures can add up to more than 100% because the analyses were done twice, once in terms of initiators and then in terms of their targets.) But once again, as valuable as military superiority has been in determining the victors in war, industrial superiority is even more valuable. For example, the side that was superior in iron/steel production emerged victorious in 74% of the cases, whereas the inferior side won the war in only 29% of the cases.

Returning once more from capabilities to allocations for preparedness, we again find that the conventional hypothesis does rather badly against the cold facts of history. That is, while the over-allocating side in terms of military personnel per capita wins in 65% of the cases, whereas the under-allocator wins in only 43% of the cases, quite the contrary occurs when we examine the percentage shares of iron/steel divided into shares of military expenditures. Using this particular indicator, we discover that the major power that was the higher allocator emerged victorious only half the time, while the under-allocator did so a full 70% of the time.

Summarizing the Results

What have we learned so far from this exercise in quantitative-scientific history? In general, we have learned that there are indeed patterns and regularities to be discovered; despite the apparent uniqueness of each case, there are enough similarities across time and place to permit generalizations. Next, we have learned that despite the *regularities,* they are not *uniformities;* world politics are too complex, and our contemporary theoretical models too crude, to expect all-or-none results. We should also bear in mind a related lesson: without systematically observed differences, there would be no meaningful similarities. For example, if all major powers put the same share of their resources into the military, we could not discover the effects of differing allocation ratios, and if all militarized disputes escalated to war, we could never discover the differences between those disputes that do escalate and those that do not.

More specifically, what have we learned about the historical relationships between military preparedness and national security as far as the major powers in the world since 1816 are concerned? First, the nations with the highest military capabilities get into militarized disputes more than twice as frequently as those with the lower capabilities, with the medium capability nations experiencing medium frequencies of dispute involvement. Military superiority not only does not enhance most

nations' ability to avoid brink-of-war confrontations, but actually makes them more susceptible to involvement in these dangerous situations. Second, and less clear, moderately high military allocation levels do not reduce involvement in disputes, but actually increase them. Those major powers that are at the very high or very low allocation levels are the least dispute prone; it is safer to keep military allocations very low or to move to very high levels, while staying close to the norm is very dangerous.

Third, the higher the nation is on military capabilities, the more frequently it will get into war; superiority is much more dangerous than *inferiority* vis-a-vis the other nations in the system. Fourth, the higher allocations are systematically the high scorers on war involvement. So much then, for the efficacy of military preparedness in keeping nations out of harm's way. Not only do military superiority and high military allocations *not* reduce the frequency with which the major powers get into militarized disputes and wars, they turn out to more often actually *increase* the frequency of these involvements in armed conflict. None of this is to suggest that all nations at all times uniformly seek to avoid disputes and wars; there are certain historical exceptions, but they seem quite rare indeed. Of course almost all nations, and especially the major powers, usually have pro-war factions, but seldom do they control the decision process.

How about avoiding defeat once these armed conflicts occur? Turning to our fifth hypothesis, we find that in militarized disputes the *militarily* superior nation prevails much less often than its inferior adversary, whereas the industrially superior one prevails considerably more often. Sixth, and similarly, the low allocators of resources to the military have their way and come out on top twice as often as those who are the high allocators. Seventh, while military superiority improves the likelihood of victory in war, industrial superiority is even more valuable. And finally, we find that those who under-allocate to the military emerge victorious much more often than those who over-allocate. In sum, our analyses point in a very different direction than we might have expected.

As we have seen, it is not merely the case that high preparedness levels are not advantageous to national security, but that in seven out of our eight hypotheses they turn out to be disadvantageous. How might we explain these surprising results?

Interpreting the Results

The most obvious explanation of our results is that we have made some serious errors in either the measurements of our variables or the analysis of the resulting data sets, intentionally or otherwise. But since my colleagues and I were quite surprised as the initial findings emerged, we re-examined the entire enterprise several times with the expectation that some procedural error would appear; we are now confident that everything was done correctly. And if there are biases in our measurement and analysis, they should be readily visible to those who have read and examined the scientific papers upon which this essay is built. As indicated in the earlier pages, we do not claim to have captured every aspect of "security" or of "preparedness" in our indicators, but those used here certainly reflect some of the more central elements of these concepts.

While more detailed investigation is necessary before we can treat our findings as conclusive—and it is not impossible that error on bias *has* crept into these early investigations—we have no choice for the moment but to take the results seriously. From a scientific point of view, every discovery remains forever vulnerable to new and different discoveries. But from a policy point of view, we cannot afford to wait for decades on the remote chance that we are wrong. If we are not wrong, and are basically right in our conclusions, then it behooves all of us to consider and act upon their implications.

Assuming, then, that subsequent research will reveal essentially the same lessons of history as these, the question is one of trying to account for what we have found. To do so, I turn to what is known in some circles as the "Singer Curve." Graphically this hypothesized curve suggests that national security can be put into jeopardy not only

by under-preparedness but also by over-preparedness. How?

We begin by reiterating that the international system remains quite anarchic to this very day, and throughout the centuries, one of the most serious scarcities in the system has been the scarcity of security. Without effective supra-national institutions, compelling legal norms, or even pragmatic incentives toward peaceful resolution of international conflicts, military force becomes the final arbiter, and military capabilities an essential instrument of national security. Of course, this need not have been inevitable, had the alleged statesmen of earlier centuries shown more foresight and courage, but by the close of the Congress of Vienna, the tradition of national sovereignty based upon military force had become so institutionalized that later efforts to move toward a more reasonable and humane international order would encounter considerable resistance. Thus, the puny efforts following each major war to bring a measure of security to global governance were easily deflected, and by 1945 it was a foregone conclusion that the "peacemakers" would emerge out of the smokescreen of diplomatic double-talk with yet another formula for preserving the status quo. And those who lead the more recently independent states have learned well from their colonial masters, saddling their people with armies and "defense budgets" that perpetuate poverty and virtually guarantee the continuation of the post-Napoleonic average of six international wars per decade.

One possible way to reduce that deadly regularity is to recognize the implications of this capability-security curve. As we see, there are two important inflection points on that curve; one reflects the transition at which increasing a nation's capability from zero begins to *add* discernably to its security. Below that level, its military forces are too weak to offer much of a deterrent to neighboring nations or other potential adversaries. To be sure, we cannot yet identify that level very precisely, given that it depends on the capabilities and the intentions of others, the weapon technology of the period and region, and its own ambitions as to what sorts of behavior are to be deterred. The other, and more important, inflection point is found

FIGURE 1   The "Singer curve": Military capability and national security

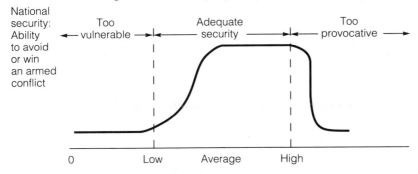

Military capability relative to other nations

at that level of increasing capability at which the *deterrent effects* begin to diminish, while the *provocation effects* begin to rise rapidly. And when the provocation effect—or more precisely, the provocation-temptation effect—exceeds the deterrent effect, it is safe to say that the nation's security begins to suffer; note, too, that while the curve rises rapidly from zero and then flattens out, it also drops rapidly once the force levels begin to exceed those necessary for deterrence. We call it the provocation-temptation effect to capture the dual and reciprocal process that is stimulated as this dangerous threshold of preparedness is approached, intersected, and exceeded.

The provocation aspect of the process is self-evident: despite its protestations to the contrary, a nation's excessive armament levels will almost always be perceived by some others as menacing. The likely expectation is that this over-allocating is preliminary to increased pressure, threats, blackmail, or even outright aggression. In brief, it is seen as provocative and typically catalyzes a reciprocal build-up on the part of those who feel most threatened. By such simple dynamics are arms races often made.

But there is another and less obvious side to this dual process: here we refer to the *domestic* effects of over-allocation. To begin, almost all nations build and maintain some moderate levels of armed force, but it takes a strong combination of a perceived threat from abroad and an effective pro-armament, hawkish coalition at home to push preparedness beyond certain accepted levels. And

with each increase in military allocation (up to some outer limit that has rarely been marked historically) there are two other increases. One is in the economic and political influence of the pro-armament coalition, coupled with the relative diminution of the influence and prestige of those opposed to such a build-up, whom we might label the owls and the doves! This, of course, makes the next year's armament increase even easier to push through than in the previous years, and as I have suggested, the process can continue for years and even decades until there are no more resources for the military and there is powerful resistance to further increases (which is quite rare) or until the dynamics of the domestic–foreign interaction process erupt into war (which is more usually the case).

The process is further exacerbated by the psycho-political consequences of continued over-preparedness. As the anti-armament doves and owls decline in influence vis-a-vis their domestic opponents, their impact on general policy also deteriorates, permitting the more militaristic elements to shape the whole range of foreign and national security. These hawks tend to commit three fundamental errors, all of which proceed from the necessary conviction that their excessive levels of preparedness are justified. To achieve that, they must first believe the "worst-case analyses" regarding the motives and behavior of the opposing nations, and if the adversary is as evil and powerful as such analyses suggest, the only way to deal with him is from that familiar "position of strength." Inexorably, diplomatic intercourse becomes a charade, one's deterrent becomes increasingly provocative, and normal modes of internation influence are replaced by acts of crude intimidation. Reciprocity from the other side should come as no surprise!

Second, these excessive allocations are justified on the grounds that they provide an effective instrument by which to deter, control, or intimidate the adversary. From this grows a routine reliance on the threat or use of military force as a major instrument of national security policy. And these unfortunate habits, even if unsuccessful, become ingrained in the foreign policy establishment, leading to a diminution of the policy repertoire: "If we have these ships, planes, tanks, and guns, why not use them?" The burden of proof ultimately shifts from the trigger-happy element to those who would advocate a more flexible, prudent, and creative foreign policy. Third, if the military instrument is not particularly effective in modifying the adversary's policies—and it usually is not—the standard response is that we need *more* of the same. Like drug addicts, the weapon addicts can never get enough, believing that just one more "fix" will bring success. Further, since the rival power is typically responding in essentially the same way, *their* policy failures will be frequent enough to create the illusion of success for "our side." To use another analogy, these hawks are like gamblers in a casino, winning just often enough to sustain their faith in their strategy.

Finally, and following from this set of distorted perceptions, we typically see two other domestic consequences. One is that more and more of the competent specialists either resign from, or are forced out of, their government positions and are replaced by loyal hard-liners. The other equally serious effect is that the nongovernmental groups go along, if not capitulate, or they become increasingly isolated and shrill in their opposition, and thus suffer further loss in their credibility, or they disintegrate and disappear from the politically relevant scene. To put it bluntly, the nation soon finds itself without a responsible, competent, and credible counter-elite in the foreign policy/national security sectors.

With the emasculation of an effective counter-elite, the tragic process becomes virtually irreversible; almost all of the internal and external incentives now reinforce one another. As result, those in power are all too likely to continue the military build-up and to weaken their economy in the process, to get into more disputes of the wrong kind at the wrong time and manage them ineptly; to suffer reverses in more and more of them; and finally, to stumble over the brink of war and into the murderous abyss from which there is no turning back until thousands or millions of their citizens have died a horrible death.

Conclusion

To be sure, the above scenario may not always unfold exactly as outlined here, nor do I claim that it rests on this solid sort of historical evidence that characterizes the central part of this essay. But it has an alarmingly familiar dynamic for those of us who have followed the costly and dangerous course of the Soviet–American cold war or have studied any of the hundred-odd enduring rivalries between 1816 and 1980, particularly those eighteen cases that were accompanied by an arms race. Furthermore, it is menacingly consistent with the findings reported in the earlier section.

What are the implications of a study such as this? First, there are lessons to be learned from history, but only if we treat the historical record as a potential data base from which quantitative analyses can be conducted in order to check our hypotheses against all the cases. As long as we exploit history for one or another set of parochial purposes, searching out only those cases that support our arguments and ignoring those that do not, we will never learn in any reliable, scientific sense of the word.

Second, the bulk of the evidence (but, to reiterate, not all of it) strongly disconfirms the conventional wisdom. Military preparedness, if carried too far, is a menace not only to the nation's adversaries, but to itself and its citizens. We have seen that, in general, it is the excessively militarized nation that gets into most of the disputes and most of the wars, and while military superiority helps to win wars, preserving the industrial base helps even more. And, perhaps most interestingly, we have seen that high levels of preparedness and ratios of allocation to the military consistently produced more defeat than victory in those numerous brink-of-war confrontations that characterize our badly governed international community.

Research such as that reported here has a lot more to tell us about international politics, and much of it runs counter to the folklore of diplomacy and strategy. Such research, however, is still in its infancy and remains under-staffed, under-funded, under-studied, and worst yet in the short run, under-utilized by those who shape and influence the security policies of the nations. It would be a crime against humanity if the lessons of history were not sought after and put to use in time to avert World War III, and all the indications are that the crime will indeed be committed.

References

Gochman, Charles S. and Zeev Maoz. 1984. "Militarized International Disputes." *Journal of Conflict Resolution* December.

Maoz, Zeev. 1982. *Paths to Conflict: International Disputes Initiation 1816–1976.* Boulder, Colorado: Westview.

Singer, J. David and Melvin Small. 1974. *The Wages of War.* New York: John Wiley.

not convincing regarding right to generalize: what about tech., neighbors, allies, internal pol, particularly considering contraventions

Deterrence Reconsidered

Richard Ned Lebow

The principal theme of *Psychology and Deterrence* is disenchantment with deterrence as both a theory of state behavior and a strategy of conflict management. Deterrence is inadequate as an explanatory theory of international relations because the growing body of empirical evidence indicates that neither leaders contemplating challenges nor leaders seeking to prevent them necessarily act as the theory predicts. We are also critical of deterrence as a prescriptive strategy because it can provoke the very behavior it seeks to prevent.

The major strengths and weaknesses of deterrence can both be said to derive from the theory's most fundamental characteristic: it is a system of abstract logic all of whose principal postulates have been derived deductively. This contributed to the theory's appeal as it facilitated the development of coherent, elegant, and seem-

Excerpted from Robert Jervis, Richard Ned Lebow, and Janice Gross Stein, *Psychology and Deterrence* (Baltimore: The Johns Hopkins University Press, 1985). Reprinted by permission of the publisher.

ingly powerful explanations for important aspects of interstate behavior. For statesmen and scholars alike, deterrence theory held out the promise of a pathway through the forbiddingly complex and increasingly dangerous maze of international relations, a pathway that began with one's own national interest and led in the end to enhanced security. This was particularly attractive in a world of nuclear weapons because it encouraged statesmen to believe that efforts on their part to reduce any uncertainties surrounding a state's willingness to defend its commitments could prevent miscalculation by an adversary and forestall the kinds of challenges that had so often led to war in the past. For this reason, deterrence continues to be seen as the principal intellectual and policy bulwark against nuclear holocaust.

Despite the obvious appeal of deterrence theory, its sometimes sophisticated but always abstract rationality fails to provide an adequate description of how states actually behave. Case studies indicate that states are both more cautious *and* more prone to risk-taking than the theory predicts (Lebow 1984). They also suggest that judgments of the credibility of another state's commitment may have little to do with its bargaining reputation. In addition, there is some evidence that the timing of foreign policy challenges may be independent of the relative military balance between the parties involved.

Any critique of deterrence must in all fairness acknowledge that deterrence sometimes seems to have been a successful strategy for preserving one's interests while avoiding war. Unfortunately, successes are much more difficult to document than failures because they generally result in inaction. In the absence of evidence detailing the deliberations of a state's leaders, it is impossible to know whether they actually contemplated a challenge of another state's commitment and, if they did, whether they decided against it because of perceptions of its military capability and resolve.

Likely examples of successful deterrence in the post-1945 period include West Berlin in the 1960s, Taiwan in the 1950s, and South Korea after 1953. Taiwan and South Korea probably would have been invaded and taken over by hostile neighbors in the absence of vigilant efforts on their part to develop the means to defend themselves. In all three cases, success also depended upon the continuing commitment of the United States to protect their independence, or existing status in the case of Berlin. It also seems evident that mutual possession of nuclear weapons has made both superpowers more cautious of each other than might have otherwise been the case. However, it is by no means clear that nuclear deterrence has succeeded in preventing a Soviet invasion of Western Europe, as is sometimes alleged. Moscow may have shied away from such an adventure even in the absence of the threat of nuclear retaliation. Nor is it apparent that the obvious reluctance of the superpowers to transgress upon each other's vital interests is in any way attributable to their respective strategic doctrines, force structures, or public statements about those interests.

There is also a class of situations in which deterrence might have worked if it had been applied. Munich is commonly cited in this regard, the assumption being that Hitler would have backed down had France and Britain remained unequivocal in their commitment to defend Czechoslovakia. Hitler, however, was furious that Chamberlain was so accommodating and even raised new demands at the last moment in the hope of forestalling an agreement (Weinberg 1970–80, p. 663). By 1938, Hitler *wanted* war. Resolve on the part of his adversaries would have been no more successful than appeasement in preventing it. Had Britain and France stood firm a few years earlier, then the future of Europe might have been quite different.

Berlin in 1948 and Korea in 1950 seem better examples of confrontations which might have been averted if deterrence had been practiced. Studies of the Berlin crisis have documented the series of contradictory measures and public statements that characterized American policy toward that city prior to the imposition of the blockade. They have suggested that this indecision and confusion encouraged Soviet leaders to conclude that the United States was unwilling to risk war to defend its position in that city (Clay 1950; Howley 1950; Davison 1958, pp. 71–78). An even more compelling case has been made that American disengagement from South Korea in 1949–50 led the North Koreans to conclude that Washington would not intervene militarily to prevent their conquest of the South (Truman 1955, pp. 2,355–65; McLellan 1976, pp. 267–70). Unambiguous American policies which demonstrated the depth of the American commitment to the status quo *prior* to both challenges might well have forestalled them.

Finally, there are a number of conflicts in which deterrence was tried but failed. The Cuban missile crisis is the most obvious example. Graham Allison called John F. Kennedy's efforts to put the Soviet Union on notice that the United States would not tolerate the introduction of "offensive weapons" into Cuba "a textbook case of responsible diplomacy" (Allison 1971, p. 42). However, Kennedy's efforts failed to deter Khrushchev from surreptitiously attempting to deploy ballistic missiles on that island capable of striking at the United States. The year 1962 also witnessed the failure of patient Chinese efforts to deter India from pursuit of its "Forward Policy" in territory contested by the two countries. Deterrence also failed in the Middle East in 1967, 1969–70, and 1973. Arab states provoked or started a war with Israel in all three instances despite Israeli military superiority and unquestioned Israeli resolve to use that superiority in defense of its interests.

The states whose commitments were challenged in the examples cited above appear to have carried out the four operations held to be essential for deterrence. They (1) defined their commitments with some precision; (2) communicated the existence of these commitments to adversaries well in advance of any challenge; (3) possessed the military capability to defend their commitments or to punish severely any adversary who challenged them; and (4) demonstrated their resolve to use force if necessary to do this. It would be a mistake to focus only on the behavior of the defender in these instances in order to find out why deterrence failed (Lebow 1981, pp. 82–97). The analyst must also inquire into the motives of the challengers in question and seek to understand how and why they misjudged the capability or resolve of their adversaries.

Case studies analyzed in *Psychology and Deterrence* and in other publications by its several authors suggest two principal explanations for these kinds of deterrence failures. The first is the existence of numerous and diverse barriers to interstate communication which can distort, transform, or altogether block out the signals states send to each other. The second is the apparent failure of states practicing deterrence to identify and address, at the same time, what may be the most important causes of foreign policy aggression.

Barriers to Signaling

The success of deterrence as a strategy of conflict avoidance depends not only upon the capability and resolve of the defender of a commitment but just as much upon his ability to communicate that capability and resolve to adversaries. When difficulties arise in this regard, deterrence theorists usually attribute them to structural causes, among them the past military weakness, internal political division, or poor reputation for resolve of the state in question. When deterrence is predicated upon nuclear reprisal, they also stress the difficulty of making this threat credible when it would entail war with another nuclear power.

Deterrence theorists tend to ignore the difficulties that are associated with the signaling process itself (Jervis 1970, pp. 18–40). They assume that adversaries, who usually speak different languages, nevertheless share common symbols that facilitate effective communication. Everyone is thought to understand, so to speak, the meaning of fierce guard dogs, barbed wire, and "No Trespassing" signs. In practice, however, this may not be so. Statesmen, moreover, frequently adopt complex and finely calibrated strategies of coercion which make quite unrealistic demands on their adversaries' interpretative abilities. A striking example of this was the American decision in 1965 to send ashore a "light" marine division instead of a "heavy" army division in order to signal to Hanoi Washington's limited objectives. The intended significance of the type of unit deployed was undoubtedly lost to the North Vietnamese for whom the salient fact was that of the deployment itself (Rosen 1982, pp. 83–113; Gaddis 1982, pp. 246–53).

A second, and probably equally common cause of insensitivity to signals, arises from the failure to understand the context in which they are made and in terms of which they take on meaning. A signal can easily be missed if it is not recognized as a significant deviation from the norm. Allen Whiting describes several such occurrences preceding the Chinese entry into the Korean War in November 1950. Peking increased both the frequency of newspaper articles on Korea and the strength of the language used to indicate Chinese interests on that peninsula. There is no evidence that the Americans picked this up or, if they did, were in any way aware of the manner in which the foreign language press especially was being used to signal intensified Chinese concern with developments in Korea (Whiting 1960).

Signals can also be misunderstood if they are interpreted in an inappropriate context. The international relations literature abounds with examples of such distortion. In 1961 Chinese soldiers surrounded Indian outposts which had been set up in contested areas of Ladakh. Having demonstrated their ability to cut off several Indian outposts, the Chinese subsequently withdrew, leaving the Indian pickets unharmed. Peking intended the action as a demonstration of resolve but one that would allow Indian leaders to back down without loss of face because violence had been avoided. However, government officials in New Delhi interpreted the Chinese withdrawal as a sign of timidity. They reasoned that Chinese forces had failed to press their tactical advantage because Peking feared the consequences of a wider conflict with India. As a result, Indian leaders became even bolder in their efforts to occupy as much of the disputed territory, east and west, as was possible (Whiting 1975, pp. 42–106).

The reason why the Chinese signal failed to have its intended effect was the belief on the part of Nehru, Menon, and their military advisers that Peking was loath to start a war with India because it feared defeat. They were also convinced that China wished to avoid being branded as the aggressor by the nonaligned bloc. As later events demonstrated, these Indian assessments were based on serious misjudgments about both the political and the military consequences of a Sino–Indian conflict. The Chinese, who were unaware of the nature and extent of these Indian illusions, behaved in a way damaging to deterrence by reinforcing in Indian minds the very expectations about themselves they sought to forestall (Lebow 1981, pp. 57–95).

Chinese awareness of the unrealistic nature of Indian estimates of the military balance would have required an intimate and detailed knowledge of privileged communications of the Indian government, something not normally at the disposal of other states, especially adversaries. For this reason, the problem posed to effective communication by asymmetrical assessment seems to be all but insurmountable in cases in which such assessments cannot be inferred from diplomatic discussions, public statements, or actual policies.

Even analysts sensitive to this problem would no doubt face great difficulties in convincing their own governments that adversarial assessments of the military or political balance were completely at variance with their own. Take the case of Pearl Harbor. The Japanese attack was predicated upon the erroneous assumption that the American reaction to destruction of its Pacific fleet would be to withdraw from the western Pacific. As Japanese leaders wanted to avoid an all-out war against the United States, a struggle they knew they could never win, their attack would make sense only if the resulting war could indeed be kept limited and short. Imagine, if you will, the difficulties of an American intelligence analyst who had succeeded in second-guessing this scenario in trying to convince his superiors of Japanese intentions. The premise upon which the attack rested—that the United States would accommodate itself to loss of its fleet instead of fighting back—would have struck American officials as so patently absurd that they would have been likely to have dismissed out of hand any warning based on it.

The Falklands conflict provides a recent and even more dramatic example of the importance of the adversary's understanding of the context as a determinant of a willingness to take risks (Lebow 1983a, pp. 5–36). There were many causes of miscalculation in both capitals, but one important one was surely the fact that Buenos Aires and London conceived of the conflict in quite different terms. From the Argentine perspective the Malvinas were national territory that had been occupied by a colonial power since 1833. British sovereignty over the islands was an atavism in a world that had witnessed numerous wars of national liberation that had all but brought the age of colonialism to an end. Viewed in this light, it seemed a farfetched notion indeed that a colonial power in the year 1982 would try to reimpose, let alone succeed, in reimposing its rule on a "liberated colony" by force of arms. World opinion, international morality, and most important of all, the constellation of international political forces all seemed to militate against it. The analogies that sprung into Argentine minds were Goa and Suez—an early invasion scenario concocted by the navy was actually called Plan Goa. The original Goa operation resulted in the colonial power, Portugal, accommodating itself to the loss of its colonial enclave on the Indian subcontinent when it was overrun by India. Suez, of course, remains the best example of how an attempt to reimpose colonial domination failed for all the reasons mentioned above.

The British conceived of the Falklands controversy in an altogether different light. Politicians, the press, and public opinion for the most part dismissed the colonial metaphor as inappropriate because the population of the islands was of British stock and wished to remain under the protection of the Crown. Majority opinion did not see the Argentine invasion as an example of national liberation but rather as an act of naked aggression carried out by a brutal dictatorship against a democratic and peaceful people. For the British, the relevant historical analogy was Hitler and the origins of World War II. Newspapers made frequent references to the events and lessons of that period. Chief among the lessons was the need to stand up to aggression lest failure to do so whet the appetites of would-be aggressors everywhere. The Thatcher government pursued this line of reasoning: it justified the need to retake the Falklands with the twin arguments that "aggression must not be allowed to succeed" and that "freedom must be protected against dictatorship."

If it was inconceivable for Argentina that Britain would go to war to regain the Falklands, it was equally inconceivable to most Britons that they would not if it proved the only way to effect an Argentine withdrawal. The different cognitive contexts in terms of which the two countries understood the conflict led not only to contrasting visions of justice but also to quite different imperatives for action. Unfortunately, policymakers in both London and Buenos Aires, while not altogether ignorant of the others' conceptualization of the conflict, seemed unable to grasp its implications for that country's behavior.

Statesmen could be educated to the importance of trying to conceptualize conflicts as they are experienced by their adversaries. This does not mean that they would succeed in doing so. The obstacles that stand in their way are both self-imposed, consisting of all the personal, political, as well as cultural obstacles to the development of empathy, and also structural obstacles, involving a function of differing conceptual contexts and of asymmetries in assessment. There is already quite a literature in psychology on empathy and techniques of encouraging it. Some of it has been useful in sensitizing people to the manifestations and effects of prejudice, thereby easing racial tensions in various institutional settings. In theory, policymakers could also be taught empathy. In practice, this is unlikely to happen, as most policymakers will have neither the time nor the inclination for such training. Their political needs are probably an even bigger barrier to empathy as the difficult kinds of decisions that political office entails would not be facilitated (quite the reverse) by greater understanding of the needs and motivations of political opponents or other groups whose interests were about to be sacrificed.

The external impediments that hinder proper interpretation of an adversary's signals are probably even more difficult to overcome. This may require an intimate familiarity with the political culture in question. However, leaders of countries themselves rarely possess any special area expertise. American presidents in particular are unlikely to have very much foreign experience. This does not mean that they lack firm opinions about foreign policy, especially when it concerns the motives of their country's principal adversary. They also tend to surround themselves with advisers who hold similar views. While this may be a lamentable practice, leaders may be no better informed when they rely on the advice of "experts." Familiarity with a country or culture is in itself no guarantee of accurate insight or prescience. It can even be a hindrance to the extent that the "old Russia hand," Arabist, or what-have-you, is the prisoner of deeply held but not necessarily accurate opinions about what goals motivate that country's policymakers or what factors they weigh when they make decisions. For all these reasons, misunderstandings and incomprehension will always be rife. Given this unpleasant fact of international political life, a strategy of conflict management based upon the premise that clear, unambiguous signaling is readily attainable seems quite unrealistic.

The Causes of Aggression

Deterrence theory assumes that commitments are most often challenged because the states responsible for them appear to lack the capability or will to defend them. Case studies of actual conflicts contradict this depiction of international relations in important ways. They indicate that the existence of a vulnerable commitment is neither a necessary nor a sufficient condition for a challenge. Vulnerable commitments may never be challenged, while credible ones may be. This phenomenon points to the existence of serious misperceptions on the part of challengers and to the presence of different, or at least additional, causes of aggression.

My own study of brinkmanship crises analyzed a class of acute international crises whose defining characteristic was the expectation on the part of the initiator that the adversary would back down when challenged (Lebow 1981, pp. 57–95). I found that much more often than not brinkmanship challenges were initiated in the absence of any good reasons indicating that the adversary lacked

either the capability or the resolve to defend this commitment. Not surprisingly, almost all these challenges resulted in setbacks for the initiators, who were themselves compelled to back down or go to war.

Faulty judgment on the part of initiators could most often be attributed to their perceived need to carry out a brinkmanship challenge. This compulsion arose from a combination of grave foreign and domestic problems which policymakers believed could only be overcome through the successful challenge of an adversary's commitment. Brinkmanship was conceived of by them as a necessary and forceful response to danger, as a means of preserving national strategic or domestic political interests before time ran out.

When policymakers believed in the necessity of challenging commitments of their adversaries, they became predisposed to see their objectives as attainable. They convinced themselves that they would succeed without provoking war. Because they knew the extent to which they were powerless to back down, they expected that their adversaries would accommodate them by doing so. Some of the policymakers involved also took comfort in the illusion that their country would emerge victorious at little cost to themselves if the crisis got out of hand and led to war.

The extent to which would-be challengers are inner-directed and inwardly focused is also a central theme of the work of Janice Stein (in Jervis, Lebow, & Stein 1985). In her analysis of the five occasions between 1969 and 1973 when Egyptian leaders seriously contemplated the use of force against Israel, Stein found that decision making departed significantly from the postulates of deterrence theory. All five decisions revealed a consistent and almost exclusive fixation by Egyptian leaders on their own political interests. They spoke in almost apocalyptic terms of Egypt's need to liberate the Sinai: to uphold the rights of Palestinians; and, above all, to wipe out the humiliation of 1967 by waging a successful military campaign. By contrast, Israel's interests, and the imperatives for action that could be expected to flow from them, were not at all salient for Egyptian leaders.

The Egyptian failure to consider the relative interests of both sides resulted in a flawed estimate, not of Israel's credibility, but rather of the scope of Israel's military response. In 1969 Egyptian leaders attached a very low probability to the possibility that Israel would carry the war of attrition onto Egyptian territory in order to maintain its position in the Sinai, a miscalculation of major proportions, given the magnitude of the punishment Israel in fact inflicted upon Egypt. In 1973 the Egyptians never even considered the possibility that Israel would invade Egypt proper as a means of reasserting its authority along the Canal and then refused until it was too late to give credence to reports that such an operation was under way.

Egypt's inability to understand that Israel's leaders believed that defense of the Sinai was important both for its own sake and as an indicator of resolve was merely one cause of its miscalculation in 1969. Stein demonstrates that Egyptian leaders overestimated their own capacity to determine the course of a war of attrition and underestimated that of Israel. They also developed a strategy to fight the war, to culminate in a crossing of the Canal, that was predicated on a fatal inconsistency: the belief that Egypt could inflict numerous casualties on Israel in the course of a war of attrition but that Israel would refrain from escalating that conflict in order to reduce its casualties.

Stein describes these self-indulgent assessments and also Egypt's toleration of logical contradictions in its expectations as evidence of pervasive wishful thinking. She believes that this was a response to the strategic dilemma faced by Egyptian planners in 1969. Egypt could neither accept the status quo nor sustain the kind of military effort that would have been necessary to alter it. Instead, Egypt embarked upon a poorly conceived limited military action. The wishful thinking and the biased estimates associated with it were a form of bolstering the means by which Egyptian leaders convinced themselves that their strategy would succeed. Once again Israel's deterrent failed, not because of any lack of capability or resolve, but because Egypt's calculations, in the words of Stein, "were so flawed that they defeated deterrence."

Egyptian decision making in 1969 provides one more example of the phenomenon that my study of brinkmanship identified as the most frequent cause of serious miscalculation in international crisis: the inability of leaders to find a satisfactory way of reconciling two clashing kinds of threat. The psychological stress that arises from this decisional dilemma is usually relieved by the adoption of defensive avoidance as a coping strategy. Leaders commit themselves to a course of action and deny information that indicates that their policy might not succeed. As has been true in many cases of crisis decision making, the Egyptian decisional dilemma that prompted defensive avoidance was the result of incompatibility between domestic imperatives and foreign realities. The domestic threat—political and economic losses—was the overriding consideration for Egyptian policymakers as it was for the Argentines.

The primacy of domestic political concerns may not be entirely attributable to the self-interest of the policymakers involved, although this factor should not be discounted. It may also be related to their ability to foresee and visualize domestic disasters more vividly than foreign ones. Because of this the domestic costs of passivity in these cases probably appeared greater and more probable than a more detached assessment might have indicated and certainly also more difficult to deny. Foreign catastrophe, by contrast, depended upon the behavior of adversaries whose political systems were less well understood than one's own and whose policies were accordingly more difficult to predict. It was simply much easier for policymakers to delude themselves that somehow their foreign ventures would succeed than it was for them to convince themselves that the domestic price of restraint would be less than horrendous. Not surprisingly, they chose to avoid what appeared to be certain loss in favor of a policy that held out the prospect of at least lower costs in the Egyptian case and the chance of substantial gain in the case of Argentina.

If deterrence theory describes an adversary's vulnerability as the catalyst for aggression, it prescribes credible, defensive commitments as the most important means of discouraging it. The empirical evidence marshaled in this study once again challenges the validity of the theory's assumptions. This is most apparent with respect to the role of military capability, and adversarial restraint is both more uncertain and more complex than deterrence theory allows.

Stein found that Egypt went to war in 1973 in spite of its leaders' adverse estimate of the military balance. The same domestic political considerations that compelled Egyptian leaders to challenge Israel also provided the incentives for Egyptian military planners to devise a strategy that compensated for their military weakness. Human ingenuity and careful organization succeeded in exploiting the flexibility of multipurpose conventional weaponry to circumvent many of the constraints of military inferiority. The Egyptians achieved a defensive superiority in what they planned to keep a limited battle zone.

According to Stein, two other considerations were crucial catalysts for the Egyptian decision to challenge Israel in 1973. These were the twin assumptions made by Sadat and his advisers that there was no chance of regaining the Sinai by diplomacy and that the longer they postponed war the more the military balance would favor Israel. Both assumptions helped to create a mood of desperation in Cairo, so much so that Sadat repeatedly purged the Egyptian military command until he found generals who were optimistic of finding a way around Israel's awesome air and armored capability.

The Japanese decision to attack the United States in December 1941 seems analogous in almost every important respect to the Egyptian decision of 1973. Like the Egyptians, the Japanese fully recognized the military superiority of their adversary, in this instance based on greater naval power and a vastly superior economic base. The Japanese nevertheless felt compelled to attack the United States in the forlorn hope that a limited victory would facilitate a favorable settlement of their festering and costly conflict with China. As the Egyptians were to do more than thirty years later, the Japanese military planners devised an ingenious and daring strategy to compensate for the adversary's advantages; they relied on air power and surprise in the hope of neutralizing American

naval power in the Pacific in one sharp blow. They too deluded themselves into believing that their foe would reconcile itself to the political consequences of a disastrous initial defeat instead of fighting on to regain the initiative, a miscalculation for which they were to pay a truly monumental price. The Japanese strategy was also an act of desperation. Tokyo opted for war only after it became clear that it could not attain its objectives by diplomacy. Japanese leaders were also convinced that the military balance between themselves and their adversaries would never again be so favorable as it was in 1941 (Butow 1961; Borg and Okamoto 1973).

These two cases suggest that the military balance, even when correctly assessed, is only one of several considerations taken into account by policymakers contemplating war. They are also influenced by domestic and foreign political pressures which push them to act, frustration with the low probability of achieving their goals by peaceful means, and their judgments about future trends in the military balance. As we have just seen, these considerations can prove decisive.

If there is any single example that drives home the point that challenges may be unrelated to the military balance it is the recent war in the Falkland Islands. The Argentine decision to invade in March 1982 was a result in the first instance of the faltering legitimacy of the military junta and its increasingly desperate need to do something to shore up its public support. Like the Japanese and the Egyptians, the Argentines had also lost all faith in the prospect of achieving their external goal, sovereignty over the islands, by diplomacy. Disenchantment with negotiations was all the more a catalyst for military action as peaceful resolution of the dispute had appeared a very real possibility until the failure of the so-called lease-back proposal in the late fall of 1981. A transfer of sovereignty had seemed so likely that the junta, both as a bargaining tactic and as a means of drumming up domestic support for itself, had actively encouraged public expectations to this effect. The Argentine military now became the prisoner of the very passions it had helped to arouse.

Had a military appraisal of the situation dominated Argentine deliberations, the junta would almost certainly have waited another year before launching its invasion of the Falklands. It was public knowledge that in the interim HMS *Invincible* would have gone to the Australian navy. *Intrepid* and *Fearless,* the two amphibious assault ships, would have been scrapped together with some of the supporting frigates. Britain, which barely possessed sufficient naval assets to retake the Falklands in 1982, would almost certainly have been unable to do so in the absence of these vessels. The junta, composed of generals and admirals, deemed political considerations more important than calculations of relative military balance, with results that were nothing short of disastrous.

Most of the twenty-odd cases examined by Lebow (1984) and Stein (1985) in their most recent studies support the conclusion that policymakers who risk or actually start wars pay more attention to their own strategic and domestic political interests than they do to the interests and military capabilities of their adversaries. Their strategic and political needs appear to constitute the principal motivation for a resort to force. When these needs are paramount, policymakers are prone to disregard the ways in which the same kinds of strategic and political needs might compel adversaries to stand firm in defense of their commitments. They may discount an adversary's resolve even when the state involved has gone to considerable lengths to demonstrate that resolve and to develop the military capabilities needed to defend its commitment.

Deterrence theory can be accused of standing reality on its head. It assumes a constant level of hostility between adversaries the expression of which is a function of the opportunity to act. Our cases point to just the reverse causation: the principal incentive for aggressive foreign policy appears to be a state's own perceived vulnerabilities which lead its policymakers to challenge an adversary even when external opportunity to act, in the form of an opponent's vulnerable commitment, is absent. Domestic and strategic needs and the perceptual distortions they engender may actually constitute the greatest threat to peace in the contemporary world. This finding has obvious and important policy implications.

Deterrence dictates that the defender attempt to manipulate the adversary's calculus of cost and gain in order to reduce the adversary's incentive to attack or to challenge an important commitment. The research described in *Psychology and Deterrence* suggests that one important reason why deterrence often fails is that defenders attempt to manipulate attributes of the situation, especially adversarial perceptions of resolve and relative military capability, that may not be critical to the calculations of the would-be aggressor. Efforts to influence the adversary may require attention to the *adversary's* strategic dilemmas, domestic political costs of inaction, and assessment of achieving at least some objectives by nonviolent means. All these factors must be considered by defenders as proper and productive targets for manipulation.

If weakness is an equal or even more important source of confrontational foreign policies than strength, it calls for a corresponding shift in the focus of efforts to prevent the use of force. Too much attention is probably devoted in theory and practice to making commitments credible and not nearly enough to trying to understand what might prompt an adversary to challenge them. A more sophisticated approach to conflict management would make use of both deterrence and reassurance. Leaders must seek to discourage an adversary's challenges by attempting to reduce both the adversary's opportunity and its perceived need to carry them out. They ought to avoid situations in which their own state is perceived as so weak or irresolute as to invite challenge but at the same time be careful not to make an adversary feel so weak or threatened that it has the need to do so.

It may be that to avoid war a status quo power has to pursue two distinct and not easily reconcilable objectives. It must maintain its own power and credibility while at the same time working to forestall the development of the kind of unstable conditions that lead to a security dilemma. In the words of Jack Snyder, the status quo power "must worry about everyone's security, not just its own" (Snyder, in Jervis, Lebow, and Stein 1985). The ideal way to accomplish this may be to deploy the kinds of forces which convey no serious threat of offensive advantage and thus avoid bringing about a situation of strategic instability.

Policymakers should also shun commitments and alliances that can be defended only by forces and strategies that pose a threat to the adversary's ability to provide for its own defense and that of its allies.

Conclusions

Deterrence purports to describe an *interactive* process between the defender of a commitment and a would-be challenger. The defender is expected to define and publicize its commitment and do its best to make it credible in the eyes of his adversary. Would-be challengers are expected to update frequently their assessment of their opponents' commitments and to probe for weaknesses with regard to their capability and resolve. The repetitive cycle of test and challenge is expected to provide both sides with an increasingly sophisticated understanding of each others' interests, propensity for risk-taking, threshold of provocation, and style of foreign policy behavior.

Several of the cases analyzed or referred to in our study cast doubts upon the expectation that repetitive interaction between adversaries contributes to a better understanding of their respective intentions and modus operandi. From the perspective of the challenger, one reason for this may be the inner-directed focus of policymakers. Leaders contemplating challenges of other states' commitments were remarkably insensitive to external realities. The Americans in Korea in the fall of 1950, Sadat's Egypt in 1973, and the Argentine junta in 1982, to mention only three examples, initiated challenges primarily in response to their domestic political needs. These internal imperatives, not their external opportunities to act, were decisive to their decisions to proceed. In the Egyptian and Argentine cases, domestic political pressures determined the timing of the challenge as well. In the Egyptian decision, the putative resolve and capability of the adversary did not figure prominently in the policy debate. When external military and political realities were considered, as in the Korean and Falklands decisions, they were on the whole subordinated to political needs; the information available was distorted or processed selectively in order to make a challenge appear feasible. Policymakers in these cases can hardly be said to have based their challenges on their judgments of the credibility of their adversaries' commitments. Their process of risk assessment differed markedly from that described by deterrence theory.

From the perspective of the defender, the picture appears much the same; repeated clashes can fail to lead to any better understanding of adversarial motivations or foreign policy style. Soviet-American relations can be cited as a case in point. The "lessons" American policymakers have drawn from the series of cold war confrontations can only in the loosest sense be said to derive from the behavior of their adversary. They seem more the result of a largely subjective learning process whereby American policymakers tended to interpret Soviet behavior in terms of their preexisting notions of the motivations behind Soviet foreign policy. I have tried to document elsewhere how the Cuban missile crisis provides a striking illustration of the way in which assumptions about adversaries can misleadingly seem to be confirmed and thereby increase their grip over the minds of the policymakers who approach international affairs in terms of them (Lebow 1983b, pp. 431–58). Afghanistan seems to have had the same effect.

The image of adversarial relationships that emerges from our study is one in which the expectations that the two sides have of each other may bear little relationship to reality. Challengers tend to focus on their own needs and do not seriously consider—or if they do, often distort—the needs, interests, and capabilities of their adversaries. Defenders in turn may interpret the motives or objectives of a challenger in a manner consistent with their expectations whether those expectations are in any way warranted. Both sides may also prove insensitive to each other's signals for a variety of political, cultural, or other reasons. In such circumstances, recurrent deterrence episodes may not facilitate greater mutual understanding. Experience may actually hinder real learning to the extent that it encourages apparent confirmation of misleading or inappropriate "lessons."

The inner direction of policymakers points to one of the ironies of international life: much of the effort made by defenders to impart the appearance of credibility to their commitments is probably wasted as challengers may not pay much attention to them. Even when they do, they may deny or simply not understand the signals being directed their way. Cultural, contextual, and organizational barriers to interpretation abound, not to speak of motivated biases on the part of policymakers already committed to proceeding with a challenge.

Partisans of deterrence admit that it may not always succeed in discouraging aggressive behavior. But they insist that it is unfair to assess the efficacy of nuclear deterrence on the basis of conventional cases. They describe deterrence between nuclear adversaries as far more effective in regulating conflict because the prospect of nuclear war is so terrifying as to frighten policymakers into behaving more or less rationally in crisis situations. Both Bernard Brodie and Thomas Schelling have at one time or another advanced this line of argument (Brodie 1973, pp. 313–14, 375–432; Schelling 1966, pp. 96–111, 246–47). Schelling's argument is worth describing because it has become something of a party line for deterrence theorists. He describes the threshold to war as generally ambiguous and difficult to define. Escalation is characterized by uncertainty, as neither side can really know just what action on its part will trigger war. It becomes an exercise in competitive risk-taking with diplomatic victory going to the side willing to take the greatest risks, assuming that war is avoided. But the devastating nature of nuclear war and the uncertainty of the threshold encourage prudence and caution on both sides. Adversaries, Schelling argues, attempt to avoid war by taking small, carefully controlled, and, whenever possible, reversible steps up the rungs of the escalation ladder (Schelling 1966, pp. 96–97).

There is another side to the nuclear coin. According to a number of scholars, nuclear weapons have had the effect of raising the "provocative threshold," that is, of increasing the number of actions that now come within the purview of

coercive bargaining, but which in the prenuclear age might have precipitated war (e.g., Kahn 1965, pp. 94–131; Osgood, R. E., and Tucker, R. W. 1967, pp. 150–57; Snyder, G. H., and Diesing, P. 1977, pp. 451–54). Snyder and Diesing point out that the observable lengthening of the crisis escalation ladder somewhat contradicts the assertion that nuclear adversaries behave more cautiously because of their fear of war: "The paradox is that the nuclear fear faces two ways; it induces caution in oneself but also the thought that the opponent is cautious too, and therefore will tolerate a considerable amount of pressure and provocation before resorting to acts that seriously risk nuclear war" (1977). The obvious danger here is that one side or the other, convinced that the step it is about to take is acceptable to the adversary, and perhaps even likely to compel the adversary to concede, will instead push the confrontation beyond the point of no return. In Premier Khrushchev's metaphor, the "knots of war" will become tied too tightly for either side to undo them.

Our own findings lend credence to the fear that such a miscalculation could occur. We saw that policymakers are prone to distort reality in accord with their needs even in situations that appeared relatively unambiguous. The more numerous and ambiguous the signals are, the easier it becomes to do this, for uncertainty is often a breeding ground, not of restraint, but of irrational confidence. It is questionable whether any situation can be so salient and stark as to preclude wishful thinking. It may be, as many deterrence theorists allege, that the most obvious kinds of vital interests backed up by a credible second-strike capability constitute such a barrier to misperception. Certainly, this is a comforting belief. It is nevertheless apparent that the variety of complex signals that constitute crisis bargaining possess no such clarity. Many of these signals are subtle or intentionally vague. Others require a sophisticated understanding of the adversary's political process or culture to be properly understood. It is in this kind of situation, when the outcome of the crisis may unwittingly hang in the balance, that wishful thinking or miscalculation is most likely to occur.

References

Allison, G. T. 1971. *Essence of Decision: Explaining the Cuban Missile Crisis.* Boston: Little, Brown.

Borg, D. and S. Okamoto. eds. 1973. *Pearl Harbor as History: Japanese-American Relations, 1931–1941.* NY: Columbia University Press.

Brodie, B. 1973. *War and Politics.* NY: Macmillan.

Bueno de Mesquita, B. 1981. *The War Trap.* New Haven: Yale University Press.

Butow, R. 1961. *Tojo and the Coming of the War.* Stanford: Stanford University Press.

Clay, L. 1950. *Decision in Germany.* Garden City, NY: Doubleday.

Davison, W. P. 1958. *The Berlin Blockade: A Study in Cold War Politics.* Princeton: Princeton University Press.

Fisher, R. 1969. *International Conflict for Beginners.* NY: Harper and Row.

——— 1973. *Dear Israelis, Dear Arabs: A Working Approach to Peace.* NY: Harper and Row.

Gaddis, J. L. 1982. *Strategies of Containment.* NY: Oxford University Press.

George, A. L. and R. Smoke. 1974. *Deterrence in American Foreign Policy: Theory and Practice.* NY: Columbia University Press.

Hoffmann, S. 1968. *Gulliver's Troubles.* NY: McGraw-Hill.

Howley, F. L. 1950. *Berlin Command.* NY: Putnam.

Huth, P. and B. Russett. July 1984. "What Makes Deterrence Work? Cases from 1900 to 1980." *World Politics* 36 (4): 496–526.

Ienaga, S. 1978. *The Pacific War, 1931–1945.* NY: Pantheon.

Jervis, R. 1970. *The Logic of Images in International Relations.* Princeton: Princeton University Press.

Jervis, R., R. N. Lebow, and J. G. Stein. 1985. *Psychology and Deterrence.* Baltimore: Johns Hopkins University Press.

Kahn, H. 1965. *On Escalation: Metaphors and Scenarios.* NY: Praeger.

Kennedy, J. F. July 11, 1963. "American University Address." *New York Times.*

Kennedy, P. 1981. *The Realities Behind Diplomacy: Background Influences in British External Policy, 1865–1980.* London: Allen and Unwin.

Lebow, R. N. 1981. *Between Peace and War: The Nature of International Crisis.* Baltimore: Johns Hopkins University Press. Pp. 270–71.

——— March 1983. "Miscalculation in the South Atlantic: The Origins of the Falkland War." *Journal of Strategic Studies* 6: 5–35.

——— Fall 1983. "The Cuban Missile Crisis: Reading the Lessons Correctly." *Political Science Quarterly* 98: 431–58.

——— Summer 1984. "Windows of Opportunity: Do States Jump Through Them?" *International Security* 8: 147–86.

Mack, A. January 1975. "Why Big Nations Lose Small Wars." *World Politics* 27: 175–200.

Maxwell, N. 1972. *India's China War.* Garden City, NY: Doubleday.

McLellan, D. S. 1976. *Dean Acheson: The State Department Years.* NY: Dodd, Mead.

New York Times. 1900–1980. Index to. NY: The New York Times.

Osgood, R. E. and R. W. Tucker. 1967. *Force, Order, and Justice.* Baltimore: Johns Hopkins University Press.

Rosen, S. P. Fall 1982. "Vietnam and the American Theory of Limited War." *International Security* 7: 83–113.

Russett, B. 1967. "Pearl Harbor: Deterrence Theory and Decision Theory." *Journal of Peace Research* 4 (4): 89–105.

Schank, R. C. and K. M. Colby. eds. 1973. *Computer Models of Thought and Language.* San Francisco: Freeman.

Schelling, T. C. 1963. *The Strategy of Conflict.* Cambridge: Harvard University Press. Pp. 3–20.

——— 1966. *Arms and Influence.* New Haven: Yale University Press.

Singer, J. D., S. Bremer, and J. Stuckey. 1972. "Capability Distribution, Uncertainty, and Major Power War, 1820–1965." In *Peace, War and Numbers,* edited by B. Russett. Beverly Hills, CA: Sage.

Snyder, G. and P. Diesing. 1977. *Conflict Among Nations.* Princeton: Princeton University Press.

Snyder, J. L. 1985. "Perceptions of the Security Dilemma in 1914." In R. Jervis, R. N. Lebow, and J. G. Stein, *Psychology and Deterrence.*

Stein, J. G. 1985. "Calculation, Miscalculation and Conventional Deterrence: The View from Cairo," and "Calculation, Miscalculation and Conventional Deterrence II: The View from Jerusalem." In R. Jervis, R. N. Lebow, and J. G. Stein, *Psychology and Deterrence*. Baltimore: Johns Hopkins University Press.

Truman, H. S. 1955. *Memoirs*. Garden City, NY: Doubleday. Vol. 2: 355–65.

Weinberg, G. 1970–80. *The Foreign Policy of Hitler's Germany*. 2 vols. Chicago: University of Chicago Press.

Whiting, A. S. 1960. *China Crosses the Yalu: The Decision to Enter the Korean War*. NY: Macmillan.

——— 1975. *The Chinese Calculus of Deterrence: India and Indochina*. Ann Arbor: University of Michigan Press.

Confining the Military to Defense

Randall Forsberg

Most arms control efforts are intended to reduce the risk of nuclear war while allowing large nuclear arsenals to be maintained indefinitely. But the risk of global nuclear holocaust cannot be substantially reduced until the capability to perpetrate such a holocaust has been virtually eliminated. To significantly lessen the terrible danger of nuclear war, we must cut the 50,000 nuclear weapons that exist today to a very small number, perhaps 500, perhaps 250, perhaps even fewer. In other words, we must eliminate 99 percent of the current nuclear arsenals.

The enormous destructive potential of even a few thousand nuclear weapons launched against military forces illustrates why such a reduction is necessary. For example, a U.S.-Soviet nuclear exchange directed at land-based missiles alone, which would involve the explosion of 2,000 to 3,000 large nuclear warheads in each country, would kill 3 to 20 million people in the United States and a like number in the U.S.S.R. simply from the downwind trails of radioactive fallout. In addition, it would destroy the ozone layer and blacken the sky with the soot and smoke from tremendous firestorms, causing drastic ecological damage. The most dire possibility is that the blocking of sunlight would create a freezing "nuclear night" which could be fatal to all forms of life.

Moreover, *very* small numbers of nuclear weapons, if launched against cities, have the potential to wreak similarly unimaginable damage. A cataclysm limited, for example, to 250 nuclear weapons exploded on cities throughout the northern hemisphere might not irreversibly destroy modern civilization, but it would cause unprecedented devastation, killing scores of millions of people, and perhaps hundreds of millions. Thus the only way to lift the shadow of nuclear war that has darkened our lives since World War II is to eliminate nuclear weapons altogether.

As people have learned of the predictable effects of nuclear war, most have concluded that the world's first order of business should be to abolish nuclear weapons. But government policies continue to be headed in just the opposite direction—toward not only more nuclear weapons but ever more "usable" ones as well. There are several reasons for this unabated production of nuclear weapons. Because the subject of nuclear arms control is technical and complicated, people assume they cannot understand it. Because it is remote and difficult, they assume they cannot influence it. This sense of helplessness has been reinforced by the fact that nuclear arms control is a matter of international negotiation; thus the positions and motives of the participating nations remain ambiguous and partly hidden. Even when people are convinced of the need for change, they have little sense of constructive policy alternatives. As a result, they give arms control issues a relatively low priority in their voting preferences. Meanwhile, those with vested interests in the continuing arms buildup are powerful and well organized.

These explanations for the arms race have long been recognized. In response to them, efforts have been made by many different groups to improve public education in order to create among the public an interest group sufficiently large and well organized to more than offset the influence of the military-industrial complex.

But there is an additional reason for the arms race, not widely recognized, that has made it impossible to reverse the nuclear arms buildup even when the majority of the public has been in favor of doing so. This obstacle is a powerful underlying motivation that leads influential elites to oppose any fundamental change in the pattern of the arms race and that creates considerable ambivalence about the need for change. What motivates the maintenance of enormous nuclear arsenals and the production of new nuclear weapons is not the desire of nations to deter nuclear attack by threatening retaliation in kind. As most people realize, relatively small, unchanging nuclear arsenals would be adequate for this purpose. What drives the continuing arms race is the desire to deter conventional warfare. This is clear in the very nature of the nuclear arsenals that have existed since 1960. Most of the 50,000 nuclear warheads are designed not to attack cities but to attack military targets in a war that has escalated from

some conventional conflict. Weapons designed for such "nuclear warfighting" include not only most "strategic" weapons but even larger numbers of short-range, "tactical" nuclear weapons intended for use on the conventional battlefield.

By posing a threat of escalation from conventional war to countermilitary nuclear attacks, U.S. and Soviet nuclear arsenals are intended to deter three forms of conventional warfare: first, the deliberate initiation of another conventional world war among the big powers; second, any conventional challenge by one big power to the interventionary use of conventional force by another; and third, conventional intervention by a rival power.

Because the functions of nuclear forces are actually deeply intertwined with the functions of conventional military forces, it has been and will continue to be impossible to make deep cuts in nuclear arsenals until we have come to grips with the problem of ending conventional warfare. This is something that past nuclear arms control efforts have not attempted to do. In fact, past arms control efforts have attempted to do just the opposite. Arguing that we ought not risk a nuclear holocaust over the issues that cause conventional war, they have ignored the inevitable link between nuclear weapons and conventional warfare. In effect, they have tried to place nuclear weapons in a class apart from all other aspects of military power and warfare.

Because it confuses what *should be* with what *is,* this approach has been counterproductive. Instead of weakening the link between nuclear weapons and conventional warfare and thereby making nuclear arms control easier to achieve, it has simply obscured the most profound causes of the arms race, muddied the genuine public policy issues, and thus weakened the case for any arms control measures.

Because the function of large, ever-improving nuclear arsenals is to deter conventional warfare, we will never be able to reduce nuclear weapons substantially until the use of conventional military forces is restrained by means other than the threat of nuclear escalation. Furthermore, we will not be able to reduce nuclear weapons to the very low numbers that would no longer threaten the survival of our societies—a few hundred weapons or fewer—until we have brought conventional warfare largely or entirely under control. Before we can hope to abolish nuclear weapons altogether, we must eliminate the prospect of conventional war among the big powers, end their intervention in developing countries, and limit all conventional military forces to small, short-range, purely defensive armaments.

These objectives can be achieved if we try to accomplish them not in one fell swoop but through a series of gradual, clearly demarcated steps each of which creates a plateau of military, political, and technological stability that can be maintained for years or perhaps even decades. At each stage of the process, we must eliminate the more provocative, aggressive, or escalatory aspects of armaments, leaving the more defensive elements for later reductions. These features will give our societies the time and the mechanisms they will need to fully internalize inhibitions against the use of military force as a tool of policy. They will also help motivate widespread and sustained efforts for change in an environment in which people despair of ever achieving a stable disarmed peace, yet in which pressures for change must be very high in order to prevail over the enormous psychological, economic, and political pressures to maintain the status quo.

By gradually confining the role of conventional military forces to defense, more and more narrowly defined, we can move safely toward a world in which conventional forces are limited to short-range, defensive armaments, in which international institutions provide an effective nonviolent means of resolving conflicts, and in which nuclear weapons can be abolished.

Not only *must* we move toward a stable disarmed peace in order to eliminate the danger of nuclear war, we *can* do so, and we can do so safely. The step-by-step approach to disarmament set forth in this article will not be quick or easy, but it has the great virtue of being much less risky than our present course. The only alternative is a permanent technological arms race between the superpowers that is jointly managed by arms control agreements and accompanied by the steady spread of nuclear weapons and independent military industries to more and more countries.

The Functions of Large Conventional Forces

Developing a feasible path to a stable disarmed peace must commence with an understanding of the functions of military forces as they are today. Because the underlying function of the nuclear arms race is to influence the use of conventional armaments, it is useful to begin by analyzing the functions of conventional military forces. In fact, the lion's share of world military spending and arms production, about 75 percent, is consumed not by the nuclear arms race but by the conventional armed forces of the industrialized countries that lie in a band across the northern hemisphere: the United States and Canada, Europe, the Soviet Union, and Japan. Not only financially, but also politically and psychologically, the large conventional forces of these countries form the root of the problem of modern armaments. Their main functions are to deter and defend against another conventional world war, to preserve the superpower spheres of influence in the northern hemisphere, and to permit superpower intervention in the Third World.

Deterring and Defending Against Another Conventional World War

More than half of world military spending and arms production is absorbed by conventional forces maintained to deter and defend against another major war in Europe. These forces include most of the conventional forces of NATO, which comprises the United States, Canada, and 14 West European countries; most of the conventional forces of the Warsaw Pact, which comprises the Soviet Union and six East European countries; and all of the conventional forces of the nonaligned European nations.

NATO and the Warsaw Pact maintain large conventional military forces—standing armies totalling close to 10 million men—on the assumption that as long as the forces on both sides are balanced neither side will start a war. The nonaligned European countries maintain conventional forces to make an invasion of their territory in the event of an East–West war too costly to be worth undertaking.

Of U.S. ground and naval forces, about half are intended to help deter and defend against a war in Europe. These ground forces comprise most of the army's armored and mechanized divisions, which are heavily equipped with tanks and self-propelled artillery and which require an operating area with an extensive industrial infrastructure. Some of these divisions are permanently stationed in Europe; others are stationed in the United States but are earmarked for use in Europe.

U.S. naval forces oriented primarily toward Europe, called "sea control" forces, are designed to secure the sea lanes so that convoys from the United States can transport supplies of tanks, artillery, ammunition, and oil, as they did during World War II. To prevent the United States and NATO from mounting a permanently sustained attack against the East, the Soviet Union has built a very large force of anti-ship submarines, whose role is to sink U.S. supply convoys. In response, the United States and other Western countries have developed extensive anti-submarine warfare capabilities. These include submarines and aircraft, which are designed to patrol the North Atlantic and sink Soviet submarines, and surface ships, such as destroyers and frigates, whose role is to escort the convoys, providing anti-submarine and anti-aircraft "point defense" in case Soviet submarines or aircraft penetrate the earlier patrols.

In comparison with the United States, the Soviet Union devotes an even larger proportion of its ground and naval forces to the function of deterring and defending against another major war in Europe. About two-thirds of the Soviet army is stationed in Eastern Europe or in the European part of the U.S.S.R., west of the Ural mountains. (The remaining Soviet divisions are stationed in the far eastern or southern regions of the U.S.S.R., with a few maintained in the central region as a

strategic reserve.) The main non-strategic role of the Soviet navy is to respond to a possible East–West war on European soil. In addition to interdicting U.S. supply convoys, the Soviet navy is designed to provide anti-aircraft and anti-submarine defense for anti-ship submarines and to defend the coasts and borders of the U.S.S.R. and Eastern Europe against amphibious assault landings or air attacks from U.S. aircraft carriers.

The tactical air forces of both superpowers can be redeployed to regions far from their permanent bases fairly quickly. But because half of the U.S. tactical air forces are based on naval aircraft carriers, not on land, this component of the U.S. military is somewhat more flexible and somewhat less narrowly tied to the European region than is that of the Soviet Union. In the event of a major war in any region of the world—Europe or elsewhere—most of the tactical air forces of both sides could be quickly moved to that region.

In the West, it is widely believed that the Soviet Union has an overwhelming superiority in conventional military forces, especially in ground forces in Europe, and this superiority is interpreted as evidence of aggressive intentions. It is true that the Soviet Union maintains approximately twice as many ground troops as does the United States: 1.8 million men to 1 million. But in Europe, Soviet troops offset not only those of the United States but also those of three powerful U.S. allies—France, West Germany, and the United Kingdom—which have ground troops totalling 800,000 men. (The remaining NATO countries have ground troops that roughly offset those of the Soviet Union's smaller allies.) In addition, a substantial part of the Soviet army (about one quarter) is based in the Far East, where it faces a Chinese force that is evenly matched in tanks but superior in manpower. In fact, overall, Soviet and Warsaw Pact conventional forces are outnumbered by the combined forces of their potential enemies. Moreover, in other respects the Soviet Union does not appear to be preparing to initiate a major conventional war. For example, the size of Soviet conventional forces has remained roughly constant for more than 20 years; Soviet ammunition stores are ufficient for only one or two months of all-out conventional war; and Soviet front-line troops include less-trained recruits and receive less practice with advanced weapon systems than is common in the West.

Nonetheless, the possibility of a Soviet conventional attack against West Germany and the rest of Western Europe still is considered the primary Soviet military threat to the West. There is a critical difference, however, between the public view of this threat and that held by experts. What the public still tends to fear most is a deliberate, out-of-the-blue Soviet attack. In contrast, most Western military experts have gradually come to the conclusion that an outright attack is far less likely than escalation from a local conflict to an all-out war in which the Soviet Union would try to mount a blitzkrieg defense. Soviet leaders see a mirror-image threat. They fear not so much a deliberate NATO conventional attack against Eastern Europe or the U.S.S.R. (although such an attack might not be so implausible if the Warsaw Pact were to disarm unilaterally), as, say, an uprising in Eastern Europe or a move toward German reunification that would spawn an all-out war and place Soviet or East European territory in jeopardy.

Thus the large conventional forces of the industrialized countries are intended less to deter and defend against out-of-the-blue, large-scale aggression by one another than to deter and defend against the escalation of a lesser conflict to a major war.

Preserving Superpower Spheres of Influence

The second major function of the conventional forces of the industrialized countries is to preserve the superpower spheres of influence established at Potsdam and Yalta in the closing months of World War II. These spheres have been extraordinarily stable since 1945. The United States still is recognized as the preeminent power among the countries of Western Europe, Canada, and Japan, and the Soviet Union still is recognized as the dominant power in Eastern Europe.

The role of Soviet military forces in preserving Soviet hegemony in Eastern Europe is widely recognized in the West. It is well known that the Soviet military interventions in Hungary in 1956 and in Czechoslovakia in 1968, supported by token forces from other Warsaw Pact countries, and the threatened Soviet intervention in Poland in 1982, replaced by the internal imposition of martial law by Polish military forces, were intended to block the emergence of East European governments whose policies might be more neutral or less pro-Soviet in military, economic, or cultural affairs.

What is less widely recognized is that Soviet efforts to preserve hegemony in Eastern Europe serve in part to maintain the military alliance by which the U.S.S.R. strives to deter a major conventional war in Europe and to provide a buffer zone that would help protect Soviet territory should such a war occur. Moreover, in the East, the survival of the Soviet state is considered essential to the defense of East European countries and their communist governments. Thus, in part, Soviet military bases in Eastern Europe support the primary military functions of deterrence and defense. But to the extent that Soviet militarily backed control over the governments and domestic policies of Eastern European countries is more intrusive than it need be to sustain the alliance— and to the extent that the East–West military blocs are not needed at all to prevent another conventional war among the large industrialized powers—Soviet occupation and intervention in Eastern Europe must be seen as an independent function of Soviet military forces, aimed at maintaining cultural and economic hegemony for its own sake, not at simply strengthening deterrence and defense.

In an analogous way, U.S. conventional forces stationed in Western Europe and Japan may do more than merely provide for deterrence and defense in these regions. Just as the Soviet Union sees Eastern Europe as a buffer zone, so the United States sees its military bases and alliances in regions bordering Soviet-controlled territory as the first line of defense for the United States. U.S. officials might attempt to maintain this "forward defense" position even if American allies felt no need or desire for U.S. protection. Moreover, U.S. companies have major economic interests in Western Europe and Japan which they might persuade the U.S. government to protect, if need be, from changes mandated by free elections.

Superpower Intervention

The third major function of the conventional forces of the industrialized countries is to provide these nations with the capability to intervene in "local conflicts," usually civil wars, in the Third World. Because the risk of escalation to nuclear war has made it too dangerous for the industrialized powers to engage in conventional warfare directly with one another, the Third World is now the only arena in which the military competition between the United States and the Soviet Union takes the form of active warfare. And as the only open-ended issue of conventional war, intervention in the Third World is, ultimately, the issue that drives the nuclear arms race. For the nuclear arms competition is a race to achieve a superior capability to threaten escalation from conventional war to nuclear war; and the most likely origin of an East–West conventional war that conceivably could lead to nuclear escalation is a direct superpower confrontation in the Third World following unilateral intervention by one or both superpowers.

In developing countries, as in Europe and Japan, the superpowers have mixed motives. In part, they seek to maintain or expand spheres of influence in order to support the primary military functions of defense and deterrence. In part, they seek hegemonic control as a means to economic and political gain at the expense of local self-determination. But while in Europe and Japan the deterrent function of conventional forces is primary and the hegemonic function secondary, in the Third World this order is reversed.

In the West, large standing armies which permit intervention are justified by invoking the specter of the spread of totalitarian communist regimes by means of Soviet military aggression. Fear of the spread of communism through Soviet armed force developed between 1945 and 1950, when the Soviet Union consolidated its control of

Eastern Europe and when communist governments took power in China, North Korea, and North Vietnam, making it seem that a "red menace" was spreading outward from the U.S.S.R. across the world.

In reality, since 1945 the Soviet Union has been extremely cautious in the use of its conventional forces for large-scale intervention. In Eastern Europe, for example, Soviet troops were already in place at the end of World War II, so they did not need to cross a border or engage in open warfare in order to establish initial control. Because of the agreed spheres of influence, the subsequent Soviet interventions in Hungary and Czechoslovakia were certain not to be challenged by the West; yet both involved about 100,000 men. Such numbers were intended to ensure that the Soviet Union could put down the very small, ill-armed insurrections in those countries instantly, again without real warfare. In Poland, where Soviet troops, even if deployed on a much larger scale, would have been far more likely to become entrammeled in a large, bloody, prolonged civil war, and where such a war might have grown into a general East–West war, the Soviet Union has worked hard to avoid intervention without loosening its political control. The only large-scale Soviet intervention outside Eastern Europe, the current intervention in Afghanistan, has been directed against one of the militarily weakest countries in the world and one with no significant ties to the West.

This analysis is intended not to condone Soviet intervention, but simply to demonstrate that it has always been limited to situations in which there was no risk of confrontation with a major opponent or of escalation to a major war. The large civil wars in China, Korea, and Vietnam, which resulted in the partition of each of these countries, were supported by Soviet funds, arms, training, and advisers, but they were fought with indigenous troops. With the exception of Afghanistan, this has remained the pattern of Soviet intervention in Third World countries since 1945. It was true in Cuba, it has been true in other Central American countries, and it has been true in Africa and the Middle East. At various times over the last 15 years, the Soviet Union has sent "military advisers" to

Angola, Mozambique, Somalia, and Ethiopia, but their numbers have been limited to a few thousand at most. The largest outside military presence in Africa and the Middle East, often described as a surrogate for Soviet troops, is the Cuban contingent in Angola, which numbers 20,000. In Egypt, the U.S.S.R. had 20,000 military advisers in 1972, but they left quietly within a month when asked to do so by President Sadat. The Soviet Union has, of course, given military aid to one side in many other Third World conflicts, but it has not sent tens of thousands or hundreds of thousands of its own troops to engage in open warfare.

Each of the superpowers has cited forms of military aid by the other to justify its own large-scale interventions—the United States in Korea and Vietnam and the Soviet Union in Afghanistan. But when evaluating and responding to the military threats posed by the other, each superpower should distinguish between military aid and large-scale direct military intervention. Both aid and intervention are intended to influence the outcome of foreign conflicts, but aid supplies only financial and material support while intervention puts large numbers of foreign troops into the balance. Thus, in comparison with aid, intervention represents an escalation of foreign presence so great that it amounts to a qualitative change.

From the point of view of Third World countries, foreign military aid and even military sales do entail a certain loss of political independence, but they are far less intrusive than direct foreign military intervention. Foreign military aid is much less able to influence the outcome of local conflicts. For in the long run, these conflicts will be decided not by the supply of funds, training, arms, and advisers to one side or the other, but by the ability of one side to mobilize preponderant popular support. While foreign military aid can subvert self-determination or slow its development, it cannot in the long run prevent its emergence. Large-scale foreign intervention can.

Direct military intervention by a superpower in a developing country entails an attempt by the superpower to use its own ground, air, or naval forces to impose its view of the desired world system on a smaller, less technologically advanced nation in an internal conflict in which the superpower faces no militarily equal opponent. Such action cannot be described as defending another country from external aggression. Indeed, it amounts to committing such aggression: using superior technology, greater wealth, and manpower in the tens of hundreds of thousands to tip the balance in someone else's war. The aggressive character of such action is the same no matter which superpower intervenes, whether the conflict is about natural resources or about the political or economic system that will prevail, whether the outcome will provide an open door for capitalism or a foothold for socialism.

For these reasons the supply of military aid by either superpower should never be considered an adequate excuse for direct military intervention by the other. If anything, the appropriate, non-escalatory response to the supply of aid by one side should be the supply of aid by the other. Even better would be an international "hands off" approach, in which the industrialized countries agreed to end *all* forms of military involvement in Third World countries.

The line between aid and intervention is crossed somewhere between a few hundred military advisers and some 5,000 to 10,000 troops. For the smallest Third World countries, it may be crossed with even fewer troops, perhaps as few as 1,000 to 2,000. But from the vantage point of each superpower, when assessing the threatening potential of the large conventional forces of the other superpower, the relevant question is this: Under what circumstance are these forces likely to be used in *large-scale* aggression or intervention? In this context, Soviet military aid, even as many as a few thousand Soviet military advisers, should not be viewed as part of a quest for world domination any more than military aid and advisers from the West should be so regarded; and the supply of aid by the U.S.S.R. cannot be used as evidence of a Soviet intent to overrun the world by the aggressive use of its large conventional forces. The only relevant indicators of the likelihood of large-scale Soviet aggression or intervention in the future are the record of such intervention in the past—in Hungary, Czechoslovakia, and Afghanistan—and the evidence of the peacetime maintenance and training of Soviet interventionary forces.

As suggested by the history of U.S. and Soviet large-scale intervention in the Third World—that is, by the intervention of the United States in Korea and Vietnam with about 500,000 troops, and by the Soviet intervention in Afghanistan with about 100,000 troops—the interventionary forces maintained permanently in peacetime by the United States are far larger than the comparable Soviet forces and can be transported over much greater distances. This has been true throughout the postwar period.

About half of all U.S. ground and naval capability is designed more for unilateral intervention in developing countries than for defending Western Europe, or any other part of the world, against a Soviet attack. U.S. interventionary ground forces include the marines and the army's infantry, airborne, and paratroop divisions. These units are all relatively lightly equipped and are trained to fight in difficult mountain, desert, or jungle terrain, where few roads exist. Able to land by air or over the beach, the interventionary ground troops are not well prepared to stand against Soviet tank armies on the West German plain. They *are* well prepared to face the weaker, lightly equipped forces of developing countries.

U.S. interventionary naval forces comprise what the navy calls "power-projection" forces, that is, forces designed to project U.S. military power to distant parts of the world. These forces include 13 aircraft carriers, currently being built up to 15, five very large amphibious assault ships, and 50 amphibious landing ships. The amphibious assault ships are designed to carry and land marines and their equipment. The carriers permit offshore air operations in regions where there is not enough popular support to provide secure access to ordinary ground bases or docking facilities. Each carrier has the ability to place 100 planes, including about 80 supersonic fighter and attack planes, in a remote region of the world. In addition, each carrier is surrounded by a task force of 10 to 15 ships, including unarmed supply ships and armed escort ships which provide anti-aircraft and anti-submarine defense. Because of the tremendous

expense of building and operating such task forces, the United States is the only country in the world that operates a carrier fleet.

Unlike the United States, the Soviet Union has no aircraft carriers capable of launching and landing supersonic combat planes. It maintains instead a small fleet of six helicopter carriers. Like the five large U.S. amphibious assault ships, these carriers weigh 40,000 tons and carry 25 helicopters and 15 subsonic vertical take-off and landing (VTOL) planes, which cannot be used against supersonic combat planes. The Soviet helicopter carriers are armed primarily for anti-submarine warfare. They provide the U.S.S.R. with about one-twentieth of the power-projection capability of the United States.

Furthermore, with two exceptions (the 13,000-ton *Ivan Rogov* class), the largest amphibious landing ships of the Soviet navy weigh 4,000 tons. One-tenth the size of the principal U.S. amphibious assault ships, they are designed to operate in the enclosed seas near Soviet territory: the Baltic, the Mediterranean, the Black Sea, the Sea of Japan, and the Sea of Okhotsk. In the event of a conflict near Soviet borders, they would allow the Soviet Union to approach the action from behind and make a beachhead landing in support of its ground forces.

Because it has no large aircraft carriers or large amphibious assault ships based overseas, the Soviet Union is not capable of staging a large-scale conventional attack in South Asia, Africa, or Latin America. Large-scale Soviet military operations are confined to countries contiguous with Soviet borders, which it can reach through direct overland routes or by short, well-protected air routes. Outside Europe, these countries are Iran, Afghanistan, Mongolia, China, and North Korea. In contrast, as a result of the greater power-projection capability of the U.S. navy, the United States is free to operate in an interventionary manner in any part of the world.

The configuration of Soviet ground forces confirms the very limited extent of Soviet interventionary capabilities. While the United States has 200,000 marines, the Soviet Union has only 14,000. And since 1945, the Soviet Union, unlike the United

States has not maintained or trained a large "swing force" for direct large-scale military intervention in the Third World. Thus the 50,000 Soviet troops initially sent into Afghanistan in 1979 were drawn from Soviet divisions permanently stationed in the southern and European regions of the U.S.S.R. to deter war with the West.

Given the current configuration of U.S. and Soviet conventional forces, overseas bases, and foreign economic interests, the Soviet Union is much less likely than is the United States to undertake any large-scale direct intervention in the Third World, outside of Afghanistan, over the next decade. At present, the United States is preparing for large-scale military intervention in the Persian Gulf and is undertaking small-scale military intervention in Central America. The growing U.S. military involvement in El Salvador, Grenada, Honduras, and Nicaragua has been justified on the grounds that the Soviet Union and Cuba are supplying military aid to the opposing side. But the Soviet Union has no capability to intervene on a large scale in Central America, and Cuban troops are not present in other countries in sizable numbers. Thus U.S. policy in Central America is yet another case of one superpower using lesser forms of military aid by the other to justify its own escalation toward direct large-scale intervention.

In explaining its Persian Gulf preparations, the United States has alluded to a potential Soviet threat to Western oil supplies that might result from a Soviet intervention in Iraq or Iran. But for at least three reasons the prospect of a Soviet interventionary threat to the oil supplies originating around the Persian Gulf is extremely small. First, a Soviet move toward the oil fields would invite a Western military response as readily as would a Soviet conventional attack on Western Europe. Yet the only large-scale Soviet interventions since World War II have taken place in areas where the Soviet Union could be certain of meeting no military challenge from the West: within the Soviet sphere of influence in Eastern Europe and in Afghanistan, a country with no military, economic, or cultural ties to the West. Second, as the world's largest oil-producing country and as a net energy exporter to Western Europe, the Soviet Union itself has no need for Middle Eastern oil. Third, if its goal were to deny oil to the West, the Soviet Union could do so far more cheaply and easily by air or missile attacks on Persian Gulf oil fields than by a logistically unsupportable overland intervention in which it attempted to seize and hold contested territory in difficult terrain far from industrial supply centers in the U.S.S.R.

Thus the expansion of the U.S. Rapid Deployment Force (RDF), which is designed to allow the United States to intervene rapidly in the Gulf area with ground and air forces, must be seen primarily as a preparation for unilateral U.S. intervention in the event of a coup or civil war in one of the Gulf countries. These are referred to as relevant potential "instabilities" in official descriptions of the RDF. Nevertheless, the Soviet intervention in Afghanistan and the slight recent buildup of Soviet naval power-projection capability reflect what may be a long-term trend in the U.S.S.R. to expand its interventionary capabilities and tendencies, following the precedent set by the United States. Every decade since 1945, Soviet conventional armed forces have become perceptibly more capable of projecting military power at a distance, and somewhat less narrowly designed to defend Soviet and East European territory. Still, the day when the Soviet Union has a major interventionary capability, comparable to that of the United States, remains far in the future. Ending the conventional arms race remains a feasible way of preventing that development. It may well be the only way of doing so.

The Functions of Nuclear Forces

Most Americans believe that the purpose of U.S. nuclear weapons is to deter a Soviet nuclear attack on the United States by threatening retaliation in kind. This is indeed one of the functions of U.S. nuclear weapons, but it is by no means the only function, nor is it the function that drives the continuing nuclear arms race with the Soviet Union. From the point of view of the United States, the purpose of the nuclear arms race, to the extent that there is any rational purpose, is to deter Soviet uses of conventional force and, implicitly, to back up U.S. uses of conventional force, with the threat of escalation to nuclear war.

The likelihood that any major conventional war which involves both superpowers will escalate to the nuclear level is the ultimate deterrent to conventional war among the industrialized countries. Nuclear deterrence of conventional war is maintained not only by the thousands of U.S. and Soviet "strategic" nuclear weapons, but also by an ever greater number of U.S. and Soviet tactical nuclear weapons. These are short-, medium-, and intermediate-range nuclear weapons deployed on the battlefield, in the air, and at sea in Europe, the Middle East, and the Far East.

In fact, the nuclear forces relied upon to deter another conventional world war are so massive, and so threatening, that their use is in some respects not credible. It is difficult for policymakers to be confident that their own leaders would initiate countermilitary uses of nuclear weapons, thereby risking escalation to an all-out nuclear war, in the event of a conventional attack. As a result, NATO and Warsaw Pact conventional forces are often described as providing a more credible alternative to the use of nuclear arms. Thus, in a circular manner, the industrialized countries maintain nuclear weapons to ensure that they do not use their conventional forces, and they maintain conventional forces to ensure that they are not obliged to use their nuclear weapons. Each arsenal rationalizes the other indefinitely, in a risky manner of avoiding what is, after all, a profound danger.

The roles of nuclear and conventional military forces have been intertwined throughout the history of the nuclear arms race. In 1941 the United States began to develop nuclear weapons out of fear that Nazi Germany already was doing so. The United States wanted to be able to meet a potential nuclear threat with a nuclear response. But toward the end of the war, when it became clear that there was no nuclear threat to the Allies, the U.S. nuclear program did not stop: it pushed ahead under its own great momentum.

The first nuclear weapons were used not to deter a nuclear attack on the United States or any other country, but to serve two ends, both related to conventional warfare. First, the U.S. government argued that dropping nuclear bombs on Hiroshima and Nagasaki would end the war in the Pacific with fewer casualties, certainly with fewer American casualties, than would be suffered if the war were fought out by conventional means. In bloody, over-the-beach invasions it might have taken 500,000 American lives to recapture all of the Pacific islands from the Japanese, the government estimated, whereas the bombs dropped on Hiroshima and Nagasaki killed, immediately, close to 100,000 persons each. Their use set a precedent for postwar military thinking about the feasibility and usefulness of "limited" nuclear war in the context of conventional warfare.

The nuclear bomb dropped on Hiroshima should have been enough—if even that was needed—to make the Japanese sue for terms of total surrender, the only terms the United States was willing to accept. Thus, in the view of some historians, there was a second purpose behind the bombing of Nagasaki, and perhaps behind the use of both bombs: to inhibit the use of conventional force by the Soviet Union after the war had ended. According to this view, the bombings were intended to demonstrate that the United States not only had a monopoly on nuclear weaponry, but also was prepared to use it if the Soviet Union employed its conventional forces in a manner that the U.S. government found objectionable.

From 1945 to 1955, the United States retained a virtual monopoly on nuclear weapons. Its policy for the use of these weapons, called "massive retaliation," was to deter Soviet use of conventional force outside of Eastern Europe by threatening a massive—in other words, a more-than-commensurate—response aimed at wiping out the major cities of the U.S.S.R. In 1950 the United States had 300 propeller-driven planes carrying 300 nuclear bombs. Not very many by today's standards and not certain of penetrating Soviet air defenses, these bombs might well have been used against Soviet cities in the event of a conventional war in Europe. For although U.S. military leaders would prefer to win by destroying an opponent's military capability rather than by committing genocide, they might have calculated that the nuclear bombers able to get through Soviet air defenses would be too few to destroy the industrial capacity of the Soviet Union to rebuild a strong conventional force. Thus the initial goal of U.S. nuclear policy was not to protect U.S. cities by threatening retaliation against Soviet cities, but to deter conventional war by threatening Soviet cities as a target of last resort.

By 1960 the Soviet Union had its own stockpile of nuclear weapons and the means to deliver them to the United States. It then had 150 strategic bombers that could reach this country, along with 500 bombers that could strike Western Europe. In the interval, the United States had deployed over 2,000 strategic jet bombers aimed at the Soviet Union: 635 long-range B-52s and 1,400 B-47s stationed at overseas bases. The United States had also built a force of about 10,000 tactical nuclear weapons aimed primarily at military targets: nuclear anti-aircraft missiles, nuclear anti-submarine torpedoes, nuclear mines, nuclear free-fall bombs to be dropped from short-range tactical aircraft, and nuclear surface-to-surface missiles to be used on the battlefield against army and air force bases and oncoming tank formations. The last included Pershing I missiles with a range of 400 miles, which could travel from West Germany to East Germany or Poland, as well as missiles with ranges of 30 to 70 miles, and even howitzers with a range of 10 to 15 miles, for use on the battlefield in West Germany.

Even though the Soviet Union could threaten a nuclear attack on U.S. cities and, even more plausibly, on European cities, the United States continued to threaten to use nuclear weapons first in the event of a major conventional war. This threat was reinforced by the deployment of thousands of tactical nuclear weapons, which were designed to deter the Soviet Union from using its conventional forces in Europe and elsewhere by increasing the risk of U.S. nuclear escalation.

Until the mid-1960s the United States retained such a marked superiority in both strategic and tactical nuclear weapons that it could continue to threaten the first use of nuclear weapons on overseas battlefields with some credibility. The United States built its original strategic missile force much more quickly than did the Soviet Union. About 1,700 well-protected U.S. land- and subma-

rine-launched ballistic missiles (ICBMs and SLBMs) were deployed between 1960 and 1967. During that time, the Soviet Union still relied on its 150 slow bombers and on 200 vulnerable ICBMs. Because these Soviet systems could not be launched on short notice, they provided only a weak and vulnerable deterrent: both could have been largely or entirely destroyed, along with the Soviet nuclear forces aimed at Europe, by a preemptive U.S. attack.

The Soviet Union first began to acquire nuclear forces that gave it an invulnerable second-strike deterrent in 1966, when it started to deploy ICBMs in steel-reinforced concrete underground silos. About 1,400 such ICBMs were deployed between 1966 and 1971. The first Soviet submarine with long-range missiles, deployed in range of the United States, was sent to sea in 1967. Ten years later, the Soviet Union had 62 strategic submarines with 950 SLBMs.

By 1970 the existence of U.S.-Soviet nuclear parity began to be widely recognized. Parity meant not that the numbers of the two sides were the same, nor that the Soviet Union could match all of the esoteric nuclear capabilities of the United States, but that for the first time the Soviet Union could match the all-important second-strike capability of the United States. It possessed so many well-protected ICBMs that enough would be certain to survive any U.S. counterforce attack to give the Soviet Union the capability to obliterate the major cities of the United States in a second strike.

Between 1970 and 1977, while the Soviet Union was still building its main SLBM force, the United States withdrew most of its original ICBMs and SLBMs and replaced them with new missiles carrying multiple nuclear warheads or MIRVs (multiple independently targetable reentry vehicles). In 1976, in a program predicted well in advance and detected several years earlier in the initial testing stage, the Soviet Union started replacing its original ICBMs and SLBMs with new MIRVed missiles. Soviet deployment of MIRVed ICBMs was completed in 1982 and deployment of MIRVed SLBMs will probably be completed in 1985.

In response to the Soviet Union's acquisition of an invulnerable deterrent force, the United States has tried to recapture the clear nuclear superiority it held before the mid-1960s. This attempt has involved a number of military programs, the most important of which are mentioned here.

First, the several thousand very accurate warheads to be deployed on MX ICBMs and Trident II SLBMs will enable the United States, at least in theory, to destroy most Soviet ICBMs, underground hardened military command posts, nuclear storage areas, and major naval bases.

Second, several thousand new, low-flying cruise missiles—if they work as intended and are able to evade radar detection—will permit an unforewarned U.S. attack against Soviet industrial targets and air force and army bases.

Third, the 108 Pershing II missiles to be deployed in West Germany, each with a 12-minute flight time to Moscow and the western U.S.S.R., when combined with U.S. SLBMs launched on depressed trajectories from near the Soviet coast, will allow the United States to "decapitate" the Soviet leadership by destroying the main underground national command posts and by cutting off major satellite and ground-based warning, navigation, and communication systems.

Finally, U.S. advances in anti-submarine warfare (ASW) will give the United States some chance of destroying Soviet strategic submarines at sea. Large sonar arrays on the ocean floor off the coast of Norway, off the Azores, and off the Japanese islands already enable the United States to detect Soviet submarines leaving their ports. These arrays are attached by cable to a giant computer-processing center, which dampens out other ocean sounds, leaving only the noise of Soviet submarines. In good weather, the U.S. sonar arrays are reported to have tracked Soviet submarines across the Atlantic. Soviet strategic submarines emerge out of two narrowly enclosed port areas, one north of Norway, the other north of Japan. These submarines are relatively noisy, and their port exits are surrounded by U.S., Japanese, and British anti-sub submarines and aircraft. Because of superior U.S. ASW technology, large numbers of Western ASW submarines and aircraft, and Western geographic advantages, the United States is probably able to detect and deploy some fraction of the Soviet

strategic submarines at sea, whereas the U.S.S.R. has no comparable capability against the United States.

By 1990 the combined effect of these programs will be to put the United States back in a position similar to that of the 1950s and early 1960s, when it could threaten a preemptive strike against all or most Soviet medium-range and intercontinental nuclear forces. But there will be two fundamental differences. Twenty years ago, the number of nuclear targets was relatively small: there were no more than a couple of hundred airfields, missile groups, command centers, and naval ports. And 20 years ago the Soviet Union could not launch its missiles on warning of an incoming attack. These conditions have changed, and they have done so irreversibly. Soviet generals now can launch their missiles, just as the United States can, when their radar screens show that the opponent's missiles have been launched: in the case of ICBMs, about 25 minutes before the enemy missiles arrive. Of course, this warning time can be reduced to 10 to 15 minutes by Pershing II and depressed-trajectory SLBM attacks against the warning and communication systems themselves. But if this threat of very rapid "decapitation" continues to evolve, the Soviet Union will probably respond by ordering the automatic launch of its missiles in the event that nationwide communications are cut off.

Moreover, current U.S. counterforce scenarios call for the use of several thousand nuclear warheads against large Soviet missile forces; and a similar number of warheads could be launched on warning or automatically against the United States. These might conceivably be aimed at U.S. strategic bombers and ICBMs in order to destroy any large residual U.S. nuclear capability. But because the United States would still retain a large invulnerable sea-based nuclear force and because most U.S. land-based weapons would already have been launched, the Soviets might conclude that this was their last chance to launch a substantial attack on U.S. cities. Thus they might order an all-out attack to obliterate the U.S. urban population. Finally, even if the Soviet response were confined to military targets and even if the exchange did not then escalate to all-out countercity attacks on both sides, the ultimate ecological effects would be unpredictable and might be equally lethal.

For these reasons, large-scale counterforce uses of nuclear weapons do not represent a rational military option. Yet the United States officially retains the option to use nuclear weapons first in a conventional conflict; it continues to deploy tactical nuclear weapons on the territory of those it is ostensibly protecting; and it is proceeding to produce and deploy a new generation of nuclear weapons that will strengthen existing U.S. strategic and tactical capabilities for massive attacks against Soviet nuclear and conventional forces.

The U.S. policy of maintaining and improving its capabilities to escalate from conventional war to nuclear war is not intended to deter an out-of-the-blue Soviet attack on American cities. If anything, the deployment of improved nuclear warfighting systems, suitable for trying to fight and win nuclear wars, actually increases the likelihood of such an attack. For by making nuclear escalation more plausible, improvements in U.S. capabilities for nuclear attacks against military targets *increase* the likelihood that the United States will actually use nuclear weapons to back up its conventional forces overseas or to respond to Soviet use of conventional force. And it is escalation from conventional war to nuclear war on overseas battlefields that represents the most likely origin of an eventual nuclear attack on U.S. cities.

The primary region in which nuclear weapons are intended to influence the use of conventional military forces is Europe. But a deliberately initiated conventional war in Europe, never likely in any case given the stability of the U.S. and Soviet spheres of influence, has become increasingly unlikely as economic development has given both sides too much wealth to be worth putting at risk. If the balance of economic and political incentives alone were not enough to prevent a deliberate large-scale attack or to ensure that a budding local conflict would be ended before it spread, then the existing capabilities for nuclear escalation would clearly be adequate to do so. In fact, in my judgment, the risk of escalation to nuclear war would be much too great for any *rational* decisionmaker deliberately to mount a conventional attack

or to permit a local conflict to expand, even if U.S. and Soviet nuclear arsenals were much smaller than they are today and even if they were much less suited to rapid battlefield escalation. And if decisionmakers are *irrational,* the deployment of improved nuclear warfighting systems is at least as likely to increase the risk of a deliberately initiated nuclear attack as to decrease the risk of a deliberately initiated conventional attack.

Where precise calculations of the relative capability of the two sides to threaten nuclear escalation may actually influence the use of conventional force is the Third World. It is there that the superpowers continue to engage in conventional warfare. It is true that in many parts of the Third World there is little or no prospect of a direct conventional confrontation between the United States and the Soviet Union: for example, in Latin America, where the U.S.S.R. has no significant conventional capability, or in Afghanistan, where the West has no significant interest. But elsewhere, particularly in the Middle East, the chance of a U.S.–Soviet conventional clash that could lead to nuclear war is all too high. If the Soviet Union sent conventional forces into Iran, for example, not to threaten the flow of oil to the West but to support one side in a civil war, and if this occurred (as is quite possible) while the United States was engaged in a civil war in a nearby Persian Gulf country, then the risk of a conventional confrontation between the superpowers would be extraordinarily high. This in turn would make thinkable the first use of tactical nuclear weapons against selected military targets in the area.

From the point of view of the United States, a theoretical advantage in capabilities for nuclear escalation gives it greater freedom to intervene in developing countries without risking a conventional challenge from the U.S.S.R., while simultaneously inhibiting comparable Soviet intervention. This does not mean that the new U.S. nuclear warfighting systems are necessarily intended to be used. In fact, U.S. military analysts calculate that if they can show on paper that a direct conventional confrontation between the superpowers might plausibly escalate to a local or an intercontinental nuclear exchange that probably would leave the

United States considerably ahead in residual nuclear weapons and surviving population, then the Soviet Union would not risk either challenging any U.S. intervention or intervening itself in any region where Western stakes are high. The dream of those who seek even greater U.S. nuclear superiority, those who want to recapture the golden era of the 1950s, is to acquire for the United States a theoretical advantage at each step of the ladder of escalation that is great enough to deter the Soviet Union from risking the use of its conventional forces anywhere, at least anywhere outside of Eastern Europe. This was the situation in 1950, when the United States crossed the Pacific to support the anti-communists in the war between North and South Korea, while the Soviet Union dared not employ its conventional forces to support the communists in a country on its own border.

The Soviet Union, for its part, attempts to match each successive new wave of U.S. nuclear developments in order to deprive the United States of any theoretical superiority in the ability to threaten nuclear escalation. From the Soviet point of view, maintaining overall nuclear parity is adequate, for this permits the U.S.S.R. to intervene abroad with the same freedom (and with the same caution) as does the United States.

this is all history

The Failure of Arms Control

Several times during this century, particularly before World War I and in the wake of both world wars, large peace movements have formed in the West that favored disarmament as the route to a stable international peace. Each time, after a brief upsurge of popular support, these movements disintegrated into small groups with little political influence. The many individuals who had briefly advocated disarmament withdrew into pessimism or resigned indifference. In general, they concluded that the best they could hope for was a relatively stable armed peace, accompanied by modest arms control agreements.

This pattern has been particularly pronounced since World War II. Between 1945 and 1960, the United States, the Soviet Union, and other countries introduced at the United Nations proposals for a general and complete disarmament. These proposals may not have been made in good faith. At best, they reflected an amalgam of disparate views among informed elites about the extent to which disarmament was truly possible and desirable. As a result, the proposals of both East and West called for reduction phases and inspection requirements that the other found to be too risky. Thus the negotiations led nowhere.

By 1960, if not sooner, a consensus had developed among international elites that the goal of worldwide nuclear and conventional disarmament was neither realistic nor desirable. In the West, influential experts concluded that a better way to prevent another conventional world war was to maintain permanently large tactical nuclear and conventional military forces. To abolish tactical nuclear weapons and adopt a no-first-use policy, they believed, would decrease the likelihood of nuclear escalation and thereby weaken the nuclear component of deterrence of conventional war. Although a significant minority has recently come to believe that U.S. reliance on tactical nuclear weapons should be decreased or eliminated altogether, most in this group make these changes conditional on the strengthening of Western conventional forces. Thus, in their view, measures to widen the nuclear firebreak and to reduce the risk of nuclear escalation must come at the price of higher military spending.

Overall, military and arms control experts believe that East–West arms control talks should seek to *limit the size* of strategic nuclear, tactical nuclear, and conventional forces, but that they should by no means seek to *abolish* any of these forces altogether, for that would weaken their joint deterrent effect. Furthermore, they hold that the weaponry with which nuclear and conventional forces are equipped—which must in any case be replaced as aging equipment wears out in training and exercises—should regularly be "modernized," that is, it should be replaced with new weapons that incorporate the latest advances in military technology. In their view, therefore, arms control

agreements should not block or inhibit modernization because this, too, would weaken deterrence.

In general, the arms control efforts supported by influential elites—politicians, experts,
top bureaucrats, and journalists—have been limited to measures that might marginally affect the
longer range East–West nuclear weapons and the
conventional ground and tactical air forces in
Europe. Arms control talks have not addressed
short-range tactical nuclear weapons, naval forces,
or troops outside of Europe, nor have they attempted to regulate or end the superpowers'
competition for military power and influence in
developing countries. In the Third World, a region
of instability and social change, Western elites tend
to see the United States as being on the defensive.
In their view, the United States is trying to preserve
the Western hegemony that has existed in most developing nations since 1945, while the Soviet Union
is promoting revolution and change to increase the
number of nonaligned or pro-Soviet governments.
U.S. military intervention in the Third World, therefore, is perceived as a means to preserve stability
and avoid wider wars, whereas Soviet intervention—and only Soviet intervention—is viewed as
destabilizing and provocative.

Within this broad context, the U.S. arms
control community has defined three objectives
for nuclear arms control efforts, with the overarching goal of reducing the risk of nuclear war in a
world where nuclear weapons are taken as a given.
These objectives, widely used to devise and assess
arms control proposals, are as follows: to minimize
"crisis instability" by preventing the introduction
of systems suitable for counterforce attacks or
nuclear warfighting; to minimize "arms race instability" by preventing futile U.S.–Soviet competition
in areas that do not change the overall nuclear
balance, thus saving funds and sparing the two
sides unnecessary uncertainty and tensions; and to
keep military spending to a minimum.

Even when judged against these limited
objectives, U.S.–Soviet nuclear arms control negotiations, under way for more than 20 years, have
failed to reduce the risk of nuclear war. They have
failed for three reasons. First, government arms

control efforts have not in fact been aimed at
reducing crisis instability, arms race instability, and
military spending. Even within the U.S. arms
control community, there has been no real consensus on what the "arms race" is, or what it might
mean to stop it. For some, the arms race means
the continued production of any nuclear weapons;
according to this view, stopping the arms race
means stopping the production of nuclear weapons. But for a larger number of experts, the
periodic modernization of existing nuclear weapons constitutes a natural, steady-state process in
our technological age; thus for them there is no
"race" to be stopped. Similarly, there has been no
consensus on which weapons are stabilizing or
destabilizing. For some, all nuclear weapons above
a minimal deterrent (a minimal second-strike
intercontinental force) are destabilizing. For others, most of the extensive nuclear panoply and its
regular modernization are stabilizing, whereas
only a few types of counterforce weapon on the
opposing side are destabilizing.

Because of this lack of consensus, the official
arms control policies of the United States have
aimed to accomplish only certain lowest-common-
denominator objectives acceptable to the military
services and the National Security Council: setting
mutual U.S.–Soviet ceilings on the numbers of
large missiles and aircraft; avoiding the production
of non-functional weapon systems; ending health
hazards; and inhibiting nuclear weapon developments in other countries. Rather than strive to stop
the production of nuclear weapons and to reduce
the likelihood of escalation from conventional war
to nuclear war, U.S. arms control policies have
merely legitimized the bilateral management of a
permanent technological competition directed at
ever-improving capabilities for escalation and nuclear warfighting.

Second, U.S. arms control efforts have failed
even to identify, much less change, the most powerful motivation for maintaining very large nuclear
arsenals, including large numbers of tactical nuclear weapons, and for continually improving the
nuclear warfighting or escalatory capabilities of
these arsenals. This motivation is the desire of

both sides to influence the potential interventionary uses of conventional forces by posing a high risk of escalation to nuclear war in the event of any direct superpower conventional confrontation. Instead of addressing the interventionary functions of U.S. and Soviet forces, the arms control debate has focused narrowly on strategic arms and conventional forces in Europe, and it has done so on the basis of the simplistic and clearly outdated assumption that nuclear forces are intended only to deter a deliberately initiated, out-of-the-blue, all-out conventional attack in Europe or strategic nuclear attack. Given the modest nuclear requirements for accomplishing these relatively easy tasks, there appears to be no reason to produce new nuclear warfighting systems. When military functions are defined so narrowly and simply, opponents and advocates of the production of new nuclear weapons talk entirely past one another. The pressure to produce new nuclear warfighting systems begins to become understandable—as do the arms control community's genuine disagreements over the necessary, feasible, and appropriate roles of nuclear weapons in the international arena—only when one takes into account the extensive, diversified nuclear requirements for accomplishing the far more delicate tasks of deterring intervention by the opposing superpower, of deterring the opposing superpower from posing a conventional challenge to one's own interventions, and of attempting to influence lesser conflicts that conceivably could develop into wider wars.

So long as no attempt is made to limit or end superpower intervention in the Third World, the possibility that a direct superpower confrontation could escalate to nuclear war will remain the only constraint on such intervention. Under these circumstances, great political and psychological pressures to retain large nuclear arsenals, including large tactical nuclear forces, and to keep improving the escalatory potential of these forces will remain intact. These pressures—largely unarticulated or only vaguely expressed— will continue to block and undermine clever arms control schemes and popular arms control proposals for a no-first-use policy, for the abolition of tactical nuclear weapons, for deep cuts in strategic nuclear weapons, and for

an end to the development and production of new strategic and tactical nuclear systems with improved counterforce and nuclear warfighting capabilities.

The third reason that arms control efforts have failed is that they have not commanded sustained popular support. The public has not been informed of the basic elements of existing nuclear and conventional policies, nor have the minimalist objectives of official arms control policies inspired the public to become more informed or involved. Gradually, the public has realized that the government aims not to end the arms race, but to manage it jointly with the Soviet Union: to develop new forces not very different from what would be developed in the absence of arms control, and to keep talking while doing so. Thus it has become increasingly clear that arms control efforts rely on the *process* of negotiation, rather than on its *result,* as the only way to reduce the risk of nuclear war. But talks that do not save funds, that do not end the production of nuclear weapons, and that do not substantially reduce existing nuclear arsenals represent too small an achievement to inspire public involvement.

Unless the long-term objectives of arms control efforts are substantially expanded and strengthened, arms control negotiations will continue to achieve exactly what they now seek: the bilateral management of a permanent technological arms race, with large standing nuclear and conventional forces, large military budgets, and periodic large-scale military interventions. The nuclear freeze movement has challenged the minimalist goals of past arms control efforts and created popular support for more ambitious efforts. But the popular freeze movement has had little impact on the goals of arms control as defined by the decisionmaking elite—politicians, top political aides and bureaucrats, military planners, and arms control experts. As a result, the prospects for progress in this area over the next decade are not bright.

The only major alternative to arms control, defined in a narrow sense, and the only approach that would substantially reduce or eliminate the risk of nuclear war is disarmament. Most people envision disarmament as an inherently unilateral or abrupt, short-term proposition. Thus is does not appear to be a realistic, safe, feasible alternative to arms control. But disarmament can be feasible if it is designed to take place over a period of decades; it can be safe if it is international, not unilateral, and if it eliminates the more aggressive and escalatory uses of armed forces first, leaving the more defensive elements for later stages; and it can be realistic if it takes into account the interrelationship between nuclear weapons and conventional warfare.

Moreover, historical trends have gradually reduced the obstacles to disarmament by reinforcing voluntary constraints on warfare. For while the scale and the horrors of warfare have increased, so have the limits on the utility of armed force as a tool of power. Over the past millennium, warfare among small groups—tribes, fiefdoms, dukedoms, and principalities—has gradually been replaced by the consolidation of larger and larger regions, the nation-states, within which the use of force by groups or individuals is completely prohibited except as needed for self-defense. Indeed, a defining characteristic of the modern nation-state is its internal monopoly on the use of force.

In this century, the use of armed force by nation against nation has itself begun to be restricted. From the 16th to the 19th centuries, nations expanded their territory by the use of force; conquest and empire were considered worthy goals, and their pursuit by military officers was an honorable profession. But in the 20th century, the surface of the globe has finally been entirely carved up into sovereign states. Since World War II, colonialism and imperialism in their raw form have ended, along with large-scale aggression, aimed at seizing and incorporating foreign territory into an existing nation or empire. Outright aggression has been replaced by the lesser impositions of intervention and hegemonic control, in which troops enter with limited goals and then depart, leaving national sovereignty largely intact. Nuclear weapons have further restricted the practical arena of warfare, making conventional war virtually unthinkable as a deliberate act of policy by any of the great powers against one another.

More recently, the growing economic and ecological interdependence among nations and the growing commitment of the populations of developing nations to self-determination have imposed further limits on the utility of armed force as a tool of policy.

In light of these historical trends, it can be argued that warfare is no more inevitable among nations than it is within them. Thus the question of the feasibility of a stable disarmed peace can be stated as follows: If we can replace warfare and violence by the rule of law *within* a disparate national agglomeration like the United States, why can't we do the same thing *among* nation-states, across boundaries of race, language, and culture?

The most obvious answer is that we *could* end warfare if we established a global counterpart of the nation-state: a federated, supranational legal authority that has a monopoly on the use of force and that uses force solely to keep the peace. Yet the League of Nations, founded in such hope in the wake of World War I, and the United Nations, similarly founded after World War II, both failed to achieve this end. The failure of world federalist efforts to create an effective world government, like the failure of pacifism and of plans for rapid disarmament to make armed forces impracticable or unnecessary, rests, I believe, not in a faulty conceptual analysis of the nature of war, but in a failure to appreciate the depth of the remaining cultural acceptance of war. To put it simply, there remain many things for which people are willing to die and kill for in war.

Thus, as world governments, the League of Nations and the United Nations were premature. The people of the world simply are not ready to turn national sovereignty over to an international decisionmaking body that might abuse its monopoly on force. The fear that others might misuse armed forces intended solely for peacekeeping is rooted in the often unarticulated knowledge that most populations still can be manipulated into going to war.

Both the federalist approach and the pacifist approach call for change that is at once too limited and too rapid. They propose to compress decades, perhaps generations, of social change into a single abrupt transformation. We need *both* institutional change, as the federalists propose, *and* attitudinal change, as the pacifists argue, and we need to allow such changes to take place in a gradual, interactive manner. Neither taken alone or attempted too abruptly can possibly succeed.

What is required for disarmament to succeed is a gradual process that allows, leads, and encourages people to internalize inhibitions against the use of force and to become convinced that others have done so. We cannot possibly abolish, or even substantially reduce, conventional military forces while they are still being used for intervention and occupation, for revolution and repression. And we cannot hope to end the system of nuclear deterrence while large nations continue to use conventional armed forces to advance their own ends. We must therefore change not merely the institutions of warfare by limiting and reducing armaments, but also the deeply rooted attitudes that condone the use of force. And we must allow time and provide ways for both sorts of change to occur.

Confining the Military to Defense

To achieve a stable disarmed peace, we must eliminate the requirements for armed forces by ending the popular acceptance of certain functions of military force and by transforming other functions so that they can be fulfilled by nonmilitary institutions. The only way to do this is to constrain the functions of armed forces gradually, eliminating the need for some first while allowing others to persist longer.

As already discussed, the main functions of armed forces today are deterrence, defense, aggression, intervention, armed repression, and armed revolution. Of these, the function most compatible with achieving and maintaining a stable peace is *defense*. If all countries maintained military forces solely for the purpose of defending their national territory, only conventional, short-range forces that provide air, coastal, and border defense would be needed. Aggression, intervention, and armed repression would then cease. Without armed repression, there would be no

need for armed revolution. And without aggression, intervention, repression, and revolution, war would never be initiated.

Furthermore, if military forces worldwide were maintained strictly for national defense, and thus were never used, people would over time begin to believe that atavistic, war-making tendencies would not resurface. Fear of war would slowly be replaced by confidence in the peaceful intentions of other nations. Gradually, the perceived need for armed deterrence to prevent war would diminish. Eventually, when trust and confidence were sufficiently great, nations might be willing to abolish even their small, national defense forces and to rely entirely on international peacekeeping forces to keep watch for any nascent remilitarization and nip it in the bud. Thus, national defense, defined in the narrowest and strictest sense, is entirely compatible with those changes in attitudes that are required to permit movement toward a stable disarmed world.

The remaining functions of armed forces, in contrast, are not compatible with such progress. *Deterrence,* for example, requires that large, long-range military forces capable of inflicting terrible damage on the homeland of potential opponents be maintained indefinitely. Because deterrence works by inspiring fear, it precludes the development of the trust and confidence needed for disarmament. And because it requires large military forces to be maintained permanently, deterrence impedes the further evolution of cultural values that reject the use of force as a tool of policy. In its current form, deterrence relies not only on large conventional forces, but also on nuclear forces which are, because of their enormous destructive capability, inherently offensive. Even if maintained exclusively for the purpose of deterring nuclear attacks on cities, a posture known as minimal deterrence, these weapons still would require public contemplation of inhuman acts of genocide carried out for revenge. Such ideas perpetuate primitive caricatures of potential opponents as one-dimensional enemies, not ordinary human beings. This perception insidiously undermines the respect for the dignity and worth of every human being which must lie at the heart of a democratic civilization. Moreover, contemporary nuclear deterrence requires the maintenance of two offsetting, militarily balanced power blocs, each a hegemonically organized sphere of influence within which allies cannot maintain full national sovereignty and independence. Thus, even though it may provide a *relatively* stable peace— as stable as any can be that is based on fear, tension, uncertainty, and animosity—deterrence cannot be reconciled with movement toward a *truly* stable disarmed peace.

The functions of aggression, intervention, armed repression, and armed revolution are even less compatible with a stable peace than is deterrence. They are, in fact, directly antithetical to its development. For the most part, deterrence is aimed at avoiding warfare, whereas these other functions involve the actual use of force. As long as they are considered legitimate and permissible by a significant fraction of the world's population and decision-making elites, a stable disarmed peace will not be possible.

Most antithetical to peace are aggression and repression. Outright *aggression*—the use of armed force to demolish defenses, seize territory, establish political control, and ultimately absorb a disputed territory into the aggressor's nation—has become impracticable on any significant scale since the end of World War II. This is in part because of the invention of nuclear weapons and in part because of the evolution of international law and more. Nevertheless, fear of aggression remains high. Although this fear is rarely articulated in a general form, most people subconsciously judge, I believe, that if nuclear weapons were suddenly abolished, aggression of the type that occurred before and during World War II might once again become common. Thus fear of large-scale conventional military aggression remains the most powerful argument for preserving nuclear deterrence and the greatest obstacle to doing away with it.

The most compelling evidence that aggressive tendencies are only barely restrained is that the little brother of aggression, *intervention,* remains widespread. For the superpowers, the use of conventional forces to establish or protect governments that support their interests in smaller,

weaker countries appears to be shaped and constrained by only two factors: whether they deem their own goals sufficiently important, politically and economically, and whether they believe they can intervene without risking a direct conventional confrontation with the opposing superpower. These criteria for deciding whether to use armed force in an interventionary manner reflect little ethical, social, or political progress over those used before 1945 in deciding whether to commit outright aggression.

Armed repression and *armed revolution* to overthrow such repression remain common in many parts of the world. Both are incompatible with a stable peace but, in the absence of evidence to the contrary, the greater burden for violating the peace must be borne by the repressive government, not by the rebelling population. For even though committed by one part of a nation's citizenry against another, armed repression on a sizable scale—the use of armed forces to jail, torture, or kill political prisoners, to enforce press censorship and the banning of political parties, and to deny other civil liberties and human rights— represents the same kind of oppression as that exercised by one nation committing aggression against another nation. Thus when repressive conditions are bad enough and have been sustained for long enough, armed revolution should be considered morally justified and politically legitimate in the same sense that armed defense against aggression is justified and legitimate.

The terrible risk of armed revolution, of course, is that it may replace one repressive government with another. In theory, the less violent the revolution, the more likely the new government is to be more democratic than the old. In practice, however, the consequences have been mixed. In America, armed revolution led to a far more democratic government. In France, it led to a series of governments that were more populist than the earlier monarchies, but not much more democratic. In Russia, armed revolution resulted in an intensely repressive state under Stalin, but one that has gradually developed more civil liberties than were permitted under the czars. More recently, revolutions in Portugal and in Spain after the death of Franco have yielded democratic governments with little or no use of force. But the essentially unarmed revolution in Iran has produced a repressive religious state. The single-party communist governments established through bloody revolutions in China, Cuba, Vietnam, and Yugoslavia suppress most civil liberties, but this repression is partly offset by their efforts to achieve a more even distribution of wealth and a more well-rounded program of economic development than were sought by the former oligarchic, capitalistic governments.

Whether in the short run unarmed revolution or gradual reform represents a feasible path to majority self-determination in countries like South Africa and Namibia is an open question. What cannot be questioned, however, is that in the long run the existence of repressive governments that use armed force to inhibit civil liberties poses as great an obstacle to stable world peace as does the system of nuclear deterrence.

In sum, we can achieve a stable disarmed peace if, and only if, we gradually eliminate the non-defensive functions of armed forces. Specifically, this means accomplishing three major changes. First, the industrialized nations must end unilateral conventional *intervention* in smaller countries—whether to back governments friendly to capitalism, to support socialist revolutions, or simply to advance their own geopolitical or economic interests. The interventionary function of armed force must be replaced by a more democratic international system in which the extraordinary size and wealth of some nations no longer give them the right or the duty to act as global policemen or to exercise militarily enforced hegemony. Second, relatively democratic governments, with well-proven, resilient institutions of civil liberties, must be developed in all parts of the world, thereby eliminating the "need" for *armed repression* and *armed revolution*. Third, *armed deterrence,* particularly nuclear deterrence, as a means of preventing aggression and keeping the peace, must be replaced by powerful, internalized inhibitions against the use of force and by effective international institutions for peaceful conflict resolution.

A Step-by-Step Approach

The non-defensive functions of armed force cannot be eliminated overnight. Instead, they must be eliminated through a series of clearly demarcated steps, each of which will create a plateau of military, political, and technological stability that can last, if need be, for decades. Each step must be durable and desirable in its own right, regardless of when or even whether any of the subsequent steps are taken. For before it can be demonstrated that any subsequent step will unquestionably increase stability and security, there must be a greater internalization of inhibitions against the use of force. Public debate that identifies and gradually overcomes opposition to the proposed next step is the primary means by which constraints on the accepted uses of armed forces can be internalized. And such debate may not reach a successful conclusion for years or even decades. Because people despair of ever achieving the ultimate goal of a disarmed peace, it would be extremely difficult to motivate widespread popular efforts for change without a set of powerfully attractive intermediate goals, each desirable in its own right. Thus a series of partial steps toward disarmament is needed to keep popular pressure for change high enough to prevail over the enormous psychological, economic, and political pressures to maintain the status quo.

In order both to strengthen inhibitions against the use of force and to win the support of the majority of the public, these gradual steps toward disarmament must eliminate the more provocative, aggressive, and escalatory functions of armed forces first, while leaving the more defensive and stabilizing elements intact. The history of the development of law and of attitudes toward violence in the domestic arena suggests that defense-oriented constraints on the use of force, far from being overly idealistic or excessively ambitious, are fully compatible with human nature. Moreover, the need for self-defense is the most fundamental human motivation for retaining military forces. Thus it should be easier, as well as ethically preferable, to abolish the less defensive functions of military forces first, the more defensive functions later. Because this process would parallel the historical development of legal and ethical constraints on the use of force within nations, domestic experience would provide a useful model for evaluating the potential uses of force in complex international conflicts. In the domestic arena, both internalized ethical standards and legal codes and procedures for the nonviolent resolution of complex conflicts are highly developed and widely recognized. Thus in international conflicts, in which the parties naturally tend to see their own cause as just and that of their opponents as unjust, the degree to which a proposed use of force is truly defensive in nature can be judged objectively by the participants themselves, as well as by neutral arbiters, if we rely on analogies from domestic affairs.

Each of the steps outlined below is desirable in its own right. Each is designed to create a plateau of stability which can be maintained for an extended period of time. And each is aimed at eliminating the least defensive, most aggressive, escalatory, and provocative aspects of the military forces and policies that remain in existence at each stage of the process. In addition, each step is designed to encourage simultaneous change in the institutions of military policy and armed forces and in the attitudes that underlie the acceptable uses of force. These steps are not the only ones that would fulfill these requirements for achieving disarmament, but they do represent one plausible route.

The initial steps involve mainly the armed forces of the large powers: the United States, the Soviet Union, Britain, France, West Germany, China, and Japan. These few great powers account for nearly 70 percent of world military spending; more than 90 percent of the development and production of conventional weapons; and nearly 100 percent of the world's nuclear arsenals and nuclear-weapon production capacity. Thus the arms race can be reversed by stabilizing and then reducing the armed forces of these nations alone. This is fortunate for, difficult as it may be to limit the warmaking tendencies of a few big powers, that is a far easier task than resolving the many passionate and thorny Third World conflicts that motivate the maintenance of more than 100 smaller armies, many of them engaged in open war.

Step 1. Stop the production of U.S. and Soviet nuclear weapons and shut down their nuclear-weapon production facilities. This step constitutes a bilateral, U.S.–Soviet nuclear-weapons freeze. By preventing the further development of dangerous preparations for nuclear warfighting, a bilateral nuclear freeze would preclude refinements in the ability of the superpowers to escalate from conventional war to nuclear war. Such refinements are not needed to deter out-of-the-blue nuclear attacks on cities, nor are they needed to deter a major conventional war in Europe. They are instead most closely associated with the least defensive contemporary use of conventional force: superpower military intervention in the Third World. A freeze on the production of nuclear weapons is the best way to begin changing the military system, for it would block those new weapons that are at once politically least defensive in their ultimate purpose and technically most threatening to human survival.

Step 2. End large-scale military intervention—the maintenance of military bases and the use of troops, air forces, or naval forces—by the industrialized countries of the northern hemisphere in the developing countries of the southern hemisphere. Such intervention represents the least defensive, most aggressive use of conventional military force in the modern world. Furthermore, each superpower fears that the other will undertake some intervention that will, sooner or later, pose a significant military threat to its own interests. Thus a sweeping halt to large-scale direct military intervention by the industrialized nations outside their perimeter—that is, in Latin America, Africa, the Middle East, South Asia, or the Far East—would allow developing nations far greater independence, sovereignty, and self-determination and would, at the same time, eliminate those uses of conventional force by either of the superpowers that the other finds most threatening.

Taken together, a nuclear freeze and a nonintervention regime would stabilize and defuse the most provocative aspects of the East–West military confrontation. Neither step involves any actual disarmament. Both not only would work in obvious ways to decrease the risk of a major nuclear or conventional war, but would do so without any subtle, offsetting increased risk of war. They would benefit not only the countries directly involved, but all countries. Yet even though they call for relatively modest changes in the existing military system, the first two steps may be the most difficult to bring about. For to accept the desirability of these steps is to admit that it is unwise, unsafe, and unnecessary to try to "manage" the existing military system indefinitely, as current military and arms control policies aim to do. Accepting the first two steps means admitting that we must begin to alter the military system in fundamental ways, so that, eventually, it can be largely or entirely eliminated. Thus the seeds of support for all the subsequent steps are contained in the affirmation of the first two.

Step 3. Cut by 50 percent the nuclear and conventional forces of the NATO and Warsaw Pact nations, plus those of China and Japan. By creating surplus tanks, aircraft, and ships, which could replace existing units when they wear out in training and exercises, this step would make it possible simultaneously to mothball the conventional-weapon industries and thereby to stop the wasteful and destabilizing technological race in conventional arms and halt the international trade in major conventional weapon systems.

By closing down the conventional-weapon industries, by ending technological advances in conventional weapons, and by stopping the international arms trade, this step would complete the process of stabilizing the major armed forces of the world. In addition, the 50 percent reductions in nuclear and conventional forces would begin the process of building confidence that war can be deterred with much smaller standing armed forces than exist today.

It is unlikely that we can take further steps, such as cutting much more than 50 percent of the nuclear and conventional forces of the industrialized countries, without first considerably changing certain nonmilitary conditions. This is particularly clear in Eastern Europe, where at least half of Soviet ground forces serve to maintain Soviet

hegemony. Before the Soviet Union will be willing to eliminate most of the conventional forces now stationed in Eastern Europe, it will probably have to accept a wide range of civil liberties in that region. And for the Soviet government to permit wider civil liberties in Eastern Europe, it must probably allow them within its own borders as well. Furthermore, it probably will not be possible to persuade either superpower to eliminate more than half of its existing nuclear weapons as long as NATO and the Warsaw Pact retain conventional forces even half their current size. With 5 million men under arms on both sides, instead of the present 10 million, the risk of a major conventional war would still appear too great for the nuclear arsenals to be reduced to, say, a few hundred strategic deterrent weapons on each side.

In other parts of the world, different but equally profound political and economic changes will be necessary before further substantial reductions of conventional armaments will be possible.

Step 4. Strengthen the economic development of Third World nations, promote civil liberties in all countries, and improve international institutions for negotiation and peacekeeping. These changes should, of course, be sought throughout the process of disarmament. But progress in these nonmilitary areas will be particularly important and feasible following the third step, which will release $300 billion per year from military spending and create tremendous political optimism and energy.

Between the third step and the fifth—each a clearly demarcated change—it might well be possible to make some further reductions in the standing armed forces of both industrialized and developing nations. Unprecedented military stability would have been created by a nonintervention regime, a halt to the technological arms race in nuclear and conventional weaponry, the end of the international trade in major weapon systems, and the 50 percent reductions in NATO and Warsaw Pact nuclear and conventional forces. Accompanied by some progress in nonmilitary areas, this stability might, for example, make it possible to reduce NATO and Warsaw Pact ground troops to one quarter of their present size and to trim down their navies and tactical air forces. Moreover, tactical nuclear weapons might be largely or entirely eliminated and strategic nuclear arsenals might be reduced to a few thousand nuclear weapons on each side.

Nonetheless, at this stage, the primary elements of the international system of armed deterrence would remain: the military alliances and mutual defense commitments; the superpower bases on foreign soil; and their long-range navies, tactical air forces, and strategic nuclear weapons. Even though these nuclear and conventional force structures would be far smaller than they are today, they would continue to help deter the outbreak of a conventional world war centered on Europe. They would continue to ensure, for example, that an internal disturbance in Eastern Europe would not lead to an all-out East-West war. They would continue to prevent the rearmament of a reunified Germany or the revolt of a chafing Eastern Europe. Only when the Soviet Union is willing to tolerate political independence and diversity in Eastern Europe, when Europeans are sufficiently secure in their demilitarization not to fear the rearmament of a reunified Germany, and when the United States is sufficiently sure that neither Europe nor the Soviet Union will rearm will it be possible to move on to the next step.

Step 5. Abolish all military alliances and foreign military bases and restructure conventional military forces to limit them to short-range border defense, air defense, and coastal defense. When the function of conventional military forces has been limited for some time to national defense, narrowly defined, so that major conventional war, both civil and international, has begun to be unthinkable, the next step can be taken.

Step 6. Abolish nuclear weapons. After all nations have had time to become sufficiently confident that armed force will not be used for any purpose other than national self-defense, and thus are sufficiently confident that force will never be used, it should be possible to take the final step.

Step 7. Eliminate national armed forces altogether and replace them with international peacekeeping forces.

Whatever the merits of this particular path to disarmament, each of the steps listed above must be a central part of the process. Of course, for logical and practical reasons, certain steps must precede others. It is obvious, for example, that the production of nuclear weapons must be stopped before nuclear weapons can be abolished. Similarly, it is likely that superpower intervention in the Third World must be ended before U.S. and Soviet bases in Europe, which each considers far more vital to its security, can be eliminated. It is also clear that truly defensive military forces cannot be created until late in the process of arms reduction; but that once military forces *are* truly defensive, it should be easy to demonstrate the stability of the system and to erase the fear of war. Only then will it be possible to think of complete global disarmament.

The proposals for a nuclear freeze and for noninterventionary conventional policies demonstrate that the most immediate obstacles to reductions in nuclear and conventional forces are not the relatively easy psychological and political obstacles associated with reducing purely defensive armed forces. The obstacles to eliminating forces still used for intervention, repression, revolution, and deterrence are far more difficult to overcome. Only when these non-defensive uses of force have been substantially or entirely eliminated will it be possible to reduce either nuclear or conventional forces substantially.

This proposed series of major, clearly demarcated steps constitutes not merely a safe, feasible route to disarmament, but also a checklist which those committed to peace can use to plan and evaluate coordinated campaigns. Each step provides a focus for action, a target for effort, and a standard to measure achievement along the way.

The defense-oriented approach to disarmament resembles that of pacifists and differs from that of arms controllers in that it is aimed, ultimately, at eliminating the military system. It differs from the pacifist approach, however, in that it concentrates on institutional change and condones the maintenance of defensive armed forces until a stable peace has been achieved. It shares with arms controllers the view that progress toward disarmament cannot be made in a single step, quickly, or unilaterally. It assumes that progress will require a series of steps taken over a period of decades through cooperative international action.

If a safe route to a stable disarmed peace is necessary and possible, as this article argues, then it is important to resume debate on disarmament, a topic neglected for 20 years. The ultimate goal of disarmament should be a stable peace established within the context of a resilient system of civil liberties and well-rounded, ecologically sensitive economic development. However difficult to achieve, this goal is of immeasurable value. By reversing the dangerous developments of the last four decades, it would ensure our survival—a minimal demand to make of our societies. But beyond ensuring mere survival, it would permit us to end the ancient, pernicious institution of warfare.

Civilian-Based Defence

Gene Sharp

A Policy to Deter and Defend

Civilian-based defence is an alternative defence policy which builds upon this improvised past experience, adding to it deliberate refinement through research, policy studies, feasibility studies, contingency planning, preparations, and training. This policy is designed to deter and defeat not only foreign military invasions and occupations but also internal take-overs. This policy may be applied (1) as a supplement to military means, (2) in place of them in special circumstances only (as against a coup d'état or when the military forces have been defeated), or (3) as a permanent and complete substitute defence policy.

Deterrence and defence are to be accomplished by civilian forms of struggle—social, economic, political, and psychological. Many kinds of political noncooperation, strikes, economic boycotts, symbolic protests, civil disobedience, social boycotts, and more extreme methods of disruption and intervention are among the weapons of this policy. These are used to wage widespread noncooperation and to offer massive public defiance. The aims are to deny the attackers their objectives and to make their society politically indigestible and ungovernable by attackers. Consolidation of foreign rule, a puppet government, or a government of usurpers becomes impossible. In addition, the civilian defenders aim to subvert the loyalty of the aggressors' troops and functionaries, to make them unreliable in carrying out orders and repression, and even to induce them to mutiny.

Deterrence against invasions and internal usurpations is achieved by a strong capacity to defend. Potential attackers are deterred when they see that their objectives will be denied them, political consolidation prevented, and that as a

From Gene Sharp, *Making Europe Unconquerable: The Potential of Civilian-Based Deterrence and Defence* (Philadelphia: Taylor and Francis, 1985). Reprinted by permission of Gene Sharp, The Albert Einstein Institution, Cambridge, MA 02138.

consequence of these struggles unacceptable costs will be imposed on them politically, economically, and internationally.

The term "civilian-based defence" thus indicates defence by civilians using civilian means of struggle. This policy has also been called "civilian defence," "social defence," "nonmilitary defence," "nonviolent defence," "popular nonviolent defence," and "defence by civil resistance."

Civilian-based defence measures are applied by the general population, particular groups, and the society's institutions. The groups and institutions most involved will be those most affected by the attackers' objectives—economic, ideological, political, or other—and therefore best situated to resist them.

In this type of conflict the defenders deliberately seek to fight by using a technique of struggle with which military aggressors cannot easily deal. This is an asymmetrical conflict situation, one in which the two sides are fighting by contrasting means of combat. Since it is foolish to choose to fight with your enemy's best weapons, to have a chance at success the defenders must stick to their own chosen nonviolent weapons system. . . .

■ ■ ■

Viable deterrence and defence by this civilian-based policy are possible because violence is not the source of power in politics. The source is, instead, the cooperation of people and human institutions—which can be refused. Auguste Comte argued in the early nineteenth century that the then popular theory that attributed to rulers a permanent, unchanging degree of power was not correct. On the contrary, he insisted, the power of a ruler is variable and depends on the degree to which the society grants him that power.[1]* Baron de Montesquieu observed that "those who govern have a power which, in some measure, has need of fresh vigor every day. . . ."[2] Even sanctions— punishments—as a source of power depend on the society. Not only does the capacity to impose sanc-

tions rest on cooperation; the effectiveness of threatened or applied sanctions depends on the response of the subjects against whom they are directed.

Civilian-based defence, and nonviolent struggle generally, can wield great power, even against ruthless rulers and military regimes, because they attack the most vulnerable characteristic of all hierarchical institutions and governments: dependence on the submission and cooperation of the governed.

The rulers of governments and political systems are not omnipotent, nor do they possess self-generating power. All rulers depend for the sources of their power—authority, economic resources, skills and knowledge, intangible factors (such as attitudes to obedience), administration, and even sanctions—upon the cooperation of the population and the institutions of the society they would rule. The availability of those sources depends on the cooperation and obedience of many groups and institutions, special personnel, and the general population. The restriction or withdrawal of cooperation and obedience will directly and indirectly reduce or sever the availability of those sources of power.

If noncooperation and disobedience against an unwanted ruler can be applied and maintained— usually in face of repression intended to force resumption of cooperation and obedience— then the capacity of that regime to rule and to maintain its position is threatened. If, despite that repression, the sources of power can be restricted, withheld, or severed for sufficient time, the result may be the political paralysis of the regime. In severe cases the ruler's power will progressively die—slowly or rapidly—from political starvation.[3] This is what occurred in Imperial Russia in February 1917, El Salvador and Guatemala in 1944, and Iran in 1979.

This insight into the nature and vulnerability of political power and the widespread experience in nonviolent struggle listed in Table 1 establish

*[Footnotes have been renumbered because this reading has been excerpted from a larger body of work—EDS.]

TABLE 1   Improvised cases of civilian struggle[4]

Cases of nonviolent insurrections and revolutions against domestic dictatorial rule

Russian Revolution of 1905

Persian Revolution of 1905–1906

Russian Revolution of February 1917

Economic shut-down and political noncooperation in El Salvador against the Hernández Martínez regime, 1944

Economic shut-down and political noncooperation in Guatemala against the Ubico regime, 1944

East German uprising, June, 1953

General strike and economic shut-down against Haitian strongman General Magliore, 1956

Hungarian Revolution, 1956–1957

South Vietnamese Buddhist undermining of the Ngo Dinh Diem regime, 1963

Sudanese civilian insurrection against General Abboud's regime, 1964

Thai civilian uprising of October 1973

Iranian revolution against the Shah, 1978–1979

Polish democratization movement by Solidarity, 1980–?

Cases of national resistance to established foreign domination

Major aspects of the Netherlands' resistance to Spanish rule, 1565–1576

American colonial noncooperation campaigns against British laws, taxes, and rule, 1765–1775

Hungarian nonviolent resistance to Austrian rule, 1850–1867

Finnish resistance to Russian rule, 1898–1905

Egyptian nonviolent protests and noncooperation to British rule, 1919–1922

Korean national protest against Japanese rule, 1919–1922

Western Samoan resistance to New Zealand rule, 1919–1936

Indian independence struggles, especially the campaigns of 1930–1931, 1932–1934, 1940–1941, and 1942

Cases of noncooperation against coups d'état and other internal usurpations

German general strike and political noncooperation against the Kapp "Putsch," 1920

General strike in Haiti against temporary President Pierre-Louis, 1957

French popular resistance, government calls for defiance, and soldiers' noncooperation against the Algiers generals' "Putsch," 1961

Noncooperation to defeat a military coup d'état in Bolivia, 1978

Polish noncooperation against the regime of General Jaruzelski, 1981–?

Cases of resistance against recent foreign invasions, occupations, and puppet governments

German government-sponsored nonviolent resistance in the Ruhr against the French and Belgian occupation, 1923

Major aspects of the Dutch resistance, including several important strikes, against the German occupation, 1940–1945

Major aspects of the Danish resistance, including the 1944 Copenhagen general strike, against the German occupation, 1940–1945

Major aspects of the Norwegian resistance to the Quisling regime and German occupation, 1940–1945

Noncooperation and defiance to save Jews in Nazi-occupied countries, 1940–1945, especially in Bulgaria, Denmark, Norway, the Netherlands, Belgium, France, and Italy

Czechoslovak resistance to the Soviet and Warsaw Pact invasion and occupation, 1968–1969 that we are dealing with a type of struggle which is not restricted by cultural or national boundaries.[5] Civilian-based defence is, therefore, potentially relevant to problems of international aggression and internal usurpation in all parts of the world.

The many improvised cases of nonviolent struggle against oppression and aggression can be viewed as applications of this fundamental insight into the nature of power. Unfortunately, sophisticated rulers and aggressors have often been more aware of their dependence on the people and society than their subjects and victims of aggression have been. People have often thought they were helpless before threatening and brutal rulers whose power was in reality vulnerable and fragile.

Resources for Developing Civilian-Based Defence

Civilian-based defence becomes possible when people come to understand the power which they and their institutions can wield against potential aggressors, and prepare themselves to apply that power effectively. Civilian-based defence is not simply improvised or spontaneous resistance, as almost all past cases of nonviolent struggle have been. Instead, this policy is to be waged on the basis of advance preparations, planning, and training. Prior research and policy studies will help in planning the defence. This will increase its effectiveness in paralysing the attackers' policies and in defeating their repression, especially against ruthless regimes. Strategies of civilian-based defence are more likely to be successful if they are based on an understanding both of the requirements for effective nonviolent struggle and also of the ways to aggravate the weaknesses of the attackers' system. This includes its political, social, and economic aspects as well as its occupation administration or system of governance.

In short, civilian-based defence aims to deter and defeat attacks by making a society ungovernable by would-be oppressors and by maintaining a capacity for orderly self-rule even in face of extreme threats and actual aggression. To the degree

that people find this policy to be effective for defence, and thereby for deterrence, it becomes possible for societies to reduce reliance on, and eventually to phase out, military means. Proponents of this policy call for thorough investigation and rigorous examination of its potential.

While civilian-based defence is nonviolent, it is not pacifism. This policy can be applied effectively by persons who have supported or used violence in the past and might again in the future under other circumstances. This defence policy simply requires that they adhere to nonviolent means of struggle as part of a grand strategy for the course of the given conflict. Some pacifists would back civilian-based defence, while others would not. Overwhelmingly, the major nonviolent struggle campaigns of the past have been waged by masses of people who were never pacifists. Whole societies could therefore shift from military to civilian means of defence without deep changes in millions of individuals. Such a transition might well be made with fewer difficulties and in less time than most people have thought.

At first glance, civilian-based defence may appear to some people to be an unreasonable proposal. It may be thought that national security would be jeopardized by giving up a military-based defence system for an alternative security system that is untried and untested. This view, however, overlooks the fact that many military weapons are themselves unprecedented and untested in combat. On the other hand, nonviolent struggle—the basis of civilian-based defence—has a long history. Its consequences, therefore, may not only be less destructive than those of the new military weapons systems, but may also be much more calculable.

For many decades, military preparations have been characterized not only by refinement of older types of weaponry but also by development of new ones, even whole new types which never previously existed. In recent decades vast economic and intellectual resources have been devoted to developing and procuring weapons that were unprecedented. Rather than a disadvantage, their novelty has been usually seen as a positive quality. Governments have been not only willing but eager to apply them in war, as in the German use of rockets against England during the Second World War, the American use of atomic bombs against Japan in 1945, and the use of several new weapons during the Falklands War of 1982.

Civilian-based defence is not so extreme a projection beyond experience as was the proposal in 1939 to President Roosevelt to explore development of a whole new type of explosive from nuclear fission. In the case of civilian-based defence, there have been . . . a number of improvised experiments with nonviolent struggle against domestic and foreign domination and for national defence objectives.

All new military weapons and all policies and strategies based on innovative weapons (including those of N.A.T.O.) lack historical verification of their ability to fulfil the intended objectives. The scenarios for N.A.T.O. defence of Western Europe against a possible Soviet sweep westward by use of theatre nuclear weapons in Europe are mostly based on untested assumptions, conjectures, and guesses, and not on carefully examined experience. The only experience with the wartime use of atomic weapons—at Hiroshima and Nagasaki—is mostly ignored and excluded from European strategic calculations. The human consequences of the atomic bombings of Japan suggest that plans for the use of nuclear weapons in Europe to defend the peoples of Western Europe are not based on serious calculations of their likely results. Supporters of present N.A.T.O. policies are, therefore, in no position to dismiss civilian-based defence categorically on the basis that there is no historical experience of its planned application by a fully trained population.

As a prepared policy to be waged by a trained population, civilian-based defence is only now being developed. It is a projection from past improvised experience to a possible future prepared defence policy. Civilian-based defence is rooted in the general technique of "nonviolent action" as it has been widely used in improvised forms in the past.[6] Nonviolent action might also be called "civilian struggle." This technique has been far more important in history than has previously been recognized. Some of the more significant cases, arranged in four groups, are listed in Table

1. Note that this type of conflict has been used not only in resistance and revolution against oppression but also in several national defence struggles.

This type of combat has almost always been launched without advance decision, planning, preparations, and training. Except for limited previous experience and restricted improvisation based on largely unknown cases elsewhere, both the leaders and participants in nonviolent struggles have always had to act without the most basic resources available to military practitioners for thousands of years. These include thorough knowledge of the technique being used, strategic principles, prior organization, weapons development, and instruction in the needed skills. There have naturally been defeats: the Korean national resistance to the Japanese in 1919–1922, for example. In other cases the results have been mixed, as in the 1923 German struggle in the Ruhr. Outright victories have also been won, such as the ousting of the military dictator of El Salvador in 1944 and the defeat of Quisling's plans for the Corporate State of Norway during the Nazi occupation.

Just as for many centuries deliberate efforts have increased the combat capacity of military conflict, so research, strategic analysis, preparation, and training should multiply our capacity to gain objectives by nonviolent struggle generally, and specifically to provide deterrence and defence by civilian-based sanctions.

Considering the New Policy

Can civilian-based defence be developed to meet the defence and security needs of Western European countries more adequately and with fewer grave problems than present policies? The answer to this question is likely to shape much of the future of Europe and to influence the international system in the decades ahead.

In recent years the civilian-based defence option has been receiving increasing attention from the general public in Western European countries. In some cases, the policy has begun to receive limited consideration by governments, for example in Sweden and the Netherlands. The degree to which this policy is explored and adopted will largely be determined by the estimate made of its effectiveness in comparison to other options. It seems probable that civilian-based defence can meet the deterrence and defence needs of Western European countries more adequately than present policies, while reducing significantly the dangers of destruction of their societies and the annihilation of their peoples. If so, civilian-based defence, by its capacity to deter or defeat a possible Soviet invasion, could provide an alternative to nuclear war.

In several countries scholars and others have begun to investigate the utility of nonmilitary forms of struggle as a possible supplement to military means or as a full alternative to provide deterrence and defence against aggression.[7] However, this work, while impressive, remains rudimentary in comparison to the results of centuries of study devoted to conventional military strategy and tactics. In this infant stage of development, civilian-based defence certainly has problems which require careful consideration. These problems will need to be compared to those of present policies. No perfect policy exists. No policy, military or civilian, is free of risks and costs, nor can the consequences of any policy be guaranteed.

Nevertheless, the risks and costs inherent in today's military and civilian-based security policies for Western Europe are not equal. The capacities and possible consequences of each policy can be evaluated and compared, with a reasonable degree of validity. Detailed evaluation of civilian-based defence will require research, analysis, feasibility studies, preparations, training, and finally, as with all policies, application in a crisis. It is possible, however, to begin here to explore the relevance of the civilian-based defence policy for Western Europe.

The policy must meet the needs of particular countries of Western Europe; their diversity must be recognized. When we speak of "Europe" and "Europeans" we lose a great deal of precision. The European nations share a common civilization and their political systems are often very similar. However, each country differs in culture and geography, and usually in language and climate. They also vary significantly in social, economic, and political conditions. They also differ in specific defence and security needs, including the degree to which the threats to national security come from internal groups or from foreign states.

The neutral and nonaligned countries—Finland, Austria, Ireland, Switzerland, Sweden, and Yugoslavia—are so different from one another that they can only be grouped together for consideration of the most general problems and needs. Individual studies are required for each of these countries on its possible receptivity to civilian-based defence and on the capacity of the policy to meet perceived security needs. Each of the minor N.A.T.O. partners—Norway, Denmark, Iceland, the Netherlands, Spain, Portugal, Belgium, Luxembourg, Greece, and Turkey—and each of the major European members—West Germany, Britain, Italy, and France (in its special relationship)—require individual consideration. The situations of the North American members—Canada and the United States—are still different.

In all these societies the motives for adopting and applying civilian-based defence would be the same as have long been the case with military means: love of one's own country; belief in the right of a people to choose its own political system and government; opposition to international aggression, internal usurpations, and foreign domination; belief in a religious or moral duty to protect one's homeland and people; conviction that however imperfect one's own society, its defence against foreign aggressors and internal usurpers is a prerequisite to building a better one; and agreement that, however much people may disagree among themselves, no outside state or internal clique will be allowed to dominate them.

Both "minimalist" and "maximalist" positions may be relevant in considering what role civilian-based defence measures might have in the defence policy of any given country. Let us look first at the policy from a minimalist perspective.

A country might add a modest civilian-based defence component to its defence policy alongside its military posture with the aims of: (1) increasing the deterrent effect of its overall policy by making visible preparations to continue defence even after occupation; (2) deterring and defeating internal or foreign-instigated coups d'état or other usurpations; (3) mollifying a strong peace movement or anti-nuclear weapons movement; (4) emphasizing the strictly defensive intent of the overall policy; (5) meeting the demand of a smaller political party needed for a coalition government; or (6) reducing the dangers of escalation to nuclear war by providing an active defence alternative when conventional military means appear or have proven to be inadequate. . . .

. . .

Dissuading Nuclear Attacks

With a civilian-based defence policy, nuclear weapons are unnecessary and even counterproductive, for they create threats to national security and survival. This is true whether nuclear weapons are provided by an alliance, are based in the country by an ally, or are independently controlled. If a country adopts civilian-based defence against conventional invasions and ends association with nuclear weapons and bases, two of the most serious dangers of nuclear attack are removed: pre-emptive strike to prevent an expected nuclear attack and escalation of a conventional war to a nuclear one.

As we have noted earlier, when a country directly possesses nuclear weapons, or provides bases for them, or even belongs to a nuclear alliance (hence bringing suspicion of regular or emergency basing), it becomes virtually inevitable that opposing nuclear powers will target that country. Deployment of nuclear weapons, or assistance in such deployment, makes a country extremely dangerous to others, whatever the actual intent. That country will be seen as a potential attacker or accomplice to a nuclear attack.

On the other hand, countries which do not possess nuclear weapons, have no nuclear bases, and are not members of a nuclear alliance, minimize the likelihood of being targeted by other nuclear powers. Zaire, Colombia, New Zealand, Sri Lanka, and Morocco do not seriously expect nuclear attack. The United States, the Soviet Union, China, Britain, France, and the countries with nuclear bases or with facilities that might be used in nuclear war do contemplate seriously the possibility of nuclear attack. They claim their nuclear capacity, or that of their alliance, is required to deter potential attacks. In fact, that capacity is a major stimulus of the danger.

Transarmament to civilian-based defence, in contrast, drastically reduces the likelihood of being targeted and pre-emptively attacked.[8]

Civilian-based defence can also reduce the danger of escalation of a conflict to nuclear war. This danger exists under both present N.A.T.O. policies and the proposals to shift from nuclear deterrence for Western European security to an expanded conventional military capacity for N.A.T.O. and for individual countries. Within the framework of military means, there is always the possibility that one side or another, fearing defeat, would resort to nuclear weapons—acquired from an ally, kept in hidden stocks, or freshly assembled. The danger is most acute under present conditions, in which both alliances are tied to dominant nuclear powers.

By replacing conventional military weaponry and nuclear weapons with civilian-based defence, the defence struggle could be kept entirely outside the military framework. This would virtually eliminate the danger of escalation to nuclear war. Nor is a nuclear attack on the country with a nonmilitary defence policy likely as a means of securing political or other goals. The normal goals of invasions—political, economic, ideological, and territorial—could not be achieved and would even be directly endangered by the use of nuclear weapons in the territory to be occupied. A nuclear attack at the beginning of an invasion would therefore be counterproductive for the attackers. Once civilian-based defence is under way against an invasion and occupation, the presence of the attackers' personnel in the country would drastically reduce or eliminate any large-scale use of nuclear weapons.

Even on the scale of Hiroshima and Nagasaki, selective atomic attacks on a civilian-based defence country to induce political submission would be

tragic. However, the small likelihood of their occurring and the relatively limited scale of the
resulting destruction and casualties need to be
compared with the results of the significantly
larger nuclear attacks to which nuclear power or
nuclear-base countries might be subjected.

The potential for small-scale use of nuclear
weapons for pure destruction or vindictive punishment of the defiant population exists, but it is
doubtful that it would occur, for four reasons. First,
once the civilian-based defence struggles are under
way, the dynamics of the conflict strongly tend to
shift the attackers' measures away from the more
blatant forms of violence and toward efforts to gain
political control. This clearly occurred, for example, in Czechoslovakia within a few days in August
1968 and extended well into the next year, even
beyond the ascent of Gustav Husak to leadership
in April.

Second, in some cases people in the attackers' homeland, repelled by a nuclear attack against
a nonviolent population, may react disruptively.
Where news can reach the general population, the
regime may suffer a general loss of legitimacy and
support, while having to deal with unrest and
demonstrations. In addition, even if public knowledge can be restricted and delayed, this use of
nuclear weapons may be used by rival factions
within the ruling élite to oust and replace the
existing rulers.[9]

Third, the use of nuclear weapons against a
civilian-based defence country is likely to provoke
serious international reactions. While some states
may be relatively indifferent to world opinion,
hostility and denunciations may nevertheless have
an impact when accompanying diplomatic and
economic sanctions threaten significant international political and economic losses. In the case of
nuclear aggression, the greatly intensified revulsion is likely to mean that such losses may be more
widespread and lasting than is commonly the case
with international sanctions. The increasing dependence of the Soviet Union and other countries
on foreign trade and food shipments increases the
seriousness with which the prospect of international sanctions will be viewed.

Fourth, because the weather and winds generally move from west to east in Europe, the Soviet
Union would also have to take special measures to
prevent unacceptable nuclear fallout from Western
Europe from reaching Eastern Europe and the
Soviet Union. Such steps as using "clean" bombs
or aerial explosions, or setting limits on the explosions could reduce this danger to the U.S.S.R. itself.
However, Soviet officials would need to be cautious
about such actions. Awareness of them might lead
the Soviet or Eastern European populations to
become alarmed and protest.

All these factors make a nuclear attack on a
Western European civilian-based defence country
unlikely.

However, just as it is necessary to face the
consequences of nuclear war resulting from the
failure of nuclear deterrence, so it is necessary to
face the question of what a civilian-based defence
country would do under threat of nuclear attack—
an extremely improbable eventuality.

Various responses to implied or explicit
threats should be examined. These should include
diverse options, even an apparent bending to
specific demands at the moment, so as to be able
later to regain the political initiative. More defiant
options are, however, potentially appropriate. If
the threat had been made quietly through diplomatic channels, in order to induce some type of
submission, then a major publicity and diplomatic
campaign could be launched, with the aim of
producing sufficient world revulsion and possibly
domestic reactions in the attackers' homeland to
block implementation of the threat. A prudent
nonviolent position in face of such threats would
be to refuse to bow even to nuclear blackmail.
Submission to a particular threat would likely be
the beginning of a series with escalating demands,
with no end in sight.[10] Refusal to submit to even
nuclear threats is part of present N.A.T.O. policy as
well, except that in it the refusal to bow is
combined with the threat of a N.A.T.O avenging
counterattack, with the virtual certainty of a Soviet
preemptive or retaliatory major nuclear strike. In
order to reduce or eliminate nuclear threats and
attacks from hostile ruthless states, it is essential

in civilian-based defence that potential attackers be made aware that even those threats will not achieve their objectives.

It is highly unlikely but conceivable that in an unusual situation a hostile foreign state might hope to tyrannize a civilian-based defence country into submission by actual selective use of atomic weapons. However horrendous that prospect may be, it must be compared to what would happen if nuclear deterrence failed: probable massive nuclear attacks to eliminate second strike capability. With civilian-based defence, the absence of nuclear retaliation would most likely prevent the rapid escalation to nuclear devastation that is probable when both sides possess nuclear weapons.

If the civilian-based defence country had been attacked selectively with nuclear weapons to induce submission, the attackers would need to suspend such bombing to determine if it had produced the desired result. That pause would provide time for the outbreak of the domestic and international repercussions discussed above and for possible reassessment by the attackers of their strategy. Much greater chances would then exist for a cessation of nuclear attacks than would be the case when nuclear retaliation followed the first nuclear attack.

Civil defence measures against fallout from such limited attacks would make much more sense than against more massive nuclear attacks, for non-nuclear countries can survive limited small-scale nuclear attacks—as did Japan.[11] Civil defence measures need to be examined carefully in this context, since limited attacks differ significantly from the annihilation likely to result from attack and counterattack between two nuclear powers. In a civilian-based defence country, civil defence preparations become another part of a purely defensive posture. This contrasts with the perception of a large civil defence programme in a major nuclear country as part of preparation for a first strike on its rival.[12]

Within the context of civilian-based defence, and beyond civil defence efforts, attention should also be given to the desirability and potential effectiveness of developing and deploying purely defensive technological measures against nuclear attacks (whether in the anti-ballistic missile form or some other). Work would be required on the likely effectiveness of such measures and their relative contribution to security, as compared with other means, alongside the civilian-based defence policy. It could be difficult to demonstrate that such research, development, and deployment were purely defensive, and that would be necessary to preclude a pre-emptive attack. (Such an attack could be based on the false belief that the defensive anti-ballistic missiles were actually disguised offensive nuclear-armed rockets.)

In summary, while civilian-based defence is not directly a deterrent against nuclear attack, the policy can by other forces of dissuasion significantly reduce the chances of such a catastrophe. The strictly defensive nature of the policy would, if accurately perceived, remove the fears which could produce pre-emptive attacks and dangerous steps of military escalation which could lead also to a nuclear attack. Recognition that this was a policy of people sufficiently strong that they did not require the threat of mutual annihilation in order to refuse to submit to nuclear blackmail could also reduce the incidence of such threats. The choice of a strictly defensive policy to deal with security threats combined with a foreign policy concerned with human rights and welfare throughout the world could contribute to a reservoir of international goodwill which also would discourage attacks. In other words, the nonoffensive nature of civilian-based defence and its other political and international influences tend strongly to dissuade massively destructive attacks by nuclear or other means.

Major work is needed to examine and evaluate such possible dissuasive effects of transarmament on the probability of nuclear attack. It is important to learn how to maximize these effects while securing a society's principles, independence, and survival. In addition, both negotiated and self-reliant ways of reducing nuclear dangers need to be continually and fully explored.

What If Deterrence Fails?

For Europe itself, transarmament to civilian-based defence potentially provides a way to reduce the

TABLE 2   Comparative difference

Deterrence Policy	Success	Failure	Possible Consequences of Failure of Deterrence
Nuclear	No attack	Nuclear war	Massive destruction and dangers of annihilation
Civilian-based defence	No attack	Defence policy implemented	Defeat and life under harsh dictatorial rule or Successful defence with free way of life restored

dangers of the continent becoming a nuclear wasteland. It could do this by providing strong means of deterring and defending against a Soviet conventional invasion without the threat or use of nuclear weapons. Deterrence by civilian-based defence of such an attack is rooted in the capacity of the society with this policy to defend itself successfully, and to defeat the attackers' efforts to gain control and specific objectives. An understanding of how the policy works to achieve defence against actual attack is needed to appreciate the deterrence potential of civilian-based defence. It is therefore important to examine more fully in the next two chapters how this policy could provide effective defence.

That topic is important for another reason as well. No deterrent—military or civilian—can ever be guaranteed to deter. Capacity to deal with its possible failure is therefore essential. The requirements, conditions, and risks of deterrence by civilian-based defence need to be fairly compared with those of deterrence by present conventional military and nuclear policies. The consequences of failure of deterrence by each policy must also be compared, along with the courses of defensive or remedial action which can then be taken. This is almost never done.

Table 2 is designed to facilitate comparison of nuclear and civilian-based deterrence of invasion. Many people compare the best possible results of nuclear weapons—successful deterrence ("no attack" . . .)—with the worst possible results of civilian-based defence—failure of both its deterrence and defence capabilities, and therefore harsh dictatorial rule. . . . This is, of course, not a reasonable comparison. Success and failure of each policy for deterrence, as well as of the respective consequences of the failure of the two deterrence policies, need to be compared with each other, as the table indicates.

Unlike failure of nuclear deterrence, the failure of civilian-based defence preparations to deter invasion of Western Europe does not bring likelihood of annihilation, but instead application for the first time of the real defence capacity.

1. Auguste Comte, *The Positive Philosophy of August Comte* (Freely translated and condensed by Harriet Martineau, with an Introduction by Frederic Harrison. London: George Bell & Sons, 1896), vol. II, pp. 222–223.

2. Charles Louis de Secondat, Baron de Montesquieu, *The Spirit of the Laws* (Translated by Thomas Nugent. Introduction by Franz Neumann. New York: Hafner, 1949). vol. 1, p. 313.

3. For a fuller presentation of this theory of power, see Gene Sharp, "The Nature and Control of Political Power," in *The Politics of Non-violent Action,* pp. 7–62, and "Social Power and Political Freedom," in *Social Power and Political Freedom* (Boston: Porter Sargent, 1980), pp. 21–67.

4. Most of these examples from before 1972 are described, briefly or at length, with cited introductory sources, in Gene Sharp, *The Politics of Nonviolent Action.*

5. See Gene Sharp "Nonviolent Action: An Active Technique of Struggle," in *The Politics of Nonviolent Action,* pp. 63–105; and ibid., passim.

6. On the nature, theory of power, methods, and dynamics of nonviolent action, see Gene Sharp, *The Politics of Nonviolent Action.*

The technique of nonviolent action on which civilian-based defense is based may be relatively unfamiliar to many readers. That technique has been historically neglected and politically misunderstood. The brief explanatory passages about its dynamics and relevant historical cases possible in this chapter are necessarily inadequate to correct past neglect. Therefore, the reader has been referred to various sections of the author's *The Politics of Nonviolent Action* (924 pp.). Extensive historical evidence of the power potential of nonviolent struggle can be found therein, along with detailed analyses supporting certain assertions in this volume.

No comprehensive history of nonviolent struggle has been written. Various cases are described in the following sources: Karl Ehrlich, Niels Lindberg, and Gammelgaard Jacobsen, *Kamp Uden Vaaben;* Barthélemy de Ligt, *The Conquest of Violence: An Essay on War and Revolution* (New York: E. P. Dutton, 1938, London: Routledge, 1937, and New York and London: Garland Publishing, 1972); Clarence Marsh Case, *Non-Violent Coercion: A Study of Methods of Social Pressure,* pp. 285–396 (New York: Century Co., 1923, London: Allen & Unwin, 1923, and New York and London: Garland Publishing, 1972); Adam Roberts, ed., *Civilian Resistance as a National Defense;* Gene Sharp, *The Politics of Nonviolent Action;* and Gene Sharp, " 'The Political Equivalent of War'—Civilian-based Defense," in *Social Power and Political Freedom,* pp. 195–261.

For bibliographies of accounts of cases of nonviolent struggle, see the brief one in Gene Sharp, "For Further Reading," in *Exploring Nonviolent Alternatives* (Boston: Porter Sargent, 1970), pp. 133–159. An extensive annotated, classified bibliography of relevant books in English is in preparation. For notification when it is available, send a postcard to Bibliography, Program on Nonviolent Sanctions, Center for International Affairs, Harvard University, 1737 Cambridge Street, Cambridge, Massachusetts 02138, U.S.A.

7. See the various publications on the topic listed in the Bibliography in Gene Sharp, *Making Europe Unconquerable: The Potential of Civilian-Based Deterrence and Defence* (Philadelphia: Taylor and Francis, 1985), from Australia, Austria, Britain, Denmark, Finland, Germany, India, Japan, the Netherlands, Norway, Sweden, and the United States of America. The literature about the policy varies, with differing primary emphases, such as problems of defence, social change, war and peace, and normative considerations.

8. For another discussion of nuclear weapons and civilian-based defense, see Anders Boserup and Andrew Mack, *War Without Weapons,* pp. 177–182.

9. The 1964 ouster of Khrushchev from the Soviet leadership has frequently been attributed in part to his colleagues' judgement that his 1962 moves to deploy nuclear missiles in Cuba were imprudent. Actual nuclear attacks on another country might produce stronger, swifter consequences within a ruling group in a crisis.

On weaknesses and factionalism in totalitarian systems, see Ernest K. Bramsted, "Aspects of Totalitarian Systems" in Adam Roberts, ed., *The Strategy of Civilian Defence* (*Civilian Resistance as a National Defense*), pp.67–69, and Gene Sharp, *Social Power and Political Freedom,* pp. 97–102.

10. For a similar view, see George F. Kennan, *The Nuclear Delusion: Soviet-American Relations in the Atomic Age* (New York: Harper and Row, 1984), p. 71.

11. See Cresson H. Kearny, *Nuclear War Survival Skills* (Coos Bay, Oregon: Nuclear War Survival Research Bureau, 1980).

12. On the contrasting significance of civil defence preparations in different defence contexts, see Dietrich Fischer, *Preventing War in the Nuclear Age* (Totowa, New Jersey: Rowman & Allanheld, 1984), pp. 59–61.

PART NINE

The Nation and the International System

The nation-state has been the fundamental unit of large-scale social organization for the past few hundred years. The nation-state is a sovereign entity, meaning that it answers to no "higher" or "greater" authority. Yet at the same time the nation-state and its inhabitants do not live in isolation. Each country is part of an international system of nation-states. If each nation-state takes its own interests to be more important than anything else and recognizes no legitimate authority greater than its own laws and institutions, then wars between nations will continue. "Nationalism" as a unifying bond between the inhabitants of nations in turn requires opposition to another people.

"The Nation and the International System" explores some of the crucial relationships concerning war and peace processes among nations. In "Nuclear Weapons and the End of Democracy," Richard Falk discusses the role of nuclear weapons in increasing the power of presidents and decreasing the role of democratic processes in determining foreign and military policies. National sovereignty in the nuclear age thus translates into the sovereignty of a handful of powerful elites, while everyone else, even in formally democractic countries, are relatively subordinate and powerless.

Yet there are possibilities for a different world order beyond the system of states threatening each other with nuclear annihilation. Dietrich Fisher, in "Conflict Resolution," expounds on the dynamics of international negotiations and the differences between negotiating strategies that succeed and those that fail. In "Peace Soldiers: United Nations Military Forces," sociologist Charles C. Moskos presents case histories of how United Nations peace-keeping forces have been used to monitor and enforce various peace treaties. These peace-keeping forces are regular military units from different countries around the world that are temporarily assigned to the United Nations. In "Successful Negotiation by the UN: Mission to Peking," Joseph Lash shows how the United Nations has used diplomacy to ameliorate some of the bitter conflicts between the Republic of China and Taiwan, former adversaries during the Chinese revolution–civil war of the late 1940s.

In "Goodbye War," Gwynne Dyer summarizes the arguments for changing the sovereignty of the nation-state and creating a different international system given the continued industrialization of war and the development of weapons that can destroy civilization: "Some generation of mankind was eventually bound to face the task of abolishing war, because civilization was bound to endow us sooner or later with the power to destroy ourselves. We happen to be that generation, though we did not ask for the honor and do not feel ready for it. There is nobody wiser who will take the responsibility and solve this problem for us. We have to do it ourselves."

Nuclear Weapons and the End of Democracy

Richard Falk

Prospects for democratic governance are definitely connected with the dynamics of hegemonic statecraft. For instance, it is notable, as Eqbal Ahmad has pointed out, that fascism flourished in the interwar period precisely in those states among the capitalist industrial powers (Germany, Italy, and Japan) that had been substantially excluded from the imperial game of colonizing non-Western peoples and expropriating their raw materials.[1] It is also notable that hegemonic leaders of the day "provoked" a lethal rivalry for colonial spoils that eventuated in general war.

In our own era there is an apparent link between post-colonial hegemonic tactics and anti-democratic interventionary diplomacy, part of an overall plan to make the world as safe as possible for multinational corporations and banks. Capital flows depend upon stable political environments that offer rewards by way of profits, and stable political environments can only be achieved, given mass discontent and mobilization rampant in the Third World, by institutionalizing repression. The widespread militarization of the internal political order of the Third World expresses the extent to which the functional requirements for order virtually require a permanent declaration of war by governing elites against restive citizenries. This hegemonic dynamic is reinforced in Third World countries by economic pressures to curtail inflation and labor demands, solicit further extensions of international credit, contain social demands for anti-poverty public services—that is, by the whole relatively recent International Monetary Fund (IMF) dimension of anti-democratic influence.

Such a geopolitical/geoeconomic array of anti-democratic pressures is generally understood, at least in progressive circles. Gino Germani was an unusually perceptive interpreter of modern threats to democracy; he was particularly aware of the anti-democratic consequences of an emergent interdependence on all levels of international life. More than almost any contemporary political theorist, Germani sensed that democracy could no longer be reconciled with the fragmentary organization of the planet into territorially separate and rival sovereign states, regardless of the political will or ideological predisposition of national leaders. Such an insight has revolutionary implications, suggesting, for instance, the absolute necessity of evolving a global perspective as a precondition for sustaining genuinely democratic modes of governance. Incidentally, a globalist outlook, as Germani also understood, need not be centralist in aspiration, but might most plausibly work toward superseding statist dominance by decentralist withdrawals of legitimacy and the formation of a world system out of relations among what Christian Bay calls "natural political communities."[2]

In this essay, my concern is with the *structural relevance* of nuclear weaponry and strategy to the future of democracy. The central contention is that the existence of nuclear weapons, even without any occurrence of nuclear war, interferes with democratic governance in fundamental ways. In other words, we don't have to wait for Armageddon to begin paying the price, as measured by the quality of democracy, for a system of international security constructed around the central imagery of nuclear deterrence. To presume this relevance of nuclear armaments and doctrines to democracy is itself somewhat unusual. For instance, one searches in vain the pages of the Trilateral Commission's notorious study, *The Crisis of Democracy,* for any reference to the erosion of democratic governance as a consequence of "the nuclear revolution"; the Trilateralists' idea of "crisis" is based on the alleged erosion of authority and stability through the undisciplined tactics of social movements demanding reform that surfaced in the late 1960s, a phenomenon described elsewhere in positive terms as the beginnings of a participatory model of democratic revitalization.[3] In the background, of course, is a concern about the preconditions for capitalist efficiency under contemporary conditions, including a fear that the work ethic, achievement syndrome, and greed impulse are being drained away by cultural developments, including a substantially alienated intelligentsia in so-called mature capitalist countries.[4]

The nuclear weapons question is inserted on the orthodox agenda of liberal democracy in a dramatically perverse way by David Gompert, overseer of an influential study, *Nuclear Weapons and World Politics,* a product of the 1980's Project of the Council on Foreign Relations. Gompert writes:

> *In the long run, the existence of nuclear weapons could fundamentally alter government-citizen relations. If, over time, the need of governments to field expensive deterrent forces is not appreciated by citizens who no longer sense a real nuclear threat, popular support for the maintenance of forces could fade*—and governments might feel themselves compelled to provide for deterrence without the consent of the governed.[5]

Evident in this remarkable passage of unsurpassed reification, is a presumed priority being accorded "the government" on nuclear military policy over and against the possible opposition of "the citizenry." Democracy is turned on its head, not out of any alleged emergency that prevents either consultation or the participation of representative

institutions, but because the perceptions of "the rulers" are favored over the adverse will of "the people" in an area of disagreement. Such a realistic vision of what has already become standard operating procedure throughout the nuclear age raises to the level of explicit ideology the dire impact of nuclear weaponry upon democratic governance.

Daniel Ellsberg, a former government official with responsibility in the nuclear policy area, confirms the extent to which American presidents were prepared to use nuclear weapons in nondefensive roles and far beyond what the American people were ever allowed to understand. He writes:

> *When I did most of my working plans in '59, '60, and '61, . . . I assumed that I was reading basically retaliatory plans . . . The generals knew better. They knew that these plans were not at all for retaliation because, on the contrary, the Russians had no ability to strike first. So all these plans were really initiative plans, first-strike plans.*

And, then, more concretely:

> *What I discovered, going back to Truman who made such threats in 1950, is that every team of every president has seen the serious recommendation by the Joint Chiefs of Staff of plans involving the initiation of nuclear warfare under certain circumstances. More significantly, at least four Presidents have secretly authorized advanced preparations for such first-use, or have actually threatened adversaries with U.S. first-use in an ongoing crisis.[6]*

Ellsberg has documented these assertions thereby suggesting that political leaders in the United States have failed throughout the nuclear age to consult with, or disclose to, the public the occasions on which the use of nuclear weapons was seriously contemplated. In this sense, the government's refusal to accept notions of public accountability in the nuclear domain has been consistent and bipartisan.

In one of the few attempts at a systematic discussion of the relevance of nuclear weapons to the constitutional processes of the United States, Michael Mandlebaum considers their impact largely as a matter of adding an "enormous responsibility" to the presidency and of producing an unavoidable increase in governmental "power."[7] Mandlebaum even hazards the view that "Perhaps the reason for delegating nuclear authority to the President is similar to the role that anthropologists have assigned to divine kingship: a means of coping with forces that seem beyond human powers of understanding and control."[8] Of course, the view of "delegation" here is very strained, as the Congress, let alone the public at large, are ill-informed about the nature of presidential authority with regard to nuclear weapons. In a formal sense it is true that this grant of authority seems consistent with the underlying consitutional conception of the President as commander-in-chief of the armed forces.[9] Yet more substantively, the actuality of nuclear weaponry is such, with its requirement of constant readiness, as to defy the moral constitutional expectation that the President must have the unchallenged authority to make battlefield decisions in wartime, an authority conceived of as pertaining only to that special circumstance of emergency and national unity that is presumed to exist during a properly declared war. As is obvious, and will be discussed later in this essay, nuclear weapons, by their very existence, forever obliterate the occasion of "peace," thereby, in my judgement, depriving a democratic polity of one of its most essential preconditions. Even those optimistic about the capacity of the modern state to uphold democratic values generally concede that governing procedures for accountability by leaders and participation of citizens are substantially abridged in the context of "war." Thus, a permanent state of war, not by the nature of political will or the character of international antagonisms, but as a structural reflection of the nature of modern weaponry, casts a dark shadow across the very possibility of a democratic polity. Citizens of secondary nuclear and non-nuclear democracies, at least to the extent that their governments take part in the geopolitics of alignment via alliance relations, have "delegated" this awesome authority over the deployment and use of nuclear weaponry to leaders of another state! Here, again, such a delegation may conform to the formal logic of constitutionalism, but it shreds the fabric of democratic substance seemingly beyond repair.

More substantively, this new grant of powers to a particular leader does entrust an awesome actual capability to a fallible, flawed human being or, at most, to a small, often hidden, inner group of advisors. Traditionally, divine right prerogatives even if pathologically abused could only produce limited damage, although of a severe sort for a given time and place. Increasingly, the leadership of the main nuclear powers possesses a capacity for destruction commensurate with what traditional religions attributed to the divine, a capacity to cause in the fullest sense a global or human apocalypse. Authority and power to inflict such results by a single process of decision suggests the extent to which the citizenry is inevitably and permanently excluded from determinations that decisively shape societal destiny.

But it is not only the upholders of constitutional legitimacy that overlook the relevance of the nuclear weapons dimension. Sheldon Wolin, in an eloquent introductory editorial to his new journal of progressive opinion, pointedly titled *democracy,* nowhere indicates that nuclear weapons may foreclose democratizing prospects in unsuspected, unacknowledged, and crucial respects. His emphasis is on "the steady transformation of America into an anti-democratic society" as a consequence of the increasingly authoritarian character "of the country's primary institutions." Similarly, Alan Wolfe in his excellent book, *The Limits of Legitimacy,* devoted to an assessment of anti-democratic pressures on the liberal state, neglects even to mention the relevance of nuclear weaponry.[10] Both Wolin and Wolfe are fully aware, of course, that nuclear weapons are crucial political "facts" that are reshaping the modern state, but they interpret political reality on the basis of traditions of political thought oblivious to the reality of nuclear weapons.[11]

Perhaps, the failure to emphasize nuclear issues partly reflects an attitude that their relevance is so manifest as to be taken for granted or so "structured" into our world context as to be beyond the domain of practical politics, however radical their intention. In either event, I believe the failure to address the issue of nuclear relevance is an important omission for any serious reflections on the current democratic prospect.

André Glucksmann writes that "Everything subtle, profound, definitive and rigorous that has been said about nuclear weapons—which means not much—was said already a century before."[12] By this provocative assertion, Glucksmann is arguing that antecedent acquiescence in "totalist thought" had completely vested in the state ample authority and modalities to subordinate ethics to considerations of state power—"The nascent order of reciprocal terror was a feature of Western culture long before the invention of nuclear weapons."[13] And, of course, such an observation is pertinent. The moral ease, for instance, with which American decision-makers adopted atomic tactics in World War II was definitely "facilitated" by belligerent policies already routinized, especially terror bombing of civilian centers of population.[14] This striving for nuclear rectitude was, in a sense, reinforced by the Nuremberg Judgment that imposed criminal punishments for the "immoral" political behavior of the defeated leaders of Germany and Japan, but neglected "the wrongs" of the victorious powers.

Taking at face value Glucksmann's contention that the secular triumph of totalist ideology had already destroyed the moral foundations of state power long before Hiroshima, I find myself unable to go along with the postulate of continuity as a way of avoiding the need for specific analysis and commentary on the distinctive relevance of nuclearism. In this regard, I agree with the important recent assessments of nuclear relevance by E. P. Thompson and Robert Jay Lifton, as well as the earlier wide-ranging analysis of Karl Jaspers.[15] Thompson, in an indictment of left/Marxist thought for its failure to highlight the nuclear issue, analyzes the contemporary political situation beneath the overarching, trans-ideological category of "exterminism," that is, as underscored in his own title, "the last stage of civilization." As is now widely known, Thompson's special concern is centered on the particular victimization of Europe as a potential " 'theater' of apocalypse" in a struggle waged by the superpowers who, in effect, seek to maintain their homelands as "sanctuaries," that is, as "off-limits" in the event of a nuclear exchange.[16] Thompson notes in passing that "a prior condition for the extermination of European peoples is the extermination of open democratic process." Underneath this assertion is the conviction that citizens would never knowingly give their assent to such a suicidal arrangement, and that therefore their rulers (not any longer mere leaders) must impair their access to knowledge and their rights to act on what they know. Repression at home, preferably by anodyne means designed to induce apathy, becomes a necessity of governance if security is to be premissed, directly or indirectly, on the logic of exterminism. Again nuclearism and democracy collide in a specific, concrete manner.

Robert Lifton, whose writings probe the psychological and cultural significance of nuclear weaponry, reaches conclusions startlingly similar to those of Thompson. As he puts his emphasis, the new capacity for totalist destruction "changes everything (fundamentally alters our ultimate and immediate relationships in ways . . .) and seems to change nothing (it is apparently ignored by much of the human race, which goes about business as usual.)"[17] Note that for Lifton, the element of continuity is maintained not by the antecedent terrorism of state power, as alleged by Glucksmann, but by the failure of most people, including leaders, to grasp the radical novelty of nuclear weaponry. This novelty centers upon the sheer magnitude of potential destruction, giving secular reality to what had previously been a largely symbolic reality associated with the apocalyptic premonitions of religious tradition.

As Lifton goes on to suggest, the special aura of urgency in the United States around atomic espionage issues during the 1950s, culminating in the incredible ritual of capital punishment enacted in response to "the crimes" of Ethel and Julius Rosenberg, was associated with guarding the unprecedented power and with anxiety about the potential vulnerability created by nuclear weaponry.[18] The full absurdity of the security pretext for internal repression became evident only two decades later when bomb designs were written up as undergraduate student exercises, and do-it-yourself bomb-producing technology became the subject matter of monthly magazine articles. What is not absurd, however, is the governmental need to frighten its own citizenry into subservience by insisting that no one challenge the awesome authority of the government to engage fully and secretly in the apocalyptic end-game of exterminism. We note the recent reflex outburst by Ronald Reagan's first National Security Advisor, Richard Allen, in reaction to the European grassroots movement against nuclear weaponry. In a rare post-1945 breakdown of Atlanticist decorum, Allen publicly castigated the emergent European mood, saying that ". . . outright pacifist sentiments are surfacing abroad. One recent incident of concern is the split in the British Labor Party. Right now the second largest party in Great Britain has adopted as part of its official platform the renunciation of nuclear weapons. We are even hearing, in other countries, the contemptible 'better red than dead' slogan of a generation ago."[19] Allen's words lend substance to Lifton's fear of "the particularly dangerous radical right embrace of *American* nuclear weapons" that "might well lead one to seek nuclear Armageddon as a way of achieving total purification."[20] The animus of the revival of anti-Soviet, anti-Communist hatred, the resumption of the Cold War and arms race, marks the current period as a peculiarly dangerous phase within the wider context of nuclearism.[21] As such, we can expect an intensification of anti-democratic institutional initiatives. Such an expectation has been confirmed in the early months of the Reagan presidency by such steps as an upgrading of the CIA, a renewed stress on the linkage between national security and broad governmental prerogatives of official secrecy and surveillance procedures, an attack on the Freedom of Information Act, and an impending proposal to reinstate capital punishment in relation to the federal crime of espionage.

A concrete instance of this attitude of sufferance toward the citizenry occurred on September 19, 1980 when a monkey wrench dropped in a Titan II silo located near Damascus, Arkansas producing a large explosion.[22] Local residents were naturally anxious to discover whether large amounts of radiation had been released. Astonishingly, the Pentagon took the incredibly arrogant position that it would neither confirm nor deny the reports that a nuclear explosion had occurred, or that there was a fallout danger. And more astonishingly, the public generally acquiesced in this display of official arrogance. Incidents of this sort, inherently revealing, are also indicative of a process whereby the citizenry is thoroughly demoralized with respect to citizen rights and duties, being subjected to an experience of learned helplessness.

One scarcely noticed dimension of nuclearism is the dubious legality of nuclear weapons.[23] In fact, the entire edifice of the law of war rests upon the central prohibition of indiscriminate killing of innocent civilians and includes separate prohibitions for weapons that cause victims "unnecessary suffering" or disproportionate damage.[24] It hardly requires a learned disquisition to comprehend the radical inconsistency between the minimum reading of the law of war and the insistence on national discretion to threaten and use nuclear weaponry. Such an inconsistency is peculiarly significant for democratic polities as their deepest pledge is to govern within a framework of law (a government of laws, not men). Furthermore, all "mature democracies" insist that every political entity claiming sovereign rights accept the obligations of the international legal order, virtually as evidence of its intention to participate as a state in international life. The hue and cry directed at the Iranian governing authorities for their failure to uphold the immunity of American diplomats and embassy premises during the 1979–81 Teheran hostage crisis was based on the apparent rejection by the Khomeini leadership of this behavioral standard.

The claims of international law in the war/peace area are particularly strong in relation to the United States' conception of political legitimacy. It was, after all, the United States that had taken the lead throughout the century to circumscribe sovereign discretion in relation to force and had, after World War II, insisted on criminal liability for political leaders who commit war crimes.

Some apologists for nuclearism contend lamely that under international law the sovereign is permitted to do everything that has not been expressly prohibited. There is some basis for such a contention in relation to certain subject matter, but it hardly seems applicable to nuclear weaponry. In this setting, law follows closely the minimum imperatives of morality; international law has since the 17th century been an uneasy blend of governmental consent for contrived rules and procedures and the natural law postulate. In our time, conventional moral outrage is concentrated upon "terrorism," the victimization of the innocent for the sake of ulterior political motives. It hardly takes a master moralist to reach the conclusion that nuclear weaponry and strategy represents terrorist logic on the grandest scale imaginable, yet the popular discussion of terrorism usually exempts nuclear weapons despite the currency of such phrases as "the balance of terror." The point here is that law and morality converge to condemn nuclearism, an acknowledgment increasingly being made by religious and cultural leaders of independence and stature.[25]

To suggest that nuclear weapons are illegal and immoral, and that leaders who threaten or contemplate their use are guilty of crimes of state, is to raise core questions about the legitimacy of *any* governance structure. Reliance on nuclear weapons is not just one of many governmental functions, it is in many ways the decisive undertaking of national political leadership, the one upon which, almost everyone agrees, all else hinges. If that undertaking is perceived by a substantial fragment of the citizenry as a criminal enterprise, then it will be impossible for political leaders to achieve legitimate authority. Deception, secrecy, and coercion will become increasingly indispensable instruments of governance, not to handle anti-social deviants, but to prevent citizens of the highest moral authority from challenging the absolutism of the state. Criminal prosecutions of those who dare expose this state secret of illegitimacy disclose the inevitable dilemma of "democratic" governments that embrace nuclearism.[26]

Either the government ignores such protests and acts of resistance despite the loss of legitimacy, or it prosecutes its clearest moral voices despite the loss of legitimacy. There is no way for a democratic political leadership to retain its legitimacy in the eyes of its citizenry for very long if a sustained campaign around the legal and moral status of nuclear weapons is mounted. Some overarching questions emerge. Can democratic forms retain even provisional vitality when their substance is so deeply perverted? Or do these forms become atrophied rituals that disguise the passing of democracy from the scene? Can the nuclear question be kept cordoned off from the overall, routine administration of state power? Responses to these questions vary from country to country and depend on the consciousness of the citizenry and the perceptions of national leaders, as well as upon the tension level of international relations. In general the higher the tension level, the greater the anti-democratizing impact of the legitimacy dilemma arising from the existence of nuclear weaponry.

The focus on the United States is not meant to exempt the Soviet Union from scrutiny, but since the Soviet system seems procedurally anti-democratic in its essence it falls outside the strict scope of this inquiry. To the extent that the Soviet political leadership relies on nuclear weaponry, a crucial dimension of authoritarian governance is added. By now, whatever may be said about its earlier ambivalence, the Soviet Union seems to be fully committed to a reliance on nuclear weapons as a means of upholding its interests.[27] Because secrecy and public participation are so curtailed in the Soviet political system, there seems to be little opportunity for citizen opposition to nuclearism, while at the same time, reliance on nuclear weapons places formidable, rarely acknowledged constraints on the possibilities of democratizing reform taking hold within Soviet society.[28]

Of course, I am not arguing that nuclear weapons nullify all democratizing impulses at the state level. It is certainly possible to alter government/citizenry relations in a democratizing direction despite a reliance directly or indirectly, upon nuclear weapons. It is rather a matter of structural constraint that bears on the most essential issue of state power in a manner that is anti-democratic in an extreme sense (here, democracy refers not only to the consent of the governed, but also to the idea of a government of laws, not men, which given shared human vulnerability has to include policies at the state level bearing on war/peace, resource use, and environmental protection).[29]

The broad implications of this analysis are two-fold: the restoration of democratizing potential at the state level depends on the downgrading and eventual elimination of nuclear weapons as an element of international political life; secondly, normative opposition to nuclear weapons or doctrines inevitably draws into question the legitimacy of state power and is, therefore, more threatening to governmental process than a mere debate about the propriety of nuclear weapons as instruments of statecraft. The Machiavellian question is foremost: can a system of sovereign states ever manage to get rid of a decisive weapon by which an unscrupulous leader might impose his will? The course of international history strongly supports a negative reply. In effect, democracy, as a political framework, seems to be a permanent casualty of the nuclear age, although democratic forms, as an increasingly empty shell, can persist, disguising for some time the actuality of their inner collapse. The trend toward authoritarian governance, although prompted mainly by other factors, may also

be, in part, a consequence of the anti-democratic influences of totalist attitudes and capabilities operative even in non-nuclear states (often reinforced by way of alliance or acceptance of "a nuclear umbrella").

Of course, there is an apparent paradox present. The erosion of democracy by way of nuclearism is, at the same time as the European movement suggests, a stimulus to democracy. It may yet be possible for citizens to organize in such a way as to exert some measure of democratic control over nuclear weaponry short of achieving its total elimination. Advocacy of a no first use declaration and posture could provide a realistic goal for democratic movements seeking to restore balance in the relationship between government and citizenry and sanity to the quest for international security.[30]

The future of democracy then is at one with two intertwined explorations: the possibility of a post-Machiavellian international political order[31] and of a post-nuclear world.[32] In central respects, safeguarding and restoring the democratic prospect for mature capitalist polities depends on a comprehensive world order solution. The beginning of such a solution may involve delegitimizing the state in the area of national security. For this reason the religious, medical, and legal campaign against nuclearism seems of vital relevance to the very possibility of a democratic revival.

---

1. Oral presentation, "Abolition of War Conference," Institute for World Order, New York City, June 6, 1979.

2. Bay, "Toward a World of Natural Communities," *Alternatives* VI: 525–560 (1981); see also Chapter III of Falk, *A Study of Future Worlds* (New York, 1975) for a presentation of a range of world order systems alternative to the present statist system.

3. For depiction of "participatory democracy" see C. B. Macpherson, *The Life and Times of Liberal Democracy* (Oxford, 1977), 93–115.

4. Michael J. Crozier, Samuel P. Huntington, and Joji Watanuki, *The Crisis of Democracy: Report on the Governability of Democracies to the Trilateral Commission* (New York, 1975); Daniel Bell, *The Cultural Contradictions of Capitalism* (New York, 1976).

5. David C. Gompert and others, *Nuclear Weapons and World Politics* (New York, 1977), pp. 4–5 (emphasis added).

6. "Nuclear Armament: An Interview," pamphlet of the The Conservation Press, pp. 1, 3, undated.

7. For discussion see Michael Mandlebaum, *The Nuclear Revolution* (Cambridge, 1981), pp. 177–183.

8. Ibid., p. 183.

9. Ibid., p. 182.

10. Alan Wolfe, *The Limits of Legitimacy* (New York, 1977).

11. It seems significant to note that Wolfe fails to enlarge the agenda even in the course of his otherwise devastating critique of the Trilateral Commission report, cited note 4. Wolfe, pp. 325–330.

12. André Glucksmann, *The Master Thinkers* (New York, 1980), p. 151.

13. Ibid., p. 150. Simone Weil and Stanley Diamond push the argument back further, maintaining that the fundamentally coercive nature of the state has been the ground for all subsequent modes of official violence. For a brief discussion of their views see Falk, *Human Rights and State Sovereignty* (New York, 1981), pp. 128–131.

14. See a careful interpretation of the decision to use atomic bombs in Robert Jay Lifton, *The Broken Connection* (New York, 1979), pp. 369–381, including consideration of the "moral" interposition by Henry Stimson, then Secretary of War, of reasons why Kyoto, because of its cultural stature, should be "spared," that is, taken off the list of approved targets.

15. See Karl Jaspers, *The Future of Mankind* (Chicago, 1961).

16. Edward Thompson, "Notes on Exterminism, the Last Stage of Civilization," *New Left Review*, No. 121, May–June 1980, pp. 3–31, and pp. 10–14.

17. Lifton, op. cit., p. 335.

18. Ibid., pp. 354–56.

19. Text of "Remarks by Richard V. Allen Before the Conservative Political Action Conference 1981," Washington, D.C., March 21, 1981, p. 10.

20. Lifton, op. cit., p. 359.

21. This danger is heightened by adoption of first-strike strategic thinking, by new weapons innovations, and by conflicts and instabilities that threaten hegemonic patterns of Western influence over resource-producing countries in the Persian Gulf and southern African regions.

22. See, report, of "U.S. Nuclear Weapons Accidents," *The Defence Monitor*, X, No. 5, 1981, p. 11.

23. Typical of this discussion is the assumption that international law currently imposes no restraints on the discretion of governments to use nuclear weapons. See, for example, Michael Mandlebaum, "International Stability and Nuclear Order: The First Nuclear Regime," in Gompert, op. cit., pp. 23–24, where such discretion is connected with the absence of express treaty restrictions and the general unenforceability of international law. For a refutation see Richard Falk, Lee Meyrowitz, and Jack Sanderson, "Nuclear Weapons and International Law" (unpublished paper, February 1981).

24. For a comprehensive treatment of this and related issues see Falk, Lee Meyrowitz, and Jack Sanderson, op. cit.

25. See, for example, James W. Douglass, *Lightning East to West* (Portland, Oregon, 1980); see also Delhi Declaration on the Prohibition of Nuclear Weapons (1978).

26. A notable instance of such civilian resistance has involved Catholic activists associated with Rev. Daniel P. Berrigan and his brother, Philip Berrigan. Their most recent undertaking involved entering a General Electric plant in King of Prussia, Pennsylvania, and damaging two nosecones intended for Mark 12A missiles. The eight individuals involved, known as the Plowshares 8, were prosecuted, convicted, and sentenced in a trial conducted in a highly emotional atmosphere in which the defendants were determined to center the case on their claim that nuclear weapons were illegal and immoral, and the judge was equally determined to rule such considerations out of order. For a brief evaluation see Falk, "Shield for Civil Disobedience—International Law—a Counterforce Weapon Against Nuclear War," Pacific News Service, August 1981.

27. See Mandlebaum, op. cit., pp. 202–3, for comments on the Soviet approach to nuclear weapons.

28. Jean-François Revel, for instance, reports that efforts by European anti-nuclear protesters to march from Copenhagen to Moscow, as well as Copenhagen to Paris, were refused, while at the same time the anti-nuclear protest was given Brezhnev's explicit blessing. Revel, "The Strange Nuclear Diplomacy of Willy Brandt," *Wall Street Journal*, August 19, 1981, p. 29.

29. For my world order analysis of these issues see Falk, *A Study of Future Worlds*, op. cit.

30. I owe the impetus for this paragraph to Robert C. Tucker, long a forceful advocate of no first use thinking. For Tucker's views on this prospect, along with the position of other commentators on international affairs, see Robert C. Tucker, Klaus Knorr, Richard A. Falk, and Hedley Bull, "Proposal for No First Use of Nuclear Weapons: Pros and Cons," Policy Memorandum No. 28, Center of International Studies, Princeton University, 1963; and Falk, Robert C. Tucker, and Oran R. Young, "On Minimizing the Use of Nuclear Weapons," Research Monograph No. 23, Center of International Studies, Princeton University, March 1, 1966.

31. Cf. Ferenc Feher, "Toward A Post-Machiavellian Politics," *Telos*, No. 42, Winter 1979–80, pp. 56–64; see also Stanley Hoffman, *Duties Beyond Borders* (Syracuse, New York, 1981).

32. The main focus of a book to be written jointly by Robert Jay Lifton and myself, bearing the tentative title *Indefensible Weapons: A Political and Psychological Account of Nuclearism*.

Conflict Resolution

Dietrich Fischer

Independent measures, which have been mainly discussed up to here, can accomplish a great deal more for the prevention of war than is generally assumed. Still, there are limits to such measures.

Certain things can be achieved only through mutual cooperation.

In this chapter, some methods of conflict resolution will be briefly explored: some ways of negotiating successfully without giving in; the role of transnational institutions; how to overcome domestic conflicts that may invite foreign intervention; some principles of fair sharing; and the role of peace research.

Successful Negotiations

The key to success in negotiations with an opponent is to come up with imaginative proposals that hold something attractive *for both sides;* for if the opponent would lose something by accepting a proposed solution, we can hardly expect him or her to agree to it.

Negotiating tactics can be divided into four basic approaches, shown in Table 1, depending on whether a negotiator seeks to satisfy the interests of both sides (position 1), of only his or her own side, (position 2), of only the other side (position 3), or of neither side (position 4). . . . Many believe that to "win" in negotiations one has to be "tough" (i.e., take a "hawkish" stand); that if one is too "soft" ("dovish"), one will lose. But that simple idea looks at the wrong dimension. The most-successful approach is that of a "peacemaker." The most-irrational position is that of the "warmonger." Yet we are far too familiar with that last form of behavior.

Some may doubt whether it is possible to meet simultaneously the interests of both sides in negotiations. But, in fact, opportunities for mutual gains are abundant. In discussing possibilities for mutually beneficial cooperation between the United States and the Soviet Union, Deutsch criticizes

> *an underlying view which hampers the attempt to strengthen cooperative bonds:* the view that anything which helps them hurts us. *Clearly, it helps them if their control over their nuclear missiles is such as to prevent accidental firings. But does this harm us? Clearly, it helps them if their children have available the Sabin polio vaccine. But does this harm us?* [Deutsch 1983, p. 28; emphasis added].

Schell (1982, p. 288) writes "for both superpowers—and, indeed, for all other powers—avoiding extinction is a common interest than which none can be greater." This common goal ought to provide a solid basis for negotiations aimed at preventing a nuclear war.

If negotiations are to be successful, they must offer each side some gain, *in each side's own view.* For this reason, for example, a disarmament proposal that requires the Soviet Union to shift its main missile force from land-based to submarine-based systems is unlikely to be negotiated successfully. It may well be that such a shift would objectively increase the security of the Soviet Union. But that is not what counts. Unless the Soviet leaders believe such a shift to be in their interest, they will not agree to it. So far, there is no indication that the Soviets have been convinced that it would be better *for them* to place less reliance on land-based missiles. A more-likely path to agreement on nuclear arms reductions may be to propose an equal, mutual ceiling on the number of warheads, and to leave it to each side to decide how it will base them—whether on land, submarines, or bombers, or on what combination of them—to make its own system least vulnerable, *in each side's own perception.* Under such a proposal, each side would likely begin to dismantle its most-vulnerable and least-reliable weapons, which would have the advantage of reducing strategic instability.

To achieve success in negotiations, it is helpful to be explicit about one's interests, but to remain flexible about the concrete solutions by which those interests are to be met. Fisher and Ury (1981) give the following example from daily life: suppose a husband and wife want to build a house together. If an architect asks each of them separately to draw his or her preferred floor plan, it will be almost impossible to reconcile the two different plans. But if he asks each to specify the number and purpose of rooms he or she needs, the architect may be able to come up with a design that meets the interests of both.

Fisher and Ury offer an application of this principle to the solution of an international conflict and show how an innovative approach may meet the interests of both parties in negotiations. During

TABLE 1   Four negotiating tactics

	Ignore Own Interests	*Promote Own Interests*
Promote Negotiating Partner's Interests	**3. "Dove":** Try to reach agreement at any price by giving in prematurely and sacrifice your own interests.	**1. "Peacemaker":** Seek imaginative solutions that can satisfy your own needs as well as those of the other side, and reach agreement without giving in.
Ignore Negotiating Partner's Interests	**4. "Warmonger":** Try to deny the interests of the other side at any price, even if this means that you have to sacrifice your own interests.	**2. "Hawk":** Promote only your own interests and fail to reach agreement because you have nothing attractive to offer to the other side.

the 1978 Camp David peace negotiations, an impasse appeared to have been reached.

> *Israel insisted on keeping some of the Sinai. Egypt, on the other hand, insisted that every inch of the Sinai be returned to Egyptian sovereignty.... Looking to their interests instead of their positions made it possible to develop a solution. Israel's interest lay in security; they did not want Egyptian tanks ... on their borders ... Egypt's interest lay in sovereignty;... after centuries of [foreign] domination, Egypt was not about to cede territory to another foreign conqueror.... Egypt and ... Israel agreed to a plan that would return the Sinai to complete Egyptian sovereignty and, by demilitarizing large areas, would still assure Israeli security [Fisher and Ury 1981, pp. 42–43].*

Fisher and Ury's example illustrates once more that if one wants the other side to agree to a proposed solution, it is in one's own interest to have something attractive for the other side in the proposal; otherwise, the other side is not likely to accept it. For this reason, if we are interested in reaching an agreement, it is to our own advantage to try to explore and understand as fully as possible the interests of the other side, as the other side

really perceives them. The real interests of our opponents need not be identical with their declared positions, but it may also be quite different from how *we* would perceive their interests if we were in their position. It will not help us to approach the other side with an attitude of "We know what is good for you." While it is helpful for mutual understanding to try to place oneself in the other's situation, for example by playing reversed roles, it is still necessary to carry out a *dialog* to explore how the other side really sees its interests.

To understand the interests of the other side does not mean that we give something away. On the contrary, it helps us to achieve what we want by simultaneously meeting the interests of the other side. This is particularly important in the field of security. Countries which have long avoided war have taken great care not to be seen as a threat by others as long as they leave them in peace. If we want to be secure, we must think of a way in which others can also feel secure, otherwise we will not remain secure for long. I once tried to discuss the problem of stable vs. unstable deterrence with a professor who teaches nuclear strategy at a U.S. military academy. He broke off the discussion by saying, "*Our* task is to defend ourselves. How the Russians are going to defend themselves is *their* problem; we cannot figure it our for them." This short-sighted attitude, which is likely to be found on the Soviet side as well, is partly responsible for the precarious situation into which we have maneuvered ourselves. The race between the superpowers to keep ahead in nuclear weaponry, without giving much thought to how the other side is going to assure its perceived security in any other way than by building up a huge nuclear arsenal, has brought us to our present predicament. To regain real national security, the superpowers will have to think of measures that improve the security of both sides at the same time.

If we want to reach a lasting agreement, it is in our own interest to leave the other side a face-saving way out of any impasse that may develop during negotiations, and not to seek to humiliate it. For example, . . . it might have been better for the United States to permit Khrushchev a face-saving withdrawal of Soviet missiles from Cuba, by agreeing formally to some reciprocal step, than to force him to back off—a humiliating response that may have contributed to the subsequent intensification of Soviet military expansion.

For an agreement to be stable, it should be firmly anchored in each side's self-interest. Each side must be convinced that if it were to break the agreement, it would *itself* lose something, not only the other side. A signature on a document does not necessarily make an agreement "binding." For many, the loss of honor or good conscience that would be associated with breaking an agreement may be sufficient to keep them from breaking it, but not necessarily for all. *It is not wise to rely on a nation to keep agreements that go against her interests.* It is not even enough that each side would lose if it broke the agreement; each side must also clearly *perceive* it that way. For example, as the course of history showed, it was objectively not in Hitler's interest to break the non-aggression treaty with the Soviet Union in 1941. But blinded by his early victories, Hitler did not see it that way. For the Soviet Union's non-aggression treaty with Germany to be effective, it ought to have been backed up by a stronger and more clearly visible defense capability. "Trust" alone is not a good basis for a lasting agreement; it is important to take precautions not to be cheated. But this does not in any way imply that one should seek to cheat or threaten

the other side. According to Deutsch (1983, p. 30), his research suggests that the approach most likely to elicit cooperative behavior, and which also appears to be most effective in reforming aggressive criminals, is a firm and self-confident, but calm and nonbelligerent, attitude.

Being cautious is not to be confused with being hostile, or with presuming the worst intentions on the part of those with whom we deal. We can very well seek friendly relations with them, but it would be unfair even to our best friends if we were to put them deliberately into a situation where they are tempted to cheat.

An agreement based on blind trust is probably worse than no agreement at all, because it may penalize those who keep it and reward those who break it. For example, when the U.S. government called for voluntary restraint in wage and price increases to fight inflation, John Kenneth Galbraith mocked that he hoped the next step would be voluntary taxes—he would be the first not to pay them. For the same reason, it is important that arms control agreements include adequate provisions for verification of compliance. This does not mean that it is necessary that verification be 100 percent reliable; it is sufficient if there is a reasonable risk that violations might be detected. For example, the detection of tax evasion is far from perfectly reliable, but cheaters are discovered and punished occasionally, and this is sufficient to induce most people to pay their taxes. Even though that system is not ideal, it is preferable to no tax system at all. Similarly, with arms control agreements, it is desirable to see constant improvements in verification procedures, but even if verification is not yet perfect, this is no reason not to keep and seek to expand existing agreements. The situation would be much worse in the absence of any agreements whatsoever. For this reason it would be useful, for example, to resume negotiations aimed at a comprehensive nuclear test ban treaty.

If two countries are engaged in a series of negotiations, it is counterproductive to begin with the most-difficult and -controversial issues. Success is far more likely if those issues are addressed first where there is the strongest common interest, and where agreement is relatively easy to achieve. As

Churchill once put it, it should be possible to settle something before settling everything.

Some people think that areas of agreement are less important and no precious time should be wasted on them, that all effort should be concentrated on dealing with the crucial points of disagreement. But such a negotiating strategy is likely to fail. Unless areas of common interest are also stressed, it will be much more difficult to find solutions in those areas where interests are opposed. On the other hand, if some agreements in relatively noncontroversial areas have already been reached, a favorable climate will have been created for negotiations on more-difficult issues.

For example, in arms control and disarmament negotiations between the United States and the Soviet Union, it is best to start with topics where there is a very strong and easily visible joint interest. One such area is the prevention of the spread of nuclear arms to more and more countries, and particularly into the hands of terrorists—a field where unilateral measures cannot achieve much. If even one country makes technology and raw materials for the manufacture of nuclear bombs available to others, nuclear bombs can spread. To prevent this, *all* potential leaks must be blocked. The common interest of both superpowers, and of most other countries, has made conclusion of the nonproliferation treaty of 1968 possible. A further strengthening of the inspection mechanism of the International Atomic Energy Commission, to prevent the dissemination of weapons-grade uranium and plutonium, particularly to terrorist groups, is an area where there seems to be little reason for disagreement between the superpowers and where an early treaty might be reached.

Another area of strong joint interest is the prevention of nuclear war by accident. Many steps in that direction can, of course, be taken independently by each side, in its own interest. But certain measures require mutual cooperation. For example, the 1963 establishment of a direct communication link between the White House and the Kremlin (the "hot line") could not have been implemented by one side alone. Agreements on similar issues, such as regular high-level or even summit meetings, could be mutually beneficial. Also, the exchange of information on how to effectively prevent technical malfunctions that could lead to false attack warnings or accidental missile firings should be noncontroversial.

A further area where negotiations could be fruitful would be the joint exploration by both the United States and the Soviet Union of measures to make their nuclear forces less vulnerable to a surprise attack.

On the other hand, the effort to achieve balanced force levels through negotiations over how many weapons of one type are equivalent to how many different weapons of the other side are almost designed to fail. Each side will claim that the weapons of the other side are more dangerous, so that the other side will have to make deeper cuts. As Johan Galtung said, there is only one way to find out with certainty how different weapons compare—by trying them out in a war. Past disarmament negotiations have not only failed easily but may even have been counterproductive by searching for a precise "balance." Each side prefers to add to its arsenal in areas where the other side has more, instead of destroying weapons of which the other side has less. Disarmament negotiations reveal where these gaps are, and may thus lead to more armament (Galtung 1984). . . . Numerical parity in weapons is neither sufficient nor necessary for security. It is far more important to avoid destabilizing weapons systems that may precipitate a war. Negotiations with the aim of establishing a perfect "balance" may divert precious energy and time from other, more-important and more-promising areas.

Since national security is an extremely sensitive area, burdened with emotions, it may be useful to spend some effort as well on other areas where mutually beneficial cooperation between the superpowers is possible. Examples are the exchange of scientific information, or direct cooperation in such areas as the peaceful exploration of space, medical research, pollution-free manufacturing techniques, and the development of new energy sources. Some joint work is going on in all of these areas, but such forms of cooperation could be greatly expanded for mutual benefit.

The Role of Global Organizations

To solve global problems that no single country can tackle alone, global organizations must take over. Some global problems entail potential dangers to human survival that are not related to military technology: an accumulation of carbon dioxide in the atmosphere caused by excessive burning of fossil fuels worldwide could lead to a greenhouse effect, warming up the earth and melting the polar ice caps. Coastal areas would be flooded, and the earth's climate and food production patterns could change in unpredictable ways. Another danger is that certain industrial pollutants could deplete the ozone layer that protects life on earth from excessive ultraviolet radiation. The result would be not only an increase in skin cancer, but also a higher rate of possibly lethal mutations, in humans as well as in animals and plants. No country can prevent such potential catastrophes alone. As long as one major industrial power continues to accumulate carbon dioxide or to deplete the ozone layer, all nations will be affected.

About six thousand years ago, one of the first advanced civilizations emerged in Egypt. A possible reason was that the irregular flooding of the Nile valley was a problem that no single farmer could attack alone. Cooperation on a very large scale was necessary to build a dam to store the water and release it in a controlled way. Similarly, the need has now arisen for the emergence of some form of global organization to deal effectively with the global problems facing all of humankind.

To deal with problems that no country can solve by itself will require the establishment of more global institutions. The first such global organization, which has operated successfully for more than a century, is the World Postal Federation, which was founded in 1875. Since then, a great variety of international organizations have developed, both at the governmental and nongovernmental levels, most notably the League of Nations and the United Nations; but a number of others are still needed. One issue that can be dealt with successfully only at the global level is disarmament.

Galtung (1984) has proposed a U.N. agency that would not only work toward the elimination of offensive arms, but also help member countries to defend themselves without becoming a threat to other countries. Maybe such an agency could be more successful than the disarmament agencies have been so far, because member countries would perceive it to be in their obvious interest to cooperate with such an agency.

Many global institutions still wait to be created. But at the same time as the need for them has increased, it has also become much easier to communicate at a global level. It is hard to imagine that when the United States was founded two centuries ago, the fastest method for a message from New York to reach Washington was via horseback and took ten days. A message to England took three months by sailboat. Today, any point on earth can be reached in seconds by telephone, and personal contacts among people from different parts of the world have increased enormously. While technology has created many global problems, it has also provided better means to solve them.

One difficulty that hampers negotiations at the global level is that the negotiators themselves do not always suffer directly from a lack of agreement, and therefore tend to prolong the negotiations. For example, at a U.N. conference negotiating a new wheat agreement, including provisions for food aid to regions in conditions of famine, the delegates failed to reach agreement but were apparently very well fed. The Catholic church has developed an efficient mechanism to achieve rapid agreement on the selection of a pope—perhaps after centuries of trial and error. The cardinals are simply locked up until they announce their joint decision. (Maybe we should lock up the disarmament negotiators in Geneva until they have reached agreement.) . . .

• • •

The forces that seek an improvement in the situation of the underprivileged can either be channeled into constructive directions and absorbed into the government, or be suppressed with violence. Suppressing them may appear as the simpler and quicker solution, but that approach only tends to postpone the problem. Unless the injustices are removed that lead people to risk their lives in order to change their society, dissatisfaction will grow and make the problem worse in the long run. The following analogy may illustrate this point. If a mountain torrent causes destruction, its power can be channeled into productive uses for irrigation and power generation, or an impenetrable dam can be built to block its flow. As the water level rises behind the dam, the dam must be built higher. But ultimately the pressure of the water will build up to such a level that it will break through any wall and cause much greater destruction than would have occurred in the absence of an attempt to block it. Similarly, if an attempt is made to block inevitable social change by force, the violence and destruction will ultimately assume much larger proportions than if the needed reforms had been undertaken in time.

If a "friendly" government in another country has lost popular support, another nation can either try to prolong its life by economic and military aid, even intervening in its support, until the inevitable bitter end occurs, at great human cost; or it can seek to build good relations with a newly emerging, more-popular government. The same two types of approaches have also been tried in the economic field, and this may give a clue as to which approach works better. European countries and the United States have tended to extend the life of obsolete industries through subsidies until they finally collapse, causing even greater economic disruption. Japan does the opposite. When an industry is no longer competitive and is in difficulty, the government helps the affected companies to move into *new,* more future-oriented industries. It might be worth trying the method Japan has used so successfully in its economic policy in the field of foreign policy as well, in choosing with which groups to build good relations. One difficulty is, of course, that there is more emotional attachment to a certain political party that may have lost its popularity than to a certain branch of industry that may have lost its competitiveness.

Fair Sharing

Some standard mechanisms exist by which disputes can be arbitrated in a fair way. A traditional method is "cut and choose." If one cuts a cake into two pieces and the other is free to choose one, neither side has any grounds for complaint. That method can be generalized to more than two participants (see, for example, Baumol 1981). Such methods would be useful, for example, in settling disputes over inheritances. Quarrels often arise among heirs over certain sentimental values, for example, who can keep the parents' house, and who receives only money as compensation. If there are two heirs, one could divide the inheritance into two portions he considers of truly equal value to him. The other heir could then choose which option she prefers. There would be no cause for argument or regret, and the income of inheritance lawyers would diminish.

The same method could be used to solve certain international disputes. Two countries may want to build a joint steel plant, to take advantage of scale economies. But each would prefer to have the plant on its own territory, to create jobs and to give greater assurance of future supply. Potentially beneficial forms of economic cooperation often break down over such disputes. A simple solution would be the following: one country estimates how much it would be worth to it to have the plant on its own soil, and how much compensation it would be willing to pay to the other country for letting it have the joint plant. It can choose the level of compensation in such a way that it is *indifferent* to either having the plant and paying the compensation, or receiving the same amount of compensation from the other country and not having the plant. Then it can let the other country choose. In this way, the dispute could be settled in a fair, amicable way, with no later regrets.

Sometimes the market can be an effective tool for conflict resolution. People need not agree with each other on the values of various goods. If people place *different* values on different goods, they can both benefit from an exchange. They would be ill-advised to try to convince the other side that their own relative evaluation is correct. For example, when the U.S. government bought Alaska in 1867 from Russia for $7,200,000 it would not have cared to argue with the czar that Alaska was really worth a great deal more.

On the Role of Peace Research

Innovative ideas and proposals for preventing or solving conflicts peacefully are much needed. Deterrence or defense, even nonmilitary defense, is only a last resort to seek to prevent a war when a conflict has already reached an acute stage. To use an analogy, to prevent a child from being a delinquent, we rely primarily on education. Detainment in a "correctional facility" is only a last resort, if education has failed. Similarly, prevention of war through deterrence or dissuasion should be only a last resort, if it has not been possible to resolve a conflict in other ways. Much more work needs to be done on the prevention of serious conflicts at a very early stage, when it is generally easiest to do something about them. An important role in this endeavor needs to be played by conflict and peace research.

At the United Nations Second Session on Disarmament in 1978, then Secretary General Waldheim appealed to all nations to make available 0.1 percent of their military expenditures for disarmament research and education. Even that relatively modest amount is not devoted to peace research in most countries. Yet research and education for the prevention of war could probably contribute a great deal more to countries' security than could marginal additions to their military hardware. The prevention of a nuclear holocaust is certainly worth a greater effort.

Peace research now depends mainly on individual efforts and voluntary contributions. Let us try to imagine the state of military defense if it depended on individual actions and voluntary donations. Still, this is no reason for despair. In the last century, the slave traders and slave owners prospered materially, while the people who freed slaves and worked for the abolition of slavery did so out of commitment to a social vision, voluntarily. In spite of their apparent disadvantage, they were successful in the end.

References

Deutsch, Morton. 1983. "The Prevention of World War III: A Psychological Perspective." Presidential address given at the Fifth Annual Meeting of the Society of Political Psychology. *Political Psychology* 4: 3–31.

Fisher, Roger and William Ury. 1981. *Getting to Yes: Negotiating Agreement Without Giving In.* Boston: Houghton Mifflin.

Galtung, Johan. 1984. *There Are Alternatives! Four Roads to Peace and Security.* Nottingham: Spokesman.

Schell, Jonathan. 1982. *The Fate of the Earth.* New York: Alfred A. Knopf.

Peace Soldiers: United Nations Military Forces

Charles C. Moskos, Jr.

A balanced and concise statement on the peace-keeping functions of the United Nations has been given by Inis Claude.[1] Peacekeeping is an interim measure, designed to forestall the globalization of a local conflict until a political solution can be devised and accepted. Peacekeeping represents an effort, not immediately to promote the settlement of disputes, but to prevent their degeneration into violent conflicts and thus to restore the possibility that practical settlements may be found. For the peacekeeping force, the positive objective of improving relations among parties already embroiled is subordinated to the negative purpose of preventing the entanglement of external powers. All United Nations peacekeeping forces have operated within the confines of a limited mandate. Or, to use a medical analogy, the military component of peacekeeping has been charged with a prophylactic role—the containment and retardation of conflict—rather than a therapeutic one—resolving the source of conflict. But rather than dwell on peacekeeping in the abstract, let us look briefly at the manner in which actual peacekeeping forces have been brought into being and have operated.[2]

The League of Nations

What appears to be the first concrete proposal to establish a peacekeeping force under the aegis and command of a genuinely international body (as opposed to a multinational allied force) occurred in 1920. At that time there was a dispute between Poland and Lithuania over the status of Vilna in Poland. Although the city was Lithuania's historic capital, the majority of Vilna's inhabitants were Poles. With the concurrence of Poland and Lithuania, the League of Nations recommended a plebiscite in Vilna which was to be supervised by an international force. Ten nations (all European) agreed to contribute small contingents to what would be a 1,500-man League force. But by March 1921, owing to Lithuania's second thoughts, Soviet objections to an international force so close to its borders, and the reluctance of the contributing states to get involved in a foreign embroglio, the idea of the plebiscite was abandoned and with it the proposal of a League of Nations supervisory force. Nevertheless, the proposed Vilna force set a peacekeeping precedent by embodying the principle of a peacekeeping force instituted by a world organization.

The League's peacekeeping activities in the South American district of Leticia created a precedent of a different sort. In 1922, this virtually uninhabited 4,000 square mile area had been ceded to Colombia by Peru. A decade later, however, the dispute was reopened when Peruvian nationals from an adjacent region drove out the Colombian officials stationed in Leticia. The Peruvian government's opposition to Colombia's efforts to reoccupy the district led to minor skirmishes between the two nations. To prevent an outbreak of a full-scale war, the League of Nations proposed that Leticia be governed by a League commission while Peru and Colombia negotiated a settlement. The proposal was accepted by the concerned parties, and in June 1933 a League commission began its administration of Leticia. Upon the departure of the commission from Leticia in June 1934, the district was peacefully returned to Colombia. Significantly, from a peacekeeping standpoint, a seventy-five-man contingent of Colombian soldiers wearing the League armband was assigned to duty under the League commission. Thus, these seconded Colombian soldiers became, albeit in a marginal fashion, the first soldiers actually to be commanded by an international authority.

A much more significant example of the League of Nation's use of a peacekeeping force to settle a territorial dispute concerned the Saar. In 1919, the former German area was placed under the administration of a League governing commission in which France initially had a dominant influence. The League's administration was to last fifteen years, at the end of which time the Saarlanders, almost all Germans, were to decide by plebiscite whether to rejoin Germany, pass to France, or remain under League control. Following the removal of the French garrison from the Saar in 1927, the international character of the governing commission became much more apparent. As the time for the plebiscite approached, the already highly charged local situation became aggravated by the belligerent German Nazi presence on the border. The governing commission requested an international force to maintain conditions of law and order before and during the voting. In December 1934, the first truly international peacekeeping force ever assembled arrived in the Saar. It consisted of thirty-three hundred officers and men: fifteen hundred from Great Britain, thirteen hundred from Italy, and two hundred fifty each from the Netherlands and Sweden. At the polls on January 13, 1935, over 90 percent of the Saarlanders voted for reunion with Germany. The international force, having successfully performed its mission, left shortly thereafter, and the Saar was reunited with Germany the following March.

The Saar international force was a remarkable accomplishment. Assembled only a month before the plebiscite and with no past experience to call upon, the force consistently operated in an efficient manner during its short tenure. Under the central command of a British major general, the force had a small British staff section complemented by English-speaking liaison officers in the Italian, Dutch, and Swedish contingents. Tactically, the force avoided deployment in small detachments and made its presence known to the population by frequent foot marches and vehicle patrols on major thoroughfares. Although troops were to come into action only at the request of the civil authorities of the governing commission, their use of weapons remained within the discretion of the military commanders. Official guidelines on the use of force were suitably pacific in tone but still sufficiently vague to allow latitude in interpretation, such as act with restraint, use only that force necessary to restore order.[3] Because of the general acceptance of the force on the part of the Saarlanders and the certainty of the plebiscite's outcome, however, there was never any instance in which the force had to resort to a show of arms. Nevertheless, what is important to note is that the League's international force in the Saar was employed in a military rather than police capacity.

Beside the proposals specifically involving peacekeeping forces mentioned here, the League of Nations, of course, took numerous other actions in situations that endangered the peace. Indeed, prior to 1930—before Japan, Italy, and Germany began their aggressive actions—the League's efforts to maintain peace were measurably successful. These generally took the form of fact-finding missions or "commissions of inquiry," which allowed the good offices of the League to serve as an instrument of conciliation between contending parties. But only in three instances—the proposed Vilna force, the pseudo-international Leticia force, and the Saar international force—did the League of Nations actually seek to establish a peacekeeping force that used military personnel.

The United Nations

With the founding of the United Nations in 1945, the prospects for international enforcement of peace seemed to revive. Unlike the defunct League, the new world organization was to have a credible military power under the provisions of chapter 7, articles 39–47, of the United Nations Charter. As originally envisioned in article 43, the member states of the UN were to make available to the Security Council the armed forces "necessary for the purpose of maintaining international peace and security." In practical terms, article 43 implied a permanent force (either in being or standby) which would fall under the command of the Security Council, in which each of the major powers had veto rights.

Furthermore, as authorized in article 47, a military staff committee, consisting of a representative from each of the Security Council's five permanent members, was to be responsible "for the strategic direction of the armed forces" and to assist the Council on all questions pertaining to "military requirements for the maintenance of international peace and security [and] the employment and command of forces placed at its disposal." The intent of article 47, then, was clearly to use "collective enforcement," as sanctioned by the major powers to deal with threats to world peace. It was assumed that the major powers themselves would provide most of the armed forces for the United Nations. It is important to note that the collective enforcement provisions of the original charter posited major-power coercion as distinct from the twinned "peacekeeping" elements of noncoercion and impartiality.

From the beginning, however, the military staff committee was unable to operate in the intended manner. The growing cold war between the United States and the Soviet Union dashed all hopes that the two superpowers would continue their World War II alliance into the postwar era. It soon became apparent that no UN force could be directed by a committee, each of whose members had a veto. Thus three decades after the framers of the Charter sought to establish a permanent UN force, chapter 7 has never been invoked for any purpose, and the military staff committee has never played a role in any UN operation (although it still goes through the motions of periodically meeting and adjourning).

When the Korean War broke out in June 1950, the United States was successful in getting the Security Council—owing to a temporary Russian boycott of the Council—to recommend that member states come to the aid of South Korea and to invite the United States, which had already deployed troops on the Korean peninsula, to head a United Nations command. Nevertheless, the United Nations presence in Korea can hardly be construed as an example of an internationally sanctioned peacekeeping operation. The misnamed "UN Command" in Korea never operated under the direction of any United Nations body, nor was it financed in any way from United Nations funds. In effect the Security Council resolution served to legitimate the reality of the American intervention on the side of South Korea in what became one of the bloodier wars of this century.

In anticipation that the Soviet Union would not absent itself again from Security Council deliberations, the United States in 1950 successfully sponsored the so-called "Uniting for Peace" resolution in the General Assembly. Passed over the objections of the Soviet-bloc minority, this resolution was an effort to give the veto-free Assembly a determining role in the authorization of United Nations military operations. In this way the United States, which at that time could command automatic majorities in the Assembly, sought to incorporate the UN in its anticommunist strategies. In subsequent maneuvers in the early 1960s, the United States also sought to enforce penalties on UN members who did not contribute to extraordinary peacekeeping expenses. This "Article 19 controversy" invoked the opposition of the strict constructionists—prominently the Soviet Union and France—who held that financial as well as other aspects of peacekeeping should be kept under the exclusive authority of the Security Council. By 1965, however, the United States had come to acquiesce in the view that no state could be compelled to support financially any peacekeeping operation of which it disapproved. In fact, as the Assembly membership became less and less malleable to American interests, the United States itself quietly abandoned the principles endorsed in the Uniting for Peace resolution. Thus, though coming at it from a different direction, the United States eventually found itself in agreement with the Soviet Union that prime determination for UN peacekeeping operations resided in the Security Council.

Another effort to overcome the failure of the military staff committee (under Security Council control) to authorize an internationalized UN military force was the 1948 proposal of Trygve Lie, the first secretary-general, to set up a permanent United Nations force recruited by the Secretariat. Lie's "UN Guard" initially envisioned a standing force of eight hundred international volunteers which would expand to as many as five thousand soldiers. The UN Guard would be used for guard duty with United Nations missions, the administration of truce terms, the supervision of plebiscites, and as a police auxiliary for cities like Jerusalem and Trieste when under international authority. Lie's proposal, however, encountered not only the expected opposition of the Soviet-bloc nations but also the lukewarm support, at best, of the United States and other Western countries. The final outcome, organizationally, was the establishment of a UN field service of unarmed international civil servants which provides administrative, clerical, and maintenance support for field missions. Nevertheless, the debate on Lie's proposal did indicate the beginnings of a United Nations consensus that peacekeeping ought to be removed from big-power participation and that the Secretariat should exercise greater initiative in the establishment and operation of peacekeeping forces.

Dag Hammarskjöld, who replaced Lie as secretary-general in 1953, sought to develop a peacekeeping machinery which could skirt the impasse over collective security procedures invested in the major powers of the Security Council. Under the guidance of Hammarskjöld, United Nations peacekeeping was to become a proper function of middle-sized powers with a commitment to political impartiality. These developments reflected both Hammarskjöld's broad definition of the Secretariat's peacekeeping responsibilities and the rapidly expanding and more heterogeneous membership of the United Nations. Moreover, even before Hammarskjöld, the United Nations had begun to acquire a peacekeeping record by monitoring cease-fires and performing related services on a variety of fronts.[4] These peacekeeping missions, though largely staffed with military personnel seconded to the United Nations from member states, were not properly a peacekeeping *force* inasmuch as they did not operate as a military organization or under military command. Typically, such peacekeeping observers were unarmed. Also, as "peacekeeping" was not a term in general use until the middle 1950s, these missions were at first simply labeled agents of "peaceful settlement," a designation which served to identify them with diplomatic rather than military activity.[5]

UNEF-1

The first employment of an international military force for UN peacekeeping occurred in the wake of the October 1956 attacks launched against Egypt by Israel, France, and Great Britain. Security Council actions to secure removal of the attacking forces were blocked by French and British vetoes. Consequently, with U.S. and Soviet concurrence, the provisions of the Uniting for Peace resolution were invoked, and the issue was transferred to the General Assembly. During the first week of November, the Assembly adopted a cease-fire resolution and authorized Secretary-General Hammarskjöld to recruit a United Nations military force composed of contingents volunteered by member nations. With the acquiescence of the disputants, a cease-fire went into effect and the Assembly created the United Nations Emergency Force (UNEF).

UNEF operated first as an interpositional force covering the withdrawal of the invasion troops. Subsequently, it served as a neutralizing presence by having nonfighting units patrol within Egypt along the Israeli borders in the Gaza Strip and the Sinai desert. At maximum strength in early 1957, UNEF consisted of six thousand officers and men drawn from ten countries: Brazil, Canada, Colombia, Denmark, Finland, India, Indonesia, Norway, Sweden, and Yugoslavia. Ten years later, UNEF consisted of thirty-five hundred soldiers from seven countries. For close to a decade UNEF served the purpose for which it was intended. But in May 1967, following Egypt's request for its termination, UNEF hastily withdrew at the secretary-general's order. This was to become one of the precipitating factors in the outbreak of the 1967 war in the Middle East. But, as Secretary-General U Thant and his principal peacekeeping adviser, Ralph Bunche, explained time and again, there was no legal way in which a UN force could remain in a territory against the will of a sovereign state. Nevertheless, the abrupt withdrawal of UNEF could not have failed to impair the credibility of United Nations peacekeeping arrangements.

ONUC

The largest and most controversial UN peacekeeping force was a product of the chaos that followed the attainment of independence by the Belgian Congo (now Zaire) in July 1960. Within two weeks of independence, the Congo suffered internal anarchy, the insurrections of its army, Belgian intervention, and the secession of its richest province, Katanga. The Congo central government requested help from the United Nations, and Secretary-General Hammarskjöld requested the Security Council to act urgently. The Council responded, with the United States and Soviet Union voting affirmatively, by authorizing the *Operation des Nations Unies au Congo* (ONUC) or the United Nations Congo Operation. The guidelines originally set forth by Hammarskjöld stipulated that ONUC could use force only in self-defense and forbade the UN troops to become a party to any internal dispute, that is, prohibited the use of armed force to end the Katanga secession.

The first UN troops arrived in the Congo on July 15, 1960; they were the precursors of a force which would eventually have over twenty thousand soldiers. Thirty-five countries contributed military personnel to ONUC, but the bulk of the soldiers came from ten African nations: Ethiopia, Ghana, Guinea, Liberia, Mali, Morocco, Nigeria, Sudan, Tunisia, and the United Arab Republic. Non-African states that also contributed sizable contingents were Canada, India, Indonesia, Ireland, and Sweden. A key airlift role in the early stages of ONUC

was played by the United States. ONUC was always plagued by poor coordination of forces, conflicting goals between various national units, and a confusing dual civilian–military command system in which sometimes the secretary-general's special representative (a civilian official) and sometimes the supreme commander of the force (a senior general) each gave orders directly to the troops.[6]

Originally Hammarskjöld seemed to have in mind the termination of ONUC military activities as soon as the Belgian troops were removed and the Congolese army reestablished. After the murder of the Congolese prime minister, Patrice Lumumba, however, the Security Council, in February 1961, passed a new resolution which urged the United Nations to take "appropriate measures to prevent the occurrence of a civil war in the Congo, including . . . prevention of clashes, and the use of force, if necessary, in the last resort."[7] On the initiative of the Special Representative, Conor Cruise O'Brien, the UN launched a full-fledged military operation against the Katanga secessionists in September 1961. However, Katanganese forces, allied with white mercenaries, inflicted a demoralizing defeat on ONUC, and the United Nations was forced to negotiate terms at a disadvantage. Dag Hammarskjöld himself was killed in an airplane crash while on these negotiations. The new secretary-general, U Thant, secured O'Brien's resignation, and the operations begun earlier in the month came to an end by September 20.

After September 1961, the UN gradually built up a stronger position in Katanga. In December of that year, reinforced UN troops coupled with air support occupied the major cities of Katanga. The UN offensive had broken the back of the Katanganese secessionist movement, and soon indigenous developments would lead to a modus vivendi among the Congo's political leaders. In appraising the UN's role in the Congo, it is obvious that what started out as a peacekeeping venture turned into a minor war. The canon of impartiality was clearly breached when ONUC employed armed force in support of the central government. Moreover, the United Nations had to bear tremendous financial burdens, suffered battle casualties, and even had some of its troops accused of committing atrocities.

Nevertheless, by the time the last UN soldiers left the Congo in June 1964, ONUC had achieved definite results; it had preserved the territorial integrity of the Congo and had removed the country from the arena of cold-war confrontation.

UNFICYP

The third United Nations peacekeeping force arose out of a March 4, 1964, Security Council resolution unanimously recommending an international force to keep the peace in Cyprus. Internecine hostility between the preponderant Greeks and the minority Turks in the eastern Mediterranean island-republic erupted into violent fighting during Christmas week of 1963. Even more serious, a war between Greece and Turkey in support of their Cypriot compatriots was threatened. The immediate task of maintaining peace fell to the British, whose troops were already in Cyprus by treaty right and who maintained a large complex of bases on the southern part of the island. After attempts to reach agreement on a NATO peacekeeping force failed during the early months of 1964, the United Nations acted in March. The mission of the United Nations force defined by the 1964 Security Council resolution was "to use its best efforts to prevent a recurrence of fighting and, as necessary, to contribute to the maintenance and restoration of law and order and a return to normal conditions."[8] The first units of the United Nations Force in Cyprus (UNFICYP) arrived on the island in late March 1964. Subsequent renewals of the Security Council have kept the United Nations peacekeeping force in being through 1975.

At its peak strength in 1964, UNFICYP consisted of approximately sixty-five hundred soldiers, a force gradually reduced to twenty-three hundred men by 1974. Contributing nations of UNFICYP's military force have been: Austria, Denmark, Canada, Finland, Great Britain, Ireland, and Sweden. In accordance with arrangements worked out between the Secretariat and the Cyprus disputants, UNFICYP was instructed to interpose itself between the Greek and Turkish sides only when such interposition would be acceptable to the disputants; to negotiate in virtually all circumstances

with the belligerents; and to restore freedom of movement throughout the island only when the right to do so had been secured by local agreements with Greek or Turkish Cypriots. Adopting in essence the mandate based on the UNEF precedent, UNFICYP was to use force only in self-defense and was thereby precluded from intervening militarily in the Cyprus dispute. Thus in several instances of fighting between Greek and Turkish Cypriots, UNFICYP either ineffectively stood by or, on at least one occasion, even abandoned its positions. Even though the potentiality for renewed conflict has remained a constant in volatile Cyprus, the island on the whole, due in some significant part to the United Nations presence, was characterized by relative calm for the ten years following UNFICYP's initial deployment. Thus, although the basic dispute between Greeks and Turks on Cyprus has remained unresolved, UNFICYP must be credited with some progress in its primary tasks of pacifying the Cypriot intercommunal war and reducing the likelihood of a major war between Greece and Turkey.

UNEF-2 and UNDOF

The fourth and fifth United Nations peacekeeping forces came about as a result of the biggest Arab–Israeli war in a generation. On October 6, 1973, Egyptian forces crossed the Suez Canal and Syrian forces attacked on the Golan Heights. After suffering initial losses, the Israelis mounted a counterattack and regained the initiative; following bitter conflict, a tenuous cessation of hostilities was reached by the month's end. After intensive diplomatic maneuvering between the United States, the Soviet Union, and the combatants, the Security Council passed an American–Soviet resolution on October 22 calling for a cease-fire in place. When the initial cease-fire in the Sinai failed to hold, Egypt proposed on October 24 that a joint U.S.–USSR force be sent to the Middle East to supervise the cease-fire. The U.S. rejected the proposal while the Soviets avoided a commitment one way or the other. On October 25, the world community was startled when America suddenly placed its military forces on a worldwide alert. For a moment the danger of a superpower confrontation was posed.

The crisis abated as suddenly as it arose, when later that same day the U.S. and the USSR joined in passing a Security Council resolution establishing a new United Nations Emergency Force (UNEF) which excluded superpower participation.

By October 26, 1973, Secretary-General Waldheim had already formed the nucleus of the new UNEF, with advance elements coming from United Nations contingents in Cyprus. The total strength of UNEF was initially projected at seven thousand men. A UN troop strength of forty-five hundred men was realized over the next several weeks with contingents coming from twelve nations: Austria, Canada, Finland, Ghana, Indonesia, Ireland, Nepal, Panama, Peru, Poland, Senegal, and Sweden (domestic needs at home, however, caused the Irish contingent to be withdrawn in May 1974). Finnish Major General Ensio Siiasuvuo was appointed interim force commander. Pursuant to its mandate, UNEF has gone through three phases: first as an interposing force and observation element between the Egyptian and Israeli forces, later in controlling the separation and disengagement process, and eventually in manning the zone of disengagement (from base camps located on the Egyptian side).

While the October 1973 diplomatic efforts had been at least temporarily successful in separating Egyptian and Israeli forces, the situation on the Israeli–Syria front was one of continued war. Aided by a virtuoso performance of U.S. secretary of state Henry Kissinger, an accord was finally reached in May 1974 which worked out a four-stage disengagement in the Golan Heights sector and the thinning of Israeli and Syrian military forces in that border region. To implement this arrangement, the Security Council on May 31, 1974, authorized the United Nations Disengagement Observer Force (UNDOF) and requested the secretary-general to take the necessary steps. Waldheim proceeded to organize a twelve-hundred-man force, drawing from contingents already assigned to the recently formed UNEF. Peruvian Brigadier General Gonzalo Briceno Zevallos was appointed interim force commander, and by June 3, 1974, UNDOF was operational. Consisting of military units from Austria, Canada, Peru, and Poland, UNDOF was eventually to occupy a three-mile buffer zone in territory nominally under Syrian civil control.

While generally following the format of previous United Nations peacekeeping forces, the authorization of UNEF-2 and UNDOF broke new ground as well. The control of these peacekeeping forces was much more directly under the authority of the Security Council. Each step taken by the secretary-general to carry out the Security Council's mandate was to be submitted to the Council itself, including the appointment of force commanders and the national composition of the forces. Very important, the new UN peacekeeping forces in the Middle East would remain deployed as long as called for by their mandates—six months, initially, and subject to renewal thereafter. In effect, this meant that the withdrawal of the new peacekeeping forces could not be on the Secretariat's initiative but must remain the decision of the Security Council (although it was hard to conceive what could be done, practically speaking, if a contributing nation unilaterally withdrew from the peacekeeping force prior to the expiration of the mandate). Also, for the first time in peacekeeping history, a member of the Warsaw Pact, Poland, was included among the nations whose troops would take part in a United Nations operation.[9] Finally, in addition to their armed military components, both UNEF and UNDOF incorporated the services of unarmed military observers transferred from the United Nations Truce Supervision Organization (UNTSO) headquartered in Jerusalem. UNTSO, the longest-lived of any UN observation mission (in being since 1948), had since 1967 been monitoring the Suez Canal and Golan Heights with unarmed observers. It was anticipated that such unarmed military observers would be used extensively under UNDOF in the Golan Heights, especially in situations where there would be need for contacts with civilian populations.

Peacekeeping Doctrine

The formation of all five of the United Nations peacekeeping forces has occurred, in the face of the inoperativeness of chapter 7 of the UN Charter, with its provisions for collective security enforced by the major powers. But this has led to the emergence of an alternate peacekeeping doctrine. The administrations of each of the secretary-generals have reflected varying political circumstances and personal styles and, consequently, varying modes of adaptation to the peacekeeping enterprise. During the secretaryship of Trygve Lie (1945–53), it early became apparent that U.S.–Soviet antagonisms would make inoperative the collective enforcement measures under Security Council control. Lie's subsequent proposal for a standing UN Guard was ill-conceived and drew support from no quarter. The situation of an anticommunist intervention in Korea under putative United Nations command, and the U.S. sponsorship of the Uniting for Peace resolution (giving peacekeeping authority to the General Assembly) could only exacerbate Soviet alarm—and that of other nations—over UN military forces. To further compound matters, the efficacy of the Secretariat was fundamentally impaired by Soviet perceptions of Lie's pro-Western stance.

With Dag Hammarskjöld at the helm (1953–61), the Secretariat interpreted its peacekeeping responsibilities most broadly and was the prime mover in the establishment of the first UNEF in the Middle East and the peacekeeping force in the Congo. In his well-known summary study of the first UNEF experience, Secretary-General Hammarskjöld enunciated certain "basic principles" for peacekeeping forces: (1) the UN can station units in a territory only with the express consent of the government concerned; (2) the UN alone will decide the composition of its forces with due regard for the desiderata of the host country; (3) major powers should not provide contingents to the UN force; (4) the force must enjoy freedom of movement within the zone of operations; (5) UN personnel cannot be a party to any internal conflict and must maintain strict impartiality; (6) a UN force is an instrument for conciliation and cannot engage in combat activities, though it may respond with force to an armed attack in exercise of the right of self-defense.[10] These principles remain in the bedrock of UN peacekeeping doctrine.

Expanding upon the principles of the secretary-general's summary study, Lester Pearson, who as Canada's foreign minister won the Nobel Peace Prize as co-architect with Hammarskjöld of the first UNEF, set forth further elaboration for UN peacekeeping forces. According to Pearson, neutral middle powers ought to "earmark" military personnel or units in their national armies for possible UN duty, and such contingents should be prepared to perform "essentially noncombatant" tasks in their peacekeeping missions.[11] Since the formation of the first UNEF, about a dozen countries have actually earmarked forces for UN peacekeeping, although the level of preparedness of such forces varies considerably. But the peacekeeping role did make major headway in the national policies of several Western middle powers, most notably, Austria, Canada, Denmark, Finland, Ireland, Norway, and Sweden.

U Thant's secretary-generalship (1961–71) began inauspiciously with a constitutional crisis arising out of the financial burdens of the UN force in the Congo. A collision course between the U.S. and the Soviet Union—the "Article 19 controversy"—was avoided only when the principle was accepted that member states need not bear the obligations of peacekeeping operations to which they do not acquiesce. U Thant declined to imitate the path-breaking ventures of his predecessor, and instead pursued a cautious course in exercising the Secretariat's peacekeeping responsibilities. Nevertheless, he was quite prepared to use energetically the Secretariat in the formation of UNFICYP. Moreover, notwithstanding the setback to the UN's peacekeeping credibility caused by his abrupt withdrawal of the first UNEF, U Thant fostered the practicality of the United Nations peacekeeping by remaining on cooperative terms with all governments.

But it was also the case that, in the wake of ONUC controversies, Thant was more careful than Hammarskjöld in seeing that the Secretariat's peacekeeping initiatives did not strain the political tolerances of the major powers. U Thant went on record as stating that he could foresee no possibility of establishing a permanent UN peacekeeping force in light of United Nations and international realities. He even stated that peacekeeping training for selected military personnel under UN auspices—a Hammarskjöld-Pearson proposal—was premature and impractical. Rather, Thant stressed reliance on a more modest program of improving procedures whereby member states would earmark elements of their armed forces for possible United Nations peacekeeping assignments.[12] It would be fair to state that where Dag Hammarskjöld was prone to take a peacekeeping initiative and then seek to build a consensus around it, U Thant was more likely to engineer a consensus before implementing peacekeeping actions.

The tenure of Secretary-General Kurt Waldheim (1972–) is yet too brief to warrant a definitive characterization. But it does seem likely that the strict constructionist interpretation of the peacekeeping prerogatives of the Secretariat followed by U Thant has been carried on by Waldheim.[13] Moreover, the Waldheim era will probably witness greater major-power involvement in the management of United Nations military forces through the mechanism of closer Security Council supervision. All this confirms a change in the peacekeeping role of the secretary-general. For those who saw in Hammarskjöld's initiatives the promise of an emerging international authority, it may seem like a step backward. But although Hammarskjöld's

successors have seemingly been less versatile, they have nevertheless been more realistic in dealing with the prevailing power. Waldheim, furthermore, has revitalized the peacekeeping responsiveness of the Secretariat by appointing Brian Urquhart, who has succeeded Ralph Bunche as the world's champion of peacekeeping forces, as undersecretary-general. It also appears that the Secretariat's ability to conduct significant peacekeeping operations—the continuation of UNFICYP and the formation of UNDOF and the second UNEF—has been facilitated by the emerging U.S.–Soviet detente and the continued support of the middle powers.[14] As the United Nations approached its fourth decade, the conditions supportive of peacekeeping forces—if not of international peace—appeared to be gaining limited favor.

In sum, the institutional framework of peacekeeping forces is still in the process of definition. Peacekeeping soldiers have performed an arduous task and, with few exceptions, performed it well. The continued volatility of the areas to which they have been deployed, however, speaks too somberly of the limitations of United Nations forces. But the profession of arms in its latest incarnation, in the body of peacekeeping forces, may yet be destined to play a stabilizing role on the international scene.

---

1. Inis L. Claude, Jr., "The Peace-Keeping Role of the United Nations," in E. Berkeley Tompkins, ed., *The United Nations in Perspective* (Stanford, Calif.: Hoover Institution Press, 1972), p. 52. Another insightful overview of United Nations peacekeeping is A. J. R. Groom, "Peacekeeping: Perspectives and Progress," *International Affairs* 47 (April 1971): 340–52.

2. Although regional peacekeeping forces are not included in the purview of the present study, special mention can be made of two such instances. In 1964, Nigerian and Ethiopian military units were sent to Tanzania upon that government's request to the Organization of African Unity. The Nigerian-Ethiopian contingents replaced the British, who had initially been called by President Nyerere to restore order following a mutiny in the Tanzania army. In 1969, following the outbreak of hostilities between El Salvador and Honduras, the Organization of American States was requested by the disputants to send a truce supervising force. In neither the OAU nor the OAS peacekeeping operations, however, did the constituent military units serve under a central command.

3. J. Brind, "League of Nations: Report by the Commander in Chief International Force in the Saar, 26 October, 1935," *IPKO Documentation No. 29* (Paris: International Information Center on Peace-Keeping Operations, 1968).

4. A listing of the more important of these United Nations peacekeeping missions follows: United Nations Commission for Indonesia (UNCI), 1947–51; United Nations Truce Supervision Organization (UNTSO), variously in Palestine, Israel, and Suez sector, 1948–present; United Nations Commission for India and Pakistan (UNCIP), 1948–49, later the United Nations Military Observer Group in India and Pakistan (UNMOGIP) in Kashmir, 1949–present; United Nations Observer Group in Lebanon (UNOGIL), 1958; United Nations Temporary Executive Authority (UNTEA) and United Nations Security Force (UNSF) in West New Guinea (Western Irian), 1962–63; United Nations Yemen Observation Mission (UNYOM), 1962–64; and United Nations India-Pakistan Observation Mission (UNIPOM), 1965–66. Not included as bona-fide peacekeeping operations are those United Nations missions whose impartiality was open to question owing to a too close association with the Western position in Cold War confrontations: United Nations Special Committee on the Balkans (UNSCOB), 1947–54 in Greece; and the United Nations Commission on Korea (UNCOK), 1948–50.

An informative account of the military observer in UN peacekeeping missions is Erling Lund, "Observation Service," in Frydenberg, *Peace-Keeping Experience and Evaluation*, pp. 147–61.

5. Fabian, *Soldiers Without Enemies*, p. 67. It is also germane to note that the expressions "United Nations Military Force" or "United Nations Armed Forces" have been studiously avoided in the designations of all UN peacekeeping forces.

6. Readable and informative accounts of the conflicts within the United Nations force in the Congo from the personal vantage points of key participants are: Connor Cruise O'Brien, *To Katanga and Back: A UN Case History* (New York: Grosset and Dunlap, 1962); and von Horn, *Soldiering For Peace*, pp. 140–252.

7. UN Document, S/4741, 21 February 1961.

8. UN Document, S/5575, 4 March 1963.

9. During the early stages of the Cyprus peacekeeping operation, the Czechoslovakian government offered to contribute a military unit to the United Nations force. But American and British pressure prevailed upon U Thant not to accept the offer. Earlier Czechoslovakia and Rumania had volunteered military units to the first United Nations Emergency Force in the Middle East, but again Western pressures precluded the Secretariat from accepting socialist bloc contingents. Cox, *Prospects for Peacekeeping*, p. 43.

10. UN Document, A/3943, 9 October 1958.

11. Lester Pearson's peacekeeping proposals are cited and discussed in Fabian, *Soldiers Without Enemies*, pp. 82–83.

12. U Thant, "United Nations Peace Force," an address to the Harvard Alumni Association delivered June 13, 1963. UN Press Release SG/1520, 12 June 1963.

13. Starting with Dag Hammarskjöld and continuing with his successors, the secretary-general and his staff have become the executors of peacekeeping arrangements. Legally speaking, the secretary-general's executive management of UN peacekeeping operations derives from Article 97 of the Charter which charges the secretary-general with being the "chief administrative officer of the Organization." But in specific peacekeeping forces, such authority also derives from the authorizing resolutions of the Security Council or General Assembly. In pursuance of the execution of enabling United Nations resolutions, several levels of peacekeeping accords must be negotiated by the Secretariat.

First, there must be a "Status of Forces" agreement with the host country. The significant precedent was established in 1956 with the first UNEF, in an exchange of letters between the secretary-general and the Egyptian government in which explicit terms were set forth on the legal status and privileges of the UN forces, including areas of criminal and civil jurisdiction. Similar status-of-forces agreements were worked out in ONUC, UNFICYP, the second UNEF, and UNDOF. Second, there are "Participating Agreements" between the Secretariat and those states which place their contingents at the disposal of the United Nations. Legal bonds, that is, have to be forged between the United Nations and states participating in peacekeeping operations through a network of bilateral arrangements. Third are the "General Regulations" which specify the command and control guidelines under which the peacekeeping force must operate. Here the subject is delimiting lines of responsibility between the secretary-general, other UN civilian officials, the force commander, and the national contingents. Finally, there are the "Standing Operating Procedures" which are developed by the force commander in consultation with the Secretariat. Such "S.O.P.'s" specify how the peacekeeping force conducts itself on a day-to-day basis, e.g. restrictions on force, nature and frequency of reports, areas of responsibility within the military command, dress and discipline of troops, and so on.

14. Since its admission to the United Nations in 1971, China has not participated in any votes in the Security Council on peacekeeping forces. Symbolically, nonparticipation in a Security Council vote falls between a veto and an abstention. This choice of action reflects China's opposition to the intervention principle implicit in the deployment of peacekeeping forces.

Successful Negotiation by the UN: Mission to Peking

Joseph P. Lash

When Hammarskjöld assumed office the UN had atrophied alarmingly. It was serving neither as an instrument for collective security nor as a center for negotiation and conciliation. Great national weeklies were carrying articles with titles like "The UN Is Dying." On a disquietingly large number of world issues the great powers were by-passing the world organization.

An opportunity to begin restoring the political prerogatives of the UN came with Hammarskjöld's first important political assignment—an Assembly resolution in December 1954, asking him to do what he could to bring about the release of American airmen held prisoners by Red China.

In late fall of 1954 the Peking regime suddenly tried and sentenced as "spies" eleven American airmen who had been shot down in January 1953, while flying a Korean War mission. The Chinese claimed the plane had violated Chinese air space; the U.S. said it had been shot down over North Korea. At the same time it was disclosed Red China was still holding in custody four American jet pilots also shot down during Korean War missions.

Since the Korean Armistice Agreement obligated both sides to repatriate all prisoners of war, a wave of anger swept the U.S. Senator Knowland wanted the U.S. Navy to impose a "tight" blockade on the mainland of China. Faced with demands in Congress and the press and from the China Lobby for retaliatory measures, which President Eisenhower warned were "acts of war" and might split a Western alliance already divided over China policy, the U.S. brought the issue to the General Assembly on December 4.

A resolution presented by the sixteen nations which had provided troops to the Unified Command in Korea, called the detention of the airmen a "violation" of the Armistice Agreement, condemned the trial and conviction of prisoners detained illegally, and then, not knowing what else to do, requested the Secretary-General to make "continuing and unremitting efforts" to bring about the release of the airmen "by the means most appropriate in his judgment."

A friend, Hans Engen, recalled how Hammarskjöld made up his mind on what these "means" might be. Engen, a buoyant, blond-haired old UN hand, was Norway's permanent delegate. Extremely helpful to Hammarskjöld at a time when the UN was *terra incognita* to the Swedish diplomat, his advice and judgment were highly valued.

Hammarskjöld was very dubious about the sixteen-power resolution, which was then only in the drafting stage. In particular he questioned the usefulness of asking the Secretary-General and the UN to do this kind of job when denying one party in the dispute access to the organization. Sending a note to China would fail and further damage UN prestige. But as Hammarskjöld talked with Engen, the creative possibilities of the assignment matured in his mind. He ended the conversation by saying: "If they do, I'll go to Peking."

Hammarskjöld's decision shocked some members of the U.S. delegation. The Administration was already under attack by Senator McCarthy for "weakness" in taking the issue to the UN. When the news got out that Hammerskjöld would go to Peking, the China Lobby group denounced it as a kind of "blood barter."

"Hat in hand, suppliant, and ready to pay a ransom to the blackmailers," was one national news magazine's comment on Hammarskjöld's decision. But there was little the U.S. could do, even if it had wished (which it did not) to stop Hammarskjöld. The resolution made him the sole judge as to the ways and means of accomplishing his difficult mission.

Hammarskjöld's first objective was to "crash the gate" in Peking. This was not at all a foregone conclusion since his mandate originated with a resolution of condemnation. "You either condemn or negotiate; you can't do both," was Hammarskjöld's view. He concluded that it would be impossible to work with the resolution and be received at Peking as agent for the Assembly's decision. He never even sent it on to Peking. He calculated that his main card with Chinese Communists was their realization that an affront to the Secretary-General would not help them gain entry to the UN, something they very much wanted at that time. A rebuff to Hammarskjöld would only slam the UN door more tightly shut and strengthen demands in the U.S. for extremist measures.

Hammarskjöld cabled Premier Chou En-lai that he would like to take up with him personally in Peking the matter of the imprisoned personnel. Chou cabled back: "In the interest of peace and relaxation of international tension, I am prepared to receive you in our capital, Peking, to discuss with you pertinent questions." But in a second cable that was received at the same time, Chou declared there was no justification for the UN to try to interfere in such an internal affair as the conviction of spies by a Chinese court. Chou obviously considered it politically advantageous to have the Secretary-General of the UN come to Peking, but it was still unclear whether he would be willing to discuss the prisoner issue with him and even less clear that there could be any meeting of minds on the issue.

But first the practical arrangements had to be made. Hammarskjöld cabled his friend Uno Willers, Librarian of the Realm, to invite him and the Chinese Ambassador to Willers' home for lunch in Stockholm. He held three meetings with General Keng Piao, discussing possible routes to Peking, the duration of the visit, the set-up of the discussions, the staff that would be needed. One meeting had to be held at the home of Willers' mother in order to avoid the press which by then dogged his every step. The less he was willing to say, the more the world's interest mounted in the movements of this unpretentious man.

It was not only the pathos and human interest of the imprisoned airmen which engaged the imagination of the world, there was the larger drama of American-Chinese relations. In September 1954, the Chinese Communists had begun to bombard the offshore islands, announcing their intention of "liberating" Formosa. Faced with what appeared to be preparations to invade the offshore islands, the U.S. concluded a mutual defense treaty with Nationalist China and President Eisenhower sought authorization from Congress to use American forces in the defense of Formosa and related areas. On both sides there were extremists who wanted a showdown. It was a delicate assignment. Peking's interest was to break out of its isolation. U.S. public opinion still was bitterly opposed to recognition of Red China.

The larger issues were reflected in the farewells to Hammarskjöld and his little group of aides. Ambassador Lodge, who had led the fight in September to prevent Assembly discussion of the issue of Chinese representation, and in October rebuked Hammarskjöld for distributing a message from Chou, was at the airfield to wish Hammarskjöld Godspeed on a journey ending Peking's post-Korean ostracism and the first leg of which would be flown in a U.S. military Constellation piloted by a major who had seen service in Korea.

The delegate of the Soviet Union which had voted against the resolution threw a party for all the permanent delegates the night before Hammarskjöld left, at which the UN chief was the honored guest. Leading the contingent of Secretariat aides who saw Hammarskjöld off at Idlewild was Ilya Tchernyshev, a Soviet Under-Secretary, whom Hammarskjöld left in charge rather than Dr. Ralph Bunche.

En route to Peking, Hammarskjöld obtained appraisals of Chou from Eden in London and French Premier Mendès-France in Paris, both of whom had negotiated with the Chinese Premier in Geneva. Both advised him there were very few negotiators in the world as good as Chou. He would find a man on whom it would be hard to get a grip. Mendès-France added that in the Chinese Prime Minister he would find a *grand seigneur*, a statesman not only conscious of his own power, but a man who spoke with the self-confidence of a family which had been part of China's ruling class for a thousand years.

It was bitterly cold in Peking when Hammarskjöld and his party arrived. The winds from the Mongolian plains blew down icily. But within the Heavenly City, Hammarskjöld and Chou talked for four days amid a growing thaw. The two men were remarkably alike. Both were patricians, one a Marxist mandarin and the other a welfare state aristocrat, and a rapport was quickly established. Their formal conversations in the Hall of the Western Flowers lasted more than 13½ hours over four afternoons. "The whole atmosphere was of great earnestness," said Dr. Bokhari, the scholarly Pakistani who served as Hammarskjöld's political adviser on the trip. "There was not a sound, not a noise of any kind in the whole room," he added, except for attendants unobtrusively serving Chinese tea in tall lidded Chinese cups.

There were also dinners and receptions in the Hall of the Purple Light with menus that included consommé of swallows' nests, Peking duck, lotus seed soup, mandarin fish. There were excursions to the summer palace and the Ming

Dynasty tombs, with Hammarskjöld walking "at a terrific pace, without a hat," according to Bokhari, a partisan of less strenuous pleasures.

The formal talks were very involved and subtle. "If I express myself in circumscribed terms, it is nothing compared to Chou," Hammarskjöld commented later. Chou used exceedingly indirect language and expected the Secretary-General to do the same. The subtlety of Chinese diplomacy made him feel like a vulgar barbarian, "and you know I am not a complete amateur at this business."

Their first problem was to find a formula to get around the difficulty of Chou's discussing a matter which China maintained was its own internal affair with an international organization from which it was banned.

The prescription invented by Hammarskjöld subsequently came to be known as the "Peking formula." The discussion was held not on the basis of the General Assembly resolution, which Peking rejected, but on the basis of the authority of the Secretary-General under the Charter. Agreement by Chou to discuss the issue of the airmen did not require prior recognition by Peking of the UN's authority or advance agreement to accept the Secretary-General's conclusions.

In cutting himself loose from the resolution, and dealing with Peking on the basis of his general authority under the Charter, Hammarskjöld was able to discuss with Chou not only the issue of the airmen but "other pertinent" issues as well. This involved the whole gamut of Far Eastern problems. Hammarskjöld took the view that if the Secretary-General find that a situation may become a threat to peace and security, he is entitled to raise the matter with the government involved to ascertain whether it might be possible to take preventive action.

In the case of the airmen, Hammarskjöld was familiar with the strength of U.S. feelings aroused by their sentencing as well as post-Korean pressures in the U.S. regarding China policy. The conviction of the airmen under Chinese law might be a domestic affair, but it could have the most serious international repercussions, he told Chou. While the Secretary-General did not have a right to mix into the internal affairs of China, he was entitled to discuss the matter in view of its international repercussions.

Chou replied that the People's Republic of China recognized the UN Charter, the Secretary-General and his concern in the matter. It was legitimate for him to bring the issue up.

That having been established, Hammarskjöld went on to place before Chou the full and complete case for the release of the convicted men.

By the time he left Peking, Hammarskjöld's conclusion was that the airmen would be freed, but it would jeopardize the outcome to say so. Peking needed time to dissociate the freeing of the airmen from any appearance of yielding to pressure. Hammarskjöld figured six months.

Secondly, Hammarskjöld felt Peking would need a peg. That was the idea of permitting the families of the fliers to visit them. The family visits were never posed as a condition, but would enable Peking to save face, being in accordance with a traditional amnesty pattern in China.

The communiqué at the end of the talks was much less communicative. It said only the talks had been "useful," would "continue," and that reference "was made at the same time to questions pertinent to the relaxation of world tensions."

No deals of any kind had been made, he told a mammoth press conference back at UN headquarters. "The door has been opened and can be kept open given restraint on all sides," which meant, he explained, no reacting "prematurely" or "blasting" away.

One hitch developed very quickly when Secretary Dulles flatly turned down the idea of family visits. A State Department announcement said that the U.S. Government could not "in good conscience encourage those who may wish to go into an area where the normal protections of an American passport cannot be offered." This was not the real issue. The UN declared publicly that "Secretary-General Dag Hammarskjöld has no doubt about the safety of those members of the families wishing to visit China to see their men." The real issue was not safety of the families, but fear on the part of the U.S. that Peking would exploit the family visits to push the U.S. further in the direction of negotiations than it was prepared to go. Dulles was persuaded it was first necessary to convince Red China that the U.S. was no "paper tiger."

"One of the most curious and most upsetting features about the present world situation is that everybody is afraid of everybody," Hammarskjöld commented at the time.

It was his duty, he thought, to explain to Peking and Washington the other side's viewpoint, "as well as one can and as deeply as you can understand them. . . . "

Many of America's allies were urging it to make some military adjustments, such as withdrawal from the offshore islands, but Hammarskjöld did not have any particular measure in mind. He sought instead to create an atmosphere which would give those in China and the U.S. who wanted a *rapprochement*, something with which to work. But he also was very anxious not to be in a position where he appeared to be prodding the Americans.

Despite the rebuff on the family visits, Hammarskjöld continued discreetly to press both sides—the U.S. to keep the door open, Peking to go ahead with the release of the airmen.

As the weeks passed and nothing happened, clamor began to mount again in the U.S. on the subject of the airmen. On April 19 he told the press at UN headquarters that he was going to Stockholm to attend a working session of the Swedish Academy.

In fact, he went to meet with the Chinese Ambassador. He had considered the matter as settled, he told General Piao, at the time he had been in Peking, except for China's need for time and a peg. The General agreed with his assessment of the situation. Time was running out, Hammarskjöld noted. What remains was the need for a peg. Was there anything that could be done?

The Chinese found their peg. A representative of the Chinese Embassy met Uno Willers at a Soviet party at about this time. He learned on inquiry that Hammarskjöld would be in Sweden during the summer and that it would be his birthday. That was "very interesting," he commented. What would Hammarskjöld like for his birthday? "Books, Chinese paintings, but, most of all," replied Willers, "release of the airmen." Twice, subsequently, the Embassy called to check the date of Hammarskjöld's birthday.

On August 1, two days after Hammarskjöld's birthday, he was at his cottage in Löderup, a small village in the south of Sweden. There he received a message from the Chinese Government that they would in a few days release the airmen, not because of the Assembly decision but in order to maintain and strengthen friendship with the Secretary-General, ending with congratulations to Hammerskjöld on his birthday. Personal courtesy was what they finally used as the peg.

Goodbye War

Gwynne Dyer

There is a terrifying automatism in the way we have marched straight toward scientific total war over the past few centuries, undeterred by the mounting cost and the dictates of reason and self-interest. We *do* know what is going to happen, and we are frightened, but we do none of the seemingly obvious things that might let us alter our course away from oblivion. We resemble a column of intelligent lemmings, holding earnest meetings to denounce the iniquity of cliffs during halts in the march. Everybody agrees that falling off cliffs is a bad idea, many have noticed that the cliff edge is getting steadily closer, and some have come to the heretical conclusion that the column's own line of march is causing this to happen. But nobody can leave the column, and at the end of each halt it sets off again in the same direction.

I do not mean this as a purely rhetorical analogy: there is a serious question as to whether civilization was a wise experiment. We were doing quite nicely without it, compared to other large land animal species, and seemed set for a successful run of some millions of years. Here we are, only ten thousand years into the experiment, facing a crisis of vast proportions which we can now see was inevitable once we took the civilized road. War and the state were centrally important elements in our strategy for gaining more control over our environment, but they have brought us inescapably to our present dilemma, which involves the potential extinction of the human species.

[The prospect of a nuclear winter] raises the stakes of nuclear war enormously. . . . A nuclear war imperils all our descendants, for as long as there will be humans. Even if the population remains static . . . over a typical time period for the biological evolution of a successful species (roughly ten million years), we are talking about some 500 trillion people yet to come. By this criterion, the stakes are one million times greater for extinction than for the more modest nuclear wars that kill "only" hundreds of millions of people.

—Carl Sagan[1]

Nature has no principles; she furnishes us with no reason to believe that human life is to be respected—or any particular species either: just look what happened to the ammonites and pterodactyls.

—Victor Hugo

High intelligence, at least in the form represented by the human species, may prove not to be an evolutionary trait favorable to survival. The potentially fatal flaw is that our intelligence tends to produce technological and social change at a rate faster than our institutions and emotions can cope with—and this tendency becomes more pronounced the deeper we get into the experiment of civilization, because innovation is cumulative and the rate of change accelerates. We therefore find ourselves continually trying to accommodate new realities within inappropriate existing institutions, and trying to think about those new realities in traditional but sometimes dangerously irrelevant terms. Our treatment of nuclear war is a striking and perhaps terminal example of this behavior.

It is very probable that we began our career as a rising young species by exterminating our nearest relatives, the Neanderthals, and it is entirely possible we will end it by exterminating ourselves, but the universe is not in the business of dealing out poetic justice. Nor are we instinctively ferocious killers of our own kind. It is not some fatal flaw in our nature that now threatens our survival, but something much more prosaic: our political institutions, and the habits of thought which support them, are adapting too slowly to stay in control of the awesome powers of creation and destruction we are now acquiring. One might have wished for something grander, but if we go under as a species that will be our epitaph.

Yet, I do not believe we could or should have refused to set out on our present course, whatever the dangers. Civilization has given us a capacity for knowledge and love we could not have had in any other way—and in any case, intelligence is our main competitive advantage as a species, so we were bound to experiment with developing its potential to the fullest. The fact that this strategy also turns us into very high rollers, in evolutionary terms, is just part of the bargain.

If we succeed, we get to dominate every other species, leave the planet, understand the workings of the universe, and even learn how to protect ourselves from natural catastrophes utterly beyond the comprehension, let alone control, of any other species. If we fail to control our powers, on the other hand, we will kill ourselves off very quickly. But, win or lose, being human is a lot more interesting than being a turtle.

■

We must get the modern national state before it gets us.

—Dwight MacDonald, 1945[2]

Justice without force is a myth.

—Blaise Pascal

The solution to the state of international anarchy which compels every state to arm itself for war was so obvious that it arose almost spontaneously in the aftermath of the first total war in 1918. The wars by which independent states had always settled their quarrels in the past had grown so monstrously destructive that some alternative system had to be devised, and that could only be a pooling of sovereignty, at least in matters concerning war and peace, by all the states of the world. So the victors of the World War I promptly created the League of Nations.

But the solution was as difficult in practice as it was simple in concept. Great nations with long traditions of absolute independence and deep-rooted suspicions of their neighbors do not easily abandon all their habits just because they have created some new institution that will allegedly take care of their security problems. The idea that all the nations of the world will band together to deter or punish aggression by some maverick country is fine in principle, but who defines the aggressor, and who pays the cost in money and lives that may be needed to make him stop?

More specifically, every member of the League of Nations was well aware that if the organization somehow acquired the ability to act in a concerted and effective fashion, it could end up being used against them. So no major government was willing to give the League of Nations any real power in practice—and therefore they got World War II instead.

That war was so bad—by the end the first nuclear weapons had been used on cities—that the victors made a second and much more serious attempt in 1945 to create an international organization that really could prevent war. The United Nations Charter was a great deal more realistic about the role of power in the world: It made the five victorious great powers permanent members of the Security Council and gave them the right to veto any U.N. action of which they disapproved. It also gave them the right to coerce any other government into submission by armed forces operating under the U.N. flag, if they could agree that its actions represented a danger to peace. These arrangements didn't work either, however, because the five great powers at once fell apart into two hostile military blocs—as victorious nations almost always do after a great war, simply because as the largest surviving military powers in the world, they automatically represent the greatest potential threats to each other's security.

> *If the permanent members [of the Security Council] had stuck together as the wartime alliance in peacetime, they would have constituted, for better or worse, a very genuine, powerful authority in the world ... but of course, there was never any chance of that.... I don't see very much sign of governments, in advance, relinquishing elements of national sovereignty to an international organization which they can't control.*
>
> *It's going to be a very long time before governments are prepared in fact to submit to limitations on their national policies by an international body. Of course, in theory they've all said they wold do that in the Charter, and they're all for everybody else doing it—but when it gets to a particular government having to do that, it's not so easy. Not least because you've got a tremendous domestic opposition to it, very often.*
>
> —Brian Urquhart, under secretary-general, United Nations

It would be futile and depressing to catalogue the stages by which the United Nations rapidly declined after 1945 from its intended role as a genuine world authority able to prevent war to its present status as a largely powerless talking-shop. It would also be misleading, because the implication would be that this was an enterprise that might have succeeded from the start, and has instead failed irrevocably. On the contrary, it was bound to be a relative failure at the outset, and that is no cause for despair. Obviously, it was always going to be extremely hard to persuade sovereign governments whose institutions have served them and their predecessors well for ten thousand years to surrender any significant measure of power to an untried world authority which might then make decisions that were against their particular interests, and progress will necessarily be measured in small steps even over a period of decades.

In the words of the traditional Irish directions to a lost traveler: "If that's where you want to get to, sir, I wouldn't start from here." But here is where we must start from, for it is states that run the world. There is no point in yearning for some universal Gandhi who could change the human heart and release us from our bondage to considerations of national interest and power. We do not behave as we do for stupid or paltry reasons: those considerations really matter. We no longer can afford to settle our conflicts by war, but there is no simple solution to the problem of war which magically bypasses the existing structure of power in the world.

That structure exists to defend the many conflicting interests of the multitude of separate human communities in the world. It is true that the present nature of the international system, based on heavily armed and jealously independent states, often exaggerates the element of conflict in relations between these communities and sometimes even creates perceptions of conflict and threat where genuine interests are not at stake, but the system does reflect an underlying reality. Namely, we cannot all get all we want, and some method must exist to decide who gets what.

At the international level, that method traditionally has been a brutally simple test of strength through war. If we now must abandon that method of settling our disputes and devise an alternative, it only can be done with the full cooperation of the world's governments. That means it certainly will be a monumentally difficult and lengthy task, but it is the only relevant one. Because it is the absolute independence of national governments, and the consequent need to protect their interests with their own armed forces, that is the source of war in the first place.

As to how governments can be persuaded to do what is now required of them, that is a more difficult problem. Some are more responsive than others to the opinions of their citizens, but the main incentive for any of them to cooperate with the United Nations is a recognition that it is in their own broader self-interest—that of long-term survival—to do so. That is manifestly true, but politics is mainly the art of managing short-term problems.

The short-term disadvantages which might ensue from a surrender of sovereignty to the United Nations have deterred every national government from making any serious gesture in that direction. Mistrust reigns everywhere, and no nation will allow even the least of its interests to be decided upon by a collection of foreigners. Some existing regimes, by their very nature, would find it almost impossible to recognize the authority of any institution which did not profess their own ideological values: consider, for example, the Soviet Union or Iran. There are other governments—with major unsatisfied claims to "lost" territories which would almost certainly be frozen permanently by a genuine world authority in the interest of peace—that could not hope to survive domestically if they gave up the right to engage in war in pursuit of their national goals. Even the majority of states which are more or less satisfied with their borders and their status in the world would face great internal opposition from nationalistic elements if they were to consider even the most limited transfer of sovereignty to the United Nations.

Although nobody is thinking in terms of a "world government" that would collect the garbage and decide on local speed limits, the nationalists of all countries are quite right to worry about what a powerful United Nations might mean. The United Nations was created to end war—"not to bring mankind to Heaven, but to save it from Hell," in Dag Hammarskjöld's words—and its founders were fully aware that in order to do that it had to be able to guarantee each country's safety from attack by its neighbors, and to make decisions on international disputes *and enforce them*. Neither order nor justice can be imposed without at least the threat of superior force, if not its actual use, so a United Nations that worked obviously would require powerful armed forces under its own command. (Indeed, the U.N. Charter makes provisions for member countries to contribute contingents to just such an armed force.)

That is why the United Nations has never worked as designed: a truly effective United Nations would have the ability to coerce national governments, so naturally they refuse to give it the powers it would need to do so. They all know what

they must do to end international war, have known it since 1945 at the latest, but are not yet willing to do it. The possibility of their own interests being damaged somewhere down the line by the decisions of a United Nations grown too powerful to resist is so great a deterrent that they prefer to go on living with the risk of war. (That is, until the risk of some particular war involving them grows too great, or a war in which they are directly involved goes badly wrong. Then national governments are very glad to use the United Nations' fictitious authority to get themselves off the hook—and this applies especially to the superpowers, who have repeatedly used the United Nations in order to back away gracefully from dangerous confrontations.)

The United Nations as presently constituted is certainly no place for idealists, but they would feel even more uncomfortable in a United Nations that actually worked as was originally intended. It is, after all, an association of poachers turned gamekeepers, not an assembly of saints. Even if the organization eventually does gain some of the authority the member states have theoretically granted it, it is certain that the collective rights and interests of those states will be preserved, especially against their own citizens.

One of the implications of a powerful United Nations which is rarely discussed by its advocates (for obvious reasons) is that a world authority founded on the collaboration of national governments would inevitably attempt to freeze the existing political dispensation in the world in the interests of its members, or at least drastically slow down the rate of change. As a result, national and ethnic communities not already possessing legitimate states of their own would lose almost all possibility of gaining them in the future, simply because they didn't make it under the wire in time. If the established sovereign states of the world had created some equivalent of the United Nations with real power in the mid-eighteenth century—a mutual protection association that guaranteed their territories—the United States might never have won its independence from Britain. If they did it today, Lithuania, Tibet, and Zanzibar could abandon all hope of recovering their independent political existence, and Eritreans, Kurds, and Basques might as well forget their hopes of ever achieving it. (Not that any of them has much chance anyway.)

Even as presently constituted, the United Nations tends to place legitimacy above all other considerations. It still recognizes, for example, the Khmer Rouge as the legitimate government of Cambodia, despite its horrific record, because it was displaced by the illegitimate method of foreign invasion. Eventually some deal will be done, no doubt, and the new reality in Cambodia will be formally recognized. But the more power the United Nations is granted by its members, the more it will have to reciprocate by acting to defend their existing interests and possessions.

The consequences would be quite oppressive to many people and some would rebel. Guerrilla wars, terrorism, and other forms of armed protest against the existing distribution of power would not only continue, but might well increase. The most that could be expected, even from a United Nations with teeth, for a century or so, is an end to large-scale international war. Internal conflict, including the use of violence in pursuit of political objectives, would not vanish from the world even if all legitimate governments signed their armed forces over to the United Nations tomorrow.

There is a further, even more distasteful, implication to a United Nations with real power: it would not make its decisions according to some impartial standard of justice. There is no impartial concept of justice to which all of mankind would subscribe and, in any case, it is not "mankind" that makes decisions at the United Nations, but governments with their own national interests to protect. To envision how a functioning "world authority" might reach its decisions, at least in its first century or so, begin with the arrogant promotion of self-interest by the great powers that would continue to dominate U.N. decision-making and add in the crass expediency masked as principle which characterizes the shifting conditions among the lesser powers in the present General Assembly. It would be an intensely *political* process. The decisions it produced would be kept within reasonable bounds only by the overriding shared recognition that the

organization never must act in a way so damaging to the interest of any major member or group of members that it forced them into total defiance, and so destroyed the fundamental consensus that kept war at bay.

There is nothing shocking about this. National politics in every country operates with the same combination: a little bit of principle, a lot of power, and a final constraint on the ruthless exercise of that power based mainly on the need to preserve the essential consensus on which the nation is founded and to avoid civil war. In an international organization whose members represent such radically different traditions, interests, and levels of development, the proportion of principle to power is bound to be even lower. But as a navy petty officer used to tell us many years ago whenever he gave us the latest piece of unavoidable bad news: "If you can't take a joke, you shouldn't have joined."

It's a pity there is no practical alternative to the United Nations, because otherwise nobody would dream of creating the kind of cumbersome and meddlesome monster that a powerful world authority will probably prove to be. Most of us already feel burdened by too much government within our own national states. Adding another layer of government above that—particularly one which would function on such a crudely pragmatic level and would have to take into consideration the views and interests of people whose traditions and priorities were radically different from our own—is a prospect that is frankly dismaying.

There is no need to panic, of course, because such a thing is not going to happen in our lifetimes. Perhaps it will be less dismaying to our descendants, who *will* have to live with it (if they live at all). But the political unification of the world, on some sort of extremely loose federal basis, is virtually a certainty in the long run; the tide has been running strongly in that direction for several centuries now. Indeed, the present political fragmentation of the world into more than 150 stubbornly independent territorial units is already an anachronism, for in every other context, from commerce, technology, and the mass media to fashions in ideology, music, and marriage, the outlines of a single-global culture (with wide local variations) are visibly taking shape. National governments naturally resist the diminution of their powers that would occur if they too were to conform to this trend, but they have no good alternatives in the long run.

> *There are two possibilities, it seems to me. The first one is that we run into another global disaster, which doubtless, if there's anything left, will finally change people's minds about the benefits of unlimited national sovereignty. The second alternative is something much more gradual and slower, which is that we convince governments that, just as they have given up sovereignty in certain specialized fields—for example, radio frequencies or postal systems or something like that—that they have to do this also in the political field.*
>
> —Brian Urquhart

We consent to all the impositions and inconveniences of a distinct and unwieldy government apparatus at the national level because, in the final analysis, its benefits outweigh its costs. For all its drawbacks, it provides us with civil peace, a measure of protection from the rival ambitions of other national communities, and a framework for large-scale cooperation in pursuing whatever goals we set ourselves as a national society. All the same arguments theoretically operate with equal strength in favor of an international authority—even more strongly, given the catastrophic consequences that await us if we do not manage to contain the military rivalries of our separate sovereign states within such an organization.

Yet it is not surprising there is no widespread popular support for the surrender of sovereignty to the United Nations in any major country in the world. Most people are reluctant to accept that war and national sovereignty are indissolubly linked, and that to be rid of one they must also relinquish much of the other. The instinctive belief in the need for complete national independence is so strong in most people that change will inevitably be very slow.

Curiously (or perhaps not so curiously), that belief tends to be less strong in governments than in the people they govern. The United Nations was not founded by popular demand. It was created by *governments* who were terrified by where the existing system was leading them, and could not afford to ignore the grim realities of the situation by taking refuge in the comforting myths about independence and national security that pass for truth in domestic political discourse. The people who actually have the responsibility for running foreign policy in most countries, and especially in the great powers, know that the present international system is in potentially terminal trouble, and many of them have drawn the necessary conclusion.

It goes against the grain to speak well of diplomats, but I suspect if they didn't have to worry about the enormous domestic political resistance to any surrender of sovereignty, the foreign policy professionals in almost every country (without regard to ideology) would immediately make the minimum concessions necessary to create a functioning world authority, because they understand the alternative. Many of the more reflective military professionals would concur for the same reason.

But it is politicians who are in charge of states, and even if they understand the realities of the situation themselves (which many of them do not, for their backgrounds and their primary concerns are usually in domestic issues, not international affairs), politicians cannot afford to get too far ahead of the people they lead. Nevertheless, progress has been made.

We are already some small distance (perhaps as far as anybody could reasonably expect) down the road we must travel if we are eventually to escape from the danger of wars that would threaten our survival. The enormous growth of international organizations since 1945, and especially the existence of the United Nations as a permanent forum where the states of the world talk about the avoidance of war (and occasionally do something about it) already has created a historically new situation. We are not moving fast enough, but there is no doubt we are beginning to adapt our institutions to the lethal new realities that were made brutally clear to us by World War II.

> *People often wonder why it is that one continues to batter away here in the U.N. In the first place, it's extremely interesting. If you want to watch the human tragicomedy, this is a terrific front-row seat, and every now and then you can do something about it. You* can *stop somebody from being executed, you* can *prevent somewhere from being destroyed. It's a drop in the bucket, but ... you can sometimes control a conflict—and the most important thing is to provide a place where the nuclear powers can get out of their confrontations.... As Hammarskjöld once said, while none of us are ever going to see the world order we dream of appear in our lifetime, nonetheless the effort to build that order is the difference between anarchy and a tolerable degree of chaos.*

—Brian Urquhart

∎

At best, we all will live out our lives amid this barely tolerable chaos, permanently poised on the brink of something infinitely worse, and the most that any of us can do is to try to push things some tiny distance in the direction they must eventually go if the race is to survive. In this effort, formal arms control agreements have a certain limited usefulness (more for their symbolic value as indications that both sides wish to avoid war, perhaps, than for any real decrease in the potential destructiveness of war they allegedly achieve). There is one disarmament measure that would have the highest practical value: an agreement to reduce the world's stockpile of nuclear weapons below the threshold (roughly 500 to 2000 warheads) at which an all-out war would be likely to trigger a nuclear winter. But because that would require the superpowers to cut their nuclear arsenals by more than 90 percent, it will be rather difficult to attain.[3]

In general, however, arms races are only responses to real or perceived strategic confrontations, and it is the attitudes which we and our governments bring to these confrontations that constitute the gravest danger to peace. In the long run institutions must change, but we would be a good deal safer in the meantime if the citizens and governments of the great powers could learn to believe in the fear of others, and stop demonizing the "enemy."

Our beliefs about the nature of fear have special relevance for the theory of nuclear deterrence, which is founded on some singularly unrealistic ideas about how human beings perceive and react to threats. It is readily observable in ordinary life that the greater an individual's own fear, the more difficulty he has believing his opponent is feeling similar fear. There is an overwhelming tendency to treat the source of our fear not as human beings like ourselves, but as a blind, malevolent force which only can be managed by threats.

Threats are the very essence of deterrence, but both sides habitually fall into the same logical trap. Any deterrent threats *we* make are justifiable and nonprovocative by definition, because our fear is real and unquestionable—but they should not produce fear in our opponent unless his intention is to attack us, because *we* know that our intentions are purely defensive. Thus when our opponent responds to our threats not with mere passivity (why doesn't he just take our word that our intentions are good?), but by making his own counterthreats, we are confirmed in our conviction of his evil intentions. Naturally, we reply by piling up yet more threats of our own— again perfectly justifiable, because *our* fear is real. Every time some proposal emerges for yet another weapon to "reinforce deterrence," we should ask: how would we react if an enemy whom we feared were to deploy this weapon against us?

As for the "peace movement" in particular, it is both a manifestation of some of those changes of attitude which may eventually enable us to escape from our present dilemma and a stimulus to further change. By and large, the peace movement in each country only can affect the behavior of its own government. Its most important long-term goal, therefore, should be creating a domestic climate of opinion which will not rebel in narrow nationalistic wrath when hard choices eventually have to be made and some elements of national sovereignty must be surrendered for the sake of survival.

If this priority is accepted, however, there are major implications for the strategy of peace movements. They should resist the naive temptation to reject all the existing structures of governmental power as corrupt and irrelevant, and recognize that they need allies at the heart of those structures. They already have some secret allies there, and what they, and others who might join them, most need is to be freed of the domestic constraint of primitive nationalism that shackles them to traditional policies.

To be effective as agents of (slow) change with a broad public appeal, peace movements must avoid a descent into sectarian dogmatism at all costs. Changing popular attitudes toward peace and war and, above all, sovereignty, is a long process that can only be accomplished one step at a time. It would be foolish to reject the support of those who are not ready to accept the ultimate objective if they are at least willing to support the next step. The peace movement needs all the allies it can get. And although the fear of nuclear weapons is its most effective means of mobilizing popular support, it should not allow itself to fall into the simplistic trap of blaming our peril on the weapons or, worse yet, the soldiers.

Soldiers are not the enemies of peace. They are there to do our bidding, and to pay the price of our ambitions and our mistakes. They probably always will be there in one form or another, for conflict and the need to impose order are not likely to disappear from the human world no matter what kind of changes we make in our institutions. But the kinds of international wars we now ask them to prepare for and fight in are destructive far beyond any rational proportion between ends and means, and so *that* form of conflict must be changed and brought under control. Relatively few soldiers can see how this might be achieved in practice (knowing what they do about the roles of force and irrationality in the world), but the military profession probably has a clearer instinctive understanding of how much such a change would cost, if it could be achieved, than most civilians.

The rest of us, most of the time, still believe that we can have our cake and eat it too: we want both peace and independence, and we talk of international security and national sovereignty as though they were not mutually exclusive concepts. The ideas are all jumbled together in our minds, and sorting them out will be a lengthy and painful process.

■

The military makes demands which few if any other callings do. And of course emotionally disturbed people talk about being trained to kill. . . . The whole essence of being a soldier is not to slay but to be slain. You offer yourself up to be slain, rather than setting yourself up as a slayer. Now one can get into very deep water here, but there's food for thought in it.

—Gen. Sir John Hackett

Go, tell the Spartans, you who pass by, That here, obedient to their laws, we lie.

—Epitaph for Leonidas and the 300 who died holding the pass at Thermopylae, Simonides 480 B.C.

The universe is so vast and so ageless that the life of one man can only be justified by the measure of his sacrifice.

By one of the miserable coincidences in which war abounds, those were the last words Pilot Officer V. A. Rosewarne wrote to his mother before he was shot down and killed, at the age of 24, in the battle of Britain. His mother sent his last letter to *The Times*, which published it on 18 June 1940. The words are now inscribed on the wall of the Royal Air Force Museum in north London.

Rosewarne probably did not say those words to himself as he fell out of the sky in his burning Spitfire, but he did mean them. Strip away all the rhetoric, and the core remains: we expect our young men to sacrifice their lives for us if war comes, and they are willing to be asked.

We cannot help believing that a sacrifice like Rosewarne's—one which hundreds of thousands of young men make every year— confers a kind of dignity on those who make it, and also on those for whom it is done. It is a deeply entrenched notion in any culture with a military tradition, and that is practically every culture on earth. However, in most wars of the past half-century the civilian dead have outnumbered the military casualties, and in a total war today there would be a hundred dead civilians for every soldier killed. The ancient compact between ourselves and our soldiers has become meaningless and we cannot go on pretending it still works.

But the essential idea of sacrifice does not become meaningless. It's just that we can no longer place that burden solely on our young men. Instead of asking them to die in war so the nation can get its way, we will all have to make the lesser sacrifices necessary to avoid war.

Lesser sacrifices, but not small ones. We will not avoid war of unimaginable destructiveness just by expressions of good will. We will have to stop trying to make ourselves invulnerable to others (not that it is possible nowadays anyway), and we will have to let all sorts of foreigners who think in strange ways have a say in what we do. It will hurt, and it will cost us dearly.

In short, we will have to give up our precious independence—not all of it, or all at once, but quite a lot of it over just a few generations. It may sound naive to talk of independent states ever relinquishing even the smallest fraction of their sovereignty, but they now have a very powerful incentive: the need to survive.

Our principal source of hope, in what is admittedly a quite desperate situation, is that the human race is not only intelligent but extremely malleable. To a large extent, we are our own invention: the values we now hold and the ways we now behave are often quite drastic modifications of those we started out with at the dawn of civilization. The changes were necessary in order for us to live in large groups within a civilized society, and we were able to make them. More changes are needed now, and we can make them, too, if we have the will and enough time. Indeed, the most fundamen-

tal change of attitude which must occur if we are to survive the present dilemma *is* already underway: large numbers of people, especially in the great industrialized states whose next war might destroy mankind's future, are gradually moving beyond "tribal" definitions of humanity.

There is a slow but quite perceptible revolution in human consciousness taking place: the last of the great redefinitions of humanity. At all times in our history we have run our affairs on the assumption that there is a special category of people (our lot) whom we regard as full human beings, having rights and duties approximately equal to our own, and whom we ought not to kill even when we quarrel. Over the past fifteen or twenty thousand years we have successfully widened this category from the original hunting-and-gathering band of a couple of hundred people to encompass larger and larger groups. First it was the tribe of some thousands of people bound together by kinship and ritual ties: then the state, where we recognize our shared interests with millions of people whom we don't know and will never meet; and now, finally, the entire human race.

There was nothing in the least idealistic or sentimental in any of the previous redefinitions. They occurred because they were useful in advancing people's material interests and ensuring their survival. The same is self-evidently true for this final act of redefinition: we have reached a point where our moral imagination must expand again to embrace the whole of mankind, or else we will perish.

Both the necessary shift in cultural perspective and the creation of political institutions which will reflect the new perspective are clearly changes that must take a very long time. We already have been immersed in this process for most of a century, and it is hard to believe we are even halfway to our goal yet.

To the reasonable objection that not all cultures are changing at the same speed, and that it would be dangerous for us (virtuous us) to get too far ahead of the rest, one can only say there is certainly no imminent danger of that happening. Perhaps, in twenty or fifty years, there will come a time when some recalcitrant countries who are still wedded to absolute national independence backed by military force will become an obstacle that compels all the others to slow down their transfer of sovereignty to an international authority. But we'll have to cross that bridge when we come to it. At the moment, when *all* countries are recalcitrant, the risks involved in trying to change things just a little—the most that can be hoped for— are incomparably less than the risks of standing pat with the present system.

As for the argument that there will never be universal brotherhood among mankind, and so any attempt to move beyond the current system of national states is foredoomed: of course we aren't going to end up loving one another indiscriminately, but that isn't necessary. There is not universal love and brotherhood *within* national states either. What does exist, and what must now be extended beyond national borders, is a mutual recognition that everybody is better off if they respect each other's rights and accept arbitration by a higher authority rather than shooting each other when their rights come into conflict.

There is no irony in the fact that the period in which the concept of the national state is finally coming under challenge by a wider definition of humanity is also the period which has seen history's most catastrophic wars, for they provide the practical incentive that drives the process of change. There would be no possibility of change without the wars, but the transition to a different system is a risky business. The danger of another world war which would cut the whole process short and perhaps put a permanent end to civilization is small in any given year, but cumulatively, given how long the process of change will take, it is extreme. That is no reason not to keep trying.

However deficient in many ways the United Nations may be, I think it's an absolutely essential organization. There is no way in which this effort cannot be made—it has to be made—knowing perfectly well that you're pushing an enormous boulder up a very steep hill. There will be slips and it will come back on you from time to time, but you have to go on pushing. Because if you don't do that, you simply give in to the notion that you're going to go into a global war again at some point, this time with nuclear weapons.

—Brian Urquhart

If we should succeed over the next few generations in transforming the world of independent states in which we live into some sort of genuine international community, however quarrelsome, discontented, and full of injustice it probably will be, then we shall effectively have abolished the ancient institution of warfare as well—and teachers of the twenty-fifth century will bore students with tedious explanations of how the Era of the Sovereign State was inevitably accompanied by ten thousand years of war. The students will pay little attention, being caught up in whatever crises trouble civilization in their own time. If we should fail, however, there probably will be no teachers, no students, and no civilization.

Some generation of mankind was eventually bound to face the task of abolishing war, because civilization was bound to endow us sooner or later with the power to destroy ourselves. We happen to be that generation, though we did not ask for the honor and do not feel ready for it. There is nobody wiser who will take the responsibility and solve this problem for us. We have to do it ourselves.

---

1. Carl Sagan, "Nuclear War and Climatic Catastrophe: Some Policy Implications." *Foreign Affairs*, Winter 1983–84, p. 275.

2. Dwight MacDonald, *Politics*, August 1945.
3. Sagan, op. cit., pp. 275–84.

References

Adams, Gordon. 1986. "Economic Conversion: A Rejoinder." *Bulletin of the Atomic Scientists* June–July: 50–51.

Arkin, William and Lynne R. Dobrofsky. 1978. "Military Socialization and Masculinity." *Journal of Social Issues* 34: 151–68.

Bahro, Rudolf. 1982. "A New Approach for the Peace Movement in Germany." Pp. 87–96, 105–109, 113–116 in *Exterminism and the Cold War,* Edward P. Thompson, et al. (eds.). New York, NY: Schocken Books.

Baker, Mark. 1982. "Making War: Soldiers in Vietnam." Pp. 35–37, 98–102, 190–191, and 230–236 in *Nam: The Vietnam War in the Words of the Men and Women Who Fought There.* New York, NY: William Morrow & Co.

Bronfenbrenner, Urie. 1961. "The Mirror Image in Soviet-American Relations: A Social Psychologist's Report." Excerpted from *Journal of Social Issues* 16: 45–56.

Broyles, William, Jr. 1984. "Why Men Love War." *Esquire* 102, November: 55–65.

Cancian, Francesca M. 1989. "A Conversation on War, Peace, and Gender." Unpublished manuscript. Dept. of Sociology, University of California, Irvine, CA 92717. Prepared for this volume.

Cockburn, Alexander and James Ridgeway. From an original speech by Seymour Melman. 1983. "The Economics of War and Peace: Is War the Only Way to Save U.S. Capitalism?" *Village Voice* 28, April 26.

Cohn, Carol. 1987. "Nuclear Language and How We Learned to Pat the Bomb." *Bulletin of the Atomic Scientists* June: 17–24.

Cooney, Robert and Helen Michalowski (eds.). From an original text by Marty Jezer. 1987. "The Power of the People: Active Nonviolence." Pp. 184–196, 191–201, 138–139, and 142 in *The Power of the People: Active Nonviolence in the United States.* Philadelphia, PA: New Society Publishers.

Donner, Frank J. 1980. "Surveillance of Peace Movements." Pp. 287–288, 293–297, 304–308, 313–314, and 317–320 in *The Age of Surveillance.* New York, NY: Alfred A. Knopf.

Dower, John W. 1986. "Apes and Others." Pp. 77–93 in *War Without Mercy: Race and Power in the Pacific War.* New York, NY: Pantheon Books.

Dumas, Lloyd J. and Suzanne Gordon. 1986. "Economic Conversion: An Exchange." *Bulletin of the Atomic Scientists* June–July: 45–48.

Dyer, Gwynne. 1985. "Goodbye War." Pp. 252–265 in *War.* New York, NY: Crown Publishers.

Eisenhower, Gen. Dwight D. 1946. "General Eisenhower as Founder of the Military-Industrial Complex in 1946." From the Henry L. Stimson Papers, Sterling Library, Yale University.

Eisenhower, Pres. Dwight D. 1961. "Farewell to the Nation: On the Dangers Created by the Military-Industrial Complex." Delivered to the Nation by television and radio on Jan. 17. From U.S. Department of State, *Bulletin* Vol. 44, Feb. 6, 1961.

Fabbro, David. 1978. "Equality in Peaceful Societies." *Journal of Peace Research* 15: 67–83.

Falk, Richard. 1982. "Nuclear Weapons and the End of Democracy." *Praxis International* 2: 1–11.

Fischer, Dietrich. 1984. "Conflict Resolution." Pp. 171–180 in *Preventing War in the Nuclear Age.* Totowa, NJ: Rowman & Allanheld.

Forsberg, Randall. 1982. "Confining the Military to Defense as a Route to Disarmament." *World Policy Journal* I: 287–318.

Friedman, Thomas L. 1987. "Making Peace With Music." *New York Times* May 3: pp. 1 and following.

Gibson, James William. 1989. "American Paramilitary Culture and the Reconstitution of the Vietnam War." Pp. 10–42 in *Vietnam Images: War and Representation,* Jeff Walsh and James Aulich (eds.) New York, NY: St. Martin's Press.

Gibson, James William. 1986. "Class and the Draft in Vietnam." Pp. 213–219 in *The Perfect War: Technowar in Vietnam.* New York, NY: Atlantic Monthly Press.

Gibson, James William. 1986. "Strategy of Warfare in Vietnam: War as a Production Process." Pp. 116–128 in *The Perfect War: Technowar in Vietnam.* New York, NY: Atlantic Monthly Press.

Gray, Colin S. and Keith Payne. 1980. "Victory Is Possible." *Foreign Policy* 39: 14–27.

Hachiya, Michihiko. 1955. "Hiroshima Diary." Pp. 1–26 in *Hiroshima Diary: The Journal of a Japanese Physician August 6–September 30, 1945.* Chapel Hill, NC: University of North Carolina Press.

Howard, Michael E. 1981. "On Fighting a Nuclear War." *International Security* 5: 3–17.

Howlett, Charles F. and Glen Zeitzer. 1985. "The History of the American Peace Movement." Pp. 5–6 and 25–41 in *The American Peace Movement, History and Historiography.* Washington, DC: American Historical Association.

Kaldor, Mary. 1981. "The Weapons System." Pp. 11–28 in *The Baroque Arsenal.* New York, NY: Hill and Wang.

Lash, Joseph P. 1961. "Successful Negotiation by the UN: Mission to Peking." Pp. 56–65 in *Dag Hammarskjöld.* New York, NY: Doubleday and Co., Inc.

Lebow, Richard Ned. 1985. "Deterrence Reconsidered." Excerpted from *Psychology and Deterrence,* Robert Jervis, Richard Ned Lebow, and Janice Gross Stein. Baltimore, MD: Johns Hopkins Press.

Miles, Sarah. 1986. "The Real War: Low Intensity Conflict." From "Getting on with the Ballgame." *NACLA Report on the Americas* XX: 18–25.

Molander, Earl A. and Roger C. Molander. 1989. "The Anti-Nuclear War Movement of the 1980s." Unpublished manuscript. Dept. of Management, Portland State University, Portland, OR 97207. Prepared for this volume.

Moskos, Charles C., Jr. 1976. "Peace Soldiers: United Nations Military Forces." Pp. 12–28 in *Peace Soldiers: The Sociology of a United Nations Military Force.* Chicago, IL: University of Chicago Press.

Preiswerk, Roy. 1982. "Could We Study International Relations as if People Mattered?" Pp. 175–197 in *Toward a Just World Order,* Vol. I, Richard Falk, Samuel Kim, and Saul Mendlovitz (eds.). Boulder, CO: Westview Press.

Roark, Anne. 1987. "Star Wars: Politicizing Science in U.S." *Los Angeles Times* April 13: Pp. 1 and following.

Ross, Mark Howard. 1986. "Childrearing and War in Different Cultures." Revised version of "A Cross-Cultural Theory of Political Conflict and Violence." *Political Psychology* 7: 427–69. Prepared for this volume.

Salzman, Jason. 1987. "Kiwis Just Say No." *Sierra* May–June: 32–6.

Sharp, Gene. 1985. "Civilian-Based Defense." Pp. 50–62 and 100–108 in *Making Europe Unconquerable: The Potential of Civilian-Based Deterrence and Defense.* London: Taylor & Francis.

Sherwin, Martin J. 1985. "How Well They Meant." *Bulletin of the Atomic Scientists* August: 9–15.

Singer, David J. 1985. "Military Preparedness, National Security and the Lessons of History." Pp. 236–56 in *Swedish Yearbook of International Affairs,* Bo Huldt (ed.). Stockholm: Utrikespolitiska Institutet.

Solo, Pam, Ted Sasson, and Rob Leavitt. 1989. "Principles of Common Security." Pp. 8–9 in *Strategy Workbook: Moving Beyond the Cold War.* Cambridge, MA: Institute for Peace and International Security.

Sommer, Mark. 1986. "Contructing Peace as a Whole System." *Whole Earth Review* Summer: 12–16.

"Statement of the International Physicians for the Prevention of Nuclear War." 1981. Pp. 241–247 in *The Final Epidemic: Physicians and Scientists on Nuclear War,* Ruth Adams and Susan Cullen (eds.). Chicago, IL: Educational Foundation for Nuclear Science.

Thieu, Nguyen Van. 1982. "Our Strategy for Guerrilla War." Pp. 18–25 in *Guerrilla Strategies,* Gerard Chaliand (ed.). Berkeley, CA: University of California Press.

Totten, Sam and Martha Wescoat Totten. 1984. "Kristina Selvig and James Muller, Anti-Nuclear Activists." Pp. 113–117 and 142–147 in *Facing the Danger: Interviews with Anti-Nuclear Activists.* Freedom, CA: Crossing Press.

Tucker, Robert W. 1971. "Socialism Is Not the Solution." Pp. 138–145 in *The Radical Left and American Foreign Policy.* Baltimore, MD: Johns Hopkins Press.

Weisskopf, Thomas E. 1974. "Capitalism, Socialism, and the Sources of Imperialism." Excerpted from Pp. 57–60, 63–73, and 74–80 in *Testing Theories of Economic Imperialism,* Steven J. Rosen and James R. Kurth (eds.). Lexington, MA: D.C. Heath.